CHICAGO PUBLIC LIBRARY
R00482 43090

D1201110

FIVE RINGS OVER KOREA

FIVE RINGS OVER KOREA

The Secret Negotiations Behind the 1988 Olympic Games in Seoul

Richard W. Pound

LITTLE, BROWN AND COMPANY
BOSTON NEW YORK TORONTO LONDON

First Edition

Library of Congress Cataloging-in-Publication Data

Pound, Richard W.
Five rings over Korea: The secret negotiations behind the 1988 Olympic games in Seoul / by Richard W. Pound. — 1st ed.
p. cm.
Published simultaneously in Canada.
Includes index.
ISBN 0-316-71507-7
1. Olympic Games (24th : 1988 : Seoul, Korea) 2. Sports and state — Korea (South) I. Title. II. Title: Five rings over Korea.
GV722.1988 P68.1994
796.48 — dc20 94-543

10 9 8 7 6 5 4 3 2 1

MV-NY

Published simultaneously in Canada
by Little, Brown & Company (Canada) Limited

Printed in the United States of America

To my family,
which indulges my love of the Olympic Movement

Contents

	Preface	ix
	Acknowledgments	xv
1	Decision in Baden-Baden: 1981	3
2	The Legacy: An Olympic Tinderbox	18
3	The Potential for Boycott and Past Lessons	39
4	Setting the Tone for Korea in 1988	58
5	Planning for the North-South Negotiations	87
6	The First Joint Meeting with the Koreas	103
7	Take Two: The Second Meeting with the Koreas	120
8	Take Three: The Third Meeting	159
9	Hiatus — The Tension Mounts: No Agreement	195
10	Once More into the Breach: The Fourth Meeting	241
11	Invitations Go Out; Acceptances Come In	258
12	Keeping the Acceptances and Chasing the Strays	276
13	Upon Reflection . . .	318
	Glossary of Terms	340
	Chronology of Events	342
	Index	435

Preface

THOUGH I may not have known it fully at the time, the idea for this book was born late in the evening of October 3, 1988.

It was the end of the Closing Ceremony of the Games of the XXIVth Olympiad in Seoul, Republic of Korea. As a vice president of the International Olympic Committee, I was in the Tribune d'Honneur at the Olympic Stadium. The ceremony had finished. All the VIPs had left. The performances were over, and the performers had returned to their homes. A few hundred athletes lingered on the field, and I was leaning on the rail of the presidential box, looking to see if I recognized any of those who, like me, did not seem to want to bring the evening to a close.

I had a lump in my throat and suspiciously watery eyes (no doubt, I rationalized, caused by the smoke from the earlier fireworks display) as the realization finally sank in that the Games had finished without incident. Not only had the Seoul Games taken place, but they had been the most successful in Olympic history. More athletes from more countries than ever before had been part of the greatest sporting event in the world. There had been triumph, tragedy, and fun. The doomsayers had been proven wrong.

The Games that many predicted would be a disaster were successful — indeed, successful beyond everyone's wildest dreams. Korea, the country that had been vilified in the media for its political instability, had pulled together in a manner that astounded the world. It had made unimaginable progress toward democracy in a very short period and under very difficult conditions, fraught with conflicting and dangerous political agendas, under the nose of one of the most repressive and heavily armed countries in the world. It wore its heart on its sleeve as it fought for acknowledgment that it had a place in the international community.

The Koreans were not alone in causing the Games to be a success. The lessening of tensions between the superpowers and the international spirit of cooperation that grew throughout the middle and late 1980s certainly contributed to the efforts of the Olympic Movement to launch the Games once more as an unparalleled experience of joy for the youth of the world.

There is no doubt that the spirit of *glasnost* that was developed by Mikhail Gorbachev in the Soviet Union also contributed to the success of the Games in Seoul. Despite difficult circumstances involving their allies and the inevitable need for rationalizing their past political behavior, the Soviets ended up being positively involved in finding the diplomatic solutions necessary for the Games to take place. Participation by the Soviets was essential to the Games. The Chinese did the same, perhaps for different reasons, but there could be no dispute that their influence, quiet restraint of North Korea, and presence were essential. The United States acted as a most effective broker in the political process and combined this persuasion with a considerable amount of muscle, including some old-fashioned gunboat diplomacy when the time for the Games drew near.

Oddly enough, the Games probably helped to draw the noose even more tightly around two of the last of the Stalinist regimes: the Democratic People's Republic of Korea and Cuba. There seems little doubt that full reconciliation of North Korea and South Korea will be impossible while Kim Il Sung, the "Glorious Leader," clings to power, but the events leading up to the Games and thereafter may well make it more difficult for him to transfer his power to his erratic son, Kim Jong Il, the "Dear Leader"; or, if such a transfer is managed, the younger Kim may find it difficult to maintain power. In Cuba, as the "Special Period" drags on and on and on, the facts of life will inevitably overcome Fidel Castro. His smoke-and-mirrors performance has been remarkable and might, but for the endemic repression accompanying it, have been worthy of admiration. His resolute identification with the brutal North Korean regime and its international state terrorism in the years leading up to the Games in Seoul have seriously weakened whatever credibility he may have enjoyed (much of it given by those who vicariously enjoyed watching someone tweak the nose of the mighty United States).

The way is being prepared for change in those societies, and when the histories are written, the Olympic Games in Seoul will be credited with accelerating the progress. The Games will have contributed to the emergence and development of Korea to an even greater extent than the 1964 Olympics vitalized Japan. They will have provided an example of what the international community could accomplish by working together. Were, for example, lessons learned by the United States in building consensus for the Seoul Olympics later applied in building an even more critical consensus prior to the Gulf War two and a half years later?

The International Olympic Committee (IOC) also had a vital, and uncharacteristic, role to play in making the Games in Seoul both possible and successful. It was the IOC that had awarded the Games to Seoul in 1981. This decision was regarded at best as risky and at worst as recklessly foolhardy, depending on one's degree of optimism and place on the political spectrum. Normally, the IOC would have concerned itself only with the physical preparation of the sports facilities and related matters, leaving political machinations to the appropriate political organs. But, faced with the prospect of the Games once again being politically damaged, and having relied on political figures, without success, to solve Olympic problems in the past, the IOC instead took a bold initiative and injected itself fully into the political process.

Acting with patience and restraint throughout the process, it brought the right blend of idealism and cynicism to the delicate negotiations that lasted almost four and a half years — from before the Soviet boycott of the Los Angeles Games in early 1984 through the end of the Seoul Games in late 1988. The IOC was led through this time by a president of remarkable ability, a former Spanish diplomat and politician by the name of Juan Antonio Samaranch, elected, coincidentally enough, immediately prior to the heavily boycotted Moscow Games in 1980. He developed and implemented the unique set of negotiations between the two Koreas, never letting the often bizarre process get out of hand or sharpen to the point where any party had an excuse to deliver an ultimatum or definitively break off the discussions.

Though Samaranch often likens his role as president of the IOC to that of the conductor of a talented orchestra, this is a serious understatement of his activities. He does conduct. And there are some talented players. But he also composes the music, recruits the players, coaches them, books the concert hall, places the advertisements for the concert, acts as protocol officer, invites the guests, chooses the menu, places the seating cards, and nibbles on the ears of the critics. I have often replied to questions about how hard he works for the IOC by saying that he works 365 days per year — plus nights!

It seemed to me that the remarkable confluence of events and talents that made the 1988 Olympic Games possible was neither well known nor understood by the world at large. There appeared to me to be a considerable risk that the Seoul Games might become just another list of statistics; 159 countries took part, which compares with other "numbers" before and after. Should that happen, there would be a loss of experiences that, in many ways, were as unique as some of the stories behind Olympic records and performances — a loss of Olympic "lore," of a vital part of Olympic history, of an understanding of the story behind the Games. The story of Seoul is one that should be told and deserves to be told.

About two years ago, I discussed my concern with Samaranch. He was skeptical at first, but as we talked, he warmed, with characteristic caution, to the idea. He finally agreed that it would be worth the effort to try to record the events for posterity. But who would do it? By rights, I said, it was *his* story to write. The only problem was that if he wrote it, the risk was that the Seoul story would become, like many other Olympic books, yet another example of how to use the first person singular pronoun 100,001 times in a single work. I thought the book ought to be *about* Samaranch, among others, in this fascinating account, but not one written *by* him. I said that I would be prepared to try to chronicle the events, which I thought I could do in a more neutral manner than any of the main protagonists could. Though I had been an "insider" in many respects as a member of the IOC Executive Board from 1983 to 1991 and again from 1992, I had not been an active negotiator in the process. Therefore, while knowledgeable on the specific elements of the process leading to the Seoul Games and an avid follower of matters Olympic, I could be somewhat detached as a reporter. Where I have felt that personal observations might be helpful to an appreciation of the background or the tactical maneuvers at any particular stage, I have resorted to the use of footnotes, to help complete the picture as I understand it. I have, in addition, included a much more comprehensive Chronology than is customary in such works, both to help the flow of the narrative and to provide greater context to the many events that are described.

To those who, knowing I have been working on this book, have asked why I am doing it, typing laboriously as I do with two fingers, my answer is that the story should be told, at least in the first instance, by someone who was there. As a member of the IOC, I accept a responsibility to ensure that a contemporary history of the role of the IOC in world events is made available for the benefit of the real historians who will follow. They deserve, as they judge the actions of the actors who made decisions at the time, under the strictures of the time and with the imperfect knowledge of the time, to have before them the perspective of contemporary analysis. These data may not change their eventual assessments of who did what and why, but they may explain how the events unfolded as they did, what was sought by whom, and why.

Richard W. Pound
Montreal, May 1993

Acknowledgments

Many people have helped with the creation of this work, and while I thank them all, it would be impossible to mention everyone by name.

Special thanks go to Juan Antonio Samaranch for agreeing to share with me much of his special and personal knowledge of many of the events recorded in the book. It would have been impossible to speak with certainty on many aspects of those events without the benefit of his help and access to the IOC files.

Thanks also for the careful review of documents and dates by Karel Wendl and Wolf Lyberg, whose encyclopedic knowledge and uncompromising attention to detail are an example to all researchers.

FIVE RINGS OVER KOREA

CHAPTER 1

Decision in Baden-Baden: 1981

BADEN-BADEN, WEST GERMANY, September 29, 1981 — For the delegations of five candidate cities and their supporters, in Baden-Baden and at home, it was an anxious moment. There were two candidates to host the 1988 Olympic Games: Nagoya, Japan, and Seoul, Korea. Three others contested the right to host the 1988 Olympic Winter Games.[1] The decision of the International Olympic Committee (IOC) would be announced in a few moments by its president, Juan Antonio Samaranch. Not even Samaranch knew the outcome of the secret ballots cast by the seventy-nine members of the IOC voting in Baden-Baden,[2] which was contained in a sealed envelope handed to him several minutes earlier by three sphinx-faced scrutineers.

The tension was almost unbearable as Samaranch entered the room and made his way to the podium. He put on his glasses, pulled the envelope from his pocket, tore it open, pulled out the result, and moved forward slightly to speak into the microphone.

The competition between the candidate cities had been all the fiercer because the two candidates were both Asian, and there was a great deal of regional "face" involved in the outcome. It was clear that both cities were perfectly capable of handling the organizational logistics of the Olympic Games, no mean feat in a complex operation involving twenty-three official sports, close to ten thousand athletes, nearly five thousand

[1] The candidates were Calgary (Canada), Cortina d'Ampezzo (Italy), and Falun (Sweden). Calgary would eventually win on the second ballot over Falun.

[2] There were eighty members of the IOC present at the Session, but Samaranch did not vote and has never voted in elections for host cities of the Games during his presidency.

team officials, six thousand members of the media, and several thousand employees of the Organizing Committee, not to mention security and other personnel.

The Japanese had organized the Olympic Games in Tokyo in 1964. The Games had proven to be very successful, not only for the Olympic Movement, but also for Japan, marking its reentry into the world as a full participant in the international community, following an extensive rebuilding period after World War II. The Games were a tangible demonstration that Japan had come of age in the industrial and commercial world and that it would be a force to be reckoned with in the years to come, as "Made in Japan" took on a dramatically new significance.

Eight years later, in 1972, Sapporo, Japan, hosted the XIth Olympic Winter Games. This was, again, a first for Asia, and the success of those Games demonstrated once more that the Japanese were more than equal to the organizational challenges involved.

More important, in the context of the current struggle, the Japanese were fully aware of the enormous prestige that comes with the hosting of the Olympic Games. The Games provide an unequaled opportunity for promotion of the host country and a showcase for its people, culture, industry, tourism, and virtually everything about it. Even better, much of the promotion is done for the host country at no cost, by domestic and foreign media desperate for material pertaining to one of the most publicized spectacles in the world. The Japanese were, therefore, determined to take full advantage of yet another occasion to be front and center on the world stage. It was unimaginable to them that they might not be successful in a head-on competition with Korea.

The Koreans, on the other hand, had never hosted the Olympic Games. Nor, for that matter, had any small developing country. The Republic of Korea (ROK) was, however, on the move economically and was in the early stages of becoming the miracle country of the 1980s. The members of its Olympic bidding committee were enthusiastic and aggressive. Definitely the new kid on the block, Seoul was an intriguing combination, both bold and cautious. Unlike their Japanese counterparts, the Koreans made no secret of their desire to win and had no compunction whatsoever about asking for a commitment from IOC members to support their bid.

For the Western members of the IOC, who predominate,[3] much of

[3] By continent, the members of the IOC in 1981 were divided as follows: Europe, 34 (including Samaranch); Asia, 13; Africa, 14; America, 19; and Oceania, 2. Of the total of 82 members, 80 were present at the Session in Baden-Baden, and 79 voted.

the historical and cultural tension between Japan and Korea went largely unnoticed during the bidding process and even during the last few pressure-cooker days in Baden-Baden.[4] They were, nevertheless, very much present in the minds of the candidates, and much of the final bidding strategy of both parties was designed to avoid the traps that each suspected the other would inject into the presentations and questions from the IOC members and any other observers.

It is the nature of the IOC's selection process when there is more than one candidate city that the members tend to approach the selection as one in which less desirable candidates are eliminated, rather than seeking the best and supporting that candidate from beginning to end. Almost every recent selection of a host city has gone the maximum number of rounds of voting before a result is reached. This is particularly nerve-racking for the candidate cities, who must concentrate, in the home stretch, not so much on continuing to promote their city as in avoiding the "fatal mistake." A wrong answer to a question during the final presentation to the IOC Session could easily decide the whole candidacy. Questions might relate to public support, government involvement, security, financial stability, transportation plans, ticket prices and allocations, accommodations for the Olympic family, media facilities, sport schedules, and a host of other things. Answers would have to be smooth and positive, and appear responsive to concerns expressed, whether or not, in the great scheme of things, they were at all important. Where neither English nor French was the principal language of either delegation, both were at the mercy of the interpreters provided by the German organizers of the Session.

The South Koreans had even brought one of their most distinguished economic planners[5] as part of the official delegation for the specific

[4] There was a long history of Japanese domination of Korea, and Japanese political domination had only been ended as a result of Japan's defeat in World War II. Though it did mean the end of Japanese rule, the "liberation" of Korea had been a mixed blessing because of the Soviet Union's continued occupation of its sphere of military influence north of the 38th parallel upon the termination of the war. This led to the creation of the Democratic People's Republic of Korea as a separate client state of the Soviet Union in September 1948. The many complications arising out of the existence of the two rival states led to the Korean War in 1950, which has still, in the technical sense, not ended. It is fair to say that the relationship between Korea and Japan has been complicated by the history of Japanese colonial policy and the effort by the Japanese to eradicate Korean language and culture, and was, generally, less than fully satisfactory; this was all the more true in 1981, at the time of this contest for the 1988 Olympic Games.

[5] This was Yoo Chang Soon, who was officially described in the delegation as an "adviser" of the bid committee and chairman of the Korean Traders Association. He had formerly been deputy prime minister in charge of economic planning for the Republic of Korea and later went on to become prime minister. His background was in economics.

purpose of responding to an anticipated question thought to have been planted with one of the international federation presidents, Yuri Titov, the Soviet president of the International Gymnasts Federation (FIG), who was clearly sympathetic to the Japanese. They were right to have done so, even though it meant that they used one of the six precious places in the official delegation, the maximum permitted by the IOC for such presentations.[6] The question *was* asked, and the answer was devastating to the Japanese, who were clearly exposed not only as having planted the question (which would probably never have occurred to the individual who posed it) but to have done so for the specific purpose of trying to embarrass the Koreans, rather than advancing the Japanese bid on its own merits.[7]

The Koreans, for their part, were handicapped by at least three major problems. The first was the state of tension on the Korean peninsula. Though the Korean War had ended in July 1953, the official status was merely a cessation of hostilities, with an artificial boundary established between the two opposing regimes along the map reference of 38 degrees north latitude.[8] Technically, a state of war still existed, although for almost thirty years, the hostilities had largely been confined to sporadic minor "incidents" along the demilitarized zone (DMZ). Nevertheless, tensions between the Democratic People's Republic of Korea (DPRK) and the Republic of Korea remained extreme, and the situation was daily capable of erupting into a major armed conflict. The 38th parallel was only thirty miles north of Seoul. The DPRK army was reputed to be the fourth largest standing army in the world and was

[6] The official bid presentation team consisted of Park Young Soo, mayor of Seoul; Cho Sang Ho, president of the Korean Olympic Committee (KOC); Chung Ju Yung, chairman of the bid committee and chairman of the Federation of Korean Industries; Yoo Chang Soon (see footnote 5); Lee Won Kyung, chairman of Hapdong Inc.; and Lee Won Hong, vice chairman of the bid committee and president of the Korean Broadcasting System.

[7] The question had been designed to try to cast doubt on the financial stability of Korea, which had recently received and was continuing to negotiate for massive capital injections from Japan. It implied that the Koreans could not handle the financial implications of a project of the magnitude of the Olympics and should not, therefore, be selected. The answer, that the loans had been for the purpose of economic development and that the same sort of loans had been made in the past to other countries, never specifically referred to Japan as a similar beneficiary of such loans. The point was, however, well noted by those present. It is a matter of some irony that, before the end of the same decade, the Soviet Union, prior to its dismantlement, would be forced to petition for and obtain the same sort of development loans from the Republic of Korea.

[8] This was the former division line between Soviet and U.S. military interests during World War II and was a useful compromise position for cessation of the military hostilities of the Korean War.

deployed on just the other side of the DMZ. It was generally recognized that the peace was effectively kept as a result of the presence of forty thousand U.S. armed forces stationed in Korea (indeed, the command of the entire military forces in South Korea was a U.S. command, albeit sensitively administered) and the threat of additional U.S. forces, should conditions warrant them.

The second problem was one internal to the Republic of Korea itself: the stability of its own government. There had, for years, been no orderly change of government in South Korea, but instead a series of coups, sometimes accompanied by assassinations and almost always backed by factions within the Korean armed forces.[9] There had been considerable chaos in Korea following the assassination of former president Park Chung Hee in October 1979.[10] Such a coup had occurred only months before the IOC decision in Baden-Baden was to be made; it was led by Chun Doo Hwan, an army general who then became president.[11] It would have been naive to think, given the track record then before the world, that such a coup and the resulting government enjoyed universal approval within South Korea or that the new regime could be assured of sufficient longevity to deliver the Games in 1988.

There was also an Olympics-related problem, since Korea was one of the countries that had boycotted the 1980 Moscow Games — although they shared this dubious distinction with many other countries, including, fortunately for Seoul's bid, Japan. However, a significant difference between Japan and Korea for purposes of the IOC members from socialist countries was that all had diplomatic relations with Ja-

[9] These coups had occurred in 1960, with the downfall of Syngman Rhee; in 1961, which led to the presidency of General Park Chung Hee; in 1979, with the assassination of Park and the installation of Chun Doo Hwan shortly thereafter.

[10] Park and his chief bodyguard were assassinated by Kim Jae Kyu, the director of the KCIA (Korean Central Intelligence Agency), on October 26. Choi Kyu Hah became acting president of the Republic, and martial law was declared.

[11] Chun had been in charge of the investigation into the assassination of Park Chung Hee. On December 12, 1979, he arrested key army officers and established control of the army by force of arms. Roh Tae Woo became head of the Capital Garrison Command. In April 1980, Chun assumed illegal control of the KCIA, by not giving up his military command before assuming control of what was intended to be a civilian organization. Widespread demonstrations called for his resignation. In May 1980, he acted to extend his control, ostensibly under the authority of the Choi government, including the extension of military law. By May 31, Chun was able to establish the Special Committee for National Security Measures, a military-civilian body fully controlled by Chun. By mid-August, Choi resigned. Within a week, Chun resigned from the army and was inaugurated as president on August 27.

pan, and none had such relations with Korea. Indeed, they were all allies of the DPRK and were, therefore, virtually certain to support Japan, rather than to embarrass their socialist ally. This meant that a considerable bloc of votes would not be available to Seoul, making the task that much more difficult.[12]

The combination of all these factors, and Japan's own conviction that it was clearly superior to the Koreans and more equipped for the bid, caused the Japanese to be overconfident. There was no doubt that they believed they would win. Everything they said and did made this quite apparent. The presentations to the IOC Session and the voting were merely formalities before returning victorious to Japan. Even the fact that hundreds of Japanese from Nagoya (or, at least, purporting to be from Nagoya) had come to Baden-Baden to protest having the Games in Nagoya on environmental and other grounds caused the bid committee no concern.[13]

As a developing country and one which was trying to get out from under domination by the Japanese, Korea had had its own doubts about hosting the Olympic Games. Early on, the Koreans vacillated between wanting to go forward whether they won or lost, and believing that the worst possible situation would be to try and fail. Studies were undertaken within Korea and with government ministries and Seoul city officials regarding the feasibility of trying to attract both the Asian Games and the Olympic Games. The initial driving force behind the bid appeared to be Park Chong Kyu, at the time president of the KOC and the Korean Amateur Sports Association (KASA).

The taste for hosting international sports events had come from the World Shooting Championships held in Korea in late September and

[12] This specific problem had been raised at the IOC Executive Board meeting immediately preceding the Baden-Baden Session by Vitaly Smirnov, one of the two Soviet members of the IOC. He warned that awarding the Games to Seoul would give rise to a great number of political and economic difficulties. In particular, he referred to the inability of Seoul to host the 1966 Asian Games because the government could not guarantee the safety of athletes and officials. The Koreans stated that at the time they preferred to use available money toward economic development. The Executive Board declined to discuss the matter.

[13] Masaji Kiyokawa, one of the two Japanese IOC members (and the 1932 Olympic champion in 100 meters backstroke) had reported to the IOC Executive Board that the opposition groups were small and unimportant and should not be taken as reflective of the level of support for the Nagoya bid, which he said was very strong in Japan. The conspiracy theorists among observers suggested that the Koreans might have financed the demonstrators against Nagoya, but no evidence of this has ever surfaced. Many thought, in retrospect, that the protests of such groups had been effective against the Japanese bid.

early October of 1978. The tentative international canvassing with respect to an Olympic bid started with the 1979 meeting of the Association of National Olympic Committees (ANOC) in Puerto Rico in 1979, after Korean president Park Chung Hee had given tentative approval for a bid.[14] The Koreans had the impression that ANOC had some influence over the IOC, a measure of their inexperience in such matters. They approached the incoming president of ANOC, Mario Vazquez-Raña of Mexico, and asked for his assistance.[15] By September 21, 1979, the president had approved plans to begin negotiations for both Games.[16] A public announcement of the bid was made by the mayor of Seoul on October 8, 1979. The plans hit a major snag when President Park Chung Hee was assassinated by members of the secret service on October 26, 1979.

Park Chong Kyu was replaced as president of the KOC and KASA by Cho Sang Ho on July 14, 1980. Chun Doo Hwan had become president of the Republic of Korea on August 27, 1980. Cho discovered that the deadline for applications to host the 1988 Games was November 30, 1980, and the process got under way again. The KOC met on November 6, and after considering the pros and cons of proceeding with a bid,[17] recommended that the government submit the application.

[14] Park Seh Jik, who was the president of the Seoul Organizing Committee from 1986 until the end of the Games, wrote in his book *The Seoul Olympics* that President Park had said, "Try to get in touch with all IOC members and related dignitaries attending the Puerto Rico convention so that Korea can win the venue for sure, because it would be worse than not even trying if we tried and failed."

[15] This approach and the conclusions drawn from it are described, with some naïveté, in Park Seh Jik, *The Seoul Olympics*.

[16] The aims that Park Chung Hee had identified, according to Park Seh Jik, were: to demonstrate Korea's strength and economic power; to improve Korea's status in the international sporting community; to promote friendship with foreign countries through sport; to create favorable conditions for establishing diplomatic relations with both Communist and nonaligned nations; and to consolidate national consensus through these international sports events, primarily the Olympic Games.

[17] According to Park Seh Jik, the potential gains in proceeding with the bid were: Korean national prestige would be enhanced; the Olympic bid proposal would help to win the 1986 Asian Games; even if the bid were to be rejected, Korea would be honored as a candidate host nation; the task itself of preparing the application would provide valuable experience to the KOC; were it to become necessary, conceding to another country at the last moment might bring benefits not now apparent; and finally, the application by itself would be important because it might be the last opportunity for any nation to apply for hosting the Games, since the IOC was seriously considering a proposal to institute a permanent venue. (This was the Greek proposal to have a permanent site in Olympia, which the IOC considered briefly but rejected.) The potential losses that the KOC identified were: Korea could lose credibility in the international sports community if it should inadvertently make any error after submitting the application; popular support in economic and

The city of Seoul was concerned about the financial implications and went on record accordingly, but President Chun Doo Hwan approved the bid on November 30, and it was submitted to the IOC as required. The KOC confirmed its support of the Seoul bid on December 1.[18] There were some "cold feet" thereafter, but Chun was persuaded to stay in the race and, in August 1981, the relatively unknown minister of political affairs, Roh Tae Woo, was assigned the responsibility of directing the entire campaign of the bid. The eventual role of Roh Tae Woo in relation to the Olympics and to his country was, of course, unknown at this time.[19]

It had been a fascinating road to Baden-Baden for Juan Antonio Samaranch, where, presiding over his first Session as the new president of the International Olympic Committee, he would announce the winners of the competition to host the 1988 Games. He had been elected president at the IOC Session in Moscow the previous year, just prior to the badly wounded Moscow Olympics, on a first-ballot win, a remarkable achievement in an organization well known for its favorite-son voting in early rounds of elections.[20]

Despite this decisive victory in the race to fill the vacancy left by the retiring Lord Killanin, president from 1972 to 1980, relatively little was known by most of the IOC members about Samaranch or his abili-

---

social areas might not be easy to attain, even if the project were to be actively promoted; and the international sporting community might consider the Korean application premature, distrusting South Korea because of the political situation of territorial division, the lack of experience in hosting an "inclusive" international sports event, and possible shortage of funds to underwrite all expenses.

[18] Under Olympic rules, the NOC of the country in which the potential host city is located must approve the bid. This is a method by which the IOC attempts to ensure that the interests of the sports organizations in such countries are taken into account when Olympic bids are launched.

[19] In the period leading up to the IOC's decision, the Koreans had done the necessary homework. A committee was formed on December 23, 1980, to prepare the answers to the questionnaire used by the IOC to help evaluate candidate cities. On February 10, 1981, the KOC and Seoul signed the agreement to execute the IOC's contract, were it to be successful in winning the Games. As president of the Republic of Korea, Chun Doo Hwan signed a guarantee on February 16 that all aspects of the Games, including entry of all accredited persons, would be properly carried out. Completed application documents were submitted to the IOC on February 28. Representatives of the IOC, the international sports federations, and the NOCs visited Seoul at the IOC's expense in the spring of 1981. The NOC representatives made a special report during the course of a meeting between the IOC Executive Board and the NOCs on September 21, 1981, regarding its inspection, declaring that both candidates were capable of organizing the Games.

[20] The other candidates for the presidency had been Lance Cross (New Zealand), Willi Daume (West Germany), Marc Hodler (Switzerland), and James Worrall (Canada).

ties. He had been quietly close to the source of power within the IOC for almost all of his fourteen years as a member, following his co-optation at the 1966 Session of the IOC in Rome. He had, in fact, been elected to the Executive Board for ten of those years.[21] There must have been some inkling regarding his potential, because he had been personally selected as a member of the IOC in Spain in 1966 by none other than the legendary and autocratic IOC president Avery Brundage and was co-opted as a member despite the IOC rule that there could be two members in a country only if that country had previously hosted the Olympic Games or if it was particularly large. Neither exception applied in the case of Spain, but Brundage, in archetypal fashion, simply caused the election to happen.[22] It would, no doubt, have been a matter of great satisfaction had he lived to see his judgment of Samaranch so vindicated.[23]

In 1977, Samaranch had been appointed Spain's ambassador to the Soviet Union,[24] a noteworthy sign of respect, since the USSR was a country of considerable importance for Europe. Even more, however, there had been no diplomatic relations between the USSR and Spain

[21] Quite apart from his elected position on the Executive Board, Samaranch had remained close to all the "important" people by virtue of his position (appointed) as *chef de protocol* of the IOC, 1968–1975 and 1979–1980.

[22] The process was as convoluted as IOC procedures can sometimes become. The first step was to decide whether Spain could have a second member. (This is a somewhat vernacular description, since the IOC theory is that it appoints members "in" a country to represent the IOC, rather than members "from" a country to represent that country within the IOC. The distinction is often hard to maintain but is a fundamental principle within the catechism of the IOC.) The vote on this first matter was narrowly won by Brundage and the next day Samaranch was co-opted as a member of the IOC. Brundage asked Samaranch to ride with him to the Vatican, where the IOC members were granted an audience with the Pope, and during this ride, Samaranch asked Brundage why he had fought so hard to get him "in" as a member of the IOC. Brundage replied that he thought one day he might become the president of the IOC. Samaranch had actually been proposed as a member of the IOC at the 1965 Session in Madrid, but Brundage stated that five new members had already been co-opted at that Session and the matter would have to be deferred until the following year. This "delay" of one year would have some implications for Samaranch. It made him subject to the mandatory retirement rule of the IOC, at age seventy-two, for all members co-opted after 1965. During Samaranch's presidency of the IOC, this age was increased to seventy-five, which would eventually allow him to stand for a third term as president in his seventy-fourth year. (IOC rules allow a member to serve out the balance of the term of an elected position even if the retirement age is reached within such term.)

[23] Brundage died in 1975.

[24] This appointment also extended to the People's Republic of Mongolia, a not uncommon combination for ambassadorships at the time. The term of his appointment was from July 17, 1977, to October 16, 1980.

since the Spanish civil war. The USSR had opposed Spain's application to join the United Nations, and it was only as part of a complicated deal that permitted three separate UN memberships from within the Soviet Union[25] that the USSR's opposition was dropped and Spain was eventually "allowed" its own membership. This appointment was particularly significant, not only for Spain, but also for Samaranch.

By 1977, it was clear to most insiders that, if Killanin was to retire after his initial eight-year term as president of the IOC, as appeared increasingly likely due to his health, Samaranch would be among the candidates for the presidency. It was only in retrospect that the thought and planning that went into Samaranch's campaign became apparent. The campaign was discreet but exceedingly thorough. The Moscow appointment may have been part of it, or it may have been serendipitous, but it certainly provided an opportunity for two elements of the campaign to be brought to fruition: Samaranch's diplomatic profile was raised dramatically, and he had the regular opportunity to be in contact with the IOC members in the Soviet bloc, particularly those in the USSR itself, whose influence at the time was considerable among their socialist colleagues. Added to this, throughout the same period, Moscow was in full preparation for the 1980 Olympic Games, so there was a steady stream of Olympic visitors, including IOC members, coming through Moscow. The situation was a candidate's dream come true.

Nor was Samaranch any stranger to the mechanics of the Olympic Movement. He had served as *chef de mission* for the Spanish Olympic teams at the 1956 Olympic Winter Games, the 1960 Olympic Games, and the 1964 Olympic Games. He had been president of the Spanish Olympic Committee from 1967 to 1970. So, this was not some outsider who had never worked up a sweat in the Olympic trenches who was poised on the edge of the presidency of the entire Olympic Movement, but someone who had seen it all, from top to bottom.[26]

Samaranch was no stranger, either, to the political world. A teacher of economics and a director of a number of companies, he started as a municipal councillor in the city of Barcelona, having responsibility for

[25] These were the USSR itself and the republics of Ukraine and Byelorussia (now Belarus).

[26] On the eve of the IOC presidential election in Moscow, the late David McKenzie, one of the two IOC members in Australia, and I were having dinner together in the restaurant of the Moskva Hotel, when Killanin's secretary, Norma Macmanaway, came in and said that Killanin was all by himself in his room and asked if we might go up and have a drink with him. We did have a "jar" and, while discussing the excitement and machinations surrounding the elections, concluded that Samaranch was virtually a certain winner. Neither McKenzie nor I knew much about Samaranch

sports. He was elected a deputy of the prefecture of Barcelona, was a delegate for physical education and sport for the entire country of Spain, and eventually became president of the Barcelona prefecture. In short, he was an experienced politician and did not come to the search for the IOC presidency under any illusion as to the need for an organized campaign for that purpose.

The penultimate step leading to the election in 1980 had occurred in Montevideo, Uruguay, the previous year. The IOC Session was held along the banks of the Río de la Plata (not far from the remains of the German battleship *Bismarck,* visible at low tide) in a quaint but wholly outdated hotel, the Carrasco. Its principal claim to fame was that the architect had apparently forgotten to include a kitchen in the designs. The critical element at this Session was to be sure that Samaranch, who had gone off the Executive Board as first vice president, in rotation, the previous year, was again elected as a member of the Executive Board in Montevideo. The apparent view was that it would be easier to be elected president from within the Executive Board than from outside this inner circle. It would also serve as a barometer with respect to Samaranch himself. Had it not been possible to elect him to the Executive Board only a year prior to the main event, there would still have been time to change the overall campaign strategy. He was, however, duly elected, and the plan remained operational.

There was no guarantee of clear sailing to the presidency, even as a member of the Executive Board. The Session was restless on a number of matters dealt with by the Executive Board, not the least of which was the whole question of China. The issue had been raised in a most unfortunate manner just prior to the 1976 Olympic Games in Montreal, when the Canadian government had refused to allow the Olympic team from Taiwan to compete under its IOC-recognized name of "Republic of China," despite assurances given to the IOC by the same government at the time the Games had been awarded to Montreal that Canada would permit free access to the delegations of all NOCs recognized by the IOC. Between the time the promise had been given, prior to the 1970 IOC Session in Amsterdam, when Montreal won its surprise victory over Los Angeles and Moscow as a result of the efforts of its charismatic mayor, Jean Drapeau, and the time of the Games in 1976,

---

and we expressed some concern over this prospect. Killanin leaned back, jar in hand, smiled, and said not to worry, that Samaranch was "much better than you think."

Canada had entered into diplomatic relations with the People's Republic of China (PRC), under terms which "took note" of the PRC's position that Taiwan was merely a province of the PRC and had no international legitimacy whatsoever.

Clearly, there had been forceful representations made to the Canadian government by the PRC that Taiwan should not be allowed to describe itself as the "Republic of China," regardless of what description the IOC had permitted in the absence of the PRC, which had withdrawn from the Olympic Movement just prior to the 1956 Games in Melbourne, where it did not participate, despite having entered, in protest over the continued independent presence of a recognized NOC in Taiwan. The Canadian government had acceded to these diplomatic pressures and maintained its position despite strong protests from both the IOC and the U.S. government, which, at one stage, appeared ready to withdraw its own team from the Games in protest.

In the end, the Taiwan team refused to participate under any other name and stayed in the United States.[27] The U.S. team participated. The Canadian government was in disgrace, at least as far as the IOC was concerned. Perhaps the most unfortunate fallout from this episode was that preoccupation with the China problem appeared to cause the IOC to misgauge the severity of a rapidly developing crisis with the African countries, which led to a boycott, on the eve of the Games, of some thirty countries (twenty-two of them withdrew their teams already in Montreal and eight, despite having accepted the invitation to participate, did not come to Montreal), a tragedy that might well have been avoided.

The China problem still rankled three years later, and Killanin was determined to have the PRC as part of the Olympic Movement, even if it meant throwing out Taiwan, which had participated regularly in the Olympic Games and had followed all the rules affecting national Olympic committees. The proposal put to the IOC Session in 1979 was, essentially, that the PRC should be admitted and Taiwan sacrificed, if necessary, but that Taiwan's athletes could be part of the PRC teams if they qualified. To the chagrin of Killanin, who threatened, in a most unpresidential fashion, that the IOC would have to find itself another president if the recommendation of the Executive Board was not ac-

[27] Their yachting team, which had been in Canada, training at the Olympic yachting facility in Kingston, Ontario, had to leave.

cepted, the proposal was, indeed, sent back by the Session to the board with instructions to find a new solution.[28]

The problem was compounded when the Executive Board sent out a mail ballot in the fall of 1979, effectively reproposing the solution advanced at the Session in Montevideo. The ballot was procedurally flawed, since it contained not just the ballot, but, on the face of it, a recommendation from the Executive Board to approve the decision of the Executive Board. This caused a further uproar from members of the IOC and led to institution of legal proceedings against the IOC by Henry Hsu, the member in Taiwan, claiming that the IOC was in breach of its own rules and had acted improperly in trying to exclude Taiwan.

It was of no particular advantage for a presidential candidate to be associated with this series of unfortunate gaffes. However, it was Killanin who attracted almost all the static, and none of the eventual candidates was particularly wounded by the resulting confusion. It would not be until Samaranch was president of the IOC that the unique solution to the impasse regarding China would be negotiated and put in place.[29]

As the IOC moved closer to its choice of Killanin's successor, other dangerous clouds loomed on the horizon.

On December 26, 1979, Soviet troops entered Afghanistan. The usual sophisticated and sophistic reasons were given for the presence of the troops, but the fact remained: the country had been invaded. The situation was complicated by Afghanistan's location so close to the Persian Gulf and the major oil supplies in the region. There was outrage throughout the rest of the world, but a clear reluctance to become involved in any military action against the USSR. There ensued a frantic search for other types of sanctions that could demonstrate the repug-

[28] This decision was made despite a singularly inept performance by the Taiwan NOC delegation at the Session. The anger over the Montreal incident in 1976 was still present, as well it might have been. The leader of the Taiwan delegation made gross personal insults about Canadian prime minister Pierre Trudeau and was severely rebuked in front of the Session by Killanin.

[29] Agreement was reached in March 1981 whereby the PRC would be identified as the Chinese Olympic Committee and would use its national flag and anthem for Olympic protocol purposes. The NOC formerly described as the Republic of China Olympic Committee would become the Chinese Taipei Olympic Committee. It would be required to adopt a different flag from its national flag for Olympic protocol purposes and use the Olympic hymn in the event that one of its athletes were to win a gold medal. In all respects, the two NOCs would otherwise have complete recognition and status.

nance of the rest of the world regarding this Soviet action, but without actually doing anything that might escalate the situation.

One of the first vulnerabilities identified in the desperate search for an appropriate response to the Soviet aggression was the forthcoming Olympic Games, to be held in Moscow during the summer of 1980. The possibility of a boycott of the Games was considered at a NATO meeting within a day or two of the invasion but was discarded as likely to be ineffective. U.S. president Jimmy Carter, who had been completely surprised by the invasion and whose foreign policy record was in shambles, took up the idea. He got almost instant emotional public support in the United States for a boycott of the Games and thereafter used the Olympic Games as the leading response of his administration to the Soviet invasion.

On January 20, 1980, Carter announced that, unless the Soviet forces were withdrawn from Afghanistan within thirty days, the United States would not participate in Olympic Games in Moscow that year; the Games would have to be canceled or moved. This message was reiterated to the IOC at the Opening Ceremony of its Session in Lake Placid, just prior to the 1980 Olympic Winter Games in February, by U.S. secretary of state Cyrus Vance, in a lecture to the IOC on the meaning of the Olympics. This political homily was received in stony silence by the IOC.[30] Carter himself did not stir from the White House and refused even to open the Games, a function traditionally performed by the head of state of the host country. He preferred to remain in Washington, doing his best to ruin the Summer Games, while the Winter Games, which included a full team of excellent Soviet athletes, were being celebrated in his own country.

There was, of course, no chance whatsoever that the U.S. ultimatum would cause a withdrawal of the Soviet troops from Afghanistan. That was never a realistic possibility. The preoccupation for the IOC and the national Olympic committees was whether the full-scale diplomatic pressure being applied by the United States on other countries would be sufficient to cause their governments to cave in and order their Olympic teams to stay home from Moscow that summer. To try to develop some solidarity in the face of this pressure, the IOC, having obtained declarations of support and confidence from the international sports federations and the national Olympic committees beforehand,

[30] So caught up was he in his political lecture, Vance neglected to carry out the very task he had been invited to perform: he forgot to open the IOC Session. Killanin had to do this himself the next morning.

unanimously resolved at its Session in Lake Placid that the Games in Moscow would proceed. This unanimity included the two IOC members from the United States, Douglas Roby and Julian Roosevelt, who were strongly opposed to the boycott.

There was a long and bitter struggle, more suited to a separate chronicle of Olympic history, between January 1980 and the end of the Games in Moscow. The Games did take place and there were great athletic performances, but they were not the joyous festival of youth that they might, and should, have been. Many scars were left within countries and between friends concerning the necessity or desirability of a boycott of the Moscow Games. They would take years to heal.

The IOC itself learned, too late, that the boycott initiative of President Carter was real, that U.S. public opinion supported it, and that this was all that was required to turn it into a major political offensive that would have far-reaching consequences for the Olympic Movement. Killanin himself never seemed to take the prospect of a U.S.-led boycott very seriously until it was too late. He was, apparently, not aware of how quickly public opinion in the United States can be translated into administration policy.[31] Like many Europeans, he was also mildly contemptuous of the Americans and, therefore, did not fully appreciate the enormous raw political power of the United States. By the time he was prepared to undertake visits to Carter and Soviet president Leonid Brezhnev on behalf of the special role of the Olympics in a troubled world, the positions of the two superpowers were cast in stone.

These events did not, in the end, affect the election of Samaranch. The preparations for his ascension had borne fruit. Now the work — and work it was — began.

Samaranch cleared his throat slightly and spoke into the microphone: "The International Olympic Committee, at its eighty-fourth Session in Baden-Baden, has awarded the honor of hosting the Games of the XXIVth Olympiad to" — he paused to read the slip he had just taken from the envelope — "the city of Seoul, Korea!"

The room erupted with the cheers of the victorious Koreans. They had won, 52–27, over the Japanese.

Samaranch thought, "What have we done?" and moved to the table where the formal contracts confirming the selection were to be signed.

[31] Presidential election years in the United States were particularly delicate with respect to the Soviet Union. Add to this the American frustration with the hostage crisis in Teheran and the picture was complete for a strong emotional reaction.

CHAPTER 2

The Legacy: An Olympic Tinderbox

IF JUAN ANTONIO SAMARANCH was worried about potential difficulties with the 1988 Olympic Games, he had good reason. Each set of Games in recent memory had attracted its own political problems, which were becoming increasingly difficult to resolve.

Not that the problems were caused by the Games themselves. After all, the rules are generally fixed for each sport, the international sport federations (IFs) are well equipped to handle the technical aspects of each competition, and, for the most part, the national Olympic committees (NOCs) can manage their delegations perfectly well. There are, to be sure, occasional questions of eligibility, doping violations, and other sport-related disputes, but the mechanisms to deal with such matters are in place and usually function satisfactorily.

The real problems, those the International Olympic Committee had not dealt with adeptly, were the externally generated matters, coming from outside the world of sport — the "political" problems. They were beyond the ability of a part-time organization having no particular international status; the IOC was not equipped, either organizationally or by disposition, to deal with such issues. Any action by the IOC tended to be in response to a crisis or to someone else's initiative; it seldom, if ever, had the advantage of making the first move. A review of even a few of the Games illustrates a range of difficulties with which the IOC had had to wrestle prior to 1988. Though the IOC's record had not been stellar, each Games did manage to proceed except for those during the two World Wars.

Germany, 1936

The IOC, for example, did not understand the extent to which Germany would use the 1936 Olympic Games in Berlin as a political platform for the new Reich established by Adolf Hitler and was left with very little it could do when the scenario became clear. To its credit, the IOC insisted that banners bearing the swastika insignia of the Third Reich (other than the national flag itself) be removed from the main stadium, despite the opposition to such action by Chancellor Hitler, which was only overcome by the threat of canceling the Games.[1] There had been talk of a boycott of the Games on account of the discrimination within Germany against Jewish athletes. (This boycott, if it had developed, would have been unusual, since it was one proposed by sportspeople, not politicians.) Despite a fairly strong movement in favor of a boycott in the United States and among left-wing sports organizations in Europe, it never became widespread, possibly due to the propaganda released by the German authorities denying that such discrimination existed and, no doubt, to some rather uncritical acceptance by sports authorities of assurances given by the German authorities.[2] Once again, by the time the truth was known, it was too late.[3] This misjudgment was not made only within Olympic circles.

[1] There had been forewarnings of this during the Olympic Winter Games in Garmisch-Partenkirchen in February that year, when the IOC insisted that signs stating that dogs and Jews were not allowed in the town be taken down. Hitler asserted that he was the one who would decide how matters were run in Germany, but the IOC refused to accept this. Perhaps this earlier stand carried some weight when the banners were ordered down in Berlin.

[2] One of the IOC members in the United States, Commodore Ernest Lee Jahncke, a German-American (co-opted in 1927), had campaigned actively against U.S. participation in the Berlin Games, on the basis that they would be controlled, organized, and orchestrated by Nazi propagandists. These racists would be wholly contemptuous of the ideals of fair play and chivalry that had animated Pierre de Coubertin in reviving the Olympic Games. His decision to make public his feelings on the matter of the political system contravened the set of values of the IOC, whose members believed they should not take strong and public political positions on controversial international issues. At the 1936 Session of the IOC in Berlin, he was expelled after refusing to withdraw his declaration. The "official" reason was his nonattendance at IOC Sessions, but since he had not attended any since his election in 1927, it was clear that the real reason had been his position regarding the Berlin Games. Indeed, this was never seriously disputed by the IOC. For a more detailed review of the activities in the United States in relation to a possible Olympic boycott and the statements of leading U.S. Olympic figures, see Moshe Gottlieb, "The American Controversy Over the Olympic Games," *American Jewish Historical Quarterly* 61 (March 1972): 181–213.

[3] In general, the members of the IOC avoided politics. It appears that they may well have completely misunderstood the seriousness of the Nazi threat, since, at the last IOC Session prior to World War II in London, June 6–9, 1939, even after Nazi Germany had annexed Austria and occupied Czechoslovakia, the IOC decided to award the Vth Olympic Winter Games in 1940 to Garmisch-Partenkirchen, the second time the Winter Games had been awarded to Germany.

The Games of 1940 and 1944

The Games of 1940 were not held, due to World War II. Ironically, they had been awarded to Tokyo. When the Japanese indicated that they could not host them,[4] the Games were awarded to Helsinki, which began preparations to host them, but the war prevented them from being celebrated. Nor, for the same reason, was it possible to organize the 1944 Games. After the war, the British were asked if they could stage the Games in London and agreed to do so.[5] Neither Germany nor Japan was invited to participate. The Soviet Union had not yet applied for recognition by such a bourgeois organization as the IOC and would not do so until 1951. It, too, was recovering from the ravages of war and was in the process of absorbing all the internal punishment Stalin's dictatorship could inflict, which may well have been worse than the war itself.

Helsinki, 1952: The Soviets Arrive

The 1952 Olympic Games brought with them the entry of the Soviet Union into the modern Olympic Movement,[6] and with it, the cold war. The tensions that would exist from that time until the 1988 Olympics in Seoul were to mark the Olympic Games as potential powderkegs for political posturing, rhetoric, and reaction, each time they occurred. Those who expected such fireworks were seldom disappointed. It started right away; the Soviet team in Helsinki would not stay in the main Olympic Village, for "security" reasons. The Soviets were not worried about security in the conventional sense. They wanted to protect their athletes from contamination by the decadent West, to lock in rather than to keep out. This mentality was given more visible form a few years later with the erection of the Berlin Wall. In retrospect,

[4] This advice was given to the IOC in a cable dated June 6, 1939, sent by the mayor of Tokyo.

[5] It is possible that there might have been some serious interest on the part of New York to organize the Games in 1948, but it was clear that the European-dominated IOC was of the view that the expenses of travel to America may have been beyond European sports budgets so soon after the war, so the preemptive decision was taken to find a host city in Europe. The Executive Board took the unusual step of recommending that the members of the IOC vote for London.

[6] The USSR NOC applied to the IOC for recognition on April 23, 1951, and recognition was granted by the IOC Session in Vienna on May 7, 1951. In addition, two IOC members were co-opted in the USSR; the first was Konstantin Andrianov, at the same Vienna Session, and the second was Alexei Romanov, at the IOC Session in Oslo in February the following year.

it might have been a good time to make a point with the Soviets, but the opportunity was allowed to pass.[7]

There was no doubt that the Soviets had, as the American expression goes, "come to play" at the Olympics. Their athletes were well prepared and performed superbly. The cold war moved, with surprising ease, onto the playing fields, and the United States was served notice that its domination of Olympic events was at serious risk.

Melbourne, 1956

The 1956 Olympic Games in Melbourne, Australia, were held in the recent aftermath of the brutal Soviet suppression of the Hungarian revolution. The world had been outraged, not just at the apparent expansion of the Soviet domination of central and eastern Europe, but at the savagery with which the dissidents in Hungary had been crushed. Three European countries boycotted the Olympic Games, protesting the presence of the Soviet Union: the Netherlands, Spain, and Switzerland.[8] As noted in the previous chapter, Spain had its own peculiar relationship with the Soviet Union, and its Olympic protest was, undoubtedly, connected with the general tensions between the two countries. Less noticed was the boycott by Iraq and Lebanon, to protest the actions by the British, French, and Israelis in Egypt during the Suez crisis. Another significant boycott occurred when the People's Republic of China, which had entered the Games, withdrew at the last minute in protest over the entry by Formosa (Taiwan). This "China problem" would require a quarter of a century to resolve.

The Games, of course, continued without the missing countries.[9] Few students of Olympic history will forget the remarkable water polo final match between the USSR and Hungary, in which much more was at stake than a mere gold medal. There has probably never been a tougher match nor so much vicarious joy shared with the Hungarian

[7] The Soviets and other socialist teams were housed separately in a second Olympic Village in Otaniemi, seven kilometers outside of Helsinki.

[8] Switzerland had, apparently, reconsidered its decision, but by the time it had done so, it was too late, it said, to make the necessary travel arrangements.

[9] The IOC Executive Board had considered the possibility of censuring the NOCs that had withdrawn, but after lengthy debate, decided not to do so. The IOC issued a couple of moderately worded press releases expressing sorrow that the withdrawals had occurred and drawing attention to the ancient tradition of an Olympic truce.

team when it emerged from the pool, literally bloody, but victorious. Hungarian pride needed nothing from the rest of the world to prove its existence, but the rest of the world rejoiced in the tangible expression of it in such a forum, where the "good guys" actually won against all odds.[10]

Rome, 1960

The 1960 Games in Rome were special, as only the Italians could make them. For the athletes, they were a delight with a particular Italian magic, tiptoeing between superb performances, near disasters — rescued at the last moment by some miracle — and outright fun. For a change, political difficulties were fairly minor and did not overshadow the event itself. They would be the last Games of innocence for some time to come. This is not to say, however, that they were devoid of political problems. Taiwan was forced to compete under the name Formosa, and in the Opening Ceremony parade, behind the bearer of the sign indicating the name of the team, marched another carrying a sign that solemnly recorded "Under Protest." The Germans were still forced by the IOC to compete as a single team, fifteen years after the end of World War II. The problem of South Africa was beginning to loom as a major issue, since the legislative machinery establishing apartheid had been enacted,[11] and the South African sporting authorities had been strangely acquiescent. In fact, although it could not have been predicted during the Games in Rome, these would be the last Games for South African athletes until Barcelona, some thirty-two years later.

Tokyo, 1964

The choice of Tokyo as the host city for the 1964 Olympics was, in a way, a quasi-political statement by the IOC, reflecting what was, by then, a worldview that Japan had served its time in the wilderness following the war and could now look forward to inviting the world to

[10] The fact that the Hungarian Olympic team was in Melbourne at all was an accomplishment of some note. The IOC had managed to get the team from Budapest to Prague, notwithstanding the political chaos, and then to Melbourne. This was, perhaps, the first manifestation of a modern Olympic truce.

[11] The legislation was complicated and took many forms, but the principal elements of it were contained in the Native Consolidation Act No. 25 of 1945, the Reservation of Separate Amenities Act of 1953, and the Group Areas Act No. 36 of 1966. There were many other statutes and subordinate legislation as well.

Tokyo under peaceful circumstances. The Japanese spared no effort to make the Games a success. It was a complete national effort, beginning as early as 1954, one that underlined the remarkable ability of the Japanese to focus on a long-term project and to work collectively for the benefit of Japan. The Games were a marvel of organization and precision, a demonstration for the world to see (on only the second occasion of widespread commercial television coverage of the Games) what Japan had become. For the close observer, it was also an intimation of what Japan was in the process of becoming.

South Africa was prevented from competing due to pressure on the IOC from the African countries, who could count on support from the Soviet Union and its allies. The decision to exclude South Africa from the Tokyo Games was not made with particular grace by the IOC, but it was nevertheless made and, with varying difficulty in succeeding years, continued in place, despite serious lobbying efforts from South Africa and its allies. Their plea: politics and sports should not mix! Coming from a regime that used deliberate political action to create apartheid in sport, and from those sportspeople who had done little, if anything, in protest until their athletes were excluded by the world, this rang somewhat hollow. Nevertheless, many supported this logical inconsistency, and each time the issue was raised, the emotional quotient of the debate was extremely high, threatening the Games with potentially massive walkouts.

Mexico City, 1968

The 1968 Olympic Games had been awarded to Mexico. That these Games would be difficult must have been foreseen by the IOC, unless it had allowed itself to become completely enchanted by the warmth of Latin lobbying. The altitude of Mexico City alone, 2,380 meters, would create a serious problem for every aerobic event lasting more than a couple of minutes. Pollution, although not yet at the present lethal levels, was already severe by any measure. Mexico was not a wealthy country and had, to the outside observer, economic and social problems immense enough to be virtually unsolvable. As the Games got closer, political unrest grew in the country. Protests began to occur, using the forthcoming Olympic Games as a focal point for generalized concerns. The culmination was a terrible riot; the Mexican authorities fired on the crowd, killing more than two hundred students. Although this did not result in a cancellation of the Games (the government reached an agreement with the students' Committee of 210),[12] the memory of this event was to mar them and to remain associated with the Olympic Games, not with Mexican political problems.

1970: Expulsion of South Africa from the Olympic Movement

South Africa had not competed in the Mexico City Games, despite the considerable efforts of IOC president Avery Brundage, riding his personal horse of "politics and sports should not mix" — by now a nag that was clearly tiring — to allow its participation.[13] At its Session in Amsterdam in May 1970, less than two years after the Mexico City Olympics, the IOC would vote to expel the South African national Olympic committee from the Olympic Movement due to apartheid in sport in that country.

The decision to expel South Africa was based on the application of apartheid to sport. The IOC has never purported to make decisions that properly fall within the jurisdiction of the political authorities in any country. Its aim has always been, however inarticulately expressed, to try to establish the autonomy of sport within the larger political environment. Accordingly, the IOC has always regarded the South African "problem" in the context of the Olympic Movement from the perspective of sport and has studied the question of discrimination within sport, not within society as a whole. This does not mean, of course, that the wider human aspects of apartheid were unnoticed by the IOC or condoned by it in any way. It merely reflects the IOC's jurisdiction of competence to act. And it did act.

The Olympic Movement, under the leadership of the IOC, was the first international organization to exclude South Africa from membership and to establish a complete moratorium on contacts with South Africa. Governments and other organizations followed but have acted, on many occasions, more with words than deeds. The sport sanctions, however, were universally applied within the Olympic Movement and were very effective in isolating South Africa for almost three decades.

[12] Agreement was reached with the Committee of 210 on October 9, 1968, and the Games were held between October 12 and October 27, 1968.

[13] There was more than the usual confusion on this occasion. A vote had been taken at the IOC Session in Grenoble just prior to the 1968 Olympic Winter Games to allow South Africa to compete, with the result that South Africa received an invitation to participate. A new vote was taken in the Tokyo Session to rescind the invitation.

Only history will provide a more reflective judgment than can now be advanced regarding the contribution of the Olympic Movement to the changes within South Africa. But, if a prejudgment can be ventured, now that the final piece of legislation in South Africa creating the legal apartheid regime has been repealed, the sports moratorium led by the IOC will be recognized as one of the most important international responses to apartheid devised by any organization. It brought home, to every South African, in a direct way that could not be explained away by politicians, the total disapproval of the world of the fact of apartheid as a political system. The Olympic Movement can, and should, be pleased with the contribution which it has made toward its dismantlement.

There is often confusion concerning the delineation between the Olympic Movement and sport in general. Not all sports are part of the Olympic Movement. Some, including most professional sports, exist and are organized quite apart from the international structure that makes up the Olympic Movement. These include, for example, sports such as cricket, rugby, golf, most aspects of professional tennis, and others. There is seldom any connection between the organizational structures that govern the Olympic sports and the non-Olympic sports. The failure to grasp this fact was to lead to a tragic mistake in judgment by the African countries just prior to the Montreal Olympics in 1976, which was compounded by a lack of sensitivity and attention on the part of the IOC.

Munich, 1972: Terrorism and Apartheid

Munich, in 1972, was intended to be for Germany what Tokyo was for Japan in 1964. Virtually the entire infrastructure of this Bavarian city had been rebuilt in preparation for the Olympic Games, and the cheering of the crowds to be heard in 1972 was to be for the performance of world-class athletes, rather than the more sinister support of the Third Reich three decades earlier. There was added excitement in Germany, since, for the first time since the war, the "two Germanies" would compete separately. The host was West Germany, and East Germany was making its first appearance as a completely independent and autonomous team, with its own flag and anthem.[14] For the crowds in Munich,

[14] The NOC of East Germany was definitively recognized by the IOC at its Session in 1965. Prior to this time, and despite provisional recognition of an NOC at the 1955 Session of the IOC, the two countries were forced to compete as a single team, reflecting the prevailing Western

there seemed to be little difference between the two teams: the athletes were German, regardless of the artificial distinction forced upon them by postwar politics.

The politics of apartheid escalated to a new level in Munich. South Africa itself had been eliminated as a factor in 1970, by the decision of the IOC to expel its national Olympic committee from the Olympic Movement. The new target became Rhodesia, no longer a British colony following its Unilateral Declaration of Independence in 1965. Many of the opponents of apartheid thought that, in essence, there was effective apartheid in Rhodesia, despite differences in its legal structures and those in South Africa.[15] Sufficient political pressure had been placed on West Germany for it to agree not to recognize passports from Rhodesia as valid for entry into Germany. There was at least some basis for such a position as a matter of international law, but it is clear that such a stand would never have been taken had the Olympic Games (and their importance to Germany) not been at stake. The "neatness" of this distinction enabled the Germans not to renege on their commitment to allow entry to all athletes to Germany on the basis of a valid passport together with the Olympic identity card that served as, in effect, a visa.

The situation became even more complicated when Great Britain indicated that the team could travel as British subjects using British passports; there was no basis for Germany not to recognize British passports. This reduced the matter to naked politics. The African countries would not participate if Rhodesia took part. The IOC was put to the choice. With the greatest reluctance, it agreed to exclude the athletes from Rhodesia. But it was clearly unconvinced that there was a complete parallel between the situations in South Africa and in Rhodesia, and it deeply resented having to make such a choice at the last minute.

---

political view that there was only one legitimate Germany, West Germany, having its seat in Bonn. A hybrid solution applied for the 1968 Games; there would be separate teams, but they would march together and have a single flag.

[15] The IOC later established a commission to look into the matter, consisting of Sylvio de Magalhaes Padilha (Brazil), Syed Wajid Ali (Pakistan), and James Worrall (Canada). The commission visited Rhodesia in April 1974 and concluded that, though there were some elements of difference between the legal systems in place in Rhodesia and South Africa, there were, nevertheless, many similarities and significant evidence of racial discrimination in sport. The report of the commission was accepted by the IOC at its Session in Lausanne in May 1975, and IOC recognition of the NOC in Rhodesia at that time was withdrawn. Recognition of the NOC in Zimbabwe was granted again in 1980.

All this was overshadowed by the tragedy that struck a few days into the Games; on September 5, 1972, Black September terrorists broke into the Olympic Village and took several Israeli athletes and team officials hostage.[16] Despite negotiations and rescue efforts by the German authorities, the incident ended in the death of the hostages. It created a new imperative for security at the Olympic Games. Prior to Munich, security generally meant crowd control, and the fences around the Olympic Village were essentially to keep the curious from bothering the athletes and, in accordance with the social mores of the time, the male athletes separated from the female. Thereafter, the security portfolio became deadly serious.

One of the principal decisions that the IOC had to make in Munich was whether the Games should be canceled in the wake of the hostage tragedy. There was some pressure for a cancellation, but the IOC undoubtedly made the right decision to have a day of mourning, coupled with a memorial service for the slain Israeli team members, and then to continue with the Games. It would have been worse to allow the terrorist action, however obscene, to have brought a world event to a standstill.

Possibly one of the most unfortunate aspects of the whole matter was the apparent equation by IOC president Avery Brundage, during his speech at the memorial service, of the terrorist act with the political action by those who succeeded in preventing the participation of Rhodesia in the Games. Though nothing can excuse Brundage from having made this wholly inappropriate comparison, it can, perhaps, be understood as the result of his personally held conviction that sport should (however unrealistic this might be) be entirely free from politics and from the fact that at eighty-two years of age and after twenty years at the helm of the IOC, he simply had lost his sense of perspective. Whatever the reason, it was not his finest moment.

It was just as well that he was to retire at the end of the Games, to be replaced by the affable Irishman, Michael Morris, The Lord Killanin. It was a mark, however, of how deeply Brundage was affected by the Munich tragedy that he told Killanin, upon turning over the reins of the IOC to him, that the Munich Olympics would be the last Olympic Games.[17]

[16] The break-in and hostage taking occurred during the night of September 4–5. Patrolling units of the security service heard the noises at 4:55 A.M. on September 5.

[17] This is recounted by Killanin in his Olympic autobiography, *My Olympic Years*.

Montreal, 1976: Costs, China, and Boycotts

Brundage was wrong, of course, but the Montreal Games in 1976 had their own set of problems that earned them a special place in Olympic history. They were to take place in the aftermath of the Munich disaster, which meant that concerns over security were heightened beyond anything previously experienced in relation to the Olympic Games.

At the press conference following the Olympic Congress organized in Varna, Bulgaria, in the fall of 1973, Lord Killanin was asked a typical endless question along the lines of "In view of the Munich tragedy and the concern throughout the world for the safety of the athletes and the concern for the future of the Olympic Games and the possibility that such an outrage might occur again in the future, have you discussed the matter of security with the Montreal Organizing Committee?" Exhausted by this question, delivered without pause for breath, the journalist fell back, waiting for Killanin's revelations. "Yes," said Killanin. The penny gradually dropped for almost everyone in the room, and there were snickers from the experienced media people, who knew what had just happened. The unfortunate journalist, still waiting for the "real" answer, pressed on, oblivious to the obvious. "But," he continued, "what have you discussed?" Killanin, himself a person with journalism in his blood, beamed and pounced. "If I told you that, it would no longer be secure, would it?" And he went on to the next question, leaving the rudderless journalist helpless in his wake.

Security was, however, a very serious matter, and the Canadian security forces, quite capable in their own right, entered into the fullest cooperation with similar forces around the world to share information and tactics that might have a bearing on the Games. The result was extremely tight security with an absolute minimum of visibility, the perfect combination of tact, discretion, and complete professionalism in a potentially difficult situation.

Though far from the least of the problems, security eventually paled in comparison with other issues affecting the Montreal Games. Montreal would soon become the example, the specter, of what could go wrong financially with the hosting of the Olympic Games and would be pointed to as the reason why cities should be wary of bidding to host them. As in all matters, there was some truth to the warnings, but also considerable fiction and some actively mischievous fabrication of "facts."

Montreal made the classic mistake of Olympic hosts by not separating the capital and operating budgets. There was a great deal of infrastructure created in Montreal prior to the Olympic Games. A stadium was built, roads were improved, the metro system was extended, and other facilities were constructed.[18] Was it reasonable to regard all such investments as applicable to the two-week event of the Games, or should they have been treated as part of the infrastructure required in a city of three million people? Most of the facilities are still in active use, and the subsequent users should bear a portion of the capital costs involved. Montreal never made that clear to the public or the media, which accounts, at least in part, for the perception that the Montreal Olympics cost more than a billion dollars. In fact, the Organizing Committee, on an operating basis, made a considerable profit, so the Games, as an event, did not involve a net cost. Also overlooked in the media enthusiasm for a disaster scenario was the fact that the Organizing Committee made capital contributions from its operating profits to help with the financing of some of the construction projects.

There were two major political problems that related to the 1976 Olympic Games themselves. One, the "two Chinas" issue, has been described in part in the previous chapter. It was not particularly well handled on the spot by the IOC, partly, no doubt, because it was raised at the last minute and partly, perhaps, because Killanin, who strongly favored the reentry of the People's Republic of China into the Olympic Movement, even on its own terms (the withdrawal of recognition of Taiwan), may not have been wholly averse to letting the continued presence of Taiwan be a thorn in the side of the IOC.

At the time this particular problem erupted, I was not yet a member of the IOC, nor even the president of the Canadian Olympic Association (COA). I was a thirty-four-year-old lawyer and had been the secretary of the COA for some eight years. My firm's office was only a block away from the Queen Elizabeth Hotel, which was the IOC hotel during the Games and the location of all its meetings prior to the Games. I was at work one morning when the phone rang, and I was informed by Norma Macmanaway, Killanin's personal secretary, that "Lord Killanin would speak with me." Following this revelation, Killanin did speak with me. What was I going to do about this mess regarding China that my government had caused? What was *I* going to do? I told him I did

[18] There was a great deal of uncertainty about whether or not the facilities would be ready in time for the Games, which added to the many other concerns surrounding the Games, including obviously burgeoning costs and project management that was less than perfectly organized.

not know what *I* was going to do. What did he *want* me to do? We agreed that I should come over to his suite at the hotel forthwith. I braved the security, which was clearly suspicious of the bona fides of anyone under the age of sixty meeting with the IOC president, and arrived within five minutes of the summons.

Killanin and James Worrall, the Canadian member of the IOC and a member of the IOC Executive Board, explained the details of the problem and the position of the Canadian government regarding China and Taiwan. The government's legal position was exceedingly tenuous, but Pierre Trudeau, the prime minister of the day, was very pro-China and simply would not budge on the issue. Taiwan was welcome but could not compete using its official Olympic name, the Republic of China NOC. It had become a complete political poker game. The Canadian government had determined that the IOC was too indecisive to impose its will and acted accordingly.

With the boundless confidence of youth, I told Killanin how I thought he could outbluff Trudeau. His secretary, I said, should call Trudeau's office and say that as a matter of courtesy she was calling to advise the prime minister's office that Lord Killanin would be holding a press conference that evening at Mirabel Airport prior to boarding an aircraft to return to Lausanne. At the press conference, she should say, Lord Killanin would be announcing that the 1976 Olympic Games had been canceled by the IOC due to the refusal of the Canadian government to honor its unequivocal commitment to allow free and unrestricted entry to all delegations. In view of the impending 1980 Olympics in Moscow, the IOC felt it had no alternative but to enforce its fundamental rule regarding access by the Olympic Family to the host country. Whatever competitions might be held in Montreal would not be the Olympic Games. The IOC would be withdrawing its imprimatur.

I said he would have to do this the same day, because each day that went by lessened the value of that threat. To this day I believe the card would never have had to be played, since Trudeau could not afford to have all the preparations for the Games go to waste. He would have told the Chinese he had done his best to accommodate them, but that it was impossible for him to destroy the Games on that single issue. Killanin hesitated until it was too late, and the Canadian government prevailed. Taiwan refused to accept the Canadian position and did not participate.

Almost unnoticed in the flood of publicity surrounding the highly visible China-Taiwan issue, an even more serious problem was fomenting. Certain African sport leaders had focused on the exchange of rugby teams between New Zealand and South Africa and wanted the New Zealand delegation to be prevented from participating in the Olympic Games as a result of New Zealand's policy of not preventing all sporting contacts with South Africa. The usual threat of a boycott was raised as the consequence of the IOC's refusal to comply with the demand. Either unknown to the African leaders, or conveniently ignored by them, was the fact that the New Zealand NOC had no control or jurisdiction over rugby, which is not an Olympic sport, nor any legal or other ability whatsoever to prevent rugby teams from participating wherever they wanted.[19] The NOC was completely powerless to bring about the isolation of South Africa sought by the Africans in relation to rugby.

The principal leaders of the Africans in Montreal were Abraham Ordia of Nigeria and Jean-Claude Ganga of Congo, both well known for their roles in antiapartheid actions. Both were intelligent and highly articulate. Nigeria was the more important country of the two, but Ganga was the better and more emotional advocate. As the positions started to harden and it became clear to Ordia and Ganga that the reasonable compromise that they, as politicians (or at least sport politicians), would have settled for would probably not occur without the IOC's intervention, they sought a meeting with Killanin. By then, they realized that their earlier rhetoric had caused the political leaders back in Africa to move closer and closer to an actual boycott of the Games, which was not what Ordia and Ganga had wanted. Their perspective changed dramatically, and they were now desperate to reverse the political momentum that they had created and to save the African athletes from being recalled by the political leaders at home.

They needed an audience with Killanin to put something in place, even if it were merely a publicly announced, best-efforts undertaking by the New Zealand Olympic delegation to appeal to the rugby authorities on its return to New Zealand and some sort of blessing of their position by the IOC. Anything. But there was a problem. Access to Killanin was made difficult by Killanin himself, who had little or no

[19] As Manfred Ewald, former minister of sport and president of East Germany's NOC, points out in the excerpt from his book in the July 25, 1992, issue of *Sport Intern* (vol. 24, no. 14), South African rugby teams played regularly in the United States and Ireland, but no calls were made for the exclusion of their Olympic teams.

use for either Ordia or Ganga. He delayed granting them the meeting that they wanted until it was too late. On the eve of the Opening Ceremony, the political instructions from Africa were received: the athletes of almost all the African countries, some of them virtually certain Olympic champions or medalists, were to return to their homes without competing. Those in transit were stopped. Only Senegal and Ivory Coast refused to give such instructions, and their athletes participated in this once-in-a-lifetime experience of the Olympic Games. It was a terrible and arbitrary penalty imposed on the athletes and for no useful purpose. The New Zealand team was in no position to do anything. The politicians should have known that.

This was the first of the major Olympic boycotts, since it was at the last minute and involved many countries. There would be others. But it would be the only Olympic boycott that had at its roots the issue of South Africa and apartheid. Both the Africans and the IOC learned from the Montreal boycott. The IOC would never again allow the representatives of any country, particularly those with an important problem on their minds, to be treated in such a cavalier fashion. The Africans learned that there were some limitations to using Olympic sport as a lever against other sports, in countries where it is not legal to suspend private activities on political grounds. The boycott strategy was continued by Commonwealth nations in response to attitudinal tendencies of the British government when the Commonwealth Games were held in the United Kingdom, but this can be regarded, to some degree, as the exercise of power by the New Commonwealth and a statement against Britain, as much as an effort toward the eradication of apartheid.[20]

Moscow, 1980: A U.S.-Led Boycott

The most serious of the Olympic boycotts was that of the Moscow Games in 1980, when only eighty-one countries took part. The political pressures exerted on many countries by the United States were enormous. The pressures exerted on the national Olympic committees by their own governments and by public opinion were unprecedented. Many of the committees were unable to resist the pressures and "de-

[20] Nigeria and Uganda boycotted the 1978 Commonwealth Games in Edmonton (Canada) on substantially the same issue as the 1976 Olympic boycott, but were not joined by other African or Caribbean countries. There was a much more widespread boycott of the 1986 Commonwealth Games in Edinburgh as a result of British attitudes toward South Africa.

cided" not to participate. In the United States, the U.S. Olympic Committee, after first agreeing to support President Carter in his boycott initiative, began to have second thoughts, but was resolutely forced by the Carter administration to come to heel, voting to boycott by a 2–1 margin. The USOC's reluctance to vote for a boycott was serious enough that President Carter was forced to declare that an Olympic boycott was a matter of "national security" to the United States, a position that, even at that time, was ludicrous.

A considerable number of diplomatic favors were called in on this venture. It would be interesting to speculate what was the real "cost" to the United States of its Olympic boycott.[21] The Soviets were, predictably, enraged by the effort, but once the Olympic Movement gathered itself together and refused to move, postpone, or cancel the Games, they became even more resolved to carry on. They were, undoubtedly, stung by the negative response but did not waver in the slightest from their adventure in Afghanistan. If the Olympic boycott was to be the high point of the world's response to Afghanistan, then the Soviets could safely conclude that they were virtually free to act as they considered appropriate in their own perceived self-interest.

The Olympic Movement learned that if it remained united, it was much stronger than most had imagined, including those within the movement itself. Even though many important countries did not participate in Moscow, their sports and Olympic bodies put up a surprisingly effective defense of their autonomy; when the euphoria of self-deception by governments that resorted to "Soviet bashing" by means of the Olympic boycott began to wear off, there came a realization that, perhaps, after all, there *was* something special about the Olympic Games that made them worth keeping as a unique occasion for international understanding, even in times when tensions were at their peak.

Los Angeles, 1984: Soviet Retaliation

Conventional wisdom had it that the Soviets would definitely boycott the Los Angeles Olympics in 1984, in direct retaliation for the U.S.-led boycott of their own Games in 1980. The only question was how many countries would follow them. This looked like a good bet: a certainty,

[21] During our time in Lake Placid during the Winter Games, the late Giulio Onesti, one of the IOC members in Italy, likened the whole political response to the Soviet invasion of Afghanistan by attacking the Olympic Games as "political onanism."

if Brezhnev were still to be in power. On November 10, 1982, Brezhnev died and his place as general secretary of the Communist Party was taken by Yuri Andropov, former chairman of the KGB. He proved to be much more equivocal on the issue, and it began to look very much as if the Soviets would participate in the Games at Los Angeles. In fact, at the IOC Session immediately preceding the Sarajevo Olympic Games in February 1984, Konstantin Andrianov, the senior Soviet member of the IOC, elected in 1951 when the USSR first entered the Olympic Movement, gave a most laudatory review of the preparations by the Los Angeles organizers. This was regarded as a signal of significant import.

Andropov had been in failing health for several months and died on February 9, during the Sarajevo Games. He was replaced by Konstantin Ustinovitch Chernenko, an old friend and ally of Brezhnev. Chernenko was not regarded as a very strong successor and was thought (or at least hoped) to be the last of the old Bolsheviks to lead the Soviet Union, as the younger generation prepared to move into power. But leader he was, at a critical time for the Soviet decision with respect to Los Angeles, and he was heavily influenced by USSR president Andrei Gromyko, a longtime hard-liner in Soviet-American relations. Gromyko was strongly opposed to Soviet participation in Los Angeles. The diplomatic wars started again, in earnest. Provocative statements abounded, on both sides. The U.S. State Department cared little about the Olympic Games, and there was insufficient communication between the Reagan White House and the State Department to impress upon the latter the importance to the United States of having successful Games. The Soviets let it be known that they had grave concerns about "security" for their athletes in Los Angeles.[22]

The first official sign of a significant shift in the winds had been a telex dated April 11, 1984, from the USSR NOC president, Marat Gramov,[23] expressing concerns about Los Angeles and requesting an emergency meeting of the IOC Executive Board to discuss "flagrant"

[22] The United States had no interest in giving guarantees for the security of the athletes. East Germany asked for similar guarantees, which they might have been able to use against the pressure from the Soviets, but these, too, were refused. Their perception at the time was that the United States was not at all sure it wanted East Germany to be present at its Games.

[23] The former president of the Soviet NOC and minister of sports, Sergei Pavlov, had been banished to Mongolia as the Soviet ambassador in early 1983 and had been replaced in both positions by Marat Gramov, an apparatchik more in tune with the new administration.

violations of the Olympic Charter by the Los Angeles Olympic Organizing Committee (LAOOC).[24] Since Gramov was also the Soviet sports minister, this was an ominous development. Samaranch did not call for a full Executive Board meeting but did organize a meeting in Lausanne on April 24 with the three IOC vice presidents, representatives of the Soviet NOC, and representatives of LAOOC. The meeting was generally constructive, and a relatively optimistic press statement was agreed to by the participants and issued, giving some hope that a crisis might be averted.

Two days later, Samaranch received confidential indications from within the USSR that Soviet participation in the Los Angeles Games was unlikely. He quickly consulted the IOC vice presidents and requested a meeting with U.S. president Ronald Reagan to attempt to get a letter from Reagan addressed to Chernenko, which Samaranch could deliver to Chernenko, regarding the support of the U.S. government for the Games and an assurance of security during the Games. A meeting was agreed to and set for May 8. A day after the meeting was set, April 27, a U.S. State Department official, Edward Derwinski, advised the USSR ministry of foreign affairs that all matters decided at the April 24 meeting had been declared "null and void." Further, the U.S. administration would not disassociate itself from the alleged anti-Soviet activities. This was hardly helpful to a delicate situation. On the contrary, it was so negative that it was either inept beyond belief or deliberately provocative.

Samaranch flew to Washington on May 8, 1984, for the scheduled meeting with U.S. president Reagan. Perhaps, knowing of that meeting, and not wanting the U.S. government to do anything that would make it more difficult to boycott, the Soviets convoked an emergency plenary session of their NOC and, on the same day, voted not to participate in the Los Angeles Olympic Games. It was, ironically, the same day that the Olympic torch arrived in the United States, to begin one of the most successful torch relays in Olympic history. With the news of the Soviet decision not to participate in the Games, Reagan was advised by Secretary of State George Shultz not to write directly to

[24] During April, the U.S. embassy in Moscow requested the Soviet NOC to submit the names of its Olympic delegation to Los Angeles for visa applications, which was a clear breach of the Olympic Charter. The Charter provides that the Olympic identity card, when accompanied by a valid passport or other identity document, is all that is required to enter the host country for the period of the Games. The request for visa applications would have been a deliberate provocation and was likely intended as such by the State Department.

Chernenko. Instead, he gave Samaranch a letter addressed to Samaranch, with the request and approval to show it to Chernenko. Written confirmation of the Soviet decision was sent to Samaranch by Gramov on May 9.

Samaranch telexed Gramov the next day regarding the decision and requested a meeting with Soviet leader Chernenko. To be sure this request was not buried, he caused the IOC to issue a press release to the international press agencies stating that he had requested such a meeting. On May 14, a Soviet delegation arrived in Lausanne to advise Samaranch that the Soviet decision regarding Los Angeles was final and that he should bear this in mind when considering any possibility of visiting Moscow. This was a diplomatic way of saying that there would be no meeting with Chernenko, although the delegation did make it clear that its advice was not the formal reply of the Soviets to the official request Samaranch had sent to Gramov.[25]

The penultimate effort with respect to Soviet participation was to hold an extraordinary meeting of the IOC Executive Board in Lausanne, May 18–19, 1984, at which representatives of the Soviet NOC, the USOC, and the LAOOC were present. There was no resolution of the matter. The LAOOC made it clear that the reported abrogation by the U.S. State Department of the agreements reached on April 24 had been stated at a very low level within the department and that the secretary of state himself had confirmed that the United States would support the decisions taken at that meeting. It was far too late for that assurance to have any beneficial effect.[26]

Finally, Samaranch did travel to the USSR on May 30–31, hoping to meet with Chernenko. He did not. Reporting on this initiative to a meeting of the IOC Executive Board held at the Sorbonne on June 23, the ninetieth anniversary of the founding there of the IOC, Samaranch said he knew there was no hope. From his personal knowledge of Soviet diplomacy, he could tell the moment he arrived in Moscow that the doors were closed. Even the level of the state guest house assigned to him conveyed its own message, as did the junior level of the officials

[25] Samaranch spoke with Gramov on May 16; during the conversation Gramov had the effrontery to state that the Soviet political authorities were not involved in the decision not to participate in Los Angeles.

[26] In June, U.S. president Ronald Reagan considered sending a personal invitation to Chernenko to attend the Games, but was persuaded by Secretary of State George Shultz that such a gesture would damage U.S.-Soviet relations.

with whom he was permitted to speak. Though he had suspected that it was a hopeless mission from the outset, he wanted the record to be clear that he had exhausted every possible means of trying to bring about Soviet participation at the Games.

Thoughts then turned to the question of damage control. Although the Soviets had announced their decision as entirely personal to the Soviet Union, due to "security" concerns, and had said that they would not try to influence anyone else not to participate, this was, of course, diplomatic nonsense. There was concerted diplomatic pressure exerted on allies and friends to support the Soviet position and to stay away from Los Angeles. The diplomatic roles were the opposite of the stances taken only four years earlier, but pursued with no less vigor. This time, the IOC was much faster off the mark and conducted, under Samaranch's direction, a spirited campaign in favor of participation in the Games in all the countries that were thought to be susceptible to the unadmitted, but active, blandishments of the Soviet Union. To its belated credit, the U.S. State Department finally woke up to the prospect of seriously damaged Games and began to work in a positive manner to help stop the spread of a boycott.

The world was tiring of Olympic boycotts. In some respects, the Olympics are a microcosm of world affairs. They have the same drama and excitement. There are winners and losers; heroes and the occasional villain; all races, colors, and political systems; egos and superstars; plots and counterplots; all the stuff of the human condition. The Olympics are a model that everyone can understand. They provide people with a concept of a world in which good things can happen. People *want* the world to succeed. They want the Olympics, as a miniworld, to succeed. There is inordinate disappointment and bitterness when the Olympics do not work out according to the idealized script.

Even in the Soviet camp, there was no great enthusiasm for support of the boycott. The Warsaw Pact countries saw no reason to support the idea. If the Soviets had a security problem, which they privately doubted, that was too bad. Nobody was after the Poles, the Hungarians, the East Germans, or any of the others. They were not worried about security. Easily said. Not so easily explained to your Soviet Big Brother. In most of the countries involved, there were major economic pressures that the Soviets could apply. And, of course, the presence of Soviet troops had a sobering effect on those countries that might have been tempted to separate sport from the usual political considerations. Even so, it was clear that the Soviet pressures were creating an unusual amount of tension within the eastern bloc countries and adding strain to an already difficult series of relationships.

In the end, the Soviets were not even able to keep all the Warsaw Pact countries in a state of comradely solidarity. In a move that astounded many political observers, Romania announced that its team would participate in Los Angeles.[27] This was a stunning propaganda victory for the Americans. Less surprising, but no less important, was the participation of Yugoslavia, the warm and charming host of the 1984 Olympic Winter Games earlier in the year. Yugoslavia had enjoyed, principally due to the remarkable character of its president, Tito, a unique, almost arm's-length relationship with the Soviet Union. Also helping to mitigate the damage was the first participation of the People's Republic of China, a further sign that not all socialist countries were prepared to follow a Soviet lead on this occasion. Their other lobbying efforts were equally unspectacular. A mere fourteen countries refused the invitation to Los Angeles on the basis of the Soviet lead.[28]

[27] It certainly astounded the delegates present at the meeting of Socialist Ministers of Sport in Prague on May 23–24, 1984. Samaranch had attended the meeting and was exposed to a litany of complaints about both Los Angeles and Seoul, coupled with announcements by the various delegations that they would not participate in Los Angeles. In the midst of this depressing dirge, President Alexa of the Romanian Olympic Committee intervened by stating that the meeting was important because of the unfortunate situation that had arisen. Sport, he said, should be used to spread comprehension and peaceful respect among peoples. Romanian athletes and officials *would* take part in the Los Angeles Games to represent sport as a means of peace. He emphasized the importance of the IOC in international understanding and peace. All the Romanian national federations were ready to cooperate with the other NOCs and IFs in the interest of consolidating the unity of the Olympic Movement and of the IOC. There was complete shock in the room; apparently there had been absolutely no prior intimation that the Romanians would "break ranks" on the boycott.

[28] The fourteen were: the USSR, Afghanistan, Angola, Bulgaria, Cuba, Czechoslovakia, Democratic People's Republic of Korea, East Germany, Hungary, Laos, Mongolia, People's Democratic Republic of Yemen, Poland, and Vietnam. Other countries that did not attend, but whose nonparticipation was probably not linked to the Soviet blandishments, were Albania, Brunei, Iran, Libya, and Upper Volta. Limited as was the Soviet success in the boycott effort, it nevertheless orchestrated its series of announcements in order to gain the maximum media coverage of each refusal. The dates of the "no" responses were: May 8, USSR; May 9, Bulgaria; May 10, East Germany; May 11, Vietnam and Mongolia; May 12, Laos and Czechoslovakia; May 16, Hungary; May 17, Poland; May 23, Cuba; May 26, South Yemen; June 1, Ethiopia; June 2, Democratic People's Republic of Korea; June 26, Angola.

CHAPTER 3

The Potential for Boycott and Past Lessons

IN 1981, conditions for the future of the Olympic Games were less than reassuring. Samaranch had a major rebuilding job on his hands. It was, perhaps, fortunate that 1981 was the year of an Olympic Congress, only the second since 1930. An Olympic Congress provides an opportunity for the whole of the Olympic Movement to be together and to examine its future. Different from the normal Sessions of the International Olympic Committee, it assembles all of the international sports federations, national Olympic committees, representatives of the media, athletes, and others to examine fundamental values and missions of the Olympic Movement as a whole.

The previous Congress had been held eight years before in Varna, Bulgaria. It had been a considerable success, despite the fact that, at the outset, no one was entirely certain what its objective was, since virtually none of those present had been involved in the last Congress, held in Berlin in 1930. Once some of the participants finished describing their own special contributions to the Olympic Movement, there were several positive conclusions, including the need to recognize that, although the IOC was the acknowledged leader of the Olympic Movement, it was time to recognize the enormous contribution of the international federations and the national Olympic committees to the movement and to give them the status that their contribution deserved. Several new coordinating committees were established, which would combine the expertise and experience of all organizations. This new coordination proved to be helpful in forming the united response to the efforts to destroy the Moscow Olympics.

The 1981 Baden-Baden Congress could hardly have been held in more beautiful surroundings. The Congress center was the splendid Casino complex, only a stone's throw from the stately and elegant Brenner's Park Hotel, surely one of the loveliest classic hotels in Europe. The Congress, organized by the West German Olympic Committee under the chairmanship of Willi Daume, president of the NOC and one of the two German IOC members, was exemplary in all respects. Interest was considerable, not only because of the selection of the 1988 host cities to be made during the IOC Session immediately following the Congress, but also because the world was curious about how the Olympic Movement would respond to the aftermath of the Moscow Games.

A welcome addition to the mix of those present was a special delegation of athletes, invited to present their views on the Congress themes from their special perspective as Olympic athletes. This innovation proved to be extremely successful. The athletes wrestled with many of the most important issues in sport and presented their views in an impressive and forthright manner. Indeed, so worthwhile was the effort that, following the Congress, the IOC created a special Athletes Commission as one of its many advisory commissions and has since added athlete representatives to virtually every important IOC commission.

But underlying the positive approach of the Congress participants was a sense of unease. Everyone knew just how lucky they had been to dodge the missile launched at the Olympic Movement the year before. The participants included those who had competed in the joyless Moscow Games and those who had been prevented from attending. There were also some present who had genuinely preferred not to attend the Olympic Games in the Soviet Union under the prevailing conditions. There was a definite undercurrent of resentment against the Soviet Union for having created the crisis. The socialist countries were similarly resentful for the insult of the refusal to attend "their" Games. And there was, for perhaps the first time, a realization that the Olympic Games *could* be destroyed, if political forces were to be aligned with that objective in mind. The Games had become an almost irresistible target for opportunists, who had no interest in the Games but fully appreciated the media attention that surrounds them.

The first widespread glimmerings of Samaranch's abilities began to become apparent to the world during the Congress in Baden-Baden. He managed the whole process admirably. The preparation of the main papers was thorough, and the distillation of the main conclusions even more so. He fought off the desire of many to make the Congress a legislative body, able to make binding decisions on behalf of the Olympic Movement, with an ease and style that made the refusal completely nonconfrontational, thereby not only preserving the IOC's place at the head of the Olympic Movement, but actually enhancing its position of leadership. He was masterful in bringing about consensus and involving more and more people in the decision-making processes and structures; this increased sense of ownership was immediately apparent and has been bolstered ever since. Samaranch began to stamp his own style on the Olympic Movement, but with the willing consent of the Movement rather than the tolerance that had accompanied the domination of Avery Brundage in his years at the helm.

An Olympic Solution for the "Two Chinas"

A sample of Samaranch's diplomatic abilities had already been given earlier in the year with the resolution of the long-outstanding problem of the "two Chinas." This had created many difficulties for the IOC and had been escalated to world news just prior to the 1976 Olympics in Montreal. The abortive efforts of the Executive Board to force a solution in 1979 had led to litigation against the IOC by its member in Taiwan, Henry Hsu. An item on the agenda of the 1980 Session of the IOC in Moscow, put there by Lord Killanin, was aimed to expel Hsu as a member of the IOC. The matter was, eventually, not raised.[1] It was my personal view that Hsu was very likely to be successful in his legal proceedings against the IOC. This would have led to further complications.

It was imperative that a solution be found. This matter became one of Samaranch's first priorities as president of the IOC, and by March 1981, the IOC's China formula was in place. Taiwan would change

[1] I had discussed this matter with Henry Hsu during the Session, and he showed me the statement he proposed to read in his own defense. My impression was that it was too wrapped up in the Chinese aspects of the debate, which carried the risk that the predominantly Western members of the IOC might be confused as to the real issue. If the issue was not crystal clear, the IOC members would be likely to follow the direction of Killanin. I offered to stay at the hotal that evening, instead of going to the Bolshoi Theater, and rewrite the statement in a manner that I thought would set out the problem, the reasons for his legal actions against the IOC, and the evident unfairness, in the circumstances, of making any effort to expel him as a member of the IOC. During a coffee break in the Session the next morning, I told Killanin I had done this and that if Hsu was unable to make himself understood by the Session, I was prepared to take on this challenge myself. Killanin asked me whether, in view of all the many other issues before us at the time, I thought it might be better not to raise the question at all. I said I thought that would be a good idea.

the name of its NOC to Chinese Taipai Olympic Committee, adopt a new flag and emblem (which would not be the national flag), and use the Olympic hymn if one of its athletes won a gold medal at the Games. Its status as an NOC would in all respects be fully maintained and respected.[2] This was a compromise that the People's Republic of China was prepared to accept. It would participate as the Chinese Olympic Committee and use its national flag and anthem. The political status of Taiwan need not be addressed directly. The existence of a separate NOC in Taiwan could be "explained" by comparisons with NOCs in other territories that fell short of full statehood, such as colonies or dependencies,[3] and by the fact that, despite the political position of the PRC with respect to Taiwan, it did not seriously assert that it actually controlled sport in Taiwan.

The IOC's formula worked and has been adopted in most, if not all, of the international sports organizations. Its implementation has been generally without incident, although from time to time some elements in Taiwan have been known to inject signs and flags of the Republic of China in violation of the agreement. The IOC has been very firm on such occasions, and the offending behavior has gradually been eliminated. Organizing Committees for the Olympic Games are regularly warned to be on the alert for possible violations of the understanding, and the Chinese Taipei Olympic Committee, together with the IOC members in Taiwan, have been put on formal notice of their responsibilities to ensure that there is full good faith exercised in the carrying out of the agreement.

Often unnoticed by observers of the international situation is that it was the Olympic Movement, through the leadership of the IOC, that was the first institution to find a solution to an international political dilemma that had troubled the world for some thirty years. No other

[2] This was not an easy compromise for Taiwan to accept. I had many discussions with Henry Hsu, urging him to use his influence with the Taiwanese authorities to get their agreement. I thought that if Taiwan were to be excluded, its NOC suspended or de-recognized, or if Hsu's litigation against the IOC were to be unsuccessful, Taiwan would never have an opportunity in the future to have a separate NOC. It was far better, I urged, to remain inside the Olympic Movement under less than ideal conditions than to be completely on the outside. It was a difficult time for Hsu, who was under pressure from all sides on a matter of great importance to all parties involved. Following the settlement of the litigation, the IOC adopted what I have always referred to as the "Hsu Amendment" to the Olympic Charter, which now includes, as part of the oath taken by new members of the IOC, the undertaking to respect all decisions of the IOC "which I consider as not subject to appeal on my part."

[3] For example, Puerto Rico, Bermuda, Hong Kong, and the Netherlands Antilles.

organization had been able to find a formula that enabled the PRC and Taiwan to exist together as independent members of similar status. By any standards of international diplomacy, the IOC's handling of the situation was nothing short of remarkable. It resolved the anomaly of not having the world's most populous country within the Olympic Movement. It did not have to sacrifice one of its existing NOCs. And it extricated itself from a messy piece of litigation brought about by its own miscues.[4]

Troubled Horizons

Consensus and unity within the Olympic Family following the Baden-Baden Congress were all very well, but there were two very difficult challenges ahead for the Olympic Movement at the end of 1981: the Games in Los Angeles and, as a result of its choice of a host city for 1988, those in Seoul. They would occupy much of Samaranch's time. By now, his term as Spanish ambassador in Moscow had finished, and he had become the IOC's first full-time president, residing in Lausanne.[5] This, in itself, was an indication that the IOC had made the right choice. It also created some significant shifts in the administration of the IOC, removing a great deal of the power wielded up to that time by Monique Berlioux, whose largely unchecked influence as director of the IOC and its senior full-time employee had grown enormously in the declining years of Brundage's and during Killanin's presidencies. The only way to reverse this trend was to be physically present and to make the presidential decisions personally, rather than by proxy. Neither Samaranch nor Berlioux was comfortable with the ensuing rela-

[4] In addition, to demonstrate that the solution was not merely a political posturing, in 1988 the IOC co-opted a new member in Taiwan, Ching-Kuo Wu, upon the retirement of Henry Hsu, who had reached the mandatory retirement age of seventy-five the previous year.

[5] His term as ambassador finished on October 16, 1980. His term as IOC president commenced officially on August 4, 1980, after the conclusion of the Moscow Games the previous evening. He took up residence in Lausanne on November 1, 1980, at the Lausanne Palace Hotel. (At the time, the IOC protocol was that the incoming president, who was elected at the Session immediately prior to the Games, took office at the end of the Session; however, the IOC was considered to be "in Session" until the Games had ended. This produced the anomalous situation of an entirely "lame duck" president during the Games and a new president who was elected, but not yet in office. The situation was unsatisfactory enough that the IOC Session followed the advice of le Comte de Beaumont, the senior IOC member in France, and extended Samaranch's first term of eight years by one year, so that the IOC president would henceforth be elected in the year following the Olympic Games. This is a far more sensible cycle of presidential elections.)

tionship. Working conditions between them deteriorated to the point of impossibility, with the result that Berlioux's employment was eventually terminated during the course of the IOC Session in Berlin in early 1985.

Los Angeles: A Special Case

Challenges always face the organizers of Olympic Games. Los Angeles was no exception. The Los Angeles problems were real, but in many respects were the sorts of problems that inevitably spring up around any Olympic Games. Of course, in 1981, the boycott by the Soviets was not yet a reality and would only become a reality in May 1984. Los Angeles had been the only bidder for the 1984 Olympics. This was taken by some uninformed observers as an indication that the Olympic Games, as an institution, were in serious, if not mortal, danger. It was, admittedly, worrisome not to have more than one candidate, not only for the message it delivered, but also because it made negotiations for the best Olympic conditions much more difficult than if there was an alternative in the wings.

On the other hand, there were other perfectly good reasons for there to be only one candidate for the 1984 Games, and for that candidate to be Los Angeles. Los Angeles had bid, in 1970, against both Moscow and Montreal, to host the 1976 Olympics. It finished third. It bid again, against Moscow, to hold the 1980 Games. It lost. By the time of its third bid, most observers thought that there was no doubt that it would win, so other potential candidates were not too keen on taking up what appeared to be a hopeless cause. There had been some speculation that Teheran might also bid. Had it done so, and had it won, there would have been some rather interesting times!

It has always been a condition of an Olympic bid that the host city agree to assume financial responsibility for the Games. The city of Los Angeles would not do so. The Games were to be organized on a private basis or not at all. Despite the best efforts of the IOC to insist on this fundamental position, Los Angeles would not budge, and Killanin had no alternative but to sign an agreement with the Los Angeles Olympic Organizing Committee (LAOOC) to that effect. It was not a popular move within IOC circles and was the forerunner to a good deal of strain between the LAOOC and the IOC. Because the Games were being privately funded, the LAOOC was generally unresponsive to many of the usual requests made by the IOC, the international federations, and the NOCs. The LAOOC staff, taking the lead from its president, Peter Ueberroth, expressed itself as far more concerned with getting the job done than in worrying about some ruffled Olympic feathers — which made the ruffles all the more noticeable. This factor would also cost Ueberroth eventual membership in the IOC, a reward he deserved and ought to have received.

Doomsayers, who were legion, predicted that the infamous Los Angeles smog would ruin the Games and damage the health of the athletes, especially those who competed in endurance events. The Games would be held over too huge an area. Traffic would be intolerable; the freeway system would become paralyzed and turn into gigantic parking lots. Security would be impossible; southern California contained, if not the head office, at least the largest branch office of every organization of "crazies" in the United States. Sites for some of the sports were unavailable, unacceptable, or inconvenient. And so it went. None of the doom came to pass. Those predicting the end of the world have moved on to the next, even more certain, deadline.

The IOC handled the usual crises on a day-by-day basis, with Samaranch making the major calls and Berlioux handling the routine. Often, the main role of the IOC in the period leading up to the Games is to act as referee between the Organizing Committee and the international federations, the latter wanting the best possible installations and some not caring either how much these installations may cost or what possible use the host city may have for them once the Games are over. This is a standard problem in relation to Olympic Games. Since they are the showcase for all of the sports, each international sports federation wants state-of-the-art facilities, with every imaginable bell and whistle, and as much spectator room as possible. Little, if any, serious thought is given to what the host city will do with the facility after the two weeks of the Games are finished. The IOC uses its influence to moderate these demands.

Relations with the mass media are very important. To some degree, the success or failure of the Games is determined by the media. They need the best possible working conditions to cover the Games and to bring them to the hundreds of millions of people around the world who are not attending the events. Handling even the press accreditations is a major task, let alone trying to make it possible for a limited number of media to cover the events when they are understaffed, overworked, and operating on deadlines that vary from continent to continent. It almost always takes the Organizing Committee until the day after the

Closing Ceremony of the Games to appreciate what should have been done.

Undoubtedly, the most complex of the media relationships is that between an Organizing Committee and the domestic media. There appears to be a virtual certainty that, in the host country (and particularly the host city) the media relations will be strained. The pattern moves along predictable lines. When the idea of bidding for the Games first appears, there will be the usual mix of those "for" and those "against." When the Games are won, there is euphoria and everything is positive. In due course, when the realization of the enormity of the task sets in, concern is expressed about the ability of the local organizers to do the job, and every action they take (or do not take) is subjected to intense scrutiny. The organizers' reaction is to resist or restrict access to the media.

Part of the resistance, undoubtedly, arises from the relations between the Organizing Committee and the local press during the preparatory period before the Games. The relationship is, more often than not, confrontational. Many of the negotiations undertaken by the Organizing Committee are confidential in nature, such as the acquisition of sites for certain facilities, discussions with sponsors, preliminary plans for ceremonies, the visual "look" of the Games, and others. The organizers tend to become secretive, usually more than is really necessary, and defensive. This inflames the media, who suspect that matters are being hidden (as opposed to merely not being disclosed) and who then look for negative information or stories to report. At the end, when the Games succeed, the media are proud to participate in the success. There is a virtually chartable pattern to local media coverage prior to the Olympic Games.[6]

The LAOOC perfected the confrontational relationship with the press. Access was severely restricted, and all statements had to be cleared at the highest level, on pain of reprimand or worse. The press was very suspicious of the LAOOC and was not persuaded that what it was told was necessarily true, either in whole or in part. One area in which utmost secrecy was maintained by the LAOOC was the financial aspect of the Games. Statements from the LAOOC, right up to the time of the Games, suggested that, if they were lucky, the Games

[6] ACOG, the Atlanta Organizing Committee for the Centennial Olympic Games in 1996, is now experiencing such unrelenting media attention. It can take cold comfort from the knowledge that it is not the first Organizing Committee to suffer from this, nor will it be the last.

might just break even financially. It came, therefore, as a considerable surprise to learn of the $250 million surplus shortly after the Games concluded.[7]

Solutions to all the problems were found, except for the boycott, but even that was so well contained that the Games were a huge success. Sports officials from the boycotting countries were present, bravely risking the security dangers to which their athletes could not be exposed, some (such as Marat Gramov of the Soviet Union and Günther Heinze of East Germany) sitting resolutely through the U.S. national anthem, demonstrating some sort of solidarity with something. Perhaps, sitting there in the California sun, even the most political of them began to wonder what they had accomplished by denying a generation of their finest athletes the Olympic experience. They may even have begun to consider whether the same thing might happen four years later in Seoul. If it did, it would mean that their athletes would be removed from Olympic competition for twelve years.

Seoul, 1988: What Was in Store?

These problems were mere child's play, compared with what loomed ahead for 1988. Dealing with Games hosted by a superpower can be unnerving at times, because whenever there is a world crisis, the host superpower is bound to be on one side or the other with its rival(s) pursuing an opposite course. It may well be a question worth asking, some day, whether the IOC could best protect itself from disrupted Games if it had a policy of not awarding them to superpowers. Korea was not a superpower, by any means, but it was certainly a super problem.

That there would be trouble created by the DPRK was a foregone conclusion. The North Korean member of the IOC, Kim Yu Sun, left the Session in Baden-Baden as soon as the result of the election was known, clearly under orders from Pyongyang to do so in the event of a victory by Seoul. The Japanese, who might otherwise have been a stabilizing force in the area, appeared to have little incentive to take an active role on behalf of the IOC, which had rejected their bid, and the

[7] At the ANOC meeting in Los Angeles in January 1983, in response to a direct question from A. O. de Sales, president of the Hong Kong NOC, regarding the possibility of a surplus that might be used to help with the expenses of some of the less affluent NOCs, Peter Ueberroth, president of the Los Angeles Organizing Committee, gave his word to the NOCs present that there would not be one cent of surplus from the Games.

Japan-Korea relationship was far from settled. The disputed presence of the United States in Korea was a sore point for the entire Communist bloc. Lack of any form of diplomatic relations with many countries would make the organization of participation by those countries much more difficult than usual. The internal political stability of South Korea was, justifiably, a matter of considerable doubt. Even the nonaligned countries were, in the case of Korea, much more likely to be aligned, and aligned against Korea. Human rights issues were matters of growing concern to the world at large, and the South Korean record was not enviable.[8]

From the South Korean perspective, the successful bid for the Games was an important step in trying to regain some degree of political stability and to establish international confidence in South Korea. Both of those goals had been damaged by the assassination of the former president in 1979 and the subsequent coup by army officers, led by the current president of the country, Chun Doo Hwan. The mere fact of beating the Japanese for the Games was an enormous boost for the Koreans. Certainly, for the regime in power at the time, it provided considerable political capital.[9]

Not surprisingly, the view from North Korea was entirely different. The first unofficial commentary was released, not without coincidence, on November 20, 1981, shortly before the Olympic Council of Asia (OCA) was to decide on the host city for the 1986 Asian Games. Its dogma was that the bid by South Korea to host the 1988 Games was aimed at perpetuating the division of the Korean peninsula, by taking advantage of the international sports event.[10] The idea of Seoul hosting the Olympics was described as a "criminal act against the Korean people

[8] It remains a surprise to many observers that the record of North Korea in the same field, which was considerably less enviable, never seemed to attract nearly the same degree of media or political attention. In January 1988, the U.S. State Department, in its annual report on human rights, named the DPRK as the worst violator in the world.

[9] Subsequent to the decision of the IOC to award the 1988 Olympic Games to Seoul, a number of other international organizations decided to hold major events in Seoul. These included the 1985 International Chamber of Commerce General Assembly (December 1981) and the 1985 World Bank–International Monetary Fund Conference (March 1982).

[10] Newspaper reports credited the reaction to the Voice of the Revolutionary Party for Reunification, a clandestine medium through which the Pyongyang authorities often gave initial reactions to policies and proposals emanating from the South. Typically, such commentary took the form of radio broadcasts meant to be monitored by or on behalf of the intended recipient of the commentary. The mythology is that VRPR broadcasts from Seoul, but it has been traced to the DPRK city of Haeju.

and international community." "South Korea, in its campaign to invite the Games, demonstrated a felonious plot of perpetuating the division of two Koreas."

By the time the reaction became official, the Olympic plot had been extended to the preparation for war and the separate entry of South Korea into the UN. There was official speculation that, since the term of the presidency of the "traitor" Chun Doo Hwan was to expire in March 1988, he was likely to place himself in the position of honorary president of an event expected after the expiration of his term in office. "Furthermore, anti-Communist confrontation and war preparations of the puppet clique would be intensified and tension will increase, which would have no good influence on peace in Asia and the world."[11]

The indications, both informal and official, had little effect on the Asian Games Federation Council, which met in New Delhi in late November 1981 to select a host city for the 1986 Asian Games. In the final analysis, a vote by the council was not necessary, because the two rival candidates contesting the prize, Baghdad, Iraq, and Pyongyang, North Korea, both withdrew their candidacies. The Iraqi bid was withdrawn because of the continuing war with Iran, and Pyongyang clearly preferred to withdraw than to lose in an election to South Korea, not only on general principles, but also so soon after Seoul had been selected as host of the 1988 Olympics. The Seoul delegation said that both China and North Korea would be welcomed and that the safety of their delegations would be guaranteed.

Helping the Seoul Games

Samaranch will never disclose how many times he thought to himself that the IOC had made a huge mistake in granting the Games to Seoul. There is, however, little doubt that he believed it, although in all public statements he was careful never to allow the slightest suggestion of his private misgivings to show. There is also no doubt that he was very worried about the Games. For some, intense worry can be paralyzing. Not so for Samaranch. Faced with the impossibility of reversing the decision, he set out to find the solutions that would make the Games

[11] This was published on December 3, 1981, in the Communist Party daily *Rodong Shinmun*. Japanese expert observers of North Korean affairs said this was a clear indication that the North would boycott the Games. The rhetoric between the North and the South has never been restrained and was seldom less so than in respect of the 1988 Olympic Games.

possible. This was no formless venture, to be pursued without foundation or method.

There was, however, an idealistic underpinning to the effort, which should not be overlooked. No matter how able a diplomat Samaranch may have been, if the "product" he was selling had not been the Olympic Games, he would not have succeeded. The values represented by the Olympic Games made the "sale" possible. An international festival of youth, the finest athletes in the world meeting and competing together, striving to do their best under equal conditions for all, removed, even if only for a short time, from the tensions of the world, sharing the same food, the same accommodations, becoming friends, building respect and friendship. This is the message of the Olympic Games. No one can *really* disagree that such an opportunity should be created, if humanly possible. All that has to be done is to prevent barriers from being put in the way, or to find a way to remove barriers that may already exist. The ideal, however, is clear.

Certain of the elements in the strategy were evident to Samaranch from the outset. Unlike in the past, the IOC would, on this occasion, have to be proactive. It had to carry its own message, and it had to ensure that the IOC and its message reached those who make the decisions. The IOC could not afford merely to react to the positions or statements of others. Nor could the IOC trust others to create the favorable conditions necessary for the Games in Seoul to be successful. It had to construct its own arguments in a manner that would convince the decision makers of their merit and to become personally committed to the solution of any problems.

By the same token, the Brundagian notion that sport and politics do not mix had to be recognized as unrelated to reality in the late twentieth century. In practice, it is evident that sport and politics do indeed mix, at many different levels. For the most part, the mix is successful and is essential, in many parts of the world, if there is to be any organized sport at all. In fact, an important message from the IOC to the constituent members of the Olympic Movement is to establish and maintain the best possible relations with governments, but also, to try to gain acceptance of the need for the autonomy of sport from governmental authorities. The two parties should be able to work together, with the legitimate objectives of each being properly served.

Ignoring the political reality would be fatal to what had to be accomplished with respect to the Seoul Games.

Some means had to be found to ensure that contact could be established between the IOC and the highest levels of government. For Olympic officials, access to such levels of government in the past had been sporadic at best and was generally ceremonial. Furthermore, if the IOC was to become effective in its political relations, such contact had to be maintained on a regular basis and expanded beyond mere formalities, such as the opening of IOC Sessions or the Olympic Games. It had to extend to the political leadership and not be confined to heads of state, whose titles might not be combined with political power. And access had to be available when it was needed; it would do no good to have to wait when an issue needed resolution. In this area, Samaranch had a particular role to play.

Unstated, but nevertheless implicit, in all dealings with governments had to be the message that boycotts of the Olympic Games are not effective tools in the political aresenal. Political leaders needed to be made to understand that the boycott of a host nation does not bring about the desired political result. Instead, it merely punishes the athletes and population of the boycotting country and has little chance of achieving the desired political outcome. Did the departure of the African countries on the eve of the Montreal Games in 1976 prevent New Zealand from competing, or its rugby teams from continuing contact with South Africa? Did the Soviet Union leave either Hungary or Afghanistan because of Olympic boycotts? Did the Olympic boycott in 1980 send a message any stronger about the world's revulsion with the intervention in Afghanistan than had already been delivered through the diplomatic structures, especially when it was clear that no military action was contemplated by any of the countries that opposed the intervention?

Of course, this was not a message that was likely to be well received by all governments, so it had to be delivered indirectly or through back-channel communication. One has to look far afield to find political figures who are prepared to admit that mistakes of judgment, other than by their political opponents, have been made. The public postures remained that each Olympic boycott had sent a "powerful" (or "unmistakable" or "clear" or "convincing" — the lexicon abounds with such diplomatically muscular expressions) message of disapproval to the offending country, and that such distasteful, but necessary, steps would undoubtedly have (or already had had) a positive effect on future conduct. Privately, the political leaders were happy to look for some way to avoid any repetition of such actions. The real cardinal sin in politics is to appear to be inept.

The message that Samaranch had to deliver was the special nature of the Olympic Games and the Olympic Movement, which made them worth protecting, even in troubled times. Following the Olympic Congress in Baden-Baden in 1981, the IOC explored the possibility of trying to organize adoption of a resolution in the General Assembly of the UN, which would have called on member states not to interfere in the Games.[12] Considerable support was generated for the idea, and draft resolutions were prepared and circulated to several governments for advice on terminology and the mechanics of achieving such a consensus.

The proposal was eventually dropped, prior to its introduction in the session of the General Assembly in 1983, because of concern that, due to the very high levels of tension in many parts of the world at the time (particularly in the Middle East), such a resolution ran a high degree of risk of being "hijacked" and used for entirely different purposes than had been intended by the IOC. Once such a resolution was introduced in the General Assembly, a forum in which the IOC had no status, there would be no means for the IOC to withdraw it if the process started to go wrong. It was decided that it would be preferable to have no resolution than to have one that was perverted in some manner.[13]

The 1984 Soviet boycott of Los Angeles was unfortunate in many ways. It was unnecessary. It probably would not have happened had Andropov not died earlier that same year. It probably would not have happened had there not been a reactive change in Soviet leadership that resulted in Chernenko and Gromyko's setting the glacial tone for the Soviet-U.S. relationship, which was not helped by the Reagan administration. On the other hand, its relative failure did begin to send the message that, perhaps, the Olympic boycott was wearing thin as a political response. It also created two unique opportunities for the IOC in its management of the Seoul Games.

[12] Samaranch appointed the author as chairman of the Commission for the Protection of the Olympic Games, which was assigned the responsibility for preparing the documentation and eliciting indications of support from governments of member states in the UN.

[13] The idea, however, was still attractive, and at the meeting of the IOC Executive Board with the NOCs in Mexico on November 12, 1984, Samaranch called upon all the NOCs to explore with their respective governments the support that might be granted for such a resolution. In the meantime, it would be necessary for the Olympic Movement to fight, as it had with respect to the Games in Moscow and Los Angeles, to be sure the Games in Seoul in 1988 would take place as contemplated. Samaranch vowed that the IOC would respect its promises and the contract signed with the city of Seoul. The Olympic Movement's credibility was at stake, not only at the sporting level, but also at the international level in general.

No IOC Sanctions for Boycotters

The first was an uncharacteristic setback for Samaranch as president of the IOC. Samaranch had been bitterly disappointed, although realistic in his expectations, by the rejection of his efforts to persuade the Soviets to participate in Los Angeles. He, with almost everyone else, was frustrated by the seemingly endless series of boycotts that plagued the Olympics. And these were his first Games as president of the IOC. During the weeks before the Los Angeles Games, the media had been calling for some decisive action on the part of the IOC to bring a halt to such actions. Boycotting countries, ran the thought, should be sanctioned in some way, to make them pay a price for their anti-Olympic behavior. Despite some opposition from within the Executive Board, Samaranch proposed to the IOC Session in Los Angeles, immediately prior to the Games, that the IOC take action against national Olympic committees that did not enter teams in the Olympic Games.

Almost immediately, the Session made it clear that this was not the way in which the problem should be faced. Led by Masaji Kiyokawa, a former vice president of the IOC, and, coincidentally, winner of the 100-meter backstroke event in the 1932 Olympic Games in the same city of Los Angeles, several influential members spoke against the imposition of sanctions at this time, just before the Games, and urged that an extraordinary Session of the IOC be held to deal with the whole issue. Quite apart from the philosophical implications of the matter, the imposition of sanctions just prior to the Games would have undoubtedly increased tensions from the Soviet boycott. No one wanted the boycott, based ostensibly on questions of security, to become a self-fulfilling prophecy. Even though the Executive Board had supported his desire to impose sanctions on the spot in Los Angeles, Samaranch read the signals very quickly, limited the debate, and suggested a special Session of the IOC to be held in Lausanne in December that same year. It was typical of his resilience that Samaranch was able to turn what might have been perceived as a rejection (and which, on this occasion, was definitely a rejection) of his policy into a chance to make a quantum leap that would operate to the benefit of the difficult forthcoming Games in Seoul.

Making the Boycotters Part of the Solution

The second opportunity was to make a decisive step in attacking the main potential problem for Seoul, namely, the hopeless political relationship between North Korea and South Korea, exacerbated by the tensions between the USSR and the United States, both of which could be said to have a client state involved in the situation. The first official trip Samaranch made as president of the IOC following the Los Angeles Games was to Moscow.[14] Probably not in itself decisive, it was, nevertheless, a clear signal to the Soviets that the IOC had a genuine understanding of the fact that a problem did exist and that the IOC was both sensitive to the problem and had a desire to involve the Soviet Union in its solution. Whether this approach to the Soviets was a result of his exposure to the Soviet Union during his ambassadorial posting or an unrelated inspiration is a matter of speculation. As a diplomatic message delivered by the IOC, however, it was significant indeed and set the stage for an ongoing relationship with the Soviet Union, which was to prove invaluable over the next four years.

The Soviet Union was fully aware that the Olympic Movement, led by the IOC, with the support of the international sports federations and an overwhelming majority of the national Olympic committees who were free to act, had saved the Moscow Games. This had been accomplished at considerable cost in many countries, so the Soviet Union was definitely in a debtor relationship with the IOC, although it never explicitly acknowledged this debt and was very difficult in the early stages of the preparations for Seoul. For Samaranch to involve them in a solution to the potential political problems in Seoul was both a realistic assessment of their importance in the matter and an implicit reminder that they had a debt to repay. One of the beauties of the diplomatic process is that none of this actually had to be expressed. The mere fact of the official visit taking place and of its being the first such visit after Los Angeles sent the two messages more clearly than a press release and, more important, in a manner that called for no formal acknowledgment, denial, or comment. The diplomatic work could be done discreetly and effectively, out of the public sight, until the fruits of the labor were ready for public consumption.

And there was work to be done. The Soviets were in a difficult position. They had been heavily boycotted in 1980 and were enraged by that insult, which had seemed, to them, to be entirely unrelated to

[14] This trip was on September 19, 1984, where Samaranch would preside over a symposium on Olympic Solidarity, attended by the presidents and secretaries-general of African, Asian, and Latin American NOCs. He also met with Soviet sports minister and NOC president Marat Gramov during the visit.

the protection of their vital interests in Afghanistan. After all, they had not seriously tried to exclude the United States from the Olympics during its involvement in Southeast Asia, or even during its arguably warlike activities in 1960, when Squaw Valley was host to the VIIIth Olympic Winter Games. They were certainly bruised from the boycott of their own Games, but, in matters of security or foreign policy, there was no question whatsoever that the priority, whatever the consequences, lay there rather than with the Olympic Games. This did not reduce their anger over the boycott, and it was this sentiment that led, with the change of power, to the decision to boycott in 1984. The combination of events left them vulnerable and, therefore, potentially more dangerous, in Olympic terms. They clearly needed some care and feeding if they were to be brought back into the fold (and a fold that presented some serious political problems for them).

Samaranch made an ostentatious point of attending each and every annual meeting of the Socialist Ministers of Sport, no matter where it was held. During such gatherings, he always addressed the full meeting of ministers with the message of the Olympic Movement in his capacity as president of the IOC. He also arranged to have private meetings with most, if not all, of the delegations present. Such one-on-one occasions served both to deliver the message in less formal circumstances than the full meeting of ministers and also to reinforce his personal relationship with the respective leaders, who came away from the meetings with the definite feeling they were dealing with someone who understood the problems of governments and who was, himself, a person of stature. This, alone, made the effort to attend worthwhile. One of Samaranch's more remarkable characteristics is that he can hold six to ten meetings an hour, and each person who meets him has the feeling that he or she has been heard, understood, and given all the time needed to make a point. Even so, it tested his stamina to conduct individual meetings with virtually every socialist sports minister over the course of each gathering.

Part of the generalized process of courting the socialist countries was to make regular official visits to them and to visibly support events held in those countries. Whenever possible, these visits were coupled with meetings with senior government officials, encouraging a positive attitude toward the Olympic Games and downplaying any lack of diplomatic relations between their countries and South Korea. When visiting socialist countries other than the Soviet Union, Samaranch knew that he was essentially playing to the chorus, since the basic policy decision would be made in Moscow. Even choruses are important, however, and the success of Romania in breaking away from the Los Angeles boycott showed that there could be some gold in the mines he was prospecting. There is no doubt that a good part of the objective was to encourage as much resentment as possible within the Soviet bloc, should the Soviet Union be inclined to favor another boycott in Seoul. But it was better to avoid a problem than to try to solve one, so Samaranch pursued both angles.

One bright spot on the horizon had been the emergence of Mikhail Gorbachev as leader of the Soviet Union.[15] Quite different in many respects from the brand of Soviet leader over the years since the Bolshevik Revolution in 1917, Gorbachev was the first of the Soviet leaders who had not been part of the old guard. Though there is no doubt that he brought some of the doctrinaire baggage with him and was saddled with a good deal more in the older and conservative elements of the Communist Party of the Soviet Union, he was certainly a man of the times and one who understood that the Soviet Union could not hold the rest of the world at bay forever. There was a definite change of atmosphere in the offing — not yet winds of change, but hints of what might be possible if Gorbachev could consolidate and hold on to power. These were the early years of the high-wire act that he managed so precariously, to the gasps of an awestruck and generally supportive world.

At least there was someone in power, however tenuous the grasp may have been, who understood the absolute necessity of bringing the Soviet Union out of its isolation and into the world. Gorbachev knew that if the Soviet Union was to remain a superpower, it had to function as a full member of the international community. He also knew and, unlike the leaders before him, was prepared to recognize publicly that the economic situation in the Soviet Union was desperate, deteriorating, and virtually unsolvable. The United States was spending the USSR into bankruptcy through military expenditures, and the Soviet coffers were empty. The Soviets needed major transfusions from outside but could not hope to attract them without significant internal changes. Gorbachev was determined to take the medicine, even though it meant exposing his leadership to enormous political risk at home, where the entrenched power apparatus had a tremendous vested interest in main-

[15] Gorbachev became general secretary of the Communist Party on March 11, 1985.

taining the position and privilege of the Communist Party. Changes on the scale contemplated by Gorbachev had brought even Peter the Great to his knees. They would eventually do the same to Gorbachev.

But whether in the Soviet Union or throughout the rest of the world, Samaranch persisted with his strategy of regular consultation with political leaders and others on the forthcoming Seoul Games. It was a perfect example of making the global decision makers part of the solution, instead of part of the problem. The IOC worked assiduously to end its own isolation from the political process. An informal partnership was in the making, whereby political figures, previously ostentatiously excluded from the celebration of the Olympics, were given a role in the creation of the quadrennial miracle.

CHAPTER 4

Setting the Tone for Korea in 1988

FROM THE MOMENT the IOC announced that the 1988 Olympic Games would be held in Seoul, the North Korean position had been all too clear. It was also entirely predictable: the IOC's decision was totally inappropriate, and the South Koreans were completely incapable of staging the Games. So unthinkable was the decision that Kim Yu Sun, the IOC member in North Korea, had been ordered home from Baden-Baden by his government even before the IOC Session ended.

The catechism of socialist solidarity was such that all of the North Korean allies were placed in a difficult situation as well. These allies, other than the Soviet Union, were generally somewhat restrained in their statements but were clearly uncomfortable with the choice and were privately long of face as they contemplated the prospect of uncertainty over the next seven years. The sports leaders were even more gloomy, since they knew full well that the ultimate decisions regarding participation were completely out of their hands and would be based on an appreciation of the political factors in play as the Games got closer and closer. The political card would likely be played only at the last minute, for whatever "points" the political leadership thought might be gained at the time. There was little evidence, based upon experience, that the sporting values represented by the Olympic Games and their possible beneficial effects on humanity would be given much weight in such final decisions.

In reality, there were two phases of the concerns expressed by the socialist countries. The first was prior to the Soviet-led decision to boycott the Los Angeles Games; the second was in the context of the

1984 boycott and the fear that there might be some sanctions imposed on the boycotting countries. The criticism during the first phase was fairly moderate, along the lines of questioning the appropriateness of the choice of Seoul. It was generally known that the socialist countries had supported Nagoya when the IOC's decision was made in Baden-Baden. In the wake of the 1984 boycott decision, however, the language grew more strident, and support was obtained from some of the lesser countries in the Warsaw Pact to bolster the Soviet position.[1]

Following the Los Angeles Games, the Soviets became much more aggressive.[2] By October 1984, there were articles in the Soviet press urging that the Games be moved, identified with well-known coaches and sport personalities. In an unusual move, the two Soviet IOC members, Konstantin Andrianov and Vitaly Smirnov, sent a strongly worded letter of complaint dated October 19, regarding the IOC's actions in relation to both Los Angeles and Seoul. The letter was so bizarre, particularly in view of the fact that one or other of the two had been a member of the IOC Executive Board throughout the entire time during which the actions complained of had occurred, that it was generally believed that the letter had been sent under orders.[3] The IOC said

[1] The Soviets had generally been treading a bit carefully with respect to Seoul following the unfortunate incident on September 1, 1983, when Soviet military aircraft shot down the civilian Korean Airlines flight 007 en route from New York to Seoul. This had a very damaging effect on Soviet prestige and made its position with respect to Korea rather delicate. There was considerable skepticism in Korea and the West as to whether this incident had been an accident. Recent disclosures at the time of completion of this work suggest the Soviets had known full well that the aircraft was civilian and unarmed. On the other hand, by July 22, 1984, SLOOC president Roh Tae Woo was prepared to indicate that the Republic of Korea was prepared to resume sport exchanges with the USSR, despite the general frigidity of the relations between them. Within the United States, shortly following the incident, the California legislature adopted a resolution to ban Soviet athletes from the Games. This was countered on December 1 by a resolution of the House of Representatives supporting the Olympic Charter and welcoming all athletes to participate in the Games.

[2] Some of this aggression must, in retrospect, be taken with a grain of salt. Despite some very strong public opposition to and criticism of the Seoul Games, the private statements and indications were that not only the Soviets, but also all the other socialist countries, were very much interested in taking part in the Games. Much of the rhetoric may, therefore, have been for the sake of showing solidarity with the DPRK. This is much easier to deduce now but would have been a risky, if not foolhardy, conclusion to draw four years before the Games. It might also have been a double feint, designed to mislead the IOC at a critical time. There is not much doubt that, had a consensus built up against Seoul among the nonaligned countries, the Soviets may well have determined that their greater vital interests were in that direction. Their options were, therefore, completely open.

[3] The letter accused the IOC of having corruptly awarded the Games to Los Angeles for 1984, against a promise of television rights of $225 million. This was complete nonsense. There had, in the end, been only one candidate for the Games, once Teheran had withdrawn, but the letter suggested that Mexico and Munich were also in the running, another complete fabrication. The

that such a position by two of its members was unacceptable. They eventually apologized and withdrew the letter, and the matter was dropped.

The capitulation of the Soviet IOC members was not mirrored by the Soviet NOC. At a meeting of the Association of National Olympic Committees held in Mexico City in November 1984, the Soviet NOC was particularly virulent regarding both Los Angeles and Seoul.[4] A good part of the reason was self-justification for having boycotted Los Angeles, which had turned out to be so successful. The Soviets felt they had to try to dampen the obvious triumph of their arch-rival, the United States. Notwithstanding this opposition, which was dutifully (and stridently) supported by Manfred Ewald, president of the East German NOC and East German minister of sport, the 155 NOCs gathered in Mexico voted overwhelmingly to support the Games in Seoul. The Soviets were not in particularly good favor following Los Angeles, and their complaints regarding security at those Games had simply not been taken seriously. Most of the other Soviet allies, while paying some lip service to what was said, were not at all enthusiastic about another boycott.[5]

IOC was also guilty of racial discrimination, it alleged, since a number of the international federations that it recognized still had relations with South Africa. The postal vote it had conducted with respect to changes in the Olympic Charter to accommodate the Games in Los Angeles was illegal. Closer links were demanded with the UN and particularly UNESCO, then enjoying the nadir of its international reputation and a close relationship with the Soviets and client states.

[4] In the time leading up to the meeting of ANOC in Mexico in November 1984, the Soviet press conducted an anti-Seoul campaign. Examples of this campaign included an article by a senior sports editor of *Sovietsky Sport* in early November in which he stated: "Really, it is not too late to correct the blunder [the selection of Seoul] made three years ago." He continued, "Is it not better to decide now once and for all in advance not to go as far as a new 'Los Angeles nightmare'?" A day earlier one of the Soviet handball coaches stated in *Izvestia* that the IOC "should not delay in transferring the Olympics from Seoul." The day prior to that, a wrestling coach had written in *Sovietsky Sport* that the decision should be reviewed. All three had apparently quoted Franco Carraro, the IOC member in Italy and president of its NOC, as saying that the Games should be in Paris or Barcelona. On November 3, 1984, Pasqual Maragall, mayor of Barcelona, had obligingly announced that Barcelona would be ready to organize the 1988 Games. It was clear that all this was to lend support to what the USSR hoped might be a decision to be taken at the Mexico meetings that month. They may have overlooked the fact that readership of *Sovietsky Sport* and *Izvestia* is somewhat limited outside the USSR.

[5] Ewald had a difficult road to follow. He was personally not much in favor of Olympic boycotts, but he did have Big Brother looking over his shoulder and monitoring the degree of his apparent solidarity with the party line. So he danced, with public rhetoric, to one tune and used all the body language possible to indicate that, whatever the reservations he might have with respect to the IOC's choice of site for the 1988 Games, he did want East Germany to be present. He may well have had genuine personal concern with Seoul, since it certainly made his job of getting athletes back into the Games more difficult than had the site been elsewhere. Upon his return

Extraordinary Session, 1984: The IOC Takes Charge

One of the first steps that the IOC undertook following Los Angeles was to try to make the political exposure of the Games as low as possible. This was an outcome of the decision of the IOC Session in Los Angeles not to pursue, at that time, the question of applying sanctions against national Olympic committees that did not participate in the Games. An Extraordinary Session of the IOC was scheduled for early December 1984 in Lausanne, to consider what should be the IOC's response to boycotts of the Olympic Games. This Session was scheduled long enough after the Los Angeles Games and far enough ahead of the Seoul Games that the heat had cooled with respect to the former and nothing overt had to be directly linked to the latter, although it would have been ingenuous in the extreme not to know what the IOC had in mind. The site, Lausanne, headquarters of the IOC, was deliberately chosen to signify that the IOC would be acting neutrally, from its own base, and that it would not be swayed by any pressures that might result from any other choice of location.

The whole issue of what to do when faced with this problem of boycotts is not without some subtle difficulties, of which the IOC was well aware. Is there, for example, a *duty,* whether express or implied, on the part of a national Olympic committee to participate in the Games?[6] After all, what is extended to all NOCs is an *invitation* to participate in the Games; it is not a command. Must one accept the invitation? What if economic or other conditions in a particular country are so serious that, as a matter of national priority, it is impossible for athletes to prepare for the Games or for the country to afford to devote any resources to sport or even to pay for the expenses of its Olympic delegation?[7] The complexity of this is increased by the provisions of the

---

from the meetings in Mexico, Antonin Himl, president of the Czechoslovakian NOC, said that although the decision to award the Games to Seoul was a mistake, he thought the socialist countries would nevertheless attend the Games.

[6] There were several IOC members who shared this view, among them German Rieckehoff of Puerto Rico, who was also president of the Puerto Rican NOC. For many, the real question was the *extent* of the duty. Was it to be mandatory, with sanctions to be applied in the case of nonparticipation, or was it to be in the nature of a moral duty to do the utmost in the circumstances of the reality in each country at the time a decision was to be made? Despite the exhortation in the Olympic Charter regarding their independence from government, many NOCs, of course, are nothing more than emanations of their respective governments.

[7] Examples of events or circumstances that might prevent participation include natural disasters, wars, religious convictions, and civil instability.

Olympic Charter, which, on the one hand, proclaim the universality of the Games, but on the other, exhort NOCs to send only athletes fully prepared for high-level competition. Should the IOC be entitled to make that sort of value judgment on behalf of some 167 NOCs that then made up the Olympic Family?

Is there a qualitative difference between not accepting the invitation from the Olympic Organizing Committee in the host country and accepting it, but, at the last moment, changing one's mind and not coming, or even leaving the host country, as was the case in Montreal in 1976? Certainly, in cases such as the latter, extra expenses will have been incurred on the basis of the acceptance of the invitation and in reliance upon the acceptance. Draws will have been put in place, tickets sold to spectators, and accommodation prepared beyond what would otherwise have been necessary. There is at least an argument that some form of recompense should be imposed in such circumstances.[8] It would be, however, an illusory exercise, since few, if any, national Olympic committees have the financial resources to pay any such penalty.[9]

In preparation for the Extraordinary Session, Samaranch had asked the IOC members to collect and forward their thoughts on sanctions, in order to have background material that could be reviewed by the members upon arrival in Lausanne. He also asked one or two of the members on the Executive Board to prepare the case for a decision that would favor sanctions for nonparticipation in the Olympic Games, whether by nonacceptance of the invitation or by subsequent boycott. Though he was not as adamant as he had been in Los Angeles about imposing sanctions, he was still quite annoyed about the treatment he had received in Moscow earlier

[8] There was a body of opinion that favored the idea that if an NOC did not participate for unacceptable reasons, it should be forced to sit out the next Games. This was a view advocated by William E. Simon, then president of the U.S. Olympic Committee. This is not surprising, since the Los Angeles Games had most recently been affected by a boycott. It was not a suggestion put forward by the USOC following the 1980 Games. It was much stronger in tone than one suggested to the IOC by the Canadian Olympic Association at a meeting of the NOCs with the IOC Executive Board in Abidjan, Ivory Coast, in April 1977, following the African boycott of the 1976 Games in Montreal. The Canadian proposal held that there was no obligation on the part of any NOC to accept the invitation to participate, but that if an NOC accepted and then withdrew at the last minute, it should, as a condition of future participation, be required to reimburse the Organizing Committee for the expenses caused by its last-minute action.

[9] In the final analysis, it makes no sense to enact a rule that cannot be enforced and is obviously beyond the power of the NOCs themselves, so this option was never seriously pursued. There can be little doubt that the NOCs clearly want to participate in the Games if they possibly can and only fail to do so when circumstances beyond their control intervene.

that year as he tried to head off the Soviet boycott of Los Angeles, and he was not prepared to let go too easily.[10]

There is considerable uncertainty regarding the role of the IOC, particularly on the fringes of matters of state. Much two-dimensional media coverage exists regarding the IOC. More often than not, it is caricatured as a moribund, antediluvian collection of aging, rich, and titled men completely unconnected with reality. Though this is not the occasion to rebut all these misconceptions, an examination of the published biographies of the IOC members will demonstrate that its membership reflects a true cross section of international experience.[11] Its role is largely unknown and its structure misunderstood. The process of co-optation of its members, who are, unlike members of most organizations, representatives of the IOC in their countries rather than representatives of their countries on the IOC, is unusual and therefore a matter of diffuse suspicion for many observers. In fact, however, it is this unique structure that has enabled the IOC not only to survive for nearly a century, but also to lead an international sports movement that has become, arguably, one of the most important social and cultural phenomena in the world today.

Virtually all the management of the IOC is delegated to its eleven-member Executive Board, the members of which are elected for four-year terms by the Session as a whole. If the Session is seen as the Parliament of the IOC, then the Executive Board is its cabinet. The Session normally occurs only once a year, and in years in which Games take place, just prior to the Olympic Games. The Executive Board meets four or five times per year. Between meetings, the president is the designated organ of the IOC, which results in an unusual concentration of power in that office. The choice of the IOC president is, accordingly, one of the most important decisions that the Session is called upon to make. A measure of the importance of this decision

[10] It was his public position that there should be some sanctions imposed. He had tried to cause the IOC session to accept that position earlier in the year in Los Angeles, but failed when several of the more senior members, led by Masaji Kiyokawa, had opposed his pressure to move directly to a system of sanctions. The strident attitude of the Soviets after the Games, as they tried to rationalize their nonparticipation, did little to soften his view, despite his diplomatic visit to Moscow in September 1984, following the Games.

[11] The average age of the IOC members when Samaranch took office in 1980 was sixty-seven years. By the end of 1992, this average had dropped to sixty-one years. When he took office, there were no women members. Since that time, seven have been co-opted: Pirjo Haggman (Finland) and Flor Isava-Fonseca (Venezuela) in 1981; Mary Allison Glen-Haig (Great Britain) in 1982; Princess Nora of Liechtenstein in 1984; Anita DeFrantz (United States) in 1986; the Princess Royal, Princess Anne (Great Britain) in 1988; and Carol Anne Letheren (Canada) in 1990.

is that the initial term of the IOC president is eight years. Subsequent terms, if any, are four years. This provides a stability of leadership that is unparalleled in most organizations, and such stability is one reason that the Olympic Movement has been so successful.[12]

Despite the concentration of power in the hands of the president, and to a lesser degree in the Executive Board, the importance of the Session itself should never be underestimated. The cross section of views and experience of the IOC members provides a collective wisdom that almost always finds the right solution to many complex and sensitive international problems.

This was demonstrated very clearly during the Extraordinary Session in Lausanne in December 1984. It is also a measure of Samaranch's flexibility as president that he not only responded favorably to the change of direction dictated by the Session, but adapted and improved upon the general sense of that advice.

First and foremost, the IOC reiterated its support of the Games in Seoul. There would be no change in the location of the Games. Second, and even more important, the IOC declared that it would not impose sanctions against NOCs that did not participate in the Games. The IOC recognized that a decision against participation in the Games was not (in almost every case) a decision taken freely by sports authorities and athletes. The Games were an opportunity for the youth of the world to come together in peace and friendship every four years; there was no creation of a *duty* to do so. It would be inappropriate to provide for means of compulsion to participate. Nor, for that matter, would compulsion be enforceable.

Similarly, the IOC was not in the business of *punishing* athletes of future generations for the decisions taken by the political authorities in their countries. That would be completely antithetical to everything for which the IOC and the Olympic Movement exists. If the politicians of a country wanted to punish their own athletes by preventing them from participating in the Olympic Games, that would be regrettable in the extreme, but the IOC was not prepared to add to such self-imposed punishment by denying the next generation of athletes from that country the opportunity to be a part of the greatest sport experience in the world.

[12] In the one-hundred-year history of the IOC, there have been only seven presidents. This count does not include Godefrois de Blonnay, who was appointed (not elected) as interim president on a caretaker basis for two years during World War I.

The decision was so "right" that, once made, it was almost unthinkable that there could have been any other. It was extraordinary, in retrospect, to think that the IOC could seriously have considered any other course. The Session had been more perceptive, or at least more intuitive, than the Executive Board when, in Los Angeles, it had insisted that no decision be taken in the heat of the moment and in response to the hue and cry in the media for an "eye for an eye" reaction to the boycott syndrome. The IOC's experience has been, in general, that when it makes a mistake, it is precisely because it has not taken the time to consider fully the implications of its decisions. This would have been a perfect example. There were already enough tensions at the time of the Los Angeles Games without adding to them with a provocative decision to sanction the absentee countries.

The philosophical ground was thus prepared. Seoul had been reaffirmed as the host city for the 1988 Games. Transposing this to a practical level, what could be done to improve the chances for the success of the Games? One of the problems in the past had been the uncertainty, until the last moment, concerning the final number of countries and athletes who would take part. This imposed logistical and other difficulties on the organizers of the Games. The IOC addressed this problem by adopting a new schedule for the entry process. The invitations would now be sent out to the NOCs one year before the Games. The NOCs would be required to indicate whether or not they would participate in the Games eight months prior to the Opening Ceremony. They would not have to give the total number of athletes at such time, but merely state whether or not they would attend. The specific team sizes would be provided much closer to the time of the Games, when preliminary tournaments were completed for team sports and selection trials had been held for other sports.

There was also a feeling that if a country chose not to participate in the Games for political reasons, the athletes from that country should not be the only ones to pay the price of that decision. Its sport officials should also share in the implications of such a decision. Sport officials from nonparticipating countries would not be accredited, and international sports federations would be urged not to use officials from such countries, provided that this did not impair the running of the competitions at the highest possible level.

A further decision was taken that was of significant diplomatic importance, especially with respect to the forthcoming Games in Seoul. Up to this time in Olympic history, the invitations to participate in the

Olympic Games had been sent to the NOCs by the organizing committees for the Games. Thus, for example, the invitations for the 1984 Olympic Games had been sent by the Los Angeles Olympic Organizing Committee, an organization within the United States. The invitations to Seoul would, in the normal course, have come from its organizing committee, known by its acronym, SLOOC. The IOC sought a means of eliminating the tension that might arise from the fact that, say, the Soviet Union would be faced with having to respond to an invitation emanating from South Korea.[13]

The solution was as simple as it was inspired. Henceforth, it would be the IOC itself that would issue the invitations to participate in the Games. The underlying rationale was sound: the Games belong to the IOC, not the hosts. The IOC responds to requests from potential hosts to stage its event, but the Games are still the IOC's Games. Again, once the decision was made, it seemed so obvious that we were all slightly embarrassed not to have thought of it before. It meant, in diplomatic terms, that a nonparticipating country was deprived of the opportunity to explain its absence by reference to an invitation from a country of which it might disapprove or with which it had no diplomatic or official relations. Refusal to attend the Games would mean the country was saying no to the IOC itself and to the Olympic Movement, a much more difficult refusal to explain.

The Session was, all in all, a very positive outcome to the difficult background of Olympic boycotts. The resolution of the problem was approved with overwhelming support of the IOC members. The decisions were certainly positive from the perspective of minimizing possible difficulties with the Seoul Games on this protocol matter.

The first public sign of what appeared to be a rather bizarre development from the DPRK in relation to the 1988 Games took the form of a letter to Samaranch from Kim Yu Sun, asking him if he would be

[13] There was ongoing activity within the socialist bloc on the matter prior to the IOC Session. Sports officials from these countries met in Prague on October 19, the same date that Andrianov and Smirnov sent their letter, and issued a statement of "concern" over staging the 1988 Games in Seoul and calling upon the IOC to ensure that "normal conditions" prevailed for the participation of all countries. On November 16, more encouraging news came in the form of a statement by Antonin Himl, president of the Czechoslovakian NOC, that the choice of Seoul was a mistake, but that the Soviet bloc would participate. Five days later, however, the main player in this area, Marat Gramov, president of the Soviet NOC and the Soviet sports minister, declared that the choice of Seoul as host city of the Games was "inappropriate" and that the USSR could not understand why the Games should take place in Seoul.

prepared to state that the 1988 Games would be held in both North Korea and South Korea.[14] Kim also requested Samaranch to state that the meeting of ANOC scheduled for Seoul in April 1986 would be held in Pyongyang instead of Seoul. Samaranch had advised the IOC Executive Board of this development on November 7, 1984. He said he would make no such announcement regarding the location of the Games and that the site of the ANOC meeting was a matter for ANOC to decide, not the IOC. It was decided not to deal with this matter at the Extraordinary IOC Session that would take place in early December.[15]

In late November 1984, there were media reports of secret discussions between the North Koreans and South Koreans that might have an effect on the Games. Not only, apparently, were the "usual" discussions of a single Korean team back on the table after many years, but also there were indications that the two sides might be considering the possibility of having some events or sports in the North as well. Nothing official was admitted, but it was clear that some contact was occurring.[16] South Korean sports minister Lee Yong Ho stated in an interview on December 6, 1984, that no official request had come from the DPRK to share the Games. Lee apparently thought it would be easier to share the Games than to have a joint team from both Koreas, but was generally noncommittal.

[14] This was not the genesis of the idea at all, but merely the first overt manifestation of it. The suggestion had, apparently, first been made by Italian foreign minister Giulio Andreotti to Korean foreign minister Lee Won Kyong, on June 27, 1984. Andreotti had indicated that in order to assure the smooth running of the Games in Seoul, it might be necessary to share some part of the Games with the DPRK. The South Korean government responded that this type of collaboration was simply not possible. A similar suggestion would be made by Fidel Castro in a letter to Samaranch dated November 29, 1984. The broad outlines of such a proposal had been informally discussed by Samaranch and Kim Yu Sun in the course of their meeting in Moscow in September 1984. Samaranch had asked Kim if the North might be ready to organize some events in Pyongyang and said that if such a proposal were to be made formally, the IOC might consider it. Kim said he would give an answer during the course of the forthcoming meetings in Mexico that November. Samaranch had kept all this very close to his vest. His personal observation was that both Gramov and Vazquez-Raña were happy with this approach because it put the DPRK in a difficult position and it would be forced to respond. If this letter was the "answer" from the DPRK, it reflected an extraordinary overleap of the extent of the discussions that had been held in Moscow.

[15] On November 30, 1984, at the IOC Executive Board meeting in Lausanne just prior to the Extraordinary Session, the Executive Board agreed with Samaranch's idea to call for a meeting of the two Korean NOCs in Lausanne, without setting any conditions for such a meeting. Samaranch had announced at a press conference in Seoul in late September that the IOC was ready to organize such a meeting.

[16] See, for exmple, the *International Herald Tribune* issue of November 29, 1984: *Tribune de Genève* issue of November 20, 1984; *International Herald Tribune* issue of December 6, 1984; *Le Matin* (Lausanne) issue of December 6, 1984; *Tribune de Genève* issue of December 6, 1984.

It appeared, at this early stage of development, that such a move might provide the Soviet Union with the necessary face-saving device to enable it to participate in Seoul. Even in the period leading up to the Extraordinary IOC Session in December 1984, the USSR NOC had continued to pronounce the choice of Seoul as host city as "inappropriate." The idea of dividing the Games in some manner between the North and the South had also surfaced among some international sports officials, including Colonel Don Hull, the American president of the International Amateur Boxing Federation (AIBA), who had sent a letter along these lines to Samaranch for his comments.[17] A further inference that this type of discussion might well be taking place came from the fact of the suggestion contained in the November 29, 1984, letter to Samaranch from Cuban president Fidel Castro, a longtime ally of North Korea, that the Games should be shared. The IOC would wait to see if any official proposal would be put forward.[18]

By now, more than three years had passed since the Baden-Baden decision awarding the Games to Seoul. Seoul was in full preparation for the 1986 Asian Games, a wonderful opportunity to test not only the facilities for the Games, but also the political waters, at least in Asia. Its new Olympic Stadium had been dedicated on September 29, 1984, at a ceremony attended by Samaranch and other leading sport figures.[19] Key to the testing on the political level was whether or not the People's Republic of China would attend the Asian Games in Seoul.[20] The Tai-

[17] Horst Dassler, then president of Adidas and a figure of some importance in international sports politics, had had a meeting with Soviet NOC president Marat Gramov on August 19, 1984. Reporting on this meeting to the Korean ambassador to France on September 17, Dassler said it was Gramov's view that all nations could compete in the Games if South Korea were to give several events to North Korea.

[18] The prospects of a single team seemed rather bleak. Intra-Korean discussions concerning the possibility of a single team had broken down after three rounds of unsuccessful talks earlier that year, on April 9, April 30, and May 25. SLOOC president Roh Tae Woo had proposed to the DPRK on November 19, 1984, that the talks be reopened. This followed earlier calls to this effect: one on August 17, 1984, by the Korean government for a fourth north-south meeting (which had been rejected by the DPRK on August 27), and a second on October 4 (which did not appear to have been answered).

[19] The People's Republic of China had a small delegation present for the opening ceremony. The USSR was not represented. Samaranch followed up on this presence with a visit to Beijing immediately thereafter, from September 30 to October 2, where he met with the prime minister and the minister of sport.

[20] During this visit to Seoul, Samaranch met with Roh Tae Woo to brief him on the developments that appeared to be shaping up during this period. This included the news arising from the trip to Moscow, which he had just completed before leaving to come to Seoul, including the discussions with Gramov and Kim Yu Sun. Roh said he was prepared to consider any recommendations Samaranch might have. It was agreed that Samaranch would announce at his press conference

wan problem, which might otherwise have had some impact, had already been solved,[21] but the political support by China of the DPRK and the cool relations between China and South Korea were a potential barrier to full success of the Asian Games. There were no diplomatic relations between the two countries. It was not even possible to travel directly between them; one had to fly from Seoul to Tokyo and then from Tokyo to Beijing. Such trade as existed was conducted surreptitiously, with no official notice being taken.

As a harbinger of what was to come only two years later, the Asian Games were, therefore, important to Samaranch, who worked tirelessly to convince the Chinese to attend both the Asian Games and the Seoul Games. There was, in retrospect, probably not too much need to persuade China to participate in the Asian Games, since, according to He Zhenliang, the IOC member in China,[22] it had always been China's intention to participate. China had, in addition, every reason to be in Seoul for the Asian Games in 1986, because it had decided to apply to host them in 1990, and it would hardly have been propitious for this venture to stay away from the preceding Games. The 1990 Asian Games were indeed awarded to Beijing by the Olympic Council of Asia at its General Assembly, held in Seoul, on September 28, 1985. Samaranch, however, was not someone to leave such important matters to chance, so he kept reinforcing the importance of Chinese participation at every possible opportunity, including a personal visit to Beijing in the spring of 1986.[23]

Nothing developed from the rumored secret talks at the end of 1984. The South Koreans did not deny that such discussions might be taking

---

in Seoul that the IOC was ready to organize meetings between the two Korean NOCs, whether in Lausanne or elsewhere.

[21] Though the overall problem had been solved and both China and Taiwan, the latter participating as the Chinese Taipei Olympic Committee, had taken part at the Los Angeles Games, Taiwan was still not a member of the organization responsible for the Asian Games. Its application for membership would finally be accepted in 1986, but not in time for it to take part in the 1986 games.

[22] He Zhenliang would go on to become president of the Chinese Olympic Committee on April 15, 1989.

[23] This was an interesting visit for a number of reasons, not the least of which was the first inkling that China might be thinking of bidding to host the Olympic Games. Another revelation was that in the forthcoming five-year plan, China had decided to focus increased attention on high performance sport, with a view to becoming more competitive on an international scale. The results of this decision are already apparent.

place but provided little detailed information on the content of the discussions. Lee Yong Ho, at the time Korean minister of sports, had said that he favored a joint team, despite the difficulties that could be expected over matters such as finances, coaching, and team selection. He even appeared to hold out some thought that some events might be organized in North Korea, the idea floated by Fidel Castro, but did not elaborate.

The North Koreans, for their part, continued to protest against the choice of Seoul as the host city. On December 17, 1984, after the IOC's Extraordinary Session in Lausanne, Kim Yu Sun, president of the DPRK NOC, sent a circular letter addressed to Samaranch, with copies to all NOC members and NOC presidents, complaining that Seoul was unfit "in every respect" to be the host of the Games. The letter contained the full range of complaints customarily directed by the North against the South. It certainly did nothing to indicate that the North was affected by the outcome or accepted the results of the special IOC Session. Indeed, just prior to this Session, Kim Yu Sun had delivered a letter and report to Samaranch, which outlined the instability on the Korean peninsula, relating to a recent incident in the DMZ, when, on November 23, there had been an exchange of gunfire, resulting in a number of deaths. He enclosed the official statement published by the KCNA (Korean Central News Agency) on November 26, which was filled with the obligatory invective directed at the American imperialists and the puppet regime in South Korea. This was, presumably, designed to suggest that the Republic of Korea was unable to guarantee the safety and stability concerns required of an Olympic host city.

Samaranch did not answer Kim's November letter, which had been delivered in Mexico, well prior to the Session. He did answer the December 17 letter and circulated a copy of this correspondence to the IOC members. He reminded Kim of the decision in Baden-Baden in 1981 and drew to his attention not only the results of the recent Session (in which Kim had participated as a member of the IOC) but also the recent declarations of support for the Seoul Games made by the international sports federations (IFs) in October and the "Declaration of Mexico" of the NOCs in November. There was, contrary to Kim's allegation, no breach of the Olympic Charter involved. The IOC did not consider that the personal safety of athletes and others was at stake, including those of the socialist countries. Samaranch offered to mediate the Korean discussions regarding a joint team, should the Koreans desire such involvement on his part.[24] The scene, despite the strident rhetoric of the North, remained relatively quiet through the end of 1984 and early 1985.

There had, earlier in the year, been the usual jockeying for diplomatic position between North Korea and South Korea. On March 30, 1984, Kim Yu Sun, president of the DPRK NOC, advised Samaranch that his NOC had sent a letter to his counterpart in South Korea dated the same day, proposing that there be a single joint team for the 1984 Olympics and suggesting a meeting at Panmunjom at the earliest possible date. This was prior to the Soviet decision to boycott those Games.

The letter of reply from the South, signed by Chung Ju Yung, president of the Korean Amateur Sports Association (KASA) and the KOC, to the invitation to participate in such talks was dated April 2. It reflected the general suspicion regarding proposals from the North and was couched in terms that made this plain and would have made it difficult for the North to accept. The opening paragraphs read as follows:

> I received your letter of March 30, and first of all, I am compelled to point out the lack of any mention about the terrorist activity in Burma last October 9. In the attempt on the life of our Head of State, most of the members of our diplomatic delegation were murdered en masse.
>
> It was not only a crime against compatriots who shared the same blood and all other peace-loving peoples of the world, but also constituted a flagrant violation of the Olympic spirit which pursues peace and the unity of all mankind.
>
> Even between athletes and officials an apology for such heinous criminal conduct, in which compatriots were slain en masse, would be appropriate. We have demanded on several occasions in the past and will demand that the north Korean authorities take appropriate measures to atone for the Burma atrocity.
>
> Nevertheless, we have decided to review affirmatively your proposal

[24] Samaranch would later back off considerably from this offer, once it became clear that the subject was so complicated that it could only obfuscate the strategy the IOC adopted for negotiations with the two Koreas. Kim Yu Sun might be forgiven for repeating a request for IOC mediation on the subject, since it was offered, in the first place, by Samaranch.

for talks between south and north Korean sports officials in the pure spirit of sportsmanship, separate from any other pending issue.[25]

The general tone of the letter was very negative, while appearing to be responsive to the North's proposal. The letter also pointed out that it had taken the Germans some two hundred meetings in order to work out the matter of a single team. It did not, however, mention the vastly different circumstances that were applicable to the German situation.

The meeting, held in Panmunjom on April 9, had broken off on the Rangoon issue, when the North Korean delegation demanded retraction of the remarks made by the South.[26] The South had sent a letter on April 12 to the North Korean NOC, urging them to return to the conference table as soon as possible to resume talks on a unified team. The North had rejected this request, by a letter dated April 14. This was followed by a letter to the North from KOC president Chung Ju Yung, dated April 17, urging them to return to the table.[27] A few days later, on April 20, the North proposed a second meeting on April 26. The South refused the date in a letter dated April 24 and proposed, instead, a meeting on April 30, which was agreed to by the North Koreans on April 28. This meeting was also unsuccessful. In fact, it was so unsuccessful that the parties never actually got around to discussing the items on the agenda for the meeting.

The South sent yet another letter, dated May 9, urging resumption of the talks and a third meeting. On May 12, the North Koreans refused such a third meeting. South Korea again requested a third meeting on May 23, in a letter dated May 18. The North responded by letter dated

[25] The letter went on to point out previous efforts by the South to have such dialogues, but which were rejected by the North. These included a proposal dated June 19, 1981, made by the KOC to have joint teams for the 1982 Asian Games in New Delhi and the 1984 Olympics. In the proposal put forward by South Korea on February 1, 1982, there had been a call for an exchange of goodwill games in the North and the South and the formation of single teams for international competitions.

[26] The South had also referred in the meeting to the recent abduction of a Korean film director, Shin Sang Ok, and actress, Choi Eun Hee.

[27] Roh reported regularly to Samaranch on the progress of these meetings, including exchanges of telexes on April 11 and 12, as well as a telex on April 14, advising of the call by the KOC for resumption of the talks on April 17. In this latter telex, he mentioned the South's special concerns regarding safety and security of South Korean athletes, in light of the Rangoon bombing and the refusal of the DPRK to provide such assurances. The language in the telex to Samaranch was analogous to that in the letter sent to the North in response to the request for meetings to discuss the joint team.

May 23, proposing that the meeting be held on May 25. The next day, the North announced it would not be taking part in the Games in Los Angeles.[28] The third meeting between North Korea and South Korea was held in Panmunjom on May 25. It, too, was unsuccessful. Once again, the agenda items were never discussed. It was a hopeless situation from the outset. Given the stated objective of the meetings as exploration of the possibility of fielding a joint team in the Los Angeles Games, it was made entirely meaningless as a result of the decision by the Soviets and their allies, including, of course, the DPRK, not to participate in the Los Angeles Games. The South made one more abortive effort on May 29 to convoke a fourth meeting, but this was rejected by the North on June 1. There was some media speculation based on comments made by certain IOC members that the Soviet boycott of the Los Angeles Games might lead to withdrawing the 1988 Games from Seoul. This was unnerving enough that on June 9, SLOOC president Roh Tae Woo issued a statement discounting such speculation as the mere private opinion of some IOC members. In that he was correct; there was no IOC consideration of such an action.[29]

This latter development had some interesting fallout for Seoul from other, and unexpected, quarters. The IOC had scheduled a meeting of the Executive Board in Paris, to coincide with the ninetieth anniversary of the founding of the IOC, on June 23, 1894, at the initiative of Baron de Coubertin. The meeting itself was held at the Sorbonne, in the very room where the IOC first met in 1894. A ceremony was held in the main auditorium at the Sorbonne, attended by many dignitaries, including François Mitterrand, president of the republic. During these ceremonies, Nelson Paillou, president of the French NOC, in his address (which should have been a protocol welcome to the attendees and a retrospective view of France's contribution to the Olympic Movement) dropped a bombshell by suggesting that the 1988 Olympic Games should be moved from Seoul to Barcelona.

Everyone was caught by complete surprise, and Samaranch was forced to depart from his own prepared text to state that the IOC had decided to award the Games to Seoul and that was where they would

[28] The official announcement of the DPRK's nonparticipation was sent only on June 2.

[29] The rumors persisted, and even Samaranch was forced to discount the possibility of changing the site in a press interview he gave in Los Angeles more than a month later on July 17.

be. It was doubly embarrassing for him because his own city was involved and, furthermore, appeared ready to participate in the suggestion. Whether the idea of shifting the 1988 Games to Barcelona was completely a result of a genuine concern for the success of the 1988 Games or merely a ploy to help both Barcelona and Paris, determined rivals for the prize of hosting the 1992 Games that only one could win, is a matter for speculation. The underlying plan appeared to be that Barcelona would back into the 1988 Games, leaving the field for 1992 relatively uncluttered for Paris. The coincidence of the proposal and the cities involved strongly suggests the latter.[30]

The north-south talks, which had broken off in May, were difficult to resurrect. On August 17, the South proposed a fourth round of talks at Panmunjom, to be held on August 30. Reporting to Samaranch on this matter, Roh Tae Woo stated that, in its letter, South Korea had not mentioned anything about the Rangoon incident and the Hong Kong kidnapping of film director Shin Sang Ok and actress Choi Eun Hee. He had, apparently, only expressed regret that South Korean athletes alone had made up the Korean team at Los Angeles because of the failure to form a unified Korean team for the Games. In its letter to North Korea, South Korea had stressed that both sides should strive to make a success of the sports dialogue in view of the "many future international sports events, including the Asian Games and the Olympic Games, that will be held in Seoul at intervals of two years from now through 1988." The North had rejected such a meeting in a reply dated August 27. On October 4, the South again proposed a fourth north-south meeting. The request was repeated on November 19. North Korea never replied. Its only action was to circulate its letter of December 16, saying how unfit Seoul was to be the host of the Games.

After Castro sent his letter of November 29, 1984, a statement was made on December 10, 1984, by Kang Sung San, prime minister of the State Administration Council of the DPRK:

> We deliver our earnest support to the constructive opinions Comrade Fidel Castro Ruan expressed in his letter. Seoul is an insecure city where

[30] The matter did not cease with this suggestion and rejection by Samaranch. On November 3, 1984, Pasqual Maragall, mayor of Barcelona, completing the bilateral nature of this proposal, announced that Barcelona could be ready to host the 1988 Games if Seoul were unable to do so. On November 28, 1984, mayor of Paris Jacques Chirac "officially" announced, to the surprise of no one, that Paris would be a candidate to host the 1992 Olympic Games.

> the danger of war is constantly lurking, and the political situation there is more strained than in any other place in the world. It is evident that an international sports event such as the Olympics, aiming for good will and harmony, cannot be held successfully in Seoul, a city dominated by a warlike atmosphere.

On December 16, 1984, Kim Yu Sun sent Samaranch his letter, referred to earlier, demanding a change of venue for the Games, in which he stated:

> Since a combat situation is ever present along the Military Demarcation Line in Korea, we urge the International Olympic Committee to take prompt and proper action specified in the Charter if the designated venue is in a state of war. *We object to the Olympics being held in the South of this country, nor do we want them to be held in the North.* [emphasis added]

The message was, therefore, somewhat confusing, given the position advanced by the North only a month earlier. The collateral "combat" line of thought was, however, to disappear from the general approach by the North, except when matters appeared to be going badly for them, when it would be resurrected as the occasion seemed to require.

Samaranch was diligent throughout the latter part of 1984 as well, in trying to ensure that there could be no cause for complaint within the international community regarding Seoul's organization of the Games. He was in regular contact with President Chun Doo Hwan, employing a combination of congratulatory statements and advice on how to keep the organization of the Games moving forward in the best possible light of world opinion. Following the Games in Los Angeles, he had written to Chun, suggesting that it would be useful for Seoul if Chun were to reconfirm the undertakings given back in 1981 when the Games were awarded.[31] Chun did so in a letter dated August 22, 1984, in which he guaranteed that the Olympic Charter would be observed, that security would be guaranteed, and that the nonexistence of diplomatic relations with Korea would not be an inconvenience for Olympics-related visitors. Samaranch acknowledged this letter, delivered by the Korean ambassa-

[31] Chun had already written a similar letter prior to the Games in Los Angeles, dated July 16, expressing full support for the Games, including the matter of security and respect for the Olympic Charter.

dor in Geneva, and observed that such an official commitment might prove "quite precious" for the IOC. The letter was a diplomatic card that Samaranch played in October, when he sent copies of the correspondence to all members of the IOC, all international sports federations, and all NOCs. The objective was to be sure there would be no gaps in the formal aspects, legal or diplomatic, of the IOC's award of the Games to Seoul, which might be seized upon by detractors. Seoul should be seen to be doing everything required of it, in accordance with the Olympic Charter and its agreement with the IOC.

1985 got off to a relatively peaceful start. There was not much tension on the Olympic front. Since the efforts of South Korea to convene a fourth north-south meeting were at a standstill, Samaranch indicated on February 1 that he was ready to suggest a north-south meeting in September, under IOC auspices.[32] This did not attract any immediate attention, so later that month, at a meeting of the IOC Executive Board in Calgary, Samaranch reported that he had sent a confidential letter to the South regarding such a meeting. The KOC replied to him on March 13, accepting the IOC's offer to hold such a meeting. The North did not reply at this stage, and it was only during meetings held in Berlin during the IOC Session in early June that Samaranch had a chance to work on the DPRK, through Kim Yu Sun, regarding a joint meeting. It was agreed that Ashwini Kumar, then a vice president of the IOC, would visit the DPRK in July to explore the possibilities of such a meeting later in the year.

Ashwini Kumar, one of the two IOC members in India, was dispatched on a visit to Pyongyang in mid-July. Preparations for the visit were worked out in close coordination with Alexandru Siperco, the IOC member in Romania, and also, at the time, an IOC vice president, who was especially experienced in dealing with the socialist countries

[32] This was, in many respects, a restatement of the offer he had made during his press conference in late September 1984 in Seoul on the occasion of the opening of the Olympic Stadium, with the addition, this time, of a specific place and a general time for the meeting. No official notice had been taken by either of the two Koreas to the original offer. Samaranch advised Roh, during the visit in September, of the various suggestions regarding cohosting of the Games. Roh said the South might be prepared to have such discussions if the North would first agree to participate in Seoul. All that had changed in the interim was that Samaranch had discussed the possibility of IOC-chaired discussions between the Koreas with Kim Yu Sun during the ANOC meetings in Mexico in November. The North was not prepared to make the requested commitment, which led to Samaranch's reiteration of the IOC offer. The IOC Executive Board had approved the idea in late November.

and who ensured that Kumar was fully briefed prior to his visit. No one involved from the IOC perspective in organizing the trip was aware, at the time, of a decision apparently already taken in the DPRK that would have a profound effect on the shape of the forces affecting the Games.

Preempting the entire process of the discussions that the IOC was attempting to initiate, Kim Yu Sun had already written to the IOC on July 6 (before Kumar arrived in Pyongyang) to say that North Korea agreed to the proposed Lausanne meeting under the IOC's auspices. Even more remarkably, however, and unbeknownst to Kumar when he arrived in Pyongyang, the DPRK had sent a proposal for jointly hosting the Games, on July 12, addressed to the IOC.

The original purpose of Kumar's visit had been to see if North Korea would agree to attend a joint meeting of the NOCs of the two Koreas, at the IOC's invitation, to be held in Lausanne later in the year. Signals had been received by Samaranch to the effect that the North might respond favorably, and Kumar was to do his best to get a commitment from Pyongyang that the North would participate in such a meeting. Dates were to be proposed for the Lausanne meeting. The IOC would be represented by Samaranch, the three (at the time) vice presidents, and Raymond Gafner, one of the two Swiss IOC members, then acting as the interim administrator (*administrateur délégué*) of the IOC following the abrupt departure of Monique Berlioux as director the previous month.

Kumar was authorized to hold out that the preliminary thoughts of the IOC were that a unified team did not appear practicable to the IOC, but the two teams could march consecutively in the Opening Ceremony. The IOC did not think, contrary to some of the third-party suggestions to the contrary, that the Games could be split between the two countries. Finally, the IOC itself would give all assurances on security and related matters to facilitate North Korea's peaceful participation in the Games. Kumar made his way to Pyongyang with this brief.

The meetings, predictably, were not easy, especially since Kumar was unaware of the steps already unilaterally taken by the DPRK with respect to joint hosting of the Games, and he was placed in the awkward position of being faced with a policy decision already taken at the highest levels in Pyongyang. Kim Yu Sun advised Kumar that his government and party were interested in having talks on the problem of participation in the 1988 Games. His party felt, and had issued a manifesto on the subject, which drew its central theme from the proposal expressed by Fidel Castro, that there should be a unified organization for staging the Games in which both Koreas would have an equal share. Kumar was, of course, not in any position to agree to this and said, instead, that the contract with Seoul could not be changed. He mentioned the prospect of the two teams marching consecutively and also the possibility of other visible symbols of Korean unity. Kim was unimpressed and said that the proposals of his party had already been circulated to the capitals of the world and a copy had already been dispatched to Samaranch.

Kumar, getting away from this aspect of the discussion, asked about how the many problems could be solved if, theoretically, the Games could be dealt with as the DPRK proposed. Kim refused to give details; his answers would be ready for the Lausanne meeting. He did, apparently, understand that the solution could not be accomplished within the existing legal structure and arrangements already in place. Everyone would have to "think along fresh lines where legal hurdles did not exist." Despite many urgings from Kumar, Kim would not discuss how his NOC would tackle the many organizational difficulties that would result from a single Organizing Committee.

After two days with Kim, Kumar asked to meet with a senior member of the party and was granted a meeting with Chol Pak Song, first vice president of the DPRK. Chol welcomed Kumar as an Indian belonging to a country that had fought colonialism and was now a leader of the nonaligned countries. His own country, he complained, was bedeviled by the occupation of more than forty thousand U.S. troops, whose sole intention was to keep the country divided and who were, for this reason, masterminding the organization of the Olympic Games to demonstrate to the world that North Korea and South Korea could never be one again and that South Korea was a flourishing independent country.

Because North Korea was celebrating forty years of liberation from colonial rule this year, its people would welcome a settlement of the question of Olympic participation. Chol felt that joint celebration of the Games would be fair and just for both regions and would prove to the world that the Olympic Games were an instrument of spreading peace and friendship. Further, it would defuse tensions, which were now almost at a breaking point. He went on to describe the military situation and the possibility of a mistake that might have disastrous effects on the peaceful celebration of the Games.

He knew that the Olympic Charter did not allow for joint holding of the Games. In the present atmosphere, there would be widespread violence and unrest in the South. Thus far the student and labor leaders had not spoken against the Games in Seoul, but if the IOC remained complacent on these issues, the common person would be made aware of them and would then take to the streets. There were still three years to go, but, he declared ominously, the course of events would definitely take a violent turn if the situation were not remedied. Kumar said the IOC was conscious of its responsibilities, as had been demonstrated in the previous three Games; it faced difficult situations without fear, because its objectives were peace and friendship.

The balance of Kumar's time in Pyongyang was spent trying to get Kim to take a more flexible attitude and not to adhere rigidly to the party manifesto. Kim said the manifesto of the party had already been forwarded; if there was any reaction to it, such reaction could be forwarded to him for study. Kumar had the impression that the North was worried, at least to some degree, about world opinion, were it to boycott. They were, therefore, looking for some way of putting the other side in the wrong by making a proposal that could appear attractive to a world not well versed regarding the Olympics.

Kumar's conclusions were that North Korea knew the IOC did not want a repetition of the boycotts in 1976, 1980, and 1984, since this would be damaging to the Olympic Movement. The DPRK was also apparently under some pressure from the socialist countries to be more positive with respect to participation and had seized on the Castro proposal as a means of demonstrating its peaceful intentions and, at the same time, providing a face-saving mechanism. If the IOC did not accept the proposal, then it could say to the world that they were really in favor of participating, but their "just cause" had been rejected through no fault of their own, and purely on legalistic grounds.

This manner of framing the North Korean case, thought Kumar, might well have a certain appeal to the person in the street, and the IOC should, therefore, be particularly careful how it handled the matter. He thought there might be some value in trying to use the Olympic torch relay to highlight the desire for Korean unity and also allowing the North to organize one or two preliminary rounds of unimportant sports. He observed that this was also the view of the Soviet and Chinese sports leaders, and if later North Korea were to walk out on the Games, not only would it be completely isolated, but also there would be full participation from the remaining socialist bloc.[33]

[33] This was excellent foresight on Kumar's part, and the IOC would eventually seize the opportunity to play off the strategy that seemed to have been adopted by the North, using exactly the same approach of maneuvering them into the weaker position. Much of the genesis of the IOC tactics can be seen in retrospect in Kumar's observations.

He recognized that the present positions of the two sides were such that there was little maneuvering room and therefore no likelihood of a quick solution. The IOC should not try to force both sides to come to an immediate agreement. The discussions proposed for later in the year could be a starting point in the search for some face-saving compromise that made a symbolic show of Korean unity. North Korea should be asked to specify the practical measures that they could suggest, to implement what was contained in their manifesto without transgressing the provisions of the Olympic Charter or the contract with Seoul. They would need time to respond, and in the meantime, there would be additional pressure from the other socialist countries for the North to agree to the symbolic gestures.

Kim's letter to Samaranch proposing the joint hosting of the Games had been dated July 12, 1985, and had, apparently, been sent by mail, arriving at IOC headquarters in Lausanne after Kumar had been in Pyongyang for his meeting with Kim. The letter was brief and somewhat peremptory, simply stating that after a thorough study of the diversity of views concerning the "Seoul Olympiad," it was deemed to be most rational to have it be hosted jointly by North Korea and South Korea. The proposal, Kim continued, would eliminate the diversity of views arising from the problems of the Games venue and could thus take the Olympic Movement out of the crisis.

Kumar had barely returned from Pyongyang to deliver his report to Samaranch when Kim appeared in Lausanne on July 28, 1985, to meet with Samaranch. The first question from Samaranch was whether the North had agreed on a date for the first meeting. Kim said that October 8–9 would be fine, and this was confirmed. Kim reported that he had spoken with Kumar as Samaranch had proposed during meetings held at the time of the IOC Session in Berlin last June, and he had told Kumar they wanted to talk about a joint organization of the 1988 Games. Samaranch said he had Kumar's written report. Kim said that in recent months the Games had been discussed in his country, and that to save the Games, they should be in both countries. He wanted Samaranch's help in this; he knew there would be many technical problems, but these could be discussed at the Lausanne meeting. The name of the Games could be the Korean Olympic Games. There could be seven or eight sports held in the North. They had already discussed this with the socialist countries.

Samaranch wanted to know if they were ready to open the border to everyone to cross by car, bus, and airplane. Kim said they could not open the border for one competition only. Samaranch replied that to divide the Games was contrary to the Olympic Charter. On the other hand, the IOC would do its best to show the world, although he was not sure how, that the goal of the two Koreas was to be united in the future and as soon as possible. Kim wanted to know what he should prepare for the Lausanne meeting. Samaranch said he should request things that were possible. Kim said he did not understand what Samaranch had in mind for the meeting. Samaranch said that his idea was to have the DPRK at the Games in 1988. This presence at the Games was very important for the athletes. He suggested that Kim arrive a day before the official meeting and that he would meet with his delegation separately prior to the meeting. Samaranch warned Kim, however, that any solutions must be in accordance with the Olympic Charter. That said, he was ready to help his country.

Kim was concerned that there would not be a result from the first meeting and that there might have to be several. They had already had three meetings with the South. The presence of the IOC would be an indication of good faith, but he did not really think that they would be able to reach an agreement. Samaranch did not think that they would find a quick solution, either. The "solution" might be to show that this was a beginning and that the two Koreas might have a later meeting. But, he said, he would never say that there had not been an agreement. Kim was worried about having a press conference if there was no agreement, but Samaranch assured him that, in the West, there was always a press conference following meetings of this nature.

Samaranch said that he would be in Kobe, Japan, at the end of August and would be traveling to Seoul from there. He wanted to meet Kim in Seoul to discuss the Lausanne meeting; Kim could come from Pyongyang to Seoul for that purpose. Kim said this was impossible; if he wanted to see Samaranch, he would come to Lausanne. Samaranch noted that the situation was difficult. What was the position of the DPRK regarding the 1986 Asian Games, to be held in Seoul? Kim said they had not yet decided. Samaranch said the delegations for the Lausanne meetings should be headed by the presidents of the two NOCs. Kim said that was fine for his side, since he was minister of sport, the IOC member, and president of the NOC. As for South Korea, the KOC president had no power. Who would be the "boss"? Samaranch said he would deal with this. Samaranch did not respond in writing to Kim's letter until July 31, and then only with a mere acknowledgment and a request for confirmation of the dates for the Lausanne meeting.

The "new" position of the DPRK with respect to the 1988 Olympic Games was released on the international scene, through one of the customary outlets for North Korean political news, the Kyoto News Agency. On July 30, 1985, the deputy prime minister of the DPRK, Chung Jun Gi, announced that the 1988 Olympic Games were *Korean* Games; Korea was a single country; the Games should be divided equally between the two parts of this divided country; the revenues from the Games, such as television rights and sponsorship receipts, should likewise be divided equally between the two parts of the Korean peninsula.

The South Koreans reacted almost hysterically. On August 2, sports minister Lee Yong Ho issued his own statement, which was expressed in the extreme language that habitually marked communications from one part of Korea about the other. "North Korea again exposed its wicked motive to use the Olympics as a political tool." The rhetoric continued:

> We cannot but conclude that North Korea's absurd demand is an anti-Korean frame-up schemed in a persistent bid to hamper the successful opening of the Seoul Olympics, and once again we express our regret that North Korea has craftily tried to sabotage the Seoul Olympics ever since Seoul was chosen in 1981 as the venue of the next Olympic Games.

Minister Lee went on to cite the many reasons why the North Korean proposal was unacceptable, each reason accompanied by derogatory statements about the North or bragging about the qualities of the South. It ended with a demand that the request from the North be withdrawn. There was little doubt that the proposal from the North had no merit whatsoever, and there was not the slightest reason, as a matter of the applicable Olympic rules and protocols, or of fairness, for the IOC to give the proposal any attention. Years ago, the IOC would simply have announced that the idea was out of time, not in accordance with the Olympic Charter, and would not be considered.

But this was 1985, and the IOC had progressed significantly in its sensitivity to political factors that might affect the Games. It was a virtual certainty, from the outset, that Games split between North Korea and South Korea would never be possible. The differences between the two regimes were too deep to be resolved within the remaining time before the Games. Kim Il Sung, shrouded in the closed society of the North, was too entrenched in Marxist doctrine to accommodate the practical implications of hosting a fully international event with complete access to press, visitors, and tourists. For the South, the Games were their showcase event and their entry ticket into the world community. They were not about to water this heady wine by sharing it with the DPRK.

One interesting byplay in South Korea's response to North Korea's proposal was the statement that South Korea had proposed "reasonable and realistic suggestions" to the North to form a single team for international competitions, to take part in the 1986 Asian Games and the 1988 Olympic Games, and to have athletic exchanges between the two parts of Korea, "only to hear insincere and poor excuses from the North." Korea followers will know that this issue had been, and would continue to be, a political shuttlecock between the North and the South, trotted out from time to time as the circumstances appeared to require. The same initiative had been proposed, this time by the North, on December 25, 1979, in a letter addressed to all national Olympic committees. The ostensible idea was to participate as a joint team in the 1980 Olympic Games in Moscow.[34] Within the Communist world, of course, this would have been seen as a subjugation of South Korea by North Korea on the "home" territory of the doctrinal leader of that world. The proposal had been sent out only a couple of days before the Soviet intervention in Afghanistan, which ultimately led to the boycott of those Games by many countries.

Despite its advance notice of the proposal, the question for the IOC was what to do in the face of it. The obvious answer was to simply state that the Games had been awarded to a city (which is the legal basis on which the decision was made), that the designated city was Seoul, that the contractual arrangements had been made, and that there was nothing the IOC could do at this late stage. There is probably not

[34] The problem was not new; it had been considered by the IOC as early as its Session in Munich in 1959. The IOC had asked the NOCs of the two Koreas to meet in Hong Kong to discuss the matter, but the meeting did not take place, as a result of the refusal of the South to take part. A partial agreement in principle on the subject had been reached in talks with the IOC in Lausanne in 1963. Meetings in Hong Kong between the two NOCs from May 17 to June 1, 1963, failed to resolve the outstanding issues. At the IOC Session in Baden-Baden in 1963, the IOC decided it was impossible to have a combined team of the two Koreas and resolved to allow separate participation effective in 1964. The major elements of the various meetings are set out in the Chronology, as is the history of the formation of a separate NOC in the DPRK and the lengthy struggle over the name that it would be entitled to use.

much doubt that twenty years earlier the IOC would have done exactly that, rejecting out-of-hand the tardy, patently unworkable, completely politically motivated, and probably insincere suggestion from Pyongyang.

Emotionally satisfying as such a response might have been, the IOC wanted to do nothing that could have the effect of destabilizing the situation relating to its overall objective, holding successful Games in Seoul. So, while privately rolling his eyes at the thought of divided Games, Samaranch took time to continue further canvassing of opinion on the matter, particularly with the Soviet Union, China, Japan, and some of the European governments that followed the situation in Asia.[35] Their advice was that he should *not* reject the possibility of divided Games and that he should offer to negotiate with the parties involved to see if there might be a mutually satisfactory solution.

The announcement by the IOC that it was prepared to discuss the possibility of Games divided between the North and the South caught most observers by surprise. It caused great concern in Seoul, which feared that it might be used as a political pawn.[36] The United States was concerned because of its special role on the Korean peninsula and the possible effects on the overall stability of the entire region. Many wondered what possessed the IOC to appear to yield to this North Korean demand, which was seen as unrealistic, presumptuous, and impractical in the extreme.

The whole idea was, essentially, a matter of buying time, first, to let the international acceptance of Games in Seoul grow, and second, to prevent countries sympathetic to or bound in a political manner to the DPRK from making any preemptive statements of nonparticipation

[35] Apart from the socialist sources, whose advice in the circumstances was quite predictable, Samaranch went back to Andreotti, whose suggestion along the lines of divided Games had been communicated to the ROK foreign minister a year previously. He also consulted a German ambassador he had met while he was Spanish ambassador in Moscow, who had a particular knowledge of security matters. Ambassador Dr. Hans G. Wieck concurred with the negotiation strategy and told Samaranch that the most dangerous time would be two years before the Games. (This happened to coincide with the 1986 Asian Games.) He told Samaranch that if the USSR and China decided to participate, then everything would be fine; in fact, once their two teams were present in Seoul, Seoul would become the safest city in the world. On the socialist front, the only real surprise, when all the decisions were eventually made in connection with the Seoul Games, came from Romania, which, in an almost complete turnaround from its enthusiasm to participate in Los Angeles, was loath to go to Seoul and participated with a much reduced team in 1988.

[36] As early as July 1984, upon learning of the suggestion by Andreotti that the Games be shared, the Koreans had advised the IOC, through their ambassador in the United States, that having the DPRK as cohost would only create opportunities to sabotage the Games.

in Seoul. It gave the Soviets and the Chinese an opportunity to build their own political consensus, since the IOC was showing itself to be not only aware of their political problems regarding the two Koreas, but also as sympathetic to the difficulties that the IOC knew they were trying to resolve. It gave both socialist countries a chance to show solidarity with the DPRK and not appear to be leaving it totally isolated, which might provoke some unilateral action that could draw them unwillingly into a confrontation with the West.[37] The DPRK was nothing if not unpredictable in such circumstances, and no one wanted to increase the likelihood of some precipitous action on its part. More time was needed to get the nonaligned nations on board, since the DPRK and some of its friends had been active for several years at this point in speaking and agitating against the Games in Seoul.

The IOC's reasoning was that if the North Koreans were involved in negotiating to share the Games, it would be inconsistent for them to continue the struggle in other forums to stop the Games from taking place. The move by the IOC to negotiate was, therefore, doubly effective: it bought time for the rest of the world to come to terms with Games in Korea, and it took the North Koreans out of the camp that might have been overtly trying to destroy the Games.

It also called their bluff. There was (and remains) a considerable body of thought that the demand to share the Games was never sincere in the first place and that it was nothing but a ploy to provoke the IOC into an outright rejection of the "offer." This could then have been used as ammunition to attack the IOC for giving the Games to only one part of a divided country that was technically still at war and to complain that solidarity among the socialist and nonaligned countries would require that the Games in Seoul be boycotted. It may well be that the North Koreans were themselves stunned by the IOC's official

[37] Private indications from the Soviet bloc had already been given that the intention of the sports leaders, at least, was to participate in Seoul despite the anticipated problems. Gramov had, for example, told Samaranch on his way to Sheremetyevo Airport in September 1984 that the USSR would compete in Seoul, but that the problem of the DPRK had to be overcome in some manner. By the end of March 1985, rumors had begun to circulate that the USSR had made the decision in principle to compete in Seoul. Some of this was linked to the policy of Gorbachev, who had just become general secretary of the Communist Party. By the end of May, wire service reports were stating that the Soviets were intending to send their best athletes to competitions to be held in the ROK and that they would compete in the Seoul Games. Experience has shown, however, that the enthusiasm of sports leaders can easily be shunted aside in the national interest, so it was far from safe for Samaranch to have relied on such assurances. They may have been comforting (assuming they were true), but they fell well short of guarantees.

response: "Well, it may be difficult to accomplish what you want, but let's discuss it."

Fortunately, as well, there had been preparations for a joint meeting of the Koreas that fall, albeit with a somewhat different agenda in mind.[38] It was thus possible for the IOC to be seen to be responding remarkably quickly, in the context of an international event, to this possible new crisis in a positive manner by bringing the two sides together under the auspices of the organization responsible for the Olympic Games.[39] These appearances were important in the political milieu, which was, suddenly, watching with great interest.

[38] This had come from the press conference given by Samaranch in Seoul the previous September, when he had indicated that the IOC was prepared to convene a meeting of the two Korean NOCs. Even that announcement had been preceded by an earlier call by Samaranch on May 4, when he had proposed a north-south meeting in Lausanne. There had been no reaction to the first announcement. The IOC Executive Board had approved the idea the previous November, and Samaranch had proposed such a meeting, again, on February 1, 1985. The KOC had already, on March 13, accepted the IOC offer.

[39] Formal announcement by the IOC of the joint meeting to be held under its auspices was made on July 24, 1985.

CHAPTER 5

Planning for the North-South Negotiations

THAT THE NEGOTIATIONS with and between the two Koreas would be difficult went without saying. That they were destined from the outset never to result in an agreement also went without saying, but for different reasons. The inevitability of failure could never be referred to in public. The IOC had to appear to be conducting the negotiations in good faith, and it did, in fact, conduct them in good faith. The fact that the IOC did not believe that the negotiations could ever result in a mutually satisfactory compromise to share the Games in an equitable fashion between the North and the South was irrelevant in the conduct of the negotiations. Had they been successful, there is no doubt that the IOC would have agreed to the split venue. The IOC also did its best to create conditions that might bring about an agreement, despite its realistic political assessment that it simply would not be possible to get the North Koreans to agree to comply with the myriad responsibilities of a host country of the Olympic Games.

As in all negotiations of an international nature, the ground rules are perhaps the most important element. The IOC was careful to establish rules designed to ensure that it remained in control of the process. The prospect of having them hijacked was always present, and the IOC wanted to make it clear who was in charge and who would make the final decision. This was a reasonable precaution to take, since the IOC was responsible for the allocation of the Games and was the final authority on all matters relating to them. If it controlled the agenda and the pace of negotiations, it could limit extraneous issues and keep the discussions focused on matters pertaining to the Games. It was important to establish and maintain the mental set that the North Koreans were petitioning the IOC, not vice versa.

Who would be the parties at the negotiating table? Here again, the IOC made an initial decision that was to stand it in good stead during the entire period: the parties, in addition to the IOC, would be the national Olympic committees of the two countries, not their respective governments. The Seoul Organizing Committee would, similarly, not be involved. Of course, it did not require a degree in rocket science to know that the two governments would, in fact, be intimately involved. Not a single position on the matters under discussion could be advanced by either side without the full concurrence, indeed, instruction, of the particular government. No concession could be made without a full study of its implications in the larger scheme of the overall relationship of the two states.[1]

But, in the convenient doublethink of diplomacy, there was no formal presence of either government nor any overt acknowledgment of such presence. Had there been, it would have ensured that no progress could have been possible. Ostensibly, therefore, these were friendly discussions between the IOC, as head of the Olympic Movement, and two of the NOCs recognized as the responsible Olympic bodies in their countries, seeking solutions to solely Olympic problems. Though just as deadly serious as the usual country-to-country negotiations, the patina of the Olympic meetings was smooth and unruffled.

The place of negotiations was equally symbolic. They would be conducted in Lausanne, at the headquarters of the IOC itself and in the boardroom used for meetings of the IOC Executive Board. The two NOCs were, therefore, negotiating with the IOC on the IOC's home ground. They had to travel to Switzerland to discuss a Korean problem. They had long lines of communication to deal with and time zones that operated against them. They had to deal with the inevitable problems of simultaneous interpretation. Everything was designed to make it possible for the discussions to occur and for positions to be fully articulated, but the North Koreans, in particular, had no authority to respond

[1] In the case of the Republic of Korea, the basic policy decisions were made by the president, Chun Doo Hwan, who communicated them directly to the SLOOC, in the person of Roh Tae Woo, who, in turn, passed them on to Park Seh Jik. The president was advised by representatives of the National Unification Board, the foreign minister, and the KCIA (and successor agency). No position would be taken without a thorough review of the implications from all perspectives represented.

except in total compliance with instructions given to them before they left the DPRK or that were relayed to them by their ambassador in Geneva. They were, therefore, constantly put in the position of not responding to reasonable compromises suggested through the offices of the IOC. This had the eventual effect, as the negotiations wore on, of eroding whatever sympathy they might have enjoyed on the international circuit, including that of their own close allies.

The chief protagonist throughout the entire period of the negotiations was Samaranch. Though he enjoyed the moral support and presence of the IOC vice presidents and one or two other advisers during the process of negotiation, their role was essentially one of being seen but not heard. Even during the informal portions of the meetings, when the IOC met on its own to consider the next steps and to give the Korean delegations opportunities to consider proposals that had been made or suggested to them, the other IOC representatives were very much directed by Samaranch. It was his show. Samaranch had the benefit of wide knowledge, gathered from an eclectic array of political and sports authorities, which enabled him to stay far enough ahead of the process to determine not only the pace at which progress would occur but also the direction the discussions would take. Although nerve-racking in the extreme because of the stakes, there is no doubt that Samaranch enjoyed the negotiations as an intellectual and political challenge. As a diplomatic exercise, it was a dream come true. Especially if it worked . . .

What of South Korea, which might, with considerable justification, have regarded itself as the meat in this particular Olympic sandwich? After all, it had followed all the rules, bid for the Games, won them, invested hundreds of millions of dollars in preparations, and entered into contracts in the expectation of hosting the Games; and all of a sudden, its unfriendly neighbor to the north wanted to share in the glory and the spoils. What was worse, it appeared as if the IOC, which had given it the Games in 1981, might now be having second thoughts. To say that the South Koreans were concerned would have been a masterpiece of understatement.

If one could point to a single element of this delicate political aspect of the eventual success of the Seoul Games, it would be Samaranch's gaining of the confidence of the South Koreans in relation to the negotiations with North Korea. As a matter of national importance prior to 1988, next to defending their territory against the ambitions of the

DPRK, nothing was more important than the staging of the Olympic Games. They were the focal point for economic, social, and cultural development on a scale unprecedented in South Korea's brief history as a separate state. There was virtually nothing they would not do to ensure the success of the Games. The thought that any portion of the Games might slip away from them, and worst of all, to the credit of the DPRK, was political agony to them.

Had the Koreans been left to themselves, the negotiations, had they occurred at all, would have been divisive in the extreme, conducted in the particular confrontational style perfected in Korea. Not a single compromise would have been offered, and everything on the political agenda would have been dragged into the process. Anecdotal reports abounded of so-called negotiations between the South and the North on other issues, in which the two sides had been unable to reach agreement even on which should make the opening statement, with the tragicomic result that the two opening statements were read at the same time. Imagine, therefore, what the South must have thought when Samaranch announced that the IOC was ready to discuss splitting the Games between the two parts of Korea? The North was even referring to the proposal as "cohosting" the Games, which, they had dared to suggest, should be referred to as the Pyongyang-Seoul Games.

Samaranch saw at once that not only had the IOC to keep the two Korean governments out of the direct negotiations, but that he had to win somehow the confidence of South Korea, to the point where it would let him make offers and commitments on its behalf.

The decision of the South Koreans to place their confidence in Samaranch will stand for years as an extraordinary gesture in many respects. In effect, the country allowed a complete foreigner to handle a highly sensitive national issue on its behalf, one that had major political overtones on both domestic and international levels and to which an enormous amount of publicity was attached. Had the eventual result been anything other than a complete success, the Korean leaders who gave Samaranch the mandate would, undoubtedly, have had to resign in disgrace, and political disgrace in Korea can be deep indeed. The country as a whole would have lost face enormously, and its single greatest opportunity to introduce itself as an important player in the industrialized world would have been squandered. Even the cross-cultural aspects of this delegation of power were significant. Generations of suspicion between East and West were overcome in the grant of confidence conferred upon Samaranch. It was a major gamble, but it worked. This was, by no means, a wholesale abandonment of responsibility and a delegation of it to Samaranch, but a hard-won, even grudging, bestowal of the power to negotiate, bit by bit as the events unfolded.

Credit for the courage to make the decision must be shared between two leaders: Chun Doo Hwan, president of the Republic of Korea at the time the negotiations began, and Roh Tae Woo, who was to become his successor in the first peaceful turnover of power in the young republic. Chun had always maintained that he would turn over power at the end of his mandate, and despite the suspicions of many that he would change his mind as the time drew near,[2] he was as good as his word. Roh was selected as the presidential candidate of the ruling Democratic Justice Party and was, in due course, elected as president of an initially somewhat shaky government.

The IOC already had some exposure to Roh, who was, for a time (1983–1986) the president of the SLOOC, the Seoul Olympic Organizing Committee. He had been a friend and supporter of Chun, one of the army generals who had been with Chun from the time he assumed power in Korea. In response to Samaranch's request for some stability among the stream of constantly changing faces within the Organizing Committee in the years following the Baden-Baden decision, on July 11, 1983, Chun appointed Roh, who very quickly demonstrated the qualities of leadership that were to mark his just-over-the-horizon presidency of the country.[3] He mastered the issues in no time and brought an ability to cut through the many problems that were the natural outgrowth of a well-entrenched vertical hierarchy typical of Korea.

This hierarchical structure in Korea was always a worry of the IOC about the Seoul Games: what would happen at the end of the road,

[2] This was a constant accusation leveled at Chun by the DPRK, in the customary intemperate language of its accusations against the ROK and the "criminal" or "puppet" Chun regime. It was also a major fear of the opposition parties in the South, who had visions of massive repression of the existing, limited political freedoms as part of the process by which Chun would retain power, were he not to retire. It is clear that there was a deep suspicion of Chun among the public and political groups in Korea. His ascension to power had been somewhat brutal, even by recent Korean standards, and he was not at all well regarded on the home front.

[3] Roh had already some familiarity with the Olympic scene, having coordinated the bid process for Seoul in 1981 from the home front in Seoul. He was already minister of political affairs at that time. The SLOOC had been established as the official Organizing Committee of the Seoul Olympics on November 2, 1981, and the interdepartmental Seoul Olympic Games Support Council, under the chairmanship of the prime minister, had been put in place the next month. In March 1982, a Ministry of Sports was established to provide administrative support for the organization of the Games, and Roh Tae Woo was appointed minister of sport.

when decisions would have to be made on a much more horizontally organized structure as the many Olympic venues came on stream during the Games? The Koreans, by philosophical disposition, operated quite comfortably within a vertical structure and seemed reluctant to act on the basis of personal initiative. During the preparatory stages, however, Roh solved the bottlenecks that had built up prior to his arrival, and the IOC was more than happy with him. He was quiet and unassuming; it seems to be a mark of authority in Asia that the more powerful the leader, the more quietly he or she speaks. One could hardly hear Roh. His subordinates, on the other hand, appeared to have no difficulty whatsoever hearing every word he said.

As the South prepared for the transition of power, which Chun had promised as part of his undertaking to serve only one term as president of the republic, the role of Roh in the history of his country started to become more apparent. In February 1985, Chun requested Roh to assume the presidency of the Democratic Justice Party.[4] Roh advised Samaranch of this appointment in a letter dated February 25, 1985, which was delivered to Samaranch by the member of the IOC in Korea, Park Chong Kyu, during a visit to New York. Samaranch wrote back to Roh on March 5, offering his congratulations, but urged Roh to remain as president of the Organizing Committee, not only because of the working relationships that had been established, but in the best interests of the Games and the international image of the country. Roh agreed, for the time being, to stay on in the capacity of chairman, which he did until early 1986, when his political duties became too demanding. The presidency of the Executive Board of the SLOOC was assumed, at the 1985 annual meeting on April 25, 1985, by Lee Yong Ho, the South Korean minister of sport.[5]

[4] This appointment had drawn mixed reviews in Korea, since it appeared to many that it was simply a matter of Chun's replacing himself with someone from precisely the same mold. Furthermore, he was closely identified with Chun's violent assumption of power. It soon became clear, however, that Roh was no mere clone of Chun. On the contrary, he had his own agenda and a much more deft political touch than Chun would ever have. If it is true that one grows into one's responsibilities, Roh became a textbook case to demonstrate such a proposition.

[5] Lee Yong Ho was removed as minister of sport on January 7, 1986, not long after the television negotiations with the U.S. television networks were concluded and a contract signed. Unrealistic expectations on the part of the Koreans at the beginning of negotiations had led to an inability to respond to lower offers and concerns that the U.S. networks were taking advantage of the Koreans. Lee purported to know more about negotiating with the U.S. networks than the North Americans and their advisers. The net cost of this intransigence was a diminution of $25 million in the rights fees. The contract with NBC was signed in Lausanne on March 26, 1986, after long and difficult negotiations. Lee's removal as president of the SLOOC Executive Board followed as a matter of course.

Approximately a year later, Samaranch met Park Seh Jik, who was introduced to him by another letter from Roh. Park was then Korean minister of sports and was also an army colleague of President Chun. In Roh's letter of introduction, Park was generously described by Roh Tae Woo as Chun's most trusted cabinet member, and Samaranch was assured by Roh that he should have no trouble confiding in and discussing with Park all the various issues and problems facing the IOC and the SLOOC. He went on to say, prophetically, that if close cooperation between the two continued into the future, he was sure that everything would work out smoothly. Roh looked forward to seeing Samaranch in Seoul at the forthcoming meeting of the IOC Executive Board with the national Olympic committees in April 1986. Park Seh Jik became the president of the SLOOC, following his appointment as acting president on March 13, 1986, and Roh assumed the honorary position of chairman. Park continued as SLOOC president through to the end of the Games, doing an excellent job in all respects.

Roh went on to become the candidate of the Democratic Justice Party for the presidency of the republic.[6] Once this nomination was made in June 1987, his time available for matters relating to the Games diminished virtually to nil, but he retained a consuming interest in the success of them and was always ready to take calls from Samaranch and to intercede to break the inevitable bureaucratic logjams that occur within a political system in the process of evolution from autocracy to democracy.

At one level, it was a disappointment when Roh was selected as the candidate to represent his party in the presidential elections in 1987. It meant that he could not continue as president of the SLOOC, despite the urgings of Samaranch, who knew full well what an asset he was as head of the Organizing Committee. The silver lining to the cloud was that Roh, should he become president of the republic, had an intimate understanding of the Games and their organization, far greater indeed than Chun had. This, too, proved to be an important factor in the eventual success of the Games. There were, however, many months of uncertainty and unrest yet to come before this would be resolved.

[6] Chun Doo Hwan made the announcement that Roh would be his candidate and successor during the course of a meeting at the Blue House on June 2, 1987. The decision was "publicly" announced on June 10 to the Democratic Justice Party Convention, which overwhelmingly and predictably confirmed the nomination. Roh immediately announced his intention to begin early discussions with opposition parties to reach agreement on constitutional amendments. Though one never knows what the future may bring, it is interesting to note that Roh mentioned to Samaranch as early as April 25, 1986, that he would be a candidate in the forthcoming presidential elections.

In the meantime, Roh and Chun had both gained an appreciation of Samaranch's abilities and, between them, agreed to let Samaranch have a certain amount of leeway with the negotiations on the "cohosting" issue.

The basic authority to negotiate was granted to Samaranch during his visit to Seoul on August 25–28, 1985. He first met with Roh on August 25, to discuss the North Korean proposal made earlier that year and to determine the degree of flexibility that could be granted during the negotiations. There was no question that the concept of cohosting was even thinkable, and Roh wanted to prevent the North from using the Lausanne meeting as a propaganda platform. This was a view expressed in forceful terms as well by President Chun Doo Hwan; in fact, he insisted that there be no events whatsoever in the North. Samaranch assured both Roh and Chun on two counts: first, there would *never* be Games in North Korea, and second, he would not permit the North to use the meeting as part of its propaganda. The IOC would control the meeting, the agenda, and the press conference. Roh, after consultation with President Chun, agreed that Samaranch could proceed.[7]

The basic strategy that was discussed and agreed between Samaranch and Roh during the course of their meetings that August was to set the tone for the overall negotiations with the North. The final decisions evolved from the discussions over a four-day period. Samaranch first suggested that the IOC preside over the meeting in Lausanne and that the meeting agenda be confined to the topic of the 1988 Olympic Games. Some proposals would be made to the North, which it might accept, such as preliminary elimination events in soccer, volleyball, and handball to be held in Pyongyang and that the cycling road race would start from Seoul, run through the North, and finish in Seoul. Only sports that were easy to organize would be candidates to be staged in

[7] This was, as indicated earlier, by no means a wholesale abandonment of final responsibility from the Koreans to Samaranch. He had asked, within the overall guidelines indicated, for the opportunity to "play" and to maneuver with the DPRK during the course of the discussions, so that the impression would be given of openness and cooperation in the entire process. He told them it would be good to offer something to the North. The ace in the hole, even assuming an agreement might be reached on the sports to be allocated to the North, was that it would eventually prove impossible for the border to be opened up to allow the necessary access to the athletes, officials, spectators, and media that are inherent in the Olympic Games. As a practical matter, this simply could never have been accomplished. The objective, overall, was to be seen to respond in a positive manner, to stretch out the negotiations, and to force the North eventually to reject reasonable proposals to be made by the IOC, rather than have the IOC refuse the North.

the North. At the time of entry into the stadium for the Opening Ceremony of the Games, the senior IOC member[8] would lead the procession, carrying the Olympic flag. The flag bearers of the South and the North would follow and be stationed behind the IOC member, to his right and left. Each team would enter in three lines behind its own flag bearer. After the Opening Ceremony, each side would field a separate team.

For the negotiation process, each delegation would be composed of six members, which must include the two NOC presidents. Other members of the delegations were to be high-status people with the right to make binding decisions. Each delegation would be entitled to bring its own advisers. Simultaneous interpretation services would be provided, with interpreters to be installed in the modern interpretation booths at the IOC headquarters. The talks would consist of four sessions. On the morning of October 8, a statement would be heard first from the North. This would be followed by a statement from the South. The IOC would then state its position. On the afternoon of October 8, the IOC would have separate meetings with the South and the North. On the morning of October 9, the IOC would hold a joint meeting with both Koreas or more separate meetings with both sides. The final joint meeting would be held on the afternoon of October 9. The IOC hoped that some agreements would be reached and even signed. A joint press conference would be held with the IOC and the two delegations after the final meeting. Most important, prior agreement between the IOC and the Republic of Korea would be needed on proposals to be presented to the North.

Roh agreed in principle with Samaranch's suggestions and, after reiterating his understanding that joint hosting of the 1988 Olympic Games would be excluded from the agenda of the joint meeting, as Samaranch had promised, agreed they should meet again on the morning of August 28.

On August 28, clearly after full study by the South Korean authorities, Roh had further comments for Samaranch on the proposal. He agreed in principle with the agenda, meeting procedures, and composition of the delegations for the meeting to be held in Lausanne. He agreed in principle, as well, with the proposed arrangements for the

[8] At the time, this would have been Kim Yu Sun of the DPRK (elected in 1978), which would have been less attractive to South Korea than their own member, Park Chong Kyu (elected in 1985).

entry into the stadium for the Opening Ceremony. Events that should be held at the main stadium, including Opening and Closing Ceremonies and athletics, could not be split and therefore could not be held at other places. Preliminary elimination matches for handball, soccer, basketball, and volleyball were possible candidates to be held in North Korea. The cycling road race might start from Seoul, run through North Korea, and end in Seoul. However, he said, if preliminary matches were to be held in the North for these events, the DPRK must guarantee the free entry and exit of the Olympic Family, as well as their security. The DPRK should open its airports and roads for the free use of the Olympic Family and the transport of their equipment and materials. Roh also said it might be acceptable for the Olympic torch relay to take place partly in the North and for North Korean runners to participate in the relay.

In this regard, it would be necessary to predicate agreement in principle with the fulfillment of certain conditions. The proceedings of the negotiations should not be open to the public. The IOC should prohibit North Korea from raising political controversies at the meetings. After each session, the IOC should announce the results, following the agreement of both sides. At the joint press conference, the delegation of the Republic of Korea, as the host nation of the Games of the XXIVth Olympiad, should be entitled to make statements. The SLOOC had designated its secretary-general as the official responsible for consulting with the IOC on matters relating to the meeting. Roh requested that Samaranch designate an IOC counterpart.

Samaranch replied to several items on this list of conditions. He thought that both sides should enter the Closing Ceremony in the same way as for the Opening Ceremony. He was of the view that, at this stage, it might be necessary to offer only two sports to the North. If the IOC were to pretend to ask the South to allow more than two sports to be held in the North, the South could make the gesture of refusing the IOC's proposal. With respect to the conditions to be imposed, it might be unrealistic to impose many difficult conditions for holding preliminary events in the North that would be very difficult for them to accept. It would be better to first secure their agreement in principle. He thought it would be almost impossible for North Korea to agree to holding only preliminary elimination events for the proposed sports, since that could be seen to make Pyongyang one of the cities of the Republic of Korea.

The proposal to be made for some preliminary elimination events to be held in the North might prove helpful, Samaranch thought, in encouraging the socialist countries to participate in the Games of the XXIVth Olympiad. If the meeting were to bear no fruit, North Korea would be completely isolated. It might be desirable for proposals regarding the Olympic torch relay and cultural festivals to be presented to the North in the course of the meeting, as possible concessions, if they were acceptable to the South. If the Olympic torch were to be relayed to the South through the North, the IOC would not object if North Korea set up an Olympic flame cauldron.

As to the results of the joint meetings, the IOC would announce the results after getting the agreement of both sides. However, when the IOC met with the sides separately, it might not be possible for the IOC to get each side's prior agreement. At the first session, the North Korean position would be heard first for one hour or less. Next, the Republic of Korea would be heard for the same period of time. Finally, the IOC would make an official statement concerning the positions of both sides. After the fourth session, the IOC would announce any agreement that had been reached. However, if no agreement were reached, the IOC would announce that positive meetings had been held and that a second meeting would be convened after six or seven months, preferably following the ANOC meeting in April 1986, rather than simply announcing the failure of the meeting. He, Samaranch, would be responsible for taking appropriate measures to prevent North Korea from bringing up political matters in the course of the session.

Samaranch would preside over the joint press conference, and he would announce the results of the meeting. If the Republic of Korea were allowed to make statements at this conference, North Korea should be accorded the same right. It would be difficult for the IOC to allow South Korea to comment unilaterally. The IOC *administrateur délégué*, Raymond Gafner, would be the IOC official designated to consult with the SLOOC on administrative affairs in connection with the Lausanne meeting. However, Roh and Samaranch should take the responsibility for making major decisions on the meeting. Samaranch asked Roh to send an aide-mémoire of the talks and agreements to the IOC in the near future.

Finally, the following agreement was reached between the two concerning the form and content of the forthcoming meeting:[9]

[9] Samaranch cleverly arranged for the Koreans to produce the document that contained the agreement between the parties.

• The agenda of the Inter-Korean Sports Meeting in Lausanne will be confined to the XXIVth Olympiad.

• Joint hosting of the XXIVth Olympiad will be excluded from the agenda.

• The Meeting will be composed of four sessions as President Samaranch suggested.

• The delegations for the Meeting will be composed of six high-ranking members with the power to make binding decisions and will include the two NOC presidents. Advisers to the delegations will not be limited in number, but cannot attend the meetings.

• At the meeting only two sports will be proposed as candidates for having their preliminary elimination contests held in North Korea.

• The possibility of the 180–200 km cycling road race running through North Korea may be presented to North Korea as a possible concession in the course of the sessions at the Meeting.

• At the time of entry into the stadium for the Opening and Closing Ceremonies, the senior IOC member will lead the procession, bearing the IOC flag. The flag-bearers of South and North Korea will follow him and be stationed behind him, to his right (South) and left (North). Each team, wearing different uniforms, will enter in three lines behind its own flag-bearer. Except for the Opening and Closing Ceremonies, each side will field a separate team.

• Some proposals regarding the Olympic Torch relay and the cultural festivals may be presented to North Korea as possible concessions in the course of the sessions at the Meeting.

• The sessions will not be opened to the public. In the sessions President Samaranch will take appropriate measures to prohibit both sides from raising political controversies.

• Following the IOC's separate meeting with either side, the IOC will announce the results at its own discretion. However, following the IOC's joint meetings with both sides, the IOC will announce their results after the agreement of both sides.

• President Samaranch will preside over the joint press conference and only he is entitled to announce the results of the Meeting.

• The Secretary-General of the SLOOC and IOC Administrator Mr. Gafner will be the designated officials to consult on administrative affairs related to the Inter-Korean Sports Meeting. However, Presidents Roh and Samaranch will continue to take responsibility for making the main decisions on the Meeting.

• The Seoul Olympic Organizing Committee will send an aide-mémoire of President Samaranch's talks with President Roh, and their agreement,[10] to the IOC.

Prior to the negotiations in Lausanne, the DPRK was organizing its own campaign. Local friendship organizations were contacting the NOCs in their countries, urging them to support the DPRK proposal. Kim Yu Sun sent a circular letter to all NOCs just prior to the start of the negotiations, dated September 30, 1985, outlining the DPRK proposal and asking for support of it. Socialist NOCs gave support and wrote to the IOC accordingly. There would, obviously, be several layers of "negotiations" and discussion conducted at the same time in this process.

Samaranch had been visited by the DPRK NOC again in Lausanne at the end of July for discussions about the forthcoming meeting. Two days after this visit, on July 30, DPRK deputy prime minister Chung announced that the 1988 Olympic Games were "Korean" Games and should be equally divided. The visit by the DPRK to Lausanne followed by a couple of days a visit by Samaranch to Moscow to attend the Spartakiade, a regular series of multisport games organized for the socialist countries. On that occasion, Samaranch met with Kim Yu Sun, who insisted on sharing the Games between the two countries. The DPRK had, he said, not decided on whether it would participate in the 1986 Asian Games. Two interesting sidebars occurred on this visit to the Soviet Union, at least from Samaranch's perspective. The first was that the KGB officer who had been assigned to him during his time as ambassador in Moscow told him that Gorbachev would make important changes in the USSR, particularly since Andrei Gromyko was no longer involved in foreign affairs. Additionally, he said, Gorbachev was one of those responsible for the Soviet boycott of the Los Angeles Games in 1984. The second was that on July 27, he visited Leningrad and discussed the prospective bid by Leningrad for the 1996 Olympic Winter Games with Mayor Khodyrev.[11] Samaranch left the USSR reassured that it was at least back in the Olympic "fold."

The president (at the time) of the Chinese Olympic Committee, Zhong Shitong, wrote to Samaranch on September 19 (prior to the

[10] The agreement referred to was this document.

[11] This was prior to the IOC decision in 1986 to change the cycle of the Games. The Winter Games, in the result, were scheduled for 1994 and 1998.

award of the 1990 Asian Games to Beijing) applauding the idea of a meeting between the two Koreas and indicating that the DPRK proposal was "worth serious consideration." If the proposal could be realized, it would help to ease the situation in the Korean peninsula, help the peaceful unification of Korea, and solve the problems that confront the Olympic Movement. It was his hope that the IOC would do something for the negotiations so that positive results might be achieved. It was not, by any means, a ringing endorsement of the DPRK proposal, but it clearly indicated that the Chinese were, for the time being, content to let the IOC manage the process.

Samaranch's reply was courteous in the extreme, thanking Zhong for both his advice and his support. He said the IOC was ready to use its best efforts to reduce tensions relating to the Games and to ensure that the Games were celebrated in accordance with the Olympic Charter, pointing out that the Charter applied equally, in relation to the Games, to the IOC, the IFs, and the NOCs. He was sure that "all parties" would discuss in the "utmost good faith" solutions to any problems that might exist and that the solutions would take into account the requirements of the Olympic Charter. He closed by saying that he was always grateful to receive any advice and counsel that Zhong might be prepared to offer on this and any other matters relating to the Olympic Movement.

The final organizational details relating to the first joint meeting were discussed with each delegation on October 7, 1985, in separate meetings. Each delegation would use its own interpreters, who would translate into English the words spoken by its representatives. They would work from the translation booths in the IOC Executive Board meeting room. The words spoken in English by the IOC delegation would be translated back into Korean by the interpreter for each delegation. Recording of the discussions would be made by the IOC alone, consisting of the original in each language and the English translation. No other recording device would be brought into the room or otherwise used. The IOC would be responsible for the minutes of the meetings.

For seating arrangements, the IOC would occupy the end of the table and the delegations would face each other along the sides of the table. A draw would be held at the start of the meeting to determine which delegation would be on the right-hand side of the table and which on the left. Only six representatives could sit at the table. Three counselors could sit behind their respective delegations but would not be entitled to speak. All others would have to wait outside the room.

Only the IOC would be permitted to make statements to the press. With respect to the bilateral discussions to commence the following afternoon, the time and the order of the meetings would be communicated at 8:00 A.M. the following morning. Each delegation was asked to refrain from making unilateral declarations prior to the end of the discussions.[12] The final press conference would be held by Samaranch in the presence of the two NOC presidents.

In the private meeting with the North, most of the time was taken up with Kim Yu Sun's explanation of the position of his delegation. The DPRK delegation wanted to use the meeting to present their proposal to jointly host the Games, taking into account the realities of a divided country. This would advance the unification of Korea and reduce the antagonism between the two countries. They would respect the advice of Samaranch and seek for points in common, rather than differences, in order to arrive at a solution that would assure the success of the Games. Samaranch said that he was pleased that Kim had agreed to the meeting and explained that the terms of the agreement they had reached last July 28 in Lausanne had been respected. Regarding the press conference, Kim could decide whether or not he wished to participate. As Kim was leaving, he said the IOC should pay attention to world public attention, which favored sharing the Games.

As for South Korea, Kim Chong Ha, president of the KOC, wanted Samaranch to take the floor immediately after the DPRK if the latter proposed to have joint Games, in order to state that this was out of the question. On the other hand, if the attitude of the DPRK was more moderate, South Korea, in its remarks, would propose the solutions that had been agreed between Samaranch and Roh during their meeting at the end of August.

Making sure that this preliminary meeting did not get away from his control even before it started, Samaranch told him that the meeting had been called by the IOC and would be run by the IOC in accordance with the agreement reached between all parties. The IOC would conduct the meeting in the manner it deemed best in order to arrive, if at all possible, at a final agreement. The DPRK would be given the first opportunity to speak and would be entitled to make any statement it chose, with the exception of political statements, in which case Sama-

[12] This fell within the category of pious wish and was not considered by anyone to be a remotely realistic possibility.

ranch would intervene immediately. The South Korean delegation would be given the next opportunity to speak, for the same length of time. Samaranch would speak last.

The first session of the meeting, he said, was not essential, since the IOC thought that the bilateral portions of the meetings later in the day and on the following day would be much more important. However, it was essential that the IOC and the IOC alone be the party that introduced the proposals that had been agreed upon by Samaranch and Roh.

The essential element of the meetings for Samaranch, he said, was that the two parties could meet together and demonstrate a spirit of friendship and cooperation. The position of the IOC was well known, and it would not go back on its word. The Games had been awarded to Seoul, and there was no question of their being shared. The IOC was trying to find and propose to the North the best possible conditions for participation so that they could respond positively to the invitation to participate in the Games. He said that the statement made by the DPRK delegation upon its arrival in Geneva had been quite reserved and appeared to indicate, for the first time, a real possibility for dialogue.

Samaranch advised the South Korean delegation to emphasize that they were in the process of organizing the Games in conformity with the provisions of the Olympic Charter and to insist that the Olympic Charter must be respected. Both the Seoul Organizing Committee and the KOC should be ready to listen to and to discuss reasonable proposals, but the Olympic Charter must be respected. Samaranch indicated that it was possible that an agreement might not be reached and that a second meeting might have to be held later. What was important, however, was that a dialogue had been opened and an important step taken for the future of the Olympic Movement.

And so the negotiations began.

CHAPTER 6

The First Joint Meeting with the Koreas

LAUSANNE, SWITZERLAND, October 8–9, 1985 — Important international meetings at this level do not just happen. As in any complicated theatrical production, there is a huge amount of preparation, so that the actors are in the right place at the right time and all the lines are known in advance, thus avoiding a loss of face that might result from extemporaneous debate. The issues were too important to be resolved at a single meeting; indeed, had they been so easily resolved, the participants would, undoubtedly, have been criticized for not having acted to reach the solution on their own initiative, and sooner. Everyone realized that the first meeting with the IOC was merely an overture, although important, and one that would give hints concerning the main themes to be developed. But still an overture.

Not one to overlook any symbolic opportunity, Samaranch had invited the *syndic* (mayor) of Lausanne, Paul-René Martin, to be present at the beginning of the meeting on October 8, 1985. Martin, befitting his role as mayor of the Olympic city, welcomed the representatives of both NOCs and hoped the atmosphere of his city would be conducive to favorable discussions on the subject of unity, the Olympic Movement, and the creation of a more peaceful world. Martin had been a longtime supporter of the IOC in Lausanne and firmly believed not only that the presence of the IOC in his city was an asset to it but also that the Olympic Movement did, in fact, contribute to a better world. Although Martin has stepped down as *syndic* of Lausanne, he remains a friend and is always included in IOC functions as an honored guest. He has become president of the foundation responsible for the new Olympic museum in Lausanne.

To make sure that no one leapt off to the wrong start, Samaranch reminded the two delegations[1] that they had each met with him the previous day and that they were, accordingly, fully aware of how the meetings would proceed. There would be separate meetings with each of the delegations, joint meetings as required, and a press conference given by Samaranch at the end of the second day. The presidents of the two NOCs were invited to join him on that occasion. For the record, he asked if there were any questions concerning the procedures. There were none.[2]

Kim Yu Sun, the president of the NOC of the DPRK and the IOC member in that country, was invited to make a statement on behalf of his delegation.[3] This was a fairly lengthy backswing, followed by the details of the request made by the North for a share of the Games. The political rhetoric was not unusual. Samaranch was first congratulated for his bringing together this meeting in the context of successful Olympic Games. The delegates from the South were welcomed "in the spirit of fervent compatriotic love." A serious difference of views and "crisis of possible split" had come up with respect to the venue of the Olympic Games. This was likely to "adversely affect" the future development of the Olympic Movement.

A minilecture followed on the lofty ideals of the Olympic Movement

[1] The DPRK delegation consisted of Kim Yu Sun, president of the NOC; Chin Chung Guk, vice president; Han Chang On; An Bok Man; Chang Ung; Cho Myong Hwang; and four interpreters. Chin was a professional diplomat, holding the rank of ambassador.

The ROK delegation consisted of Kim Chong Ha, president of the KOC (he had been elected president on May 1, 1985); vice presidents Chang Choon Sik and Choy Man Lip; members Lee Chong Ha, Yim Tae Soon, and Nam Joung Moon; and two interpreters.

[2] The North Korean propaganda machine had been active until the last moment before the first joint meeting. In the North Korean Workers Party newspaper *Rodong Shinmun* of October 7, 1985, there was a barrage of accusations against the South with respect to the Games. The charge that the South was unfit to host the Games was repeated, as was the assertion that it was trying to use them for "sinister political plots." The South was ritually described as "a colony and military base of the U.S. imperialists," and it was observed that "never in the history of the Olympic Movement spanning nearly 100 years have Olympic Games been hosted by a puppet in a colony." By staging the Games, the South hoped it would be recognized as an independent sovereign state and thus "freeze the division of Korea and legalize the U.S. imperialists' military occupation of South Korea and the colonial fascist rule."

[3] I have elected, in order to give the best possible "flavor" of the negotiations and to illustrate the frustrating nature of the process, to describe the negotiations in detail, rather than merely to summarize the progress that was achieved on each occasion. Therefore, the substance of each meeting, based upon the official records, is described using much of the vocabulary, sentence structure, and repetitiveness of the various parties.

and the adherence thereto by the DPRK. This led to a brief review of the history of Korea, a homogeneous nation having a five-thousand-year history, now suffering the misfortunes and agonies of a forty-year "tragic division."[4] North Korea and South Korea are parts of an artificially divided country, and "the compatriots of the north and south are the single-blooded kindred and brotherhood." To their regret, however, one side of the divided Korea had been designated to host the Olympic Games, contrary to the desire of their people for national unity and reunification.

Kim Yu Sun continued by saying that a considerable number of the IOC members did not fully understand the specific reality of their divided country at the time Seoul was designated as the venue for the Games. They must not have been aware of what difficulties the decision would bring to the Korean people's desire for reunification and what antagonism and confrontation it would entail between north and south. "Subsequent developments"[5] had "manifestly" shown that failure to take "epochal" measures with regard to the Games would lead to a situation that would be exceedingly harmful to the sound development of the Olympic Movement.

Moving more directly to the political aspects, Kim warned that a great many governments, the press, the public, and sports figures had voiced their views that the choice of Seoul was "irrational" and that either the alteration of the Olympic venue or other new "epochal" measures would be indispensable in order to avert a serious crisis. If the Games were to take place as now contemplated, "not a small numbers" of countries without any diplomatic relations with "south Korea"[6] would refuse to participate in the Games. All these facts, he said, gave a serious lesson that the Olympic venue was not merely a working matter of sports and that it required further thought and consideration, particularly in the case of holding the Olympic Games in a divided country.[7]

The guiding principles that should apply, and in the context of which

[4] The genesis of the tragic division was not described.

[5] These were unspecified.

[6] In all its written material, the DPRK studiously avoided capitalizing *south* when referring to South Korea.

[7] No reference was made to the 1972 Munich Games, which were, arguably, held in a similarly divided country.

the proposals from the North would be made, were, first, that the Games in 1988 should be a great international festival for all countries to participate in; second, that the Games should be Games of friendship and cooperation, not antagonism and confrontation, for détente, not tension, for reunification and not separation; and, third, to organize and hold the Games to serve the interests of all member organizations of the Olympic Movement and not "encroach" upon the interests of "a certain member" organization or a few or several member organizations.

After serious study and search, said Kim, the North had come to the conviction that the most realistic and reasonable way was for North Korea and South Korea to *jointly* host the 1988 Olympic Games. Their specific proposal had ten elements:[8]

> (1) The north and south will jointly host the Games and field a single team of the north and south to the Games.
> (2) The Olympic Games are to be named the "Korea Olympic Games" or "Korea Pyongyang-Seoul Olympic Games."
> (3) The disciplines of the Games will be allotted "equally half" to Pyongyang and Seoul.
> (4) The opening and closing ceremonies for the allotted disciplines will take place respectively in Pyongyang and Seoul.
> (5) It shall be guaranteed (by the host cities) that all the necessary preparations for the Olympic Games will be completed in the "shortest time" in compliance with the rules and bylaws of the IOC and the international sports federations.
> (6) Regarding the free exchange of visits:
>
> > (a) Adequate conditions will be provided for the athletes, officials, journalists, and tourists to freely travel between Pyongyang and Seoul by land, sea, and air;
> > (b) For such a free exchange of visits, roads and railways will be connected between Pyongyang and Seoul, and passenger liner service will open to traffic between the Nampo Port linked with Pyongyang by highways and the Inchon Port linked with Seoul by highways;
> > (c) For the maximum convenience and expeditious travels [*sic*], passes will be issued by the respective sides at the crossing points, instead of visas, for the athletes, officials, journalists, and tourists entering the respective areas of the north and south;

[8] This was the first official exposé of the DPRK plan for the jointly hosted Games.

(d) The authorities of the north and south will issue in advance their respective statements on guaranteeing the security for the travelers and carry them out.

(7) With respect to the television rights, the televising [*sic*] rights will depend on the contract, and the profits from the televising rights will be allotted reasonably through consultations;
(8) The formation of a standing body for the joint hosting of the Games was proposed:

(a) A north-south standing body will be organized for the successful joint hosting of the Games;
(b) The north-south joint standing body will be named the "Joint Organising Committee of the Korea Olympic Games" or the "Joint Organising Committee of the Korea Pyongyang-Seoul Olympic Games";
(c) The above-mentioned Joint Organising Committee will consist of the two Co-Chairmen representing the north and south respectively and of a necessary number of its standing members;

(9) Other details will be separately worked out for agreement of views;
(10) A document of agreement will be drawn up on the north-south joint hosting of the Olympic Games and entering a single team into the Games.

Having dropped this piece of work on the meeting, Kim Yu Sun went on to say that there were solid material and technical foundations for the joint hosting and adequate facilities already in place.[9] He reiterated that their proposal for joint hosting of the Games was the most appropriate and realistic proposal for successful Olympics. The proposal was in "full accord" with the lofty ideals and principles of the Olympic Movement aimed at peace and friendship, harmony and cooperation, but "also reflects our sincere position to glorify the Olympic Games as the greatest sports festival without any turns and twists." The balance of his opening statement was directed mainly at the north-south situation in Korea and the contribution that the proposal could make to the development of friendly relations.

Samaranch then invited Kim Chong Ha, president of the Korean Olympic Committee, to make an opening statement.[10] South Kim's re-

[9] This was not true; almost all of the facilities and infrastructure would have had to be built.

[10] Since the presidents of the two NOCs have the same family name, I have referred to them, for purposes of convenience from time to time in the description of events and dialogue, as "North Kim" and "South Kim."

sponse was much shorter than North Kim's statement. He had no counterproposal whatsoever. Apart from the opening courtesies, South Kim made a point of referring to sports meetings held on a bilateral basis between North Korea and South Korea the previous year, just to underline that this present process, though novel, was not the only effort made to try to resolve the general situation.

South Kim's presentation was essentially a combination of history and the legal position of the South in relation to the 1988 Olympic Games, to make it a matter of record for the IOC that the IOC would have to break its rules and contracts in order to split the Games in any way.[11] He recalled that, since its recognition in 1948, the Korean Olympic Committee (KOC) had participated in the Olympic Games on nine occasions.[12] He pointed out as well that, following the IOC's decision to award the Games to Seoul, the KOC had established the SLOOC as the formal organizing committee for the Games, had undertaken the necessary construction of the sports facilities, and was in constant cooperation with the various international sport bodies in connection with the proper organization of the Games.

Driving home the legal position, he noted that the IOC had, officially, entrusted the KOC and the city of Seoul with the authority necessary for organizing the Games. In accordance with the Olympic Charter, a detailed agreement had been signed by the IOC, the KOC, and the city of Seoul. It was, therefore, an "established fact" that Seoul had been given the right to host and organize the Games. The KOC wanted to make it clear that it would faithfully fulfill its duties, enjoying the privileges provided by the IOC.

Moving from the legal position, Kim Chong Ha said that when Seoul was chosen in 1981, it was on the basis that IOC members, the international sports federations, and the national Olympic committees who had visited Seoul were satisfied that Seoul was the most suitable venue for the Games. All remained satisfied and were pleased with the preparations. The main Olympic Stadium had been dedicated the previous year,[13] on September 29, 1984, and the celebratory competitions had

[11] This was the approach that Samaranch had recommended he adopt for purposes of his opening statement.

[12] They had, not surprisingly, considering the U.S. influence in the Republic of Korea, "supported" the Carter boycott of the 1980 Games in Moscow.

[13] The minutes of the meeting incorrectly refer to the previous "month."

attracted athletes from China, the Soviet Union, East Germany, Poland, Hungary, Yugoslavia, and many other countries allied with the DPRK. All such events had been a great success.

Not only that, he observed, but the delegates to the General Assembly of ANOC, the organization grouping all the NOCs of the world, had, in late 1984, adopted the so-called Mexico Declaration, which called on all NOCs to proclaim their loyalty to the Olympic Charter and the Olympic ideals, to contribute to the success of and participate in the Games to be held in Seoul (and Calgary, for the Winter Games) in accordance with the decision of the IOC in Baden-Baden in 1981 and declaring the opportunity to compete in the Olympic Games as the fundamental right of the athletes and that to guarantee this right is the fundamental duty of the NOCs. The Extraordinary Session of the IOC in December of the same year had also resolved that all NOCs should participate in the Games in Seoul. The report by the SLOOC to the 1985 Session of the IOC in Berlin had been well received. In short, the Seoul Games were sure to be "the most brilliant success in the history of the Olympics."

As for North Korea, "the door is wide open for North Korean athletes to freely participate in the Seoul Olympiad, as athletes from the rest of the world will." South Kim expressed the sincere hope that North Korea would participate in the Games awarded to Seoul by the IOC Session and discuss the matter, respecting the Olympic Charter and the right of the South to host the Games. He hoped that all participants at the meeting would confer, respecting the above decision (the award of the Games to Seoul), the Olympic Charter, and the spirit of the Olympics.

Hardly a promising beginning, but no one had thought it would be easy. The positions were at opposite poles, whatever the merit of each, and there had been not the slightest indication that any form of compromise might be in the offing. Samaranch terminated the meeting with both delegations, in order to meet separately with each later in the day and to have a chance for the IOC to review its own position and role.

During the IOC's internal meeting[14] after the two delegations had left, Samaranch observed that the Games had been awarded to Seoul

[14] The IOC delegation at the first joint meeting consisted of Samaranch; vice presidents Berthold Beitz, Ashwini Kumar, and Alexandru Siperco; Raymond Gafner; Sheik Fahad Al-Ahmad Al-Sabah, IOC member in Kuwait and president of the Olympic Council of Asia; and Alain Coupat.

and that Seoul was properly carrying out its obligations in that regard. A great deal of work was being done, and considerable investment had been made by the South Koreans. The DPRK had always had a negative attitude toward the Games, but it was now thought, said Samaranch, that the DPRK wanted to share in the prestige that Seoul might reap from hosting the Games. He noted as well that this was the first *official* proposal from the DPRK to share the Games. The world would be focusing on the outcome of the meetings, and the IOC should be seen to be doing its best to facilitate some sort of agreement between the two Koreas. The other IOC delegation members were, not surprisingly, in agreement with this assessment. The very divergent views put forward at the opening session gave no basis for a possible compromise. In particular, there was no counterproposal whatsoever from the South.[15] The initial plan had been to meet first with the North, but this was changed, in order for the IOC to see what the South might be prepared to offer.

Following the plan that he had made with Roh Tae Woo, Samaranch suggested that there were some areas that could be put forward to be discussed with the South, such as having the teams of the two Koreas march together during the Opening Ceremony, the DPRK being invited to stage some cultural events during the Games and some minor events or preliminary rounds of some team events, and, possibly, even some finals in the DPRK.[16] The general plan was to see what the South might be prepared to agree to do, then present this to the North as a possible compromise to which the South might agree, at the IOC's urging, in the interest of accommodating the North.[17]

After lunch, the South met separately with the IOC. Samaranch assured the delegation that the IOC would honor its obligations under the contract it had signed with Seoul back in 1981. However, the active

[15] This was hardly surprising, since it was the first time the North had officially set out its proposal. In addition, the nature of the opening session of the negotiations was simply opening statements by each side. It would not have done for the South to appear to be eager to do anything to accommodate the North's request to jointly present the Games. Apart from that, Samaranch had advised South Kim not to make any counterproposal at this initial stage.

[16] The idea of finals was new.

[17] The idea of doing whatever was necessary to keep the door open for continued negotiations was very important to Samaranch and reflected the advice he had received from European NOCs to the effect that if this did not occur, many of them could face difficulties with respect to participation in Seoul.

participation of the DPRK in these Games should be promoted to the greatest possible degree. He asked Kim Chong Ha if he had any proposals in that regard.

Kim said it was no easy matter to make changes at this stage. Detailed competition schedules had been prepared and accepted by the international federations and approved by the IOC, quite apart from the whole matter of the adherence to the Olympic Charter. Nevertheless, he was prepared to consider the possibility of having some preliminary events in handball and volleyball held in North Korea. Finals would, of course, be held in Seoul. This would all be subject to the agreement of the IOC and the international federations concerned. Many other related questions would have to be investigated, such as transportation, access to competition sites, communication networks, and a host of other essential logistical issues.

Samaranch, coaching a witness who seemed to have forgotten some of his lines, asked whether Kim Chong Ha had any proposals regarding soccer. The South was ready to consider suggestions, since it is usual to spread the preliminary matches in the Olympic soccer tournament around to various cities in the host country. Kim would review the possibility of having two groups of the soccer tournament play preliminaries in the North. Semifinal and final matches would be in Seoul. The questioning continued. What proposals might Kim have with respect to individual sports? Perhaps the cycling road race could be staged to involve both the North and the South, such as by beginning the race in North Korea and finishing in South Korea. Cooperation between the two NOCs in organizing this event would symbolize the genuine effort toward understanding and peaceful reunification.

As to the Opening Ceremony, Kim Chong Ha proposed simultaneous entry of the two teams into the stadium. They would march under separate flags, and each team would have its own uniform. The South Korean team would march on the right side of the track and the North Korean on the left. (This is not without protocol importance, since the team on the right is the closest to the crowd and is the most visible to the audience in the stadium and, even more important, to the billions who would watch the event on television.) Samaranch made no comment on this, but asked what role the North might play in the cultural events at the Games. After a ten-minute break for consultation, Kim said that the cultural events were very important aspects of the Games, and they would be prepared to welcome active participation from the North in such events.

Kim reiterated that athletes and officials from the North would have no difficulties regarding entry and participation. As to the subject matter of the current discussions, he wanted to be sure the IOC was firm in its commitment to the principle that the Games were awarded to a city and that, also in principle, the competitions should be held in that city. He recognized that some events might well take place in stadiums outside Seoul, but that generally it was understood these events would be in that territory under the jurisdiction of the host NOC. If some events were to be held in North Korea, special authorization would be required from the IOC, and the other aspects of facilities and logistics would have to be reviewed before South Korea would ask the IOC to give its final approval to such a scheme. He urged that extreme caution be exercised in all reports issued to the press, in view of the delicate situation.[18]

Dealing with the latter point first, Samaranch said that he would issue a report at the official press conference the following day, after further talks with both NOCs. He then thanked Kim Chong Ha for his willingness to cooperate, reviewed the areas of compromise that had been discussed, and terminated that portion of the meetings.

Later the same afternoon, the IOC met with the North. The usual kind and flattering words were expressed as everyone settled down in preparation for the real discussions. Samaranch began by saying that the IOC could not accept the proposals made by North Korea, since they were contrary to the Olympic Charter. The Games had been awarded by the IOC to Seoul in 1981, and the IOC now had to stand by its decision as well as to respect the contract it had signed with the KOC and with the city of Seoul.

However, the presence of the delegation from North Korea indicated that they were realistic and that they wanted to have the best possible participation for the Games. This had led to the convening of the meetings in Lausanne under the aegis of the IOC. Though the IOC could not accept their proposal, it might, nevertheless, be possible to arrange for the organization of some events in the North. Samaranch wanted to know if the North was ready to discuss such a solution.

As was to be the case during most of the negotiations, Kim Yu Sun

[18] This, of course, was at the very heart of the political problem for both Koreas. The South wanted it to be clear that it was the host nation and that anything it might give to the North should be seen as just that — an accommodation made by the official host of the Games. The North, on the other hand, was desperately afraid of being maneuvered into a position that would be manifestly subservient to the South.

did not answer the question directly. Instead, he revisited most of the same points he had made during the morning session. Joint hosting was the key to the whole position. He said that many countries were considering refusing to send teams to the Games, but that support for joint Games had been voiced. It was clear from his remarks that what was at issue was recognizing that the North had an involvement of sufficient importance to be able to refer to themselves as "hosts" and not be described with some lesser appellation. Kim urged the IOC, once again, to understand the North's proposals and to consider them favorably.

Samaranch thanked him for his comments. Kim Yu Sun then proposed that the following sports be staged in North Korea: archery, judo, track and field, gymnastics, weight lifting, volleyball, table tennis, wrestling, handball, shooting, and swimming.

A break of ten minutes followed.

Samaranch reiterated that, to be very clear, the IOC could *not* accept the proposal, but that to try to provide the best possible conditions for the participation of the DPRK in the Games, the IOC wanted to know if they were ready to begin discussions regarding the possibility of organizing some events in the North. If the delegation needed more time to consider the position, Samaranch said the IOC would be prepared to wait until the following morning for a response.

Kim Yu Sun did not let go. He said that the IOC had initiated and organized the meeting, as a result of which his NOC had started its own discussions regarding the various problems.[19] That was the reason they had set forth the proposal during the morning session and why separate discussions were being held with the IOC during the afternoon. Since Samaranch, as president of the IOC, had stated that some events could be staged in Pyongyang, the North had considered that the IOC had agreed to the Games being shared between North Korea and South Korea.[20] That was the reason his NOC had officially proposed that it stage certain events. If the Games were not held jointly,

[19] This is not wholly consistent with what the DPRK had already done, such as distributing the manifesto on its position regarding the Games even before it had officially agreed to the joint meeting with the IOC.

[20] It was never clear exactly to which statement by Samaranch he was referring, but it may have gone all the way back to the meeting between Kim Yu Sun and Samaranch in September 1984 in Moscow. Samaranch had asked Kim at that meeting if the North would be prepared to organize some events in Pyongyang, and Kim had said he would reply at the November meetings in Mexico. It was, however, a considerable "jump" to conclude from any such discussion that the concept of "cohosting" was thereby on the table for discussion.

Kim submitted, the Olympic Charter would be contravened.[21] His proposals had been reasonable and rational; the IOC should reconsider them.

Samaranch countered by saying that the IOC had considered the North's proposals very carefully and could not accept them. The IOC had no power to alter its 1981 decision to award the Games to Seoul. No "joint" Games could be held, as this would contravene the Olympic Charter. What the IOC was now asking was whether the North was ready to discuss the possibility of organizing some events. If they needed some time to study such a proposal, the IOC was ready to grant it. Kim Yu Sun, continuing the dialogue of the deaf, said that his NOC had proposed the events that it wished to hold and hoped that the IOC would study this proposal once more. His delegation would provide the IOC with a response to its suggestions the following morning. DPRK NOC vice president Chin Chung Guk said that both the IOC and the NOC should reconsider each party's proposal prior to the morning meeting.

The next morning showed that, clearly, not much progress had been made overnight.[22] Samaranch stated the purpose of this further meeting. North Kim restated that cohosting was the most efficient way of ensuring the success of the Games. The Baden-Baden decision had not taken sufficient account of the realities of the situation in Korea. The Olympic Charter was all very well, but it was not always strictly adhered to, as was the case with the 1956 Olympics, when the equestrian events had to be held in Stockholm, rather than in Melbourne, due to the quarantine regulations in Australia.[23] Similarly, at the 1984 Los Angeles Games (which the North had not attended) there had been two Olympic Villages, whereas the Charter stipulated that there be only one.[24] His proposal for cohosting the Games should be reconsid-

[21] Though this might be seen as an attempt to refute the legalistic approach taken by South Kim at the morning session, North Kim did not make any attempt to specify how there would be a contravention of the Olympic Charter were his proposals not to be adopted.

[22] Each of the parties had been in contact with the press, the North warning of massive boycotts if its proposals were not accepted, and the South stating that the award of the Games to Seoul was irrevocable. The North would not be satisfied with symbolic treatment, and the South said the North's demands were unreasonable and more extensive than they had expected.

[23] Once again, North Kim omitted any reference to the 1972 Munich Games, in which his NOC had participated.

[24] In fact, separation of Olympic Villages is relatively common. Yachting events have often been widely separated from the other Olympic events, and many Olympic Winter Games have had separate Olympic Villages. Also not mentioned was the separation of the Olympic Villages in Helsinki, in which the Soviet Union had insisted its athletes be separately quartered.

ered, since it reflected the Olympic ideals of peace, harmony, and friendship.

Samaranch stressed that the proposal for joint hosting was not acceptable to the IOC. The Games had been granted to Seoul and should be organized by Seoul. However, certain agreements could be reached in order that all Koreans should participate to the greatest possible extent in these Games. Both the IOC and the KOC were prepared to consider organizing some events in the North, a contribution to the cultural program, and a joint parade of Korean athletes at the Opening Ceremony. These proposals could be reduced to writing in a few days, and at a subsequent meeting North Korea could present its reactions. North Kim thought that the cohosting proposal should be further studied.

After a short break, Samaranch, escalating the diplomatic language, said that the IOC "rejected" the proposal for joint hosting of the Games. The IOC would forward a letter to the North Korean NOC advancing certain ideas that would involve them more actively in the Games. These ideas could be studied and comments brought forward at a further meeting, to be held on January 8–9, 1986. North Kim said he would be pleased to study the proposals. Samaranch said there would be a further joint session later that afternoon and a press conference following the meeting, which North Kim was welcome to attend.

North Korea's departure was followed by the arrival of South Korea. Samaranch said the meetings had been progressing "smoothly," although the position of the North was "very different" from that of the IOC. The North had made a proposal that the IOC could not accept, since it was contrary to the Olympic Charter and to decisions taken by the IOC subsequent to the awarding of the Games to Seoul in 1981. He advised that after the meeting held with the South, the IOC had proposed to the North that it organize certain events, parade jointly at the Opening Ceremony, and take part in the cultural program. He felt, however, that this was not the right moment for the NOC of the North to discuss such a proposal.[25] Accordingly, he had decided to send a letter to North Korea during October 1985, and to suggest a further meeting in January of the following year.

Before writing, Samaranch wanted to know whether the KOC had studied the possibility of fielding a joint team for 1988. He was aware that talks had been held in recent years, but wanted to know what the

[25] Not only was it clear that the North would need time for consideration and the receipt of instructions, but also the idea of stretching out the negotiations was most important for the IOC.

NOC thought. Kim Chong Ha of South Korea said that this matter had been discussed continually between North Korea and South Korea, the first meeting having occurred in June 1981, when his NOC had discussed sports exchanges between the two countries and had proposed fielding a single team for the 1984 Olympics.[26] No reply had been received until five months before the Games, at which time it had not been possible to enter a joint team.[27] Kim also pointed out that the socialist countries had joined the USSR in its boycott of Los Angeles. Three meetings had been held,[28] all of which were unsuccessful. He also said that (presumably in the context of the DPRK boycott of the 1984 Olympics) the North had said it would never again discuss the question of a single team with the NOC of the South.

If, however, the IOC recommended such a solution and the NOC of the North agreed, his NOC would discuss the matter directly with the NOC from the North.[29] He noted, in tempering the agreement to discuss the matter, that from his perspective, the fielding of a single team would mean, to North Korea, the cohosting of the Games and that the North would take the position that it was cohosting the Games should this occur.[30] Apart from this, they would treat the proposal

[26] No such talks actually took place in June 1981. There had, however, been a proposal from the president of the Korean Amateur Sports Association on June 19, 1981, directed to the DPRK, which suggested sports exchanges and the formation of a single team for international events. According to then KOC president Chung Ju Yung, the first communication of what might be considered a response to that suggestion of June 1981 had been a letter from Kim Yu Sun dated March 30, 1984.

[27] The DPRK proposal suggesting a single joint Korean team for the 1984 Olympic Games was made on March 30, 1984. Kim Yu Sun advised Samaranch by telex the same day. The call for a north-south meeting to discuss the proposal was accepted on April 2 by the KOC, which proposed the date and agenda. KOC president Chung Ju Yung advised Samaranch of his acceptance of the request for the meeting by telex dated April 3, which included the text of his response to Kim Yu Sun. SLOOC president Roh Tae Woo also advised Samaranch separately of this development and drew specific attention to that portion of the KOC response that referred to the Rangoon bombing in October 1983. The DPRK accepted on April 6. On April 7 and 8, the KOC and the DPRK named their respective delegations. The first of the series of meetings was held on April 9 at Panmunjom. In addition to the Rangoon issue, the DPRK decision to boycott the 1984 Games doubtless put an end to the necessity of considering the matter at that time.

[28] The two additional meetings were held, all at Panmunjom, on April 30, 1984, and May 25, 1984. A fourth had been proposed for August 30, 1984, but did not take place.

[29] The most recent call for north-south meetings had come from the South, in a letter from the KOC to the DPRK dated July 25, 1985. It appeared to be the nature of the relationship that if one side wanted such a meeting, the other did not. The ebb and flow of this dynamic had long marked such dialogue.

[30] In the larger political context of the matter, this would obviously have created major problems for the South.

seriously and were ready to discuss it directly with the North. Samaranch agreed that this was a matter that should be pursued directly between the two NOCs, without the IOC's involvement. It was evident that such discussions, if they occurred at all, had no prospect whatsoever of success. They would also involve collateral matters, into which the IOC did not wish to be drawn. Hence the rapid agreement from the IOC that these discussions be bilateral.[31]

Samaranch's other question to Kim Chong Ha during this portion of the meeting was whether the South was prepared to offer any other events to the North. It was not.[32] It considered that the North would only be satisfied with organizing exactly half of the Games. Samaranch said the IOC would study the possibility of offering other events to the North, since the IOC's idea was to allow them to stage some events and also to facilitate their participation in Seoul. He said that a copy of the letter sent to the North would be sent to the South. Would the KOC be prepared to meet again in January? The IOC would not offer any additional events to North Korea without first consulting South Korea. The IOC's position was clear; it would respect the Olympic Charter and the decisions taken since the Games were awarded. The Games had been awarded to Seoul and would take place there, but the IOC was attempting to offer "something" to the NOC of the North to enable the North to take part in 1988. That was the whole purpose of the meeting.

By the standards of this negotiation, South Kim's reply was ragingly positive. He appreciated Samaranch's confirmation that the IOC would respect the charter and the decisions taken regarding the choice of Seoul as the venue for the Games. They were prepared to offer something to the North in order to pay tribute to the efforts of Samaranch to ensure wide participation in the Games. If the NOC of the North respected the Olympic Charter and the decision to award the Games to Seoul, his NOC would be prepared to participate in the January 1986 meeting.

The final meeting of the first round of negotiations was held the

[31] There was certainly no incentive for the IOC to get drawn into the entire range of north-south issues that would inevitably arise during any such discussions. Samaranch was consistent throughout the entire negotiations with the two Koreas that the matter of a joint team was one for the Koreans to deal with on their own. This was, however, at variance with his initial position on the matter, in which he had offered the IOC's services for just such negotiations. The latter decision was clearly the better course.

[32] This refusal was consistent with the contents of the negotiating strategy agreed upon between Samaranch and Roh.

afternoon of October 9, 1985, and involved both NOCs. Samaranch thanked both delegations for their constructive attitudes during the negotiations. He was sure this meeting would prove useful in obtaining an agreement that all Koreans would be involved in the 1988 Games. Before making his final statement, he gave the floor to the two NOC presidents.

North Kim had a statement. He reiterated his proposal for joint hosting of the Games as one that was, he said, constructive and that of a single team as the most appropriate for the Korean situation and in accord with the world's desire for "smooth development" of the Olympic Movement. He continued with, essentially, the content of his opening statement, almost as if the entire process that had occurred had never existed. He noted that they would be returning home without any "good result" from the joint meeting that could "satisfy their expectation and desire" but held out a generally expressed hope that "if we seriously consider the prevailing situation before the Olympic Movement and display the spirit of unity and cooperation, bearing in mind the hope of the world people and sportspeople, we will be able to have a good result."

If ever one wonders why diplomats are driven, on occasion, to drink, this meeting is a perfect example.

South Kim had no prepared text. He thanked everyone for the meetings and their participation and the serious manner in which the parties had conducted the discussions. His NOC felt very firmly that all the Korean people should participate in the 1988 Games. Within the framework of the Olympic Charter, his NOC was prepared to offer some events to North Korea, and he hoped they would respond in a positive manner to such a gesture and that successful dialogue would ensue. Although no final agreement had been reached, South Kim expressed the wish that all Koreans should "honorably" be able to participate in the Games to be hosted by *his* NOC.

At the press conference, the IOC issued a rather vague communiqué outlining the meeting that had just occurred. Part of the communiqué made it very clear that the IOC was not wavering from its decision to give the Games to Seoul. Another made it clear that it would be looking equally hard, in the interests of those very Games, at how to get the widest possible involvement from the Korean people. Though some progress had been achieved, the IOC felt that further discussions were necessary before an agreement could be reached; the IOC had proposed they be held in early January of the following year. The parties had agreed to such discussions. The communiqué pointedly mentioned that the meeting had been called at the initiative of the IOC.

Had the reaching of an eventual agreement been essential to the successful staging of the Games, this would have been a most discouraging meeting, since the North had shown no flexibility whatsoever. The concessions agreed to by the South were real, but in the context of a negotiation that was predicated by the DPRK on a cohosting concept, they fell far short of what would be required to bring a level of satisfaction to the other side. On the other hand, both sides had accepted the authority of the IOC to decide the questions at issue, with the exception, fortuitously for the IOC, of the single team in the Games. Both had agreed to come back to the table in a few months, and neither had felt pushed to the point of breaking off the discussions.

This was particularly important to the IOC in its overall strategy of containing the DPRK, which would expose itself as a fraud were it to be negotiating to cohost the Games at the same time that it tried to encourage a boycott of these very Games. Since there was no proposal of the IOC actually on the table at the conclusion of the first meeting, North Korea could not be in a position to reject an offer that had not yet been made. It could only wait to see what was offered and then respond at the next meeting.

Thus, though no agreement had been reached, it was, nevertheless, a good two days' work for the IOC. It certainly had been *work,* since the parties involved were very entrenched in their positions and brought an enormous amount of institutional enmity to the table. The formal positions put forward by each side contained a series of traps for the unwary, which could easily have led the IOC off into political swamps from which there was no return and into which it would have been folly to enter. It was only by sticking to a narrow range of discussion, on which it held the high ground and on which it could be more knowledgeable, that the IOC avoided these traps. This would continue in later discussions, in which the IOC would be lured by the prospect of finding solutions to the unsolvable; but, like Ulysses and the Sirens, it managed to resist these temptations. One should never underestimate the arcana of the problems that exist between North Korea and South Korea or, perhaps more contemporaneously, that existed at the time the Olympic negotiations were conducted.

CHAPTER 7

Take Two: The Second Meeting with the Koreas

LAUSANNE, SWITZERLAND, January 8–9, 1986 — The IOC's objective was to keep both the momentum up and the pressure on the Koreas by having the second joint meeting very shortly after the first. By the standards of international organizations, particularly when the issues are complex and sensitive, having a second meeting so quickly smacked of almost unseemly haste. Add to this the usual end-of-year doldrums, and it may well be asked why Samaranch wanted to pursue the negotiations so assiduously.[1]

The answer was simple. There was great interest in the outcome of the discussions on several levels. On a world media and political level, there was a certain fascination with the drama that was being played out, which was increased by the dearth of "hard" news emanating from the parties to the discussions. The normal economic rules of supply and demand applied; the less news there was, the greater the demand appeared to be. Not much useful or substantive information relating to

[1] This was also a variation on the schedule of the meetings that had been agreed to between Samaranch and Roh in August 1985. At that time, the second meeting had been expected to be sometime after the ANOC meetings scheduled for April 1986 in Seoul. On October 11, 1985, almost immediately after the meeting, the Australian Olympic Federation issued a statement objecting to the DPRK proposal to stage half the Games. Samaranch simply reported on the meeting at the IOC Executive Board meeting in Lisbon with the Executive Council of ANOC on his visits to Korea and stated that if the political situation in the world were to be delicate, there could be problems for the Games.

the negotiations and the progress therein was coming from the IOC itself.[2] Also having a direct bearing on the Olympic Games were matters of interest other than the general political issues between the two Koreas regarding the hosting of events in both territories, important as they may have been at this early stage of discussion.

Early reaction at the political level seemed to be confined to New York, where separate interviews were given on October 21 by DPRK and ROK officials. The DPRK foreign minister said that the DPRK would urge Communist countries to boycott Seoul if the events were not evenly divided between North Korea and South Korea. The ROK chief of mission merely stated that cohosting was technically and logistically impossible.[3]

In his letter of October 23, 1985, to Kim Chong Ha, Samaranch reassured him that, as pointed out during the first discussions, there was no question of the IOC's reopening discussion on the awarding of the Games to Seoul. To call this into question would be fundamentally contrary to both the Olympic Charter and the contract with the city of Seoul. The matter did not, therefore (and this was an important signal), even figure in the proposed agenda for the second joint meeting. On the other hand, he said, it was obvious that the IOC would support and associate itself unreservedly with any understanding to which the

[2] Press conferences given by Samaranch are deliberately bland, so much so that they are generally excruciatingly dull to attend. That is his intention; he believes there is nothing to be gained on such occasions by appearing to be brilliant. Nor does he permit a series of questions from any single member of the media. He will always move on after each question to another person in the audience. He may, on occasion, deliberately answer a different question from the one that has been asked.

[3] Castro had, by now, gotten on his own bandwagon. In March 1985 he had given an interview to U.S. congressmen on the 1988 Olympics, in which he was critical of the IOC, the Games, and certain sports personalities. Samaranch had returned the compliment on July 23, criticizing the comments made by Castro in the March interview. On September 6, the Cuban media carried reports that the foreign ministers of the nonaligned nations had endorsed the Cuban proposal that the 1988 Games be jointly organized. On December 1, in an open letter to Samaranch, Castro attacked the IOC's choice of Seoul as the host city for the Games and said that the Games should be split between North Korea and South Korea. By February 4, 1986, he was stating (at the Third Communist Party Congress) that Cuba would boycott unless the DPRK and ROK cohosted the Games. He also reinterated the complaint that Cuba was prevented from hosting the 1987 Pan American Games by reason of a $25 million bribe from an unidentified multimillionaire. Most assumed this was a reference to Mario Vazquez-Raña, president of PASO. During the same Congress in Havana two days later, DPRK vice president Pak Sung Chol called for other nations to "wage a dynamic struggle" for the DPRK to get a share of the Games. Pak visited with the president of Nicaragua the next day, and Daniel Ortega said that Nicaragua would not participate in Seoul if the DPRK proposal for cohosting was not realized.

two NOCs might come with respect to participation of the DPRK in the Games.

Maintaining his practice of attending such meetings, Samaranch accepted the invitation of the president of the Vietnamese NOC, Ta Quang Chien, to attend the annual meeting of the Socialist Ministers of Sport during November 14–16, 1985, in Hanoi. It came as a disappointment, but little surprise, to learn, upon his arrival and following the dinner on the evening of November 14, that the DPRK was attempting to influence the other participants to adopt a very categoric resolution against the Games in Seoul. Only the Cubans, however, appeared to be strongly supportive.

The following morning, Samaranch was invited to address the delegates at the meeting. He was careful not to say anything that might lead to a polarization of positions. He gave his customary address of solidarity, unity, the success of the Olympic Movement to date, and the agreements necessary to work for the future.[4] Following his remarks, each of the delegations spoke regarding its position.

The first was the Cuban minister, Conrado Martinez, who strongly attacked the IOC, complaining that there had been a great deterioration within the Olympic Movement. Montreal and Moscow bore witness to this situation; Los Angeles in 1984 compounded the discredit and raised to "fantastic levels" mercantilism, commercialization, anti-Sovietism, and antisocialism. There was now the unpopular decision to allocate the next Games to Seoul, capital of South Korea, the capital of disrepute, where there was repression by aggressive militarism and the humiliation of the people, who reject the grotesque and illegal North American military presence.

Martinez continued his diatribe against the IOC by raising the fury of Cuba at having lost its bid for the 1987 Pan American Games to the U.S. city of Indianapolis. These games, he said, belonged to Cuba "by right," and Cuba had been "arbitrarily" deprived of the chance to host them. They had thought there would be a possibility of appealing to the IOC and had done so. They had thought the IOC would defend a "just cause" and avoid the "crime" constituted by such disregard of Olympic standards and principles. The denunciation of these irregulari-

[4] Samaranch has mastered the successful politician's maxim regarding delivery of a message: Keep It Simple — Say It Often.

ties and the actions of the "unscrupulous" Mario Vazquez-Raña, president of the Pan American Sports Organization (PASO), to the IOC had been "simply useless."[5]

Today's situation was more serious. At stake were the Olympic Games and the decision as to whether the Olympic Movement saved itself or perished. He referred to Fidel Castro's letter to Samaranch dated November 29, 1984, and the proposal to share the Games approximately equally. It appeared, he said, that Samaranch had not grasped the contents of that letter. He should bear strongly in mind that many "progressive" countries shared the Cuban reservations concerning Seoul.

Martinez was followed by Kim Yu Sun of the DPRK. He thanked the IOC for its efforts to find a solution, but thought that the results of the first joint meeting the previous month were deceptive. He said the solution proposed by his NOC had the support of the socialist countries. He deplored the agenda for the January 1986 meeting (which did not deal with the issue of cohosting) as not reflecting their "objective view" of the situation. He made no reference to the active efforts the DPRK had been making at this meeting to garner support for its position.

Each of the others spoke briefly. Antonin Himl of Czechoslovakia supported the idea of organizing some events in the North. Lia Manoliu of Romania merely reaffirmed the loyalty of Romania to the Olympic Movement and to the IOC.[6] Günther Heinze of East Germany, then a member of the IOC, hoped the 1988 Games would help the unity of the Olympic Movement and thought the meetings in Lausanne between the two Koreas were positive and would lead to positive results. Trendafil Martinski of Bulgaria wanted to avoid the problems that arose in 1980 and 1984. Marat Gramov of the USSR spoke generally and expressed a number of thoughts and ideas, but was not particularly insis-

[5] This was a nonsensical position, of which everyone was aware. The 1987 Pan American Games had had to be re-awarded by PASO when, initially, Santiago, Chile, and later the alternate sites of Quito and Guayaquil had abandoned the games. There was a competition between Havana and Indianapolis, which was won by Indianapolis. The Cubans were furious and extremely bitter about the loss. They accused PASO president Vazquez-Raña of treachery in the matter, although it was clear to all present at the meeting where the decision was made that Vazquez-Raña had done as much to support Cuba as he could possibly have done. An appeal to the IOC against a decision of PASO, a continental association of NOCs, was simply impossible; the IOC had no standing whatsoever to interfere with a decision of PASO.

[6] Romania had been the major failure of the Soviets to enforce their boycott of the 1984 Games in Los Angeles.

tent that they be adopted. Marian Renke of Poland, who had been very strident at the previous year's meeting, was much less so on this occasion, saying that the decision to award the Games to Seoul had been taken, and it was not possible to go back on that. He thought the NOCs should have a greater role in the choice of the host cities of the Games[7] and pointed out the importance of the forthcoming ANOC meeting in Seoul the following April. Istvan Buda of Hungary repeated much of what had already been said, and the Mongolian representative expressed support for the position of the DPRK.

Samaranch's reply was quite brief. He read the letter of October 25 that had been sent to the DPRK NOC following the first joint meeting, calling for a second joint meeting in Lausanne the following January, together with the agenda, so that there would be no doubt about what was planned. He reiterated that the IOC could, under no circumstances, accept that the Games be cohosted. He reminded the delegates of the resolution adopted by ANOC in Mexico the previous year in support of Seoul.

Kim Yu Sun intervened again to raise a minor point with respect to the agenda of the January 1986 meeting, that of a single Korean team, without which there could be no question of the DPRK's participation. Samaranch's reply to this was uncharacteristically brusque: the position of the IOC was to offer the best possible conditions so that the DPRK could participate. Period. His impression was that this was well understood by all present. He refused to enter into any discussion on the issue of a single team for the two Koreas.

During the afternoon, Samaranch had brief meetings with each of the delegations. He gained the impression that all of them were pleased that he had come to the meeting to stand up to the DPRK and to make sure that the final communiqué was as neutral as possible. The position of the DPRK was generally unsupported, and, except for Cuba, it appeared that none of the delegations wanted to get too close to the DPRK attitude.

Samaranch had not responded to the diatribe by Martinez of Cuba during the full meeting. That would have been a waste of effort and would, undoubtedly, have merely increased tensions. He did, however, have a lengthy and laborious meeting with him in the afternoon. After

[7] This is an emerging issue driven by both the international federations and some of the NOCs, which has led to more than the usual level of demagoguery within the Olympic Family.

about an hour and a half, he thought he had at least succeeded in getting Martinez to understand what the IOC was trying to do and to reduce some of the ill feelings toward the IOC. He asked Martinez to transmit this position to Fidel Castro and to express that he was ready to come to Cuba at any time to meet Castro, if he was invited to do so.

All in all, it had been a useful meeting. Samaranch's presence had reinforced the position of the IOC in the conduct of the negotiations with the two Koreas and allowed a dialogue to be resumed with a number of influential persons within the Olympic Movement.[8] In the airplane on the way back to Geneva, Samaranch prepared a letter to USSR president Gorbachev and U.S. president Reagan, who were due to arrive in Geneva for a summit meeting, as well as a press release from the IOC. These were released on November 17. Samaranch believed the Olympic Movement should not be on the outside of such an important event.

Samaranch had a meeting in Lausanne on December 6, 1985, with South Korean sports minister Lee Yong Ho to discuss a number of matters relating to the Games.[9] He first learned that the IOC member in Korea, Park Chong Kyu, had died of liver cancer that had been diagnosed very late, only four weeks before his death. Lee reported that he had recently been to a meeting of the Olympic Council of Asia and had been encouraged by positive meetings with representatives from Vietnam and what was then North Yemen. He thought both countries were ready to participate in the Games.

They discussed the recent meetings of the Socialist Ministers of Sport held in Hanoi. Samaranch said that this could have been a very dangerous meeting for the Seoul Games, but that his presence there had resulted in a very moderate final communiqué. Lee said he had

[8] In the press conference following the Hanoi meeting, Samaranch stated that the Games had been awarded to Seoul and would be held in Seoul. If the DPRK proposal to cohost the Games was meant to split the Games in two, the answer was no. That was not possible.

[9] On November 11, before a parliamentary commission, Lee had stated that sharing the organization of the Games with the DPRK was "totally out of the question" and that the ROK had merely offered to share some preliminary events with the DPRK in the spirit of national reconciliation. At the end of the previous month, the SLOOC had asked for government help to stop the manufacture and sale of caps and T-shirts that criticized the USSR, such as those bearing pictures of bleeding polar bears and the 1983 downing of KAL flight 007, as contrary to government policy of attracting the USSR and Eastern European countries to the Games.

met the vice president of the North Korean NOC in Bahrain and that the latter had spoken only of the possibility of a joint team and the cohosting of the Games. That was, confirmed Samaranch, maintaining his control of the meeting, the same position the North had adopted at the Hanoi meeting. With respect to the joint team, that was a matter for the two Koreas to discuss, without the IOC's being involved.

Lee also wanted to know when the late General Park would be replaced with a new IOC member in Korea. Would there be a second Korean member, in accordance with the Olympic Charter, following the Games? In addition, he wanted to know whether the SLOOC could be represented on the IOC Executive Board. Lee was personally very aggressive, and it was clear at the time that he had designs on becoming an IOC member himself. He hoped to use his position as sports minister to lever his candidacy. Samaranch put him in his place immediately by saying that it would be the IOC that would decide on both the identity of and the timing of the election of the new member to replace Park.[10] He did not respond to the suggestion of a second member.[11] As to the IOC Executive Board, it was made up of IOC members only. The SLOOC would report to it in April and October of 1986.

They also discussed the difficult television negotiations that were in progress with the U.S. networks, by then with NBC. The Koreans had been particularly awkward in these negotiations, due mainly to unrealistic expectations concerning what the rights fee might be. These expectations, when not realized at the first negotiations in September 1985, where the highest offer was $325 million, had led those present, including Lee, to such a state of indecision that the negotiations had had to be suspended.[12] When they were resumed, the price for the

[10] This would be Kim Un Yong, president of the World Taekwondo Federation and a vice president of the SLOOC, who was co-opted at the October 1986 Session of the IOC in Lausanne, following the 1986 Asian Games.

[11] Not only was the idea premature, but even to raise it at this stage of the discussions between the two Koreas showed an astonishing lack of understanding about the enraging effect it would have had with respect to the DPRK. The Olympic Charter is very clear that the maximum number of IOC members in any country is two. The appointment of a second member in the South at this time would have been, whatever else might have been concluded as a result of such an appointment, a complete repudiation of the contention of both Koreas that they were parts of a divided country that hoped to reunite, if only the right formula could be found. Lee knew perfectly well that there can be a maximum of two IOC members in any country. Two in the South and one in the North was simply not possible.

[12] The IOC (I was chairman of the IOC Television Negotiations committee) had strongly urged Lee to accept the offer of $325 million that had been made by NBC, since this offer, in our view, was the best that would be forthcoming. The SLOOC negotiators in the room had no authority

rights had dropped by $25 million. The Koreans, and Lee in particular, felt they had lost face and were being extremely critical of the IOC and NBC, the network that had been the highest bidder. It seemed clear that Lee was under pressure at home, and it was, in fact, not long before he was removed as minister. The meeting was difficult, and the atmosphere very disagreeable.

So bad, in fact, was the relationship at this stage that a week later, on December 13, 1985, the Korean ambassador in Geneva came to Lausanne to meet with Samaranch to see what could be done to restore the good relations between the IOC and the SLOOC. Samaranch did not pull his punches. He said he had previously expressed his concern about this problem and that what had happened simply confirmed his fears. The present problem was much more important for Korea than for the IOC, since it involved the international credibility of Korea. The second problem was the lack of direct communications between the SLOOC and the IOC and principally between himself and Roh Tae Woo. Samaranch thought that he and Roh should meet two or three times per year in Seoul and once or twice in Lausanne, in order to make important decisions. He was also annoyed with the attitude that the Korean press seemed to have adopted with respect to the IOC. The IOC had done everything possible to make the Games a success and was, he said, still not perceived in a positive light in Korea.

The ambassador agreed to transmit the concerns to Seoul. He ventured the thought that perhaps the Koreans were nervous about the possibility that the North would use the Lausanne meetings as a political platform. Samaranch assured him that the IOC was extremely vigilant on that point and that it would not permit such actions. He had

---

to agree, since the real negotiators were Lee and Park Chong Kyu, who did not want to appear to be the negotiators and therefore stayed out of the room. During discussions between the IOC and the SLOOC, Lee was intransigent and considered that he knew how to negotiate with Americans better than we did. At the time, the arrangement between the IOC and the Organizing Committees was that the television rights were negotiated "jointly," so the IOC was not in a position to insist. As a result of the experience with Seoul, the IOC now fully controls television negotiations. The unrealistic expectations had come as a result of the abnormally high price paid by ABC for the U.S. rights to the Calgary Winter Games during negotiations held in January 1984. The Koreans appeared to have used the traditional ratio of rights fees between Summer and Winter Games and had reached a figure between $700 million and $800 million as the expected rights fees. This attitude had been encouraged by statements of former IOC director Monique Berlioux, who had said that failure by the international federations to adjust competition schedules might cost the IOC as much as $500 million and that the IOC expected to receive between $500 million and $700 million for the U.S. television rights. The Koreans had come to the negotiations with instructions not to accept any offer less than $550 million. Without approval from the highest levels in Seoul, no one at the negotiations was prepared to accept responsibility.

little hope that there would be an agreement, but every attempt should nevertheless be made.[13] In that regard, the meeting in Hanoi had been very useful. What would happen at the 1986 Asian Games was most important and could provide a good indication about what would happen in 1988.

The day after his January 6 meeting with South Korean minister Lee, Samaranch had a meeting, together with Alexandru Siperco,[14] with Kim Yu Sun of North Korea and his NOC vice president, Chin Chung Guk. He explained that the forthcoming joint meeting would be conducted in the same manner as the first. The North confirmed that it had received the material for the meeting, the agenda, and the overall program for the meetings.[15] Samaranch said that the agenda items would only be discussed during the bilateral portions of the meetings. They could be discussed in any order, but he wanted a detailed discussion so that progress could be made.

The North wanted to know whether, during the bilateral portions of the meetings, the IOC and NOC delegations could face each other across the table, rather than having the IOC at one end and the NOC on one side. Samaranch said that as president of the IOC, which was presiding over the meetings, he was obliged to sit at the head of the table. If this posed a problem, the layout of the meeting could be changed. The North did not insist.

Kim said his delegation would do its best to resolve the differences at the meeting. Should, however, this not occur, would it be possible to extend the discussions? Samaranch said it would be possible, in view of the travel difficulties to and from Pyongyang, which he himself had visited on two occasions.[16]

North Korea returned for another informal meeting on January 9,

[13] The same month, on December 19, the Korean deputy foreign minister, Lee Sang Ock, advised his Japanese counterpart, Kensuke Yanagiya, that the Koreans were prepared to make some limited concessions to the DPRK if the DPRK were to accept Seoul as the principal site and host city of the Games. Another Japanese official referred to cohosting as unrealizable.

[14] Siperco carried much of the burden of dealing with the DPRK on a day-to-day basis and was subjected to endless harangues and meetings, which he bore with remarkable patience and restraint throughout the entire process.

[15] Kim Yu Sun had written to Samaranch on November 25 with his comments on the agenda for the meeting, with which he was not happy, but he confirmed that the DPRK NOC delegation would attend the second meeting.

[16] One occasion had been for the regular annual meeting of Socialist Ministers of Sport in September 1983. The other was an earlier visit in March 1982.

1986, with Samaranch and Siperco. They had reviewed their previous proposal to stage eight sports during the Games. During the informal meeting they were prepared to make their position clear regarding the staging of events. During the formal part of the meeting, however, their position would remain unchanged for the present time.

Samaranch stressed that there should be no misunderstanding between himself and Kim Yu Sun, since there had been talks between them in Moscow two years earlier.[17] He believed that the delegation had spoken with Siperco the previous day and had reached a conclusion. Siperco reported to Samaranch, following his meeting with the North, that their delegation had been favorable to the proposal of three full sports events, one of which could possibly be soccer, being staged in Pyongyang.

North Korea explained that it was intending to participate in the Games or it would not be taking part in the discussions. The issue of a single team was raised again, and again Samaranch insisted that this was a matter for the two Koreas to resolve. If a conclusion was reached for a joint team, the IOC would accept this decision. If not, the IOC's proposal for the joint parade of the two teams in the Opening Ceremony would still be valid. The North proposed that the three sports be soccer, table tennis, and archery or shooting. Samaranch said he could not make a commitment without first speaking with the relevant IFs.

The IOC, he said, would honor its contract signed in Baden-Baden for the staging of the Games in Seoul. It was, nevertheless, possible for some events to take place in Pyongyang, but only upon the agreement of the North Korean NOC to participate in the events being held in Seoul. The North raised the name of the Games, requesting that they be called the XXIVth Olympic Games Pyongyang-Seoul, or Seoul-Pyongyang, depending upon whether it was written in the North or in the South. This proposal was, said Samaranch, under no circumstance acceptable to the IOC. The discussion was left with the agreement in principle that the Games would be the Games of the XXIVth Olympiad in Seoul. The IOC would study the possibility of substituting Pyongyang for Seoul for those events being held in North Korea.

[17] There was every likelihood that there had, indeed, been some confusion during that meeting in September 1984. Samaranch had spoken Spanish, which had been translated into Russian, and the Russian had, in turn, been translated into Korean. Communication from Kim Yu Sun had followed the same path in reverse. It would have been a miracle had there not been some loss of meaning or precision in this exchange.

The North wanted to have a joint Organizing Committee with the same number of participants on each side. This was neither possible nor acceptable to the IOC. It would be necessary to have a special Organizing Committee for the events to be staged in Pyongyang.

They discussed the prospect of a further meeting to continue the talks. Samaranch thought there should only be three delegates from each NOC. North Korea did not want to have the next meeting in Seoul during the forthcoming IOC meetings in Seoul that April, preferring, instead, to come back to Lausanne on June 10–11, 1986. Samaranch suggested an informal meeting in March to discuss various matters prior to the June meeting, and it was agreed to have this on March 7. There were many matters to be considered on both sides. Samaranch requested the North to send him a memorandum prior to the March meeting, raising all points to be discussed; he would, for his part, send a similar memorandum to the North.

Samaranch tried once more to get a clarification of North Korea's position regarding participation in the Games in Seoul. Kim Yu Sun, in a non sequitur response, said that as the Games were occurring on Korean territory, it was not correct for North Koreans and South Koreans to participate against one another. Samaranch pointed out the obvious; Koreans from both sides had been competing against each other in competitions throughout the world.[18] The North Korean NOC should be ready to participate in Seoul with its own team. Finally, Samaranch advised the North that it should attend the meeting of the NOCs in Seoul in April. Failure to attend might have serious consequences, regardless of the political difficulties that they themselves might undergo in order to attend the meeting.

At 6:00 P.M. on January 9, Samaranch met with Kim Chong Ha of South Korea; Chang Choon Sik, vice president of the KOC; and ROK ambassador Park. He told the South Korean delegation that he really did not know whether or not North Korea was ready to take part in the Games in Seoul, but he had advised them that it was in their best interest to be present in Seoul for the April meetings. Kim Chong Ha thought that a delegation from the North would attend the meetings and perhaps also the Games.

Regarding the joint team, it appeared that the North strongly favored a united team, but Samaranch had been cautious and had taken the

[18] To be fair, the situation here was somewhat different, but there was nothing to be gained by getting onto that particular tangent, so Samaranch chose to overlook the subtleties of the position.

position that this was purely a Korean problem, to be solved by the two sides, and the IOC would not preside over the discussions on that subject. Kim thanked him for his cooperation in this matter. The Seoul Games were the first to take place in the Korean nation, and the Korean people would be very disappointed if Korean teams entered the stadium without their national flags or the names of the countries. He thought that the best solution for both sides would be to use both flags and names, but march together. He thought that the North wanted to have a united team so that they could compete in every event, without having to qualify in the usual manner.[19] The single-team concept might work if political leaders in both Koreas agreed. However, North Korea could cause problems by prolonging the negotiations for a single team, which would make the organization of the Games very difficult. This was a tactic, he said, employed by the North in all joint discussions between the North and the South.

What sports, asked Samaranch, did Kim Chong Ha think could be given to North Korea to organize? Kim had thought about this during the previous night. Table tennis was one possibility, and he intended to propose this upon his return to Korea. There was no qualifying event, and the North was strong in this sport. He had also thought of canoeing, as there was a river that ran between the two countries. Samaranch pointed out that the SLOOC had already spent a great deal of money on a special site for the canoeing and did not think this would be a good solution. He thought the sports to be offered should be ones that were easy to organize.[20] Kim was not so keen on Samaranch's suggestion regarding archery, since the South was better at this sport, but he would think about it.[21]

Samaranch stated that he was not optimistic, and much would depend upon the meeting between the two Korean leaders at the summit meeting in March.[22] The IOC would keep the door open but would

[19] The host country is entitled to an automatic entry into the final round of all team sports in the Games, without having to qualify in the normal manner through elimination tournaments.

[20] Quite apart from not being certain about the ability of the North to organize events at the level required for Olympic competitions, there was the obvious fail-safe consideration of being able to stage them in Seoul on short notice, were any agreement with the North to disintegrate at the last moment.

[21] He was certainly prescient on that point: Korea swept the women's individual competition, won a silver medal in the men's individual event, and won both the men's and women's team events.

[22] Efforts were under way to try to organize such a meeting. It did not take place.

always support the contract awarding the Games to Seoul. It was important to see what happened with the Asian Games. A more encouraging sign was that during several recent international events, Soviet teams had participated.[23] He told Kim that a delegation from the North would be coming to Lausanne in March to hold private discussions. Kim said that his NOC did not intend to push or reject North Korea, since they were afraid of repercussions. They would maintain a flexible attitude, and both the SLOOC and his NOC would put their trust in the IOC.

Nineteen eighty-six was a bellwether year for Seoul and its Olympic Games. In April, a regular meeting of the Association of National Olympic Committees (ANOC) was scheduled to take place in Seoul. This is a regular occurrence on the Olympic calendar, which provides the NOCs (167 in 1986) with a chance to examine, in the host city itself, the progress being made by the host city in the organization of the Games and to give the leaders of the NOCs a firsthand exposure to the host city, which is often necessary for proper planning of the participation of their teams two years later. Similar meetings were held, for example, in Los Angeles and would be held in Barcelona two years before their respective Games.

This meeting would, by reason of the countries attending or not attending, give the IOC a straw count of what might be expected in 1988, so it was important to be able to demonstrate to all NOCs that the IOC was pursuing the Korean discussions as quickly as possible to find a solution to the north-south conundrum. If the IOC were to be perceived as lagging, this might be interpreted as an indication that it was not serious in its efforts, which, in turn, could give some countries an excuse to stay away from the meeting and thereby cast further doubt on Seoul's ability to organize successful Games.

A much more tangible test of the eventual success of the 1988 Games was also in the offing for 1986. The 1986 Asian Games were scheduled to begin on September 20 and to end in early October, the period selected for the Olympic Games two years later.[24] The Asian Games

[23] Among these events were the World Judo Championships in Seoul during 1985, the Thirty-third World Archery Championships in October 1985, and the Fifth World Cup of Boxing in late October and early November of 1985.

[24] The Olympic dates would later be slightly changed, to back up the date of the Opening Ceremony to September 17, 1988, at the request of the Organizing Committee. This was to increase the statistical probability of good weather for the Opening Ceremony. It worked.

were, of course, to be held in Seoul. It was vital for the success of the Olympics that all, or virtually all, of the Asian countries participate in the Asian Games. Though it would have been ideal were the DPRK to participate in these Games, there was little hope that this could occur without a "deal" on the Olympics — but this issue was, essentially, a sidebar. What was essential was China's participation and that the potentially volatile Arab countries attend in support of the Games. The IOC's ongoing efforts had to provide the necessary comfort, to all these countries, that everything possible was being done to bring about a compromise between the two Koreas.

At 10:10 A.M. on January 8, 1986, Samaranch called to order the second joint meeting of the two Korean NOCs with the IOC.[25]

The necessary control of the process was established at once. Samaranch would make an opening address, to be followed by one from each delegation. The IOC would then meet with North Korea, then with South Korea, and later with North Korea again. There would be an official dinner in the evening, and on the following day either joint or bilateral meetings would be held, depending on the decisions Samaranch would make during the first day. Complete flexibility was entirely in the hands of the IOC.

Even the agenda operated in favor of the IOC's control of the meeting and any progress that might, or might not, be made. Apart from the welcome and the final topic relating to follow-up, there were only four items:

> (a) joint parade of the two delegations on the occasion of the Opening Ceremony of the Games of the XXIVth Olympiad;
> (b) examination of the events which could be held on the territory of the NOC of the Democratic People's Republic of Korea;
> (c) examination of events which could be held using the territory of the two NOCs; and
> (d) participation of the NOC of the Democratic People's Republic of Korea in the cultural programme of the Games of the XXIVth Olympiad.

This was not an extensive agenda and was, in itself, a signal that

[25] Apart from Samaranch, the IOC delegation consisted of two of the three vice presidents, Siperco and Beitz; the president of the Olympic Council of Asia, Sheik Fahad Al-Ahmad Al-Sabah; and Raymond Gafner.

the IOC was not going to revisit the philosophy of joint hosting the Games, although it was inevitable that the North would raise it again at the first opportunity.

Samaranch was fairly short in his introduction of the meeting. He reminded them that the desired result had not been obtained at the October 1985 meeting, but that it had nevertheless been important to have had such communication between the two NOCs through the IOC. This was merely a positioning statement, underlining the central role of the IOC in the process. He then said that he wanted to follow the agenda of the meeting very closely, to facilitate the reaching of an agreement. He reviewed the position of the IOC with respect to the Seoul Games, which meant honoring the contract with Seoul, as had been the case with Moscow and Los Angeles. As a matter of IOC tactics, this was a point worth having on the record at each stage of the negotiations, since it demonstrated that the IOC had protected the Games in a socialist country with at least as much vigor as it had with respect to Games in one of the Western countries.

Having said that, the IOC was aware that Korea was a divided country, a "special" country,[26] having two official states. The IOC was doing its best on behalf of the entire Olympic Movement to offer the best conditions to the North to facilitate the latter's acceptance of the invitation to take part in the Games. It was these conditions that would be discussed during the course of the meeting. Although a comprehensive agreement might not be reached, the mere fact that the discussions were taking place would show the world that progress was being made.

If no positive results were obtained from the meeting, it would be difficult for the IOC to convene a third joint meeting. Having spoken to both delegations, Samaranch said, he knew that each NOC was ready to make great efforts to try to reach an agreement. The meeting was very important, not only for the Games of the XXIVth Olympiad, but also for both of the Koreas. The delegations were asked to bear in mind their own countries and their youth in order to obtain an agreement.

Kim Yu Sun of North Korea was invited to speak.[27] It was a set

[26] *Special* is a word used by Samaranch in many situations, to convey a multitude of characteristics, almost none of which are "good."

[27] The DPRK delegation consisted of Kin Yu Sun (North Kim), Chin Chung Guk, Han Chang On, An Bok Man, Chang Ung, and Cho Myong Hwang.

piece, which he read. The usual thanks were expressed and fraternal greetings extended. His delegation was in Lausanne in the hope of meeting the desire of the entire Korean people and the peoples of the world for friendship, harmony, and cooperation by achieving a "good result" in the interest of the Olympic ideal from the first days of this year, the year of peace.

He recounted how, during the first round of the discussions, respective views had been exchanged, and they had presented their proposals and ideas on the subject, so that the XXIVth Olympic Games as a grand world sports festival would no longer follow in the footsteps of the previous "troublesome" Olympic Games. His delegation had presented its detailed ten-point proposal, proceeding from the sense of heavy responsibility they had assumed from the sportsmen and people in the north and south of Korea, as well as all the sportsmen and people in the world and from their conviction that the "identity of our minds and joint efforts," if achieved, would help to find a solution.

As expected, though not on the agenda, the cohosting issue was not dead. North Kim reminded the IOC that the joint hosting proposal and the idea of a single team had been presented after a serious consideration had been given to the present situation of the Olympic Movement and the specific realities of their divided country. He said this was why, since the announcement of their proposal, many governments and sports and public organizations had extended "their high appreciation of and full support and favorable response" to their cohosting proposal as a "realistic and reasonable" way to strengthen the Olympic ideal and principles, to "save the Olympics from the imminent crisis," and to contribute to the reunification of Korea. He said that the support and solidarity among the world people in favor of their proposal "is ever increasing."

However, said North Kim, to their regret, there had been no serious discussion of any of the problems at the first joint meeting, and there had been no appreciable news to please the "world people" watching the meeting for success. Nonetheless, he continued, the world people interested in sports and the Olympics have been encouraged by the tripartite agreement to deeply study the various proposals and meet again for discussion, and they are still hoping for the success of the current joint meeting.

Regarding the agenda of the meeting, North Kim said that they had seriously studied it. As far as the proposed subjects were concerned, there was some similarity as well as differences in the respective viewpoints. If all were to put forward their respective ideas and try to discuss them sincerely, they would be able to reach an agreement. Naturally, some differences existed among the three parties, but the common desire for a solution would bring the joint meeting to a successful conclusion.

At the end of this preamble, North Kim got to the agenda. Regarding the events to be held in the North, his delegation had already made its specific proposal and declared its readiness to ensure free travel between North Korea and South Korea. Therefore, on that question, he thought it should be possible to reach an agreement if the parties displayed the spirit of mutual understanding and cooperation.

As to the joint parade at the Opening Ceremony, the North had different views. In its desire to prevent national division and achieve reunification, they had proposed to jointly host the Games and to form a single team of the North and the South to take part in the Games. Their proposal on the formation of a single team was to prevent the athletes of two parts of one nation from entering the Games as two teams, but, instead, to parade as a single team in the same uniform, under a single flag, and to take part in the events as a single team as well. This, he said, was what the "entire people" in the North and in the South "unanimously" wished, and it was also the desire of all the sportspeople and people in the world.

Since both the IOC and the South Korean "side" had previously proposed, "on several occasions" the formation of a single team, this problem could be discussed easily under the auspices of the IOC. Since this had been one of the many subjects previously mentioned, Samaranch noted it for later discussion. It did not go unnoticed by South Kim, either.

North Kim finished his opening statement by saying that, besides the subjects proposed for discussion by the IOC, there were other important problems that must be discussed and solutions found. He said that all the problems that had been raised for the success of the Games should not be excluded (from the agenda) but should be discussed one by one in a sincere manner for their solution.

South Kim spoke next.[28] His greetings were more perfunctory. His approach, not unlike the first time the parties met, was essentially

[28] The KOC delegation consisted of Kim Chong Ha (South Kim), Chang Choon Sik, Choy Man Lip, Lee Chong Ha, Yim Tae Soon, and Nam Joung Moon.

legalistic: the IOC had granted the Games to Seoul; there was a contract; Seoul had observed the terms of the contract; approvals had been given; and the doors were wide open for all countries to compete freely in the Seoul Games without constraints, including athletes from the North. He repeated, virtually word for word, the part of his opening address at the first joint meeting regarding the dedication of the Olympic Stadium on September 29, 1984, and the attendance of socialist countries on that occasion.

The preparations were nearing completion. With pride and confidence, they were determined to make the Seoul Olympics the most successful in Olympic history. They were working hard, within the Olympic Charter regulations, to share this honor among all Korean people. Sounding a warning to the IOC, he carried on to observe that the Olympic Charter and the decisions of the IOC Sessions had been respected. Were this principle to be disregarded or changed, the Olympic Games would be placed "in great danger." From this perspective, they had proposed to the IOC some feasible suggestions in relation to participation by the North in the XXIVth Seoul Olympiad. These had been based on the expectation that the North would take part in the Games, respecting the Olympic Charter and the decision of the IOC Session.

His delegation had expressed their willingness to discuss the matters identified at the previous meeting, but not disclosed to the North at that time, namely: joint entrance in the Opening Ceremony, holding some preliminaries for men's handball, men's volleyball, and soccer; discussion of a sport that could be held to link the South with the North, and, finally, participation by the North in the cultural programs. The question of which was the host city was not open for discussion.

In partial rebuttal to North Kim's observations on the single-team concept, South Kim said his country, the Republic of Korea, had hoped for many years to form a single team with the North for participation in international events and had hoped to hold meetings to discuss the matter. Talks had, indeed, been proposed, and the formation of a joint team suggested. In addition, many conferences had been held to deal with those issues and inter-Korean sports interchanges. The issue of a single joint team did not concern only the Games. It was not on the agenda for this meeting and should be resolved by the two sides at a separate meeting. The door was, of course, open for the North to take part in the Seoul Games.

In a brief finale to this portion of the meeting, Chin Chung Guk, a vice president of the North Korean NOC, wished to know if the South would be prepared to take part in the 1988 Games with a single team composed of athletes from both territories. South Kim replied that this question had been raised at the last meeting, following which the North Korean NOC had "withdrawn" its proposal. There was no further comment from North Korea.

The meeting, having followed an all-too-predictable course in the opening stages, adjourned for the time being. The positions were of no surprise to the IOC; progress in such matters is seldom, if ever, expected to be made in the public portion of meetings. Rather, it is left to the hard negotiation that seems best to occur in private.

Half an hour later, the North returned to the table with the IOC. Samaranch turned to the agenda. The matter of the joint parade had been raised by the IOC, since both NOCs were striving for the reunification of the two states in the future, once political conditions made this possible. The IOC believed that, since the Opening Ceremony was watched by spectators worldwide, a joint parade would provide an ideal opportunity to display a spirit of goodwill and would express the mutual desire of the two states for cooperation. Both teams could march together under their individual flags, with, perhaps, the Olympic flag at the forefront of the delegations.

Kim Yu Sun was not buying. He said that at the previous meeting, his NOC had put forward a proposal advocating a single Korean team for the Games. Such a joint team would promote reconciliation and unity and, furthermore, would encourage participation at the Games by socialist and third-world countries. The Korean people strongly favored the reunification of Korea, and the formation of a single team was in full conformity with the aims and ideals of the Olympic Movement. In the past, talks had been held between the two NOCs with a view to sending a single team to the Olympic Games, under the same flag, wearing the same uniform, and with a common national anthem. Unfortunately, these talks had broken down, despite great effort and initial enthusiasm on both sides.[29] Kim was of the opinion that it was now appropriate for such talks to be resumed and proposed that discussions to that effect be held under the auspices of the IOC. He was sure that the IOC was in support of this suggestion of a joint team.

[29] They had, in fact, broken down most recently because North Korea did not wish to continue them. In earlier talks, it was South Korea that had been particularly unwilling to consider the prospect of a joint team.

Samaranch ducked. There were two NOCs, and Korea had participated in previous Olympic Games and international events as two separate teams. Talks had been held, twenty years ago, in order to consider forming a single Korean team of athletes, but these had not been successful. The question had been further debated by the two Koreas and subsequent meetings held during the course of 1985. The IOC was prepared to encourage the South Korean NOC to resume talks and suggested a meeting that could be held in the North, followed by a further meeting held in the South. But, he said, the IOC's view was that this was an internal matter, to be resolved by the two Korean NOCs. If an agreement were to be reached favoring a joint team, the IOC would be pleased to receive such a proposal. If no agreement could be reached before 1988, Samaranch suggested that the IOC proposal should be implemented. He reiterated his views concerning the beneficial effects of following such a course.

Kim Yu Sun persisted. Since the Games were to be held on the Korean peninsula, it was "essential" that a single team represent the two Koreas. It was necessary that the subject of a single, joint team be debated at this meeting, with the guidance of the IOC. Representation of the two Koreas in this manner would "guarantee" the success of the Games in 1988 and would symbolize the hope of the peoples of Korea for reunification. Samaranch pointed out that three meetings had been held the previous year to discuss the possibility of a joint team without the advice of the IOC having been sought. The IOC was ready, should an agreement to this effect be reached, to accept that a joint team would participate in the Games. But the matter was an exclusively Korean matter, and the IOC would intervene only to encourage the South Korean NOC to continue dialogue in this respect. Now, Samaranch said, he wished to have the opinion of Kim on the specific suggestion regarding the joint parade of the two delegations. Kim merely repeated that discussion of the possibility of the participation of a single team should be held in the context of the present meeting. Since the Games were to be held on the Korean peninsula, the IOC's intervention in the matter was particularly appropriate.

Samaranch bailed out of this agenda item. He said he had made the IOC's position very clear. The IOC was bound to honor the Baden-Baden decision and the contract it had signed with the South Korean NOC. The IOC was endeavoring to offer the best conditions with respect to participation in the Games by North Korea. He requested the cooperation of the North Korean NOC so that an agreement could be reached. He would inform the South Korean NOC of the proposal for a joint team. He suggested that the respective presidents meet during their stay in Lausanne to discuss when the bilateral, inter-Korean talks might be resumed. This particular agenda item would be considered at a later stage of the meeting between the IOC and the North Korean NOC.

It was not a promising beginning.

The next effort concerned the events that might be held in North Korea. Samaranch reported that agreement had been obtained from the South Koreans that several team sports events in basketball, handball, volleyball, and soccer could be held in the North. Kim merely referred back to the statement he had made at the previous meeting. His NOC felt that it would be appropriate to allocate twelve sports to the South and eleven to the North. After a detailed examination of the situation following the first meeting and the statements issued by the IOC, he proposed that the following sports be staged in the North: soccer, athletics, gymnastics, archery, judo, weight lifting, volleyball, table tennis, wrestling, handball, and shooting.

Samaranch said the proposal was unacceptable to the IOC. The IOC would not agree to cohosting of the Games, nor that the Games become the Pyongyang-Seoul Games. It was not an easy matter to gain the support of the IOC Session, the international federations, and the SLOOC for proposals that some team sports events be held in Pyongyang or elsewhere in the North, since this was in direct contradiction to the terms of the Olympic Charter. The IOC was, however, striving to offer to the North Korean NOC the possibility of organizing some events.

Kim Yu Sun argued that the success of the Games was closely connected with the issue of the reunification of Korea. He wished, above all, that the Games be those of peace and friendship. Hence his proposal that eleven sports be staged in North Korea. Such a proposal had been formulated after careful consideration of the realities of a divided country and a detailed review of stadium facilities. He requested that each NOC examine the ideas put forward and that discussion of this point be resumed later that afternoon or the following day.

Samaranch replied that if Kim retained his present standpoint, it would be difficult for the IOC to work toward an agreement. Although the IOC was perhaps contravening the Olympic Charter by offering to the North the organization of some events, he thought he could get the approval of the IOC members, the international federations, and the

Seoul Organizing Committee. He urged Kim to take a more realistic stance, since in the present circumstances it was improbable that a mutually acceptable solution could be reached.

With no success on either of the first two issues, the meeting moved on to a consideration of what events might be staged in both North Korea and South Korea. Samaranch thought that only one sport would be suitable for this, namely, cycling. He thought it might be possible to hold three or four races across both territories, with the races starting in the North and finishing in the South. The offer to share certain events would play a very important part in the success of the Games.

There was a somewhat unexpected response from Kim Yu Sun at this juncture. He said that though his delegation had great interest in this item on the agenda, it had not expected a statement by the IOC at this time. He thought that both the marathon and the long-distance cycling races could cover both territories. Were this to happen, many of the barriers to the reunification of the Korean peninsula would be broken down. It was his opinion that it would not be fair if the events were to start in the South, cross to the North, and then finish in the South. Both territories should be used to break down barriers. He proposed that the marathon start in the North and finish in the South and that one of the long cycling races start in the South and finish in the North.

This suggestion was given short shrift. Samaranch stated that the crossing of the border would be possible only in cycling. The idea of the marathon crossing the border, he said, had already been discussed with the International Amateur Athletics Federation (IAAF) and had been found to be technically impossible.[30] Cycling would be the only possible sport; the location of starts and finishes could be discussed at a later date.[31] He added that the concept of finishing in the North did not really tally with the IOC's ideas on the matter.

The final subject on the morning agenda was the participation of the North in the cultural program of the Games. Samaranch led off by stressing the importance of the role played by the cultural program in the success of the Games. He knew how important culture was to

[30] Oddly enough, on October 6, 1985, the IAAF had actually suggested a variation of such an event (a relay marathon) in connection with the 1987 Seoul World Cup Marathon.

[31] Some cynical humor poked fun at the cycling road race: if the race started in the North and finished in the South, by the time the Olympic cyclists got to the 38th parallel, there would be 100,000 North Koreans in the "race" to the South.

North Koreans and felt that they should make a substantial contribution to any such program.[32] Kim Yu Sun agreed that participation in the cultural program would certainly help reunification. He was ready to agree to the concept, as long as the program was organized by the IOC with equality for both countries. His delegation would never agree to the idea of the cultural program's being organized by one country with the other playing a secondary role.

Samaranch avoided the issue, saying that it was not up to the IOC to arrange the cultural program. This was the responsibility of the SLOOC. Samaranch was prepared to guarantee that participants from the North would be closely observed and treated fairly by the IOC. Just before adjourning for a well-earned lunch, Samaranch told the North that unless both parties moved closer to agreement in the afternoon session to follow, it would be very difficult for him, as president of the IOC, to call for a third joint meeting. The IOC was trying everything to facilitate agreement, but it required the cooperation of the delegations. A third meeting would be impossible, he said, unless North Korea offered proposals that were more realistic. He invited the delegations to meet among themselves and return later that afternoon.[33]

At 3:00 P.M., the IOC met with the South. Samaranch started by asking whether or not the South would agree to fielding a joint team with the North, but with different uniforms. It was not clear what he was trying to accomplish with this question, unless he was referring only to the people at the Opening Ceremony. The idea would have been unfeasible for actual competitions. He advised that the North had expressed great interest on many occasions in having a joint team, including during meetings in Lausanne and Hong Kong several years previously.[34] Both sides had had numerous meetings since then, particularly during 1985, but no agreement had been reached. The IOC would be happy if an agreement could be reached between the two NOCs. Was South Korea prepared to resume the talks that had been broken off in 1985? Samaranch wanted to know if he could advise Kim Yu Sun that South Korea

[32] The North was generally regarded as the part of Korea that had the greatest interest in preserving the traditional Korean cultural heritage.

[33] No such meeting occurred.

[34] This reference was to the meetings in 1963.

would be willing to resume the talks in the near future and suggested that the two presidents meet to decide on a date for such talks.

Kim Chong Ha did not answer directly. He simply said that the issue of a joint team had been tried out in the past, but that as far as the 1988 Games were concerned, it was the responsibility of the two NOCs to find a solution to the problem. With regard to a date for talks on the matter, this could be arranged according to the schedule of Red Cross and economic talks taking place during 1986. In the same measure of nonresponse, but with the obvious intention of moving the matter forward in some manner, Samaranch said he wanted to advise Kim Yu Sun that the South was prepared to resume talks in the near future, but without specifying a date.

Concerning the joint parade at the Opening Ceremony, Kim Chong Ha said that if the North accepted the IOC's recommendations, then it would be willing to accept the possibility of parading together at the Opening Ceremony. He proposed that three columns of the South's delegation parade on the right in their own uniforms and behind their own flag, and three columns from North Korea parade on the left in their uniforms and behind their own flag. Such a joint parade would demonstrate Korea's wish for unity. No response was made by the IOC.

Instead, Samaranch moved on to the events that might be organized in the North. At the previous meeting, the South had agreed to allow some preliminary events in basketball, soccer, handball, and volleyball to be staged in the North. The IOC was now proposing that the North be permitted to organize all competitions, preliminaries, and finals, in one of these four sports, in order to convince North Korea to accept the invitation to take part in the Games.

Kim Chong Ha called for a brief time-out to confer with his delegation. He was neither ready nor authorized to make such commitments and was undoubtedly put off balance by the speed with which Samaranch seemed to be moving.

His response was that under the Olympic Charter, the Games were awarded to a city six years prior to the Games' being celebrated, which was why Seoul had been awarded the Games in 1981.[35] This time

[35] There was no specific date set out in the Olympic Charter for the awarding of the Games to a host city, although the IOC normally did this approximately six years prior to the Games. In fact, the Seoul Games were awarded seven years in advance of the Games. The current system is to award the Games approximately seven years in advance. Sessions held in odd-numbered years will choose the site for Games, and Sessions in even-numbered years will be held on the occasion of the Games themselves, under the new rotational schedule for Summer Games and Winter Games.

period was required in view of the extensive preparations needed for the Games, which were constantly expanding. More than four years had now passed since Seoul had been awarded the Games, and it would not be easy to relocate some of the preliminary events. Furthermore, his NOC was not aware of the facilities available in the North nor which of the sites were most suitable for the various sports. His NOC had received no reply from the North regarding the preliminary events it had proposed to stage in the North. All things considered, therefore, it was not opportune for his NOC to consider granting additional events to North Korea.

Samaranch emphasized that the IOC had organized the two meetings to date in order to try to help the Games in Seoul. The IOC's position was clear and firm: it supported the Games in Seoul, sharing the same desire as the KOC for the Games to be successful. The main danger facing the Games was the position of the DPRK NOC. The IOC was trying to convince the North to accept the invitation to take part in the Games, an invitation that would be sent out by the IOC itself. Offering the North Koreans the possibility of organizing all competitions in a team sport might encourage them to participate in the Games. Putting the idea in another way, he said that the IOC supported the Games, which belonged to the IOC, and he was trying to ensure their success. The proposal for the organization of one sport in the North emanated from the IOC, not from the North. Realizing by now that Kim Chong Ha needed time to get instructions from Seoul, Samaranch suggested that his delegation comment on the proposal the following day.

Kim Chong Ha went a bit further at this stage than might have been expected. He appreciated the efforts being made by the president (and the other IOC delegates, to be sure, he added diplomatically) and realized that the South and the IOC shared the same goals. It would not, however, be worthwhile to give more concessions to the North. But, he held out, the proposal could be accepted if the North Korean NOC withdrew its demands for cohosting the Games and naming them the Seoul-Pyongyang Games. Samaranch thanked Kim for his usual helpful attitude toward the IOC. He confirmed that the IOC had long since rejected the claims of the North for cohosting the Games. In fact, he said, these claims had not been discussed at that morning's meeting with North Korea.[36]

[36] This was not entirely correct, since the North had raised the question of the eleven sports it wished to host, in the context of the cohosting proposal made at the previous meeting. On the other hand, Samaranch had rejected the request, so it was, arguably, not "discussed."

If progress was to be made, Samaranch requested that the IOC's proposal be kept in mind, should the North be considering participation in the Games under certain conditions. If not, the situation would remain unchanged. Kim Chong Ha confirmed that his NOC had not changed its position regarding the staging of some preliminary events in the North. The following day, he would advise whether or not his NOC would accept the IOC's proposal and allow North Korea to organize one team sport, provided it withdrew all claims for cohosting the Games.

Closing the circle on the events that might be held on both territories, Samaranch stated that, originally, it had been proposed to hold the marathon in both the North and the South, but that this was not possible for technical reasons, so the only possible events would be in cycling. The technical director of the SLOOC, Shin Hyun Taek, was invited into the meeting and explained that the only cycling race that could be organized to use both territories would be the men's team road race.

Regarding the cultural program of the Games, Samaranch was not aware whether the South had studied this item or if it was ready to propose a program to the IOC. He also wanted to know if South Korea would be ready to share the Olympic torch relay with North Korea. South Kim said that exchange visits between the two territories had already taken place through the Red Cross, involving cultural troupes, and further exchanges were planned. For the Games, all NOCs would be invited to take part in the cultural program in order to make it a success, including the North. As far as sharing the Olympic torch relay was concerned, if the North withdrew all its claims for cohosting the Games, his NOC would positively consider such a possibility.

Samaranch advised Kim Chong Ha that his delegation would be invited to the meeting the following day and that a third set of meetings might be convened, if necessary. Kim thanked Samaranch for arranging the talks between the two sides but felt that they should be more productive. He requested that the IOC consult his NOC before setting a date for a third joint meeting, in view of the busy schedule for 1986. In response to a question from Raymond Gafner concerning the latest date at which the program for the Games could be altered, should an agreement be reached, Kim said they would need the final details prior to June 1986. North Korea, however, would first have to withdraw its various demands.

Samaranch digressed somewhat to speak of other matters. It was hoped that the U.S. television rights agreement with NBC would be signed at the next IOC Executive Board meeting on February 12, and Samaranch requested Kim Chong Ha to ask Roh Tae Woo, as president of the SLOOC, to come to Lausanne to sign the contract on behalf of the Organizing Committee.[37] He felt that he and Roh should meet more often. Since Samaranch would be in Seoul twice during 1986, he suggested that Roh visit Europe twice, the first time in February. When the SLOOC had been created, relations with the IOC had been close, and many problems had been solved. During this most important period, regular meetings between Samaranch and Roh could only prove advantageous. This was probably an unrealistic expectation but the mere suggestion was sufficient to exert some pressure on the South Koreans to be more responsive on a broad range of matters.

Regarding the U.S. television contract, Samaranch recalled that the IOC had advised the SLOOC to accept NBC's offer at the first round of negotiations in September 1985. When the offer had finally been accepted in November 1985, the minimum guarantee had been $25 million less than originally offered, although the overall figure had been substantial.[38] The IOC, he said, had vast experience in dealing with television networks and was aware of each network's limitations. The IOC's aim, moreover, was the same as the SLOOC's: to achieve as high a figure as possible.

The SLOOC had, said Samaranch, received bad advice that the contract would amount to between $500 million and $800 million, figures that had appeared in the press, which led to disappointment when the final figure of $300 million was learned.[39] This was, however, the

[37] The contract was eventually signed on March 26.

[38] For all the disappointment expressed by the Koreans, the contract eventually signed was the largest contract ever entered into for the television rights to the Summer Olympic Games. Even the Games in Los Angeles, on U.S. territory only two years previously, had brought only $225 million. What appeared to rankle their pride was that the U.S. contract for the 1988 Olympic Winter Games in Calgary had been signed for $309 million. They had not understood the aberrant dynamics of that particular negotiation, nor that the price had been excessive. They had also managed to negotiate a much larger share of the total rights than the normal agreement would have given them. The IOC formula at the time was to give the Organizing Committee 20 percent of the rights fees to help provide the host broadcast and international broadcast functions. Samaranch had agreed with Roh that the SLOOC would get an amount based on a theoretical rights fee much higher than the actual contract amount. The SLOOC was, therefore, receiving a subsidy from the IOC.

[39] Samaranch has always been convinced that the unrealistic figure expected from the U.S. television negotiations resulted from bad advice given to them by their television consultants, TWI International of New York. Barry Frank, who acted on the SLOOC's behalf, insists that no such advice was ever given, although he did think that the eventual figure would be higher than $300 million. The final contract was expressed, in face-saving terms for the Koreans, as a minimum payment of $300 million and a maximum of $500 million, depending upon advertising sales. The

highest figure ever paid for the Summer Games, higher than the $225 million paid for the Los Angeles Games, and the time difference between Seoul and American prime-time viewing was considerable. Samaranch warned the SLOOC to choose its advisers carefully, since the success of the Games represented a great deal to the Republic of Korea. The Games would be more than just a sports event. The Republic of Korea was a small country but had vast organizational capabilities.

In order to ensure that the Games would be successful, perhaps the most successful in Olympic history, all NOCs had to be encouraged to take part, including the DPRK. He urged the KOC and the SLOOC to trust the IOC's advice. Samaranch sent his best regards to General Roh, hoping to see him in Lausanne the following month, and sent his wishes for success to the new sports minister, Park Seh Jik. Both the KOC and the SLOOC would always be supported by the entire Olympic Movement. Kim Chong Ha thanked him for his words and said he would transmit the request to Roh. The meeting adjourned.

Half an hour later, the IOC met once again with the North. Samaranch asked for the results of their study of the IOC's proposals. North Kim said he was happy to see that four events proposed by the IOC were among the eleven proposed by his delegation. His delegation had discussed the situation and was now ready to propose that *eight* (down from eleven) events take place in North Korea: soccer, table tennis, gymnastics, volleyball, judo, archery, wrestling, and shooting.[40] His delegation was in agreement that cycling could be held in both territories. They wanted a single team for the Games; it would be most unfortunate if two Korean teams should compete against each other, all the more so as the Games were to take place on Korean soil.[41] Any discussions regarding a joint Korean team should take place under the auspices of the IOC. He understood that the South was not opposed to discussion of this point and asked the IOC to include it on the agenda for the next meeting of the two delegations with the IOC. As to the cultural

---

prospect of additional revenues was completely illusory, since NBC sales were based on price levels that assumed a rights fee payment of $300 million, and not more.

[40] In this proposal, athletics, weight lifting, and handball had been removed from the original list.

[41] This was his response to Samaranch's observation that Korean teams had competed against each other for years in international competitions. The distinction was drawn between competitions abroad and competitions at "home."

program, it would be impossible for his country to hold one of its mass displays if the whole cultural program was to take place in Seoul. He proposed that there be two separate cultural programs, one in Seoul and one in Pyongyang.

Samaranch thanked him and said that he would go through the agenda item by item. Regarding the Opening Ceremony, it was the intention of the IOC that there be a joint parade of the two teams. The ceremony would be watched by more than two billion people and would be a good opportunity to show the world the goodwill of both states. The IOC agreed that there should be meetings between the delegations on this point, and the IOC would accept any solution that might be found. He ignored the effort made by Kim Yu Sun to get the IOC to accept a mediation role in any such discussions of a joint team. It was the clear wish of the IOC, he said, that both delegations should parade together at the Opening Ceremony.

Regarding the eight sports, their proposal was still unacceptable. Preliminary competitions in four team sports and one complete sport, including the finals, could be held in the North. Samaranch said he would try to convince the IOC Session, the international federations, and the SLOOC of the advisability of this idea and stressed that, in so doing, the IOC was already going further than the rules allowed. There appeared to be no major problems with regard to cycling races taking place across the border.

With respect to the cultural program, Samaranch suggested that the North might be able to organize the mass display at the beginning of the one sport that could take place entirely in North Korea. He had in mind, however, a contribution that the North Koreans might make to the program organized by the SLOOC. The IOC would honor its commitment to Seoul but would try to give the North the best possible chance to accept the invitation to participate in the Games. The IOC would also be ready to offer the North a part of the Olympic torch relay across the Korean peninsula.

He invited the delegation to consider the proposals and to return the following day. Kim Yu Sun replied that his delegation had already made "great concessions" and urged all the parties to appreciate fully the opinions and positions of others. His delegation was totally opposed to holding only preliminary events in the North and the delegation would refuse to discuss the matter. Samaranch responded that the IOC had shown that it was very respectful of the position of the North and that it had already been very patient. The IOC would adhere to the Olympic

Charter and honor all contracts. The IOC and the Olympic Movement would fight to ensure that the Games would be very successful. The IOC would meet with the delegation the following day.[42]

The meeting with the North the following day was short.[43] Samaranch said that agreements in principle had been reached on the events that could be held in both territories and with respect to the cultural program. The joint parade and the sports to be held in North Korea were still pending. As to the former, the IOC was willing to accept any solution proposed by the two NOCs and encouraged both sides to resume the talks held in 1985. Further time was needed to study the North's proposals regarding the events to be held there.

A third round of talks was proposed for June 10 and 11. In the meantime, the different positions of the North and the South would be studied, and he hoped it would be possible for the IOC to submit a final proposal, acceptable to both parties, at the third joint meeting.

North Kim considered that some progress had been made at this second round of talks despite the complicated problems involved. The success of the meeting, he said, was due to the IOC's efforts. Nevertheless, problems remained that still required further discussion, and he hoped that the IOC would further study his proposal and prepare itself for the third joint meeting. If the Games of the XXIVth Olympiad were cohosted by the two Koreas, it would show the unity of the Korean people to the world. The IOC's efforts would then be appreciated by the Korean people. Costaging the Games would ensure their success and contribute to the future development of the Olympic Movement.

[42] During the day of the meeting in Lausanne, a press conference was held in Moscow by Mikhail Kapista, a deputy foreign minister. His statements continued the enigmatic position of the Soviet Union, which could be taken as support for the DPRK, while keeping open the participation of the Soviets in Seoul. The customary criticism of the IOC's decision in 1981 was repeated: "The decision was cynical because everyone knows that a large group of states, including the Soviet Union, does not recognize and does not intend to recognize the South Korean regime. We are against this and are still opposed to holding the Olympiad in South Korea." He said, however, that once the decision had been taken, it had become necessary to find a compromise. He made it clear that if the IOC proposal were to be accepted, the Soviets would take part in both Pyongyang and Seoul, but he did not address the possibility of what might happen if no agreement were to be reached.

[43] In the interim, both sides had continued their negotiations through the press, with statements being delivered following the end of the previous day's negotiations. Each party knew that Samaranch would have all the news agency reports on his desk before the meetings began on the second day, so they knew this was an additional opportunity to "negotiate" with the IOC and to make statements that they might not otherwise dare to make in the presence of the IOC itself. Apart from that, they had to make appropriate noises for consumption on their respective home fronts.

Moreover, it would encourage a greater number of NOCs to take part in the Games. He requested the IOC to do its utmost to guarantee the success of the Games by facilitating his NOC's participation.

Samaranch requested the delegation to be present at a joint meeting of the two delegations at noon. The afternoon press conference would be given by the IOC alone. Both Korean delegations were welcome to attend as observers but would not take part in it.

There was a brief meeting with South Korea. Samaranch said that at the end of the meetings between the two NOCs, the results achieved were not outstanding, but a certain amount of progress had been made. The North Korean NOC was gradually revealing a change in its initially unyielding attitude. The IOC's position remained unaltered, and full support was offered to the KOC; the IOC would stand by the commitments that it had made. It was a question of the IOC and the KOC working together in order to try to ensure the participation of the North in the Games. Samaranch believed it essential to continue the dialogue with North Korea and suggested a third series of joint meetings to be held on June 10 and 11 in Lausanne, as there was still the possibility that an agreement could be reached. He proposed that Kim Chong Ha of South Korea, accompanied by one or two of his delegates, should meet with him privately at 6:00 P.M. that evening.

Kim said that if North Korea withdrew its proposals advocating cohosting the Games and the participation of a single Korean team, and if an agreement could be secured that the agenda of a future meeting would be strictly adhered to, his NOC would be in favor of the organization of a third series of joint meetings in Lausanne. In addition, if the North Korean delegation were to show a more realistic and practical attitude, the South would be prepared to study the possibility of allocating the organization of all the competitions in one sport to the North.

Samaranch thought that by June 1986, the political situation would have improved even further and that this would facilitate talks.[44] In addition, the meeting of the IOC Executive Board with the NOCs would take place in April 1986 in Seoul, so that the position of the DPRK could be monitored before the meeting to be held in Lausanne. Whether or not the North participated in the gathering of NOCs in Seoul would be indicative of their stance. He would also be meeting with government representatives in Korea and hoped that such encoun-

[44] This was a possibility suggested to him by Kim Un Yong.

ters would work favorably toward an agreement between the two Koreas. As before, the IOC would prepare an agenda for the June joint meeting and provide it in advance to each delegation. He gave the same admonishment to the South with respect to the press conference.

Kim Chong Ha was alert to the conversation and had picked up on one of the statements by Samaranch. What, he asked, were the details of the change in attitude of the North to which Samaranch had alluded? Samaranch replied that during the first series of meetings, the North had continually insisted that the Games awarded to Seoul become the Pyongyang-Seoul Games and that the sports be divided equally between the two Koreas. Now, the claim that it was essential that North Korea cohost the Games had been dropped, and the North Koreans were now requesting that several sports be allocated to them. He was of the impression that relations between the two delegations were improving and that communication had become easier.[45]

Kim Chong Ha repeated that, should the North reveal a positive attitude that satisfied both the IOC and the South, it was not too late to consider allocating a full sport to the North — either one of the four team sports that had previously been mentioned, or even another sport. Samaranch believed that it would be advisable to award one of the four team sports to which reference had already been made, but that it was not the right time to begin a detailed examination of such a question at the present meeting. His main concern was that relations between the two NOCs should improve. If relations on a political level were good, this would be reflected in the type of agreement that could be formulated in order to ensure participation of athletes from North Korea in the Games.

Kim Chong Ha agreed that it was necessary to keep open the possibility that an agreement could be reached. Samaranch asked for the trust of the delegation in the policies of the IOC, which fully supported the Seoul Games. He advised that the North was convinced that a joint Korean team should participate in the Games, but that this was a matter for discussion between the two NOCs. If an agreement could be reached to send a single team, this would be acceptable to the IOC. Should no agreement be reached, the IOC would be favorable to the

[45] This was considerably more positive than the actual state of affairs, but Samaranch did not respond with any particulars of the discussions with the North in this meeting with the South. Whatever else may have happened, the North had never abandoned the concept of cohosting; indeed, it was the fundamental negotiating position from which everything else flowed.

participation of two separate Korean teams, as had been the case at previous Games. Kim Chong Ha said that his NOC placed full trust in the IOC, its president, and its members and that Samaranch's assessment of the situation was correct. They adjourned prior to the final joint meeting at noon.

The wind-up gathering was brief and pro forma. Samaranch led off by thanking both delegations for their collaboration and stressed that their collective task was not simple. All three parties were doing their best to reach positive agreement in order to ensure the greatest possible success of the Games. Some progress had been made over the past two days, but they were still some way from full agreement. The IOC was satisfied with the results of the second in this series of meetings. Communication between the parties was much improved and had now been put on a much more friendly basis.

He thought that the meetings should be continued and proposed that the third joint meeting should be in Lausanne on June 10 and 11. He hoped that such a meeting would be the last and that an agreement would be reached that would allow North Korea to accept the invitation to participate in the Games. He repeated the IOC's position. It would respect the decision taken in Baden-Baden and honor the contract with the city of Seoul. The IOC would do everything in its power to ensure the successful celebration of the Games in Seoul. He closed his remarks with the customary thanks to both delegations.

North Kim thanked Samaranch and his colleagues and congratulated them on the sincere efforts that had brought about the meeting. He felt that his delegation had made every effort during the meeting and had advanced the most realistic and practical proposals. He considered that his delegation's generosity might contribute to the success of the Games and to the eventual reunification of the peoples of Korea. He thought that there had been progress made in some areas and that the way was now clear for the possibility of full agreement in the future. He hoped that all proposals would be discussed and that the most forward looking solutions would be adopted.

South Kim offered his thanks and appreciation to Samaranch and the members of the IOC delegation for arranging and presiding over the meeting. He thought that his delegation was doing its utmost to allow the participation of the North. The proposals made by his delegation had been very realistic and should be acceptable to the other delegation. He felt sure there would soon be a positive response from North

Korea and that as long as the Olympic Charter and the decisions of the IOC were respected, there should be no problems with their participation at the Games. He congratulated Samaranch for his goodwill and devotion to the development of the Olympic Movement.

Samaranch closed the meeting and prepared for the press conference later that day.

The North Koreans did not return to Pyongyang right away; they stayed in Lausanne for further private meetings with Samaranch on January 13 and 15. Kim Yu Sun did not take part in these meetings. The North was represented by its vice president, Chin Chung Guk, and Kim Deuk Kil, described as a member of the NOC. There was also an interpreter from the DPRK mission in Geneva. They needed more "clarifications" regarding certain elements of the discussions on January 8 and 9. They said that telexes and telegrams had already been sent to the government of the DPRK, but it would be necessary to make a report upon their return.

They needed to know what, apart from soccer, would be the other two sports to be proposed by the IOC. There would be discussions on this in March, but they wanted an answer as soon as possible. Their delegation was aware that Samaranch saw little chance for a united team but felt that if both sides were favorable, it was not unfeasible. They would follow his advice and pursue the discussions. They requested that Samaranch or a vice president of the IOC attend the discussions for a joint team. It would not be necessary to be present during all discussions, just at the opening and any crucial moments. They also wanted to follow up on what they had understood to be Samaranch's proposal to describe the Games as the XXIVth Olympic Games in Pyongyang and have confirmation of this. How, too, would North Korea be involved in the Olympic torch relay?

Samaranch said he would need some time to consider these questions and would see the North Koreans two days later.[46]

[46] An interesting and cogent observation regarding the meetings to date was made by a Swiss journalist, Eric Walter, in the January 13, 1986, edition of *La Suisse:* [author's translation] "What is important in this affair is not so much whether preliminary events will be held in the North and whether the North will present cultural programs in Seoul, but rather the evident desire for dialogue between the two countries with sport as the pretext. Thanks to the Olympic Games and the efforts of the president of the IOC, one notes some progress, some possibilities of rapprochement, and perspectives for negotiations in other domains. Of course, there is always the question of a terrible political iron fist, but sport is playing its role of catalyst. It is to be hoped that it will emerge as a winner from this new test, since it really cannot afford a new defeat. The Olympic Games — whatever may be their impact — cannot stand four successive boycotts."

On January 14, the official Workers Party newspaper in the DPRK, *Rodong Shinmun,* published an article following up on Kim Il Sung's New Year's message that it would be necessary to have three-way talks involving the United States, the DPRK, and the ROK before a summit meeting on the matter of reunification of Korea called for by Kim could occur. The presence of U.S. troops was characterized as an obstacle to reunification and the usual demand to the South was made to refrain from organizing the annual Team Spirit military exercises. Prior to summit talks between North Korea and South Korea, it was "imperative to create an atmosphere of national reconciliation and trust through many-sided talks."

Samaranch answered Chin's questions on January 15. The three sports that had been mentioned by the North during the informal meeting on January 9 had been soccer, table tennis, and archery. Samaranch would not be able to contact the relevant IFs before the North confirmed its intention to participate in the Games in Seoul. The North, he reminded them, had advised Siperco that a definitive reply would be given on January 10, but the IOC was still awaiting this confirmation. The talks on a single team should commence as soon as possible between the two Koreas. If the first joint meeting failed, the IOC would consider appointing an IOC representative to be present at the discussions.[47] The exact itinerary of the torch relay had not been fixed, but it could probably be arranged to have it pass through North Korea. As to the name of the Games, it was his belief that, for the competitions held in Pyongyang, it would be possible to call them the XXIVth Olympic Games in Pyongyang, but there were many small matters subject to study by the IOC. Much work would have to be done by the IOC to get the agreement of the IOC members, the IFs, and the Seoul Organizing Committee, and there were still many questions to be resolved and discussed.

Samaranch said he was ready to meet with the North Korean delegation as many times as was necessary. A further meeting was arranged for January 20. The North wanted to know whether the KOC had given its approval for the staging of three events in the DPRK. Samaranch replied that this was a problem for the IOC to solve, and it was first necessary to have the firm commitment from North Korea and

[47] This was a reversion to the original position, in which Samaranch had offered the IOC as an arbitrator on this matter.

then to contact the IFs. The North wanted to know if the number of sports could be increased. Samaranch said that the organization of three full events was already very difficult to arrange.[48] He again advised the North to be present at the meetings in Seoul in April. Failure to attend could result in the isolation of their NOC.

On January 20, the same cast duly reappeared. Chin said he had reported to his government regarding Samaranch's call to the president of FITA, the IF governing archery, and the possibility of a meeting with the FITA president in Rome.[49] Chin thought that the government's response would be favorable. Samaranch said he would arrange for an invitation to be sent by FITA.

Chin then delivered a number of statements. His delegation had already mentioned the desire to cohost the Games and its desire to participate with a single team. This had been done at the first joint meeting. At the second joint meeting, it had been indicated that some sports could be held in Pyongyang and that a special Organizing Committee could be established for this purpose. His delegation had considered that this was a sincere effort on the part of the IOC president for the success of the Games in 1988. However, his delegation could *not* accept the condition that it must first of all declare its participation in the Games in Seoul. If the IOC maintained this position, it could jeopardize the previous discussions. In the opinion of his delegation, the intention of the meetings in Lausanne was not to seek means for the participation of the DPRK in the Games, but to seek a way to cohost the Games. The DPRK was ready to participate in the Games in Pyongyang and Seoul with one team, and the condition of participation in Seoul was irrelevant.

He continued. Three sports were insufficient. His delegation returned to its original position of at least eight sports. He wanted to know the position of the South regarding the sports to be staged in Pyongyang, as this would enable the delegation to follow up its discussions with Samaranch on March 7. He reinterated his delegation's view

[48] Again, Samaranch gave the impression that much more progress had been made than was actually the case. It was one of the advantages of the separate meetings, since the nonattending party relied entirely on the IOC to provide the data at each successive step of the process.

[49] Samaranch had discussed this with Francesco Gnecchi-Ruscone, the president of FITA, and the proposed arrangement was satisfactory to FITA; the women's event could be held in Pyongyang. FITA was in one of its periodic difficulties with the IOC and wanted some concessions from the IOC concerning the Olympic archery program, so it was quite cooperative on this matter.

that the Games be called the XXIVth Olympic Games in Pyongyang-Seoul, or the XXIVth Olympic Games in Seoul-Pyongyang, respectively. North Korea was interested in participating in the torch relay but requested more precise details in order to study the matter.

Samaranch said that he regretted the statements made by the delegation; they were not very encouraging. Under these conditions, he was not "able" to contact the IFs. It was necessary to have the confirmation of the DPRK NOC that it would participate in the Games in Seoul. He suggested that the delegation speak with Siperco, who had been acting as the IOC's adviser on this matter, and a meeting was arranged for later that day. Chin said that the conditions placed on his delegation were not diplomatic ones and that the DPRK NOC could not be asked to recognize the SLOOC. Samaranch merely stated that he was speaking on behalf of the IOC. There would be a further meeting on March 7.

Siperco's meeting that evening included the North Korean ambassador as well as the delegation that had met earlier with Samaranch. The tone of the meeting was rather tense. The Koreans were very critical of Samaranch's position that they had to confirm that they would take part in Seoul as a condition of the allocation of events to the North. The description of the portion of the Games in Pyongyang was unacceptable. Samaranch was merely expressing the position of the South. And so on.

A good deal of the three-hour meeting was spent going over old ground, not unlike the formal meetings themselves. The North Koreans regarded their proposals as part of a package and were reluctant to break this package into separate portions for discussion and negotiation. That was why, Chin said, in view of Samaranch's attitude, they continually reverted to their original proposal. They wanted an answer to the proposal from South Korea and from the IFs before they carried on with the negotiations.

Siperco answered the criticisms directed at Samaranch. He reminded them that the proposal for three sports and the name of the Games had been a result of the meeting that he, Siperco, had had the night before with the North Korean ambassador and the NOC delegation. The position of the ambassador had been that he was personally in agreement, but that he needed the approval of his government. Siperco said it was an unfortunate insinuation by the North that Samaranch had expressed the South Korean viewpoint. It was not Samaranch's intention to impose an ultimatum; the conditions for participation would flow from the agreements that would be reached as a result of the negotiations. It would not be possible to start the discussions with the IFs and the South Koreans and to make public in this manner different proposals, given the North's request that the negotiations be kept confidential, until agreement had been reached on the problems that were being discussed.

Nobody, not even the IOC president or the IOC Executive Board, could take the responsibility for proposing to the IOC Session, which was the only body able to decide, solutions that were unreasonable. To arrive at an acceptable formula, account would have to be taken of the dates that were significant in the overall organization of the Games. These included the Executive Board meeting in February, the meeting of NOCs in April, the meeting of the IFs in September, the Asian Games in September, and the IOC Session in October. Samaranch, he said, was also very dissatisfied with the North's continual revisitation of matters that had already been settled. They should understand that if they continued with this tactic, Samaranch would not be disposed to carry on with the negotiations. Even the meetings planned for March 7 with the North and the joint meeting proposed for June would be pointless.

Finally, there appeared to be an agreement that the North Koreans would stop trying to deal with the matter as a complete package and would try to explore possible solutions, point by point, which would not be made public until agreement had been reached on all questions. They reviewed all the points discussed in the January meetings, once again agreeing on the three sports and the name of the Games. The participation of the North at Seoul was linked inseparably, they said, to the formation of a single Korean team. This was absolutely critical to North Korea. Without a joint team, they would not participate. Siperco discussed with them, on a hypothetical basis, assuming the South rejected the idea of a joint team, the possibility that the North Korean athletes might participate only in the events held in Pyongyang. The North Koreans thought this would be difficult but appeared ready to consider it. Samaranch, once advised by Siperco that this variation had been discussed, refused even to consider the possibility.

The North Koreans still wanted an IOC presence during the discussions with South Korea regarding a joint team, but if this was not possible, they would like the IOC to make encouraging noises about the prospect of a joint team and receive some encouraging signs in that regard from the South. They promised to give a definitive approval on the three sports upon the return of the ambassador from Pyongyang in two weeks. The IOC should not, in future discussions, expressly link the participation in the Games in Seoul with the reaching of an agreement. Such participation was possible only if a joint team was to be formed. Once the government had approved the sports to be held in the North, Samaranch would start discussions with the IFs and the South. Discussions regarding the joint team would be pursued as soon as possible.

In the Soviet Union, on January 23, the usual mixed signals were given. IOC member Konstantin Andrianov, interviewed by *Sovietskaya Rossiya,* suggested that even though the Soviets disagreed with the choice of Seoul, it was likely that they would participate, since the South Korean government had given guarantees of security to all countries, including the socialist countries. "The train," he said, "has already gone too far." To maintain the balance, Tass issued a communiqué the same day, reiterating support for the organization of the Games in both North Korea and South Korea.

CHAPTER 8

Take Three: The Third Meeting

LAUSANNE, SWITZERLAND, June 10–11, 1986—With the marginal progress apparent from the outcome of the second joint meeting, there was little optimism that any major step forward could be contemplated before the next meeting in Lausanne, scheduled for June 10–11, 1986. The IOC's focus for the short term became one of following the bilateral talks between North Korea and South Korea, which were to be held in March, and to do whatever could be done to make the meeting of all the NOCs with the IOC Executive Board in Seoul as successful as possible. The greater the success of this meeting and the more countries there were present, the greater would be the pressure on the North to come to some realistic agreement regarding the Games. Failure to do so would increase its isolation and reduce whatever sympathy might otherwise exist.

On the Olympic level, Samaranch met separately with both the North and the South in Lausanne on March 7.[1] Discussions had continued between the North Koreans and Siperco since the meetings in January. At the February IOC Executive Board meeting, Samaranch

[1] External dialogue had continued in the meantime. On February 19, in an interview in *Army Times*, General William J. Livsey, commander of the ROK-U.S. Combined Forces Command, was reported as warning that the DPRK might stage an armed provocation against Seoul to disrupt the Games. At the Asian Winter Games in Sapporo, Japan, ROK sports minister Park Seh Jik stated that joint hosting of the 1988 Games was "out of the question." This was countered by DPRK NOC vice president Pak Myong Chol, stating that the DPRK expected a positive response from the ROK to the DPRK cohosting proposal at the third joint meeting. On March 11, Kim Il Sung, addressing a rally in Pyongyang in honor of Castro, who had arrived on March 8, said that the 1988 Games were a political issue and that the DPRK would not sit idly by. In coordination with this, in Havana, sports minister Conrado Martinez called upon the nonaligned countries to support the DPRK's demand to cohost the Games.

reported that he had advised the DPRK delegation that he would not contact any international federations until he had the guarantee that the DPRK would take part in the Games. He asked He Zhenliang for a briefing on the Chinese attitude with respect to the Korean problems.

At the March 7 meeting,[2] Kim Yu Sun of North Korea stated that both his government and his NOC were pleased with the results of the first two joint meetings and had given instructions to begin the construction of an Olympic Village in Pyongyang. He said that preparations had also begun for the staging of the three sports of soccer, archery, and table tennis. They had followed up on Samaranch's suggestion to meet with the president of the archery federation, had had discussions with FIFA, the international federation responsible for soccer, which seemed disposed to accept a proposal from the IOC to stage soccer in North Korea, and had had positive discussions with the table tennis federation. Given the construction being undertaken, the government of the DPRK and the NOC wished to propose the sports to be offered to them by the IOC be extended to include wrestling, gymnastics, and judo. He reiterated their proposal for the naming of the Games as well as the proposal for a special Organizing Committee to be located in Pyongyang.

There were, said Kim Yu Sun, still divergences of opinion regarding the formation of a joint team. Previous summits on this question had failed. If the discussions could be held in the presence of a representative of the IOC and be directed to the Olympic Games, rather than international competitions generally, they would be more fruitful. The IOC presence was all the more important, since the participation of North Korea in the Games was being discussed. There had been contacts with South Korea, and two joint meetings had already taken place, one in Hong Kong and one in Lausanne, in the presence of an IOC representative.[3] The possibility of a single Korean team would be good for the image of the Games, the promotion of peace, and unification.

[2] Samaranch and Siperco were present for the IOC; Kim Yu Sun was accompanied by Chin Chung Guk, Kim Deuk Kil, and Jin Youn Myeung, the latter first secretary of the DPRK mission in Geneva.

[3] These were the abortive attempts in 1963 to form a single team for the 1964 Games in Innsbruck and Tokyo. The IOC had only been involved in the Lausanne meetings; the Hong Kong meetings were bilateral. It was clear from the discussions and behavior of the South Koreans that they were much less interested in coming to an agreement at that time on a joint team than was the North.

North Korea maintained a flexible attitude and was willing to have a "partially joint team" with a combined team in only some sports.[4]

Samaranch thanked Kim and his delegation for their efforts. Although there had been a step forward, no agreement had been reached, and it was essential that a solution be found at the forthcoming joint meeting in June. He would reply to the points raised by Kim but stressed that no firm agreement could be given by the IOC until the June meeting.

The construction of the Olympic Village and the sports facilities was a matter for the government and the NOC to decide. Samaranch only wanted to point out that no agreement had yet been reached. As to the sports, he reiterated his previous position: he would only be prepared to speak to the IFs when a firm confirmation was received from the DPRK NOC regarding its participation in the Games in Seoul. Up to now, therefore, he had not contacted the IFs. The request for three more sports would be studied by the IOC Executive Board, as would the designation of the Games. He agreed that, in principle, if sports were to be staged in the North, a special Organizing Committee based in Pyongyang would be set up to organize these.[5]

The joint team was not a problem to be resolved by the IOC, but by the two Koreas. He observed that the IOC had participated in the two inter-Korean meetings in Lausanne, but this had not been positive, and the IOC would no longer take any part. The IOC would encourage the staging of a meeting between the parties but would take no responsibility for the organization of it. Samaranch drew their attention to the fact that there were only three months left before the next joint meeting in June and that it would be necessary to find a solution by this date. There were many details to be resolved. The delegation should continue its discussions with Siperco.

Kim Yu Sun thanked Samaranch for his comments and hoped the IOC would study their proposals in a favorable manner. Participation of the DPRK in the Games would be considered if it was possible to

[4] This rather bizarre proposal, which would have been difficult to rationalize by either of the two Koreas, given their respective views of themselves and of each other, was not explained.

[5] The thought of having a North Korean "branch" of the SLOOC was hopeless. If anything was to come of the negotiations, it would be essential for the IOC to have control of whatever activities might occur in Pyongyang through a direct relationship between itself and the North. The likelihood of inter-Korean cooperation on the scale necessary to coordinate the logistical aspects of the Olympic Games was, at best, illusory.

have a partially joint team. Samaranch referred to the meeting he had had with them on January 20, when he had clearly stated that he was only prepared to contact the IFs upon confirmation of the DPRK's participation in Seoul. Ambassador Kim had said that this was not diplomatic. The IOC's position was still the same, said Samaranch, and he was still awaiting a reply regarding North Korea's participation, which had been promised by January 10.

Kim Yu Sun then said that since the events in Pyongyang and Seoul would be held at the same time, the DPRK would, therefore, be taking part in Seoul. The underlying logic of this assertion was, unfortunately, not explained. Ambassador Kim said that the North had the same goal as the IOC, to have as many delegations as possible taking part. Now that a firm answer had been given regarding participation, would the IOC be willing to grant three more sports? Samaranch said that this was the first time an answer had been given regarding the DPRK's participation in Seoul, and he would be in a position to commence discussions with the relevant IFs.[6] He did not think it would be easy to convince the IFs, but he would do his best.[7] As far as the increase in the number of sports was concerned, he thought that six was too many, but he would have to consult with the Executive Board.

The North Koreans requested an answer as soon as possible and asked if the joint meeting could be advanced, perhaps to mid-April.[8] Samaranch said he would have to consult the South before changing the plans. He once again urged the North to attend the NOC meetings in Seoul in April.

The meeting with the South dealt mainly with progress in relation to the April meetings and a discussion of television negotiations in

[6] Though it was difficult to imagine a less firm "answer" to the question, it was not inconvenient to act as if such an answer had actually been given.

[7] Of course, Samaranch had done nothing of the kind and would not do anything of a formal nature for several months, other than the preliminary contact with Gnecchi-Ruscone of FITA in early January 1986, after the second joint meeting.

[8] The DPRK obviously wanted to have some result in hand prior to the ANOC meeting later in April; Samaranch wanted to keep the pressure on them and to continue to give them more opportunities to isolate themselves. The more it could appear that the IOC was doing everything to be reasonable in the face of unreasonable conduct, the more likely it was that the NOCs would be sympathetic to its efforts. The more irrational and unreasonable the DPRK could appear to be, the better it would be for this process. North Korea resolutely took advantage of every such opportunity to lose the backing of those who might otherwise have been inclined to support its position.

various countries. It was a further occasion for Samaranch to meet with Park Seh Jik, who was then the South Korean sports minister, having replaced Lee Yong Ho, and who was slated to become the next president of the SLOOC.[9] No discussion took place on the content of the meeting with the DPRK.

The bilateral political talks in March had been the expected non-event. Indeed, with the political uncertainties in South Korea, it would have been very difficult for the government of the day to do more than render lip service to the idea of reunification; it simply would not have been possible at that stage to be seen to be caving in to the pressure of some of the opposition parties. That would have been a recipe for domestic political disaster. By the same token, it seemed to be recognized, at least tacitly, and probably by both sides, that so long as Kim Il Sung, the "Glorious Leader," was at the helm in North Korea, it would be impossible actually to reach any significant agreement. So the usual banalities were uttered, the usual accusations exchanged, and everyone went back to their respective, heavily armed solitudes.[10]

To try to make it more difficult for the North to refuse to participate in the NOC meetings in Seoul in April, Samaranch had pressed the South for an indication that the North Koreans would be welcome at the meetings and that additional meetings might be possible. He got a statement from the sports minister, Park Seh Jik, on April 1, delivered by Ambassador Park in Geneva. It did say that North Korea would be welcome and that meetings between sports officials would take place. It went on, however, to urge Samaranch strongly to persuade the North Koreans to attend the meetings "unconditionally." If the North were to state publicly that it would participate in the April meetings scheduled for Seoul, Park said, the South might consider a meeting prior to the NOC meetings. Such a meeting could be held anywhere. The South would only consider a meeting when it knew the intentions of the North and whether the North Koreans would use it as an opportunity to stage propaganda before the meetings. South Korea was skeptical. Park

[9] Park would later signal that the DPRK would be welcome at the April meetings of the NOCs and that if it were to be present without conditions, there could be additional meetings prior to the scheduled meeting with the IOC in mid-June.

[10] Lee Ki Baek, the Korean defense minister, issued a statement on March 20 that there was a danger that war could break out at any time between then and 1988.

observed that the DPRK had apparently circulated a propaganda document at the UN in New York, saying that there were more than ten thousand AIDS victims in South Korea, with an intention to scare off participants at the Asian Games and the Olympics. These were false allegations, and the minister asked Samaranch to warn the North Koreans against this sort of propaganda.

The North sent its chargé de mission, Sin Hyonrim, to see Samaranch on April 3. He said that although he had not been present at previous meetings, he had carefully studied the Olympic dossier. His country wanted to accelerate the work toward common preparation of the Games. At the first meeting, the DPRK had proposed organizing three sports. At the second meeting it had proposed three more. The IOC had said it would contact the IFs. The DPRK wanted to know the outcome of these contacts.

Samaranch said he was not then in a position to give a response, since the discussions were then under way. A reply would be available at the beginning of May, which would be well before the third joint meeting in June. He also commented that, at the last meeting, the North had asked him to see if a meeting between North Korea and South Korea could be arranged. He was now able to say that if the North Koreans attended the NOC meetings in Seoul, the South was ready to have a bilateral meeting in Seoul during their visit. If the DPRK were to make a public statement that it would participate in the NOC meetings, the South was ready to have a meeting sooner, at a time and place to be decided. This was not a proposition of the IOC, but of the South. He expressed no opinion on the idea but noted that any meeting of this sort appeared to be positive.

Sin said that when the DPRK delegation had last met in Lausanne, it had urged the IOC to have the third joint meeting as early as possible, because it wished to start the preparations for the events confided to it if an agreement were to be reached. That was why they wanted the responses from the IFs. Samaranch was now saying that the responses would not be available until May, so there seemed to be no point in an earlier meeting. Samaranch replied that he had presented the idea of the meetings between the two Koreas because it was the DPRK that had asked for the bilateral meeting.

Whether he had not been properly briefed or whether he just lost his head, Sin blurted out that his country considered the third joint meeting as very important. To prepare the part of the Games that would be given to the North, the DPRK needed to gain time. But if there were no responses from the IFs, it was useless to have a meeting. Samaranch told him to calm down; the IF responses would be ready in May, and the third joint meeting would be held in June as already planned. Sin repeated that the IOC was very important in this process and urged Samaranch to do everything necessary to get the IF approvals. Before leaving, he said that the DPRK team would participate in the Games only if the IOC gave the North six sports.

It was, clearly, an unsatisfactory meeting; enough so that it was followed, on April 9, by a visit from the DPRK ambassador in Geneva, Kim Hyong. The ambassador brought with him an invitation to Samaranch to visit Pyongyang on a private basis; during the visit matters of mutual interest could be discussed. He thanked Samaranch for all his efforts during the first two joint meetings and for the preparation and advancement, if possible, of the third. The DPRK was ready to resolve the problems necessary to ensure the success of the Games. There were many such problems, even on the eve of the NOC meetings in Seoul and of the third joint meeting, which the ambassador wanted to review and to pass on the official position of his country before examining the participation of the DPRK at the NOC meetings and the third joint meeting.

Three points in particular required an answer: the number of sports to be awarded to Pyongyang, the description of the Games, and the composition of the Organizing Committee. If the DPRK could have the assurance and the guarantee of the South Koreans and the IOC on these three questions, it was ready to take part in the NOC meetings in Seoul. Samaranch said that it was important to recall that it was the DPRK that had asked the IOC to arrange a bilateral meeting with the South. The IOC was now in a position to reply to that request. The ambassador, he said, was aware, from his chargé de mission, Sin, that this meeting had been arranged. If the DPRK attended the Seoul meetings, this would be a good opportunity to have meetings between the two sides. All the important NOCs would be there, and the absence of the DPRK would be most regrettable, but this was a decision that could only be made by the DPRK itself. With respect to the number of sports, he had already advised Sin that an answer would be available at the beginning of May. Regarding the invitation to Pyongyang, he had already been there twice but was prepared to go again. Dates would have to be agreed upon.

The ambassador wanted to clarify one of the answers given by Samaranch. The DPRK had no interest in having bilateral meetings with the South unless there was a representative of the IOC present, which would allow a more general discussion of all the issues relating to the Games. As the final authority on matters Olympic, an official presence of the IOC would have a beneficial effect at any such meeting. Samaranch said that if the DPRK was present at the NOC meetings in Seoul, he would be prepared to delegate a member of the IOC Executive Board to chair a meeting between the Koreas.[11] The ambassador said his country was ready to go to the Seoul meetings, but on condition of having the guarantee from Seoul concerning the number of sports to be organized in Pyongyang.

Samaranch repeated what he had just said: the answer could not be given before the early part of May. He reminded the ambassador that it was the DPRK that had asked for the meeting with the South. The answer was yes, and the meeting would be chaired by a member of the IOC Executive Board. The ambassador declared that the DPRK had never wanted anything other than to advance the date of the third joint meeting and had never spoken of having a meeting in Seoul. He stated that the DPRK had now made a new offer to participate in the NOC meetings and hoped that Samaranch would make this understood in the South. Samaranch said that he had already replied to all of these points and had nothing further to add. Further contact could be maintained through the IOC secretariat or with Siperco. Siperco noted that, on his way to the April meetings in Seoul, he would be spending some time in Beijing, where he could easily be reached.

Seoul was delighted with the turnout for the meeting of the NOCs in April. The NOCs met first in the context of their international organization, the Association of National Olympic Committees (ANOC). This was followed by the biennial meeting of the NOCs with the IOC Executive Board. Both meetings have a useful purpose in forming consensus on major issues that affect the Olympic Movement, and the IOC has been active in supporting both ANOC and these regular meetings. If for no other reason, they are helpful in providing a forum in which even the smallest NOCs have direct access to the IOC Executive Board to raise their concerns. Similar meetings are held annually with the IFs.

Apart from the general success of the meetings and the organization

[11] This was a clarification concerning the possibility of an official IOC presence at bilateral meetings. Samaranch did not offer to preside over any such meeting himself. In all likelihood, he would have selected Ashwini Kumar; Alexandru Siperco might have been seen as too close to the DPRK to be acceptable to the South.

of them by the South, there were several "signals" of particular interest to the IOC in relation to the Games. The Chinese attended. They were not particularly vocal, but the implication of their presence was loud and clear. Apart from the DPRK, no important Asian countries were absent. This was propitious for the Asian Games that September, as well. The Soviets were also present. What is more, this meeting marked the first time that a Soviet minister had been present in Seoul since the Korean War. The president of the USSR NOC, Marat Gramov, was (at the time) the Soviet minister of sport. This was a major political triumph for the South and equally reassuring for the IOC, since it was evidence that its restraint in dealing with the North Koreans was proving effective in reducing the tensions that might otherwise have prevented Gramov from attending a meeting in the Republic of Korea. In all, only eight of the 167 NOCs did not attend. One of these was Cuba,[12] which was no surprise.[13]

Samaranch had two particularly significant meetings during this visit to Seoul. One was after the reception hosted by the IOC on April 25, and involved Roh Tae Woo and Park Seh Jik. At the end of this meeting, he got a commitment that South Korea was ready to offer two sports to North Korea on the condition that North Korea declare it would respect the Olympic Charter and the decisions taken by the IOC at its Baden-Baden Session in 1981. This commitment was given by Roh and Park, they said, to reinforce the power and authority of Samaranch.

The outcome of the meeting was particularly pleasing to Samaranch because it meant that he had now achieved the means to accomplish his objective in the negotiations: any *no* to participation in the Games would have to come from the DPRK, because the South had made a constructive gesture and one that was not at all easy for them to make.

The second meeting on that occasion was with Chun Doo Hwan, in

[12] Cuba suffered a diplomatic setback on the Olympic question prior to the Seoul meetings when its resolution calling for cohosting of the Games was rejected after five hours of debate on April 12 at an economic meeting of the nonaligned countries in New Delhi.

[13] The April 22 issue of *Rodong Shinmun* carried a particularly hysterical statement, obviously in contemplation of the diplomatic rout implicit in the massive turnout for the Seoul meetings. It declared the holding of the 1986 Asian Games and the 1988 Olympic Games to be an "adventure" since war "might explode at any moment" in the ROK. The present situation in South Korea was stated to be reminiscent of the situation in 1950, when a "fascist clique started a war of northward invasion, engineered by the U.S. imperialists." The next day, Park Seh Jik, reporting to the IOC Executive Board, advised the IOC not to overreact to threats and pressures from the DPRK, nor to overestimate the DPRK's position. He discounted military intervention and assured the IOC that the ROK was fully capable of handling terrorism.

which Samaranch raised the question of the presidential elections during the Olympic year. Chun was not prepared to change the date of the elections nor to approach the opposition parties to seek agreement on such a change.[14] Chun assured him that nothing would happen as a result of the elections and that even if the opposition parties were to win, this would not affect the success of the Games.[15]

This meeting with Chun Doo Hwan had followed one held in Switzerland between them, only a few days earlier, on April 19, 1986, during the course of a visit by Chun to Europe, which included a brief visit to IOC headquarters in Lausanne.[16] The discussions on that occasion centered around the Korean problems and Samaranch's fears that the North might do something to destabilize the Games. The DPRK was doubtless aware that, at least for the moment, the majority of the socialist countries, particularly those in Europe, were disposed to participate in the Games. On the other hand, the DPRK had Cuba on its side. Fidel Castro was enormously respected, he said, by these countries, and they were unlikely to do anything that would disrupt their good relations with him.

For that reason, Samaranch asked Chun to look into the possibility of conceding some sports to the DPRK. Its demands had diminished dramatically. The first position had been to refuse to accept Games in Seoul; this was followed by wanting to share 50 percent of the Games; and now the request was to organize five of the twenty-three sports. He said that perhaps two or three would be sufficient, but that the IOC could only move forward in this direction with the prior agreement of the Republic of Korea. Thus, this discussion with Chun was of supreme importance.

Chun approached the matter by saying that there was a fundamental question for him; namely, was there any authority, country, or organiza-

[14] Indeed, given the overall political climate, the public's suspicion of Chun and the skepticism regarding the sincerity of his promise to leave political office at the end of his term, it would have been political suicide for him to have been seen to try to alter the election schedule in any manner whatsoever.

[15] On April 26, Samaranch advised the IOC Commission for the Olympic Movement that he was more optimistic about the outcome of the third joint meeting after his discussions the previous day and that he believed a worthwhile solution could be found. He repeated the statement in his press conference following the meetings.

[16] The April 19 meeting was private, with only Chun, Samaranch, and Kim Pyong Hoon, Chun's chief protocol secretary, in attendance. Chun had also paid an official visit to IOC headquarters in Lausanne on April 12, but no serious discussion had occurred on that occasion.

tion (in relation to the Olympic Movement) higher than the IOC itself? He had understood that the IOC was the supreme authority and that the whole world must respect its decisions. He said he knew that the organization had the best intentions, but the threats of North Korea worried him. The IOC must, he said, give nothing; it should not allow provocations; it should pay no attention to threats. That was what worried him most.

Chun's military background showed clearly in his subsequent comments. He said it was true that North Korea had more arms than South Korea, but that they did not have the means to fight against South Korea and the U.S. forces based in his country. "President Kim Il Sung knows that he cannot attack us," he asserted, "and I know it and he knows that I know it. Neither the USSR nor China would allow North Korea to attack the South. The North is not in a position to attack us. If we were to give them three sports now, afterwards they would ask us for five," he interjected, as an aside. The problem of the danger of war depended, he continued, on whether the USSR was inclined to fight against the United States in his region. The reply was quite clear: no. The second was the position of China. He assured Samaranch that China did not want war either. Without the support of these two countries, North Korea could do absolutely nothing, and if it were to do something, that would be an act of self-destruction. If they wanted a fight, they would have it, but it would be suicide on their part.

"The sole reason," said Chun, "that I am explaining all this to you is to give you the support that you need. You believe they are much stronger than they really are. Let it be well understood: North Korea was opposed in principle to the South's Olympic Games; afterwards, they wanted divided Games, then they changed their demands at least two or three times before asking, as you said, for five sports. My question is this," he continued. "Through whom did they ask for it?" Samaranch replied that they had done so directly and also through China, the USSR, Cuba, Ethiopia, and many other countries. In addition, these points were discussed during the joint meetings held in Lausanne.

Chun continued to tell Samaranch that he should understand the reality of the military situation in the peninsula and also the situation within North Korea, a country that did not understand and did not want to understand the Olympic Charter nor to follow the IOC's instructions. "You show," he said, "dignity, consistency and leadership. You are respected by the whole world, but if you give in to the claims of North Korea, you will lose your credibility and that of the organization of which you are president. The North has a domestic problem arising from the fact that they lied to their people.

"President Kim Il Sung and his son said that Seoul could not organize the Olympic Games and that there is nothing in Seoul but beggars in the streets," he stated. "It was only propaganda and I know it, but when they realized that these Games could be a success, they became very nervous. They can only get out of this problem with threats. They can do nothing to stop Seoul. Time is passing, and," he repeated, "you and your organization are greatly respected, and you may be assured that North Korea cannot win the battle against the IOC. There is a very important principle: North Korea does not wish to respect the IOC's resolutions if it does not get anything out of them. Before making any requests, they should state clearly that they respect the Olympic Charter and the decisions of the IOC. If North Korea states that it absolutely agrees to respect the Olympic Charter and the IOC's decisions, then we could discuss in Seoul in a few days' time the possibility of giving them some sports. I am favorably disposed to do what you desire to help the IOC, not North Korea, but I insist on the principle that the IOC should not feel affected by the threats of North Korea."

Chun continued by saying that before he left Seoul, he was visited by U.S. secretary of defense Caspar Weinberger and high-level American and Korean figures. Weinberger gave him a personal letter from U.S. president Ronald Reagan, in which Reagan expressed very clearly his country's wish to maintain peace in the Korean peninsula and to help the Olympic Games to take place normally. The United States had recently taken action in Libya, but Chun assured Samaranch that in Korea the reaction would be much stronger. If North Korea attacked, it would be destroyed. This was being told to Samaranch in strict confidence. His final statement on the issue of the two Koreas was that Samaranch should not take seriously the threats of North Korea. They were not in a position to do anything against the IOC. He could believe Chun just as Chun believed him. He should say to North Korea that they must respect the Olympic Charter and all the decisions taken by the IOC. "If they do so, tell them that we can help them," he concluded.

The question of the elections was raised by Samaranch. Chun reminded him that he had raised the matter the previous year in Seoul. He was sure nothing would happen but said it could be discussed shortly when Samaranch was in Seoul. This was a fairly clear brush-off, which made it clear that there was not likely to be any change in the electoral schedule. Samaranch also asked directly about the possible co-optation of Kim Un Yong as a member of the IOC, but Chun asked that the matter be deferred until they met in Seoul, which led Samaranch to conclude that he had another candidate in mind.

In Seoul, a week later, at the April 25 meeting, there was general satisfaction with the presence of so many NOCs for the ANOC meeting and the subsequent meeting with the IOC Executive Board. Samaranch began the meeting by recalling the recent visit to Europe by Chun and congratulating him on having selected such an opportune time to pursue economic relations between his country and Europe. It had, indeed, been excellent timing on his part. Chun replied that he had been happy to meet with Samaranch during his visit to Europe and to have had the chance to discuss the problems between North Korea and South Korea. He cut directly to the point: was there anything new?

Samaranch replied that the great success of the meetings with the NOCs in Seoul was a very positive step for the success of the Games in 1988. He reminded Chun that when they had discussed matters the previous week, Chun had said that if North Korea was ready to respect the Olympic Charter and the decisions of the IOC, in particular those taken in Baden-Baden, he was ready to open discussions with North Korea. Samaranch asked Chun directly whether he was ready to give some sports to the North.

Chun's first response was to congratulate Samaranch on the great success of the meetings in Seoul and for the record number of NOCs present, which would have been impossible without him. He reminded Samaranch of having said in Switzerland how much he had appreciated his personal efforts. He added that Samaranch had traveled the world to help the Olympic Movement, and above all, the Seoul Games, and that he, as well as Roh and Park, were very grateful for all this work. Therefore, and because of his extraordinary effort to defend the Olympic Movement, it was impossible for him to say no to Samaranch's request, but on the conditions he had outlined in Switzerland. What Chun wanted from the North was not a favor; he required only that it respect the Olympic Charter and the decisions of the IOC. He was concerned, in any event, that even if matters of principle could be settled, once the matters of detail were addressed, there would soon be too many people involved in the decisions. There would be a huge number of legal, technical, organizational, and political issues to be addressed.

Everyone knew perfectly well, Chun said, that North Korea was making all these efforts simply to harm the South and to prejudice the Seoul Games. He knew that the people of Korea were with the government and supported it on this matter. They knew, as well, that they had invested a great deal of effort and money in the Games, and, accordingly, it would be very difficult for him to convince the people to share the Games with North Korea. Samaranch should be very careful. They knew the North Koreans very well and knew that if they were given even one sport, they would cause South Korea enormous problems. It was impossible to expect, on their part, any kind of goodwill or cooperation. But, he said again, it was impossible for him not to accept the request put to him by Samaranch as president of the IOC. The bottom line was this: he was prepared to give the North two sports, but on the condition that North Korea respected the Olympic Charter and the conditions determined by the IOC.

Samaranch replied that, as president of the IOC, he thought the solution was a good one, since it left the responsibility of saying no to North Korea, if there was to be such an answer. It was difficult for Samaranch to believe that North Korea would be able to open its borders to more than ten thousand journalists and all the members of the Olympic Family. Chun agreed with this analysis. He said the real reason for his decision was so that Samaranch could demonstrate to the socialist countries that he had achieved a positive result from South Korea on this matter.

In principle, and Chun said he would not say so publicly, it would not be at all easy to share the Games, and sharing would create major problems. North Korea must absolutely guarantee security for everyone and accord to everyone all necessary facilities and freedom of movement. "We have to be very careful; when you give the North a finger, they want the whole arm." He was sure that the North would also want to share in the money. Finally, it was very important that if a sport were to be granted to the North, there should be direct communication with the SLOOC and the freedom to go to North Korea whenever necessary. He was not sure whether the North was prepared to accept all these conditions, but, Chun repeated, he was acceding to Samaranch's request to reinforce his status as president of the IOC.

Samaranch said that splitting the Games was not new, since, in 1956, the equestrian events had been held in Stockholm instead of Melbourne. He said that what had been agreed to was a very important step toward the success of the Seoul Olympic Games. Chun was not impressed by the comparison with 1956.[17] He said the situation of Seoul was entirely different from that of Melbourne. The equestrian events had been held in Stockholm because of difficulties faced by the Organizing Committee, whereas in Seoul, the IOC faced no difficulties whatsoever with the SLOOC. He repeated his offer for a final time and insisted that it was for the purpose of helping the IOC and its president.

The final matter discussed was the question of Roh Tae Woo's continuing connection with the SLOOC. Park Seh Jik would be taking over the presidency of the SLOOC in a few weeks, and Samaranch suggested to Chun that Roh be named chairman, which would produce a structure similar to that used in the Los Angeles Organizing Committee, in which Paul Ziffren was chairman and Peter Ueberroth was president. Samaranch did not want to lose Roh completely within the SLOOC, not only because they had developed good personal relations, but also because he was convinced that there would be need for his presence in the future. This was later put in place.

Leading up to the third joint meeting, Samaranch suggested, during an interview in Evian, France, on May 6, that the IOC might have some new elements to propose to the DPRK at the forthcoming meeting.

It was interesting to note the opinion, prior to this meeting, expressed by U.S. sports columnist Howard Cosell in an article published in the May 25 edition of the *Miami Herald,*entitled "Why the '88 Olympics Won't Be in South Korea," which quoted former USOC president William E. Simon as saying, "There is not a prayer of the Summer Games being held in South Korea," and "Juan Samaranch, the IOC president, has been quietly negotiating for some events to be held in the North. North Korea will not accept the offer. I learned from long experience with Samaranch that he is a macho man living with the outmoded maxim 'sport and politics don't mix.'" The headline for the same article published in the *Daily Sports News* read "South Korea Games? Forget It!" and the subhead was "'88 Olympics may not come off unless alternate site is planned."[18]

[17] In 1954, the IOC Session in Athens had decided that due to Australian quarantine regulations regarding importation of horses, the equestrian events for the 1956 Games would be held in Stockholm. This portion of the Games had been held on June 10–17, 1956. They were opened by King Gustav VI Adolf of Sweden and were attended by twenty-one IOC members.

[18] Samaranch thought the best revenge for this piece of work would be to send each author and source a copy of the Official Report of the Games once they were over, with no covering letter, but simply his "compliments" card and a copy of the article.

One step taken by Samaranch in preparation for the third joint meeting in June 1986 was to have a draft contract prepared, dealing with the formation of an Organizing Committee in Pyongyang, should there be an agreement reached at the meeting. The IOC already had a formal contract with the KOC and the city of Seoul, executed when the Games had been awarded in 1981.[19] This draft would be the basis of an additional contract between the IOC and North Korea, setting out their responsibilities in relation to those sports and events taking place in the North.

During this time we were in virtually daily contact regarding a variety of matters pertaining to the Seoul Games. Samaranch sent me a confidential draft of this contract on May 28, asking for comments, which I returned the same day. It was clear from the matters to be covered in this draft that even if there was to be agreement on the points to be discussed at the forthcoming joint meeting, the negotiation of such a contract with the North could take, literally, years. It was, however, a measure of the preparation for the joint meeting that the next hurdle to disruption of the Seoul Games by the DPRK would already be in place, in the unlikely event of a breakthrough in the discussions. It was never necessary to resort to this draft contract.

There was a brief meeting with North Korea on June 9, the day before the third joint meeting. It was, largely, a matter of protocol. Samaranch welcomed Kim Yu Sun and Chin Chung Guk and said he was certain that everyone would do their best to reach at least an agreement in principle. The Games were now only two years away, and an agreement, in whatever form, should be reached as soon as possible. He reminded them that any agreement would require the approval of the IOC Session in October. He was delighted to have this contact with the DPRK delegation and would reserve discussion of the substantive matters until the following day.[20]

[19] As the complexities of organizing the Olympic Games increase and the need to combine the efforts of both the public and private sectors increases in turn, the legal and organizational responsibilities of the various parties must be described in more and more detail. It is no longer feasible to leave such matters with general references to the Olympic Charter or guidelines, which are not filled with detailed requirements. The form that this has taken in recent years is a contract between the IOC and the host city and the local NOC. Such contracts are becoming very sophisticated. The dynamics of the relationships between the IOC and Organizing Committees have changed considerably as the IOC has become more active in defining the elements of its Olympic "franchise."

[20] On June 6 in Moscow, USSR NOC president Gramov had stated during a press conference in relation to the Goodwill Games that he would wait and see what happened at the third joint

Kim Yu Sun expressed a similar hope for the success of the meeting, based particularly on the outcome of previous bilateral meetings. He wanted to know how the third joint meeting would be conducted. Chin mentioned that at the time of their meeting with Samaranch in Beijing, during Samaranch's visit there following the meetings in Seoul,[21] there had been discussion of a document and of concrete proposals to be discussed at this time. Samaranch said that in the course of the meeting with the DPRK alone on the following day, such proposals would be presented. The first part of the meeting would be a matter of protocol declarations only, to be followed by in-depth discussions with each side. If there was to be agreement on the proposals to be put forward by the IOC, then the next step would be to prepare a document to reflect the agreement. It was unlikely that a document would be prepared at this meeting, since each side would need to have consultations with the appropriate authorities in their countries. This might entail a further month or month and a half. He did not want to go into details in the absence of the IOC vice presidents. Replying to Chin, he said that the IOC proposals would address the number of sports, the nature and structure of the Pyongyang Organizing Committee, and, particularly, the guarantee of the DPRK to open its border without any conditions.[22]

The third joint meeting of the IOC with the two Koreas started at 10:05 A.M. on Tuesday, June 10, 1986. After welcoming the two delega-

---

meeting in Lausanne. The following day, Radio Pyongyang announced that the DPRK had the support of the Soviet Union, China, Poland, Cuba, and Ethiopia for its cohosting proposal and that organization of the Games only in the South would be an intolerable defeat of the sacred cause of the reunification of Korea. In Paris on June 8, Samaranch had said that the IOC had something new to offer to the DPRK to help come to an agreement in principle. He thought a fourth joint meeting might be required to come to a full agreement and that a fundamental condition would be the full opening of the border between the ROK and DPRK.

[21] Samaranch had been in Beijing on April 27–30, 1986, and met with Chin on April 30. Chin was aggressive as usual and wanted the entire soccer tournament to be held in the North. He also demanded that the South stop its propaganda attacks on the North. Samaranch brought this particular diatribe to a speedy conclusion by handing Chin a transcript of a Radio Pyongyang broadcast filled with lies and insults about the South, which he had obtained from the Spanish ambassador. He also met on at least two occasions with sports minister Li Menghua and IOC member He Zhenliang to bring them up to date on the discussions with the two Koreas. Both were cautiously supportive but did not want to get too involved. Although they wanted to participate in the Games in Seoul, they did not want to create any problems with the North.

[22] All these matters were included in the draft agreement already prepared, but for strategic purposes, Samaranch did not want the North to know that the document existed. Had they known it was available, they would have wanted to study it and would have seen the additional problems to be addressed. This might well have led to a breakdown of the negotiations, which the IOC was at pains to avoid.

tions and introducing the IOC representatives,[23] Samaranch outlined the program for the two days, which was almost identical to that of the previous meetings. The sessions would, as usual, close with a press conference, to which the delegations were invited, but which would take the form of an official IOC declaration. He invited introductory comments from each delegation.

North Kim gave what was, by now, his standard opening.[24] He thanked the IOC for its assiduous preparation for the meeting and recognized the efforts of Samaranch, the vice presidents, and other IOC officials for having made every effort to cope with the difficulties lying in the way of the Games and to assure their successful hosting. He said that they had "patently" showed to the people of the world, through the previous two joint meetings and various contacts, that they had a common desire to make an excellent spectacle of the Games, "come what may." This single common desire was an important guarantee to enable the third joint meeting to be successful.

Typical of the statements he made was the following:

> The broad segments of the athletes and the peace-loving people all over the world who treasure the Olympic Movement hope that at this meeting we shall agree sincerely to all the relevant proposals one by one, thus opening up a new epochal milestone in the history of the Olympic Movement.

He recalled that certain progress had been made in the discussion of the proposed problems through the first and second meetings, but that they had fallen short of a complete agreement. For reaching agreement at the present meeting, it would be necessary to "earnestly approach" the meeting, cherishing one goal and the desire to get over the present difficulties.

That is why, he continued, the meetings are not allowed to impose any one side's will and demand on the other and, moreover, should not "commit such a thing as to create artificial difficulties in the way of the joint meeting by offering to the opposite whatever unjust condi-

[23] The IOC delegation consisted of Samaranch, Ashwini Kumar, Berthold Beitz, Raymond Gafner, Samuel Pisar, Alain Coupat (Samaranch's *chef du cabinet*), and Howard Stupp, the IOC director of legal affairs.

[24] The DPRK delegation consisted of Kim Yu Sun (North Kim), Chin Chung Guk, Chang Ung, Han Chang On, An Bok Man, and Cho Myong Hwang.

tions."[25] It was thought, he said, that each side should concede and show magnanimity and sincerity, having considered problems in view of general interests of the Olympic Movement, thus narrowing differences of views and reaching agreement. At the previous joint meetings and the bilateral talk with the IOC on March 7, 1986, he said, the North Koreans had made clear their proposals on sharing the events in the North and the South, and the main related problems, such as the appellation of the Games, the Organizing Committee, the cultural program, and other Olympic functions. He was convinced that when the fundamental problems arising in the organization of the Games were solved, on the firm basis of the Olympic spirit, the other auxiliary problems could be solved easily. His proposals were the realistic and elastic ones, which had been put forth by taking into full account the positions of the IOC and South Korea.

The North was ready to discuss sincerely any proposals, no matter which side might propose them, if they were suggested in the true sense of ensuring the success of the Games. He expected that at this meeting the South Koreans and the IOC would put forward realistic and concrete proposals. They, from the North, would do their best, conscious of their noble task and heavy responsibility, and unanimously desirous of making this third meeting a success at any cost. He was convinced that at this meeting the IOC and the South Koreans would seriously consider their proposals and respond positively to them.

South Kim had the same basic lead-in to his remarks, but with some early diplomatic sting.[26] He made an understated point of saying what a pleasure it was to see the North Korean delegates again, five months after the last meeting. The barb was not fully apparent until the next paragraph of his written statement, when he recalled the great success of the ANOC meeting in Seoul in April of the same year.[27] He thanked the IOC for its part in making the meeting such a success.

He restaked his Olympic territory, observing that, during the meetings in October 1985 and earlier that year, South Korea, as host of the

[25] It was assumed that this was a reference to the IOC's insistence that the North Koreans must first agree to participate in Seoul as a condition to allocating any events to the North.

[26] The South Korean delegation consisted of Kim Chong Ha (South Kim), Chang Choon Sik, Choy Man Lip, Lee Chong Ha, Yim Tae Soon, and Nam Joung Moon.

[27] The North Koreans had not attended, despite the IOC's urging. South Kim did not mention their absence but merely drew attention to the success of the meeting, which the North Koreans recognized only too well.

Games, in "faithful" observance of the Olympic Charter and its agreement with the IOC, was making meticulous preparations, including competition facilities and operational plans. He reiterated the South Korean position that the door was wide open for all member countries to participate freely in the Seoul Games without any constraints. They would heartily welcome their brethren under the same conditions. In particular, they had expressed their willingness to discuss the positive participation of the North, within the framework of the Olympic Charter, in order to make the Games more successful than any other and to share with the entire Korean people the honor of hosting the Games, which was entrusted to the city of Seoul.

In that context, he said, the South had fully cooperated with the sincere mediation efforts made by Samaranch and the IOC, and, in conformity with the agenda set up by the IOC, South Korea had exerted its utmost efforts to present and implement very reasonable proposals for athletes from North Korea to join the Games in a more meaningful way. Urging the North Koreans to take part in the Games without any conditions (respecting the Olympic Charter and the IOC Session's decision in Baden-Baden in 1981), they had shown their sincerity to discuss a joint entrance of the two Korean teams at the Opening Ceremony, allocation of some preliminary events to the North, linking the South and the North in the cycling team road race, and more significant participation of the North in the various cultural programs. Were these problems to be settled, the Games would provide a historic occasion for mutual accommodation, trust, and peaceful relations between South Korea and North Korea.

He continued by saying that their extensive and meticulous preparatory work for successful Games was nearing completion, and he was convinced that they had exerted every possible effort for their brethren athletes to join the historic Seoul Games in a meaningful way. He was convinced, as well, that such efforts would win the support and understanding of all international sports federations, world sports leaders, and the IOC. He noted again, for the record, that this conviction was confirmed at the ANOC General Assembly in Seoul that April, where, in the presence of all the delegates from the two main pillars of the Olympic Movement, the IOC and the NOCs, all participants expressed their great satisfaction after witnessing their thorough preparations for the Games. Furthermore, he noted, they voiced unanimously their support and understanding for the position of the South Korean NOC in attending the present meeting in Lausanne.

In order to bring about positive results from the third joint meeting, all present should humbly consider the aspirations of the world sports community and respect the Olympic Charter and the decisions made by the IOC Session. He had no doubt that if the North Korean NOC showed positive response to the South's position, this third joint meeting would make progress. He wished to make it clear that through positive cooperation and with the kind efforts of mediation by the IOC, South Korea would put forth its best efforts to make the proposals they had already presented a reality.

Samaranch gave perfunctory thanks to each delegation for its remarks, and the meeting recessed.

The first of the delegations to be called back for the real work of the meeting was North Korea. Samaranch had listened to the speech made by Kim Yu Sun and was pleased to learn that the North was willing to discuss concrete proposals with a view to reaching a solution. He gave the usual reminder that the IOC had awarded the Games to Seoul, that it had to respect this decision, and must adhere to the Olympic Charter. The IOC delegation present could only reach agreements in principle, since the IOC Session's approval would be required. There was to be a Session in Lausanne in October 1986, at which, should agreement be reached, such approval could be sought.

Samaranch wanted to discuss, first, which sports or events could be held in the North, and second, the matter of free circulation between the North and the South, this latter question being a matter of the utmost importance. The IOC had had lengthy discussions with the KOC regarding which sports or events could be offered to the North. A compromise had been reached but not without difficulty. Samaranch outlined that the IOC could propose the organization of one group of the Olympic soccer tournament in Pyongyang, but that this would not be easy, since the deadline for the entry of teams in this competition had already passed. FIFA, the governing international federation, had recently forwarded the list of 108 participating teams, and the IOC had been surprised to see that the North Korean NOC was not among them.[28]

[28] The qualifying tournament for the Olympic soccer event begins almost two years prior to the Games, with a series of regional eliminations designed to reduce the field for the final round to the maximum number of teams that will take part in the Games themselves. The DPRK was not on the preliminary list of participating teams. They later applied to enter the qualifying tournament, and should have played in qualifying matches in March 1987. They did not attend, claiming that as the host country of the Games, they were entitled to an automatic entry into the final round of the tournament.

The IOC had, furthermore, proposed that two or three cycling races start in the North and end in the South. The IOC was prepared to offer the North one complete sport, either archery or fencing, including the staging of the victory medal ceremonies, as well as the organization of table tennis, again including holding the victory ceremonies in Pyongyang. Samaranch noted that the North had had experience in organizing international table tennis competitions, having hosted the 1979 World Championships. He had personally convinced the international federation that the 1988 Olympic tournament should be staged in Pyongyang, but only after difficulty, in view of the fact that athletes from two countries (Israel and South Korea) had not been granted visas to North Korea immediately prior to the 1979 championships, despite the fact that the International Table Tennis Federation had been assured by the DPRK that all countries would be granted access. He reviewed, again, the access to the cultural programs and the joint parade at the Opening Ceremony.

Samaranch urged the North to bear in mind that it was the first time in Olympic history that the Games would be split, although the equestrian events had been held in Stockholm in 1956 and the rest of the Games in Melbourne. This was, however, a different case, as the Australian quarantine regulations had not permitted the staging of the equestrian events. For 1988, South Korea was ready to stage all the sports on the Olympic program, all facilities having been completed. After much discussion, the IOC was now extending a gesture to the North by offering the organization of certain events, provided the IOC Session confirmed the agreement that would be reached to this effect.

Kim Yu Sun did not respond directly. He said he had listened carefully to Samaranch's words. He pointed out that at the previous two joint meetings and on other occasions, the question of forming an Organizing Committee in the North had been raised. He wanted to discuss this and all other related questions at this meeting. The North wanted to host various significant events in order to make the Games a great festival. It was prepared to send a single team to the Games, provided it could organize all preliminaries and finals in soccer, table tennis, archery, wrestling, gymnastics, and judo.

He stressed that this would be the first time that a team from the North would take part in sports competitions in the South, but it was his NOC's desire to render Samaranch's efforts worthwhile. The question of the appellation of the Games had already been raised at the previous two meetings. Since the Games would be shared between the two Koreas, there should be a common appellation for the Games. In view of the objections voiced by the South and bearing in mind the IOC's position, he suggested that for those sports and events staged in Pyongyang, the Games be called the XXIVth Olympic Games-Pyongyang, a solution he believed would be acceptable to all.[29] A separate Organizing Committee would be set up in North Korea. Other details could be settled once the questions of principle had been dealt with.

Samaranch stated that he did not wish to discuss the appellation of the Games or the creation of a separate Organizing Committee until the question of which sports or events would be offered to the North and the question of free circulation between the two countries had been settled. He repeated that great effort had been made by the IOC in order to be able to offer to the North the organization of two complete sports and partial staging of others in Pyongyang. Did the North Korean NOC wish to accept the IOC's proposals as such? It was not possible to offer the North any other conditions.

Escalating the stakes somewhat, Samaranch said that once the question of the sports and events was settled, he wanted to know the procedure to be adopted by the North to ensure the free circulation, before and during the Games, of approximately twenty-five thousand members of the Olympic Family accredited in Seoul, including athletes, officials, NOC delegates, and nine to ten thousand journalists and radio and television representatives.[30]

This led to an intervention from North Korean vice president Chin, asking some questions to which Samaranch responded. It was an interesting dynamic, since the negotiations had, suddenly, reached a point at which a direct answer could have resulted in a complete impasse, and Kim Yu Sun was apparently not prepared for it. Chin acted to defuse the moment by asking for details of some of Samaranch's earlier statements. Samaranch reiterated that appellation of the Games and the formation of a separate Organizing Committee could be discussed only after an agreement had been reached regarding the sports or events to be held in the North and free circulation between the two Koreas. Chin stated that his NOC had hoped to be able to organize certain

[29] This had already been suggested by Samaranch as a possibility.

[30] One can imagine the consternation with which the DPRK must have considered the prospect of such a flood of media from the rest of the world. This was always one of the prime reasons why the IOC was so confident that it was virtually impossible for a final agreement ever to be reached in the negotiations.

sports in their entirety. Samaranch said that as far as the 1988 soccer tournament was concerned, the North would be able to organize one group of this, but not all four groups. Nor would North Korea be able to stage the finals.

Chin insisted that the North wished to stage the entire soccer tournament and stated that it had been his NOC's understanding that the IOC would grant it the right to do so. They would not be able to accept the IOC's proposal for preliminaries of certain sports to be staged in the North and the finals in the South. He thought that the IOC and his NOC should jointly study the problems of organizing the Games in the North. There were twenty-three sports on the Olympic program, and the North could not accept the IOC's proposals to allow it to stage two complete sports only. His NOC wished to hold six sports in their entirety. This was down from the previous demand for eight sports, but Chin did not specify which two were being abandoned. He urged, once again, that the IOC reconsider the position of the North, its staging of certain sports, the appellation of the Games, and the formation of a separate Organizing Committee.

Samaranch repeated the IOC's offer, stating that this was the last proposal. If North Korea did not wish to accept it, then discussions could not continue, as no solution would be reached. He also said that the question of free circulation had to be settled before dealing with the appellation of the Games and a separate Organizing Committee. The respective positions of North Korea and the IOC differed greatly, and, he emphasized, it had been difficult to convince South Korea that certain conditions should be offered to facilitate the participation of the North in the Games.

Chin said that his NOC would require time to study the IOC's offer. He suggested that perhaps women's volleyball could be held in the South and men's volleyball be held in his country. The North could accept the IOC's offer to stage table tennis and archery but also wished to hold other sports in their country, including preliminaries and finals. Samaranch emphasized that the IOC wished to receive details regarding free circulation between North Korea and South Korea.

Kim Yu Sun had, by now, recovered and reentered the discussions. He said that the free circulation issue had been discussed at the second joint meeting in January 1986, at which time the North had made it clear that all measures would be taken to ensure free circulation. Furthermore, his NOC had understood from Samaranch that it would be able to organize the whole 1988 soccer tournament and had contacted FIFA accordingly. His NOC was ready to stage sports in their entirety if the respective IFs agreed. He urged the IOC to reconsider the matter and to hold further discussions in order to find a solution to the problem. He commented that he was under the impression that the IOC wished to impose its proposals on the North.

Samaranch retorted that the IOC was not imposing any conditions on them. He stressed that the North had to understand the IOC's position and that the IOC had to stand by its decision to award the Games to Seoul and to respect the Olympic Charter. The IOC was doing its best to ensure the success of the Games by trying to encourage the participation of all NOCs. In view of the division between the two Koreas, for the first time in Olympic history, the IOC was offering special conditions to the North Korean NOC to facilitate its participation. Responding to the soccer situation, Samaranch said that he had never stated that the North would be able to hold the entire tournament. He wondered why they wished to do so, in view of the fact that the North had not even entered a team.

Before adjourning the meeting until later that day, Samaranch said he wanted greater clarification with regard to the matter of free circulation. At present, there was no communication between the two Koreas, and he wanted to know if the accredited members of the Olympic Family would be permitted access to North Korea from South Korea, and, if so, whether or not the Olympic identity card would suffice.[31]

Despite what had already been said, Kim Yu Sun stated that the North had already clarified its position at the last meeting with regard to circulation between the two Koreas. First and foremost, however, his NOC wanted to discuss the appellation of the Games and the formation of a separate Organizing Committee, in addition to which sports would be staged in the North. With a sigh, Samaranch adjourned.

At the beginning of the meeting with the South Koreans that afternoon, Samaranch explained that he had proposed that all the competitions in

[31] The expression "Olympic Family" in this context referred to athletes, officials, and media accredited through the IOC. The significance of the reference to the Olympic identity card is that such card serves as a "visa" for purposes of the Olympic Games when it is accompanied by a valid passport or other document establishing the identity of the bearer. This is designed to bypass the customary and often politically charged process of having to apply for visas to enter the host country, having the host country "consider" such applications, and wondering, often until the last moment, whether the host country would be disposed to issue such visas. It is a special feature of the international comity surrounding the Olympic Games that the host country agrees to bypass the customary procedures for entry. This is not to say that the theory is always applied, but in an overwhelming majority of cases, it is applied and works remarkably well. The United States is generally the most reluctant of host countries to accept this procedure.

two sports be allocated to the North. Mention had also been made of matches in one of the four groups of the soccer tournament and the suggestion that some cycling races might start in North Korea and finish in South Korea. He had emphasized the exceptional nature of such a division of the Games. The case was not the same as Melbourne in 1956, as Seoul was fully prepared for the organization of all the events on the Olympic program.

The North Korean delegation had wished to discuss the appellation of the Games, but the IOC had made it clear that this topic could not be considered until an agreement regarding sports and events to be held in the North had been reached. The IOC had stressed that confirmation regarding the free circulation to and from the North would be required for all properly accredited persons during the entire period of the Games. North Korea was still requesting the allocation of six sports: soccer, archery, judo, wrestling, gymnastics, and table tennis. The IOC had declared that this could not be granted; there had been many negotiations between the IOC and the South in order to reach an agreement over the possibility of competitions in two sports being held outside the South. He wanted comments from the South Koreans and gave the delegation ten minutes to consult among its members.

Kim Chong Ha reiterated the necessity for the delegates from the North to confirm the participation of their country's athletes in the Games before an agreement could be reached. During previous discussions, the question of allocating preliminary events in volleyball, handball, and soccer had arisen, provided the North were to guarantee respect of the Olympic Charter. The delegates from the North had refused to consider seriously this proposal and appeared to refute the right of South Korea to stage the Games. Only after participation of North Korea had been confirmed, and after consultations with the relevant international federations, could sports or events be allocated to the North. It was also essential that the North affirm its respect of the Olympic Charter and of the Baden-Baden decision to award the hosting of the Games to Seoul.

Should the North be granted the right to hold all the competitions in two sports, organizational matters must remain under the control of the SLOOC. In accordance with the Olympic Charter, the SLOOC was the sole body responsible for organizing the competitions, and it had made great efforts in order to advance preparatory work. His NOC proposed the sports of table tennis and fencing. The North should then agree to proper inspection of the venues by the international federations, free transfer of officials, transportation of sports equipment, entry of media representatives, and so forth. The proposal to modify the appellation of the Games was unacceptable and was, moreover, contrary to the provisions of the Olympic Charter, which stipulated that the Games' organization should be entrusted to one city.

At the previous joint meeting, it had been proposed that the team road race in cycling should begin in the North and finish in Seoul. This would create an atmosphere of harmony within the Korean peninsula. The South Korean NOC also retained its proposal that a joint parade mark the Opening Ceremony, with each delegation parading in columns, each column having its own flag, and each athlete wearing the uniform of his or her own country. The North was fully welcome to participate in the extensive cultural program that was planned in the context of the Games. The South was not prepared to allocate more than two full sports to the North. Nor was Kim Chong Ha in a position to agree to one of the groups of the soccer tournament being held outside the South.

Samaranch underlined the fact that any agreements reached were with a view to securing maximum participation of NOCs at the Games, hence the success of the Games. During his recent visit to Seoul, he had had talks with the head of state of the republic, and it had finally been decided to offer, through the intervention of the IOC, the sports of table tennis and archery to the North. The South Korean sports minister had since informed him in writing that the proposal had been modified and was now for table tennis and fencing, rather than archery. Samaranch said that he had previously contacted the international federations responsible for table tennis[32] and archery, and in principle, approval had been obtained for holding competitions in the North. He understood that, apart from suggestions concerning certain cycling races and some soccer competitions, the South was not ready to consider the allocation of further events to the North at this time.

Samaranch requested the full cooperation of the South, as a decision had to be made. A breakdown in negotiations could threaten the success of the Games. Kim Chong Ha fully appreciated that the current talks affected the Games and that it was in the interests of the South to reach an agreement. He guaranteed his full cooperation. He explained that to deal with the observation made by Samaranch concerning the

[32] Written communications between Samaranch and the president of the ITTF had occurred on May 24, 1986, with a reply sent to Samaranch on June 5, 1986.

change of sports, the decision had been made to change archery for fencing because archery was then a developing sport in the South, and it had been felt that this should be taken into consideration.[33]

There were no further comments, so Samaranch adjourned the meeting to prepare for the next session with the North, scheduled for a half hour later.

When the delegation from the North entered, there were no preliminaries; Samaranch wanted to know its position regarding the IOC's proposals put forward that morning. Kim Yu Sun would not be rushed. His NOC had already expressed its point of view regarding the main problems and pointed out that it believed the question of the sports and events it hoped to stage were closely linked with the formation of a separate Organizing Committee and the appellation of the Games. He appreciated the IOC's offer of the full archery and table tennis competitions, but his committee could not accept only one group of the preliminaries of the soccer tournament. If the IOC was not prepared to offer the organization of the entire soccer tournament, the North wished to stage two of the following sports in their entirety: judo, wrestling, shooting, or weight lifting. These would, of course, be in addition to archery and table tennis. The North also wanted to stage women's volleyball, men's basketball, and women's handball. With respect to cycling, he proposed that two races start in the North and end in the South and that two more start in the South and end in the North. He also thought that fencing was worthy of serious study.

North Kim said his NOC envisaged holding a separate cultural program. The North had expressed its position with respect to free circulation between the two Koreas on a previous occasion, and he confirmed this stance, guaranteeing that there would be no restrictions for athletes and the media as far as access to the North was concerned. Unfortunately, he said, no details had been received from the South on that subject. He asked for the IOC's position vis-à-vis the appellation of the Games and the formation of a separate Organizing Committee.

Samaranch replied that many other problems had to be solved besides the appellation of the Games. None of these could be discussed until an agreement had been reached regarding which sports could be staged in the North. The IOC had already proposed that the North organize

[33] As indicated earlier, the Korean results in this sport made it easy to see why it was a matter of interest to the South.

two full sports, one group of the soccer tournament, and three cycling races. He felt it would be unlikely that the North Koreans' new proposal would be accepted by the South. It might be possible to make slight changes to the IOC's proposal, and he said that IOC vice president Alexandru Siperco or he himself would be ready to meet with them at any time to try to reach an agreement. No other points could be discussed until it had been agreed which sports would be held in North Korea.

North Korean vice president Chin once again entered the discussion to urge the IOC and the South to review the North's new proposal and to consider substantial changes to the IOC's own proposal. His NOC would again study the IOC's offer, but he stressed that any competitions held in North Korea should be called the XXIVth Olympic Games in Pyongyang.

The appellation of the Games would be discussed, said Samaranch, only after an agreement had been concluded regarding the sports to be held in the North. The IOC could not accept the new proposal, since it called for the staging of too many sports competitions in Pyongyang. The IOC had already expended considerable efforts to convince South Korea to make the offer that had been made, an offer that North Korea should consider seriously. He or Siperco was prepared to meet the delegates while they were in Lausanne or, if necessary, to convene another meeting.

Kim Yu Sun said that after the first and second joint meetings, his NOC had seriously considered the organization of the entire soccer tournament. As a result of the efforts of Samaranch, it had decided not to request the staging of the whole tournament[34] but now wished to hold two other full sports, in addition to archery and table tennis, and also part of the volleyball, basketball, and handball competitions. Their new proposal had been made after serious study of the question in order to try to reach a solution to the problem. The issues of the appellation of the Games and the formation of a separate Organizing Committee should be raised when discussing the question of the sports to be staged, because the problems were closely linked. He again queried the IOC's stance with respect to the Games' appellation and the formation of a second Organizing Committee. His delegation proposed that all compe-

[34] This was the first time that the DPRK had backed away from its claim to host the entire soccer tournament. It was clear that FIFA would never have agreed to this in the first place, as their discussions with FIFA must have indicated. The North would later come back and insist on the right to stage the whole tournament.

titions in the North be called the XXIVth Olympic Games in Pyongyang and that the Organizing Committee be called the Pyongyang Organizing Committee.

Not to be outdone by this repetition, Samaranch said that the appellation of the Games and the formation of a second Organizing Committee could only be discussed once the problem of the sports had been settled. The IOC was, nevertheless, prepared to study slight modifications to the proposal it had made that morning, with a view to finding a solution to the problem. Four cycling races between the two Koreas could, perhaps, be staged, providing the South agreed. The South was unlikely to agree to the granting of an additional two full sports and other events to the North. The IOC's offer, he also reminded them, was conditional upon ratification by the IOC Session.

At this stage, Han Chang On, a member of the North Korean delegation, speaking for the first time during the negotiations, expressed his colleagues' appreciation for the IOC's efforts relating to the success of the Games. Many details had to be solved in order to reach a final agreement at a later date. Already, he said, on previous occasions, views had been exchanged relating to the sports competitions to be held in the North, and it had now been decided that the Games would be shared between the two Koreas. After great efforts, both sides were narrowing their differences of opinion. The North had agreed to organize archery and table tennis but had now put forward a further proposal, which he thought would be "easily acceptable" to all parties.

The North was aware of the IOC's position but hoped that the IOC would consider its new suggestions for the benefit of the Games and with a view to reaching a final agreement. Various problems relating to the Games, all of which were closely linked, had to be solved. Han urged the IOC to consider carefully the question of sports in order to hasten the conclusion of an agreement. Views could also be exchanged on other aspects, such as free circulation and the Olympic torch relay. The North was ready to discuss any points the IOC considered to be of importance, in addition to the issues that it felt should be raised. Han pointed out that the delegates had traveled a great distance from their country, where they worked for the benefit of the Olympic Movement and their national athletes and thus had great expectations when coming to Lausanne.

Samaranch said he understood the position of the North. He was also aware of the distance between their home country and Switzerland and realized that the representatives were all very busy. He repeated, however, that it was of the utmost importance to settle in principle the question of sports to be staged in the North. If the delegation agreed to do so, then the IOC would be willing to discuss other matters in the next few days. No such matters would be discussed until the North agreed on which sports it would organize. There was a twenty-minute break.

Continuing, the North Korean delegation was advised that it must realize that the IOC was trying to help it and trying to reach an agreement. Proposals such as those made by the IOC had never been made before in the history of the Olympic Movement. The IOC understood North Korea's position, but a solution could be reached if North Korea accepted the IOC's offer, which could, perhaps, be amended slightly. The IOC would then be willing to convene a fourth and last joint meeting prior to the October 1986 Session of the IOC in Lausanne, with an established agenda containing points that the North wished to raise. The delegation could provide the IOC with its reply the following morning at 11:00 A.M. A special meeting, presided over by Samaranch or Siperco, could be held, if requested, after the press conference. North Kim said his delegation would be present the next day.

At 10:00 A.M. the following morning, the IOC met with the South. Samaranch said that a trilateral meeting would be held later that morning, the timing of which would depend on how long the 11:00 A.M. meeting with the North might run. With respect to the business of the meeting, he stressed that the IOC was striving to gain the agreement of the North to participate in the Games and to propose that some events be hosted in the North. There was great pressure from the NOCs of the socialist countries for an agreement with the North to be concluded. He mentioned that the secretary-general of the U.S. Olympic Committee, George D. Miller, had recently been in Cuba and that President Castro had said that his country would not take part in the Seoul Games unless an arrangement had been made with the North. In addition, many telexes had been received at IOC headquarters from socialist countries' NOCs, as well as a letter from Marat Gramov, president of the USSR NOC, all pushing for an agreement regarding the Games.[35]

[35] Gramov's letter was dated June 5, 1986. It was expressed as a personal letter and indicated a degree of confidence in the political and diplomatic talents of Samaranch to find a solution to the problem. It also contained the usual rhetoric about the impropriety of awarding the Games to Seoul in the first place. "The choice of this city to host the Olympics has caused a number of problems. Without debating the point, I would like to underline that in this case the decision to grant the right to host the 1988 Olympic Games to Seoul appeared to be an act of a purely political character, whatever the motives of those who voted for this decision."

It was essential, first, to decide how many full sports could be granted to North Korea. Once this matter had been settled, later discussion could focus upon logistics and organizational issues such as free circulation of accredited persons, television coverage, and other matters. These questions would require detailed examination by experts in both countries. The IOC would draw up a paper proposing that competitions in conjunction with two sports and also several events be held in the North. This would be forwarded to both delegations, and a deadline fixed for response. After the previous day's discussions, it was proposed, apparently ignoring the South's desire to retain archery, to allocate all events relating to table tennis and archery, one tournament group of soccer competitions (which would not include the team representing South Korea), and some cycling events.

Samaranch emphasized that the IOC's aim was to guarantee the success of the Games and to gain the full support of the NOCs of the world. Referring to the recent ANOC meetings in Seoul, he said that these meetings had been planned for Seoul with a view to assessing NOC attendance.[36] Only a few NOCs had failed to be present, one of which was the NOC from the North. If an agreement between the two Koreas was to be reached, a further meeting would be held in Lausanne in order to discuss concrete details. Much preparatory work would have to be undertaken, and an agenda for the meeting drawn up and worked through methodically. Samaranch asked for a more flexible attitude on the part of the South Korean delegation.

Following a ten-minute pause, Kim Chong Ha expressed his appreciation for the work of the IOC and the effort to reach an agreement. He apologized for any lack of diplomacy that he might have shown the previous day. He felt, however, that it had been necessary to make clear the stance of his NOC in order that a compromise could then be sought to the mutual satisfaction of both parties. He wondered whether the delegation from the North was reacting positively to the suggestions being put forward.

There was no objection to two full sports being allocated to North Korea. Although mention had been made of archery and table tennis, he would prefer fencing and table tennis. Discussions on this could be deferred to a later date. The proposal concerning the cycling team road

[36] This was not entirely true; such meetings regularly occur in the host cities of the Games, usually two years prior to the Games. It was, however, a tactically useful assertion in the course of these negotiations.

race was also acceptable. Concerning the allocation of one group of the soccer tournament, it might be difficult to achieve a national consensus over this, since soccer was a particularly popular sport in South Korea. He added that the DPRK NOC had not yet submitted entries for the regional preliminaries.[37] Nevertheless, if allocation of one group of the preliminaries would help toward the settlement of an agreement with the North, he would be in favor of this.

Samaranch noted that it would amount to only six matches being held outside the South. Considerable progress had been made; the North had initially requested cohosting the Games, followed by twelve sports, then six sports.[38] Two sports were now being offered, and he was sure that an important step had been achieved. An official letter would be prepared and sent to both delegations, asking for approval of the proposal before the end of June. If approval from both sides was to be gained, further meetings would be held to examine the other questions. He thanked the delegation and prepared to meet once again with the North Koreans.

There had been a meeting with the North, in Samaranch's office, earlier that morning, before the "official" meetings, so at this session, Samaranch was quite brief. He wanted to know whether his understanding was correct: namely, that the North would accept the IOC's offer regarding the sports to be staged in the North, provided the IOC agreed to the denomination Games of the XXIVth Olympiad in Pyongyang, to the setting up of a separate Organizing Committee in Pyongyang, and to a further meeting.

Kim Yu Sun did a lateral arabesque. He replied that his delegation wished to ensure the success of the Games by satisfying the wishes of the entire Korean people. Although little progress had been achieved, certain views had been exchanged. However, other important points had not been discussed. He felt that, at this bilateral meeting, the IOC and his NOC should discuss important points such as the proposals

[37] He may not have been aware that the deadline for entries was April 30, 1986, or that the DPRK had entered but had failed to show up for the scheduled preliminary matches.

[38] Actually, the North had asked for eleven sports, reduced this to eight, and then to six. It was often difficult to keep track of the various permutations and combinations, which appeared and disappeared during the negotiations, particularly since some discussions related only to partial sports, to disciplines within sports, to events, or merely to preliminaries. The imprecision was not unhelpful in keeping the parties off balance.

regarding sports to be held in the North. Further views should be exchanged and decisions taken in order to narrow the differences of opinion. Moreover, the appellation of the Games and the formation of a separate Organizing Committee should be discussed at this juncture.

He had understood, said Samaranch, from what Kim had previously stated, that if the IOC agreed to support the suggestion made by North Korea to call those sports and events staged in North Korea the Games of the XXIVth Olympiad in Pyongyang and to set up a separate Organizing Committee, they would be ready to accept the IOC's offer. Kim Yu Sun requested time to meet privately with his delegation.

After ten minutes, he said that at previous meetings, the IOC had stated it would give his NOC three full sports to organize, but that now it was only offering two. His NOC required further time to study the proposal regarding sports and events both seriously and carefully.

Samaranch reiterated that the North was well aware of the IOC's proposal. The delegation would be receiving an official letter from the IOC following the joint meeting specifying the offer. The North would have until the end of June to study it and reply. If it replied positively and unconditionally, then the IOC would be prepared to study, together with the NOC, such items as the denomination of the Games, the formation of a separate Organizing Committee, free circulation, and television coverage. The IOC would also convene a fourth and final joint meeting between the two NOCs, prior to the forthcoming IOC Session in October, perhaps at the end of July. He asked Kim Yu Sun to inform the authorities in the DPRK that the IOC (including himself and the vice presidents) would do its best to support the request that the sports and events in North Korea could be called the Games of the XXIVth Olympiad in Pyongyang and that a separate Organizing Committee could be set up to deal directly with the IOC.

A joint session would now be held, at which the IOC's press release would be read to the delegations. This did not require their approval as it would be issued by the IOC alone. The IOC would then hold a press conference to which they were all invited.

The meeting then moved into joint session, shortly before noon. Samaranch reviewed the logistics regarding the letters that would be sent, the delays for response, and the prospect of a future meeting. Regarding the press conference, he asked both delegations not to speak at length with the media, as such action could have adverse effects on the work accomplished thus far. He said that, gradually, a solution was being reached and asked for the press release to be read.

The press release was drafted in the IOC's customary banal style. There were two introductory paragraphs describing who was present at the meetings and reciting that the meetings had taken place at the IOC headquarters, at the initiative of the IOC, and under the chairmanship of Samaranch. This was simply a method of staking out the "ownership" of the process. The remaining paragraphs are reproduced.

> In the course of extensive discussions which took place in a cooperative and cordial atmosphere, the differences between the parties were narrowed considerably, both NOCs stressing their sincere desire to ensure the success of the Games of the XXIVth Olympiad in 1988.
>
> With this fundamental objective in mind, the IOC delegation, in the spirit of the Olympic Charter and the decisions taken at the 1981 Session in Baden-Baden, proposed to both parties that a number of events on the programme of the Games of the XXIVth Olympiad be delegated to the NOC of DPR Korea. Specifically, the organisation of two full sports would be entrusted to the NOC of the DPR Korea to be held in its territory.
>
> The IOC has also proposed that certain additional events be partly located in the DPR Korea, and that cultural manifestations connected with the Olympic Games be organised in both parts of the Korean peninsula.
>
> The two Korean NOCs have undertaken to study this proposal and to communicate to the IOC their willingness to accept it in principle by 30th June 1986; they have already confirmed to the IOC that free access of all members of the Olympic Family to the relevant Olympic venues in the North and South would be ensured. The IOC will then convene a new meeting in order to settle all necessary organisational and operational aspects.

Samaranch reinforced the deadline for responses and observed that this was the last possibility for the question to be solved in order to ensure the success of the Games.

North Kim stated that his NOC also wished to ensure the success of the Games by fulfilling the desires of the Korean people. Views had been exchanged on certain matters for the benefit of the Olympic Movement and for the success of the Games. The painstaking efforts on the part of the IOC (and particularly the president) were commendable, and he was convinced that if both NOCs studied each other's positions, the next meeting would prove fruitful. The North, he said, had shown magnanimity and flexibility in many respects and would do its utmost to secure successful Games in 1988. He hoped that the IOC and the South would do likewise.

South Kim, not to be outdone, remarked that the meaningful participation of the North in the Games had been discussed seriously during this third joint meeting. He expressed similar gratitude to the IOC and to Samaranch for the constant efforts and support in order to ensure successful Games. His NOC had also shown magnanimity and sincerity in presenting new proposals. Thanks to the IOC's efforts, the third joint meeting had provided momentum for further progress. If all sides continued their discussions with determination, the fourth joint meeting would bear fruit.

Samaranch thanked everyone present and hoped that the meetings would be recorded in history as a step toward international friendship and understanding.

CHAPTER 9

Hiatus — The Tension Mounts: No Agreement

THE LETTERS were sent to the two NOCs on June 11, immediately following the conclusion of the third joint meeting. Samaranch asked for confirmation of the principle of the IOC's proposal by the end of June. Upon receipt of such confirmation, he would convene another formal meeting of the two delegations "in order to settle the numerous organisational and operational questions that arise." "Needless to say," he said, "the IOC will actively lead these discussions."

It was no accident that, four days later on June 15, Kim Il Sung issued a statement that athletes, foreign journalists, officials, tourists, and guests would receive a warm welcome if the DPRK were to be named cohost of the Games. These Games, he stated, were not merely "a simple sports event. They are a serious political issue affecting the reunification of Korea." To participate in the Games in South Korea, he continued, meant approving the U.S. occupation of South Korea and would give encouragement to authorities that were "scheming for 'two Koreas' and a permanent division of our country." The Republic of Korea was not fit to be the sole host of the Games because the "danger of a new war is always present."

On June 19 in New York, the ROK minister for national reunification, Park Ton Jin, said Korea might respond favorably to the IOC request that the DPRK organize some events, out of respect for the IOC and to create an "atmosphere of reconciliation by accommodating in some way" the DPRK. There was some resistance in Korea concerning the concept of giving anything whatsoever to the North, to the point that the KOC was criticized as having backed down in the face of the

DPRK by allowing even two events to be organized in the DPRK. This prompted DPRK NOC vice president Kim Duk Jun to issue a statement on June 21 criticizing the elements in the ROK that had taken such a position. He stated that "it was not to hold one or two games in our area that we proposed the cohosting of the Olympics." The IOC proposal made after the third joint meeting was described as "preposterous." The Korean ambassador in Geneva was quick to send Samaranch a translation of the statement of June 23.

South Korea responded with a one-sentence letter dated June 27, 1986; Kim Chong Ha simply stated, "I would like to inform you that the Korean Olympic Committee accepts your proposal dated the 11th of June."

Kim Yu Sun responded by letter dated June 28, 1986. The letter was, predictably, both a yes and a no. He started with an agreement to the staging of table tennis and archery but pointed out that these events were too small in number in relation to the total of twenty-three events in the Games. He wanted Samaranch to continue his efforts to assign the events proposed by the North at the third joint meeting in Lausanne. He also wanted to discuss the organizational aspects and the name of the Games. Samaranch replied to North Kim on July 3, 1986, reminding him that this was not the unequivocal answer he had sought.

The South's one-liner was followed up on June 30 by South Kim, who sent a letter and cable on the same date. The Korean ambassador in Geneva, Park Kun, transmitted the response to the IOC, also the same day.[1] The day's article in the DPRK *Rodong Shinmun* denounced the insistence of the ROK on being the sole host of the Games and pronounced that the Olympic Movement "must never be abused for the perpetuation of the division of Korea." It went on to state that the Games must be cohosted by the North and the South and that, to this end, their "elementary demand" for such basic questions as the title of the Games, division of events, formation of the Organizing Committee, and the Opening and Closing Ceremonies "must be accepted."

It was important for the IOC to maintain contact with, and the confidence of, at least, the USSR and China. Marat Gramov, as Soviet sport minister and president of the USSR NOC, had sent a letter to Samaranch immediately prior to the third joint meeting, urging him to find

[1] Representatives of both NOCs met separately with Samaranch in Lausanne on July 2, the North first, followed by the South.

some way to hold the Games in both parts of Korea. The letter was somewhat doctrinaire, particularly in its criticism of the decision to award the Games to Seoul, which was characterized as an interference into the peaceful dialogue and into the process of unification of the two parts of the country, since it put the South into a privileged position, providing it with moral, political, and economic advantage, all of which aggravated the schism and contradictions between the two parts of the country.

Having said this, the balance of his letter was quite mild in comparison with his previous diatribes on the selection of Seoul as the host city for the Games.[2] He was not aware of all the details of the negotiations, he said, so it was rather difficult for him to indicate concrete means for solving any particular problem. He was, however, convinced that it was possible to hold the Games in both the South and the North. This would not only enable the Olympic Movement to find a way out of this difficult situation but would also provide for a better mutual understanding between the two parts of Korea. He could imagine how difficult the problem was, but, as Voltaire said, "There are no great deeds without great complications." His meetings with Samaranch, he said, allowed him to maintain that with Samaranch's diplomatic and political talent and his authority and devotion to the Olympic Movement, he was quite able to accomplish this difficult task.

Samaranch demonstrated at least the first two of these qualities in a telex to Gramov at the conclusion of the joint meeting on June 11. He acknowledged Gramov's "timely" letter and expressed appreciation for the frank and open way in which he had expressed his point of view. The letter, he said, was most useful in helping him prepare for the third joint meeting with the two Korean NOCs and enabled the IOC to elaborate a proposal that the IOC thought was fair and should be acceptable to both parties. He included a copy of the official communiqué and said he would send further details in due course. The following day, Samaranch reported on the meeting to Li Menghua, the Chinese sports minister and NOC president. In each case, though the recipient of the reports was a minister, Samaranch was careful to address the communications to them in their NOC capacities, which achieved the dual purpose of keeping the negotiations one step removed

[2] It was, perhaps, not without significance that Konstantin Andrianov was in failing health and that there would soon likely be an opening for a new IOC member in the USSR. Such possibilities tend to have a calming effect on anti-IOC rhetoric.

from the naked politics they obviously were and of preserving the authority of Samaranch as IOC president in matters pertaining to the Olympic Movement.

Political statements continued to flood in from DPRK allies and the "friendship" organizations favoring the joint proposal, with the accompanying complaints about the unjustness of having awarded the Games to Seoul in the first place.[3]

The verbal jockeying with the North for "position" continued in an escalating correspondence between Samaranch and Kim Yu Sun during the summer of 1986. Kim responded to Samaranch's letter of July 3 on July 19. He appeared to chide Samaranch to some degree, saying that the points he raised in his letter of June 28 could hardly be strange and new, since they stated positions he had "clarified" more than once in previous official talks and personal conversations with him. He had readily agreed, he said, to organizing table tennis and archery and the cultural programs in Pyongyang. But the notion of staging only two full events in the North was contrary to the positions they had expressed thus far in the negotiations, and, therefore, he considered that the problem of increasing the number of events to be organized in the North and other matters, including soccer and cycling races, would have to be further negotiated and adjusted. He believed that if the three parties were again to get together "to seriously discuss these problems with all sincerity," they could reach solutions.[4]

Samaranch replied on July 28. He said that the reply from the North was not fully responsive to the IOC's letter of July 3, which had asked for clarification of the original response of June 28. He had specifically asked whether North Korea accepted "without modification" the IOC's proposal following the June 11 letter. In the absence of a clear response, he said, he could not see the utility of yet another meeting of the three parties. Such a meeting and further discussions would only be meaningful on the basis of the June 11 proposal. North Kim's "uncondi-

[3] The tone of these communications was fairly routine and clearly reflected a campaign organized and encouraged by the DPRK. Most of the groups involved were of marginal, if any, importance.

[4] A delegation from the DPRK met privately with Samaranch in Lausanne on July 21. This happened to be the same date that Gorbachev made his Vladivostok Declaration, signaling the beginnings of the new policy of détente. The following day, the DPRK ambassador in Geneva, Kim Hyeung On, announced that the DPRK wished to stage at least ten disciplines in the 1988 Games.

tional acceptance" of the IOC's proposal was a prerequisite for any further progress.

The North Korean ambassador in Geneva, Kim Hyeung On, appeared at the IOC headquarters in Lausanne on August 13.[5] Samaranch was not present; he was met by Raymond Gafner, *administrateur délégué* of the IOC, and Alain Coupat, the president's *chef du cabinet.* After the usual salutations, the ambassador recalled the first negotiations under the auspices of the IOC in the 1960s for a unified Korean team, to avoid the present situation. He underlined the goal of the IOC for the success of the Games, for the benefit of the sportspeople of the world, and, of course, the sportspeople of Korea. The Korean people knew and appreciated the efforts of the president of the IOC to assure the success of the Games and greatly appreciated the results he had already accomplished in this regard. The DPRK supported the harmonious development of the Olympic Movement under the presidency of Samaranch and wished to cooperate closely with him and his colleagues.

As to the position of the NOC of the DPRK regarding the IOC's letter of June 11, the ambassador said that Kim Yu Sun had already sent two letters to Samaranch on this subject. The IOC had advised them that these replies had not constituted the clear responses requested by the IOC. Hence, the DPRK had requested this meeting to advise Samaranch on the matter through a meeting with Gafner. In Kim Yu Sun's response to the IOC, the DPRK had given its agreement on the question of two sports, without condition. Gafner observed that this had been only part of the IOC's proposal. The ambassador continued. In his letter of June 11, Samaranch had proposed to the North one group of the soccer tournament and an event of cycling. This was why Kim, in his response, had emphasized that the number of events was too few. Samaranch had indicated, through Siperco, that it was not possible to discuss an increase in the number of sports, but that it might be possible to discuss the number of events at the fourth joint meeting of the parties.[6] It was on this basis that Kim Yu Sun had

[5] On August 6, *Rodong Shinmun* published an open letter from Castro stating that if the Games were not cohosted by North Korea and South Korea, Cuba would boycott. This position was reinforced by a statement made by Alberto Juantorena, the Cuban delegate to the IAAF Congress in Stuttgart on August 25.

[6] There is a technical distinction, in Olympic terms, between a sport, a discipline, and an event. A sport would be, for example, cycling, a discipline the road racing (as opposed to track cycling), and an event the 160-kilometer road race.

indicated his desire to discuss an increase in the number of events during the fourth joint meeting.

North Korea was in agreement with Samaranch's proposal to award two sports to them and to award one group of the soccer tournament and a cycling road race, with departures in Pyongyang and Seoul, but it had further hopes from a fourth meeting. Up to now, they had requested five or six sports; the IOC had decided on two sports. In the circumstances, the DPRK wished to discuss an increase in the number of events, as expressed by the IOC president through the good offices of Siperco.

Gafner was not about to be drawn into this quagmire. He said that he would need more details regarding the cycling event described by the ambassador, noting that the IOC had never discussed anything other than a race starting in Pyongyang and finishing in Seoul. The ambassador suggested that during the course of the last meeting, Samaranch had proposed that one group would start in Pyongyang and another in Seoul. Gafner said he had no information of this nature, but that the IOC had always said that there could be discussions with respect to partial sports. He reminded the ambassador that Samaranch had also said that there would be no question of a fourth joint meeting unless there was a complete and definitive agreement on the sports program. The position of the IOC was very clear: no fourth meeting before an agreement on the sports involved and no discussion on these sports during the fourth meeting.

A long discussion followed, in which there appeared to be confusion deliberately created and during which the ambassador tried to contradict what Gafner had said during the meeting, speaking in Samaranch's name, with what Siperco might have said, also in the name of Samaranch. The issue seemed to be whether discussions regarding an increase in the number of events might be possible during the course of the fourth joint meeting. It seemed obvious that the ambassador had strict instructions to ensure that such discussions could, indeed, take place, and with some chance of success, at the fourth joint meeting. He was evidently quite troubled by Gafner's declaration that no such discussion could take place and suggested that this revelation cast doubts on Samaranch's sincerity from the very outset of the negotiations. He did not seem to understand why negotiations should abruptly change from tripartite to bilateral.[7] He thought the IOC's position was

[7] Presumably, he meant the present series of talks in which the IOC appeared to be pressing the DPRK for commitments prior to agreeing to hold a fourth joint meeting.

in the nature of an ultimatum: if there was no agreement on the two sports and the two partial sports, there would be no fourth meeting.

The situation did not improve. Gafner said that there was a possibility of negotiating within the confines of the two partial sports but that any such negotiations would have to take place before the fourth joint meeting. The ambassador again tried to show that there was a difference between what had been said regarding the position of Samaranch as expressed by Siperco and by Gafner. Gafner simply said that only the president of the IOC could speak for the IOC and that the ambassador could, therefore, request to meet with Samaranch directly, if he chose to do so. Gafner said he could only present the position of the IOC as he knew it and said that the discussion was open. The ambassador professed to be astonished at the essential differences in position and said that Siperco had said that his mandate had come directly from Samaranch, to discuss the possibility of increasing the number of events during the fourth joint meeting. He was stunned that Olympic officials were expressing different views of the IOC president's position.

Gafner said he was not aware of what had been said during the course of the meeting with Siperco. He, however, took full responsibility for what he had said during the course of the present meeting, to which he had agreed at the request of the DPRK. If the delegation wanted to speak with Samaranch, it could request a meeting with him upon his return to Lausanne. The North Korean ambassador appeared to lose his composure entirely. This whole situation was a travesty and an unacceptable imposition. To state that there could be no fourth joint meeting unless the North accepted two full sports and two partial sports, even allowing that the two partial sports could be discussed, meant that the IOC had required that they accept only two partial sports.

That was, said Gafner, the position of the IOC as far as he knew it, but he added that there were often some delicate and subtle questions of interpretation that could lead to confusion. Only Samaranch was in a position to give an official explanation of the situation. The parties then reverted to the normal diplomatic jargon, and mutual protestations of sincerity and genuine efforts to ensure the success of the Games were exchanged.

It was left that Gafner would transmit to Samaranch the question of whether or not it would be possible to have a fourth joint meeting without a complete understanding on the question of the partial sports. Samaranch had made many efforts with respect to the Games, but if this was his final position, the DPRK would have to consider other possibilities. The system of tripartite meetings had been established from the start; it would be illogical to change at this stage. Gafner said there was no question of a change. In any event, bilateral discussions and negotiations had occurred along with the tripartite discussions thus far. What the IOC was proposing at this stage was no different. He would advise Samaranch of the meeting and the discussions.

The involvement of West German ambassador Dr. Hans G. Wieck as a source of guidance for Samaranch has already been mentioned. It was always Wieck's view that the most dangerous time for the Seoul Games would be two years prior to the Games. This, as it happened, coincided with the Asian Games in 1986.[8] He provided a memorandum to Samaranch on September 1, 1986, outlining his thoughts. It was a very thoughtful and perceptive review of the situation, as one might expect from a senior German diplomat. The mediation of the IOC in June 1986 was seen as a very helpful step in the avoidance of a boycott of the Games, at least at this stage, by the North Koreans.

Wieck shared the general informed political view that South Korea was moving in the direction of political reform and that the chief dangers to a smooth transition were the radical students, possible intervention by the military, and the danger of precipitating an action by the North. The latter was not considered too likely, and there was consensus that the major allies of the DPRK would exert restraining influences on it. The unknown factor was the high state of readiness of the North Korean troops and the sense of whether the North perceived any weakness in the South that could be exploited on a preemptive basis.

In the latter part of September and early October, the Tenth Asian Games were held in Seoul, starting precisely two years before the date of the Opening Ceremony originally scheduled for the 1988 Olympic Games.[9] Though the weather during the Opening Ceremony did not cooperate, the cold rain did not dampen the spirits of the participants, and there was, with the exception of the DPRK and Chinese Taipei,

[8] In this respect, his concerns were fully justified, since on September 14, only a few days prior to the Asian Games, a bomb explosion occurred at Kimpo Airport in Seoul, killing several people. Security precautions were maximized, so much so that there was a noticeable level of discomfort among visitors concerning the severity and inflexibility of the arrangements. These concerns were successfully addressed by the Koreans at the time of the Olympic Games, where the security was first class and not too intrusive.

[9] The DPRK announced on September 2 that it would not participate.

a full house, including China, Iran, and Iraq. The Asian Games were an ideal opportunity for the bugs to be worked out of the system. There were a few, which was to be expected, but the Koreans learned their lessons very well, and the subsequent adaptations from this experience to the Olympic Games were exemplary. It is classic Olympic lore that the day an Organizing Committee knows everything it needs to know about running the Games is the day after the Closing Ceremony.

The IOC Session in Lausanne in October, following the Asian Games, was dominated by the election of the two host cities for the Games in 1992, with Barcelona winning the Summer Games and Albertville the Winter Games. Each of those host cities would eventually be beset by serious problems, but, in 1986, there was general satisfaction that Samaranch had been honored for his work as IOC president with the selection of his native city as the host for 1992. There was less satisfaction with the choice of Albertville, but the IOC membership appeared to regard this as a consolation prize for France and a silver medal for the charismatic Jean-Claude Killy and Michel Barnier, as well as for French prime minister Jacques Chirac, whose virtual solo performance on behalf of Paris as a candidate for the Summer Games had been brilliant, so much so that it threw the Spaniards into confusion and grave concern about their own chances. Their performance in presenting the bid to the Session, even with the belated participation of Prime Minister Felipe Gonzales, had been flat, at best.[10]

Regarding the 1988 Olympic Games, the Session was advised in general terms of the negotiations that had occurred to date and the background to the situation. This consisted of a review of the negotiations, the most recent developments in the position of the parties, and the efforts of the IOC to bring about a solution to the problem. The

[10] It was only late in the process, apparently, that the Barcelona delegation decided to call upon Gonzales to be part of the official presentation. The relationship between Barcelona and Madrid has a particular social and political background, and it is quite likely that the Catalonians were willing and prepared to win the Games without overt assistance from the central government. I had discussed this with Samaranch shortly before the Session, and he asked me if I thought it was necessary for Gonzales to be there. My advice was that it could well be fatal to the Barcelona bid if the prime minister were not present, and that, if Samaranch were in a position to influence the decision, he should do everything in his power to arrange for Gonzales to participate in the presentation. The eventual delegation consisted of Gonzales, Jordi Pujol (president of the government of Catalonia), Pasqual Maragall (mayor of Barcelona), HRH Alfonso de Borbon (president of the Spanish NOC), José Miguel Abad (who would become the chief executive officer of the Organizing Committee), and Leopoldo Rodes, without whom, even with the active support of Samaranch, Barcelona would never have won the Games.

Session was advised that the North had begun a vast campaign of protestation against the awarding of the Games to Seoul immediately after the eighty-fourth IOC Session in Baden-Baden. This campaign had been considerably increased after the 1984 Games, and a number of NOCs had expressed their support for the North. The activities of the president and the vice presidents were described, as well as the joint meetings in Lausanne. A proposal had been sent to both North Korea and South Korea on June 11, 1986. The South had accepted; the North had agreed in principle, under the condition of allocation of a greater number of sports to it. The IOC had requested clarification of this in its letter dated July 3, 1986. Samaranch had met with Kim Yu Sun in Moscow on July 9, 1986, and had given him a delay until July 20 to provide the clarifications. These had been provided on July 19 but were a rehash of the original reply. Samaranch had re-sent the proposal dated June 11 in a letter dated July 28, asking for an unambiguous reply. This had been received in a letter dated August 1, in which the North abandoned its request for additional sports but wanted additional events or disciplines.

On August 21, Samaranch had proposed a personal meeting with Kim Yu Sun (or his vice president, Chin) to clarify the situation, since meetings with the DPRK ambassador in Geneva had been unfruitful.[11] A meeting with Chin had occurred on September 8, at which Chin said the North had already given its approval in principle to the June 11 proposal on three occasions; it was thus necessary to establish a fourth joint meeting as soon as possible. The increase in the number of events and disciplines could be discussed at that time. Samaranch had requested an official written reply to the June 11 proposal. A second meeting was fixed for and held on September 11. Chin said that the fact of his presence obviated the need for a written response. Samaranch insisted on a written reply. Chin would transmit this to his president. No reply had been received to date. It was felt that these discussions and the IOC proposal had greatly facilitated the participation of certain socialist countries in the Tenth Asian Games in Seoul earlier that year.

The Executive Board proposed that the Session grant it the mandate "to approve the organization on the northern part of the Korean penin-

[11] In the face of many of the statements made by the DPRK, Samaranch had issued his own statement on September 18, to the effect that the DPRK must accept the IOC proposal before further discussions could occur. He also said a boycott by the DPRK would not hurt the Games and that the socialist countries would participate even without the DPRK.

sula of the table tennis and archery competitions in addition to certain events, as mentioned in the president's letter of 11th June 1986" and "to settle in the best interests of the Olympic Movement the detailed arrangements arising from the execution of the above-mentioned decision, with the agreement of all parties concerned." This proposal was unanimously approved by the Session.

There had been some concern expressed during the Executive Board meeting prior to the October 1986 IOC Session that the approval sought might be too restrictive to permit the Executive Board to improve the offer to the North, should that become necessary; but, on balance, it was decided that somewhat restrictive terms of reference might well make it clear to North Korea that it should be responsive when it considered its own position. Any significant changes would thus have to go before another IOC Session for approval. The additional element of pressure that this put on North Korea was that, if it were not responsive to the negotiation process, it might be faced with a decision of an IOC Session, which might well not be as flexible as the Executive Board.[12]

After the Session, the North persisted with its requests for a fourth joint meeting.[13] Kim Yu Sun wrote to Samaranch on December 22, 1986, asking that such a meeting occur as soon as possible. This was followed up by a further request on January 11, 1987.[14] It led to an appearance of a delegation from the North at a meeting of the IOC

[12] During the Executive Board meeting, Samaranch reported that Castro had said he would contact the DPRK to encourage them to attend a further meeting. The IOC would, for its part, be willing to make minor changes to its proposal.

[13] On October 14, DPRK NOC vice president Chin Chung Guk demanded that eight sports be granted to the DPRK. Samaranch had further meetings with him in Lausanne on October 18 and 20. At the latter meeting, Chin said that the DPRK would prefer to wait until after the ROK presidential elections in December before continuing the negotiations.

[14] There had, in the interim, been a number of fairly positive developments. Samaranch had met with East German president Erich Honecker in Berlin on November 12, who told him that East Germany was preparing for the 1988 Games. On November 18, following the meeting of Socialist Ministers of Sport in Berlin, Samaranch stated that he was pleased with the results of the meeting and that all socialist countries would attend the Games. In a somewhat leavening counterstatement, Hungarian sports minister Gabor Deak announced the following day that the socialist countries had a common position supporting the DPRK bid to cohost the Games. On November 26, the Polish sports minister and NOC president, Boleslaw Kapitan, said that Polish athletes were training for and would compete in the 1988 Games. The same day, East Germany named its preliminary roster for the 1988 team, but still said it supported cohosting of the Games, to avoid problems.

Executive Board in Lausanne on February 12, 1987.[15] Kim Yu Sun and his delegation had met with Samaranch and Siperco on February 10, during which meeting Samaranch had said that if the IOC offer of the previous June were to be accepted by the North, the IOC was prepared to call for the requested fourth joint meeting. At such a meeting, the parties could discuss the matter of free circulation between the two Korean territories and the formation of a second Organizing Committee.

The North Korean delegation requested an informal meeting with the IOC prior to the meeting with the Executive Board. In the course of this meeting, the IOC tried to make the North understand, as it were, some of the facts of life. The North was advised that the appearance before the Executive Board would be decisive and that the conclusions to be reached would depend on reaching some form of agreement. The position of the South Koreans, the IOC said, was much stronger after the ANOC meeting in Seoul the previous April, at which almost all the sports leaders were present, and after the Asian Games that fall. There could be no question that the South would not be interested in offering any more than they already had.

The North's continual insistence, in their diplomatic efforts, meetings, and press releases, on the idea of cohosting, the common Organizing Committee, calling the Games the Games of the XXIVth Olympiad in Pyongyang, and demanding a minimum of eight sports served only to damage their own interests. These postures were unrealistic and unacceptable and cast doubt upon the North's genuine intentions to take part in the Games. There was no time to have a new series of negotiations, since, apart from the IOC Executive Board meeting in Istanbul in May, there were no other meetings before September, when the invitations to participate in the Games would be sent. The North risked, therefore, being in the same position as any other NOC, namely, of having to decide whether or not to accept the invitation without conditions.

It was likely that in the Executive Board meeting they would be asked a number of questions and that they would be expected to give precise and unequivocal answers. The answer to the question of free circulation would be of great importance to the members of the Executive Board. There would be no fourth joint meeting convened unless it appeared certain, in advance, that it would be successful. A fifth joint meeting was categorically unacceptable.

[15] The IOC announced on January 21 that the DPRK NOC would meet with the IOC Executive Board to give explanations regarding its responses to the IOC's offer of events the previous June.

The North's position, as it emerged from the discussions, was an energetic rejection of any suspicion of hesitation on their part concerning participation in the Games. They repeated that they had decided to participate in the Games, that they had begun preparations, and that their presence in Lausanne, even in the face of the very restrictive conditions imposed by the IOC, was proof of this. They did not appear, during this meeting, to be putting too much emphasis on the number of sports, but said, instead, they accepted in principle the IOC proposals, while being very interested in the indicated minor adjustment regarding such sports and events.

They reiterated their agreement to assure free circulation for some twenty-five thousand persons accredited by the IOC and insisted that during the course of the Red Cross negotiations in 1982, it was North Korea that had requested the opening of the border and South Korea that had rejected it. Accordingly, they insisted that South Korea state that it was also ready to assure free circulation. Apart from this, their main preoccupation appeared to be with matters of prestige and perception. They seemed to have abandoned the idea of cohosting and were now asking only for a separate Organizing Committee, reporting directly to the IOC. The name of the Games remained an issue: what had been discussed with the South was the Games of the XXIVth Olympiad *in* Pyongyang, rather than *of* Pyongyang.

They appeared to want some definitive agreement to result from the meeting and were most worried about losing face in case they declared that they agreed with the IOC proposals but then found themselves faced with a refusal on the part of South Korea to agree and new claims from the South. The solution to this difficulty, proposed by Samaranch, was that the North would state formally to Samaranch their definitive agreement with the IOC proposals, but their agreement would remain confidential and conditional upon the formal and definitive agreement of the South, given to Samaranch. Under these conditions, the IOC would call for the fourth joint meeting, during the course of which this agreement would be publicly announced.

The North Korean delegation obviously had no authority to agree to anything. Following the meeting with Samaranch and Siperco, they asked for a delay of twenty-four hours before meeting with the Executive Board, in order to consult with the relevant authorities.[16] Samaranch thought the North Korean delegation was somewhat intimidated

[16] Their appearance had originally been scheduled for February 11.

by the prospect of the forthcoming meeting with the Executive Board, but he had explained that the IOC Session had given authority to the Executive Board to settle the matter. This had led to the present opportunity of appearing before the Executive Board. Later, when the Executive Board met in preparation for the appearance of the North Korean delegation, Samaranch encouraged members of the board to ask questions of the delegation, to show that the entire board was involved in the matter, not just himself.

Samaranch suggested that one line of questioning might be the matter of free circulation between the two territories for all Olympics-accredited persons. This was obviously one of the main hurdles to be overcome and was likely, whatever the outcome of the discussions regarding the number of sports to be allocated to North Korea, the point on which any effort to put into practice the theoretical agreement on sports would inevitably founder. Though the North had confirmed that the airport would be opened to north-south traffic, the roads had also to be opened, and they were, if nothing else, in need of significant repair.

Ashwini Kumar reported that the DPRK ambassador in New Delhi had recently advised him that the North Koreans wished to participate in the Games, provided that they were offered more sports, in order to "save face." Vitaly Smirnov reported that the USSR Sports Committee had met with the DPRK NOC in Moscow on several occasions. The North had some new proposals, and Smirnov urged the Executive Board to be flexible in its attitude, to avoid presenting the North Korean delegation with an ultimatum. He agreed, however, that the IOC's decision not to accept all of the North's original requests had been correct. The apparent purpose of the fourth joint meeting, which the North wanted, was for purposes of taking the necessary decisions regarding the infrastructure required for the Games. He suggested that since Kim Yu Sun was a member of the Central Party Committee, and thus of the government, he might have the necessary power to make commitments. Samaranch said simply that if there was no agreement with the IOC's offer, there would be no fourth joint meeting.

When the North Korean delegation[17] appeared, Samaranch welcomed them to their first Executive Board meeting since the decision

[17] The delegation consisted of Kim Yu Sun, vice president Chin Chung Guk, secretary-general Chang Ung, and secretary Kim Deuk Kil. In addition to the Executive Board, for the IOC, there were present Alexandru Siperco, whose term on the Executive Board had expired, François Carrard, Samuel Pisar, and Alain Coupat.

PHOTO: P. HABANS

Moscow, August 4, 1980. Lord Killanin, outgoing president of the International Olympic Committee, handing over the keys to IOC headquarters to the new president, Juan Antonio Samaranch. Monique Berlioux, IOC director, and Vitaly Smirnov, IOC vice president, look on.

PHOTO: IOC

Pyongyang, October 1983. President Samaranch visit to North Korea, with local guide.

Pyongyang, October 1983. Samaranch with local guides and interpreter.

PHOTO: EPA

Berlin, May 6, 1985. IOC ninetieth Session. IOC president Samaranch presenting the Olympic flag to Roh Tae Woo, president of the Seoul Olympic Organizing Committee (SLOOC).

PHOTO: IOC

Seoul, August 26, 1985. Samaranch and South Korea's president, Chun Doo Hwan.

PHOTO: IOC

Seoul, August 26, 1985. Samaranch at dinner with Roh Tae Woo (an interpreter sits between them).

PHOTO: RIETHAUSEN

Lausanne, October 8, 1985. First joint meeting of North Korean and South Korean delegations. Back row (left to right): Alexandru Siperco, Paul-René Martin, Juan Antonio Samaranch, Berthold Beitz. Front row: Chin Chung Guk, Kim Yu Sun, Kim Chong Ha, Sheik Fahad Al-Amah Al-Sabah, Choy Man Lip, Chang Choon Sik.

PHOTO: RIETHAUSEN

Lausanne, January 8–9, 1986. At the second joint meeting. Left to right: Kim Chong Ha, president of the Korean Olympic Committee (South Korea); IOC president Samaranch; Kim Yu Sun, president of the North Korean National Olympic Committee.

Below, left to right: IOC vice president Berthold Beitz, Kim Chong Ha, Samaranch, Kim Yu Sun, IOC vice president Ashwini Kumar

PHOTO: RIETHAUSEN

PHOTO: RIETHAUSEN

Lausanne, January 8–9, 1986. Preparing to begin second joint north-south meeting at IOC headquarters in Lausanne.

PHOTO: RIETHAUSEN

Lausanne, January 8–9, 1986. IOC and Korean delegations at joint meeting.

PHOTO: IOC

Seoul, April 22, 1986. Audience given by the Korean government on occasion of the IOC Executive Board meeting with the national Olympic committees. In the center, South Korea's president, Chun Doo Hwan.

PHOTO: RIETHAUSEN

Seoul, April 27, 1986. Members of the SLOOC report to the IOC Executive Board. Left to right: Cho Sang Ho, acting SLOOC president Park Seh Jik, Kim Un Yong, Chang Ju Ho.

PHOTO: RIETHAUSEN

PHOTO: RIETHAUSEN

Lausanne, June 10, 1986. Joint meeting, IOC with North and South Korea.

Above: Meeting in progress at IOC headquarters.

Left: Kim Chong Ha.

Below: IOC president Samaranch has double handshake from Korean national Olympic committee presidents. Left to right: Raymond Gafner, IOC *administrateur délégué*; Alexandru Siperco, IOC vice president; Kim Chong Ha, president, Korean Olympic Committee; Samaranch; Kim Yu Sun, president, North Korean National Olympic Committee; Ashwini Kumar, IOC vice president; Berthold Beitz, IOC vice president.

PHOTO: RIETHAUSEN

PHOTO: RIETHAUSEN

PHOTO: RIETHAUSEN

Lausanne, June 10, 1986. Joint meeting, IOC with North and South Korea.

Above: Kim Chong Ha and members of the South Korean delegation.

Left: Kim Yu Sun.

Below: Seoul, September 1986. IOC Executive Board meeting with the Association of Summer Olympic International Federations. Samaranch with Mr. and Mrs. Park Seh Jik at the SLOOC dinner.

PHOTO: RIETHAUSEN

PHOTO: ASL

Seoul, May 1988. IOC president Samaranch with South Korean president Roh Tae Woo.

PHOTO: IOC

Seoul, September 1988. Samaranch with Roh Tae Woo at the Blue House just prior to Olympic Games.

PHOTO: IOC

Seoul, September 25, 1990. IOC president Samaranch awarded the Seoul Peace Prize.

of the IOC Session to give the Executive Board the mandate to negotiate with the North with a view to enabling the North to participate in the 1988 Olympic Games. Positioning the discussions, he said that the IOC Executive Board was empowered to negotiate within the framework of the historic offer made the previous June. The IOC would do all it could, but the historic nature of the IOC's offer should not be underestimated.

Kim Yu Sun had his usual set piece. He referred to the previous joint meetings, which he said had been taken very seriously by his NOC, and thanked Samaranch for all his efforts in that regard. He said the progress made in the talks had created possibilities for the successful holding of the Games. All had agreed on the sharing of the Games and the official holding of cultural events by North Korea and South Korea. Views had been exchanged, to a certain extent, on a series of practical problems, such as the apportioning of events, the name of the Games, and the consitution of the Organizing Committee. These successes constituted a solid basis, enabling the work of the Lausanne meetings to be brought to a positive conclusion.

However, to their great regret, the fourth joint meeting had not yet taken place, despite the fact that seven months had gone by since the last such meeting in June, thus bringing about an impasse in the progress of the talks. Since members of the Executive Board, he said, were aware of the reasons why the tripartite talks had to be interrupted, he would not go into details. They had met with Samaranch two days ago to talk about ways to overcome the present difficulties.

The obstacle to progress lay in the differences of opinion concerning the modalities of negotiation, which had come to light during the talks. Given that serious misunderstandings and mistrust existed between the North and the South as a result of forty-one years of division, only frequent meetings and serious discussions of the problems between the two sides, with the IOC as mediator, would make it possible to achieve a solution more quickly.

For example, he said, South Korea attached more importance to the apportioning of the Games, whereas North Korea attached as much to the other problems of principle, such as the name of the Games, the composition of the Organizing Committee, and so forth. In such conditions, if each party saw only the problem of its own interests as being of absolute importance and was mistrustful of the other, it would be very difficult to find a solution. Because of this, it would not be possible to bring the negotiations to a satisfactory conclusion in the near future unless the three parties concerned got together again and deliberated "open-heartedly" on the points of agreement, reducing the points of divergence to a minimum.

Kim Yu Sun was of the opinion that the different interpretation of the IOC's June 1986 proposal was obstructing the negotiations. As they had reiterated many times, the North had accepted the IOC's proposal in principle. They agreed entirely with the organization of the two sports, table tennis and archery. With respect to the partial events, namely one of the four groups of qualifying matches in soccer and the cycling race linking the North and the South, their opinion was that this problem could be submitted for discussion and impartial coordination by the North and the South.

But, in proportion to the twenty-three complete sports and 237 events in the Olympic Games, the two complete sports proposed were too little. They were of the opinion that the number of sports and events for them to host should be increased. He was sure those present would understand that if the North were to host only the disciplines proposed by the IOC, the competitions held in Pyongyang would become annexed competitions of the Seoul Olympic Games, and Pyongyang would be in danger of being considered as a provincial town of South Korea, and above all, that could give rise to a political danger, giving the impression that South Korea represented the Korean peninsula.

That was why they asked for at least five or six more disciplines,[18] to reflect the demographic proportions, should half the number of disciplines not be possible. It was public knowledge that they were doing all they could to arrive at an agreement as soon as possible. As they envisioned an agreement this year, they had been building, since last year, various modern sports facilities, including a soccer stadium with a capacity for 150,000 people. The ambiguity of the Lausanne talks placed them in a difficult position as far as increasing the investment and its effectiveness was concerned.

In the course of the three previous meetings, North Korea had, he said, taken a series of steps of concession, taking very much into account the attitude of the South Korean side and the IOC, and had demonstrated their goodwill by sparing no effort in the interests of the success of the meetings. Samaranch and the vice presidents who took part in the meetings were very much aware of this. If the North took such

[18] This expression was clarified during the meeting to mean that the North was, indeed, discussing sports or partial sports, not disciplines in the technical sense of that expression.

measures and presented new proposals, it was as a result of their desire to see the Olympic Movement contribute to peace, friendship, and solidarity among young people and nations of the world and at the same time of their aspiration to the reunification of their country. That was to say, to make the Olympic Games, by their contribution, favor the work of reunifying their divided land.

He therefore proposed that a fourth joint meeting be convened as soon as possible.

Once the DPRK delegation had left the meeting, Samaranch said that he had been prepared to convene a fourth joint meeting on the basis of written agreement in principle to the IOC's June 1986 proposal. Thus far, such agreement in principle had been given only orally. Samaranch had been insistent throughout that the North must accept in writing. It seemed clear that this was unlikely to be achieved.

It was, by now, becoming clear to everyone that such an impasse could well become a stumbling block, as much for the IOC as for the Koreans, and a means had to be found to get around this situation. Vitaly Smirnov (USSR) expressed the view that the main desire of the North Korean delegation was to bring about a fourth meeting. It was, in his view, important not to terminate the discussions but to remain in contact. Ashwini Kumar (India) said that, as the delegation had agreed in principle, there was every reason to keep the door open. He Zhenliang (China) thought the concern of the North was to ensure that the Republic of Korea did not have the Games to itself and to avoid appearing to play a subsidiary role. The delegation had expressed its agreement in principle to the IOC's proposals, and it would be best to accept that as an official statement and agree to a fourth meeting. Kéba MBaye (Senegal) was of the view that a recorded declaration by the head of a delegation had the same value as a written statement.

A consensus developed that the best way to break the deadlock would be to treat the situation as one in which the IOC would accept the declarations by the North Koreans as the "acceptance" that the IOC had requested and to proceed with calling a fourth joint meeting. All agreed that it was much better, at least at this stage, to keep the discussions going, rather than to risk a definitive rupture of the dialogue. This was certainly true, since the possibility of the IOC's being forced to reinstitute the discussions at a later date under potentially different conditions might well result in its being in a much weaker position. As it was, the IOC was in the relatively strong position at present of merely responding to a request to continue a series of discussions that it had already instituted and in respect of which it was in full procedural and moral control.

The position to be adopted by the IOC would, therefore, be that it was pleased to have the acceptance in principle of its June 1986 proposal and that a fourth joint meeting would be called to discuss the details of the proposal and its implementation,[19] under the chairmanship of the IOC, of course. The details of the meeting would be contained in the agenda that would be prepared for purposes of the meeting. The North Korean delegation was invited back into the Executive Board meeting, and the text of the IOC decision, as stated by the president, was read to it.

> On behalf of the Executive Board, I am very happy to note your will to cooperate.
>
> We have taken note of your acceptance in principle of our proposal as expressed in our letter of June 11, 1986.
>
> Within this framework, and for the purpose of advancing the detailed arrangements, I inform you of the IOC's intention to convene a fourth meeting in Lausanne between the NOCs of the Republic of Korea and of the Democratic People's Repubic of Korea under the chairmanship of the IOC.

Ambassador Chin asked when the proposed meeting would be held. Samaranch said that no date had as yet been set but that all parties concerned would be informed as soon as possible.

At a press conference given by Kim Yu Sun following the meeting with the Executive Board on February 12, he insisted that, despite the agreement in principle with the IOC's June 1986 proposal, the North still wanted more sports to be held in Pyongyang than had been offered to date by the IOC. Samaranch, at his press conference the next day, following the Executive Board meeting, stated that the IOC could not offer more to the DPRK. Assurances had been received from the highest levels of the socialist countries that they would participate. Furthermore, he said, the IOC would never "close the door to negotiations with the North Koreans."

Although the decision was taken without any particular difficulty, it did not reflect any real optimism within the Executive Board that there had been any significant progress toward a meaningful agreement

[19] This had some of the earmarks of the strategy adopted by U.S. president Kennedy during the Cuban missile crisis in 1962, when he chose to reply to the "softer" of the two letters sent by USSR general secretary Khrushchev and to completely ignore the harsher one.

with the North. The continued refusal of the North Koreans to give a definitive written response to the IOC proposal was troubling, though hardly surprising. Indeed, it would have been remarkable had such an unequivocal response been forthcoming, in the circumstances. There was also, in the background, a concern that the South might be upset, were the IOC to appear to lean too favorably toward the North Koreans, and that it might well refuse to agree to further concessions.

There was, as well, the fact that the North, despite its relatively soft language, had not withdrawn at all from its demand for at least a third of the overall sports and events to be held in North Korea. Though not a great deal of emphasis had been placed on it by Kim Yu Sun during his presentation, it was nevertheless clearly mentioned and still very much on the table so far as the North Koreans were concerned. The South Koreans had been quick to jump on Samaranch's statements at his February 13 press conference. On February 17, on the eve of his departure to visit Eastern European countries to gain support of the Games, South Korean sports minister Lee Sei Kee stated that the DPRK demand for more sports was unacceptable. March 3 brought forth a statement by DPRK NOC vice president Chin that there be cohosting of the Games and the allocation to the North of eight sports. This was duly noted by the DPRK Central News Agency the following day. Counterpoint was provided by ROK sports minister Lee's return from his fifteen-day trip to Eastern Europe and the announcement by him that Czechoslovakia, Yugoslavia, and Hungary were ready to participate in the Games. While in Tokyo on March 25, the speaker of the People's Chamber of East Germany, Horst Sindermann, declared at a press conference that East Germany would participate in the Seoul Games whether or not the DPRK cohosted them.

Keeping the pot simmering, the Cuban news agency reported on April 5, on the basis of an interview with Kim Il Sung, that Kim believed that more than a third of the sports should be allocated to the North, in its capacity as cohost. Reports were issued on April 14 stating that the DPRK NOC secretary-general agreed to have both the Opening and Closing Ceremonies in Seoul, but that the DPRK should have more events. DPRK NOC president Kim Yu Sun telexed Samaranch April 18, trying to confirm rumors that a fourth joint meeting might be held in June 1987 and urging that it be held as soon as possible.

Announcement of the dates of the fourth joint meeting was made by the IOC on April 22. The South Korean delegation was to meet with Samaranch the next day. The DPRK demands were also announced on April 22. South Korean sports minister Lee Sei Kee responded immediately by saying that no more sports would be offered to the North. Kim Chong Ha merely stated that the KOC would stand by the IOC formula.

While these actions were occurring with respect to the negotiations, another set of negotiations was foundering in Korea. Constitutional discussions between the government and opposition parties had become particularly polarized, principally over the issue of direct presidential elections but with many other issues on the table as well. The give-and-take of such discussions was not something to which President Chun Doo Hwan was particularly well suited. By the early part of April, his vestigial patience was exhausted; on April 13, Chun issued a statement postponing any modifications to the constitution until after the Olympics, including any further negotiations with the opposition parties. So far as can be determined, this decision was taken on the advice of the security authorities, including Chang Se Dong, then head of the National Security Planning Agency (formerly the KCIA). It appears that no political input from Roh Tae Woo and his colleagues had been obtained before the announcement was made.

Apart from a rather unfortunate linkage of constitutional amendment with the Olympics, this was a decision that would eventually lead to the most serious political crisis since Chun had assumed power in Korea. It very quickly led to major tension and violent demonstrations that troubled not only Korea but also its allies and friends. On the narrower Olympic front, it increased concerns as to the ability of the Koreans to provide a safe and stable environment for the Games.

On April 26, 1987, Samaranch sent a telex to Kim Yu Sun of North Korea, stating that the IOC Executive Board, at its meeting of February 12, had "taken note" of his NOC's acceptance in principle of the IOC's proposal contained in Samaranch's letter of the previous June. He advised Kim that on the basis of that acceptance, the IOC intended to call a fourth joint meeting in Lausanne on July 14–15, 1987, under the chairmanship of the IOC.

He said that in so doing, the IOC Executive Board had proceeded on the basis of two minimum assumptions: first, that the borders and designated passageways between the two states would be open to all accredited members of the Olympic Family, and, second, that the athletes of North Korea and South Korea would both fully participate in the competitions held in the northern and southern parts of the Korean peninsula, including the official Opening and Closing Ceremonies in

Seoul. He noted that, though agreement must be reached on a number of outstanding points, the Executive Board was certain that both parties proceeded from these assumptions, as, otherwise, the holding of the fourth joint meeting would be pointless.[20]

To ensure that the fourth joint meeting would result in positive and final decisions, the IOC Executive Board considered that prompt and careful preparation was now necessary. With that in mind, on May 6, Samaranch advised that he had asked Alexandru Siperco to visit the North Korean NOC in Pyongyang, on May 26–30, 1987, accompanied by a small delegation. Siperco would discuss with them a number of specific questions to enable Samaranch to be in a position to conduct the fourth meeting. Upon receipt of confirmation of the visit, he would submit a list of the questions to be considered prior to the delegation's arrival.[21]

He asked that the delegation be shown the sites and facilities that the North proposed for holding the competitions allocated to them as well as the points to be discussed and the ways of passage between North Korea and South Korea. At Samaranch's request, the delegation would then proceed from Pyongyang to Seoul for a meeting with the authorities in the South. He would be most grateful if Kim Yu Sun would arrange for the delegation to cross from north to south at the line of military demarcation at Panmunjom; he was asking the South to extend the same Olympic courtesy.

This latter, among other features of the communication, was brilliant. It forced the North to demonstrate whether or not it was sincere on the matter of free circulation; it was a request by the IOC, not the South; and it was asked as a matter of Olympic courtesy. It put the North Koreans into a real corner but left them plenty of room to comply without any further political consequences.[22]

[20] The counterpoint to this was the urging by Kim Chong Ha to the DPRK on April 28 that it stop demanding more events, or risk having none at all. On May 1, in a speech given to launch his new political party, the Party for Reunification and Democracy, Kim Young Sam compared the Seoul Olympics to the 1936 Olympics in Nazi Germany under Hitler. This produced a very strong reaction from Kim Chong Ha and a warning to all opposition politicians not to use the Games to try to create political tensions.

[21] The next day, May 7, the DPRK NOC issued a statement, monitored in Tokyo, demanding the cohosting of the Games and cited a clash between the North and the South as a serious threat to the Olympic Movement. On May 8, however, its vice president, Chang Ung, announced it would consider the possibility of a visit by an IOC delegation.

[22] This idea could be traced back to a letter to Samaranch from Kim Un Yong dated July 13, 1983, in which the existing border situation between North Korea and South Korea was explained. The suggestion had been made that the IOC propose opening the border to the DPRK (and

Not unexpectedly, the IOC request threw the North Koreans into great confusion. It took Kim Yu Sun almost three weeks to give a formal response, and it was not until May 17 that Samaranch had a reply, one that was unresponsive to several of the principal issues in the telex. Pleasure was expressed at the reopening, due to Samaranch's efforts, of the joint meetings after a year's interruption. However, Kim Yu Sun thought July would be too late; the "due arrangements" for large-scale preparation for the Games were then in "full swing." They were facing great difficulties in this regard because they were not sure what sports or events on which they should concentrate for purposes of providing the necessary facilities as a result of there being no final agreement arising from the Lausanne meeting. Time was against them. The meeting should be held earlier.[23]

The meeting should also "completely discuss and decide the very question arising in cohosting the XXIVth Olympic Games by North and South." For that reason, they welcomed the IOC delegation's visit to their country. What was most important at this stage was that the South must accept their proposal regarding cohosting, and this question should be dealt with during the delegation's visit. They could not, he said, "but wonder" about the fact that the South Korean NOC continued to insist on its original position and had declared that there would be no change in the future. The sense of the next sentence of Kim Yu Sun's response was not entirely clear but seemed to address the idea that this position on the part of the South revealed an intention to make the North's portion of the Games subservient to those in the South and at the same time, to reject the idea of cohosting the Games. This put great difficulties in the way of the fourth joint meeting. For the meeting to be a success, the South Koreans "must give up their obstinate position and express a goodwill and sincerity toward the meeting."

Kim Yu Sun continued that the North had already made public, on several occasions, that once the North-South cohosting agreement had been realized, appropriate measures would be taken to open the military demarcation line to allow the members of the Olympic Family to come

---

possibly to China). The Republic of Korea would agree to such a proposal. No dignitaries had ever passed through the DMZ, except for some North Korean and South Korean delegates some ten years previously during official discussions. Though this letter antedated the negotiations and even the idea of such negotiations, the prospect of the implicit political capital it contained was not forgotten.

[23] Kim's concern on timing was that the later the meeting the less time would remain before the IOC sent the invitations to the Games.

and go freely between North Korea and South Korea. This had been put forward at the first joint meeting in Lausanne, and he believed there should be no ground to wonder about it. What was interesting to them at this time was to find a solution to cohosting the Games between North Korea and South Korea, including the competition of eight sports or events, rather than the question of means of passage for the IOC delegation at Panmunjom. To settle this question was fundamental. He could not understand Samaranch's position of proposing the question of crossing the military demarcation line (not a border line of one country, he pointed out) by the IOC delegation when the fundamental question of the North Koreans had been set aside. The question of passage was one to be discussed *after* the fundamental question of cohosting had been solved. He wanted to know, soon, the questions that the IOC delegation wanted to discuss with them, "carefully taking into account our above-mentioned position."

Samaranch replied on May 19. He expressed deep disappointment regarding the DPRK's unwillingness to enable the IOC delegation to cross the demarcation line from North to South.[24] If such a simple gesture of goodwill could not be extended at this advanced stage of the discussions, he asked, what hope was there to ensure the movement of large numbers of people both ways, preparatory to and during the Games? It was an unprecedented opportunity for the IOC to generate political capital for itself at the expense of the DPRK.

In order to render the fourth joint meeting constructive and decisive, given the limited amount of time left for the preparation of facilities and logistics, he had stressed the importance of the preparatory work that needed to be done and had asked for Kim Yu Sun's full cooperation. He had the uncomfortable feeling, he stated, that this cooperation was not forthcoming. He was, nevertheless, prepared to send the IOC delegation, which would travel by way of Beijing to Pyongyang. The delegation would consist of Siperco and Coupat. He requested that the necessary visas be delivered in Beijing.

In a clear delineation of the mandate of the delegation, he stated that it must be competely clear that the delegation would not be in a position to discuss "any conditions departing from the assumptions of

[24] Samaranch had already prepared his own exit from any political corner on this issue, in a statement on May 12 to the effect that an IOC delegation would still go to Pyongyang even if it were not to be allowed to cross the line of military demarcation as had been requested. He also said that though September 17, 1987, was a very important date (the sending of the invitations to the Games), it was not the "limit."

the Executive Board as stated in my letter of 26th April, or from the terms contained in our letter of 11th June 1986 which you have accepted in principle."

On May 20, the IOC sent the list of subjects to be discussed with the North when the delegation arrived in Pyongyang. The list was comprehensive in nature and was designed to identify problem areas that were certain to arise. Among the most important were: guarantees from the government of the DPRK that competitions would be organized in full conformity with the Olympic Charter; guarantees that the North would participate in the events organized in the South and the reciprocal guarantee that the South Koreans could compete in events in the North; provision of transportation facilities for travel between the two parts of Korea and inside the DPRK; free entry of all sports and technical equipment and facilities, including those required by the television and radio networks, journalists, and photographers; entry, accreditation, transportation, and accommodation of athletes and officials from the IOC, the IFs, and all recognized NOCs; questions relating to broadcasting, Olympic marks, and symbols; and others.[25]

On May 22, Kim Yu Sun responded to the telexes of May 19 and 20. His answer was not promising. Their great desire was to achieve a north-south cosponsorship of the Games. He deemed it urgent, therefore, and important, to discuss the basic problems such as allocation of the numbers of sports and events in the forthcoming Pyongyang meeting with the IOC delegation and the meeting in Lausanne. He had expected the IOC delegation would visit, armed with realistic proposals for the problems, in order to make a practical contribution to the success of the fourth Lausanne meeting. Instead, he could not help but be surprised by the fact that the IOC had "turned the face from our proposals and accepted the South Korean side's as the established one," whose intention is to allocate only two full sports and two other partial sports to their territory. He expressed regret at the IOC's seeming distrust with respect to the Panmunjom crossing, which, he said, was not a fundamental question at this stage.

He could not but worry about the progress of the fourth meeting

[25] Samaranch was careful to issue a press release outlining the process and, in particular, the fact of the DPRK refusal to respond affirmatively to the IOC's request "as a gesture of courtesy and mutual goodwill" that its delegation be allowed to cross the demarcation line between the two Koreas at Panmunjom. Such a gesture "would, in fact, have been considered as demonstrating a true willingness for dialogue with a view to reaching an acceptable solution for all." It also set forth the fact that Samaranch had informed the DPRK NOC "that he was extremely disappointed by their unwillingness to grant this authorization, which seemed not to be very encouraging for the continuation of the negotiations."

after receiving Samaranch's telexes. He could not understand what the IOC would discuss at the meeting, if it excluded fundamental questions such as the sports and events already discussed at previous meetings. As for the list of questions to be discussed, they were the questions that the North Koreans had already officially raised and clearly answered in meetings with the IOC. They were not "imminent" questions but merely further duties that would be carried out in accordance with the Olympic Charter when the cohosting agreement had been achieved. Therefore, Kim Yu Sun officially proposed to discuss the following items with the IOC delegation: allocation of sports and events, name of the Olympic Games, constitution of Organizing Committee, Opening and Closing Ceremonies, TV rights, and others.

The gauntlet had been clearly thrown. Samaranch responded the same day. He was angry enough that he responded in French, rather than the English that had been used to date in the negotiations. At the present stage of negotiations, he said, it was preferable not to react to the manner and tone that Kim Yu Sun had used to address the IOC. Certain terms were unacceptable in substance and in form. He observed that a certain confusion prevailed in communications. He did not consider it useful to pursue the exchange, since the IOC delegation that was coming to Pyongyang would be in a better position to discuss with him the best way to prepare for the next meeting.

He drew once again to the attention of Kim Yu Sun that the mission of the IOC delegation was to prepare for the fourth joint meeting to be convened by the IOC in mid-July, by taking note of the positions of the North Koreans on matters that had not been studied in depth during earlier meetings, but which nevertheless represented essential elements of an eventual agreement.

Kim Yu Sun had the right, of course, to raise with the IOC delegation, in addition to the twelve points on the IOC agenda, any questions he wished. Samaranch observed, however, that Kim Yu Sun appeared to be calling into question the basis of the previous discussions, the principles of which had been clearly set forth in the IOC's letter on June 11, 1986, and which Kim had accepted in principle in February of this year.

On May 23, DPRK president Kim Il Sung had a three-hour meeting with Chinese premier Zhao Ziyang, which was described in the official communiqué as "cordial, friendly, and sincere." It followed an official reception of Kim the previous day by Deng Xiaoping in his capacity as chairman of the Chinese Communist Party. He Zhenliang reported on the meeting to Samaranch on June 9. To prepare the media for the

IOC delegation's visit to Pyongyang, the IOC issued a press release on May 25 outlining the state of the negotiations with the two Koreas. This release recounted the decision to have a fourth joint meeting, the refusal of the DPRK to allow the delegation to cross at Panmunjom, its request for eight sports, and previewed the visit of the IOC delegation on May 27–29.[26]

The IOC delegation arrived in Pyongyang on the evening of May 27 and departed by train for Beijing at noon on May 29. The DPRK refused permission for Siperco and Coupat to pass from North Korea to South Korea via Panmunjom. The meetings were led, from the North Korean side, by Ambassador Chin, vice president of the NOC. Kim Yu Sun participated only on the last afternoon, stating on that occasion that he had been occupied with ministerial obligations.

The two days of laborious discussions were interrupted only by one visit to sports installations then under construction in Pyongyang.[27] The North provided a document that clarified its position and set out its obligations in the event that the IOC accepted its proposals. In order to avoid any misunderstandings, each point was recorded verbally, but officially, by both parties on tape recorders during the final meeting, at which Kim Yu Sun was present. This would, if nothing else, at least enable the discussions at the fourth meeting to begin with a full awareness of the North's position. The IOC delegation did not sign any document but did send a written version of the recorded session to the North.[28]

[26] The next day, Park Seh Jik stated that the refusal of the DPRK to allow passage through the DMZ by the IOC delegation went against the Olympic spirit.

[27] Siperco was an ideal person to lead the IOC delegation, since he was thoroughly familiar with the background to the negotiations and the style of negotiations in the socialist world; he was able to deal with the particular dialectics without becoming, at least visibly, enraged. Once given his brief by Samaranch, he was more than able to carry it out and to avoid the traps set for him by Ambassador Chin. Samaranch's cross-check on the discussions came in the form of the separate presence of Coupat, as his *chef du cabinet*.

[28] The transcript of the discussions is agonizingly tedious, and it is a tribute to the patience of Siperco and Coupat that they were able to persevere in the face of an obstinate refusal by the North Koreans to recognize the reality that faced them, their attempts to twist the facts of the international situation, the rationalization of their acts thus far, and the repetition of the same arguments that had been made on this and other occasions. Coupat makes an interesting observation to the effect that, at one stage of the discussions, it appears as if an agreement might actually be reached, and it was only when the DPRK negotiators realized this possibility that they found an insurmountable problem (the prospect that the South Korean flag might be displayed and its anthem played if one of its athletes were to win a medal), which then prevented an agreement from being put in place. He concluded that this was evidence of two aspects of the situation: first, that the North Koreans had never studied the full implications of what they had proposed, and,

The North was not in a position, at the time of the meeting, to say whether or not it would permit the flags of all participating countries, including the Republic of Korea, to be flown in all the stadiums. Nor would it commit to raising the South Korean flag and playing its national anthem should an athlete from South Korea win a gold medal. Its answer on such questions would only be given on the occasion of the fourth joint meeting. The IOC delegation did not make any counterproposals to those submitted by the North, despite considerable pressure from the North Koreans that it do so.[29]

Concerning the crossing of the line of military demarcation, the delegation again expressed the disappointment of Samaranch regarding the refusal to allow passage. The North said that no non-Korean had ever been authorized to cross at Panmunjom, not even the secretary-general of the UN, who had expressed a desire to do so.[30] Passage would, however, be open at the time of the Games. North Korea was very interested to know how the IOC delegation planned to travel to Seoul. The reply was that, because of the North's refusal to allow passage, the delegation would not go to Seoul on this occasion but would return to Lausanne and receive instructions from Samaranch.

The construction of facilities was reasonably impressive. A vast sports complex with approximately ten stadiums or sports halls having an average capacity of two to five thousand spectators was almost ready in the outskirts of Pyongyang, as was an "immense" accommodation complex for about twenty-five thousand persons, which was ultimately destined for the people of the North. A new open-air stadium with places for 150,000 spectators was also nearing completion.[31]

---

second, that they never had any intention to stick to anything they might have promised during the negotiations.

[29] They were clearly searching for some proposal by the IOC, off which they could play at the fourth joint meeting or in the general political and propaganda scrum. Siperco was careful to define his mandate as one of taking note of the DPRK position with respect to the IOC offer of the previous June, which the DPRK had purported to accept in principle in February. He held out the possibility that Samaranch might, personally, try to sweeten the offer slightly and to convince the IOC Executive Board to accept it but stressed that this was a personal undertaking by Samaranch and nothing more. Nor would he say what the "extra" might be; that was a matter for Samaranch to decide.

[30] There was a somewhat garbled reference to a crossing at Panmunjom on the occasion of the *Pueblo* incident, when the "criminals," the American aggressors, after having been excused by the DPRK for their intrusion in DPRK territorial waters, passed through Panmunjom.

[31] Siperco was reasonably fulsome in his praise to the DPRK of its facilities, to the point of saying that he had confidence that the North had the capability, one day, of organizing something as complex as the Olympics on its own. He did not comment, with good reason, on the likelihood that the DPRK would ever be given the opportunity to do so.

In their report to Samaranch, Siperco and Coupat emphasized that the North insisted that the absolute minimum satisfaction of its requirements was imperative: organization in the North of one-third of the Games, with all the consequences and prerogatives flowing therefrom, in the domains of sport, protocol, finance, press, and marketing.[32] The North Koreans repeatedly insisted that the successful completion of the Games depended on the successful completion of these negotiations. There were complaints that the IOC had turned its face on their proposals and had accepted the South Korean proposals as the established proposals.[33] Collaterally, on the matter of soccer, the decision of FIFA to eliminate the DPRK from the preliminary qualifying tournament for the Games was being formally contested. North Korea considered this decision to be without grounds and asked the IOC to assist it in its interventions with FIFA.[34]

The formal position of the North, as recorded and subsequently sent by the IOC to the North as a record of the meeting, contained five requests and eight commitments from the North Koreans. The requests were:

(1) That a total of eight sports and disciplines be organized in the North: table tennis, archery, judo, soccer, wrestling, gymnastics, women's volleyball, men's basketball, and women's handball;

[32] Perhaps another measure of the impossibility of ever reaching an agreement was this aspect of the demands. Even the DPRK, which might be excused for having a less than state-of-the-art knowledge of commercial sponsorship and television arrangements, must have been aware of the practical considerations implicit in the amending of arrangements already in place and, in many cases, already paid for by contracting parties.

[33] These were reiterated by the North during the meetings, notwithstanding the hostile reaction from Samaranch to the accusation made by Kim Yu Sun. They got no better reception from Siperco and Coupat.

[34] The explanations given by the North in respect of its behavior on this issue bordered on the incomprehensible. The decision by the FIFA committee was unjust, it said, since the DPRK was fully entitled to take part in the final tournament. This was because the question of hosting the tournament was under discussion with the IOC, and, therefore, it was impossible for them to have entered the preliminary tournament. The matter had to be viewed as being in suspense, since it was the IOC that decided everything to do with the Olympic Games. It was not the same as, having entered, to have withdrawn. (In fact, they *had* entered, and although they may not have withdrawn in a formal sense, they did not show up for the scheduled preliminary matches, which amounted to the same thing, if not worse.) So, since they had not applied, there was still the possibility that FIFA could provide them with the entry forms, and all could be made well. Siperco simply called attention to the fact that the DPRK had entered the preliminaries and then had not appeared at the appropriate matches. There were clearly two different versions of the facts, so Siperco left it that he would report this view to Samaranch, and the IOC would get the official position from FIFA.

(2) That the denomination of the competitions organized in the North be Games of the XXIVth Olympiad Pyongyang;
(3) That the Organizing Committee for the part of the Games to be organized in the North, which would be established by the North Korean NOC, be responsible only to the IOC and benefit from all the rights, privileges, and duties of an Organizing Committee, equivalent to those of the Seoul Organizing Committee. It would be given the name Organizing Committee of the Games of the XXIVth Olympiad Pyongyang;
(4) That the part of the Games organized in the North be opened by the IOC president, an Olympic flame be lit and burn throughout the duration of the Games, and the Olympic flag be flown. The Opening and Closing Ceremonies of the Games in Pyongyang and Seoul should be equivalent.
(5) That regarding television, the North was ready to ensure broadcasting "by its own means." The television rights and revenues for the sports and events taking place in North Korea will be in accordance with the Olympic Charter. The North Korean Organizing Committee would wish to contract by itself with the television broadcasters concerned.

If the IOC were to accept, in totality, the requirements of the North as set out above, then the North Korean NOC would engage to:

(1) Obtain from its government the written engagement that all the stipulations of the Olympic Charter would be strictly observed;
(2) Accept entry on its territory of all those accredited by the IOC in accordance with the Olympic Charter, upon sole presentation of the Olympic identity card, and to offer all means necessary for the crossing of the demarcation line from its side;
(3) Organize the events or sports granted to it in accordance with the requirements and regulations of the IFs concerned and in close collaboration with them;
(4) Respect the stipulations of the Olympic Charter, particularly regarding accommodation, transportation, and services provided for the members of the Olympic Family;
(5) Not to permit any "legal dispositions" to oppose the requirements of the Olympic Charter, especially regarding material, importation, and use of any necessary equipment by the media;
(6) Participate in the competitions organized in South Korea, in the

official Opening and Closing Ceremonies in Seoul, and in the cultural program, authorizing in return the South Korean NOC to participate in the competitions, ceremonies, and cultural program organized in North Korea;

(7) Ensure that the flags of all the delegations participating in the Games, without any exceptions, are flown on all Olympic sites in Pyongyang and that each winner's flag is hoisted in the stadium while that delegation's national anthem is played.[35] Regarding the delegations and the athletes of the two parts of Korea, a final decision would be taken, following discussions, on the occasion of the fourth tripartite meeting; and

(8) Appeal to the Court of Arbitration for Sport in case of litigation.

This remained on the table pending the outcome of a similar meeting with the South. No comment was made by the IOC at this time.

On June 11, Samaranch proposed to the South Koreans that the IOC delegation visit Seoul from June 25 to June 28 or 29. Writing separately to Park Seh Jik, the president of the SLOOC, he asked if the delegation might meet with him personally during the visit in order to report on its visit to the North and to raise some matters in relation to that visit. He also asked Park to arrange for the delegation to meet privately with the chairman of the SLOOC, Roh Tae Woo.[36] Copies of both letters were forwarded to Kim Un Yong, who had been elected a member of the IOC at the October 1986 Session in Lausanne.[37]

This was not an easy period for South Korea's domestic politics. Starting on June 10, there was a severe political crisis for the government of Chun Doo Hwan, which included civil demonstrations in Seoul and throughout the country, riots, and confrontations with the police.

[35] This issue appeared, as a matter of the record of the meeting, to have been solved, despite the problems that had occurred when the implications of it were first "discovered" by the DPRK negotiators. It is fair to say that the IOC placed little faith in the content of the undertaking.

[36] Roh Tae Woo had, by this time, been officially designated as the candidate of the Democratic Justice Party to succeed Chun Doo Hwan and was on the eve of making his famous Eight Point Proposal, which was issued on June 29. It was an extremely busy time for him.

[37] There had been no shortage of "volunteers" to replace the deceased Park Chong Kyu and considerable lobbying within Korea for the nomination. As a practical matter, the new IOC member in Korea needed the tacit, if not overt, support of the president of the republic. Samaranch had insisted to Chun that he wanted Kim Un Yong, despite considerable opposition within Korea, and Chun eventually gave his approval to the appointment of Kim.

The evident concern was that the existing electoral college system virtually guaranteed that the government controlled who would become the next president of the country when Chun stepped down. Interestingly enough, the DPRK was somewhat restrained in taking advantage of the unrest as it began to develop. Kim Il Sung made no reference to it during an interview given on June 11 on the occasion of a conference on cooperation of nonaligned countries in Pyongyang. Similarly, two days later, the DPRK foreign minister, Kim Yong Nam, made no reference to political unrest in the South during an interview with foreign delegates to the same conference.

Such restraint was not shown in all quarters. Jesse Jackson, then engaged in his campaign for the U.S. presidency, suggested on June 17 that the United States might boycott the Seoul Games unless South Korea were to make significant progress in human rights and free elections. USOC president Robert Helmick, returning from a visit to Seoul, stated the same day that though he hoped that those responsible for the Games would be successful, the United States would not participate in the Games if there was a security risk. Samaranch was forced to issue a statement from Toronto, also the same day, where he was visiting the Toronto bid for the 1996 Games, that the IOC had no change in plans to hold the 1988 Games in Seoul.

Roh Tae Woo met with President Chun, also on June 17, to discuss the crisis. The Yugoslavian news agency Tanjug, emerging from a posture of restraint, had quoted DPRK officials as saying they were building facilities to host the entire 1988 Games if the political situation in the Republic of Korea deteriorated. Roh, emerging as a leader, urged Chun to reverse his April 13 decision to suspend constitutional discussions and led the confrontation with those government leaders who advocated force and the imposition of martial law to suppress the demonstrations. In this, he was assisted by delivery of a letter on June 18 by U.S. ambassador James Lilley from President Ronald Reagan urging moderation in dealing with the crisis. Secretary of State George Shultz similarly urged an end to the eight days of protests and a resumption of dialogue.[38]

Roh chaired a special meeting of the Democratic Justice Party on June 21. Chun agreed to meet Kim Young Sam three days later, but

[38] In a related move, Senator Edward Kennedy and four other legislators introduced draft legislation on June 18 calling for economic sanctions against Korea. Congressional leaders called instead for political dialogue between the government and opposition parties.

Kim later described the meeting as a failure. In the meantime, secret meetings were being held with the Soviets in Tokyo, where, on June 24, SLOOC vice presidents Kim Un Yong and Kim San Hoon agreed with USSR vice minister Viacheslav M. Gavrilin on security measures for Soviet athletes and agreed to allow the Soviets to anchor in the Korean port of Inchon during the period of the Games. This was a major breakthrough with the Soviets, who have traditionally had such an agreement with the Olympic host country. There was certainly a Soviet ship in the Montreal harbor during the 1976 Games, and the Los Angeles Organizing Committee had agreed to allow this in Los Angeles, prior to the Soviet decision to boycott the Games in 1984.

Samaranch maintained an extensive network of contacts in relation to the Korean problem and was in constant communication with these contacts. One sports leader who enjoyed a special relationship with the North and who appeared able to discuss matters more openly than most others was Ichiro Ogimura, the Japanese president of the International Table Tennis Federation. Ogimura reported to Samaranch on a visit he had made to China and the DPRK in mid-June 1987. On the occasion, he had met with the Chinese NOC and Chinese deputy minister for sports Xu Yinsheng, and had, when in the DPRK, been shown both sports facilities and the famous Nampo water basin, the latter to demonstrate that North Korea had no intention to inundate South Korea. In the DPRK, he met with Li Chang Son, vice chairman of the Sports Commission; Chang Ung, secretary-general of the North Korean NOC; and Li Jong Ho, deputy president of the Asian Table Tennis Union.

Ogimura reported that there was general appreciation for Samaranch's efforts and that the North was trying its best to reach an agreement. The sports facilities were fine. They were already in contact with foreign suppliers of equipment but were hampered by not being certain of what sports they would be staging. Their broadcast facilities were capable of transmitting anywhere in the world, and they were members of a number of satellite systems. He reported that they had already accepted the concept of free access at the first meeting, and a second airport would be ready in the spring of 1987. The crossing at Panmunjom, clearly a sore point, was explained again. There had been foreigners allowed into the demilitarized zone, but only the UN Commission members from Switzerland, Sweden, Czechoslovakia, and Poland. Access had never been extended to even the Swiss ambassador or any other foreigner in any other capacity. The North said it had proposed that the IOC delegation fly from Pyongyang directly to Seoul but that had been refused. The North was very worried about the time problem. The official invitations to participate in the Games would be sent out by the IOC on September 17. They were worried that the tactics of the South Koreans were to delay and let the time expire. They suspected that Samaranch might have the same tactics.

Ogimura thought the North was serious, not only because they said they were, but because they had built the facilities, their Youth Festival in 1989 would not have a sports component, and, perhaps most important, they would lose too much face if they were not to host the Games. They had spent a great deal of money preparing and had even co-opted soldiers from the army to help with the labor. If the fourth meeting was to be a failure, he thought there would be a strong possibility that with a year to go before the Games, the DPRK might move to a diplomatic attack. The question of face was not without importance, since, as a closed society, the DPRK was not too concerned about loss of face with respect to the outside world; it was the internal face that mattered. Ogimura said that when Japan was a closed country for some 260 years, it did not worry about its face to the outside.

What the North needed to save face was the image and outlook of cohosting the Games, so that it could be explained to the people of the North. The situation was good for a compromise because of the time limit before sending the invitations to the Games and because the South had some internal political uncertainties of its own, which might well be helped if an agreement with North Korea could be reached. North Korea could not accept anything that would make it appear subservient to Seoul or that Pyongyang was a part of Seoul in any way. South Korea should agree to giving the image that the North wanted.

He was concerned to some degree with China's perception that there was a possibility that the Soviet bloc might not participate if the North was not present. This was a message given several times by He Zhenliang, the IOC member in China. The visit of Kim Il Sung to China had been a success, although the Chinese leaders had avoided having any detailed discussions about the Games.[39] North Korea was realistic enough not to expect any assistance from the United States, which they

[39] This had occurred between May 21 and May 26, 1987, and had involved meetings with all the senior Chinese leaders, including Deng Xiaoping, chairman of the Chinese Communist Party Central Advisory Commission; President Li Xiannian; and Premier Zhao Ziyang.

expected would continue with its "two Koreas" policy. They did not think they would get much help from the Japanese government, either; they had been advised that Prime Minister Nakasone had been working hard during his visit to Eastern Europe to promote participation in the Seoul Games.

The IOC delegation's visit to Seoul was relatively uneventful, although not without some difficult negotiations with the South Koreans. At the end of the visit, a memorandum was prepared, dated June 30, 1987, outlining the position of the KOC and the SLOOC regarding the list of requests that had emanated from the North. It was expressed, however, as being in response to the requests made by the IOC. In it, South Koreans:

- renewed their commitment to accept the participation of a delegation from the North in the official Opening and Closing ceremonies, in the sports competitions and in the cultural programme in the South and the reciprocal commitment with respect to participation in the same activities in the North;
- undertook to guarantee, for their part, the provision of the necessary means of transport between the two parts of the Korean peninsula;
- requested that the North refrain from referring to the "co-hosting" of the Games, but, rather, employ the term "sharing" and indicated that it would propose an appropriate name for the competitions to be held in the North when they came to the fourth meeting in Lausanne;
- undertook to accept the establishment of an ad hoc Organizing Committee, under the auspices of the IOC, responsible for the organization of the competitions and ceremonies taking place in the North and responsible for all matters relating thereto, the name of which committee would be proposed at the joint meeting;
- wished to remind the IOC that the only Host City of the Games was the City of Seoul, which accepted to share this privilege with the City of Pyongyang;
- pointed out, in consequence, that the only official Opening and Closing ceremonies of the Games could be those organized in Seoul;
- undertook to guarantee free access and entry into the South for all persons accredited by the IOC and coming from the North and likewise for all sports or technical material, including that of the media which would be necessary for its work;
- undertook to grant, in every way possible, the assistance which might

be requested of it by the IOC for the successful staging of the Games in both parts of Korea;

- agreed to guarantee that the flag and anthem of the North would be used without restriction in all cases as stipulated by the Olympic Charter, including the stadia, parades of the delegates and medal ceremonies;
- were studying a possible amelioration of the offer made by the IOC on June 11, 1986, regarding the sports or events to be organized in the North; and
- requested that the questions of television broadcasting and the marketing programme regarding the part of the Games to be organized in the North should not affect the contracts already in process on the part of SLOOC.

The memorandum was not signed by South Korea (the same procedure as adopted for North Korea) in order to allow for some reevaluation during the course of the forthcoming fourth joint meeting.

Reporting separately to Samaranch from the formal summary of the meetings, Siperco and Coupat thought that the meetings contributed to a better appreciation on the part of many of the South Koreans of the dangers to the 1988 Games of not getting the domestic situation under better control and establishing social tranquillity. The IOC delegation had met with Kim Chong Ha, Park Seh Jik, sports minister Lee Sei Kee, Kim Un Yong, Roh Tae Woo, the media, and many others, including representatives of the departments of reunification and security. The delegation was somewhat insistent in meeting with Park Seh Jik, who had not, apparently, intended to be part of the discussions, and even more so with respect to Roh Tae Woo, who was very heavily involved in crucial political initiatives at this time.[40] It was a constant part of the message to everyone they met that the political instability then rampant was very dangerous for the Games. It was crucial for the South to find ways of defusing the situation.

There was a noticeable difference between the positions of Kim Chong Ha, who was inclined to seek compromise, and Park Seh Jik, who had a much tougher approach to North Korea (as befitted a former army general). There was considerable jockeying for position by many

[40] The delegation had a personal message to Roh from Samaranch and insisted on personal delivery of it, despite many attempts on the part of Roh's staff to obtain it for subsequent delivery to him. The meeting eventually took place on June 30, the day after his epochal declaration.

of the South Koreans in relation to the IOC delegation, with each trying to imply that he was expressing the "official" position of the highest political authorities. Park presided over the discussions from the Korean perspective, and although the final memorandum was fairly mildly expressed, it represented a good deal of laborious work on the part of the IOC delegation to achieve this. Park's apparent inclination had been to backtrack somewhat from the position that South Korea had already appeared to have reached in previous discussions.

The initial position of the South had been to refuse to consider any change to the offer, not even to replace the preliminary soccer matches that had been on the table from the outset of the discussions and that, in all probability, would fall by the wayside as a result of the North Korean mismanagement of the issue. There was resistance to the idea of a separate Organizing Committee in the North. This was on the basis that what was really being discussed for Pyongyang were separate local competitions (not unlike, conceptually, the yachting events in Pusan) and that all events had to be under the control of the SLOOC. Wrestling with this, the South Koreans went through a variety of proposals, starting with the creation of a subcommittee in North Korea, under the control of the SLOOC; to a subcommittee linked with the IOC, which would serve as an intermediary for the transmittal of the SLOOC's decisions; to a subcommittee under the control of the IOC, but obliged to consult the SLOOC for each decision; and, finally, agreement that a separate Organizing Committee, independent from the SLOOC, could be formed under the full control of the IOC. Regarding the name of the Games, they first refused even to consider it but eventually agreed to study the matter.

The tensions within the Korean group were sufficiently high that Kim Chong Ha, in a separate conversation over coffee with the IOC delegation, set forth a position that was far more conciliatory in tone than Park's. He said that if the North Koreans were to renounce the idea of cohosting and to accept a lesser concept such as "sharing with Seoul" or "in association with Seoul," assure the free circulation between the two parts of Korea, and participate in the Opening and Closing Ceremonies in Seoul, the South would be prepared to offer, at the fourth joint meeting, a replacement for soccer and one or two disciplines more. They had considered among the possibilities rhythmic gymnastics, synchronized swimming, diving, freestyle wrestling, modern pentathlon, slalom canoe, women's volleyball, and women's handball. As to the name of the Games, he thought a formula along the lines of

Games of the XXIVth Olympiad in Pyongyang could probably be acceptable. Regarding ceremonies, North Korea could organize different Opening and Closing Ceremonies from those in Seoul, which the IOC president could attend, if he so wished.

Kim Chong Ha claimed that he had received the authorization to present this offer to the IOC delegation directly from President Chun Doo Hwan, and that it was he, Kim Chong Ha, who had been charged with settling the problem of the DPRK in relation to the organization of the Games. He advised the delegation about the composition of the South Korean delegation to the fourth joint meeting, which, he said, grouped the representatives of the different authorities in Seoul and those, in particular, that were responsible for DPRK matters. His intention was to present these proposals to Samaranch during their meeting on July 13, as the limits of the compromises that South Korea was prepared to make, but only at the end of the discussions. Siperco urged him to make the proposals at the beginning of the meeting, which might unblock the situation and create an atmosphere more conducive to concessions from the North, or, at least, should the proposals be refused by the North Koreans, would be evidence of good faith on the part of South Korea and the IOC.

The meeting with Roh Tae Woo was in his capacity as honorary president of the SLOOC.[41] Siperco delivered the verbal message from Samaranch to the effect that the IOC had always shown full confidence in the success of the Seoul Games, even in the most difficult times.[42] He referred to the pressures to change the site of the Games and to Samaranch's public statements, at the moment of greatest political tension, of support for the Games in Seoul and for the SLOOC itself. The appreciation of the IOC president was transmitted in respect of the positive solution that Roh had brought to the political life of the country and his confidence that with these new conditions, the Games would proceed with even greater success.

Roh was, as always, very courteous with the IOC delegation and conveyed his respects to Samaranch as well as his personal undertaking to help the SLOOC find the best solution to the problem of the participation of the DPRK in the Games. His statement on the occasion was

[41] Attending the meeting were Kim Chong Ha, Kim Un Yong, and Cho Sang Ho, both of the latter in their capacities as vice presidents of the SLOOC.

[42] Coupat also privately delivered a personal letter from Samaranch to Roh, of which Siperco was not aware.

not as polished as some, but reflected his view that the political crisis was coming under control, a matter in which he could take some justifiable satisfaction.

> I would first like to express my deep thanks for the kind message of President Samaranch and for his unswerving support in times of difficulty. I would also like to extend my warm regards to all friends in the IOC including Mr. Siperco and Mr. Coupat for their effort to make the Seoul Games a great success.
>
> From the very beginning, I was sure we can overcome the political difficulties. Now with the dramatic means of democratization, all the Korean people are united in one and they can now redouble their efforts for the success of the Seoul Olympiad.
>
> Our people has [*sic*] a great deal of political desire, and there were political conflicts before the Asian Games last year. But during the Games' period, every citizen contributed to the successful hosting.
>
> Now that we have reached a 100% consensus, the Olympic Games will surely be a historic success.
>
> In fact, it is true that even when we had demonstrations in the street, our export continued to increase, which is a proof of the diversification of our society.
>
> As to the allocation of some sports to North Korea, basic principles were set up between me and President Samaranch when I was active SLOOC President. I always believe that this matter should be settled in faithful accordance with the Olympic Charter. However, in spite of our sincere efforts, the north has continued to impair our preparations for the Games and tried to propagate their political purposes.
>
> There have been other official and unofficial contacts between the south and the north apart from the sports talks, and I know something more than you know. In the sports talks, north Korea should never repeat their contention of "co-hosting". The allotment of some sports to the north has been pursued in order to give some cause for them to join the Seoul Games and to foster trustful friendship with them.
>
> The fourth talks should also be conducted within this context. I am not in a position to make a decision on more concessions to the north. We have here relative officials including SLOOC president and they will consult with the government. In that process, I will also help them to make a good decision.
>
> It is my wish that the fourth meeting will proceed smoothly and fruitfully in compliance with the Charter. I would like to take this

opportunity to pay tribute to all your efforts for the Seoul Olympiad, and sincerely wish that we will share the fruits and the glory of making the greatest-ever Olympiad in history.

One of the most intriguing byplays in the entire process of the negotiations was the manner in which North Korea played itself offside with respect to the soccer tournament. The North, despite having entered the competitions, had failed to show up for the qualifying matches in Kuala Lumpur.[43] As a result, FIFA, after reviewing the circumstances, ruled that the DPRK would be excluded from further participation in the competition, that the DPRK soccer federation was to cover the losses or lost profits of the Malaysian soccer association, the bill for which would first be submitted to and approved by FIFA, and that the case would be further studied by the FIFA Executive Committee. The preliminary recommendation had been made by FIFA's Subcommittee for Matters of Emergency of the Organizing Committee for the Olympic Football Tournament, which had met in Zurich on March 26, 1987.[44] A feature of particular interest was that this subcommittee was presided over by a Soviet, Dr. Viacheslav Koloskov.[45]

The FIFA Executive Committee met on June 11, 1987, to consider this report and the request for a reconsideration by the DPRK soccer federation.[46] Not only did the Executive Committee confirm the deci-

[43] Though the DPRK had not shown up on the preliminary list of 108 countries that Samaranch had received from FIFA prior to the third joint meeting, South Korean soccer officials observed on June 24, 1986, that the DPRK had applied to compete in the regional preliminary rounds of the Olympic tournament, according to the FIFA bulletin. The draw was scheduled to be made on June 27, in Mexico, during the World Cup.

[44] Press reports on March 13 had already commented on the DPRK's refusal to play in the Asian qualifying rounds of the soccer tournament on the basis that it was the cohost of the Games and, therefore, did not have to qualify.

[45] Samaranch was quick to jump on this opportunity. On March 28, he stated that the Olympic authorities totally supported the FIFA decision to expel the DPRK from the Olympic soccer tournament, as a "technical" matter, which was outside the jurisdiction of the IOC. This was a most convenient distinction to be able to draw. The international sports federations are responsible for the rules affecting the sports, such as playing rules, equipment, and qualification. This was an opportunity to reinforce the autonomy of the international federation, FIFA, and for the IOC to absolve itself of any of the responsibility for expelling the DPRK. There was always the opportunity for the IOC to intervene in the future, to reach an accommodation with FIFA, were an agreement with the DPRK to be reached regarding cohosting of the Games. The credit for a solution would then redound to the benefit of the IOC, though any blame if there were no such accommodation would rest with FIFA.

[46] The DPRK Football Association had urged FIFA on April 11 to reconsider its decision.

sion of the subcommittee in all respects, but it imposed an additional fine of SF 5,000 on the DPRK federation for unsporting conduct, which was to be paid not later than July 31, 1987. The decision was said to be final and without appeal. Though the FIFA Executive Committee decision was not known by the North Koreans at the time of the visit of the IOC delegation at the end of May, the matter had already been ruled on by the subcommittee, and the North was obviously concerned. No doubt this was a reason for requesting the IOC to intervene in the matter.

Samaranch had written to Joao Havelange, president of FIFA and a member of the IOC in Brazil, on June 18 to inquire about the matter, presumably in response to the request of the North Koreans, and asked for whatever documents might be available in relation to the decision, since this was undoubtedly going to be a matter of some importance at the forthcoming meeting with the two Koreas scheduled for July 14–15. On July 3, Josep Blatter, secretary-general of FIFA, responded to Samaranch, explaining the process that FIFA had followed in reaching a decision. Apparently, the North had argued that it had never registered for the tournament, but the tournament organizers had established that this was not the case and that the North Koreans had shown an evident desire to particpate in the preliminaries. Futhermore, registered or not, the North would have lost all its rights to participate in the final tournament. That situation would remain unchanged, even if one of the groups in the Olympic soccer tournament were scheduled to play in Pyongyang.[47]

Perhaps the most significant moment in the entire political process leading up to the Games in Seoul was the preemptive declaration made by Roh Tae Woo on June 29, 1987. It is commonly referred to as his Eight Point Proposal. The declaration was all the more remarkable because it had evidently been made by Roh on his own initiative as the prospective presidential candidate of the Democratic Justice Party, a candidate regarded with considerable misgivings by many among the Korean population. Many saw in Roh nothing more than another army general, ready to achieve political power by force if the limited democratic process in Korea at the time did not produce the "correct" result. It caught the opposition parties completely off guard and took almost every breath of the proverbial wind from their political sails.

[47] Samaranch knew that it would be impossible that FIFA would permit the DPRK to be readmitted to the Olympic soccer tournament. Without a team from the DPRK competing in the tournament, it was absurd to think of soccer matches being played in Pyongyang.

Through his declaration, Roh put forward certain plans and undertakings that he proposed to follow as a candidate. Furthermore, he said that if these were not acceptable to President Chun Doo Hwan, he would retire from political life and would not be a candidate in the forthcoming presidential elections. First and foremost, Roh stated that the presidential elections should be direct elections, rather than the existing electoral college system that effectively stacked the voting in favor of the party that had the most seats in the National Assembly. Such an electoral college system virtually guaranteed that the Democratic Justice Party candidate would become the president. Attacking this system was a major plank in the political platforms of the opposition parties, who had clamored for a system of direct presidential elections with not inconsiderable public support. Roh's declaration deprived them of this opportunity to attack the Chun government and the Democratic Justice Party as perpetuators of such a system. He also tied this change generally to speedy constitutional revision through agreement with the ruling and opposition parties, designed to lead to the direct elections prior to the February 1988 date when Chun Doo Hwan's term of office was to expire. Laws were to be revised to guarantee free and fair presidential elections.

Roh also declared that a large number of political prisoners, including Kim Dae Jung (the best known of the opposition leaders, who was under house arrest, and who had been the target of an assassination attempt by the Korean Central Intelligence Agency), should have their political rights restored, except for those charged with violent crimes. A free press was to be permitted, including allowing newspapers to base correspondents in provincial cities. A guarantee of respect for human rights was proposed. Political parties were guaranteed the right to carry out legal activities unfettered, in order to foster a political climate in which dialogue and compromise could prevail. He proposed institution of autonomy at local and campus levels, with the principles of independence and self-reliance guaranteed for all levels of society. He proposed a nationwide campaign against violent crime and corruption. In addition to the specific proposals, he issued a generalized call for "bold social reforms."

His declaration was a complete political coup. It caught the opposition by surprise. It adopted most, if not all, of the planks in their own platforms, severely limiting their abilities to build campaigns on an "anti-Roh" basis, since there was no longer any appreciable difference between them on the substantive issues. Most important for Roh, it served to position him as his own man, not simply the next incarnation or generation of Chun Doo Hwan. This established an entirely new level of personal credibility for Roh, and respect, however grudging, for his political courage. It showed him as someone prepared to listen to the people and not as an ascetic removed from the rigors of ordinary political life, as Chun had been.

More important, Roh's declaration had been made at the height of escalating public demonstrations against the Chun government, principally, but not exclusively, by students and in the face of increasingly sympathetic public support of the students. Matters had reached a point where a crisis could have developed with very little difficulty. There was a considerable calming effect produced by his declaration, and the level of demonstrations dropped significantly in the days following its release, as the population digested its implications. The declaration had predictably little effect on the more radical student groups, who continued to agitate, but over time, public and even student support for the extremists diminished markedly, and the radicals became marginalized. This state of affairs would generally remain true up to and during the Games, although the media continued to give inordinate coverage to the dissidents throughout the entire period.

The level of such attention to the political crisis and violence in Korea at this time was considerable. Speculation had become rife in the media that the site of the Games would have to be changed. As a vice president of the IOC in North America, I received many requests to comment on such speculation. One network show, *Meet the Press,* was typical of such occasions. I appeared on June 21 to face a panel that was convinced a change of site was necessary and equally convinced that the IOC had a plan to go to one of the cities that had indicated it could be ready in time, such as Barcelona or Los Angeles. My purpose in agreeing to appear on the program was to make it clear that the IOC had no alternate site and was neither discussing nor considering an alternate to Seoul. The Games would be in Seoul, or there would be no Games. It was also to try to send the message that the IOC was confident that the Koreans would solve their political issues in their *own* manner well before the Games and that the Games would be held successfully in Seoul as scheduled.[48]

[48] Though there were some economic considerations involved in the cost of the applicable premiums, it had always been my view that the IOC should not, in all the special circumstances of Seoul, attempt to insure its share of the television revenues from the Games, and, in the end, we did not. I thought the IOC should stand at risk, just as Seoul was, so that there would be a complete mutuality of interest in making the Games a success.

A further problem to be addressed was that all the media speculation about the stability of Korea and the need to change sites was occurring some fifteen months before the Games. This was a completely unrealistic time frame for such a decision. When pressed for a possible time frame, were it to become necessary to make such a decision, I repeated that I did not think we had to change sites, but that if the situation were still unsettled perhaps three months before the Games, it might be necessary to ask the SLOOC and the government whether they thought the conditions were such that the Games could properly be held and then to take our decision on the basis of such advice. The objective was to deflect the current attention away from a period that had no relevance for making such a decision.[49]

Regardless, I said, of any divisions that might exist at a domestic political level, one thing was certain: namely, that all the Korean people were united in their desire to host successful Games in 1988, including the students, opposition parties, and the government.[50] I also spent more time persuading major television networks from giving any play at all to the speculation, including David Brinkley of CBS, and the CBC National News. My line with them was that they might not wish to look foolish on a matter as important as this, but that if they insisted, I would be happy to appear on their programs to support the IOC position in favor of Seoul as I had on NBC and ABC. Both decided not to pursue the matter and were, I expect, delighted not to have done so in light of the subsequent events, including the relative calm that descended a week or so later, following Roh's declaration.

Roh Tae Woo, at this stage still using the SLOOC letterhead, wrote a personal and confidential letter to Samaranch on the date of his announcement of his democratic reform package. He was responding to

[49] The following evening, on ABC-TV's *Monday Sportsnite,* I clarified this aspect of the three-month period, since some media reports fixed on the specific number of months rather than the removal of the issue from the fifteen months that now remained. The point was that the IOC should not be seen to be vacillating on the choice of an Olympic city some fifteen months before the Games, when there was no demonstrated likelihood that there would be trouble at the time of the Games. We were not searching for an alternative site, despite the "offers" from cities like Los Angeles, Berlin, and Barcelona.

[50] The SLOOC was nervous enough about the press coverage of the problems in Korea that, seeing newspaper reports of the interviews, Park Seh Jik called Samaranch to express concern that I was wavering in support of Seoul. I was surprised and disappointed enough about such an interpretation that I wrote a lengthy letter to Park Seh Jik on July 3 explaining just how supportive I had been.

a letter from Samaranch dated June 25, which had contained comments on the political situation in the Republic of Korea. Roh made the polite sounds that one would have expected in respect of advice coming from someone with both a wide grasp of world politics and a genuine interest in the future of Korea in particular. Samaranch's ideas and proposed political agenda had been examined, he said, very carefully by him and his colleagues, and they fully grasped the meaning of the outline that Samaranch had presented.[51] However, earlier that day he had announced to the Korean people his reform package and wanted to inform Samaranch of this.

Roh's explanation of this package and the implications for the future included these statements:

> Under our new proposal, we will endeavour to undertake immediately the revision of our current Constitution to allow for direct Presidential elections by the end of this calendar year to be followed by the scheduled transfer of executive power in February next year. Other reforms proposed include the expansion of press freedom; greater institutionalized protection of the rights of the individual citizen, specifically to include the release of Kim Dae Jung and the restoration of his political rights; and increased local autonomy through local elections.
>
> This package, I feel, offers the Korean people a substantial democratic opportunity and a system that can best meet their needs and dreams as we strive to create a better future for the generations to come. As you are well aware, part of the brighter tomorrow for Korea is next year's Summer Olympic games in Seoul — an event whose spirit has swept this nation.
>
> Much to the credit of our citizenry, the Olympics have remained far above the back and forth that has gone on among our political parties over the past months. Guided by the brilliant leadership of the IOC and by our pride as Olympic hosts, the Korean people have never veered from the path that leads us to the 1988 Games. This consensus of opinion in Korea that welcomes the Games, combined with the consensus of political opinion that has seemingly been generated by today's announcement, creates a solid foundation in my country for a peaceful and spectacular

[51] Samaranch, along with many others, had been gravely concerned by the recent levels of demonstrations and violence in Korea. He thought they posed a potential threat to the Games and could not be ignored. He had twice proposed to Chun that the elections be postponed by common agreement with the opposition until after the Games. He proposed to Roh that the presidential elections proceed in accordance with the current constitution, but that they be followed in 1989 with direct elections.

> Olympics. It should also put to an end the wave of negative publicity about the Seoul Olympics that has been a by-product of our political difficulties.
>
> I must tell you that, personally, I have always been confident that our political differences would be settled in a manner that Koreans could be proud of and that other nations, friend and foe alike, would respect. I am determined not to fail in this endeavour and today I feel that we are on the verge of such a breakthrough.

It was a wonderful and encouraging letter, especially from someone who had staked his entire political future on a single bold initiative.[52] Already, as a political candidate in an election for the presidency of the country, which he had opened up to direct elections rather than to the electoral college process, which he could have been certain of winning, Roh had shown the qualities of statesmanship that would make him, by the end of his eventual mandate, one the most important leaders in the history of his country. His preemptive action on June 29, 1987, made possible the transition from military-based rule to democracy within a time frame that few would have believed possible. To the IOC and the rest of the diplomatic world, Roh's action was a most significant step, not only for its inherent wisdom but also as a signal that he was not a mere disciple of the autocratic Chun Doo Hwan.

The election campaign itself would be marked by unprecedented freedom of debate and speech, including the excesses that often mark the transition from little freedom of expression to democracy. There needs to be some exposure to such freedoms before the limits of self-discipline, rather than externally applied discipline, come into play. In the end, although the usual cries of "foul" were issued by the losers, it appeared that even they did not have much faith in the existence of significant injustice in the process and were, in the issuing of the ritual recriminations, simply (to adapt the famous line near the end of the classic film *Casablanca*) rounding up the usual suspects.

On July 9, just prior to the fourth joint meeting, Mario Vazquez-Raña, president of ANOC, telexed Samaranch to confirm that he had, at

[52] There is an interesting byplay in Roh's letter, which may belie a portion of the apparent gamble he took in breaking from the Chun Doo Hwan mold and the threat to resign if Chun did not agree with his position. He states to Samaranch in the letter: "Taking all of this [the contents referred to] into consideration, let me pass on the assurances and warm wishes of His Excellency Chun Doo-Hwan, who has learned of your letter *and concurs in this response*." [emphasis added] It suggests a higher degree of orchestration than the public statements of the day asserted.

Samaranch's request, sent messages to both the North Koreans and the South Koreans, urging them to seek ways to find a compromise in the interest of the youth of the world, which would enable the Games to proceed in tranquillity. A solution to the problem would be a historic solution that would be an example of the power of the Olympic Movement. The NOCs were confident that the IOC would be able to find a solution. In case, however, that an agreement could not be reached to celebrate the Games in both Koreas, due to nonsporting reasons, he had asked all concerned to give their complete support to Seoul so that the Games could take place within the framework of the Olympic Movement.

Only three days before the fourth joint meeting with the Koreas, Samaranch received a message from U.S. assistant secretary of state Gaston Sigur, complimenting him on his strong public statement of confidence in Seoul as the site of the Games. He gave Samaranch some assessments based on his recent visit to Korea. Sigur had found a significant change in the attitudes of Koreans toward political change and a growing likelihood that there would be an open, more democratic, system. Although there would undoubtedly be hard bargaining between the government and the opposition in the months to come, the prospects for an acceptable compromise seemed bright.[53]

There was no doubt that the dramatic declaration of Roh Tae Woo on June 29 had been a vital step in this process. The effect of his declaration, in defusing the impending crisis at that time, was to be a major factor in his election as president of the Republic of Korea. His proposals were welcomed by virtually everyone, including the opposition, despite the undoubted fact that they encroached heavily on their own political territories.

With this confluence of events, the Olympic stage was set for the fourth joint meeting.[54]

[53] The Korean sports minister, Lee Sei Kee, also sent Samaranch a letter dated July 8, 1987, thanking him for his stand on suggestions for a change of location for the Games and observing that the process of democratization in Korea was making others uneasy about the situation. He thought, however, that the process that was unfolding was one the Korean people knew how to solve, and which they would solve. He was sure the joint meeting under Samaranch's presidency would proceed favorably.

[54] On July 10, Chun Doo Hwan announced his resignation as leader of the Democratic Justice Party. Kim Chong Ha met with Samaranch on July 13 so that Samaranch could reveal to him the strategy to be followed for that meeting.

CHAPTER 10

Once More into the Breach: The Fourth Meeting

LAUSANNE, SWITZERLAND, July 14–15, 1987 — Samaranch could be forgiven if his introductory statements at the beginning of the fourth joint meeting in Lausanne on July 14, 1987, were delivered with some weariness of spirit.[1] The players were the same; the gulf between the two sides was still enormous; the likelihood of agreement was slight enough to be illusory. But the show had to go on. There was more at stake than the two Koreas. The real audience, to which everyone continued to play, was ensconced in the political capitals of the world, particularly in Eastern Europe and in the nonaligned nations. It was in these capitals that the reviews would be published and the determination made concerning whether the Olympic Games in Seoul were a show that would make it to Broadway or one that would close in New Haven.

He started by reminding the parties that the meeting was vitally important, since the opening of the Games was in a mere fifteen months' time. An agreement with the North was needed as soon as possible. The IOC had clearly decided at Baden-Baden in 1981 that Seoul was to organize the 1988 Games. No objections had been made until requests had been received from the North Koreans several years after the IOC's decision. The IOC had agreed to talks in view of the special situation in the Korean peninsula and had offered conditions under

[1] The IOC delegation consisted of Samaranch; vice presidents Berthold Beitz, Prince Alexandre de Mérode, and Richard W. Pound; and Kevan Gosper, Alexandru Siperco, Sheik Fahad Al-Ahmad Al-Sabah, Raymond Gafner, François Carrard, Samuel Pisar, Alain Coupat, and Howard Stupp.

which the participation of North Korea would be possible. This was, one must not forget, an important, historic offer whereby Pyongyang would stage two full sports and two events.

Both parties were urged to try their utmost to reach an agreement. The rest of the world was watching Lausanne, hoping that, in the name of sport, solutions not normally reached in other areas of life would be found. The IOC, after certain problems during the Los Angeles Games in 1984, wanted the whole of the youth of the world from 167 countries to come together in 1988. Samaranch renewed his plea for goodwill on both sides and said that, although he would be disappointed if no conclusion were to be reached, he did not expect that the task would be easy. He reminded the delegates that September 17 was the date on which the official invitations to the Games would be dispatched. Although no final date had been set, it would be most convenient if the delegates could agree on the number of sports and events that the North would organize and, in addition, on matters such as television coverage, a separate Organizing Committee for the North, the appellation of the Games in North Korea, the Opening and Closing Ceremonies, and participation of sportspeople in both Seoul and Pyongyang.[2] He closed his speech with a plea to both delegations to be sensitive to the responsibilities they shared. An important issue was at stake, of consequence not only to the Olympic Movement but also to both the Republic of Korea and the Democratic People's Republic of Korea.

Kim Yu Sun of North Korea was invited to respond.[3] He expressed the thanks of his delegation to Samaranch for the continuing efforts of the IOC to ensure the success of the Games. He thought the long-awaited fourth round of talks was most important in order to discuss and settle completely all the problems relating to the Games. In the previous talks there had been many differences, but in the course thereof, views were exchanged on a series of problems, and certain progress made. Had this meeting been held earlier, more "remarkable" progress would undoubtedly have been made.

[2] The list was extensive enough to make it impossible to reach agreement at this meeting. It must have been apparent to everyone participating at the meeting that this would be the case.

[3] The DPRK delegation on this occasion consisted of Kim Yu Sun, Chin Chung Guk, Chang Ung, Han Chang On, Cho Myong Hwang, and Pak Chun Il.

Although the meeting was being held somewhat belatedly, his delegation earnestly hoped that at this time all the problems would be discussed seriously and good results achieved to meet the expectations of the world, which wholeheartedly wanted settlement of the problems of the Games cohosted by the North and the South. To this end, it was necessary, first of all, for all parties to the talks to adhere to the principles of settlement of the proposed problems, to put forth specific plans, and to show the spirit of sincerity and cooperation to reach agreements. From the outset, his delegation had made it clear that the problems of the Games should be solved to suit the Olympic ideal for peace, friendship, and unity and to accelerate the accomplishment of the reunification cause of his divided country. This had led to the request of the cohosting of the Games by the North and the South.

His delegation had set forth specific proposals on the allotment of events, appellation of the Games, composition of the Organizing Committee, rights to television, free travel between the North and the South, and other fundamental problems. It had showed flexibility and magnanimity to take into full account the opposite side's views. He then proceeded to review his position. Concerning events, the North and South should host them half and half; otherwise, one-third of the Games, at least, should be held in North Korea, in view of the respective proportions of the population in North Korea and South Korea. They had put forward their eight-event proposal in consideration of the positions of the IOC and the South Koreans' opposition to the sponsorship of the events half and half.

The proposal allotting them only two full sports (table tennis and archery) and two partial sports (one group of preliminary soccer matches and cycling road races) was welcomed insofar as the two full sports were concerned, but they were not satisfied with the two partial sports. No one could say that they had been given two other events by being given one of four groups of soccer and some cycling events crossing the North and South. Therefore, they could say that the number of sports allotted to them was not four, but only two. That was why one of the most important problems of the meeting was to enable them to host eight full sports, including soccer.

Next, since the Games were to be cohosted by North Korea and South Korea, the appellation of the Games, the composition of the Organizing Committee, and Opening and Closing Ceremonies should be fairly solved to suit such conditions. They proposed to call the Games to be held in Pyongyang the XXIVth Olympic Games, Pyongyang[4] and create the Pyongyang Olympic Organizing Committee separately on their side and insisted on carrying out the Opening and Closing Ceremonies equally in Pyongyang.[5] Their position on these subjects remained unchanged, and they wanted agreements to be reached at this time on such matters.

Besides this, there were still many outstanding problems, including cultural programs agreed upon in principle at the last talks, and television rights, on which there had been "a great deal of views exchanged." Final agreement should be reached at this meeting on these basic problems. The Games were only a year off. The IOC had already declared to all member organizations that the deadline for the talks was September 17, the date for sending the invitations to the Games.

Siperco and Coupat had visited their country last May and had seen, firsthand, the gigantic sports establishments under construction. If the parties failed to reach agreement this time, and invitations were to be sent in September, all their labors would have been in vain. This would discourage the people of the North and the South very much, as well as the people of the world who have cherished desire and interest in this meeting, wanting a decisive realization of the cosponsorship of the Games. Therefore, everyone present assumed heavy responsibilities. If all parties had an intention to solve the problems of the Games completely this time, to ensure the sound development of the Olympic Movement, and contribute to the alleviation of the sorrows and hardships of the separated Korean peoples, there were many possibilities to reach agreements.

North Kim considered that for their success, it was most important for all sides to display a spirit of understanding and cooperation on the principle of mutual respect and equality. It was also necessary for all parties to put forth specific plans on all the problems. Frankly speaking, he said, they did not know of any other proposals except those the IOC made public for the first time at the third joint meeting. He hoped

[4] It is a mark of the dialogue of the deaf that was occurring for the North Koreans to persist with this request. Siperco had explained, ad nauseam, during the meetings in Pyongyang in May, that the 1988 Games were, decidedly, *not* the XXIVth Games at all, but the Games of the XXIVth Olympiad. They would be only the twenty-first Games actually held, due to cancellations of the Games, due to war, in 1916, 1940, and 1944. The North Koreans appeared to be resolutely obtuse on this point, despite asserting a "perfect" knowledge of the Olympic Charter during the May meetings.

[5] This, too, had been firmly rejected during the May meetings as completely incompatible with the Olympic Charter.

that the South would desist from its intrinsic position and advance constructive proposals at these talks. He thought that to reach final agreement at this important meeting, it would be imperative to break free from the existing form of the talks and hold "various" talks. He proposed, therefore, at this time to hold bilateral talks between representatives of the North and the South, at the presidential and vice-presidential levels. Because only two days were available at this time, by doing so they could make effective use of the precious time and solve many problems. His delegation would sincerely make every effort and acquit itself well in reaching final agreement at this meeting.

Kim Chong Ha of South Korea was given the opportunity to reply.[6] He thanked the IOC and Samaranch for the continued effort and unwavering support toward the successful staging of the XXIVth Olympiad in Seoul. He had just listened to the speech made by Kim Yu Sun and was surprised to note some unexpected conditions presented. He had become very concerned about the possibility of having positive results from this fourth meeting. He would, however, continue to cooperate with the IOC in order to bring about a fruitful conclusion.

The sports talks that were proposed and presided over by Samaranch had, thus far, encountered various complications. Nevertheless, it was very meaningful that the talks had resumed after a year of suspension, during which the South had tried to develop and substantiate the proposal of the IOC. At the previous three talks, his NOC had exerted sincere efforts with generosity and patience in the belief that the Seoul Games should be more successful than any other previous Games. In particular, at the third meeting, the IOC made its mediatory proposal to allocate two full sports and some events of two other sports to the North Koreans. Although it was not easy for them to accept this proposal, they did so without any conditions out of respect for the authority of the IOC and its efforts. In fact, the North Koreans' acceptance in principle, if somewhat belated, was very fortunate for the progress of the talks.

Now what they should do was discuss and settle practical and technical problems on the basis of the IOC proposal, such as free travel of the Olympic Family between the South and the North, Games organization, and operations in relation to the staging of some sports in Pyong-

[6] The KOC delegation consisted of Kim Chong Ha, Choy Man Lip, Lee Chong Ha, Yim Tae Soon, Park Soo Chang, and Kim Sam Hoon.

yang. He expected, therefore, for North Korea to make clear at this meeting that it would participate in the Games, ensure free travel of the entire Olympic Family, and attend the official Opening and Closing Ceremonies in Seoul, thereby contributing to a positive conclusion of these talks.

They heartily welcomed the participation of the North in the Seoul Olympiad and would guarantee their maximum safety and convenience. Furthermore, Kim Chong Ha once again made it clear that the South would send its athletes to the competitions to be held in the North. Since the visit of the IOC delegation to Seoul last month, he had repeatedly announced their specific position on all matters related to the early settlement of the IOC proposal. The issue of organizing and operating the Games to realize the IOC proposal could be settled without serious difficulty if the South Koreans and North Koreans could discuss these matters with each other, within the framework of the Olympic Charter and all other agreements.[7] To realize the IOC proposal, the IOC, South Korea, and North Korea should have serious discussions in conformity with its basic spirit and contents. There were only fourteen months before the opening of the Seoul Olympiad. He ended his speech by expressing the wish that the IOC proposal be further specified and developed during the fourth meeting.

Before adjourning to begin the one-on-one meetings, Samaranch read the July 9 telex from Vazquez-Raña and mentioned that many telexes had been received in support of the IOC, including those from Primo Nebiolo, president of the Association of Summer Olympic International Federations; Ichiro Ogimura of the International Table Tennis Federation; and Chiharu Igaya, a member of the IOC Executive Board in Japan. These were not random selections that Samaranch just happened to mention: nothing he did during the negotiations was done by chance. Each of these communications bore a definite message to the participants and, of course, the international gallery. The IOC had the support of all the NOCs. It had the support of the IFs. It had the support of the IF president most closely connected with the North, in the person of Ogimura. It had the support of its highly placed Executive

[7] Each of the delegations clung to its doctrinal imperatives concerning the proposals. The North reintroduced the concept of cohosting, and the South reiterated the legal and contractual basis on which the Games had been awarded to Seoul. The full soccer tournament was raised again, despite earlier semiagreement that only one group was being considered for staging in the North. The North Koreans had little alternative but to press on with this, since it was the only way to generate even the slightest hope of regularizing their situation with FIFA.

Board member in Japan. Japan was a country with a special relationship with Korea, and many of the Koreans in Japan had come from North Korea.[8]

As had become the custom, the IOC met with the North first. Samaranch expressed his disappointment during recent months with the reaction of the North Koreans regarding the possibility that two full sports and two events be staged in the North. He reminded the delegates that, following the third joint meeting in Lausanne, the North Koreans had agreed in principle to the IOC's proposal. Thus, the request to organize eight full sports was not acceptable. However, should the North Koreans be prepared to accept the IOC's initial proposal, it would be possible to consider some adjustments regarding the events to be staged in the North.[9] The IOC was fully prepared to examine the question, particularly in light of the difficulties that had arisen with certain IFs with respect to organizing Olympic competitions in the North.[10]

The IOC felt that the North Koreans had adopted an inflexible position in recent months. It was essential to bear in mind that the IOC had striven to find a solution acceptable to the North Koreans and to ensure that they would be able to participate in the Games. The IOC was also disappointed that the IOC delegation had been refused authorization to cross the Panmunjom "border" into the Republic of Korea in May. The granting of such permission would have been considered a gesture of goodwill and an indication of the possibility of a compromise between the North and the South in the context of the Games. Before any detailed discussion of points raised during the delegation's

[8] In some respects, this was as broad as it was long. There was, indeed, a "special" relationship between Japan and Korea, but, given the history of the relationship, it was not necessarily a positive factor. Despite this, however, the Japan-Korea relationship was nevertheless important on a current basis to both the North and the South, and it was worth putting it on the table at this time.

[9] This was intended to telegraph a final "sweetener" for the North Koreans, but also to indicate that there was not much left to offer. The IOC thought it should be seen to be adding something to the North Koreans' position at each meeting and not to give the impression that the IOC was intractable. This prospect had already been mentioned on other occasions, the most recent being the visit by Siperco and Coupat to Pyongyang in May, but this was to put it on the record.

[10] This was an oblique reference to the problem with FIFA, which had also been discussed during the May meetings in Pyongyang. From the IOC's perspective, it was useful to be seen to be trying to address a problem that could not possibly be solved on the basis of soccer matches in the North. By trying to steer the North Koreans away from this fixation on soccer, the IOC could not later be accused of leading them down a hopeless path.

visit could take place, it was necessary that the North accept the proposals advanced by the IOC.

Kim Yu Sun was pleased to attend the fourth round of discussions between the IOC and the two Korean NOCs and stressed the importance of reaching an agreement since time was short before the celebration of the Games. The visit by Siperco and Coupat to the DPRK had been most constructive and had allowed an extensive exchange of views. The report compiled by the IOC delegation reflected the position of his NOC, and he felt it was not necessary to repeat it.[11] Samaranch reiterated that before the discussion could proceed, the agreement of the North Koreans was required with respect to the organization of two full sports and two events in the North.

The North Korean position was, said Kim, unchanged. It welcomed the possibility of staging two full sports and also the possibility of modifying the initial proposal relating to two events. However, they felt that two full sports were insufficient and requested that the number be increased. They were disappointed that the IOC had espoused the viewpoint of South Korea. It was hoped that the IOC would put forward new, constructive proposals in order that the North and the South could host events on a fair basis.

Samaranch emphasized that the proposal made following the third round of talks was put forward by the IOC and not by the South Koreans. The IOC was prepared to undergo further negotiations and to modify the offer of two sports and two events. Moreover, there was a possibility of allocating full sports, rather than isolated events, as in the original offer, as it might be impractical to organize separate events. But the talks could only continue if the North Koreans agreed to accept the proposal in principle, so that a final decision could be made regarding the sports concerned.

Chin, ever the professional, picked up on the new element. What was the precise nature of the adjustments to the original proposal to which Samaranch had referred? Any modifications would require, cautioned Samaranch, discussion with the IF concerned. He suggested withdrawal of the preliminary group of soccer, particularly in view of the difficulties encountered by the North Koreans with FIFA, and in its place, allocation of the full women's volleyball tournament, which would include the presentation of medals, to the North. In addition,

[11] See Chapter 9.

the cycling road race could take place entirely within the North, rather than crossing the border, as previously proposed.[12]

Kim Yu Sun said his NOC welcomed the possibility of an increase in the number of sports to be staged in its territory. But he wished to emphasize that the NOC had worked toward the goal of staging soccer competitions and that large stadiums had been constructed with that in mind. The efforts of the North Koreans had concentrated upon soccer competitions being allocated to North Korea. Soccer was a popular sport in the North, and the North Koreans had repeatedly requested that soccer should be allocated to them. The DPRK had not presented its application for the preliminary rounds of the soccer tournament in the Asia region as a result of the "abnormal conditions" prevailing at the time.[13] A full eight sports, including soccer, should be allocated to the North.

Samaranch referred to the situation that had arisen in connection with the soccer preliminary rounds and to the fact that the FIFA committee responsible for such matters had decided to disqualify the team from North Korea for not having participated. It was impossible for soccer as a full sport to be organized in the North. However, should the North Koreans still be interested in retaining one of the preliminary groups, this could be discussed and a decision reached before the close of the present meeting. An agreement in principle was still required to the IOC's offer of staging table tennis, archery, the women's volleyball tournament, and the cycling race before the IOC could study the details relating to the soccer group.

Chin said he hoped the IOC would reconsider and allocate to the North the full soccer tournament. This proposal had been put forth during the second round of joint talks. Allocating only one group of the preliminaries to North Korea showed, he said, discrimination against the North. Samaranch, clearly annoyed by this, said that the term *discrimination* was unacceptable to the IOC, since the Games had been awarded to the city of Seoul, which had applied for them. Pyongyang had not put forward a candidature for the Games. The IOC hoped,

[12] This, too, was a new development. Previous discussions always had included this as one or more events that would start in one country and finish in the other. This was, viewed objectively, a rather forlorn hope that read well but would have been impossible to execute properly.

[13] These were, naturally, not described. Clearly, what had happened was the realization by the DPRK political authorities that entry in the qualifying tournament might have been perceived as incompatible with the claim to be cohosting the Games, due to the automatic free entry of the host country in the final round of the tournament, that is, the sixteen teams that actually participate in the Games themselves.

with the current negotiations, to further relations between two parts of a divided country through the celebration of the Olympic Games. The North Koreans should study the IOC's suggestions. They would meet again later that day.

After lunch, the IOC met with the South Koreans. Samaranch said that in the last meeting with the North Koreans, that morning, an important offer had been made, although the North had persisted with its request to stage one-third of the Games. Before discussing this problem, however, he wished to pose some questions regarding recent events in the South, to determine whether or not they would affect the Games.[14]

Kim Chong Ha stated that democratization in the republic was a fairly recent development. With respect to the conflicts between the ruling Democratic Justice Party and the opposition, the president of the republic had agreed, on June 19, 1987, to allow measures of democratization that had been agreed on by the government. There would be no further conflicts and demonstrations on the political front. He reminded Samaranch of some concern before the Asian Games, which had proven unfounded, as everyone in the republic had been in favor of the 1986 Asian Games. A similar consensus existed with respect to the Olympic Games in Seoul, and the internal political situation would in no way hamper them.

Samaranch, constantly worried about "signals" that might have some deeper meaning, asked Kim Chong Ha about media reports that the Olympic flag, which had been flown over the city hall building in Seoul, had been removed during a recent demonstration. He also asked about the position of the opposition parties regarding the Games. Some had been quoted as having said that they wanted democratization first and the Games second. Kim Chong Ha said that the incident regarding the Olympic flag had been wrongly reported. He believed that on July 9, during a demonstration for a student who had been killed, a flag of mourning had been raised in place of the Olympic flag, but that the Olympic flag had been rehoisted at the insistence of the people. Everyone was in agreement over protecting the Olympic Movement. With respect to the opposition leaders, the two main figures, Kim Young Sam and Kim Jong Pil, had no objection to the successful staging of the Games. Presidential elections were to be held before the Games, so

[14] These related to the recent political turmoil in the ROK, which, although abated as a result of Roh Tae Woo's declaration of June 29, continued to trouble Samaranch all the way up to the time of the Games.

that democratization would come first, without any impact on the Games at all.

Given the present status of the political situation, Samaranch asked if it would be appropriate to continue with plans for his visit to Seoul in November of that year, since it might come at a politically sensitive period before the elections. Would it be better to reconsider the timing of his visit, in spite of the fact that it was conveniently linked with visits to the People's Republic of China and to Japan? Kim Chong Ha said that, as far as he knew, Samaranch's visit had nothing to do with internal politics. He would not be obliged to meet with political leaders, although they would be invited to the reception that the KOC would give in Samaranch's honor. Samaranch concluded that he would proceed with the visit as planned.

Turning to the matter at hand, he advised Kim Chong Ha that he had told the North Koreans that only minor adjustments could be made to the IOC's last offer, which consisted of staging the women's volleyball tournament and the whole of the cycling road race, which was originally to run through the North and finish in the South. This was considered prudent, in view of the refusal to let an IOC delegation cross the border between north and south. He would continue to refuse further demands from the North Koreans for eight sports. He wished, nevertheless, to show that the IOC was dealing fairly with the North. He thought it best to offer something more to them. The original offer had encouraged many countries, particularly socialist ones, to agree, albeit unofficially, to take part in the Games in Seoul. These countries were now urging the IOC to concede more to the North, which the IOC wished to do, so that if certain countries did not eventually participate, it was because they did not really wish to do so.

Would the South Koreans support the IOC in this matter? The South already had an abundance of proof of the IOC's help and support, especially during the past few weeks when there had been rumors of the Games going to another city. Samaranch had clearly stated that the Games would be held in Seoul or not at all. Kim Chong Ha replied that he had been deeply impressed by Samaranch's support in the past and was greatly appreciative of the interview he had given the previous week in Zagreb, on the occasion of the FISU (International University Sport Federation) University Games. He wanted to confirm where, if he had understood Samaranch's proposal that the cycling road race was to be held in the North, the end of the race would be. Samaranch said that the North would organize the race in and around Pyongyang. In the IOC's opinion, it would be easier for one of the two countries to organize the race in the present situation.

Kim Chong Ha backtracked a bit. In his view, technical details remained to be settled during this round of discussions, but the speech by North Kim had been disappointing and threatened to eliminate any progress made in the negotiations and proposals. The claim to be cohosts of the Games and to have an Organizing Committee of equal status to the SLOOC was a direct renunciation of what it had agreed to in principle during the third round of talks.

Samaranch agreed that the speech had been disappointing, but he wished now to discuss the reaction of the South to the proposals made by the IOC to the North Koreans that morning, namely, to keep the previous offer of two sports and to add the team road race and women's volleyball. Kim Chong Ha requested a five-minute recess.

Upon reconvening, he said he believed the cycling race would lose its symbolic significance if it did not run through both Koreas. This signified the freedom to travel of the Olympic Family. He was also concerned that the location of the race might be dangerous if such travel conditions were not granted. Samaranch repeated that the race would be better organized by one of the two countries. Kim Chong Ha asked whether this was the IOC's final offer to the North, or whether something else might be added later.

Samaranch was not prepared to state categorically that this was the final offer. The IOC was trying to help the Republic of Korea. Though it would have been easy to determine that all sports events should be held in Seoul, certain socialist countries might have refused to participate. He believed a further gesture was necessary, so that all countries would realize that they were doing their best to find a solution.

Kim Chong Ha thanked Samaranch for his support. If, he continued, the North withdrew its claim to cohost the Games, if it complied with the Olympic Charter, attended the Opening and Closing Ceremonies (which should be held only in Seoul), participated in the Games in Seoul, and guaranteed unrestricted travel over the border, his NOC would study the proposals in a very positive way.

The answer would be needed, at the latest, by the following day, said Samaranch, as otherwise these talks would have produced no result. Kim Chong Ha said he realized time was short and would give the answer as soon as possible. Seoul was always in support of the IOC and positive in its relations toward it. He wondered whether IOC-accredited persons would be able to cross the border, and he anticipated problems for foreigners with tickets to the archery and table tennis events. Samaranch agreed that there was a great deal to discuss in connection with all these matters, but that it was futile to do so until the number of sports to be given to the North had been settled. He added that he supported the position of Siperco and Coupat during their recent visit to Seoul.

Later that afternoon the North Korean delegation returned. It was asked to advise the IOC of its reaction to the IOC offer made that morning. Kim Yu Sun referred back to the first joint discussions in October 1985, in association with which details had been given regarding free circulation between the North and the South. It was proposed to open roads, railways, and airways to ensure the possibility of free travel for all those concerned in the Games. The question of free circulation was of vital importance to the successful staging of the Games in both parts of the Korean peninsula. He hoped this would clarify the position of the North Koreans, as doubt seemed constantly to be expressed about whether free circulation would be feasible, and he did not want this issue to be an obstacle to the continuation of the discussions. He expressed, for his own delegation's part, concern that the authorities in the South had not thus far guaranteed free circulation to athletes, officials, and journalists from North Korea. Referring to Samaranch's request for the IOC delegation to cross to South Korea at Panmunjom, a telex had been forwarded to the IOC that clearly stated why the request could not be granted.

He thanked Samaranch for the adjustments made to the IOC's original proposal and appreciated this gesture as a contribution toward fruitful discussions and a step toward the progress to be achieved. His delegation had considered carefully the allocation of sports to be granted to the South and the North. Only as a result of cohosting the Games could a contribution be made toward the development of the Olympic Movement and the reunification of Korea. His NOC had clarified on various occasions the number of full sports that it hoped to stage and had put forward "flexible alternatives" that took into account the viewpoint of the South Koreans. However, out of a total of twenty-three sports and 237 events, North Korea wanted to host a minimum of eight full sports, since allocation of fewer sports would be meaningless and would "subordinate" organization of events in Pyongyang to those hosted in Seoul.

With regard to soccer, his NOC had, from the outset, attached importance to the staging of soccer competitions in the North and had, in fact, approached FIFA in respect to this. The delegation hoped sincerely that soccer would be one of the sports allocated to the North. Chang Ung, secretary-general of the NOC, intervened at this point to provide some further clarifications regarding soccer, since the question had been broached. Their NOC had hoped that the allocation of sports and events would be decided upon during the second round of talks with the IOC, but this had not been the case. The deadline for applications for the preliminary tournament in the Asia region had been set at April 30, 1986. If their NOC had put forward an entry, this would have been interpreted as a withdrawal of its proposal to host the soccer tournament in the North. In response to FIFA's inquiry concerning why it had not entered its team, North Korea had reiterated its wish to host the soccer competitions.[15] He felt the North Koreans should be given the responsibility of organizing some of the more popular sports and sincerely hoped that soccer might be given to the North.

Samaranch said they would be informed of the IOC's position the following morning.

The first meeting on the morrow was with the South Koreans. Samaranch said the IOC had decided to maintain the offer made the previous day to the North. Kim Chong Ha wanted to be sure that the offer was the same as it was the previous day. It was.

Kim Chong Ha expressed deep gratitude for the IOC's efforts and cooperative gestures to date, the time that had been devoted to his delegation, and the good advice and encouragement it had received. It was their intention to try to make the Games the greatest in history. In the bilateral meeting yesterday, they had been asked to consider the possibility of granting women's volleyball and the cycling road race to the North. This fourth round of talks could produce fruitful results if the parties dealt with the practical aspects on the basis of the IOC's proposal. The North was virtually ignoring the IOC's proposals and was asking the South to make unrealistic concessions. In the circumstances, Kim Chong Ha was only prepared to reconfirm his position and to state that they would study the proposal in a positive way, if the North was to withdraw its claim to cohost the Games, to open up its borders, and to agree unconditionally to take part in the Opening and Closing Ceremonies in Seoul.

This was a sufficient basis upon which Samaranch could proceed. The South Korean delegation had the full right, Samaranch said, to consider the matter. He asked for a written reply by the end of August.

[15] This explanation is not consistent with the facts as determined by FIFA, which showed that the DPRK *had* entered the tournament and simply failed to show up for its scheduled match.

The sending of the invitations to the Games was to be on September 17. That would not necessarily mean an end to the discussions, but it was a "very important" date for the IOC. The delegation would receive an official letter from the IOC containing the statement issued at the end of the meeting. Several meetings were scheduled for the same day the invitations were to be sent. The invitation ceremony would be held at 12:00 noon, and both the KOC and the SLOOC were invited to be present in whatever numbers they wished.

Ten minutes later, the North arrived for its final bilateral meeting of the fourth talks. Samaranch reiterated the revised offer; if the North Koreans were to accept this proposal, the IOC would call a fifth joint meeting to discuss other issues such as free circulation, formation of an Organizing Committee, television coverage, and so forth. The IOC would not issue a deadline for receipt of acceptance, but asked the North Koreans to bear in mind the "significant" date of September 17 for the sending out of invitations to the NOCs for participation in the Games. The IOC "recommended" that a reply be forwarded as soon as possible before that date.

Samaranch once again drew the attention of the North Korean delegation to the fact that the IOC was sensitive to the point of view that the delegation had expressed and was, in allocating the organization of sports to the North, going against the principles laid down in the Olympic Charter. Its proposal was historic in that, for the first time, and contrary to the rules in the Charter, the Games would be celebrated in two countries. The IOC was disappointed that the North Koreans did not seem to attach sufficient importance to the possibility of organizing Olympic competitions in the North. They were urged to study the IOC's proposal attentively and to provide an answer as soon as this was possible.

Kim Yu Sun said that his delegation had attached great importance to the fourth round of negotiations in the expectation of reaching an agreement in principle on this occasion. During the visit of the IOC delegation in May, views relating to the denomination of the Games, the composition of an Organizing Committee, television rights, and Opening and Closing Ceremonies were "not far opposed."[16] The ques-

[16] It is impossible to imagine how he could have gained this impression, particularly since he had already acknowledged that the report prepared by Siperco and Coupat reflected the discussions that had occurred. In any event, the IOC delegation had merely been exploring what the DPRK wanted, insofar as it wanted anything, and had certainly not been negotiating on behalf of the IOC.

tion of allocation of sports and events remained the most difficult problem. His delegation was grateful for the new proposal that had come out of the meetings and appreciated Samaranch's and the IOC's efforts toward an initiative that would be a landmark in the development of the Olympic Movement. His NOC hoped that the Games would be cohosted by the North and the South.

They recommended that the IOC not restrict the deliberations to practical concerns of whether or not to increase the number of sports and events to be organized in the North, but should ensure a broader basis for discussion, such as Korea as a divided nation and the possibility of a new development in the history of the Olympic Movement. North Kim hoped that the IOC would study the requests made by his NOC and work toward a final agreement in light of this. Samaranch took note of the delegation's appreciation of the IOC's efforts.

Ambassador Chin intervened to say that he thought that there should be no conditions attached to the calling of a further round of discussions. He said that all the issues connected to the celebration of the Olympic competitions in the North should be examined, since they were interlinked. It was his view that the discussion should not focus upon the sports or events that would be awarded to the North, since this represented only one facet of the issue. By imposing conditions to which agreement must be granted before negotiations could proceed, the IOC was creating unnecessary obstacles to the progress of the talks.

Samaranch was brief and to the point: North Korea must accept the IOC's proposal regarding the sports and events before discussion of any other points could begin.

The final portion of the meeting with both delegations was, essentially, a matter of protocol, in which everybody thanked everybody and the IOC read out to the parties the statement that would be released to the press shortly thereafter. The closing speeches were short and, by now, entirely predictable. South Kim referred back to the Baden-Baden decision and supported the IOC in its position as mediator. North Kim thought the amendments were a step forward, that his NOC had advanced concrete suggestions advocating cohosting of the Games, and he hoped that all parties would study the recommendations set forth by his delegation, leading to further talks to be held in a spirit of cooperation toward a fruitful conclusion.

The press communiqué issued by the IOC set out, of course, the elements of the new proposal but was principally designed for the real audience on the diplomatic sidelines. It contained, therefore, a number of messages that the IOC wanted to be sure these observers would understand. The first sentence made it clear that the meeting, as was the case with the previous meetings, had occurred at the IOC's initiative and at its headquarters in Lausanne. The man in charge was Samaranch. The delegations were the respective NOCs of North Korea and South Korea. The discussions were held in a cordial and constructive atmosphere. The parties exchanged their points of view, while both emphasized their efforts to ensure the complete success of the Games. North Korea, too, was co-opted into this joint exercise.

The IOC called specific attention to its commitment made in Baden-Baden in 1981, in accordance with the Olympic Charter, to the city of Seoul, which was entrusted with the honor of "holding"[17] the Games. The IOC drew to the attention "of all concerned" its tireless and continual efforts to ensure the success of the Games and the participation of all NOCs. It pointed out that the IOC had adjusted its previous proposals, taking into consideration the evolution of the discussions during the four meetings, the observations made by the IOC delegation following its visits to Pyongyang and Seoul, and the IOC's recent consultations with the IFs and NOCs. The proposal was then outlined.

The acceptance of the IOC's proposal by the two parties concerned should be received at the IOC headquarters in Lausanne as soon as possible, given that the invitations to take part in the Games would be sent out "by the IOC" to the NOCs on September 17. The clear implication of this statement was that if there was no agreement in place with the North, the invitations would refer only to Seoul. Upon the IOC's receipt of the acceptances from the two parties, the other questions relating to the organization of these competitions would be the subject of meetings that would immediately be convened upon the direction of the IOC.

Finally, the IOC "points out and stresses" the exceptional and unprecedented character of its proposal in the history of the Olympic Movement. For the "real" audience, this was not a subtle message. The IOC would expect a quid pro quo flowing from them.

[17] The expression "hosting" was avoided on this occasion as one that was too politically charged in the circumstances.

CHAPTER 11

Invitations Go Out; Acceptances Come In

IT CAME as little surprise to anyone that no agreement was reached between the two Koreas before the IOC was to send out the invitations to the 1988 Olympic Games on September 17, 1988.

On August 10, 1987, Kim Yu Sun of North Korea sent a response to Samaranch following the fourth joint meeting.[1] Samaranch had kept the pressure on by sending a letter on July 16, containing the IOC proposal, so not to have any gap in the IOC's efforts to keep matters moving forward.[2] The text of Kim's letter was faxed to him the same day, which was just as well, since the letter itself did not arrive in Lausanne until August 20.

Kim Yu Sun regretted that there had been no agreement reached at the fourth joint meeting, contrary to their expectations. He was concerned with the public statement of "some people concerned directly" with the talks that they could not change their "intrinsic positions" at all "nor were there any possibilities to promote even in case of agree-

[1] This was followed by a press conference on August 11, indicating the DPRK's dissatisfaction with the IOC proposal and a demand for a fifth joint meeting.

[2] On July 27, the DPRK ambassador to Beijing, Sin In Ha, gave a press conference at the DPRK embassy and stated that the USSR, China, and other Communist countries supported the DPRK's desire to cohost the Games but stated that they had not promised to boycott the Games if they were held only in Seoul. Coincidently, on the same day, an Olympic delegation from the USSR NOC was in Seoul to begin meetings with SLOOC officials and review preparations for the Games. On August 4, the DPRK indicated its dissatisfaction with the IOC proposal and demanded a fifth joint meeting prior to September 17. Assistant Foreign Minister Park Soo Gil responded for the South on August 6, saying that the South might be willing to accept proposals to transfer additional events to the North if it were to accept the IOC proposals made at the fourth joint meeting. The DPRK ambassador in Beijing held another press conference on August 10, for Communist journalists, to explain the reduced demands by the DPRK.

ment being reached." He carried on to say that the only way out to overcome the difficulties was "for all parties to this to show each other magnanimity and elasticity in the spirit of sincere cooperation."

On the basis of "serious study" of the IOC's adjusted proposal, his NOC had a new proposal: it proposed to host five full sports and one partial sport by "drastically reducing" the demand for eight sports. This meant, he said, that they "fully agreed" to the IOC proposal (table tennis and archery, full sports; and women's volleyball, partial sport). In addition to this, however, they demanded three more full sports, including soccer. They wanted the full soccer tournament because only one group of the tournament was "too partial" and wanted the individual cycling road event to be replaced by another. On top of that, they wanted another full sport.

Secondly, in order to "create an atmosphere of trust and cooperation" and to "promote the process of agreement," they wanted to discuss at the next joint meeting all the important problems such as the events, denomination of the Games, composition of the Organizing Committee, Opening and Closing Ceremonies, television rights, and "so on."

Thirdly, they wanted the fifth joint meeting to be held in August, if possible, or before September 17, the date on which the invitations to the Games would be sent by the IOC.[3]

Samaranch replied on August 24. It was a short letter. He simply stated the obvious: Kim Yu Sun's letter could not be considered an answer to the proposal made on July 15 as confirmed in the letter of July 16. The IOC would be pleased to call a fifth joint meeting but only upon receipt of the DPRK's full acceptance of the IOC's "important and historical" proposal. He expressed himself as fully confident that the parties, working in the best interest of the Olympic Movement, might still be able to reach a final agreement "in time."[4]

[3] The usual number of background activities had preceded this exchange. On July 23, the DPRK had proposed that the two Koreas and the United States meet in Geneva to discuss mutual arms reductions. This did not receive much support from South Korea; on August 3, Park Soo Gil proposed that the two foreign ministers meet but rejected the DPRK proposal as a "typical propaganda piece." The formal statement was more neutral and simply indicated the points that South Korea wanted to discuss, without discussing the DPRK agenda. New York was proposed as the place for the meeting, where both would be present for the opening of the UN session; the Olympics were not mentioned.

[4] It was an interesting period in the entire exercise. There were already some signs that the international sports organizations were not wholly pleased with the prospect of events in North Korea. As early as June 22, a spokesperson for FILA (the international wrestling federation), Toshimisu Azuma, had stated that there would be no wrestling competitions in the 1988 Olympics if they were to be held in North Korea. By August 22, the president of FIAC (the international cycling federation), Valery Syssoev (a Soviet), telexed Samaranch to advise that because they had

Kim Yu Sun did not respond until August 30, 1987; the fax of the message reached the IOC on August 31. He regretted the condition established by Samaranch for the holding of the fifth joint meeting. He said there was no doubt about the differences between the parties to the talks, but that the meetings held under Samaranch's chairmanship were "in the course of coming near the certain agreement." Such a meeting gave him the confidence that they might manage even now to find a key to "slash differences and reach a final agreement," were the parties to sit together once again and discuss the matter in a "cordial and open-minded way, respecting the views of each other." He urged Samaranch to call another joint meeting as soon as possible.

If it was impossible for Samaranch to call the meeting before September 17, "for some unavoidable reasons," he asked him to put off sending the invitations to the Games until such a meeting could be held.[5]

Samaranch responded on September 4. He regretted that Kim Yu Sun had not found it appropriate to accept the IOC's important and historical proposal of July 15, which would have enabled the IOC to call a fifth joint meeting quickly. He acknowledged Kim's kind remarks about his efforts to find a solution and assured him the IOC would continue to make every effort to achieve that goal. If Kim Yu Sun was ready to accept the IOC's offer, Samaranch was ready to convene a meeting with the DPRK delegation in Lausanne on October 7 in order to establish the points that could be discussed at a possible fifth meeting between both Korean delegations. Finally, Samaranch was sure that Kim, as a member of the Olympic Family, would understand that it was absolutely impossible to postpone the ceremony on September 17, since the date was stipulated in the Olympic Charter.

Kim Yu Sun's rejoinder was dated September 15. He claimed that a "due answer" was again not given to their "earnest proposal" to convene an early fifth joint meeting, in respect of which he expressed great disappointment and regret. He presumed that the inability to accept

---

learned the DPRK had renounced holding any Olympic cycling events, the FIAC Congress scheduled for two days later planned to advise all national federations that all competitions would take place in the South. This response from the IFs was as broad as it was long; on the one hand, it showed support of the IOC in its efforts to help the Seoul Games and the consensus in favor of the Games. On the other, it was potentially disquieting for Samaranch, since he did not want the individual sport federations taking unilateral actions that might interfere with the process he was managing so delicately, and that might force North Korea into a corner too early and provoke precipitous action on its part.

[5] A press conference was held by the DPRK NOC on August 31, to advise that it had requested the IOC to postpone sending the invitations.

the proposal was "connected to some extent with the disagreement between us and the South Korean side." Therefore, he considered it necessary to hold bilateral talks between the two NOCs concerned.

The telex was, to say the least, somewhat garbled. It stated:

> Therefore in our endeavours to seek various ways of solution we came to conclusion that it is necessary to hold bilateral talk represented by the NOCs of the North and South of Korea which are directly concerned in Lausanne joint meeting for having arranged solution decisive of convocation of the 5th joint meeting before the deadlock of the joint meeting imbued with our painstaking efforts will become worse. Motivated by this we sent South Korea a letter containing our proposal on holding immediately North-South bilateral talk in the frame of the tripartite meeting for narrowing different views in Lausanne or other convenient places, followed by the 5th joint meeting for reaching final agreement. Once difficult problems are solved at the North-South bilateral talk, it will be much easy for three parties to reach final agreement at the 5th joint meeting and help the IOC in its work to a certain extent.[6]

Kim Yu Sun hoped that Samaranch would actively help the north-south direct negotiation. He reiterated his request that the sending of the invitations to the Games be put off; this would be one of the "good conditions" of the talks.

In Korea, on August 15, President Chun Doo Hwan, during his Forty-second Liberation Day message, called for resumption of the suspended north-south dialogue and urged the DPRK to participate in the 1988 Games. On August 21, he warned that he would not tolerate any more major social or economic upheaval that might sully the Republic of Korea's record of achievement under his administration. By September 3, Roh Tae Woo and Kim Young Sam had agreed on dates for direct presidential elections. These would be held on December 16.

[6] This effort was part of a flurry of activity generated by the DPRK as it became evident that the IOC would be sending the invitations to the Games as scheduled. On September 9, an article in *Rodong Shinmun* warned of increasing tensions if the Games were to be held only in South Korea. On September 10, the North Koreans suggested that the real deadline for successful negotiations might be January 17, 1988 (the date replies were due from the NOCs), rather than the date the invitations were to be sent. On September 11, North Kim said he would be sending a letter to the KOC, requesting bilateral meetings between the Korean NOCs prior to the fifth joint meeting. On September 12, South Kim announced he would pick up the letter at Panmunjom on September 15. South Korea was in no hurry to start such negotiations, was suspicious of them, and, in any event, was going to do nothing to interfere with the sending of the invitations to the Games on September 17.

* * *

The invitations to the Games of the XXIVth Olympiad were sent from the IOC's headquarters at Château de Vidy in Lausanne on September 17, 1987, exactly one year prior to the Opening Ceremony, as called for in the Olympic Charter, in accordance with the decision made by the IOC in its special Session held in Lausanne in December 1984. Both the SLOOC and the KOC were present. The DPRK was not.[7]

South Korean president Chun Doo Hwan had transmitted a message to Samaranch for the occasion, bearing the same date, assuring him of the successful staging of the Games. He thanked Samaranch and the members of the IOC for their support and assured them that all aspects of the Games were well under way, including security,[8] facilities, organization, and management, through the concerted efforts of the people and government of the Republic of Korea.

Samaranch made a brief speech at the ceremony, in which he reviewed the efforts of the people of Korea since the decision of the IOC in Baden-Baden in 1981 when the Games were awarded to the city of Seoul. He noted that they and the SLOOC had totally dedicated themselves to ensuring the greatest success of the Games and were preparing unparalleled facilities so that all athletes could take part under the best possible conditions.

In referring to the political dimensions, he stated:

> As you are all aware, during the last three years, there have been many discussions in this respect, particularly in order to provide all members of the Olympic Family with the best possible conditions to take part in the Games. Under the auspices of the IOC, there have been four joint meetings in Lausanne between the delegations of the NOCs of the Republic of Korea and the Democratic People's Republic of Korea. Last year the IOC made a generous and I would even say a very important and historical offer to this country.

[7] Only five days prior to sending out the invitations, Samaranch was on an official visit to Syria to attend the Tenth Mediterranean Games. While there, he announced that the IOC would keep negotiating with both Koreas and would not "close the door." This was a propitious place from which to counter a radio report that had emanated from Radio Pyongyang, monitored in Tokyo on August 5, in which it was reported that Syrian vice president Abdel Halim Khaddam had declared to DPRK minister of foreign affairs Kim Yong Nam during the latter's visit to Syria in July that Syria might boycott the Games.

[8] This was the first aspect noted, in response, no doubt, to the alleged concerns that had led to the Soviet boycott of the Los Angeles Games, the previous withdrawal of the 1966 Asian Games from Korea, and the general concerns related to the situation in South Korea, both domestic and in its relationship with North Korea.

> We have not yet reached a final agreement, but the ceremony today should not be misinterpreted as meaning there will not be one. I can assure you that the IOC will always keep the door open until the very last moment, as we should be more than pleased to see all 167 NOCs of the world taking part in these historical Olympic Games.

Following the ceremony, Samaranch replied to Kim Yu Sun's telex of September 15. He said that though the IOC appreciated the opportunity for continued communication with his NOC, the IOC was still waiting for a positive response to the important and historic proposal of July 15. He also advised North Kim that, in accordance with the provisions of the Olympic Charter, the IOC had sent the official invitations to all 167 NOCs to participate in the Games of the XXIVth Olympiad that day. The invitation was signed by Samaranch as president of the IOC. He had also included with each invitation an accompanying letter referring to the negotiations, under the auspices of the IOC, between both NOCs on the Korean peninsula and the possibility of an agreement that might be reached in the future regarding events to be organized in the territory of Kim's NOC. He was sure this would demonstrate the IOC's continued willingness to discuss the matter and to keep the door open for agreement until the last moment.

Kim Yu Sun did not reply until October 2, when he referred to a meeting with Samaranch in Soukhoumi[9] and welcomed Samaranch's mention of a bilateral meeting between the IOC and the DPRK NOC. He thought, however, that North Korea and South Korea were so far apart on the matter of cohosting and that the failure to reduce the differences between them was due to the fact that the South "has been obstinate in opposing our proposal." They had proposed, on September 12, a bilateral meeting, but the South had turned down the idea in a letter dated September 24.[10] As North Kim stated: "She said that the

[9] This was the thirty-sixth meeting of Socialist Ministers of Sport, held in Soukhoumi, USSR, on September 21–23. At this meeting, the DPRK had denounced the IOC's sending of the invitations to the 1988 Olympic Games. Samaranch had attended this meeting, in accordance with his normal practice. The meeting, as might be expected, endorsed the idea that the Games should be shared between North Korea and South Korea and that a positive solution to the matter should be pursued. The press communiqué issued upon the conclusion indicated that this was the seventh time Samaranch had attended such meetings and that he had explained in person the progress to date in the meetings of the two Korean NOCs under the auspices of the IOC. Notwithstanding the terms of the communiqué, the USSR was very pleased with the actions of the IOC. Samaranch had read the entire IOC proposal in response to the DPRK criticism.

[10] The sending of the DPRK letter of September 12 had been preceded by an announcement by North Kim on September 11 that he would be delivering a letter to the KOC at Panmunjom the

holding of the bilateral talk might have embroiled the problem worse confounded." He said the North had once again suggested to the South that a bilateral meeting be held and asked Samaranch to wait until they heard from South Korea.[11]

Samaranch replied the same day, simply stating that the IOC was still waiting for an answer to the letter of September 17 and reminding Kim Yu Sun that time was passing very quickly.

In separate political developments at the time, the U.S. assistant secretary of state advised the Korean foreign minister Choi Kwang Soo on September 14 that, during a visit to Moscow the previous week, he had asked Soviet officials to use their influence over the DPRK to cause the DPRK to accept the IOC's proposal to stage some of the events of the Games in the North. During an interview with the leader of the Japanese socialist party on September 26, Kim Il Sung expressed the hope that direct dialogue with the United States might occur. On September 28, the powerful European Broadcasting Union, holder of the European television rights to the Games, advised Samaranch that organization of events in the DPRK could have serious logistical and financial consequences for broadcasters of the Games. And, in early October, the Japanese Red Army issued a statement saying that the Games were being used as part of the new Japanese imperialist strategy for Asia.

During the course of his visit to Korea in the middle of November 1987, Samaranch attempted to arrange a meeting with the leaders of

---

next day. South Kim had advised Samaranch on September 22 that he would be sending a letter to North Kim on September 24. The letter urged the DPRK NOC to accept the IOC's latest proposal. The KOC had advised the IOC that it accepted the revised proposal arising out of the fourth joint meeting on August 17. The KOC view of the proposal was that negotiating in the absence of the IOC was intended by the DPRK to weaken the South's position. This was a view shared by Chun Doo Hwan, who wrote separately to Samaranch on the subject.

[11] North Kim announced on October 2 that he was sending a letter to the KOC, which could be picked up on October 3. South Kim indicated that he would receive this letter on October 12. North Kim acknowledged the new date on October 6 and agreed to change the date for receipt of his letter. North Kim's letter urged the KOC to agree to a second meeting between the two NOCs, as proposed by the IOC. On October 15, South Kim said he would send a letter to the DPRK NOC to be received at Panmunjom on October 16. This letter would urge the DPRK NOC, once again, to accept the IOC's revised proposal. In a memorandum sent to Samaranch on the same date, the KOC expressed its thanks that he had insisted on the acceptance by North Korea of the IOC proposal before agreeing to have a fifth joint meeting. It also expressed the view that the recent push by the DPRK NOC for bilateral talks had the ulterior motive of dividing the IOC and the KOC, since there was no "important information" as alleged by the DPRK to be brought to the IOC. The KOC wanted no more events to be allocated to the North. The DPRK NOC said the letter would be received on October 20 at Panmunjom. On October 23, the DPRK NOC issued a statement proposing postponement of negotiations for the cohosting of the Games. Little occurred after this, other than a press conference by the KOC on November 26, in which it urged the DPRK NOC to accept the IOC's proposal.

the opposition political parties, but this was not made possible by the Korean authorities. He did, however, have a secret meeting with Roh Tae Woo, Park Seh Jik, and Kim Un Yong. At the end of the trip, while in Guangzhou on November 20, Samaranch had a meeting with North Kim, who promised an answer to the IOC proposal by mid-January of 1988. On November 24, Osamu Maruoka, described as second in command in the Japanese Red Army, was arrested in Tokyo, and his plans were stated to be to travel to Korea via Osaka on December 7.

Such tensions as there were suffered an increase when a Korean Airlines aircraft was destroyed over Burma on November 29, killing all 115 passengers on board. Subsequent investigation tied the bombing to agents of the DPRK, one of whom confessed to the bombing as well as being an agent of the DPRK. Ties went as high as the "Dear Leader," Kim Jong Il, son of Kim Il Sung. From the Olympic perspective, it served to increase the isolation of the DPRK, and such support as they might have garnered, even among the socialist countries, evaporated significantly thereafter. This was reflective of the international reaction generally, even among the countries that normally gave at least vocal support to the DPRK. No one wanted to be associated with such criminal behavior.[12]

In the early part of December 1987, the United States and the USSR had a summit meeting in Washington.[13] During this meeting, the Olympic Games were discussed, and following the meeting, Deputy Assistant Secretary of State for East Asian and Pacific Affairs William Clark briefed the Republic of Korea officials on the content of the Olympic discussions.[14] On December 9, U.S. secretary of state George Shultz had explained the U.S. position that the 1988 Olympic Games

[12] I spoke with Samaranch on November 30, after his return from Japan and China, and he said he had had assurances from the top leaders in China that China would participate in Seoul. On the matter of the KAL bombing, in a conversation on December 3, I suggested that this tragedy, if linked to the DPRK, might, in a macabre way, actually help the chances of successful Games in Seoul.

[13] Samaranch had sent his by now customary telegrams on behalf of the Olympic Movement to both Reagan and Gorbachev on the eve of the summit meeting.

[14] Samaranch and I had watched the signing ceremony on television in his hotel room in Lausanne on December 8. During the evening, Samaranch said that he had suggested sanctions against nonparticipating countries in the course of his recent Far Eastern trip but had later withdrawn the idea. We had a long discussion on the issue, and he said he wanted to discuss the possibility at the Executive Board. I told him I was opposed to the idea of sanctions in the circumstances, and he asked if I would mind not speaking to that effect too early in the Executive Board discussion.

should be held without any trouble with the participation of all member countries. In response, USSR general secretary Mikhail Gorbachev mentioned briefly that the allocation of several sports to North Korea could help the Olympic Games to be held in Seoul smoothly.

During the working group meeting on regional issues, the director of policy planning staff of the U.S. State Department, Richard Solomon, expressed the hope that the Soviet Union would participate in the 1988 Olympic Games. The reply from the director of the Soviet Institute of World Economy and Internal Affairs, Primakov, was that the Soviet Union was apparently 95 percent in favor of participating. The final decision would be made in January 1988, but Soviet athletes had been in training with the intention of participating. He also noted that North Korea had proposed cohosting of the Games and expressed the hope that a number of sports would be held in North Korea, but he did not appear to link the Soviet decision on participation to the North Korean cohosting proposal.

This information was relayed to Samaranch by Ambassador Lee Sang Ock of the Permanent Mission of the Republic of Korea in Geneva on December 14, 1987. Samaranch passed on the contents of this message to the Executive Board members the next day without comment, other than to say that the information might be of assistance.

The presidential elections in the Republic of Korea were held on December 16, 1987. These were to mark the first step in the peaceful transmission of power since the republic was created. Roh Tae Woo became the president-elect, in direct elections.[15] International observers of the elections expressed themselves as satisfied that the elections were, with very few exceptions of no significance, properly carried out.

On December 23, 1987, German Rieckehoff, the IOC member in Puerto Rico, sent a telex to Cuban president Fidel Castro, urging him to use his best efforts to ensure that Cuba would participate in the Games. He reminded Castro that the Olympic Games, imperfect as they may be in some respects, were nevertheless almost the only opportunity in the world where all peoples could meet together in a spirit of

[15] Roh won with approximately 37 percent of the popular vote, which was, in the circumstances of so much political division in the country at the time, a healthy, if not overwhelming, plurality. Samaranch was so nervous about the outcome that he had Kim Un Yong call him every half hour with the results up to that point. My recollection is that Samaranch called me in turn about three or four times to pass on the latest results.

human solidarity. Samaranch, who received a copy, thanked him for his effort, which he thought was very good.

Still writing as chairman of the SLOOC on December 26, 1987, Roh Tae Woo sent greetings to Samaranch in a letter delivered through Kim Un Yong, the IOC member in Korea and a vice president of the SLOOC. Kim was delegated to discuss with Samaranch not only the preparation for the Games but also matters of international relations, including a visit of SLOOC officials to China and Eastern Europe. Roh assured Samaranch that although he was faced with an enormous amount of work and responsibilities, he would give his "utmost effort" for the success of the Games and the cause of the Olympic Movement, for which they both stood.[16]

Samaranch met with Kim Un Yong and replied to Roh on January 6, 1988. He was particularly satisfied with the state of preparations for the Games. As of the time of writing, the IOC had received confirmation of participation in the Games from 138 NOCs and was endeavoring to convince the remaining twenty-nine to participate.[17] He said he would help the SLOOC with its relationships with the socialist countries.[18] Finally, Samaranch wished Roh success upon taking office as president of the Republic of Korea on February 25, 1988. He suggested a meeting with Roh prior to the Games, preferably after the forthcoming parliamentary elections.[19]

[16] A Soviet delegation was present in Seoul on December 27–30 to agree on the accommodations to be allocated to the Soviet team, as well as on certain consular functions to be performed in Seoul. At a dinner on December 28, the Soviets predicted that 160 countries would participate in the Games.

[17] Two days previously, Soviet NOC president Marat Gramov had stated in Frankfurt that the USSR did not intend to boycott the Games; the problem of the DPRK remained to be solved, but the IOC had left the door open for further talks.

[18] Samaranch had also spoken on January 6 with the vice president of the Cuban Council of Ministers, José R. Fernandez Alvarez, to review the IOC's efforts to ensure the participation of the DPRK. Fernandez had agreed to discuss the matter with Castro, but in view of the "privileged" relationship with the DPRK, it appeared difficult to accept anything short of sharing the Games between the two countries. On January 8, Samaranch sent Fernandez a copy of his telex to Kim Yu Sun of January 6, together with the number of acceptances to date, and reminded Fernandez that the latest offer to North Korea had been based on the recommendation made by Fidel Castro.

[19] It was also helpful on the domestic Korean front that Kim Young Sam, the runner-up in the December 1987 elections, stated on January 6 that his party would do its best to make the Olympic Games the "greatest festival in the world." This was a welcome change from some of his earlier statements as a political candidate; he was, perhaps, leaving open his political options as a future (successful) presidential candidate.

* * *

1988 was not without some potentially explosive opportunities on the Korean peninsula. One example was the regular Team Spirit military exercises, involving U.S. and Korean forces. This was specifically mentioned in the New Year's message of North Korean president Kim Il Sung, which included the following:

> In view of South Korea's internal situation as well as the North-South Korean relations, not a few people are currently expressing deep concerns that 1988 may turn out to be the most tense and complicated year. Under the watchful eyes of the whole world, we should transform this year's situation of the Korean peninsula into a decisively favourable one for the cause of peace and peaceful reunification.
>
> Out of these aspirations, we maintain that through a dialogue we should resolve such issues as the termination within this year of large-scale military exercises including the joint military exercises of Team Spirit, preparation for multilateral arms-reduction talks, co-hosting of the Games of the XXIVth Olympiad by the North and South and ceasing of mutual recriminations and slanderings. Through the resolution of the above-mentioned pending issues, the North and South should make this year a historic one which will mark a new turning point for national reconciliation and solidarity.
>
> For the above purposes, we propose holding a North-South conference in which representatives from all political parties, social groups and various circles including the authorities of the two sides will participate. This joint conference between the South and North will bring down barriers between the two parts of Korea and bring about a new phase conducive to hastening the era of peace and peaceful reunification.[20]

Undoubtedly, one of the most difficult aspects of managing a complicated situation, as Samaranch was attempting in relation to the Games, is dealing with the mass of often conflicting data that bombards the

[20] During breakfast in Samaranch's room on January 26, he professed to be very worried about the DPRK, even to the point of fearing that there would be "war" if there were no eventual agreement on the Olympic question. He had sent Roh Tae Woo a letter urging that the annual Team Spirit exercises be canceled, or at least postponed until after the Games. The previous week he had met with USSR foreign minister Eduard Shevardnadze and explained the IOC proposal. Samaranch also told him that the level of the DPRK delegation was very low, having no power to negotiate, and that the IOC was willing to try to find a solution. Shevardnadze appeared to have been somewhat surprised at the level of negotiations and said he would look into it.

decision makers. Consider the letter Samaranch received from the IOC member in Malaysia, Datuk Setia Raja Tan Sri Datuk Seri Hamzah Abu Samah, dated December 23, 1987, which reached him on December 31. In this letter, Hamzah recounts a recent meeting with the South Korean ambassador in Kuala Lumpur, who was a former chairman of the dialogue between North Korea and South Korea. He reported that the ambassador had said that the South Koreans might agree to the sharing of the Opening and Closing Ceremonies, to the idea of having joint teams, to the sharing of television rights, and so on, in the forthcoming Games in Seoul. To the ambassador and many South Koreans, to have a successful and noble free Olympic Games was more important than anything else.

It was not clear whether the ambassador was expressing his personal view, a governmental view, or that of the SLOOC. The ambassador assured Hamzah, however, that this view had been expounded by all the candidates in the last general election, including Roh Tae Woo, whom Hamzah had known since the IOC Congress in Baden-Baden when Seoul won the bid to host the Games.[21]

Hamzah said that when he was in Pyongyang two months earlier, the North Koreans had been prepared to give way if they were awarded the whole of the soccer tournament. He did not think that FIFA would agree to this, but since the two Koreas were willing to have joint teams, the problem could be sorted out, and they would be happy with the preliminary tournament. They would, he said, also welcome the possibility of South Korea's wanting to concede on the question of joint Opening and Closing Ceremonies.

Hamzah offered to help solve the problem confidentially, since he was close to both parties in his capacity as Asia Football president and as a former president of the Olympic Council of Asia. Samaranch acknowledged the letter, thanked him for the information, and said he would not hesitate to let him know if he could be of assistance in resolving the question.

The proof of the pudding regarding the IOC efforts to deal with the Korean situation would come by January 17, 1988, the date when acceptances to the IOC's invitation to participate in the Seoul Games were

[21] Hamzah's recollection on this latter point does not appear to be correct, since Roh did not attend the IOC Session in Baden-Baden. He had stayed in Seoul to coordinate the efforts relating to the bid from the capital as minister in the government.

due. Reminders were sent on November 18 to ninety-one NOCs that had not yet replied. Further reminders were sent on December 18 to the forty-nine NOCs that had not replied by that date. On January 5, a reminder was sent to the twenty-one NOCs that had not yet accepted, and on January 10, the IOC sent a reminder that the last date for acceptances was January 17 to the ten NOCs that had still not replied.

It was a matter of some relief to Samaranch that East Germany accepted to participate in the Games and officially notified the IOC by letter dated December 21, 1987, of its decision. Manfred Ewald forwarded the acceptance and in his covering letter said the announcement was made on the assumption that the Games would be organized on the basis of the Olympic Charter and would contribute toward strengthening the unity of the Olympic Movement, understanding between nations, and the maintaining of world peace. His NOC would, furthermore, support the efforts of the IOC aimed at making it possible to hold the Olympic events in both parts of Korea.

Typical of the communications that Samaranch was receiving at the critical period in early January, prior to the official deadline for notification of participation, was a telex received from President Kenneth David Kaunda of the Republic of Zambia dated January 6, urging him to allocate a reasonable number of sports to the North. Copies of this message were sent to presidents Chun Doo Hwan and Kim Il Sung. (Samaranch later got a letter of the same date delivered through the Zambian embassy in Bonn, in which the copies of the letter were shown as having been sent to Kim Il Sung and Roh Tae Woo as president-elect of South Korea.) Kaunda did not hesitate to note that one of the many capacities in which he sent the message was as chairman of the Frontline States and the Organization of African Unity.

Samaranch replied on January 11, thanking Kaunda for his interest in the matter and congratulating Zambia for having accepted the invitation to take part in the Games. He assured him that the IOC would do everything in its power to enable every country to take part. He reviewed the two years of negotiations, the proposal made by the IOC in July 1987, and the fact that the IOC was still waiting for a reply from the DPRK. He noted that 144 NOCs had confirmed their participation, already a record, and that the IOC expected still more before January 17.[22]

[22] Both the USSR and China announced their participation in the Games on January 11. The USSR statement still supported the sharing of the Games but said the number of sports to be allocated to the North was for the IOC to decide. The DPRK situation had, the statement said, not been discussed by the Soviet NOC. South Korea followed these announcements with supportive

* * *

Everyone was watching the count of acceptances as the deadline approached. Lord Killanin wrote to Samaranch on January 5, saying how delighted he was that Marat Gramov, president of the USSR NOC and Soviet minister of sport, had followed East Germany and Hungary by indicating acceptance. He would be keeping his fingers crossed until all the acceptances were in. Samaranch, he said, had had a "very trying and difficult time," and he hoped that the pessimism Samaranch had expressed would not be justified.[23] He felt that Samaranch had done "more than enough in regard to North Korea as the Games were allotted to Seoul." He would see him the next month at the Olympic Winter Games in Calgary.

That there would be certain refusals to attend was known to almost all the close observers of the situation. Cuba had made it clear it would not participate unless the north-south situation was resolved. The DPRK was clearly not going to attend unless the negotiations were successful from its perspective.[24] It was also likely, because of the relationship between Cuba and Nicaragua, that the Cuban influence would result in nonacceptance by Nicaragua. Sure enough, on January 16, Moises Hassan, president of the Nicaraguan NOC, telexed Samaranch to advise him that his NOC would not participate. He cited as reasons for the decision the lack of concentration on sport due to the hostilities in his country, nonqualification of their best athletes through the Pan American Games, and the bad economic situation in the country.[25]

Samaranch replied to the telex the next day, stating that even a

---

announcements of its own. It said that it would permit the USSR and other socialist countries with which it had no diplomatic relations to transport athletes and officials on their own planes or ships. It confirmed the previous secret arrangement that the USSR would be permitted to bring a ship to Inchon and to use it as its "main supply base" for its Olympic athletes. The USSR published the decision of the DPRK not to participate in the Games without comment. Politically, the Korean opposition parties and the U.S. State Department all welcomed the Soviet decision to participate.

[23] Samaranch was resolutely pessimistic regarding the Seoul Games. It was as if he did not want to allow himself to believe that the matters were under control in case that might cause him to relax and be caught unaware if something unexpected were to develop. He was similarly pessimistic about Sarajevo, Los Angeles, Calgary, Albertville, Barcelona, and Lillehammer. He is well along the way to being pessimistic about Atlanta and Nagano. By the time of publication, he will already be mildly pessimistic about whichever host city has been chosen for the Games in the year 2000.

[24] The DPRK NOC issued a statement of its intention to boycott the Games on January 12.

[25] The actual letter from Hassan did not reach the IOC until March 22. In his reply to the letter, Samaranch merely repeated the contents of his telexed reply described in the next paragraph.

symbolic presence of Nicaragua would be very positive. He found it strange that Nicaragua would have participated in the Games in Los Angeles, the Central American and Caribbean Games, and the Pan American Games the year before, while the country was in the same circumstances as the present. He reminded the NOC that through the IOC program of Olympic Solidarity there were funds available for at least eight persons as well as a grant for equipment and supplies. He asked them to reconsider their decision once again and reminded them that the NOC would not share in any of the Olympic Solidarity funds for the period of 1988–1992 if it did not participate in the Games. He was certainly not prepared to let stand without comment such a feeble rationalization of a political decision not to participate. The request had no effect.[26]

The DPRK decision not to participate was officially communicated to Samaranch in a letter dated January 11, 1988, signed by Kim Yu Sun. Samaranch, to keep the pressure on the DPRK, had sent a special telex to Kim on January 6, reminding him that Ambassador Chin had asked, during his meeting with Samaranch on October 19, 1987, for a delay until mid-December to answer the IOC proposal of July 16. Samaranch had agreed to wait but now wanted a reply. The letter from Kim Yu Sun was received in Lausanne on January 26.[27] He stated that they could not participate in the Games to be "singly" hosted by the South Korean side and that this being the case there was no possibility for them to accept the invitation. He was sorry that this was the outcome, but it was the only measure they could take "because of the failure of agreement on the cohosting question we ardently desired for." However, he went on to say: "But we do not think that it is our last effort to effect the Olympic cohosting and inform you that we still have hope for its possibility."

Kim Yu Sun referred to the New Year address of the respected leader Kim Il Sung and his call for a north-south joint conference to discuss "some immediate problems for national reunification and détente in-

[26] A broadcast by Radio Pyongyang, monitored in Tokyo on March 24, 1987, stated that following a visit by Nicaraguan president Daniel Ortega to Pyongyang, Ortega had declared to the DPRK vice president and minister of foreign affairs that Nicaragua would not take part in the Games unless they were cohosted by North Korea and South Korea.

[27] The news, as such, of its decision not to participate was derived from the press announcement by the DPRK on January 12.

cluding the problem of north-south cohosting of the XXIVth Olympiad." He thought that if this conference were to be held and would take measures for the solution of the cohosting problem, a subsequent joint meeting in Lausanne might lead to a final agreement. Interestingly enough, North Kim appeared to acknowledge that the DPRK had not answered the IOC's July 1987 offer: "We hope that you will also await our answer to the IOC's proposal requested in your telex dated July 15 [*sic*], until the north-south negotiation will be held."[28]

On January 28, Samaranch replied, saying how disappointed he was with the decision. The IOC was, however, willing to further await their reply to the historic and important proposal made on July 15, 1987. He emphasized and drew North Kim's attention to the fact that time was passing very quickly and that each day gone rendered the possibility of any agreement more and more remote. He reiterated the statement made at the IOC press conference on January 18 that, even though the deadline for inscriptions had passed, the IOC was still ready to reach an agreement that would enable his NOC to participate in the Games.

The Cuban decision was communicated by Castro himself in a letter dated January 13, 1988. It was a full three pages, rehashing the earlier efforts on his part to bring about some sense of compromise, acknowledging Samaranch's efforts in the same direction, commenting on the political situation in South Korea (which he decried), and concluding with the decision not to attend.[29]

> The National Olympic Committee and government of Cuba have decided not to enter, that is to say simply not to commit ourselves to the Games. Although we deeply regret this unavoidable decision, our people and our athletes, whose conduct is always governed by profound ethical considerations and a deep sense of honour, will not be disheartened and will continue to train for the Olympic Games in Barcelona in 1992, assuming

[28] On January 19, after all the acceptances were received, SLOOC president Park Seh Jik announced that the SLOOC would continue to keep the door open for the DPRK to participate in the Games.

[29] Samaranch told me in a conversation on January 7 that he had spoken with Manuel Gonzales Guerra, the IOC member in Cuba, and Conrado Martinez, the sports minister, who had appeared to want to participate in the Games. The final decision, however, would be made by Castro himself.

> that no punitive action is taken against us for having behaved in such a dignified manner. We wish nevertheless to inform you, dear friend Samaranch, that taking into account your great interest in our participation, should the miracle of ensuring a safe and non-violent celebration of the Games in Seoul happen, and should you with your characteristic tenacity manage to achieve a co-hosting of the Games, we should be prepared to reconsider our decision, provided that, in those circumstances, the IOC would esteem the humble participation of Cuba to be worthwhile.
>
> I should like you to know that for Cuba, the moral principles of the people are of more importance than the excitement of the Olympic Games and the gold medals to be won.

Castro's letter did not arrive in Lausanne until January 21, and Samaranch waited until February 16 to answer, which he did from Calgary, Canada, where he was attending the Olympic Winter Games. The reply was only one page. He was sorry that the decision was made, since once again Cuban athletes would not be present at the greatest sporting event in the world. He reminded Castro that after their last conversation, he had improved the offer to the DPRK as Castro had requested, but that this had not brought about a definitive solution to the problem. He said he intended to go to Pyongyang himself to see if he could make a last effort to achieve a solution. He said that even though the deadline had passed, the IOC was continuing to leave the door open, although the time was passing very quickly and a solution would have to be found as soon as possible. He urged Castro to reconsider his own position.

By the time of the deadline for acceptance of the invitations to participate in Seoul, 161 of the 167 NOCs recognized by the IOC had accepted. It was, by any measure, a stunning accomplishment for the Olympic Movement and for the Republic of Korea, in its struggle for the international recognition that it had sought in hosting the Games.

Acceptances were one thing, however, and actual participation in the Games another. How "soft" were some of the acceptances, and how many had been sent in simply to preserve flexibility rather than as definitive promises of attendance? For that matter, how was the new Roh government going to fare in the elections for the National Assembly later that year? Would public opinion in Korea rally behind the Games as they grew nearer? Would the volatile DPRK be kept under control, either on its own initiative or under "counsel" from its Chinese and Soviet allies?

It was certain, regardless of one's view of the eventual outcome, that the work was far from over. The initial "sale" of the Seoul Olympics had been made from an attractive catalog, but the "goods" had neither been paid for nor delivered. Both the IOC and the Republic of Korea would have an anxious eight months ahead of them.

CHAPTER 12

Keeping the Acceptances and Chasing the Strays

THERE WAS TIME to draw breath, once the acceptances were in, but only just. As is often the case when fighting a perceptional battle, the small things that go wrong assume an exaggerated importance, out of all proportion to the vast majority of successes. Thus, the few NOCs that did *not* accept the invitation drew almost all of the media attention, not the 161 that had agreed to participate. The IOC had little alternative but to play in the same ballpark and to try to grab its share of the headlines that might result from the "conversion" of those who had not accepted the invitations in the first place. It mattered little that the nonacceptances, with the exception of Cuba, were by countries having marginal importance as sporting nations. The DPRK was, naturally, a special case and could be expected to have a few good athletes, as might Ethiopia. Nicaragua, Albania, and the Seychelles would not have been noticed at all.

Several of the Latin American countries were offended by the Cuban decision to boycott the Games. It had been generally thought that the gesture by PASO, the regional organization of NOCs in the Americas, in awarding the 1991 Pan American Games to Havana, carried with it the concomitant understanding that Cuba would participate in the Seoul Olympics.[1] Many of the Latin American delegates who participated in that decision were of the view that it was all part of a single

[1] Even Samaranch had allowed himself some hope in this regard. Reporting to the IOC Executive Board on December 12, 1986, he thought that with the award of the 1991 Pan American Games to Havana, it would be much more difficult for Cuba to justify a boycott of the 1988 Olympic Games to the countries in the Americas.

package. There was talk of a boycott of the Pan American Games in Havana in retaliation.

The Korean ambassador in Uruguay reported that he had met with the Uruguayan NOC president and chief of the Uruguayan Sports Directorate, Julio Cesar Maglione, on February 29, who had said that the vice president of the Cuban NOC would be visiting Montevideo to ask for the participation of Uruguay in the Pan American Games. Maglione said that Uruguay would not attend those Games unless Cuba participated in the Seoul Olympics. Furthermore, there would be a PASO Executive Board meeting in Argentina in the latter part of March, and at that meeting the possibility of boycotting the Pan American Games by the Latin countries would be discussed if Cuba did not change its stand on the Seoul Olympic Games.[2] It was evident that the Cubans were aware of or worried about the possibility of removal of the Games, since on January 20, Cuban minister José R. Fernandez Alvarez issued a statement that there was no reason to suppose this would happen, either at the hands of PASO or the IOC.[3]

Ethiopia was another country that refused to participate in the Seoul Olympics, as it did in the Los Angeles Games in 1984. The South Korean reports on this suggested that the Ethiopians may have miscalculated on their boycott but were not sure how to get out of the box into which they had placed themselves.[4] Their ambassador to Ethiopia

[2] Nothing would come of this possibility regarding the 1991 Pan American Games. All the Latin American countries participated. Samaranch explored the possibility of encouraging a boycott of the Pan American Games with both Canada and the United States, but there was little interest in such action, which, if it occurred at all, should have been seen to be a Latin action directed at other Latins, not by the two large non-Latin northern powers in the Americas. Apart from this, there was a risk that this sort of action might accelerate into an action-reaction process at the time, which could have been dangerous and counterproductive. From a technical sport perspective, the Pan American Games were also qualifying competitions for some sports in the Olympic Games, which would have had an adverse effect on the Seoul Games. That there was no support for this among the Latins was evident from the statement by PASO president Mario Vazquez-Raña on January 16, 1988, to the effect that he thought the 1991 Pan American Games would still be in Havana despite the Cuban boycott of Seoul.

[3] This concern was still present later in the year. On May 21, the Cuban NOC issued a declaration that its hosting of the 1991 Pan American Games was not linked to its participation in the 1988 Olympic Games. It added to this that, in an offense to Cuba, in 1985 it had been "deprived" of its right to host the 1987 Pan American Games. More follow-up occurred on September 11, when Fidel Castro wrote to Samaranch urging that a solution be found, indicating that he would try to help prevent the DPRK from being "carried away from what is, after all, its obvious right."

[4] There had been several occasions on which this decision had been telegraphed, so it was not a matter of great surprise when it was eventually announced. In an address to the African Continental Association of NOCs (ANOCA) on December 18, 1985, the president of the Ethiopian NOC and commissioner for sports and physical culture, Tsegaw Ayele, warned of an Olympic boycott

had met with the Ethiopian ambassador to Geneva when the latter was present in Addis Ababa in late February 1988. The decision not to participate had been taken by the Party Central Committee. In view of public opinion, a considerable number of the Ethiopian leadership now regretted the decision and was searching for some pretext to modify its stand. Apparently the decision not to attend had been taken some two years previously and had not taken into account the change in stand of the other socialist countries. The Ethiopian government was closely watching the tripartite discussions and other international developments. Its statement regarding nonparticipation was amplified on January 19, to indicate that reconsideration of the decision was possible if the cohosting proposal of the DPRK were to be accepted. They were well offside and were quite aware of the corner into which they had painted themselves.

Though it was clear that Ethiopia's relations with the DPRK and its public commitments had a major influence on the decision not to participate, it was also true that Ethiopia was concerned about its reputation among the nonaligned and socialist countries. Chinese influence was greater than that of the Soviet Union and other Eastern European countries, as evidenced by President Mengistu's proposed visit to China in June 1988. On learning this, Samaranch immediately telexed He Zhenliang, the IOC member in China, suggesting that in view of this proposed visit and the possibility of a change of mind on the part of the Ethiopians, a discussion of the matter "at the highest levels" might be useful.[5]

It was important to keep the United States and the USSR firmly behind the success of the Seoul Games and to involve them in the solution to

---

if the Games were not cohosted. Samaranch had been present at the same meeting and had praised the African participation at Los Angeles, while urging the African states to avoid being manipulated by their "adversaries" to stage Olympic boycotts. On April 10, 1986, the Ethiopian head of state, Colonel Mengistu Haile Mariam, stated that Ethiopia would boycott the Games if they were not cohosted by both North Korea and South Korea. Samaranch had telexed Ayele on March 13, 1987, asking for the text of the statement that threatened a boycott. The Ethiopian statement issued on January 19, 1988, confirmed the decision not to participate, said the reason for the decision was the failure to have joint hosting of the Games; if the Games were to be staged in both countries, Ethiopia would reconsider its decision.

[5] The Chinese remained very cautious about attempts to influence countries not to follow the North Korean lead. They were perfectly well aware that any such efforts would immediately become known to the North Koreans, and they could see no advantage in souring their relationship any further than their own decisions to participate in the Asian Games and Olympic Games had already accomplished. This was certainly true in the case of a small country such as Ethiopia.

any problems that might develop in the seven or eight months leading up to the Games. On January 19, Samaranch was careful to issue a statement thanking both Reagan and Gorbachev for their efforts to lower world tensions and to acknowledge that their efforts in that direction had been at least in part responsible for so many acceptances to the Games. The gesture was not only politic but an accurate reflection of reality. The next day, while in Madrid, he met with the Soviet foreign minister, Eduard Shevardnadze, to discuss matters relating to the Games and to enlist his help in making sure that all countries would be able to participate. On January 23, Samaranch stated that he would like to meet with Soviet general secretary Gorbachev to enlist his help in solving the problem with North Korea. Each of these efforts was intended to make it difficult for the Soviets to criticize the continuing attempts of the IOC to find a solution to the problem, since on the two recent occasions, it had been asked to help in a matter that was important to one of its client states. It was made evident that their support was not merely being taken for granted; after all, it was eventual participation in the Games that really mattered.

In Korea, during the immediate postacceptance period, the complicated tango between the two sides continued. In what was his first foreign media press conference since taking office as president, Chun Doo Hwan stated that he believed that the North would gradually change its hard-line policy and agree to commence peace talks as early as 1989. A week later, on February 6, North Korean NOC secretary-general Chang Ung repeated that the desire to share the Games was part of the whole question of the reunification and that it could not be discussed except in the context of this larger issue. The SLOOC response to this the next day was simply to urge, once again, that North Korea participate in the Games. On February 8, the United States announced that it would be sending naval forces of at least one carrier group to the Sea of Japan area for exercises during the period of the Games, to discourage the North from taking any actions that might disrupt the Games.

The 1988 Olympic Winter Games were held in Calgary during February 1988 and were successful to the point of earning the ritual statement by Samaranch that they were the "greatest" Winter Games in Olympic history. On this occasion, this happened to be true. At the IOC Session immediately preceding the Games, the IOC resolved to do everything in its power to ensure full attendance at the Games in

Seoul.[6] The SLOOC itself agreed to keep the "Olympic door" open for the uncommitted NOCs. At a press conference in Calgary, the South Korean ambassador, Roh Jae Won, stated that Korea expected more violence from the North and that the proposed American naval maneuvers were fully justified. The following day, on February 11, North Korean secretary-general Chang Ung called the ambassador an "idiot" for making such a remark.

Former Japanese prime minister Nakasone met with president-elect Roh Tae Woo in Seoul on February 11 and pledged Japanese support for a terror-free Olympics and offered the services of Japan to help improve relations between South Korea and China. There was, at this time, quite a considerable effort by the Japanese to improve the difficult relationship between Japan and South Korea. Most initial visits came from Japan to Korea, and the return visits, if they occurred, seemed to require initial pilgrimages by Japanese leaders to Korea. The significance of this was not lost on either the parties or external observers. On February 16, Roh indicated that relations might be expected to improve. The same day, in the UN Security Council, Japan supported the Korean case that the blowing up of KAL flight 858 on November 29, 1987, was a clear act of state terrorism by North Korea.[7]

Roh Tae Woo was sworn in as president of the Republic of Korea on February 25, 1988. The transition of power had been accomplished peacefully, and tensions in Korea were markedly reduced. In his inaugural address, Roh stated that the door of dialogue would be kept open for the North for the sake of peace and unity on the Korean peninsula. A few days later, in his Samil Independence Day message on March 1, he said that the North would be welcomed to the Games. Within a week, U.S. assistant secretary of state Derwinski confirmed the presence of U.S. naval forces of one or two aircraft carriers at the time of the Games as a "very timely practical coincidence" in a statement made on March 6.[8]

* * *

[6] Consistent with this, Samaranch reminded Kim Yu Sun on February 10 that, though the deadline for acceptances had been January 17, the door would be kept open.

[7] On February 13, the South Koreans had issued a statement addressed to the North, demanding an apology for the bombing. In Olympic developments the same day, DPRK NOC secretary-general Chang Ung, still in Calgary, stated that the DPRK might reconsider its previous stance if the meeting proposed by the DPRK were to take place on February 19.

[8] The customary North Korean condemnation of the annual U.S.-Korean Team Spirit exercises was issued on March 23, accompanied by the imprecation that these were a serious threat to

One of the advisers in whom Samaranch continued to place great confidence throughout the period leading up to the Games was Giulio Andreotti, at the time the Italian minister of foreign affairs. They spoke and corresponded regularly, and Samaranch has always been deeply appreciative of the counsel he received. Typical was Andreotti's correspondence in late March 1988, in which he advised Samaranch of the information he had been able to glean, through diplomatic channels, regarding participation in the Games by Cuba, Albania, and Ethiopia. Samaranch thanked him warmly on March 30 and sent him a copy of his latest correspondence with Castro.

March was relatively quiet. Rumors were published on March 18 by the Hungarian Yonhap News Agency that Cuba might be rethinking its position on the Olympics. On March 24, the PASO Executive Committee gave its president, Mario Vazquez-Raña, a mandate to try to reverse the decisions of Cuba, Nicaragua, and the DPRK. Although the DPRK was clearly outside the territorial application of PASO, were the North Korean position to change, then it would naturally follow that there would be no reason for Cuba and Nicaragua to boycott. The U.S. Olympic Committee removed some of the pressure on Cuba in this regard by its announcement that it would likely attend the 1991 Pan American Games in Havana even if Cuba did not participate in the Seoul Games. This appeared to lead to further speculation from Hungarian sports officials on March 26 that Cuba might reconsider its position on participation. Vazquez-Raña visited Cuba in April and met with Castro to discuss Cuban participation. He offered to go to the DPRK for the same purpose.

On March 21, South Korean foreign minister Choi Kwang Soo advised his Japanese counterpart, Sosuke Uno, who was present in Seoul on an official visit, that the Republic of Korea would continue its efforts to ensure participation in the Games by the DPRK. Meetings were also arranged for Uno with president-elect Roh Tae Woo and with prime minister Lee Hyun Jae. April got off to a somewhat more tense beginning when, at the 442d meeting between the UN Command and the DPRK forces, called by the DPRK, DPRK major general Li Tae Ho

---

peace in Asia and the rest of the world. On April 1, the complaint was continued during the course of the 442d meeting between the DPRK and the UN Command, the meeting having been called by the DPRK. Tensions were attributed to the DPRK. On April 7, the U.S. commander in chief of forces in Japan stated that given the unpredictable nature of the North Koreans, the possibility of DPRK actions during the Games could not be ignored and stated he was ready to send additional troops if necessary.

protested against the annual Team Spirit maneuvers, claiming that such exercises could easily switch to war when the signal was given, and stated that the DPRK armed forces were on full alert. U.S. rear admiral William Pendley replied that if tension existed on the Korean peninsula, it was the fault of the DPRK.

On April 24, following a meeting of the IOC Executive Board, Samaranch announced that though the door was still open, it was now too late for those NOCs that had not accepted the invitation to the Games to participate in the team sports. Participation in individual events was still possible. On April 25, following up on an agreement reached in February in the meeting between Roh Tae Woo and Noboru Takeshita, Japan and South Korea began a two-day meeting in Tokyo to cooperate regarding possible terrorism at the Games.

On April 26, 1988, elections were held for seats in the National Assembly. Though Roh Tae Woo's Democratic Justice Party won the largest number of seats, it did not win a majority. Within two days, however, the opposition party leaders agreed with Roh's call for an Olympic truce. They agreed that there were many problems to be solved in South Korea, but there was no compelling reason why some of the solutions could not wait until after the Games. This statement, at this stage, was a very helpful and welcome indication that there would not likely be any serious disruption of the Games within South Korea or, at least, none sanctioned by any of the mainstream political parties. This was no indication that radical student groups would necessarily comply with the idea of such a truce, but it left them as marginalized as they had ever been and without any significant public support.

Perhaps because of the increased support from Japanese authorities on matters of security, there appeared to be a slight shift in the public utterances from South Korea regarding the perception of threats from North Korea. The meetings with the Japanese were critical, since it was from Japan that the easiest ingress to Korea could occur, whether from Japanese would-be terrorists or from North Koreans disguised as Japanese or South Koreans. The higher the level of security in Japan, the less likely that such intruders could make it as far as Seoul. Given the efforts to improve relations between Japan and South Korea, it was definitely in the best interests of Japan that no terrorist entering Korea be traced back to entry through Japan. A healthy mutuality of national interests had developed. The South Korean authorities began to discount the prospect of North Korean intervention and stated that their security net would be sufficient to guard against terrorism.[9]

The summer of 1988 was hot. And it seemed longer than usual, as time crawled forward toward the date of the Opening Ceremony of the Games. The focus of those concerned with the Olympics was on holding the apparent consensus together. The leverage of the countries who were not attending seemed much greater than that of the vast majority of those which were expected to participate. There were many groups having nothing to do with the Olympics, who had entirely non-Olympic political agendas, who did not hesitate to try to use the forthcoming Olympic Games as leverage to achieve their own particular objectives.

The most vociferous were radical student groups, whose primary objective was to topple the government of Roh Tae Woo. Although relatively small in number, these groups were virulent and violent in their protests and actions, trying whenever possible to provoke police response, which translated into media coverage of the worst kind for South Korea, and resorting to firebombs and other projectiles upon almost any pretext. It was only a gradual dawning of the fact that they had very little public support that led them to diminish the protests and to restrict them mainly to university campuses as the time of the Games drew near. In the interim, however, they did considerable harm to the confidence surrounding the Games and to the perception of South Korea as a stable country trying to work its way into becoming a modern democracy.

On May 14, the worst student violence since Roh Tae Woo became president occurred, ostensibly over the issue of cohosting the Games with North Korea. The violence was quelled, but the situation remained tense and uneasy. SLOOC president Park Seh Jik offered to go to North Korea to brief officials in the North about progress in the organization of the Games, if the North accepted the IOC's offer, which was still outstanding. Opposition leaders, taking no chances with public opinion, but adding little of value to finding a solution, urged the gov-

[9] Statements were made to this effect on May 4, 1998, by Yook Wan Sik, chief of Olympic Security Coordination and Control. This tendency was not atypical of the views of Olympic security chiefs. The similar official at the Calgary Olympic Winter Games had been less worried about entry into Canada of known terrorists than of more "routine" security risks. Since the unfortunate incident at the Munich Games in 1972, the degree of knowledge and cooperation among international and national security forces has increased enormously and, though the danger can never be ignored, it now seems to be at a manageable level. This relative calm was disturbed slightly on May 10, when Japanese Red Army member Yashiro Shibata was arrested in Japan and records showed, according to the media, that he had recently visited the DPRK.

ernment to resume talks with the objective of persuading North Korea to participate in the Games. The only leader who stepped way out of line was Kim Dae Jung, who publicly supported the DPRK proposal to cohost the Games. It is not clear what opportunistic urge led to this position, but it evoked such a storm of criticism from the government, sports leaders, and opposition leaders alike that he was forced into an ignominious retraction of the suggestion on May 23.

Despite a Japanese ban on DPRK officials as a result of state-sponsored terrorist activities on the part of North Korea, Japan allowed a DPRK delegation to enter the country to participate in the Asian Table Tennis Championships. This delegation left Japan in protest on May 21, after Japanese authorities refused to allow the delegation to attend a political event. On May 24, Japanese foreign minister Sosuke Uno stated that Japan would continue to urge the DPRK to participate in the Olympic Games, despite its boycott of the table tennis event in Japan. It was not evident what the DPRK had hoped to accomplish by this evident provocation of the Japanese authorities; it certainly did nothing to endear it in the direction of the DPRK or to improve the already tenuous relations between the two countries. In any event, the Japanese were not greatly moved by the departure of the DPRK delegation and simply ignored it as a factor in Japanese support of the Seoul Games.[10]

Samaranch has never been shy about injecting himself and the Olympic Movement into world events. The U.S. and Soviet leaders were in the process of their fourth summit meeting in Moscow at the end of May 1988. The meeting was scheduled for May 29. On May 27, Samaranch issued a press release from Lausanne, sending his greetings, on behalf of the entire Olympic Movement, to the two leaders. The text of the message was not earth-shattering, but it was designed to keep the Olympic Movement in front of the superpowers on that occasion.[11]

[10] This particular circle was completed on June 7, when the International Table Tennis Federation revoked the berths reserved for DPRK players in the Olympic tournament.

[11] This was nothing new; he had done so prior to each of the previous summits. More to the point, perhaps, was that political leaders within the United States, like Senator Ted Stevens of Alaska, working with sports leaders, were urging that the summit meeting produce a statement supportive of the Olympic Movement, an objective that was accomplished on this occasion. Although the author believes that Senator Stevens would have acted in this manner in any event, to complete the record, it was a fact that Anchorage, Alaska, was a candidate for the 1994 Olympic Winter Games, the decision for which would be made by the IOC at its Session in Seoul in 1988, immediately prior to the Games. Stevens has a track record of supporting sport and the Olympic Movement in the United States and was one of those most responsible for the steering of the Amateur Sports Act, 1978, through the U.S. Congress.

> In this Olympic year, 1988, only a few years from the celebration of the first century of restored Olympism, the whole world shares our wish that your fourth historic meeting will advance the cause of world peace.
>
> For several years now, the hundreds of millions of members of the Olympic Movement throughout the world have followed with increasing expectation the efforts that you are making towards this goal, and they send you their warmest and most cordial encouragement.
>
> Brotherhood, friendship, international understanding and world peace are the intangible ideals which each and every human being hopes will one day be realized. This fourth meeting between the supreme leaders of the Soviet Union and the United States of America is a sign to everyone that such a hope is not in vain.
>
> The entire Olympic Movement sends its sincerest wishes that this immense hope of Peace will at last be attained, and assures you of its unqualified support in pursuit of this aim.

The message was well enough received by the two leaders that they included a brief statement on the Olympic Movement in the joint statement that they issued on June 1, 1988, in Moscow.[12]

> Noting the rapidly growing sports ties between the two countries, including their National Olympic Committees, the two leaders expressed their support for the International Olympic Movement, which promotes international cooperation and understanding through athletic competition.[13]

Leading up to the summit, the usual activities were occurring in and around Korea. Kim Il Sung, no doubt not wishing to upset the

[12] This was a significant breakthrough, since, on the occasion of the previous summit meetings, though the Olympics had been dealt with as part of the briefings given by officials present at the meetings, there had never been anything explicitly mentioned about the Games in the official statement issued by the two leaders.

[13] It would be naive to think that this statement was included simply because Samaranch had been sending messages on the occasion of each summit meeting. Much collateral effort was being generated by friends of the Olympic Movement in the United States, who had the necessary access to those who would decide on the content of the final statement to be issued by the two leaders. Though there were many who undoubtedly contributed to this effort, two persons in particular should be singled out. Donna deVarona, an Olympic swimming champion and president of the Women's Sport Foundation, worked tirelessly on both the principle of the statement and suggestions about the content. And Senator Ted Stevens, a longtime friend in high places of the Olympic Movement in the United States, wrote a persuasive letter to Secretary of State George Shultz on March 25, 1988, urging that the joint statement express support of the two leaders for the Olympic Movement. Shultz replied on May 23, saying that he would urge the leaders to do so. The many contacts of the IOC lawyer, Samuel Pisar, were also very useful in this direction.

Soviet Union, nor, for that matter, China, declared on May 24 that the DPRK boycott of the Seoul Games was still in place but denied any intention on the part of the DPRK to disrupt the Games. This was a statement not unlike that made by the USSR about its boycott of the 1984 Games in Los Angeles. It portrayed a swanlike indifference to the actions of others but hid the furious paddling going on underneath the surface. For the sake of international balance, on the very same day U.S. assistant secretary of state Derwinski issued a statement to the effect that North Korean terrorism posed an "extraordinary potential threat" to the Games, but that security forces were ready to prevent outbreaks of violence.[14] He also tossed off a statement that Cuba's decision to boycott was the result of Castro's "screwed up" sense of priorities, not a particularly helpful comment in the circumstances.[15]

The DPRK announced on May 25 that it planned to host a major meeting of socialist leaders on September 9 to celebrate forty years of the DPRK. It was said that USSR general secretary Gorbachev would be Kim Il Sung's guest on this occasion. Most Asian and Western diplomats doubted very much, and correctly so, as it turned out, that Gorbachev would accept any such invitation. In Tokyo on May 26, Japanese prime minister Takeshita assured the Korean ambassador, Lee Won Kyong, that Japan would cooperate fully to ensure that the Games would be safe. The quid pro quo was a statement by the ambassador that President Roh Tae Woo had found the February talks between the two leaders to have been useful. On May 27, Kim Il Sung was hard at work trying to convince the secretary-general of the Czechoslovakian Communist Party, who was visiting the North, to support the cohosting of the Games. Czechoslovakia was one of the many Eastern European socialist countries that had already accepted the invitation to Seoul and had, furthermore, been one of the first out of the block in indicating that it would go to Seoul with or without the DPRK.

While this was under way, Samaranch was off on another one of his international trips. His stamina has become almost legendary, and the agenda for the trip was particularly ambitious. He left Lausanne on

[14] On May 26, press reports were published stating that U.S. spy satellites would be redeployed to keep special watch on military movements in the DPRK for signs of a buildup or other potential threats.

[15] Cuba's prospects of becoming involved in the Games took a technical turn for the worse on May 25, when it was scratched from the volleyball tournament by reason of failing to meet the entry deadline of May 24. The effect of the decision may, perhaps, be measured by the fact that at the Barcelona Games in 1992, the Cuban women's team won the gold medal.

May 29, met briefly with the Korean ambassador in Geneva, and boarded Swissair for a flight to Zurich en route to Bombay, then to Hong Kong, where he met briefly with the Spanish consul, then to Seoul, arriving midafternoon, local time. There was the usual official welcome and a press conference at Kimpo International Airport. He met with Park Seh Jik, president of the SLOOC, and Kim Un Yong at the airport and left for the hotel. Upon arrival, he met for the next hour and fifteen minutes with various Olympic and SLOOC personnel and the Spanish ambassador.

The following day, May 31, he left for a tour of the Olympic Center and meetings with President Park and SLOOC officials. After this he went to the city hall to meet the mayor and political leaders of Seoul, followed by an official lunch and film presentation. He returned briefly to the hotel before departing once more for the Olympic Center and three more hours of meetings with SLOOC officials. The day was completed with an official dinner hosted by Park Seh Jik.

On June 1, the day began with the inauguration of the new Olympic swimming complex and the inauguration of the Olympic Village. This event was attended by ROK president Roh Tae Woo; Samaranch had a meeting with Roh, and a reception at the Olympic Village hosted by Roh followed. Then came an official lunch given by the minister of sport and a visit to the Olympic Park and the open-air sculpture exhibition, a return to the hotel, and a meeting with a candidate city representative. A book presentation by the author of a work on Seoul preceded departure for the residence of President Roh, an hour's private meeting with Roh, a reception and dinner hosted by Roh, and a final return to the hotel.[16]

June 2 brought with it an even more brutal schedule. It began with a breakfast reception for the three main opposition political leaders, Kim Dae Jung (People's Democratic Party), Kim Young Sam (Unification Democratic Party), and Kim Jong Pil (New Democratic Republican Party), together with the president of the ruling Democratic Justice Party, Yoon Gil Joong, for which occasion the press and television were on hand. Park Seh Jik and Kim Un Yong of the SLOOC attended as well. There was a two-hour working breakfast, at the end of which a short press statement was issued. The press release outlined the fact

[16] On June 1, Korean foreign minister Choi Kwang Soo announced that Olympic "attachés" accredited under the Olympic Charter (as interfaces between the Organizing Committee, SLOOC, and the various NOCs) from countries without diplomatic relations with Korea would be allowed to perform consular functions and would be granted consular protection and supervision of their property in addition to their purely Olympic functions.

that Samaranch had first been officially received by President Roh the previous day and that the present meeting had been called by Samaranch.[17] It went on to state:

> President Samaranch recalled and detailed the efforts made by the IOC, the International Federations and the National Olympic Committees to enable all members of the Olympic Family to attend the Games awarded to the City of Seoul in 1981. The political leaders of Korea unanimously re-assessed their unfailing support to the Games of the XXIVth Olympiad in Seoul and commended the IOC and the Olympic Movement for their outstanding efforts in order to ensure the broadest possible success of the Games which had led to a record participation of 161 NOCs.
>
> To answer the strong wishes expressed by all participants in the meeting, the President of the IOC had therefore decided to publicly appeal once more to the authorities of North Korea to urge them to reconsider the unique and historical offer made by the IOC to share part of the Games with the City of Pyongyang.
>
> With only 107 days remaining before the opening of the Games, the President of the IOC repeated his willingness to immediately answer any invitation to visit the DPR of Korea to meet the Head of State, in order to discuss with him all possibilities for the North Korean athletes to be present in Seoul while the South Korean athletes would participate in the events organized in Pyongyang.
>
> The IOC strongly urges all those in charge to do their best in this period where all tensions in the world seem to ease, to contribute to this very important development in international relations, thus fulfilling the aims of the Olympic Movement, i.e., fraternity, comprehension, friendship and Peace among all people of the world.

This accomplished, Samaranch left for the International Broadcast Center, where there was an official inauguration and a tour of the building. Lunch was hosted by the president of the Games Operations Bureau. Returning to the hotel after lunch, Samaranch then gave several television interviews and recorded a televised statement. There were discussions after this with SLOOC officials and the signing of

[17] The meeting had, indeed, been requested by Samaranch, since it was important to have the support, publicly expressed, of the opposition leaders. Arranging such a meeting had proven very difficult and had required considerable effort by Samaranch, Park Seh Jik, and Kim Un Yong to get it organized. It was particularly important for this meeting to have occurred and for it to have been successful, since the student demonstrations at the time were attracting a great deal of attention, and the situation was potentially quite volatile.

assorted agreements. He also received representatives of the 77 Democratic Organizations of Korea, a student organization that had requested a meeting only a couple of hours earlier on the same day. He then left for the airport, where he gave a press conference for forty-five minutes and departed for Tokyo en route to Anchorage and Paris.[18]

In Tokyo, he met with Chiharu Igaya, the IOC member in Japan, and with the Japanese press and departed an hour later. Owing to the time change, he arrived in Anchorage the same day for an official visit of approximately twenty hours.[19] This involved arrival at the Evan Congress Center; an Alaskacom teleconference; visits to the Alaska Performing Arts Center, the figure skating venue, the University of Alaska, a regional training center, potential accommodation sites, Providence Hospital; a helicopter tour of the sites for downhill skiing, bobsled, and luge; and, finally, for that Endless Day, a reception given by the Anchorage bid committee. The following morning, he visited the Museum of Anchorage, attended a demonstration of local sports, gave a press conference, got back on the plane, and left for Paris, to attend the French Open tennis matches at Roland Garros.

It was never clear what a visit to Pyongyang by Samaranch might accomplish. Little, if anything. It was, however, something that Samaranch had indicated, in his meetings with the Korean delegations, he was prepared to do. He had, moreover, confirmed this intention in his correspondence with Castro, so he kept the matter percolating, although he cleverly shifted the onus to call for such a visit from himself to the North Koreans.

On June 2, 1988, the date on which he issued the press release in Seoul, he had Raymond Gafner, the *administrateur délégué* of the IOC, forward to Kim Yu Sun, but from Lausanne, a copy of a press release issued by the IOC that day. It was preferable to use this neutral routing, although the North Koreans were perfectly aware that Samaranch was in Seoul at the time.

Kim responded within two days, by telex dated June 4. He was

[18] The South Koreans used the occasion of this visit to announce liberalization of curbs on public debate regarding the issue of reunification of Korea, increase of trade, and family visits. This was a considerable break from the position on these matters during the Chun Doo Hwan administration. The Korean prime minister also called upon the DPRK to participate in cabinet-level discussions on trade and exchange visits, as well as the Olympic Games, but the North refused to accept the letter at Panmunjom.

[19] Anchorage was a candidate city for the Olympic Winter Games to be held in 1994, the decision for which would be taken at the IOC Session in Seoul prior to the Games. The competition was won by Lillehammer, Norway.

obviously not fooled by the change in emphasis. He replied to Gafner that they did not understand the intention. They complained that they had invited Samaranch to come to the DPRK on several occasions, and, each time, Samaranch had not responded. Thereafter, he had never made a direct proposal for a visit but only through third parties. They had already clarified their position and thought Gafner was well aware of it. What was the purpose of doing all this through a press release? The bottleneck was not the relationship between them and the IOC but between the North and the South on the issue of cohosting. Was the South prepared to cohost in name and in reality? If this problem could be settled, they would be willing to meet with Samaranch at any time to settle the problems of cohosting.[20]

Samaranch replied on June 7, saying that the information had been sent while he was abroad[21] and had been done in that manner only to save time and to keep Kim Yu Sun informed. He was shorter in his substantive reply, perhaps because the ploy had been identified, and stated that Kim Yu Sun as a member of the IOC was aware (as Samaranch himself had always stressed) that the Games are awarded to a city and not to a country, and it was on this basis[22] that the IOC had been able to make this unique and important historic offer to organize some events in Pyongyang. He reiterated that he was prepared to visit Pyongyang at any time to meet with the head of state and discuss this question with him following the meeting with Vazquez-Raña and Rieckehoff.[23] He awaited his prompt reply.

[20] Radio Pyongyang, unwittingly falling into the trap set by Samaranch, had announced on June 4 that Samaranch would *not* be invited to Pyongyang. Once again the DPRK had put itself in the position of appearing to refuse an offer designed to help find a solution to the problem. After all, Samaranch could not issue his own invitation to visit the DPRK; he could only indicate that, were an invitation to be received, he would be favorably disposed to accept it.

[21] He did not mention that "abroad" was, in this instance, the Republic of Korea. Technically, he had been in other countries as well, so use of the general term was perfectly justifiable.

[22] It is not entirely clear on what "basis" this was, but in the dialogue with the two Koreas, there was always some degree of license in the purely logical application of some of the principles involved. Samaranch refers to this as the "Olendorf Method," which involves responding to any statement or question with something entirely off-point and completely unrelated to the topic at hand. The result is chaos, a condition that was often a feature of the negotiations with the two Koreas.

[23] This meeting had followed a meeting in Havana on the evening of June 1 and morning of June 2 between Vazquez-Raña, Rieckehoff, and the Mexican ambassador to Cuba, on the one hand, and Fidel Castro, Minister Fernandez, and Manuel Gonzales Guerra, the Cuban member of the IOC and president of the Cuban NOC. The meeting had been subsequent to a visit by Vazquez-Raña and Rieckehoff to Pyongyang. Each had reported separately by telex to Samaranch on June 4. They appeared to be encouraged by their visits to both Cuba and the DPRK and reported Castro's personal opinion that the DPRK was likely more interested in the symbology of having

Kim Yu Sun replied on June 10, acknowledging the telex of June 7 and stating they welcomed his intention of visiting their country "expressed directly to us this time." He hoped to see a "fine fruition" to the visit, but the present situation did not show "such symptom." This was because the South Korean authorities "stubbornly oppose the cohosting, while suppressing with force the strong demand of the broad sections of South Korean people for the cohosting of the Olympiad and the composition of the North-South single sports team." He doubted, therefore, that a visit by Samaranch would be successful; if it was not successful, it would be good for neither party. Falling directly into the trap set for him by Samaranch, Kim Yu Sun recommended that Samaranch wait until the north-south dialogue was completed before coming.[24]

In his telexed reply the same day, Samaranch reiterated his readiness to come to Pyongyang but said he would rely on Kim Yu Sun to find the right moment. He drew, once again, the attention of Kim to the fact that only ninety-nine days remained before the opening of the Games and that it would become more difficult with each passing day to implement any agreement.

On June 14, North Kim acknowledged this telex and thanked Samaranch for his understanding of their stand. He urged that they make joint efforts "to ripen earlier favorable condition" for Samaranch's visit to their country, as Samaranch had agreed in his telex. However, continued Kim, there were some points raised by Samaranch in his press conference in Barcelona on June 9 that they did not understand, and they would inform him separately of their opinion on the matter.

Samaranch replied on June 16. The comments he had made to the press were in reference to the "important and historical offer" made by the IOC the previous July, and he had stated that he had not had a response to that offer. In addition he was referring to his telex of June 6, which repeated the proposal sent on June 2 and expressed to Kim Yu Sun on many occasions, also without response. He continued, with respect to the other remarks of Kim, that he had often declared to Kim, his NOC delegation, and the world press, and was repeating again, that one of the most important elements of any possible agreement with

---

events in the DPRK than in the relative importance of such events. The author has some doubts that Castro was correct in this particular assessment in light of the Korean situation generally, quite apart from the question of whether the DPRK wanted any events in the first place.

[24] On June 9, a statement from the DPRK Central News Agency, monitored in Tokyo, said that the DPRK would not participate in singly hosted Games and would continue to work for cohosting.

the IOC regarding the Games of the XXIVth Olympiad was full respect for the conditions set down in the Olympic Charter and in particular free entry for all members of the Olympic Family.

The IOC had always been told by the DPRK side that "this would not be a problem once an agreement is reached." Samaranch wanted to point out here, as he had done before in their meetings and publicly, the IOC's deep concern over this issue. With only ninety-three days remaining before the opening of the Games, the entire Olympic Family was extremely worried over the fact that there were no adequate points of entry into his country to meet this demand, without substantial improvements in the possibilities of travel across the demarcation line.

Finally, as a personal body blow, Samaranch reminded Kim Yu Sun that he hardly needed to draw his attention, as an IOC member and president of his NOC, to the fact that the IOC governs the Olympic Movement and owns the rights over the Olympic Games. To claim that his request was none of the IOC's business, but a matter to be settled only between North Korea and South Korea was, therefore, totally incomprehensible. Samaranch was confident that Kim would appreciate that the most important responsibility for all members of the Olympic Family was to try to the last minute to reach an agreement. The IOC hoped and expected that he would examine the IOC offer to share the organization of some events in Pyongyang, as preparations urgently needed to be initiated if they were to be effectively implemented.

Kim Yu Sun replied on June 21, stating: "As we have already made clear, once the cohosting is realized the problems you are apprehending on the XXIVth Olympiad would be naturally solved." The important thing now was to make the South Korean side accept the cohosting. He hoped Samaranch would make "efforts" with them for the realization of the cohosting.

Samaranch replied on June 24, increasing the pressure:

> After having stretched our rules to the limit in order to offer you a unique and historical proposal, we cannot understand what you intend to obtain through "co-hosting."
>
> We would appreciate at least receiving a clear and complete explanation from your side on what you imply by the word "co-hosting" point by point. For us, implementing the IOC's proposal to organize five sports or events in Pyongyang, effectively means to co-host the Games.
>
> We would also like to stress once again that time is running out very quickly. Concrete preparations must be undertaken very soon if adequate

conditions are to be offered for crossing the border to all members of the Olympic Family as we have always requested and in accordance with the Olympic Charter.

It will very soon be too late to meet with this request, which would render the whole discussion absolutely futile.

This was a serious blow to the North, as can be seen from the content of Kim Yu Sun's response to Samaranch's telex, sent on June 27.

> You must have been well aware that the topic under our discussion at the Lausanne joint meetings and on many other occasions including the visit to our country by the IOC delegation on May 1987 was the question on the North-South co-hosting of the 24th Olympic Games.
>
> Nevertheless you are now requesting us the explanation of the co-host, at which we wonder why.
>
> As for the matter of sports and events you mentioned, we have already made clear more than once that it is no more than a component within the framework of the co-host and it also went down with everyone.
>
> We consider deeper attention should be paid to seeking for the methods for the co-host under the condition that the Olympic Games is to be held in the Korean land and the spirit of supporting the co-host is surging higher among the South Korean people out of the desire towards the national reunification.
>
> The fundamental matter at present is the agreement of the South Korean authorities upon the co-host.
>
> We also follow the stand of the South Korean side, being irritated over the fast passage of time.
>
> I hope the IOC will have understanding of such stand of ours and cooperate with us in finding out all possibilities for the realization of the co-host.

Samaranch wasted no time in replying to this somewhat hysterical response from Kim and, in his telex of June 27, backed Kim even further into the diplomatic corner.

> Further to our many efforts in order to seek a solution to this matter, I fully agree that the question of the number and type of events was to be only an element or component of any further agreement and am happy to see that our opinions are similar in this respect.

In addition, I should like to reiterate what has always been pointed out during all of our meetings, either privately or during the official meetings: there are many other elements to be considered and solved in order to reach an agreement. I have repeatedly stated that one of the most significant of such elements would be the full compliance of your side with the requirements of free travel of all members of our Olympic Family, namely the possibility for nearly 30,000 people to cross the demarcation line at Panmunjom.

I should also like to stress once more that the decision to award the Games of the XXIVth Olympiad to the City of Seoul is final and cannot be questioned. I have repeated this at every meeting since nearly four years and you should be fully aware of it in your capacity of IOC member and the oath taken by you to abide by our Olympic Charter.

Consequently, as we are in agreement on all these points, I am wondering the reasons which refrain [*sic*] you from giving a clear answer to my last telex, instead of speaking regarding the supposed attitude of other parties which do not play any role in the reaching of an agreement. As IOC member, you know that the only responsible body is the IOC, the owner of the Olympic Games.

I cannot see the differences between what we offer, that is to stage part of the Games of the XXIVth Olympiad in Pyongyang and your claim to be "co-host" of the Games.

Finally, I would be particularly interested to know the truth regarding the statement made by ambassador Chin while in Berlin at the Conference on De-Nuclearized Zones, in which he claimed that I would never be invited to come to the DPR of Korea.

I should therefore appreciate your full and unrestricted cooperation in the long and difficult process by at least endeavouring to set out in writing which elements you consider to be unsolved in what you persist in calling the "co-hosting" of the Games.

The North could not keep up with this level of pressure and the turnaround time that the IOC consistently demonstrated. Kim had no alternative but to reply, but did so by post, rather than by telex, to benefit from the delay that this would afford. His letter of response was dated July 7 and reached the IOC only on July 19. It was the customary jumble of generalities and repetitions.

I gladly received your telex dated June 29th, 1988. Through your telex I came to be better aware of the energetic efforts you are making even at this moment when the appointed day is in the offing to carry into effect the sublime desire for the north-south co-host of the 24th Olympic Games thereby making it successful sports festivity.

I feel happy over this and send a reply as you requested.

I avail myself of this opportunity to reaffirm you that our position remains unchanged towards the question of opening the MDL[25] you propose and our co-hosting.

If you again consider our telex dated June 15th, 1988[26] and the documents containing our co-host demand which was given to the IOC delegation on a visit to our country in May 1987, they will give a clear answer to all matters you raised.

Besides, as for the interview our Vice-President had with the KYOTO correspondent in Berlin in June last, we consider that the original text of the KYOTO news dated June 23 will help your correct understanding and dispelling of misunderstanding.

Convinced that esteemed Mr. President will express your deep understanding of our sincere efforts for the strengthening and development of the Olympic Movement, I wish you good health and success in your noble work.

Two could play the same game. Samaranch replied on July 19, also by mail. It was equally general and inconsequential, concluding with the by now routine observation that time was running out very rapidly.

On June 17, while this jousting between Kim and Samaranch was going on, Raymond Gafner telexed Kim to advise him that his invitation to attend the ninety-fourth IOC Session in Seoul from September 15 to 17 was being sent to him that day through the DPRK embassy in Switzerland.

Fencing of a similar nature continued on other fronts during June 1988. The U.S. State Department stated on June 6 that it had assurances from the Soviet Union that it would use its best efforts to prevent trouble during the Games. The DPRK indicated the same day that it might, after all, be ready to consider cabinet-level meetings with the South as a preparation for future bilateral meetings. The following day, U.S. secretary of defense Frank Carlucci said, while in Seoul for an annual security conference, that U.S. armed forces would be ready to

[25] Military demarcation line.

[26] Presumably the telex dated June 14, 1988.

crush any disruptions of the Seoul Games. Japan and Korea continued their liaison meetings regarding security matters relating to the Games. The DPRK continued its statements that it was continuing to press for cohosting. Students in South Korea were stopped from marching to meet North Korean students at Panmunjom. Calls were repeatedly made by leaders in the South for the North to participate in the Games, including at the UN in New York on June 10.

The White House issued a statement, also on June 10, confirming that it had asked the Soviets to use their influence to see that nothing would happen during the Games. This was not new, but the message was undoubtedly worth repeating. The statement generated a response the following day from the DPRK ambassador to the UN, Pak Gil Yon, who declared that there was nothing to worry about "because we are all brothers." On the other hand, he fired his own warning that the military buildup was a problem that would not go unchecked. The Seoul Olympics were the Olympics of War, and he compared them (however inaccurately) to the Berlin Games in 1936. The South Korean ambassador merely repeated the call for boycotting countries to participate in the Games. The DPRK response on June 13 was to criticize the "negative attitude" of the United States toward the DPRK proposals for summit talks with the South. Radical students made their customary helpful contributions by burning a few Olympic flags and throwing incendiary bombs at Japanese cultural centers and other public buildings.[27] Government and opposition parties agreed to establish a special committee in the National Assembly to discuss the whole question of unification.[28]

On June 15, a number of important signals were sent and received concerning the Games. Thirteen Asian and Pacific countries met in Tokyo to agree on security measures designed to reduce the threat of terrorism at the Games. Press reports indicated that a leading member of the Chinese politburo, Li Ruihuan, had recently met with Kim Il

[27] By June 15, radical students were again rioting in Seoul, this time in protest against military training. A minor firebomb attack was made against the Democratic Justice Party headquarters in Seoul, and some riots occurred in Taejon to protest the breaking up of the planned march to Panmunjom on June 10, which had been intended as a meeting of students from the North and the South to discuss cohosting of the Games.

[28] This was a further instance of the improvement in openness within South Korea, which followed upon the reforms proposed almost a year earlier by Roh Tae Woo. A joint committee on this subject would have been almost unimaginable under Chun Doo Hwan. It was an overt recognition that the matter of reunification was something beyond mere party lines and that a solution to any Olympic problem was conceivable only against the larger background, in which all parties had an important stake.

Sung in Pyongyang and had delivered a very polite, but nevertheless very firm, message that China wanted the Seoul Olympics to run smoothly.[29] U.S. secretary of state George Shultz announced that the Soviet authorities were certain that there would be no North Korean terrorist activities directed at the Seoul Games. On the other hand, the following day, Shultz expressed concern regarding some rather aggressive military moves by the DPRK, including deployment of SAM-5 anti-aircraft missiles within range of Seoul.[30]

The level of general international governmental support in favor of smooth Games was quite heartening as the summer approached. The G-7 countries met in Toronto in the latter part of June and supported the request of Roh Tae Woo, brought forward by Japanese prime minister Takeshita, that Western governments support the Games in Seoul. This gesture was doubtless part of the complicated mating dance then in progress between Japan and Korea. Only five days earlier, Roh had said he was looking forward to visiting Japan to express his gratitude to various parties, after the Games had been completed. On June 24, the United States again announced that its naval presence off the coast of Korea would be increased. It also stated that the United States did not believe the Soviets thought the SAM-5 missiles in the possession of the DPRK would be used against Soviet athletes at the Games. This was, of course, a double message. It reminded the Soviets that they bore a certain responsibility for having supplied the missiles to the DPRK in the first place,[31] and it reminded the DPRK that it had better be careful in biting the hand that fed them with the weapons.

Efforts continued to collect some of the strays during this same period. These efforts reflected a concern by the IOC not only with the geopoliti-

[29] In the circumstances, this represented a major commitment of support from China. Both the fact that it was made by Li Ruihuan in Pyongyang and its timing provided particular weight to the message.

[30] FIFA president Joao Havelange stated on June 16 that it would no longer be possible for the DPRK to stage any part of the Olympic soccer tournament. Two days earlier, Australian officials had added some unnecessary uncertainty to the situation by publicly announcing that they had plans for emergency evacuation of their Olympic team in the event of disturbances in Seoul.

[31] The United States was not, as might be expected, pleased with the supply of such weaponry to the DPRK by the Soviet Union and continued to object to such activity. Its complaints continued at least to July 18, when Secretary of State Shultz "regretted" the supply of military aircraft and missiles to the North but softened the stance in the context of the Games by saying that he doubted the weapons would be used to affect security at the Games.

cal implications, but also for the benefit of the athletes, even of small countries, who would be affected by adverse decisions. Madagascar, for example, was another doubtful starter. Its participation had also been linked with cohosting of the Games by the DPRK.[32] On June 17, Samaranch wrote to Jean-Claude Ganga, IOC member in Congo, who was at the time minister of tourism, sport, and recreation, asking him if he might, with the approval of the Congolese head of state, undertake a mission on behalf of the IOC to be sure that Madagascar understood the implications of a decision not to participate in the Games. Samaranch thought that the relations between the Congolese leader and his colleague, President Didier Ratsiraka of the Democratic Republic of Madagascar, might make this a worthwhile effort. Ganga was unable to go.

This was not the only avenue explored by Samaranch. He had met with Federico Mayor, director general of UNESCO, in Lausanne on June 17. During this meeting, Mayor agreed to have a UNESCO official, Charles Randriamanantenasoa, visit Madagascar and attempt to ensure that Madagascar would not withdraw from the Games. Randriamanantenasoa visited Madagascar between June 23 and 26. He explained in a letter dated June 25 that Mayor had authorized him to undertake this mission on behalf of the IOC to seek a means of having Malagasy athletes take part in the Games. He had become acquainted with the position adopted by the Joint Ministers/Supreme Councillors of the Revolution Committee, namely, that participation by Madagascar was to be conditional on cohosting. He referred to the provisions of the Olympic Charter regarding allocation of the Games to a city and pointed out that these provisions were not to be contravened.

Despite this, he continued, the IOC had on four occasions endeavored to organize meetings between representatives of the two countries. He outlined the five sports proposed to be allocated to the North but confirmed that no agreement had been signed between the two parties. He noted that the countries of Eastern Europe that had confirmed their participation in the Games had declared their conviction of the IOC's good faith and their appreciation of the efforts undertaken by the IOC. Madagascar was one of only six [*sic*] countries, out of a total of 167, unable to take part in the Games. He thought that, in spite of every-

[32] On June 13, DPRK sources announced that Madagascar would boycott the Games and that its previous acceptance had been conditional upon cohosting by the DPRK. This was not the first such statement by the DPRK. On January 15, it had claimed Madagascar would not participate, and the IOC had issued a denial of the claim on January 20.

thing, Madagascar could still change its decision; if so, sanctions[33] could be avoided against its athletes, who were, at that time, in France, training for the Games.

He put forward two proposals. The first was that Madagascar's Joint Committee might meet again to decide, in the need for clarity, to disassociate sport from politics. In this way, he suggested, the efforts of the commission responsible for seeking reunification of the two Koreas would be furthered, and participation by athletes in the great youth sporting event in Seoul would at last be unreservedly confirmed. Part of this effort would be to include Madagascar among the Eastern European countries that were to take part in the Games. The second proposal was to inform the comrades in the DPRK of these decisions and to explain that they were taken solely in the interest of the Malagasy athletes. This, he thought, would be seen in the DPRK not as a withdrawal of support from them, but rather as the expression of their constant concern to help their young people. He was sure they would understand and even give the Malagasy athletes their blessing.

He concluded with a plea to the president. He had carried out his mission in a spirit of complete receptiveness because, like the president, he cared about young people and about the athletes of his country. Why not give them the chance to compare themselves in sport with other young people? Why not offer them the joy of taking part in the Olympic festival? There they would have the opportunity to meet other young people with the same tastes and aspirations, to draw closer to them, to promote alongside them both peace and mutual understanding between individuals and countries, and, perhaps, to discover solutions to the international problems that the world now faces. He thanked the president in advance for his valuable assistance to the young people, who needed him, his wisdom, and his decisiveness very much.

This letter had been prepared after Randriamanantenasoa's arrival to Antananarivo, Madagascar, on June 23. That day he had met with the president and the secretary-general of the Malagasy NOC, the director of sport and leisure, and the director of physical education. The following day, he met with the minister of population, youth, and sports, and at later meetings, the secretary-general of the presidency

[33] If he meant sanctions to be imposed by the IOC, he was misinformed, since no sanctions of this nature had been contemplated. If he meant that Madagascar would not benefit from funding provided through the IOC Olympic Solidarity program, he was correct. In the larger sense of sanctions meaning a disadvantage to be suffered by the athletes who had prepared for the Games and who would be deprived of the chance to participate, he was certainly right.

of the republic, who was also the chairman of the commission responsible for the reunification of the two Koreas, and the director of protocol of the president of the republic.

On the basis of these meetings, Randriamanantenasoa concluded that the NOC had no autonomy whatsoever with respect to the governmental authorities. The reason given for the decision at all levels (the cohosting) did not appear to be the real reason, which he thought was that Madagascar wished to take advantage of the excellent opportunity afforded by the Olympic Games to increase international awareness of the need to reunite the two Koreas. On the political level, the president seemed unable to withdraw his support from the DPRK. The decision had been taken, it seemed, by the Joint Ministers/Supreme Councillors of the Revolution Committee. Although certain officials were not in favor of the decision, including the minister of population, youth, and sports, none dared to make any other suggestions to the president, who alone appeared to have the final word.

After discussions with the secretary-general of the presidency of the republic on June 25, he prepared the letter referred to above, which was given to the president the same day.

At an official reception given on June 26 to celebrate the twenty-eighth anniversary of Madagascar's independence, Randriamanantenasoa was able to have a brief meeting with the minister of foreign affairs and also with the president of the republic. The president told him the "question" would be reexamined. In his report to Mayor dated June 28, he said that without wishing to prejudge the final decision of the president of the republic, he thought he had succeeded in making the Malagasy authorities aware of the need for Madagascar to take part in the Games. Rather than listing all of the negative consequences flowing from nonparticipation (about which all authorities at all levels were aware), he had cited the positive benefits that Madagascar could stand to gain though participation. He noted that Madagascar was to host the Games of the Islands of the Indian Ocean in 1989. Mayor forwarded a copy of the report and other documents to Samaranch on July 1.[34]

An important event occurred in Lausanne on June 21, 1988. The IOC hosted a meeting under the rubric of Olympism Against Apartheid at its headquarters, to which all African sports leaders were invited, to

[34] Madagascar did not participate in the Games.

reaffirm the IOC position against apartheid in sport. The timing of this gathering was not entirely coincidental, even though the subject matter was an important issue within the Olympic Movement. Samaranch wanted to remove the issue of apartheid as a factor in the 1988 Games and thereby eliminate a possible area of instability within the Olympic Family as part of the equation for the last three and a half months leading up to the Games. The meeting produced a firm declaration on the subject and, in retrospect, may be seen as the genesis of the eventual work to readmit South Africa to the Olympic Movement four years later.

By the end of June, the circle around North Korea was becoming rather tight. On June 25, following a visit by Kim Un Yong to Moscow,[35] it was announced that the Soviet Foreign Ministry had decided to open a consular office in Seoul during the Games and that there were plans to extend this initial contact to economic and cultural spheres thereafter. On June 27, Japan announced that thorough immigration checks would be instituted at all airports and seaports starting July 1 in order to deter terrorists from entering and leaving Japan. On June 29, representatives from seven governments announced special aviation security measures relating to the Games. By now, the DPRK was reduced to repeating demands relating to cohosting the Games that were rapidly becoming absurd: cohosting meant not only the events to be staged in the North, but also the name of the Games, a separate Organizing Committee, Opening and Closing Ceremonies, a joint team, and sharing the television and other revenues. Its position was moving from the unrealistic to the surreal.

On July 2, more than one hundred members of the National Assembly, both government and opposition, introduced a resolution calling for North Korea to participate in the Games, stating that this would help the cause of reunification. A proposal was made by the National Conference of Literary Writers to have prominent cultural persons meet prior to the end of the year to help create the conditions that could lead to reunification. North Korea, for its part, announced that a letter dealing with a proposed meeting of students at Panmunjom would be

[35] The visit was, ostensibly, in his capacity as president of the General Assembly of International Sports Federations (GAISF) and in, therefore, a sport context, but he had at least one direct governmental mission. This was not unusual, since he had been part of the Korean diplomatic mission in the United States several years previously.

delivered on July 4. On July 4, for the first time, the South Korean government allowed dissident students to march. The usual "Death to . . ." slogans abounded, but there was little, if any, indication of public support for the students. North Korea launched another verbal attack against the South, saying that its refusal to accept the North's cohosting proposal was aimed at continued division of Korea and accused it of refusing to open the border.

One of the major policy initiatives that President Roh Tae Woo was to make early in his presidency was his July 7, 1988, Special Presidential Declaration for National Self-Esteem, Unification, and Prosperity. This declaration was intended to set forth the basic policy directions of the Republic of Korea, but perhaps most important, it addressed the major issue of the intra-Korean relationships that occupied so much of the political dialogue in each part of Korea and between the two Koreas. It reflected, as might be expected, a growing tendency on the international political scene to search for areas of détente and showed that Roh was not only aware of the trends but also wanted the Republic of Korea to be part of the current efforts in that regard. It was a very astute piece of political work, both for domestic and international consumption.[36]

Viewed solely from the perspective of its effect on the 1988 Olympic Games (which is to do it some injustice, since the ramifications were much broader), the declaration had the effect of demonstrating to the international community that the South was much more attuned to the political realities of the world, that it was much more creative and flexible in its approach to political issues, that it was, in effect, taking charge of the need to find a solution to an internal Korean problem, and that the real "dinosaur" in the equation was the DPRK. This could only reinforce the conviction of those countries that had agreed to accept the invitation to the Games that they had made the right decision.

Internally, within the Republic of Korea, the declaration had an even more salutary effect. It added a much-needed third dimension to the carefully propaganda-created image of the North as an archenemy

[36] The declaration had, in some respects, been foreshadowed by previous statements and comments by Roh. In the first press conference following his inauguration, given on April 21, 1988, he had said that he would make the rest of his term a period to pave the way for peaceful reunification by promoting reconciliation and cooperation between the two sides. Similarly, in meetings with the leaders of the opposition parties on May 28, 1988, he made it clear that his government would pursue a unification policy in a way that would help create a national community in which all Koreans could live well.

having no redeeming features whatsoever and no justifiable existence as a separate entity. Unrealistic as the propaganda position may have been in the past, there can be little doubt that it reflected the political reality and that however crude the caricature might have been, it was nevertheless effective on the intended domestic audience. It probably suited the ruling parties as well, for somewhat different purposes. Roh's declaration effected a significant change in the perception of the South with respect to the North and gave the South a greater sense of responsibility for bringing the two countries together. This would have to be done through negotiation, cooperation, and understanding, in a desire to involve the North as a responsible member of the international community.

The Declaration itself consisted of six basic points:

(1) Promotion of exchanges between the people of the North and the South and opening the door to visits by overseas Koreans to both parts of Korea;
(2) Positive arrangements for finding out the fates and whereabouts of dispersed families, exchange of letters, and mutual visits;
(3) Opening of doors for north-south trade;
(4) Cessation of opposition to nonmilitary trading by allies;
(5) Hope for free inter-Korean contacts and cooperation in the international community; and
(6) Willingness to cooperate in the improvement of the North's relations with allies.

Against the background of the past forty years, the declaration was a brave start, but it reflected only an intention or will and would require careful handling to make sure that the genuineness of the desire was properly communicated to and understood by the North.[37]

Roh Tae Woo reported on some of these developments to Samaranch on July 20. He also referred to Samaranch's letter of June 30, delivered to him through the Korean representative in Geneva, which contained a proposal that had obviously created some difficulties in South Korea.

[37] Efforts would include trying to resume the suspended South-North Red Cross Conference (proposed on July 13, 1988), rejected on July 16 by the North, and supplemented by an offer from South Red Cross for a three-month period (August 12–November 12) of efforts to locate missing families. Other efforts were to try to have meetings of North Korean and South Korean education officials (proposed July 15, 1988), rejected by the North on July 17, and publicizing a new foreign policy on July 16, 1988, which gave specific substance to Roh's declaration as it affected the "new" view of the north-south relationship.

The reply was, as always, very restrained and courteous, but on this occasion it was clear that the South Koreans were rather vexed. The proposal was one prepared on May 24, 1988, by Samuel Pisar, the IOC's outside counsel on the Korean matter, and Samaranch had been careful not to get too close to it, though still being identified with it if the Koreans were agreeable. He stressed that it was the private opinion of Pisar and not an official stance. It made no sense for Samaranch to burn his bridges with them.

The proposal was positioned as a Proposal for a Further Initiative Between South and North Korea and read as follows:

> The I.O.C. has managed to resolve the immense problems of the two Germanies and the two Chinas. On the eve of the XXIV Olympiad we cannot lightly abandon a last minute effort to resolve the seemingly insoluble problem of the two Koreas.
>
> The challenge is not only to prevent confusion, indeed, violence during the games; I do not think this will happen. It is to avoid increasingly serious incidents in the next few months, and dispel the cloud that hangs over Seoul '88 as a dangerous, unpredictable place one should stay away from. Summit declarations of support for the Olympics do not necessarily help. I believe they tend to be counter-productive, confirming the existence of a growing risk of turbulence. Yet there is an underlying international equation that could still make the Seoul games the most universal and exciting ever.
>
> East and West are in a posture of détente: neither Washington nor Moscow want incidents that might poison the improving climate. Beyond that, the Soviets seek normal games because their athletes (after the West's absence from Moscow in 1980, and the East's from Los Angeles in 1984) are in danger of becoming demoralized. Their allies have expressed discontent and a determination not to be drawn into new controversies and boycotts. China has also signified its desire that all go well in Seoul. In addition, South Korea is moving to develop commercial relations with Russia and Eastern Europe, and receiving favorable responses. Even Fidel Castro, who has stubbornly stood by Pyongyang, is manifestly uncomfortable in his isolation and unpopular exercise of authority to deny Cuban athletes the right to compete. The fact remains, however, that none of these powerful forces seems able to bring Pyongyang to participate, or control its determination to rob Seoul of an expected triumph.
>
> Having participated at President Samaranch's side in all of the I.O.C.'s contacts and negotiations with the two Koreas, I am convinced that the key to the solution, if it still exists, is now with ROK. The

central issues are not which and how many events are allocated to North Korea (that has pretty much been decided, and the games are unalterably Seoul's) or whether Pyongyang will "co-host" (this is an essentially semantic issue: holding any event in the North is inevitably a "co-hosting"); or how many tens of thousands of Olympic Family members will cross the demarcation line (a much smaller number might be enough if the Pyongyang events were held in a small Olympic enclave).

To my mind the situation calls for an imaginative act of statesmanship *à la Sadat* by the South Korean leadership. I am not suggesting that President Roh travel to the North, or take any of the physical or political risks assumed by the Egyptian leader. But I believe that if Sadat and Begin could develop a momentary dialogue leading to a truce, and eventually peace over the Sinai, Roh and Kim Il Sung could do something similar at least as regards the games, if not reunification.

My suggestion is that President Roh undertake an audacious initiative by addressing Kim Il Sung directly, to suggest a physical and psychological truce, whereby military threats and political invective would be suspended for the duration of the Olympiad, as in ancient Greece, so the games can proceed on a "co-hosted" basis in the historical interest of all the Korean people. Such a truce (with a lowered military profile by all concerned) may later help to open a more permanent dialogue between the two divided parts of the peninsula. It would not be the first time that sport and sportsmanship contributed to a diplomacy of reconciliation and peace.

For such an unconventional move to succeed, the address to the North must be nonpolemical, putting it momentarily as a co-equal on center stage. (I can imagine the diplomatic skill and literary eloquence with which it could be formulated.)

The current South Korean mentality appears to be cast in marble: "Let's humiliate the North with a highly successful Olympics in the South; then we will be able to negotiate from strength." This attitude should be shelved, at least for the time being. It seems to me wiser, given the enormous stakes for which South Korea is playing, to try a more flexible approach, leading to athletic and other contacts in limited areas. An approach of this type could, with luck, calm the students and radicals in the South, and consolidate Roh's political stature in Korea and the world. I believe Washington would not be opposed to such a stance: indeed, I have reason to believe that it would encourage it. Castro (not to mention Moscow and Peking) might also jump on it to ease North Korea toward moderation vis-à-vis the games.

While this may be too much to expect, the best way to move toward

> a denouement would be an urgently arranged meeting between two specially empowered and highly authorized emissaries of South and North Korea, perhaps even the two leaders in question, preferably in the presence of President Samaranch. Messengers of peace, with ready access to Roh, Kim Il Sung, Castro, Washington and Moscow are, fortunately available and can easily be activated for such a mission.

The extent of Roh's disenchantment, as president of the republic, with the Pisar proposal was evident from the tone of the second paragraph, in which Samaranch was chastised for attempting to change the ground rules rather late in the game:

> However, as you are well aware, the co-hosting of the Olympics as demanded by North Korea poses problems because it is always shrouded in a semantic equivocation. Since the idea presented in Mr. Pisar's report appears to be a departure from the fundamental position of the International Olympic Committee with regard to the vexed issue of co-hosting, we feel the concept in the report needs to be spelled out in unequivocal terms.

He continued:

> You will agree, Mr. President, that since Seoul was awarded the Olympic Games in 1981, the Korean government has made every possible concession to North Korea in order to encourage its participation in the Games, and, furthermore, we would spare no effort in the coming months to that end, in that the Seoul Olympics with North Korea's attendance prove to be a great opportunity for national reconciliation.

Regarding his recent declaration, he advised Samaranch:

> I have expressed on several occasions my sincere hope for a meeting between the highest authorities of Seoul and North Korea, and, guided by that spirit, a special declaration was issued on July 7, designed to help the two parts of Korea do away with confrontation and explore venues for mutual cooperation. The Korean government will take various practical measures for an inter-Korean reconciliation keeping in line with the declaration, and it is our earnest hope that North Korea come to this historic festival of peace and harmony for mankind.
>
> I believe that a recent resolution urging North Korea to join us in

> the Seoul Olympics, which was unanimously adopted by the Korean National Assembly, well represents the deep aspiration of the Korean people for North Korea's participation.
>
> We will continue our efforts in close collaboration with the International Olympic Committee, while keeping the door open for North Korea until the very last minute, in the same manner as we have done during the past seven years.

Samaranch replied to Roh's letter on July 24. Roh's message had been perfectly well understood, and it was time to back away from the change in position. The wording of his response was extremely conciliatory. He included the following comments with respect to the Games.

> This gives me yet another opportunity to reconfirm the full and complete support of the International Olympic Committee in the efforts to ensure the greatest possible success of the Games of the XXIVth Olympiad in Seoul.
>
> As I look back on our efforts since Seoul was designated as the host city for these Games, almost seven years ago, I am more and more convinced that these Games will be the best in our Olympic history and involve the participation of a record number of National Olympic Committees.
>
> May I also take this occasion to say how much the IOC Executive Board, meeting in Lausanne today, and I personally, appreciate the recent initiatives taken by you on 7th July 1988 and by the National Assembly on 1st July 1988. These are steps of statesmanship and understanding which we hope will bear fruit.

Roh understood that a shift in policy as significant as that disclosed in his July 7 declaration had to be followed up on a regular basis, lest it be ignored, or worse, be perceived as just another step in the confrontational process that had typified the north-south relationships for so many years. In his August 15, 1988, message on the forty-third anniversary of national liberation, Roh proposed that he and DPRK president Kim Il Sung meet as soon as possible to discuss ways and means of achieving unification. He attached no conditions regarding venue or agenda. A personal response was forthcoming from Kim Il Sung himself on September 8, the day before the fortieth anniversary of the DPRK. Kim mentioned both the North and the South, suggested

Pyongyang as the venue, and referred to a nonaggression pact, establishing a confederal government (not a new proposal), and establishing a "peaceful unification committee." There was no evidence of a change in the North's strategy.[38] Roh would again call for such a meeting with Kim on October 4, 1988, in his policy speech to the 144th Regular Session of the National Assembly, as well as in his address to the UN General Assembly on October 18, 1988.[39]

On July 12, Soviet Olympic officials announced that Soviet athletes would live in the Olympic Village in Seoul and not separately on ships. On July 16, China announced that it would send its largest Olympic team ever to the Games in Seoul. Around these very positive announcements from the major allies and sponsors of the DPRK, North Korean officials in France were stating that there would be no trouble, while, at the same time, the UN Command was criticizing the North for trying to undermine the Games by making war threats and contriving tension in the area. U.S. secretary of state Shultz gave kudos to South Korea on July 16 for "impressively struggling to put this democracy on the road" and expressed confidence that the Games would be safe and successful.

The resolution of the Korean National Assembly adopted earlier that month[40] calling upon the North to take part in the Games was transmitted to the North on July 17. This was the same day the Soviet Olympic attaché said he was sure the Games would be safe; otherwise the Soviets would not have agreed to participate. The next day, somewhat to everyone's surprise, the DPRK accepted delivery of the letter, the first com-

[38] Such a change would have been remarkable in the circumstances, and it was generally considered that a genuine breakthrough in the North's policy would have to wait for Kim's death or removal from political life. It would likely also depend on the North's being able to escape the imposition of "Dear Leader" Kim Jong Il, as part of the nepotism and personality cult that appeared to have taken hold in the North. The anomaly of such a succession in a Communist regime seemed to have escaped the notice of the North.

[39] Though this work is not the place for a detailed analysis of Roh's address to the UN, it was an able piece of statesmanship and one in which he was careful to give credit to the developments occurring in the USSR and in China, without which it would have been doubtful at best if South Korea could have made such remarkable progress. The success of such openness can be seen in the degree to which socialist countries almost immediately began to pursue and extend diplomatic and quasi-diplomatic relationships with the South.

[40] The twentieth plenary meeting of the 142d Extraordinary National Assembly adopted a resolution on July 9, calling for participation in the Games by the DPRK. Polls published the same day showed a significant majority of Koreans supported Roh Tae Woo's declaration aimed at peace on the Korean peninsula.

munication from the South that it had accepted since Roh Tae Woo had become president on February 25. Within three days, the North suggested a joint north-south parliamentary meeting to discuss questions of nonaggression.[41]

The response from the North Koreans was enough of an apparent breakthrough that wildly optimistic rumors began to spread that North Korea and Cuba might well participate in the Games, although there was no objective evidence to that effect. The source of the rumors had, seemingly, been linked to the opposition parties and to Derwinski of the U.S. State Department, which was compelled to issue a statement on July 25 that there was no evidence to support the rumors. The following day, the DPRK suggested the idea of cohosting the Games might be included on the agenda for the proposed parliamentary talks. On July 27, South Korea agreed that this could be included on the agenda. Samaranch expressed his satisfaction with the prospect of the talks and hoped the Olympics could benefit.

These developments prompted a number of reactions within South Korea. SLOOC president Park Seh Jik made a last-ditch appeal to the North to participate and, at the same time, urged dissident student leaders to keep a low profile during the Games. The same day, July 28, government party politicians stated it was now too late, for all practical purposes, for any events to be staged in the North. And Kim Il Sung, calling for the parliamentary discussions to take place at the earliest possible moment, renewed his demands for cohosting the Games while, at the same time, denouncing the plans of the United States to reinforce its military presence in and around Korea during the Games.

On August 1, South Korea called for a preliminary meeting to discuss the agenda for the proposed parliamentary talks. Samaranch stated in an interview that same day that it was now too late for any of the team events to be held in the North, even if the North were now to accept the proposal. Two days later, the South Korean foreign minister officially announced the opening of a Soviet consular office in Seoul and stated that this would help to improve relations between Moscow and Seoul. Special security measures were announced for flights between Tokyo and Seoul through to the end of the Games. Radical student leaders

[41] This was unusual enough that Samaranch expressed the cautious thought to the IOC Executive Board on July 24 that recent developments in Korea might be helpful. This was compounded by a recent visit by Mario Vazquez-Raña and German Rieckehoff to the DPRK following meetings with Fidel Castro. Samaranch still did not think Cuba would participate, since the communications he had with Cuba in that regard had come directly from Castro.

denied any concept of an Olympic "truce."[42] On August 6, the Japanese government announced that it would invalidate the passports of any persons suspected as terrorists who might try to disrupt the Games in Seoul. This was the first time that the Japanese government had acted in such a manner with respect to the Games and the first time that it had ordered passports returned in this manner for Japanese security interests.

The North indicated on August 8 that it would respond the following day with respect to the South Korean proposal for a preliminary meeting. The response was delivered as promised, and the North agreed to a meeting at Panmunjom on August 17. The meeting would eventually be held August 19. The North continued to press for a five-day parliamentary meeting to start on August 26. In the context of these exchanges, Samaranch caused the IOC to issue a press release on August 11, calling for participation by the DPRK in the Seoul Games and reiterating the IOC's earlier requests for a joint parade of the teams from the North and the South in the Opening and Closing Ceremonies. This call was immediately supported by Park Seh Jik on behalf of the SLOOC and by the KOC. A full briefing was given on August 12 by Park to President Roh, the opposition leaders, and other prominent figures in South Korea, all of whom promised full support for the Games.

Roh followed up his assurances in this regard by calling for a "ceasefire" on all violent student demonstrations in the period leading up to the Games.[43] He urged that the wisdom of the country be pooled for the success of the Games and that "family quarrels" be put aside until after the Games. Cho Sang Ho, now minister of sport, issued a statement that the door remained open to the North, but that entries would have to be received not later than September 2.[44] Within two days of Roh's call for a ceasefire concerning violent student demonstrations, the

[42] By August 7, however, the radical leaders, faced with no public support, were forced to state that demonstrations during the Olympic period would be confined to university campuses. Such time was, however, not yet upon them, and the next day some students left Seoul campuses for a cross-country march toward Panmunjom to meet with DPRK students for unification talks. DPRK students began their own march to Panmunjom for the same purpose. Clashes occurred on August 10 when the South Korean students were turned back by police.

[43] On August 5, the Law for the Preservation of the Peace of the Olympics was proclaimed in Korea.

[44] In Paris on August 1, Samaranch had been quoted as saying that it was now too late for team events to be staged in the DPRK, even if the IOC's proposal were to be accepted.

South Korean police began to take a much tougher stance in breaking up such demonstrations. On August 15, Roh stated that the people and government of Korea would not forgive violence that threatened the Games. Students were again prevented from marching to Panmunjom to meet with their northern counterparts. The government's position was that the north-south issue was a matter for government to solve.

In his message on August 15, celebrating forty-three years of freedom from Japanese rule, Roh Tae Woo called for a meeting of the top leaders of the North and the South to meet for a dialogue. On the following day, the DPRK advised the IOC that its proposal for joint marching of the teams from North Korea and South Korea was rejected. The North would be in touch with the IOC following the meeting scheduled for August 19, if the results of that meeting were to be positive. In North Korea, the Cuban ambassador was reported as confirming the Cuban position of nonparticipation in the Games in a speech on August 17, at the end of a month-long celebration of "solidarity with the Cuban people."

The preliminary meeting to discuss the agenda for the planned parliamentary meeting took place on August 19 and continued through August 20, but no progress was reported on matters pertaining to the Games. At the end of the meeting, the South had proposed that the Olympic matter be discussed at a meeting to be held in Pyongyang on August 29, but this idea was rejected by the North on August 22.

Japanese assistance for the Games continued even as these meetings were being held between the North and the South. On August 18, the Japanese minister responsible for the postal services announced that special security measures would be instituted for parcels destined for Korea. The North Koreans had demonstrated a decided penchant for bombs, and the Japanese had supported the UN Security Council resolution condemning North Korea for state terrorism. Four days later, special security measures were announced to protect foreign athletes training in Japan, as well as foreign diplomatic establishments and prominent persons. Concurrent concern was expressed in Japan that Japanese passports stolen two years earlier in Madrid might be intended for use by terrorists.[45] Emerging from a year-long cessation of publication, the Japanese Red Army *Political Review* (no. 29) strongly criticized

[45] Ten Japanese passports had been stolen from a group of Japanese tourists on February 18, 1986.

the ties between Japan, Korea, and the United States and called for a fight against them.

Another breakthrough for the South Koreans occurred on August 23, when China granted permission for KAL to overfly Chinese territory for Olympic-related flights from Tripoli and Zurich. It was announced that Korea hoped such permissions might continue after the Games and that it would negotiate for such concessions.[46] The same day, on only forty-five minutes' notice, North Korea requested continuation of the meetings in Panmunjom. The South said this was impossible, but suggested August 24 instead. Though the North agreed to this, the meeting was not held until August 26. This meeting produced the customary nonresult, and the only matter of consequence was that the negotiators agreed that the discussions would not be continued until October 13, after the Games in Seoul would have finished. To the surprise of no one, the North Korean delegates to the meeting accused the South of deliberately blocking the North's participation in the Games.

It was clear that the South Korean authorities were not entirely certain they had solved the potential problems with student demonstrations. It was a constant worry of Samaranch's as well. Indeed, he was hypersensitive to media reports of demonstrations and was constantly badgering the Koreans to find some way to stop them, occasionally without full reflection concerning the political costs involved. Beginning on August 23, "Peace Zones" were established in Korea, in which no political rallies were to be permitted from that date until October 31. Two U.S. activists were arrested that same day and ordered deported from South Korea because of their participation in radical political meetings. The deportation proceedings did not put any damper on the relationship with the United States, since the next day, Assistant Secretary of State Derwinski announced that the combination of public opinion and security measures would deter terrorists, that the Games would be a triumph, and that the radical students did not appear to have any public support. On August 26, Seoul was declared to be a Peace Zone, in which unauthorized gatherings and manifestations were prohibited. The combination of all this appeared to be enough for the students,

[46] Similar concessions had been requested of the Soviet Union, and Samaranch had been asked to support such requests on behalf of the Koreans. He waited, however, until the Chinese had made their announcement of consent before writing to Soviet NOC president Marat Gramov to ask for his assistance in the matter, in a telex dated August 28. Earlier discussions had occurred on this matter. Earlier in the month, Cho Choong Kun, president of KAL, had visited Moscow to request permission to overfly the Soviet Union for flights with Olympic participants. Permission was granted by the Soviets.

who indicated that demonstrations during the Olympic period would be confined to university campuses.[47]

On August 27, the Japanese authorities ratcheted up security measures again, announcing that airport security would be increased and that armed guards would be placed on all ferries operating between Japan and Korea. Some 80 percent of its coast guard strength would be assigned to the Sea of Japan, to prevent the smuggling of arms and explosives into Korea. As September approached, it appeared as if most of the risk pertaining to the Games had been adequately contained. The security measures would, naturally, have to be carefully executed, but confidence was growing that the plans were satisfactory and that the foreseeable contingencies had been factored into the plans.

Samaranch made a special effort on August 29 to persuade Kim Yu Sun to attend the IOC Session in Seoul prior to the Games, while knowing it was all but impossible for this to occur. He also expressed his disappointment that no solution had been found, although he was still ready to discuss some kind of agreement, in the interest of the athletes involved. In the Soviet press of August 30, Yuri Titov, who, almost seven years previously, had posed the "set-up" question on behalf of the Japanese, was quoted as complimenting the preparations for the Games. On September 1, the Bolshoi Ballet performed in Seoul. There could, in the circumstances, hardly have been a clearer stamp of Soviet commitment to the Games than this. Nor a clearer message to North Korea.[48]

To avoid a problem similar to one that had arisen during the 1986 Asian Games, when an Iranian athlete defected, Park Seh Jik announced on September 3 that no political asylum would be granted to any persons from the third world during the period of the Games. Samaranch arrived in Seoul the next day, to stay until the Games were finished. He was greeted upon arrival by a telex from Kim Yu Sun, in response to his message of August 29, that the DPRK had left no stone

[47] An unhelpful statement, attributed to former IOC director Monique Berlioux, was published on August 27, saying that security measures in Seoul would "kill the very soul of the Games."

[48] Park Seh Jik, in his own account of the Games and their organization, states that on September 2, four individuals, including Kaneko Eiko, an international terrorist connected with North Korea and the Japanese Red Army, attempted to infiltrate Korea with forged passports. He also stated that special action had to be taken in connection with advice received that North Korea was planning to blow up chartered planes transporting Soviet and Chinese athletes to the Games. On September 4, he reported, an individual traveling to Korea on an Iranian passport had refused to allow his baggage to be inspected. During a stopover in Bangkok, he had been observed purchasing batteries and wires.

unturned at the parliamentary meetings between the North and the South to solve the cohosting problem. The effort had failed owing to the unjust position of the South. His NOC would not participate in singly hosted Games.[49]

The first Soviet plane to land in Korea arrived on September 6 with part of the Soviet delegation for the Games.

By this time, Samaranch could easily afford to continue playing the game with Kim Yu Sun. He simply announced on September 7 that the door was still open to North Korea to participate in the Games. The North remained offside in the eyes of the world and remained in the position of having refused a reasonable offer from the IOC. Doubtless, it mattered not to the North Koreans at this stage, since their performance was directed to a captive audience at home, not the rest of the world. The IOC announced that it had accredited some Cuban journalists, but that sports officials would not be accredited. Any results published in Cuba, despite the editorial perspective that could be expected to be vigorously negative, could only drive home to the Cuban leadership the cost of the futile boycott. The Chinese announced that they would double the press coverage of the Seoul Games in comparison with the previous Games in Los Angeles. And the radical student leaders announced that they would refrain from street demonstrations but would definitely topple the Roh government by the end of the year.[50]

In a meeting with President Roh Tae Woo on September 8, Samaranch outlined his plan to keep the door open to North Korea until the Closing Ceremony. Though nothing would come of it, the tactic of never having closed the doors could only help and not hurt the situation. The same day, in one of the symbolic gestures of which he is a master,

[49] The DPRK formally announced its boycott of the Seoul Games on September 4 and stated that it would do nothing to disrupt the Games.

[50] Despite this declaration on September 7, there was a minor battle with police by radical students on September 8, close to the Shilla Hotel, where Samaranch and the IOC were staying. Apart from a further incident with other radical students the following day, there were few, if any, other demonstrations of this type. Samaranch was unamused, despite the assurances of Park Seh Jik that it was a small demonstration, unreflective of the sentiment of the Korean public. He insisted that measures be taken to prevent this kind of action, since he thought the media would focus on it and give the Games a bad reputation. Park maintained that taking forceful action would be worse than merely containing the demonstrations. Samaranch nevertheless insisted that his views be brought to the attention of the Korean government. Most of the IOC Executive Board agreed with Park and, in any event, Park was not about to let Samaranch make decisions of that nature in Korea.

Samaranch dined in the Olympic Village with the leaders of the government and opposition parties.[51] He arranged for Marat Gramov, the Soviet NOC president and would-be IOC member,[52] to issue a call for all countries to participate in the Games.

September 9 was a date of further loss of face for Kim Il Sung. In the first place, he received a telex, delivered through Kim Yu Sun, from Samaranch, extending greetings for the anniversary that day. It was the fortieth anniversary of the founding of the DPRK, to which Kim Il Sung had invited the leaders of all the socialist countries, including Mikhail Gorbachev of the Soviet Union. As had been widely predicted by Asian and other diplomatic observers, Gorbachev did not attend. Nor did Andrei Gromyko. What was even more telling, however, was the choice of its representative: Viktor Chebrikov, head of the KGB. This was taken by most as a deliberately low-level presence of the Soviet Union and a signal to the North Koreans regarding the Olympic Games. The customary mass rallies were held, and Kim Il Sung trotted out a repeat of earlier calls, going back to 1980, for unification of the Korean peninsula on a confederal basis. The South had regularly rejected this approach in favor of direct parliamentary elections.[53]

By September 10, the focus of attention turned, at last, to those athletes who were in Seoul, rather than those who were not. Mario Vazquez-Raña reported that Castro was "very, very sad" that matters had not been resolved and that the Cubans would not be able to participate in the Games.[54] North Korea, in one of the more unusual moments of the long campaign, urged all the socialist countries attending the

[51] There was a minor concern about security generated when some DPRK propaganda was found in the Olympic Village on September 8. The South Koreans were, however, sufficiently relaxed about the matter that on September 9, the Ministry of Culture and Information was prepared to state that books brought into the country by eastern bloc athletes and tourists would not be confiscated and that the new policy of the government was that publications on communism would be opened to the public, as long as their contents did not violate the constitution.

[52] He would replace Konstantin Andrianov but only remain an IOC member until 1992, when his membership would lapse, owing to the "disappearance" of the country in which he was a member, namely the USSR. The other member in the USSR, Vitaly Smirnov, was confirmed as IOC member in Russia.

[53] This was not an altogether surprising position, given both the democratic tendency of the South and its considerable numerical superiority were such elections to have occurred.

[54] This sadness did not stop Castro's criticism, on September 24, of all the other socialist countries for having attended the Games.

Games to refrain from political actions that the South might use to its political advantage.

The IOC Session began on September 12. It was largely uneventful. There was a brief flurry of activity at the behest of the IOC member in Libya, Bashir Attarabulsi, who requested help in drafting a message to Gadhafi to assist in making sure the Libyan team got the proper authorization to travel to the Games. This took a few days, but the Libyan team did arrive in time for the Games, though not in time for the Opening Ceremony, where Libya was represented on that occasion by a few journalists outfitted in appropriate garb for purposes of public presence. The IOC also allowed the television signal of the Games to be made available, at no cost, within North Korea. On September 13, South Korea and Hungary announced their agreement to exchange permanent missions, and, in an interview on NBC, President Roh expressed the view that full democracy in Korea would follow the Games.

On September 14, South Korea indicated it would agree to talks in Pyongyang provided there would be no interference with the Games. Kim Il Sung responded to Samaranch's greetings delivered in relation to the anniversary celebrations by stating that a symbolic participation on the part of North Korea was not possible. He urged Samaranch to cause the South Korean authorities to change their position on cohosting. The first part of the message was understandable, but the second was plainly absurd, coming three days before the Opening Ceremony.[55] Though most messages from most leaders are written for them, it is difficult to imagine what the author of this suggestion had in mind. It accomplished nothing except to cause the "Glorious Leader" to appear hopelessly out of touch with the reality of the situation. The day before the Opening Ceremony, on September 16, Mikhail Gorbachev delivered a major foreign policy address in Krasnoyarsk, proposing a seven-point peace plan for the Asian and Pacific regions. The times were propitious.[56]

[55] Cuba denied rumors, which continued to pop up here and there, that it would participate in the Games, as late as September 14. Such a rumor had been published in the *Shinmun* newspaper in Seoul on August 12, and they kept circulating from time to time. Cuba added to these denials the statement that the 1991 Pan American Games were not in doubt, because, unlike the United States in 1980, Cuba had not exerted any pressure on other countries not to participate.

[56] This statement was followed shortly thereafter by a remarkable development in Soviet foreign policy. On September 27, in an address to the UN General Assembly, Soviet foreign minister Eduard Shevardnadze announced the de-ideologization of Soviet foreign policy, stating: "Class struggles have come to an end in the international society and ideology can no longer become the basic principle of international relations."

* * *

September 17, 1988, could not have been brighter, and the weather augured well for the Opening Ceremony of the Games of the XXIVth Olympiad. The Games got off to a magnificent beginning that was a testimony to the planning and preparations so assiduously carried out by the South Koreans for so many years.

I remember particularly, among the many brilliant elements of the ceremony, the symbolic portrayal of how the forces of conflict come together at the last moment into a unity of effort and will.[57] It seemed to me a striking image of what we had seen happen in the course of this long adventure.

[57] The only significant possibility of political catastrophe came from an inadvertent identification, during the Opening Ceremony, of Jerusalem as the capital of Israel. The Arab nations were most upset and threatened to pull out of the Games. This was avoided at the last minute when the SLOOC apologized for the error.

CHAPTER 13

Upon Reflection . . .

THIS IS NOT A BOOK about what happened on the fields of play during the 1988 Olympic Games. Others have described the Games more ably than I could hope to do. In any event, much of the Games themselves are portrayed in the thousands of images of grace, beauty, effort, failure, triumph, and courage. The Olympic Games are an amalgam of the individual stories and personal quests of the athletes who come to test themselves, to see how they will fare in the ultimate crucible of competition. The final measure of the Olympic Games rests deep in the hearts of the athletes who have come there to do their best and who know, inescapably, in the recesses of their souls, whether they have competed with honor and to the best of their own abilities on that occasion. We can watch, as spectators, and share in what are the tips — albeit beautiful — of thousands of personal icebergs.

This work has been, instead, an attempt to explore some of the factors that made it possible for those athletes to have had the opportunity to participate in the 1988 Olympic Games. It is an effort to show that the Games, as an institution in our society, are more than a mere series of athletic competitions that simply "happen" every four years. The Olympic Games are much more important than this. They have become a microcosm of the world itself, expressing its tensions in an intellectually and emotionally manageable theater. A theater, perhaps, in which the willing suspension of disbelief gives life to the idea of what could be possible if only all the latent goodwill of humanity could be harnessed.

South Korea

What, after all, was this small country of South Korea, which aspired to be host to the world? What motivated it to take on the Olympic Games, one of the most challenging events imaginable, clothed with its own inherent tensions and saddled with considerable international political baggage? Did Korea have something to offer or something to prove? What were the risks it incurred by daring to audition, in 1981, for one of the biggest parts in international theater? What motivated it to make the move from Japanese understudy to Korean star, in a face-to-face confrontation with the internationally acknowledged Asian leader? For most of the world, with the exception of a hazy recollection of the Korean War in the early 1950s, Korea tended to be a footnote on the international scene, a small but unsolvable problem in which there was little interest.

The fact of the matter is that Korea possesses a long and culturally rich history. It has had rather a difficult last century, in which it has been dominated and overrun by Japan, Russia, the Soviet Union, and the United States.[1] There is an immensely strong feeling of nationalism, rivaling similar Chinese sentiments, but one that is perhaps not so diffuse as that of the Chinese, since its territory is much more concentrated.[2] This feeling is sufficient to make the concept of reunification strong enough that political leaders on both sides of the 38th parallel dare not avoid including the matter as part of the active political agenda, regardless of how unlikely achievement of the objective may be in the foreseeable future.

As it approached the 1988 Olympic Games, South Korea was in an evident state of transition. The transition was not as apparent when the campaign for the Games was begun, since a presidential assassination and a subsequent military coup intervened in the process, although these may well be seen, in retrospect, as symptoms of that transition, violent as they were. In the years leading up to the Games, there had been astonishing economic progress in South Korea, and it appeared that the populace was generally content to trade some, even significant,

[1]The scope of this work does not permit a full exploration of this history, but it may serve, in part, to explain why the thought of preempting Japan as host of the Olympic Games might have been, despite the risks, particularly satisfying to the Koreans.

[2] Some observers have suggested, and not without a grain of truth, that today's China is, perhaps, a civilization that is trying to be run as a country.

political freedom for the increases in the standard of living. There was (and remains) a sense of the Confucian concept of national harmony, which occurs under a strong and hierarchical leadership. This is evident in many aspects of Korean society and has been maintained in the middle class, which expanded with the economic success of South Korea. The philosophical tendency, however strong it may have been, was also reinforced by the military, which was powerful, disciplined, and conservative.

On the other hand, increased economic prosperity, coupled with the broad base of education in South Korea, brought with it the inevitable desire for more freedom of expression, whether of thought, economic activity, or political action. The seeds were sown, and it could only have been a matter of time before they germinated and eventually flowered. The political leadership, at the time derived from the military, was not unaware of this but was intensely concerned about the pace and direction of any change. It was not completely opposed to change but did not want undisciplined or precipitous change and was prepared to intervene with such force as might be necessary to prevent it. By the time Seoul was awarded the 1988 Olympic Games by the IOC in late 1981, the presidency was held by Chun Doo Hwan, a former army general, who had seized power following the assassination of Park Chung Hee, himself a military figure, in a coup that involved its own share of bloodshed.

In that respect, there was not much to distinguish the Chun regime from many other military governments, even though Chun went through the ritual cleansing of retiring from the military before assuming office. Few believed, however, that he threw out all his uniforms when he became president, nor that, behind his civilian presidency, the military had an entirely benign disinterest. The combination of his Confucian mental set and military conservatism made Chun an unapproachable figure, unattractive to the population at large. Coupled with the muscular legal framework that made full political expression in Korea difficult and dangerous for those who opposed government policy, the Chun government was regarded with both distaste and fear.

Change was, nevertheless, in the wind, and in some respects this was appreciated as much by the military as by any segment of Korean society. Its concerns were not so much change as such, but its management, together with an overriding commitment that it be accomplished without exposing the republic to the adventurism of North Korea. With something in the order of one million armed troops along the borders of the two Koreas, the possibility of misadventure was considerable, and the history of the North gave little reason for relaxing vigilance in the slightest. As a priority, therefore, the military was prepared to intervene if the process of change were to get out of control or expose the South to a military intervention from the North. This imperative was known by the political leaders on all sides. Its full implications were not necessarily appreciated by student leaders, who, with the energy of youth unsupported by experience, occasionally pushed too far too fast, with all too predictable reaction. The more radical student leaders had different objectives. They wished to provoke such responses, preferably excessive responses, and attempted, whenever possible, to do so. Anarchy is an absence of form. Political vacuums are created in order to be filled. By the radical students, of course.

Chun had indicated, regardless of the cynicism with which this indication was observed, that he would leave office at the end of his term. He had, with occasional lapses, indicated that he would condone the amendment of the constitution, if the ruling Democratic Justice Party and the opposition parties could agree on the amendments. Chun had not gone as far as giving up the built-in advantage of the ability of the leading party to load the National Assembly with its own appointees, but a change in this direction was only a matter of time. Nor had he agreed to direct presidential elections, since this squandered the same built-in advantage his party already enjoyed. But this, too, was inevitable, and the hand-picked candidate to succeed him, Roh Tae Woo, had conceded this within two weeks of being confirmed as his party's candidate in the presidential elections. Chun endorsed this decision and may well have known the concession would be forthcoming at the time of choosing Roh. Roh benefited from this recognition of the current political reality as well as from the political immaturity of the opposition parties, which fragmented prior to the elections and allowed him to emerge through the middle as the winner, in effect, by default.[3]

The South Koreans had many reasons to bid for the Games.[4] Having done so successfully, the focus and the onus shifted dramatically. They were still sensitive about having to concede that they were unable to host the first Asian Games they had been awarded and had now, deliberately, placed themselves in a situation in which they had sought and won not only the 1986 Asian Games, but the biggest prize of all, the

[3] It was interesting to note that Samaranch, accompanied by Mario Vazquez-Raña, visited Chun at his home on October 3, after the Games were over, to thank him for his support during his presidency.

[4] See, for example, Chapter 1, footnote 16.

Olympic Games. For South Korea, nothing could stand in the way of successful hosting of both events. These were entré to international recognition, acceptance, and membership in the family of nations. This was a feeling shared by all South Koreans. The depth of this feeling was underestimated by many foreign observers, who thought that the domestic or family political squabbles would prevail. The observers were wrong from the outset. The Koreans would *never* have countenanced losing face on their own account. If external circumstances intervened to prevent the full accomplishment, that would have been painful indeed and a matter of national sorrow. But the thought of fouling their own nest was complete anathema to them.

In some respects this desire made them vulnerable. They probably accommodated a considerable number of unjustified and unnecessary requests from persons and organizations preying upon the insecurity that existed prior to the Games. For the most part, this was likely a minor annoyance and not much of an expense, given the stakes for which they were playing. On the other hand, the desire to succeed served to focus a great deal of national attention and to apply a great deal of talent to the two projects, with the result that they were, in the end, immensely well organized and a demonstrable credit to Korea. The initial objectives were entirely achieved.

In the process, there can, in retrospect, be little doubt that the evolution of democracy was accelerated considerably as a result of the efforts of South Korea to respond to the expectations of the rest of the world. This was made easier by the confluence of international events that had eased tensions between the superpowers, but there was, in addition to this, a distinct Korean response. There was a great deal of international help in the move toward an acceptable form of democracy, but one of the difficulties inherent in receiving such advice and pressure is that each of the donors believed its form of democracy was the best and argued for its application in Korea. Overlooked, perhaps, in the desire to provide counsel was the fact that each society must develop in its own way and that democracy is not a mass-produced suit of clothing to be bought off the rack, nor a suit that can be put on and taken off at will.

South Korea had its Confucian background as a consideration, with the tradition of the strong leadership that goes with it. They were experimenting with the democratic process and really only got full encouragement to proceed as a consequence of the June 29, 1987, declaration of Roh Tae Woo. This, in itself, took some time to digest, and the early part of the period of new freedom was infused with political hormones, as the limits of the new freedom were tested. It must have been a matter of some comfort to the public at large that the freedoms were proposed by one of the military politicians and approved by a military president. The risk of attempting to accelerate the process would have been appreciably greater without the backdrop of this particular element in their society. There seems little doubt that the democratization would eventually have occurred, but similarly little doubt that the military would, equally, have intervened if social disruptions arising out of it could be seen to have created (or even potentially created) an instability to be exploited by the North.

One of the main areas of help in the process of democratization within South Korea was the restraints put on the North by its Chinese and Soviet allies. Neither wanted war with the United States. They would have been placed in a particularly difficult position were the North to become involved in any significant military activity in Korea, since there was no doubt that the United States, with some forty thousand troops in Korea at the time, would immediately have been engaged and would have been required to accelerate such engagement as much as necessary to protect its troops and interests in Korea. Indeed, the United States, for many reasons affecting its Asian policy, would have had no alternative but to commit to such action. There was, therefore, a complete congruence of national interests among the three superpowers to prevent any incidents on the Korean peninsula. There can be little doubt that the appropriate messages were conveyed both by China and the Soviet Union to the DPRK in their roles as allies. However unpalatable to the North they may have been, they appear to have been both received and understood.

North Korea

The 1988 Olympic Games must have been very difficult for the North Koreans. Having never been fully recognized as a country by most of the world and, even where recognized, only receiving such status as an accommodation to China or the Soviet Union, or to annoy the United States, the North had both a chip on its diplomatic shoulder and increasing anxiety that it was on the verge of losing, once and for all, the struggle to overshadow the South. The judgment had been largely made already by most of the world, but successful Olympic Games in Seoul would be conclusive evidence on a scale impossible to ignore. The dilemma was clear, and the horns on which the North found itself were sharp. However absurd its position and rationalizations may have seemed to observers, the situation was deadly serious to the North. It was this very seriousness that caused everyone, including its allies, to treat the North with caution, lest it respond to the mounting pressure with some intemperate action that might have serious implications for others.

In the beginning, North Korea had sought to deny the likelihood that the world would choose Seoul for the site of the Games. When the choice was made, it tried to ridicule the decision, but no one seemed to listen. Even its allies did not seriously object to the choice, until the Los Angeles boycott in 1984, when it became much more convenient to do so, not only to draw some attention away from their own anti-Olympic actions, but also because there was increasing fear that the political situation in 1988 might be such that another boycott could become inevitable. The United States was such a recognized sponsor of South Korea and the Soviet Union such a recognized sponsor of the North that it would be almost as if one or the other of the superpowers would "win" or "lose" a diplomatic battle over the site of the Games, even before their proxy warriors took to the fields of presumptive battle.[5]

The North suffered the additional humiliation of having to withdraw from the competition to host the 1986 Asian Games, in the face of certain victory by the South in that contest within Asia itself. It would have been an unacceptable loss of face to receive the numerical judgment of a vote, so withdrawal of its candidacy at the last moment was the only political solution. As the preparations proceeded, it became increasingly clear that the South was likely to succeed with both ventures. This called for a reassessment of the stand-off policy to date and an exploration of the second possibility, which was to let the regional Asian Games proceed without comment, while doing whatever presented itself as an opportunity to destabilize the situation, and to develop a strategy to dilute whatever success the South might achieve through the main event of the Olympic Games.

There was probably little thought directed at the Games themselves, other than as a means to the political end of not losing relative position

[5] It has always been something of a mystery that the Games have been seen as a substitute for war in many media circles. They have been denigrated as such, with such intensity of feeling (if not profound thought) that, it appears, the observers would rather have a real war than the surrogate war they identify. If ever it could be demonstrated that the Olympic Games have taken the place of a real war, their existence could be justified, on that basis alone, forever.

to the South in the internecine political struggle for dominance on the Korean peninsula itself. It did not seem to matter much to the North how inept it appeared during the process starting in 1984 and ending after the Games in 1988. Its audience was at home, under highly controlled conditions. The population of the North could not be allowed to come in contact with the rest of the world in less than fully controlled circumstances. The arrival of the world, in the form of the people and media accompanying the Olympic Games, could not be controlled. The prospect, therefore, of the North's actually playing host to these multitudes was slight enough to be negligible. It was impossible that the border between north and south could be opened to the level of free passage necessary to accommodate the Olympic Games.

What, then, was this laborious process of negotiation all about? It was, first of all, an opportunity for the North to keep the Olympic question before its public and to portray its authorities as battling the perfidious South in the name of national reunification and fighting against the imperialist United States. It was, in this respect, hoping to be able to portray itself as a patriotic Korean David against the Goliath of the capitalist world. There was the secondary purpose of drawing attention away from the fact that the 1986 Asian Games were in Seoul. The Olympic negotiations overshadowed the preparations and successful staging of this event. There was the bombing at Kimpo Airport just prior to those Games, attributed by the South to the North, which was a clear attempt to destabilize the South at this critical time. Whether or not the North was responsible, it more than suited the South to make such a public attribution of blame as part of its overall strategy of dealing with the North in preparation for the 1988 Games.

The negotiations would, however, have to end at some stage. There would either be an agreement or there would not. The negotiations were a strategy designed to lead to an attribution of eventual blame, not a means for ensuring that an agreement would be reached. Nobody thought an agreement would be reached, except, perhaps, the South, which feared that through some miscalculation the parties might find themselves faced with the existence of an agreement despite the efforts not to do so.

From the outset, the IOC had assured the South Koreans that no agreement was possible. From the outset, as well, the North had been so outrageous in its demands and so intransigent in its negotiations that it was evident it did not expect there to be an agreement. One half of the Games in the North was not possible. Less than one half would make it clear that the North accepted the dominant position of the South. That was not possible. A clever variation on the theme was developed as a fallback position that could appear to save face, namely, that the number of sports in the North could conform with the distribution of the population on the peninsula, which is what gave rise to the proposal for hosting eight sports that appeared during the negotiations. This would have been impossible for the South to accept, for the same reason that it might have satisfied the North.

The negotiations regarding the Olympic Games were all conducted within the context of the highest policy levels of the respective governments and their attitudes toward the policy of reunification. All Koreans appear, as a matter of nationalism, to want reunification. They cannot agree on the appropriate terms, given the enormous gap between the political systems in each country. There seems little room for compromise, given the recent history. Though there have been significant leadership changes in the South, none have occurred in the North, and the system is such that until Kim Il Sung steps down, is deposed (of which there appears no likelihood), or dies, there will be no change in the position advanced by the North. It remains one of the few remaining political systems of its discredited model.[6] Barring a breakthrough in the overall negotiations, the Olympic matter was too important to be considered in isolation.

With no prospect of resolving the problem of the Games, the matter, from the North's perspective, became one of trying to get the South to make a mistake in the negotiations, which would lead either to political instability in the South of such magnitude that concerns regarding security would lead to moving the Games from Seoul[7] or to creation of sufficient sympathy for the "just cause" of the North that the IOC would be pressured by its own constituency to change the site in order to avoid massive boycotts. In the event that neither of these results could be achieved, then at least the South had to be seen as the reason

[6] The DPRK's actions in withdrawing from the Nonproliferation Treaty in the face of outside insistence that its nuclear facilities be inspected to determine if its activities include the preparation of weapons-grade materials is a matter for some concern in respect of a country with an aged despot who has lost every military, economic, and political encounter with the archenemy to the south. The uncertain stability of the presumptive successor to Kim Il Sung, his son Kim Jong Il, is a matter of even greater concern, as the nuclear drama continues.

[7] This had happened with respect to the 1966 Asian Games, although a modicum of face was saved by South Korea's surrendering the Games rather than having them withdrawn.

why the negotiations failed and as responsible, therefore, for yet another perpetuation of the national division.

The first possibility foundered almost at once, when the IOC stepped into the process and took charge of the Olympic discussions. This deprived the political leadership, on both sides, of both a direct forum and the complete agenda of issues and recriminations. It also took the politicians themselves out of play and left the discussions to surrogates who had limited, if any, flexibility with which to negotiate. This served to make the negotiators less effective and to leave increasing control of the pace, agenda, and initiative in the hands of the IOC. By affecting even something as minor as the order in which individual sessions of the joint meetings were held, the IOC was able to influence which side was placed in a strong or weak position at any given time. Knowing this, each of the parties came to rely more and more on separate discussions with the IOC in order to try to get some idea of how it should respond in succeeding stages of the negotiations. The referee had taken over the match and was writing the rules as the match progressed.

The second objective was never achieved because the negotiations were so protracted that the urgency of making a deal never became acute. Nor did the actions of the North, in almost every significant respect, Olympic and otherwise, lend themselves to much sympathy, even from its allies. Indeed, they were embarrassed by the acts of international terrorism carried out by the North, and, but for the fact that these might continue or escalate if the North were further cornered, they would have been delighted to wash their hands of the DPRK altogether. They certainly did not want to send a diplomatic message of implied support through identification (other than through the most modest of lip service) with a North Korean initiative to ruin the Olympic Games. The Soviets had been boycotted in 1980 and had returned the favor in 1984; they now wanted to get back in the Games. The Chinese were back in the Olympic Movement and were in the process of gearing up for major commitment to international sport, and so long as the Soviet Union was not itself trying to displace Chinese influence in North Korea on this Olympic issue, its interests coincided with those of the USSR.

Cuba

It fell to Cuba to be the only significant sports power to side with the DPRK. It was the second time in a row that Fidel Castro had prevented his country's athletes from participating in the Games. Although he was wont to describe these actions as being out of loyalty, in the first instance, to the Soviet Union, and in the second, to the DPRK, the fact of the matter is that he was desperate for the financial support he was getting from each of them. The Cuban economy was, and remains, in appalling condition. The country is not self-sufficient and relies on massive injections of outside capital and supplies. At the time of the Los Angeles Games, the main paycheck was written by the Soviet Union, so when it said, on the boycott issue, "Jump," the only question for Castro, despite posturings to the contrary, was "How high?" By 1988, the DPRK was supplying an increasing level of its outside support; the Soviet Union had decided, under increasing pressure from the United States, as well as on its own account, that economic support of Cuba was a luxury it could no longer afford, and Castro had, as a pauper, no other alternative but to act as his banker requested.

Left to his own, there could be little doubt that Castro would have attended both Los Angeles and Seoul. Sport is important in Cuba, and there were many world-class athletes who would have been Olympic medalists in both Games. There is little doubt that the final decision in both cases was made by Castro himself, and, probably, with some regret. Apart from an interest in sport and a desire to see his small country perform against the superpowers, it was a reminder that, as a bankrupt, he could decidedly not afford the luxury of being nonaligned. He had taken the Queen's shilling and now was expected to do his duty. With the 1988 situation, he had somewhat more flexibility to move, although the eventual bottom line would be the same, if the DPRK insisted that he toe that line. He was among the first to realize that if there were to be a boycott by North Korea, he would be part of the meat in the sandwich. This undoubtedly led to his formulation of a proposal for holding part of the Games in the North, which had appeared early in the process.[8]

It is difficult to know for certain whether Castro thought there was any realistic possibility that such a proposal could work. He remained wedded to it thoughout the entire period of the negotiations and even after the formal discussions between the two Koreas and the IOC had

[8] It was never entirely certain whether Castro came up with the idea on his own or merely adopted the idea first voiced by Andreotti. His proposal certainly postdated the original expression of the possibility. On balance, it seems likely that the idea would have been communicated to him through the DPRK prior to November 29, 1984, the date he wrote to Samaranch.

wound down. As late as June 1988 he appeared still to be persuaded that the North wanted to proceed with organization of part of the Games and that a symbolic attribution of events would be sufficient. His earlier counsel to Samaranch had been to the same effect. He also appeared to believe, even three months before the Games, that if Kim Il Sung were to be made aware of Castro's personal opinion, this would have some influence on Kim and the DPRK policy on the matter. In these perceptions, he seems to have been completely wrong. On the other hand, he may have been committed to the idea of cohosting the Games simply because it was his idea, and he was not prepared to walk away from the idea regardless of how impractical it might have become when exposed to the light of Korean political reality.[9]

The United States

The United States could not be faulted in its support of South Korea in relation to the Olympic Games. It ensured that, unlike its actions in respect of its own 1984 Games, its full diplomatic machinery was activated in Korea's favor. This went as far as the summit meetings between Reagan and Gorbachev and extended to assigning significant elements of its Pacific fleet to the Sea of Japan immediately before and during the Games. Though on occasion some of its actions might seem contradictory, the United States also put enormous pressure on the South Koreans to speed up the process of democratization. Much of this was generated in Congress and through the media, which appeared to cover, with evident relish, every antigovernment demonstration involving more than one person. It is also fair to say that the administration was in high-level discussions with Chun Doo Hwan and his officials to press for progress in the liberalization of the existing regime. There can be little doubt that these representations had an effect, if not on Chun, then certainly on Roh Tae Woo.

On balance, the United States seems to have accomplished much of what it hoped in South Korea and was able to use the 1988 Olympic Games as both a carrot and a stick in the process. Speedy and significant progress was made in democratizing the country; the profile of its ally shone at the expense of the DPRK; the United States was seen as effective with the USSR in discussions pertaining to the Games, the success of which would harm the Soviet's client state; and the United

[9] Even after the Games had begun, Castro criticized the other socialist countries that participated.

States had a relatively benign opportunity to show the effect of its military presence in the Far East.

The Soviet Union

By 1988, Gorbachev was beginning to feel the pressures of an unsolvable economic situation in his country. Despite taking some steps that were necessary and long overdue, the momentum of decades of inefficient central planning, hopeless distribution channels, demoralized labor, misapplication of valuable resources, and corruption was such that the economy continued a precipitous decline. The only possible salvation, and even this was doubtful, had to come from the Western democracies in the form of massive capital injections. This required better relations than had previously existed between them and the Soviet Union. The cold war and the arms race had to end.

It did not matter whether the Soviets still had the same philosophical reservations about the West or not; the inescapable fact was that they could not afford to continue to act as they had in the past. The Olympics were a small pawn in this game, but pawns have their uses and, properly maneuvered, pawns can occasionally capture queens. There was no point in antagonizing the United States on this matter. Besides, the Soviets had not been in the Games since Moscow, and there would be no support among the public for a boycott over, of all places, the DPRK. In addition, it would be very difficult to impose another boycott on the Warsaw Pact allies, and to ask for one and be refused would be extremely awkward. So the best policy in the circumstances would be to appear to support the idea of sharing the Games, to keep the North Koreans relatively happy, but to attend whether the North Koreans were happy or not. The Chinese seemed to feel the same way, which was reassuring.[10]

China

China had its own priorities to consider. It was fortunate for the 1988 Olympic Games that the Chinese interests were such that support could be given to the South Korean initiative, since without such support, it

[10] Samaranch was careful to telex Gorbachev on October 7, congratulating him on the Soviet team's successful Olympics and, in particular, for his contribution to the internal aspects of such success as well as in his summit meetings with the United States.

is extremely unlikely that the Games could have been such a success. China, too, along with the Soviet Union, had to walk something of a political tightrope with North Korea. Clearly, it did not want there to be any significant hostilities into which it could be drawn; if there were such hostilities, it would likely have been inevitable for Chinese involvement to have been required. Unless, of course, the Soviet Union could be finessed into taking the responsibility for shoring up the North. But even this would have had its political downside, were China not to be seen as supportive of its Asian ally.

Instability in the region was in nobody's best interests, so the preferred course of action was to try to avoid an escalation of tensions to the point of any precipitous action. The source of any such miscalculation was properly assessed as more likely to be the North than the South, so appropriate dampers had to be placed on the North. It was assumed, as much by the Soviets as the Chinese, that the North would probably not start something serious without being relatively certain of backing from at least one of its major allies. In that respect, the assessment of Chun Doo Hwan regarding a major military intervention was undoubtedly correct. On the other hand, even minor skirmishes, non-threatening in themselves, might easily get out of hand and rash decisions be made at field level that could give rise to more serious implications.

The decision to have negotiations under the auspices of the IOC was, in many respects, exactly the type of solution that the Chinese favored. They were indirect, but nevertheless meaningful from an Asian perspective. More important, they were polite and not confrontational, since it was unthinkable to be rude to an organization such as the IOC, which was doing its best to find a satisfactory solution. So long as the negotiations continued, there could never be sufficient loss of face to require preemptive action to save or recover face. The time consumed by negotiations could also defuse the need to resort to other actions. In the process, the North could certainly judge the warmth of support from the Chinese by reading its "body language." What it could see was far from encouraging.[11]

[11] On the other hand, the Chinese were careful to accord to DPRK president Kim Il Sung all of the trappings appropriate to a head of state of a valued ally. This included a state visit in September 1982, where he was given very high-level treatment, to the evident annoyance of the USSR. The Soviets responded through a meeting of one of their senior officials in the Ministry of Culture, G. Popov, with ROK president Chun Doo Hwan at the Blue House, during the course of a visit to Seoul in November of the same year for a conference of the World Council of Museums. Popov and three Tass correspondents were the first Soviets to visit Korea on official ROK visas. There

The Chinese were in the process of experimenting with a modified form of socialism, one that was moving cautiously away from full centralized planning, not without trepidation, through a series of, to use a Western marketing term, test markets. They were not certain how this would work and were having some difficulty in adjusting to the international requirements of full participation in market-driven economics. Even the relatively minor forays into this world had consequences that had to be absorbed, assessed, and adjusted for, prior to moving another step or two. There was clearly major concern on the part of the Chinese leadership that its economic readjustment and the inevitable corresponding social fallout had to be controlled. The thought of uncontrolled change was anathema. Even today, the Chinese are horrified with the results of the uncontrolled process that brought the Soviet Union to collapse. There was no wish to add the further strain of chaos to the area by hostilities, even if confined to the Korean peninsula.

Within the Olympic world, the Chinese were seen to be supportive of the Olympic Movement. Beijing had bid for and won the right to host the 1990 Asian Games; it was in its best interests, therefore, to support the same games in Seoul in 1986. It was in the process of mounting a bid for the Olympic Games in the year 2000, which provided additional impetus to be supportive of successful Games in Asia. There could have been little realistic hope from the North's perspective that China would be fulsome in defense of efforts by them to disrupt the Seoul Games if no agreement were to be reached at the negotiating table with the IOC. China might urge, as it did, the reaching of an agreement to share the Games, but only at the absolute minimum level that might be expected from an ally. Quite apart from the differences in cultural "style" between the North Koreans and the Chinese, the North Koreans were not likely to bite the hand that might feed them.

Chinese-style indications of such reticence had been given on several occasions, even as early as the 1984 Olympics in Los Angeles, which the Chinese attended despite the socialist boycott. Meetings between sports officials indicated support of negotiations with the IOC for a share of the Games for the North, but, at the same time, indications were given of Chinese interest and intention to participate in the Games wherever they might eventually be held. And, once it became reasonably certain that all chances for an agreement had foundered, the final,

---

was another such visit by Kim Il Sung closer to the Games in 1987, when he undertook a five-day trip, May 21–26. On this occasion, he met with Deng Xiaoping and had a lengthy meeting with Premier Zhao Ziyang.

unmistakable message that China wanted no problems with the Games in Seoul was delivered to the North in mid-June 1988 by politburo member Li Ruihuan. This tracked the similar message from the Soviet Union. The circle was completed around North Korea, and it would have been foolhardy for it to engage in any overt disruption of the Games.

Regardless of its motivations, there can be no question that the quiet support of the Chinese was instrumental in the success of the Seoul Games. The Olympic conduct of China cannot be faulted in any way. It supported the process of negotiation until the very end of that process and then supported the decisions of the IOC to proceed with Games organized only in the South.[12] It acted with restraint, given its importance, and then participated fully in the Games, all without causing irreparable damage to its relations with its ally, North Korea. It also took the additional significant step of allowing KAL to overfly its territory for purposes of the Games. And it sent the appropriate diplomatic signals to South Korea that it was ready to discuss a fuller series of trade and diplomatic ties when the time was ripe.

Japan

Japan, too, provided comprehensive assistance to the South Koreans, once it recovered from the pique of losing the Games to Seoul. There is no doubt that a great deal of thinking had gone into the whole nature of Japanese-Korean relationships between 1981 and the time of the Games in 1988. These were, as indicated in the narrative, complicated and not without a number of inherent difficulties and attitudinal prejudices. But the national interests of the respective states and the interrelationships in the modern commercial and economic world required adjustments, and these were accomplished. Japan could not afford to be isolated from a major economic power in the region, particularly one with such close ties to a world power like the United States and one

[12] The South Koreans, for their part, had also done what they could to have the best relations possible with the Chinese. An incident had occurred in 1983 that was to help ease the possibility of tensions. On May 5, 1983, the hijacking of a Chinese plane provided the opportunity for the beginning of relations between the ROK and China. The Korean handling of the situation was regarded as "correct" by the Chinese, and an agreement was signed on May 10, containing a provision that both parties would maintain the spirit of mutual cooperation in matters of emergency involving them in the future. This led to later development of correspondence between Chun Doo Hwan and Deng Xiaoping, through the good offices of Pakistani president Zia Ul Hag. By March 1984, ROK athletes competed for the first time in the People's Republic of China, in Davis Cup tennis preliminary matches.

that China was showing signs of accepting as well. To maintain its standing as a power and influence in Asia, it had no choice but to face the new reality. It also had to take the initial steps in regularizing the relations. This was an important message, one well understood within Asia and noted elsewhere.

The national interests of Japan were engaged in yet another manner. As the obvious jumping-off place for entry into South Korea, it would have been disastrous were the source of any trouble with the Games in Seoul to be traced to Japan and any lapse, deliberate or accidental, in Japanese security precautions. Once it was on board, Japan spared no effort to ensure that nothing went wrong from that perspective, and its cooperation was superb. The same was true of its diplomatic effort. It was a demonstration of Asian solidarity, much appreciated by the South Koreans, and has undoubtedly paid dividends to the Japanese in the management of the process of adjustment between the two countries.

The performances by the various political powers were, therefore, generally not out of character. Each promoted and protected, as best it could in the circumstances, its national interests. If the Olympic Games happened to be a positive or important feature in such national interests, they attracted the requisite attention and were used accordingly. If they were not of interest, they were ignored.

The International Olympic Committee

The only truly aberrant performance among the international organizations and interests represented was that of the International Olympic Committee, which eschewed its traditional role of avoiding political action and injected itself into a question that had, at its foundation, nothing whatsoever to do with sport. The creation of conditions propitious to successful Games in Seoul was, instead, a nakedly political issue, which had been a thorn in the side of the entire world for some forty years.

The IOC's atypical behavior in the context of the 1988 Games was demonstrated, arguably, from the moment of its decision to choose Seoul in the first place, and continued in its efforts to participate in the political process that then became inevitable. The IOC's history in political arenas was less than impressive. As an international organization, meeting only once per year (except in Olympic years, when a Session is held immediately prior to the Games, for a total of two meetings), it was not suited to the daily demands of a negotiation process. Even its Executive Board seldom met more than quarterly. If negotiations were to be held against a rapidly changing political background, in which the political agendas were complex and interrelated, they would, of necessity, have to be conducted by the president.

Looking at presidents of the IOC over the last three or four decades might have given cause for concern. Avery Brundage would have been unsuited to the task, first, because of a tendency to speak in the form of Commandments, and second, because he refused to accept the reality that political forces not only could, but did, have a direct effect on the Games. His style, based on the latter years of his presidency, would have been the stating of (to him) self-evident Truths about the separation of sport and politics, which would have served only to polarize any delicate situation.[13] His successor, Lord Killanin, on the other hand, would have been far more flexible on a personal level but less likely to get fully involved in the minutiae of a complicated process and lacking in both the range of the established international contacts necessary to get information and the credibility to meet at equal levels with the diplomatic and political powers. The starting point for the IOC was, therefore, very close to ground zero.

In the event, however, neither Brundage nor Killanin was involved in the Seoul process. It fell to Samaranch to make the decision. His nature is proactive. His background was one of seeking compromise.[14] He prefers to walk a mile to avoid a problem rather than to be called upon to solve one. That a problem would be likely to develop over Seoul was a virtual certainty. If it developed on a global scale, then, like the situations in 1980 and 1984, it would be difficult, if not impossible, to undo. The choice was, in some respects, Hobson's choice. He had little alternative but to act and to bring the IOC along with him. This latter step was generally after the fact, but he was scrupulous in making sure that authority was granted by the IOC before any binding commitments were made.[15] His suggestions and negotiating positions were, however,

[13] This conclusion, though in the author's opinion correct in respect of the latter years of Brundage's term as president of the IOC, does not do justice to his much more politically realistic approach in earlier years, when he displayed considerable subtlety and deftness in such areas.

[14] Though personally quite impatient with slow-moving or obtuse individuals, he has, nevertheless, enormous institutional patience. This includes an ability to listen to endless repetitions of the same arguments and a corresponding ability to repeat the same message to the same people whenever required.

[15] Or, that commitments made would have to be ratified by the IOC Executive Board or Session, as the case may be.

well ahead of the approval curve, and most of the IOC members had little knowledge of the detailed state of negotiations at any particular time. They were, however, confident that the IOC was in good hands at all times.

Samaranch moved with considerable speed to establish the credentials necessary to play the role. Consultations with political leaders were designed to try to make them part of the solution and to accept that the Korean situation, as it related to the Seoul Games, might well be best addressed within the structure of the Olympic Movement, where there were at least some rules of engagement and an authority accepted, at least in theory, by the Olympic parties. Other political work could be done in parallel, in the direction of lessening general tensions, while the Olympic issue could appear to remain separate and to benefit from the results of whatever international efforts were also progressing. Once the political authorities had the measure of Samaranch as someone who could be relied upon not to do anything precipitous, there developed a degree of confidence that he could be left to reach an internationally satisfactory accommodation.

The IOC's decision to act was fraught with risk. A decision not to act would have been equally risky. At least by acting, the IOC had a chance to protect its own territory and to conduct a campaign on its own terms. It could probably, or at least arguably, not be worse off by seizing the initiative than by reacting after the fact to political decisions taken elsewhere. If world conditions were to be such that matters escalated to the highest levels of politics, that would happen whether the IOC might wish it or not.

But, if the process could be conducted by the IOC in a sensible manner and with sensitivity to the political imperatives, then the IOC might be left to act on its own. This would permit the political powers to get on with the more complicated arrangement of the new and emerging relationships between the superpowers without the noisy complications of an old cold war situation to divert their attention. The suddenly precocious IOC might serve a useful function by diverting attention to the Olympic negotiations while the more serious work went on behind closed doors.

A mutuality of interest developed, and the IOC played its role exceptionally well, earning a new level of respect in political circles. This mutuality of interest continued right through the process to the eventual result. The world powers wanted peace and a lessening of global tensions. In Olympic terms, this was reflected in full participation in the Seoul Games. The few holdouts were not significant. The sponsors of the holdouts would see to it that their charges did nothing to increase tensions, while leaving them sufficient room for their exculpatory propaganda.

It would be naive to think that the Olympics were a fulcrum from which the world was moved. In the ultimate application of realpolitik, the self-interest of states will override an event even as important as the Olympic Games. Samaranch is right when he says that if the political situation in the world at the time of the Games is calm, we will have good Games, and if it is bad, the Games can be adversely affected.

This "absolute" has been tempered to some degree by a dawning political recognition that Olympic boycotts have a tendency to hurt the boycotter more than the intended target country, even if the target is the host country. An Olympic boycott can annoy, enrage, or send a signal to the target country, but since it relates to an event that only occurs every four years and for a period of sixteen days, its effectiveness is limited.

The permanent damage is suffered by the boycotters themselves and their citizens. Thus, for example, the United States was not affected by the Cuban boycott as much as Cuba and its athletes. South Korea was not affected by the Cuban boycott of its Games as much as Cuba and Cuban athletes. There is a growing realization that Olympic boycotts are ineffective in accomplishing the stated political objectives. Political leaders who resort to Olympic boycotts are increasingly regarded as inept, because they punish their own people for no political gain. But for the general knowledge that he was bankrupt and had to sing from the songsheet provided by his bankers, Castro would be judged politically inept for imposing two successive Olympic boycotts on his athletes.

In the final analysis, in the late 1980s the world was ready for an easing of tension, and the 1988 Olympic Games provided a convenient opportunity to demonstrate that an international consensus was developing. Both ends of the political spectrum cooperated, each with its own set of values and styles, to bring about the desired result. The few renegades were identified as such and their absences noted, with regret, but without much sympathy, except for the sacrificial athletes who were the meat in a rather stale diplomatic sandwich.

The Olympic Movement emerged from the process leading to the Seoul Games, and from the Koreans' superb organization of the Games themselves, stronger than ever before. All the leaks in the Olympic bucket were repaired, and the water that had escaped in Montreal, Moscow, and Los Angeles was replaced. The minor spillage of the absent countries in Seoul was simply that; they would almost certainly be back in the fold by the time of the Barcelona Games in 1992. The organizational abilities of the South Koreans had given added value to an event already recognized as the best in the world and had established awesome standards for the organizers of future Games. The IOC had been able to rally all the elements of the Olympic Movement together in support of and in defense of the movement, making certain that each element was both important in the process and, more significant, recognized as important.

The IOC itself recovered whatever ground it may have lost and moved on to a significantly higher level of international respect. It demonstrated a hitherto unknown (or at least unrecognized) capacity to handle itself with dexterity in complex international situations without merely resorting to its own catechism and sports vocabulary. Furthermore, its president acquired an international profile normally reserved in the media for political leaders and the respect, among political leaders themselves, attributed to heads of state. This was to prove helpful in 1992, when the IOC managed to gain some "Olympic" relief from the UN Security Council Resolution 757 directed at portions of the remnants of Yugoslavia and thereby make it possible for at least some of the athletes from that country to participate in the Barcelona Olympics.

That there will continue to be problems of a political nature surrounding the Olympic Games in the future is a virtual certainty. Human nature cannot be expected to undergo a dramatic change. Nor can the objectives of political leaders be expected to diminish in priority; if something more important is at stake than the Olympic Games, then it would be naive to think that perceived national interests will be sacrificed for the benefit of an international festival of youth and sport. The world appears to be in an accelerating state of differentiation, in which ethnic and other groups are focusing on their differences rather than their similarities. The greater the number of moving parts, the greater the likelihood that something will break. One hopes that the inevitable conflicts will be regional in nature, rather than global.

The Olympics will be forced to live in the world political environment as it exists at various times. The IOC can, perhaps, be more sensitive to the choice of host cities, but it is very difficult to predict political conditions some seven years in advance of the event to be awarded. A single permanent site is not the answer. For one matter, the Games belong to the world, not to a single country, and no country should be permanently estopped from aspiring to host the Games some day. For another, who can predict what the conditions might be in a permanent site from one Games to the next? Even Greece, which has often been proposed as a permanent site, has gone through political changes of considerable proportion, which might not be palatable to many other countries and which might invite nonparticipation. Further, the Olympic facilities and installations must be absorbed into the daily usage of the host countries, not just maintained as white elephants to be dusted off every four years. The economics of such a situation would be untenable.

The record of the Olympics, however, is such that one can face the future and all its unknown challenges with some considerable degree of confidence that they will be overcome. There is a momentum of positive reinforcement of the Olympics as an institution; they really do represent the best of the human condition. They do demonstrate that international cooperation is possible if there is a common element of goodwill and a desire to succeed. Hundreds of millions of people throughout the world work toward the goals represented in dramatic form by the Olympic Games. These people and the Games themselves deserve the chance to fulfill themselves. Seoul was a wonderful demonstration of what is possible. The success was the result of millions of people working for a common objective, each working in his or her own manner, and it was shared by each and every one involved in making them possible. Even more, the joy was shared by hundreds of millions in addition, for whom this Olympic miracle became proof of what can be possible.

The world is ready and accepts the fundamental Olympic values. The greater challenge for the future may well lie within the Olympic Movement itself: Can it live with its success? Can it demonstrate these values in its own activities? Can it honor its own ethics? The Olympic Movement should, perhaps, consider the words of advice given by Polonius, in Shakespeare's *Hamlet,* to his son Laertes:

> This above all: to thine own self be true,
> And it must follow, as the night the day,
> Thou canst not then be false to any man.

Glossary of Terms

AENOC	Association of European National Olympic Committees
ANOC	Association of National Olympic Committees
ASOIF	Association of Summer Olympic International Federations
DJP	Democratic Justice Party (ROK)
DMZ	Demilitarized Zone
DPRK	Democratic People's Republic of Korea (North Korea)
FIFA	International Association of Federation Football
FISU	International University Sport Federation
FITA	International Archery Federation
GAISF	General Assembly of International Sports Federations
IAAF	International Amateur Athletics Federation
IF	International Federation
IOC	International Olympic Committee
ITTF	International Table Tennis Federation
KASA	Korean Amateur Sports Association
KCIA	Korean Central Intelligence Agency
KCNA	Korean Central News Agency (DPRK)
KOC	Korean Olympic Committee
LAOOC	Los Angeles Olympic Organizing Committee
NOC	National Olympic Committee
OCA	Olympic Council of Asia

PASO	Pan American Sports Organization
PRC	People's Republic of China
ROK	Republic of Korea (South Korea)
SLOOC	Seoul Olympic Organizing Committee
USOC	United States Olympic Committee
WTF	World Taekwando Federation

Chronology of Events

15 Aug. 1948	Republic of Korea (ROK) established; U.S. military government ends.
1948	National Olympic committee (NOC) in ROK, Korean Olympic Committee (KOC), recognized by International Olympic Committee (IOC).
9 Sep. 1948	Proclamation of establishment of Democratic People's Republic of Korea (DPRK); president is Kim Il Sung, who has spent several years in USSR.
12 Dec. 1948	UN General Assembly recognizes ROK as only lawful government in Korea; recommends occupying forces withdraw as soon as practicable; USSR withdraws troops in late 1948.
1 Oct. 1949	People's Republic of China (PRC) established under leadership of Mao Zedong.
25 June 1950	Armed invasion of ROK by DPRK marks start of Korean War; Seoul captured within three days.
25 Nov. 1950	China enters Korean War in force; troops have been entering Korea since mid-October.
23 April 1951	USSR applies for recognition of its NOC.
27 July 1953	Armistice declared in Korean conflict; signed at Panmunjom.
1955	Graduating class of 1955 at Korean Military Academy in-

cludes Chun Doo Hwan, Roh Tae Woo, and Chong Ho Yong.

14 June 1956 IOC Executive Board notes that DPRK has created new NOC and has applied to IOC for recognition; IOC chancellor instructed to reply that only one NOC per country is allowed and to suggest solution similar to that for Germany (subsequent to World War II, IOC had recognized one NOC for all of Korea, which had its seat in Seoul; this NOC now has no contact with the North because of current formal state of war).

11 Nov. 1956 DPRK's new application for recognition of NOC considered; reply to IOC suggestion of June 1956 had been that it was impossible to consider same solution as for Germany.

22 Nov. 1956 Spain, Holland, and Switzerland boycott Melbourne Olympic Games, November 22–December 8, in protest over Soviet intervention in Hungary; Iraq, Egypt, and Lebanon boycott due to actions of British, French, and Israelis in Egypt; PRC withdraws because entry of Formosa Chinese accepted.

1957 IOC Session in Sofia grants provisional recognition to NOC in DPRK, valid only for internal affairs (but not on international basis) on understanding that it would only be possible to compete in 1960 Games as a combined team from Korea; new NOC required to send constative documents to IOC; difference between Koreas and Germany noted (Koreas still at war).

22 May 1959 IOC Executive Board again considers problem of two Koreas; matter to be discussed with international federations the following day.

25 May 1959 Fifty-sixth IOC Session in Munich, May 25–28, considers possibility of joint Korean team; reports are reviewed of meeting to be held between Koreas in Hong Kong.

12 Feb. 1960 Korea problem again considered by IOC Executive Board; no position taken.

Feb. 1960 IOC president Avery Brundage reports to IOC Session in San Francisco that DPRK accepted a meeting in Hong Kong, but that ROK refused; discussion regarding Korea to be continued at Rome Session later that year.

Aug. 1960	IOC member in USSR, Konstantin Andrianov, insists on immediate decision regarding Korea so that DPRK can participate in Rome Olympics; IOC president Avery Brundage reports that all efforts to unite the two Koreas have been unsuccessful; a possible change in the ROK government might produce a different result; decision postponed until 1961.
25 Aug. 1960	Olympic Games in Rome, August 25–September 11. Taiwan required to compete under the name Formosa; these will be the last Games in which South Africa will compete until 1992 in Barcelona.
15 June 1961	IOC Executive Board rejects DPRK NOC application for recognition.
June 1961	IOC member in Romania, Alexandru Siperco, speaks at IOC Session in favor of recognition of DPRK NOC; Brundage agrees that statutes are in order, but without an agreement with ROK it is impossible to accept DPRK; decision postponed until 1962 Session at request of KOC.
2 Mar. 1962	KOC letter requesting delay of five or six months to submit recommendations about formation of unified team considered by IOC Executive Board.
March 1962	IOC Session decides to place NOC of DPRK on official list of IOC recognized NOCs and to send letter to KOC asking its opinion with regard to participation in Games of unified team; reply due by September 1, 1962; if negative reply received, North Korea will be invited to participate in 1964 Games as independent team.
24 Jan. 1963	Meeting in Lausanne of IOC with two Koreas results in quasi agreement in principle for combined Korean team for both Games in 1964; details are to be worked out between the two Koreas; the IOC will study the matter of the flag of the combined delegation.
25 Jan. 1963	DPRK NOC delegation sends letter to KOC delegation in Lausanne complaining about refusal by KOC to continue talks due to impossibility of communication in Korea and proposes further talks on bilateral basis in Lausanne the next day.
6 Feb. 1963	Second meeting in Lausanne between two Koreas results in

agreement on all details except flag to be used; IOC suggests solutions.

7 Feb. 1963 IOC Executive Board learns that DPRK has accepted one of the solutions proposed by the IOC, but KOC has not; options proposed by IOC were: white flag with Olympic rings and inscription "United Korean Team" or white flag with map of entire Korea, separated in the middle by the Olympic rings.

17 May 1963 Meetings begin in Hong Kong between two Korean NOCs and will last until June 1; four days of discussions are required to agree on agenda of meeting; no substantive agreements reached.

13 June 1963 DPRK NOC reports to IOC on discussions held in Hong Kong between the two Korean NOCs; it has suggested further meeting at Panmunjom on June 26 or in Rangoon if venue not acceptable to KOC.

26 July 1963 Further meeting between Koreas scheduled for Hong Kong; it does not occur.

18 Aug. 1963 IOC president Avery Brundage meets with KOC in Lausanne regarding joint Korean team for 1964 Olympics; KOC refuses to participate in joint meeting scheduled for following day and leaves.

19 Aug. 1963 Brundage meets with DPRK NOC in Lausanne, advises that KOC had no authority to discuss agenda matters and has left Lausanne; Brundage sets deadline of August 31 for KOC to state whether it will resume discussions on matter of joint team; if positive reply is received, IOC will decide on dates and places for future meetings; advises DPRK representatives that KOC delegation feared strong public reaction if united Korean team at Games in Tokyo.

14 Oct. 1963 IOC Executive Board prepared to recommend to IOC Session that there be two Korean teams in 1964 if negotiations for a combined team break off; this would exclude the use of any flag by the teams.

Oct. 1963 IOC Session decides that there will be no combined Korean team in 1964 Games; DPRK NOC will be allowed to compete separately; names of NOCs will be Korea and North Korea.

25 Nov. 1963 IOC confirms to DPRK NOC the use of the flag and hymn

to be used by its delegation in Games in Innsbruck and Tokyo; confirms the names of the Korean delegations as Korea and North Korea.

25 Jan. 1964 Problem with badges worn by DPRK NOC delegation on uniforms reported to IOC Executive Board; DPRK referring to itself as "Korea."

29 Jan. 1964 DPRK NOC participates in Olympic Winter Games in Innsbruck, January 29–February 9, but with flag that does not conform with decision of IOC Session in 1963; DPRK wanted permission to use nonconforming flag and different name (Korea); requests refused.

4 Oct. 1964 IOC member in USSR, Konstantin Andrianov, protests at IOC Executive Board meeting that neither DPRK nor India received invitations to the meeting of NOCs prior to Tokyo Games; IOC president Avery Brundage replies that invitations sent, but defects in postal systems probably responsible.

Oct. 1964 DPRK NOC protests suspension by international federations of six athletes who had participated illegally in GANEFO Games (Games of the Newly Emerging Forces) in Djakarta and threatens withdrawal of entire team; no exceptions granted by IOC Session.

10 Oct. 1964 Olympic Games in Tokyo, October 10–24; North Korea and South Korea compete separately.

1965 Juan Antonio Samaranch of Spain proposed to IOC Session in Madrid for co-optation as IOC member; decision deferred for one year since five new members had already been co-opted at this Session.

1966 Juan Antonio Samaranch co-opted as member of the International Olympic Committee at its sixty-fifth Session in Rome; result of one-year delay makes Samaranch subject to IOC rule that members co-opted after 1965 must retire at age seventy-two; age limit increased to seventy-five during Samaranch's presidency, eventually permitting him to stand for third term in 1993 at age of seventy-three.

2 May 1967 DPRK NOC requests change of name for its NOC; IOC Executive Board takes no decision.

Feb. 1968 DPRK NOC requests that IOC accept the name it had chosen for the NOC (DPRK rather than North Korea); IOC Session rejects request, 31–21.

30 Sep. 1968 IOC member in USSR, Konstantin Andrianov, says to IOC Executive Board that it is discrimination not to comply with request of DPRK NOC to change its name; IOC president Avery Brundage to meet with NOC to find solution (this issue also affected East Germany and Taiwan).

Sep. 1968 IOC Session, at urging of Andrianov and despite resistance of IOC member in Korea Chang Jey Young to discussion prior to union of two Koreas, decides to allow DPRK NOC to use its desired name, but only with effect from 1972; solution had been agreed by all parties "in an Olympic spirit to allow free competitions"; all express pleasure that "the thorny problem that had existed for twenty years finally had been settled"; despite agreement, DPRK refuses to compete in Mexico Games.

1 Jan. 1969 Report of disagreement about IOC action with respect to Koreas in Mexico City; deferred to 1970 IOC Session for discussion, since Andrianov not present at meeting.

1969 At IOC Session in Warsaw, IOC member in ROK Chang Jey Young questions whether decision of Session in Mexico in 1968 to allow DPRK to use full DPRK name was conditional on DPRK taking part in Mexico or was final that new nomenclature was to be effective November 1, 1968; decision is that name change was final (28–15–2); Chang protests, but is overruled [Chang was correct, since IOC had issued press release October 14, 1968, stating permission to be called DPRK NOC had been withdrawn since North Korea had not participated in Mexico]; DPRK cables thanks and states that henceforth it will participate in all Olympic activities.

May 1970 IOC Session in Amsterdam expels South Africa from Olympic Movement; Montreal and Denver selected as host cities for 1976 Summer and Winter Olympic Games; Denver will later withdraw due to domestic political and environmental issues and will be replaced by Innsbruck.

April 1971 PRC competes in World Table Tennis Championships in Nagoya, Japan; nine U.S. athletes also participate.

6 April 1971 PRC table tennis team invites U.S. team to visit China;

	U.S. Table Tennis Association president requests advice from U.S. ambassador in Tokyo, who recommends acceptance of invitation.
14 April 1971	U.S. table tennis players received by Chou En-lai, giving indirect signal that diplomatic initiatives between United States and PRC might now be welcome.
6 July 1971	U.S. president Richard M. Nixon makes speech praising Chinese people and predicts PRC will be one of eventual five major powers; détente appears to exist with USSR.
16 July 1971	U.S. secretary of state Henry Kissenger completes talks with Mao Zedong and Chou En-lai that will lead to visit of President Nixon to China.
25 Oct. 1971	PRC admitted as member of UN; Republic of China (Taiwan) excluded.
21 Feb. 1972	President Nixon visits China for eight days, the longest visit of a U.S. president to a foreign country; first time a U.S. president has ever negotiated in a country with which United States had no diplomatic relations.
1974	ROK advocates cross-recognition of two Koreas by United States, USSR, PRC, and Japan; DPRK denounces idea.
	Assassination of ROK president Park Chung Hee's wife, Yuk Yong Su, during assassination attempt on him.
1975	Korean influence-peddling scandal exposed in United States, including illegal activities of KCIA.
17 July 1976	Montreal Olympics begin, finishing August 1: African countries boycott on basis of New Zealand participation following rugby tours by New Zealand teams to South Africa; Iraq and Guyana also boycott for same reason; only Senegal and Ivory Coast participate from Africa; major diplomatic problem results from Canadian government's reneging on promise to admit all NOCs recognized by IOC by refusing to admit NOC of Republic of China (Taiwan) under that name.
April 1977	Canadian Olympic Association proposes to IOC Executive Board in Abidjan, Ivory Coast, that, though no NOC has obligation to accept invitation to participate in Games, if NOC accepts invitation and withdraws at last moment, it should be excluded until previous Organizing Committee

has been reimbursed for expenses resulting from withdrawal.

17 July 1977 Juan Antonio Samaranch appointed ambassador to the USSR and People's Republic of Mongolia; he is first Spanish ambassador to the USSR since Spanish civil war.

Dec. 1978 United States and PRC establish full diplomatic relations.

Jan. 1979 Deng Xiaoping (elected chairman of Communist Party in China in March 1978) visits U.S. president Jimmy Carter in Washington.

16 March 1979 KOC president Park Chong Kyu forwards feasibility study regarding 1988 Olympic Games to ROK Education Ministry.

3 April 1979 KOC president Park Chong Kyu asks Seoul city government for relevant data to assess possibility of attracting Asian and Olympic Games to Korea.

April 1979 IOC Session in Montevideo rejects IOC Executive Board proposal to remove recognition of NOC in Taiwan as precondition of reentry of PRC into Olympic Movement.

Aug. 1979 ROK president Park Chung Hee authorizes KOC to sound out prospects of support for ROK bid for 1988 Games at ANOC meeting in Puerto Rico; KOC believes it has support from Mario Vazquez-Raña, incoming president of ANOC.

19 Sep. 1979 ROK National Physical Education and Sports Council agrees to bid for 1988 Olympic Games.

21 Sep. 1979 ROK president Park Chung Hee agrees to going forward with a bid for 1988 Olympic Games; apparently more interested in bidding for Tenth Asian Games as prelude, but both ventures approved.

8 Oct. 1979 Mayor of Seoul announces candidacy of Seoul to host 1988 Olympic Games to the people of ROK.

26 Oct. 1979 ROK president Park Chung Hee and chief bodyguard assassinated by Kim Jae Kyu, director of KCIA; Choi Kyu Hah becomes acting president and declares martial law; Olympic bid shelved for time being due to political crisis.

Nov. 1979 IOC Executive Board circulates mail vote on question of

China and Taiwan; ballot defective due to recommendation of Executive Board on ballot itself; IOC member in Taiwan, Henry Hsu, institutes legal proceedings against IOC to prevent vote from being acted upon; proceedings not settled until March 1981.

12 Dec. 1979 Chun Doo Hwan, in charge of investigation into death of Park Chung Hee, arrests key army officers and establishes control of army by force of arms; Roh Tae Woo becomes head of Capital Garrison Command; Chong Ho Yong is special forces commander.

20 Dec. 1979 Radio broadcast from DPRK proposes meeting with ROK on January 17, 1980, to discuss single team for 1980 Moscow Olympics.

DPRK NOC president Kim Yu Sun writes to KOC president Park Chong Kyu suggesting joint team for 1980 Moscow Olympics and proposes meeting on January 20 at Panmunjom to discuss.

24 Dec. 1979 ROK NOC says it has not received DPRK's proposal of December 20.

25 Dec. 1979 DPRK NOC suggests joint Korean team for 1980 Olympic Games in Moscow in letter to presidents of all NOCs.

26 Dec. 1979 Soviet troops invade Afghanistan.

DPRK NOC broadcasts announcement that message for proposal of joint team will be delivered at Panmunjom on December 27.

27 Dec. 1979 DPRK NOC message regarding proposal for joint team in Moscow Olympics received by KOC at Panmunjom.

9 Jan. 1980 KOC announces that message for DPRK will be delivered at Panmunjom on January 11.

11 Jan. 1980 KOC replies that DPRK offer cannot be implemented; proposes goodwill matches between the two sides; welcomes DPRK to international matches in Seoul in 1980; proposes meeting after Moscow Games.

20 Jan. 1980 U.S. president Jimmy Carter announces U.S. boycott of Moscow Olympics if Soviets do not withdraw from Afghanistan within thirty days.

12 Feb. 1980	IOC, with support of IFs and NOCs, decides unanimously that Moscow Games will continue.
14 July 1980	Cho Sang Ho replaces Park Chong Kyu as president of Korean Amateur Sports Association (KASA) and KOC.
17 July 1980	At IOC Session in Moscow, Juan Antonio Samaranch is elected president of IOC on first ballot, replacing Lord Killanin.
19 July 1980	Moscow Olympics begin, finishing August 3: U.S.-led boycott in protest over Soviet invasion of Afghanistan results in only eighty-one countries participating.
4 Aug. 1980	Samaranch takes over keys to Château de Vidy, IOC headquarters in Lausanne.
6 Aug. 1980	Ceremony in Lausanne to celebrate arrival of Samaranch as IOC president.
22 Aug. 1980	Chun Doo Hwan resigns from army.
27 Aug. 1980	ROK president Chun Doo Hwan inaugurated.
Oct. 1980	DPRK president Kim Il Sung proposes reunification of Korea through confederation of the North and the South.
	Revised Constitution approved in ROK through plebiscite.
16 Oct. 1980	Samaranch's term as ambassador to USSR and Mongolia ends.
1 Nov. 1980	Samaranch takes up residence in Lausanne at Lausanne Palace Hotel.
6 Nov. 1980	KOC meets to reconsider bid for 1988 Games; agrees to recommend that bid proceed.
27 Nov. 1980	Temporary problem develops for Olympic bid when city of Seoul advises that it has insufficient financial resources to carry on; ROK president Chun Doo Hwan gives instructions to proceed.
30 Nov. 1980	ROK president Chun Doo Hwan reconfirms decision to proceed with Seoul's bid for 1988 Olympic Games.
1 Dec. 1980	KOC notifies IOC of its support for bid by Seoul for 1988 Olympic Games.
23 Dec. 1980	Coordinating committee formed in Seoul for purposes of

preparing answers to IOC questionnaire for candidate cities.

Jan. 1981 ROK president Chun Doo Hwan calls for summit talks with DPRK.

Feb. 1981 Chun Doo Hwan runs for presidency of ROK under new Constitution approved in October 1980 and is elected.

2 Feb. 1981 ROK president Chun Doo Hwan is first head of state to visit Reagan White House; this fuels suspicion of Korean students that United States was involved in suppression of Kwangju riots.

10 Feb. 1981 KOC and city of Seoul sign undertaking addressed to IOC regarding signature of host city contract with IOC if Seoul bid for the 1988 Olympic Games is successful.

16 Feb. 1981 ROK president Chun Doo Hwan guarantees to IOC that his government will allow access to all accredited persons and will provide all financial and administrative support in connection with 1988 Olympic Games.

28 Feb. 1981 Seoul and KOC submit completed application to IOC in respect of bid for 1988 Olympic Games; proposed dates are September 20–October 5, 1988 (Nagoya will propose October 8–23, 1988).

March 1981 IOC negotiates agreement to allow both PRC and Taiwan to be full members of the Olympic Family after arranging matters such as name of each NOC, flags to be used, and anthems to be played during victory ceremonies; IOC is first international organization to achieve such a result with the "two Chinas."

10 March 1981 IOC invites IFs and NOCs, at IOC expense, to send representatives to report on candidate cities of Nagoya and Seoul.

30 March 1981 NOC representatives Richard W. Palmer (Great Britain) and F. Don Miller (United States) visit Seoul through April 4 to inspect and report to IOC.

4 April 1981 IOC Enquiry Commission visits Seoul through April 8 to inspect and report to IOC Session; commission consists of Giulio Onesti (Italy), Pedro Ramirez-Vasquez (Mexico), and James Worrall (Canada).

June 1981	ROK president Chun Doo Hwan renews call for summit meeting with DPRK.
10 June 1981	IF representative Adriaan Paulen of the International Amateur Athletics Federation (IAAF) visits Seoul through June 12 to inspect and report to IOC; representative Frederick Holder (IAAF) is able to visit Nagoya, but previous commitment prevents him from visiting Seoul.
19 June 1981	KASA president proposes sport exchanges and formation of single team for international events to DPRK, including 1982 Asian Games and 1984 Olympic Games.
Aug. 1981	ROK president Chun Doo Hwan assigns minister of political affairs Roh Tae Woo responsibility for leadership in Olympic bid.
21 Sep. 1981	NOC commission of inquiry into candidate cities of Nagoya and Seoul reports in meeting of NOCs with IOC Executive Board that both candidates are capable of organizing 1988 Olympic Games.
29 Sep. 1981	IOC awards 1988 Olympic Games to Seoul at its eighty-fourth Session in Baden-Baden.
2 Nov. 1981	The SLOOC established as official Organizing Committee for 1988 Olympic Games.
20 Nov. 1981	Voice of Revolutionary Party for Reunification in DPRK calls Seoul's hosting of 1988 Olympics a "criminal act against the Korean people and the international community" (VRPR is a clandestine broadcaster that announces it is from Seoul, but has been traced to the DPRK city of Haeju).
28 Nov. 1981	Asian Games Federation Council selects Seoul as host city for 1986 Asian Games after Pyongyang (DPRK) and Baghdad (Iraq) both withdraw candidacies.
3 Dec. 1981	Article in DPRK *Rodong Shinmun* ridicules award of 1988 Olympics to Seoul.
Dec. 1981	Seoul Olympic Games Support Council founded, composed of prime minister and other government ministers to take appropriate actions on measures necessary for the Games.

	Seoul selected as site for 1985 International Chamber of Commerce General Assembly.
1982	ROK president Chun Doo Hwan issues specific proposals for talks with DPRK and possible reunification.
1 Feb. 1982	KOC proposes exchange of goodwill games with DPRK and formation of single team for international competitions.
March 1982	Ministry of Sports established in South Korea to provide administrative support for organization of Olympics; Roh Tae Woo is minister of sport.
	Seoul selected as host for 1985 World Bank–International Monetary Fund conference.
28 March 1982	Samaranch visits Moscow, meets with USSR NOC president Sergei Pavlov and IOC members Andrianov and Smirnov.
29 March 1982	Samaranch visits Pyongyang, meets with prime minister and Kim Yu Sun, DPRK NOC president and IOC member in DPRK.
30 March 1982	Samaranch visits Beijing, meets PRC vice president Deng Xiaoping and Li Menghua; gives press conference March 31.
7 April 1982	Samaranch visits Seoul, April 7–9; meets with KOC, SLOOC, ROK president Chun Doo Hwan, minister of sports Roh Tae Woo, ROK minister of education, and mayor of Seoul, Park Young Su.
25 April 1982	U.S. vice president George Bush visits Seoul, April 25–27.
30 April 1982	Roh Tae Woo appointed home affairs minister.
6 May 1982	*Rodong Shinmun* article states ROK incapable of hosting Olympics due to economic problems.
6 July 1982	SLOOC meets Samaranch in Lausanne, July 6–7.
17 Aug. 1982	ROK president Chun Doo Hwan leaves for tour of four African countries to improve ROK's diplomatic contacts with third world nations.
Sep. 1982	DPRK president Kim Il Sung visits Beijing and is given very high-level treatment, to evident annoyance of USSR.

25 Oct. 1982	Samaranch attends thirty-first meeting of Socialist Sports Ministers in Havana, Cuba.
Nov. 1982	Senior Soviet official in Ministry of Culture, G. Popov, visits ROK for conference of World Council of Museums, meets with President Chun Doo Hwan in Blue House; thought to be in response to visit by DPRK president Kim Il Sung to Beijing; three Tass correspondents also in Seoul for this occasion; these are first Soviets to visit on official ROK visas.
17 Nov. 1982	Samaranch attends Tenth Asian Games in New Delhi, November 17–22.
19 Nov. 1982	Samaranch meets with Ambassador Kim and delegation from the SLOOC and numerous Asian NOCs in New Delhi.
24 Nov. 1982	Samaranch receives ROK ambassador in Lausanne.
18 Dec. 1982	Samaranch in Moscow; meets with Sergei Pavlov, USSR NOC president, IOC members Andrianov and Smirnov, and International Gymnastics Federation president Yuri Titov.
4 Jan. 1983	Samaranch meets Vietnamese chargé d'affaires in Lausanne.
5 Jan. 1983	Kim Un Yong, president of World Taekwando Federation (WTF), visits Samaranch in Lausanne.
11 Jan. 1983	Japanese prime minister Yasuhiro Nakasone visits Seoul on first official foreign visit to establish closer links between Japan and ROK; DPRK reacts negatively to "plot" between United States, Japan, and ROK.
13 Jan. 1983	Samaranch meets with delegation from SLOOC while in Los Angeles; further meeting planned in Lausanne in July.
5 May 1983	Hijacked Chinese plane provides opportunity for beginning of relations between ROK and China; ROK handling of situation was "correct" and agreement signed on May 10, containing provision that both parties would maintain the spirit of mutual cooperation in matters of emergency involving them in the future; later correspondence developed between ROK president Chun Doo Hwan and Chinese leader Deng Xiaoping through Pakistani president Zia Ul Hag.

5 July 1983	Kim Un Yong, president of WTF, visits Samaranch, who requests information on north-south border matters.
8 July 1983	Samaranch telexes Roh Tae Woo, congratulating him on forthcoming appointment as president of SLOOC.
11 July 1983	Roh Tae Woo becomes president of SLOOC.
13 July 1983	Kim Un Yong writes to Samaranch, explaining border situation and suggesting that IOC propose opening to DPRK and possibly PRC; ROK will agree to allowing border to open; no dignitaries have ever passed through DMZ except north-south delegates some ten years previously during official discussions.
1 Sep. 1983	Soviet military aircraft shoots down civilian KAL 007 passenger plane, which had strayed off course over Sakhalin on flight from New York to Seoul.
Sep. 1983	U.S. State Department, reversing previous policy, allows U.S. diplomats to converse on matters of substance with DPRK officials who initiate such discussions in neutral settings.
15 Sep. 1983	Samaranch attends Chinese National Games in Shanghai, September 15–19; meets with PRC vice president Ulanhu and minister of sport Li Menghua.
21 Sep. 1983	Samaranch attends thirty-second meeting of Socialist Sports Ministers in Pyongyang, DPRK, September 20–25.
23 Sep. 1983	Samaranch visits Beijing, meets with PRC president, Li Xiannian.
24 Sep. 1983	Samaranch visits Seoul, September 24–27, meets with SLOOC president Roh Tae Woo and ROK president Chun Doo Hwan.
8 Oct. 1983	DPRK proposes to U.S. government through U.S. embassy in Beijing the setting up of three-nation talks between United States, DPRK, and ROK.
9 Oct. 1983	Four cabinet ministers and fourteen senior ROK officials killed and fourteen more injured by remote-controlled bombs at Aungusa Mausoleum in Rangoon, Burma (now Yangon, Myanmar): bombing tied to DPRK.
10 Oct. 1983	Burmese government arrests suspected DPRK national Chin Mo as suspect in Rangoon bombing.

11 Oct. 1983	Burmese government arrests second suspect in bombing, Kang Min Chol; both suspects are Korean, but not yet identified as from the North or the South.
Oct. 1983	U.S. State Department reverses September decision with respect to bilateral discussions with DPRK officials.
4 Nov. 1983	Burmese government severs diplomatic relations with DPRK and orders all diplomats out of country within forty-eight hours.
1 Dec. 1983	Countering resolutions by California legislature, U.S. House of Representatives passes resolution supporting Olympic Charter and welcomes all athletes taking part in Games; California resolutions to ban Soviets followed shooting of KAL 007 passenger airliner.
Jan. 1984	East German sports minister Manfred Ewald gets evasive answer from USSR NOC president and sports minister Marat Gramov concerning Soviet participation in Los Angeles; Ewald speculates that USSR concerned about being beaten by United States and East Germany in the Games.
17 Jan. 1984	ROK president Chun Doo Hwan expresses wish to prevent intense confrontation between ROK and DPRK.
Feb. 1984	Olympic Winter Games in Sarajevo; Soviet IOC members enthusiastic regarding forthcoming Games in Los Angeles.
3 Feb. 1984	SLOOC reports to IOC Executive Board in Sarajevo; delegation headed by Roh Tae Woo.
9 Feb. 1984	General secretary of Central Committee of Communist Party of Soviet Union, Yuri Andropov, dies and will be succeeded by Konstantin Chernenko.
March 1984	ROK athletes compete in second round of Eastern Zone Davis Cup Preliminaries in Kunming, China; this is the first time ROK athletes have competed in PRC.
30 March 1984	DPRK NOC suggests single joint Korean team for 1984 Olympics and early meeting to discuss; sends notice of such communication to Samaranch.
April 1984	PRC responds to ROK athletes being present in PRC in March by sending athletes and officials to participate in

Eighth Asian Youth Basketball Championships and Second Asian Swimming Championships in Seoul.

U.S. embassy in Moscow requests USSR NOC to submit names of its delegation to Los Angeles Games for visa applications, in violation of Olympic Charter.

2 April 1984 KASA and KOC president Chung Ju Yung accepts proposal for north-south meeting and proposes date and agenda; notification of this and text of reply sent to Samaranch.

5 April 1984 Roh Tae Woo and KOC president write separately to Samaranch regarding proposed meeting and the raising of the Rangoon bombing as an issue in such meeting.

6 April 1984 DPRK accepts time and place of meeting and composition of delegations for purposes of discussing joint team.

7 April 1984 ROK announces names of delegation for meeting to discuss joint team.

8 April 1984 DPRK announces names of its delegation for same meeting.

9 April 1984 First north-south sports meeting held at Panmunjom; meeting unsuccessful.

11 April 1984 SLOOC requests IOC approval to change dates of Games from September 20–October 5, 1988, to September 17–October 2, 1988.

USSR NOC president Marat Gramov telexes Samaranch to express concern regarding Los Angeles and requests a special IOC Executive Board meeting to discuss "flagrant" violations of Olympic Charter by Los Angeles Organizing Committee (LAOOC).

Roh Tae Woo telexes Samaranch regarding north-south meeting and unsuccessful outcome.

12 April 1984 ROK proposes second meeting regarding joint team for Los Angeles Games to be held April 18.

Samaranch telexes Roh Tae Woo in response to latter's report concerning north-south meeting.

14 April 1984 DPRK rejects proposal for second meeting to discuss joint team for Los Angeles Games.

17 April 1984 KOC president sends letter to Kim Yu Sun, president of DPRK NOC, urging return to negotiations.

18 April 1984	Roh Tae Woo advises Samaranch by telex of developments regarding north-south meetings to discuss joint team for Los Angeles Games.
24 April 1984	DPRK proposes second meeting to discuss joint team to be held on April 26.
24 April 1984	Meeting between Samaranch and IOC vice presidents, representatives of USSR NOC, and LAOOC in Lausanne; relatively optimistic press statement agreed to by all participants, giving some hope that a crisis may be avoided.
	ROK proposes date of April 30 for second meeting.
26 April 1984	Samaranch receives confidential indications from USSR that USSR not likely to participate in Los Angeles.
	Samaranch consults IOC vice presidents and requests meeting with U.S. president Ronald Reagan to see if he can get letter from Reagan to USSR president Chernenko stating U.S. government's support for Games and giving assurances regarding security; meeting set for May 8, the day Olympic flame due to arrive in United States.
27 April 1984	U.S. State Department official Edward Derwinski advises USSR Ministry of Foreign Affairs that all matters decided at April 24 meeting have been declared null and void and that U.S. administration will not disassociate itself from alleged anti-Soviet activities.
28 April 1984	DPRK agrees to meeting to discuss joint team for Los Angeles Games on April 30.
30 April 1984	Second north-south meeting to discuss joint Korean team for Los Angeles Games held at Panmunjom; meeting unsuccessful.
May 1984	SLOOC reaches agreement on basic program of events with all international federations except FIG and IAAF; such agreement important for purposes of television negotiations.
	DPRK president Kim Il Sung visits Moscow.
4 May 1984	Samaranch proposes north-south meeting in Lausanne.
8 May 1984	Plenary session of USSR NOC meets in Moscow and decides not to participate in Los Angeles Olympics.

	Samaranch meets with U.S. president Ronald Reagan and Secretary of State George Shultz in Washington; gets letter from Reagan addressed to him urging Soviets to reverse decision, to be delivered to USSR president Chernenko.
9 May 1984	USSR NOC president Marat Gramov telexes Samaranch to advise of USSR decision not to participate in Los Angeles.
	ROK proposes a third north-south meeting to be held in mid-May to discuss possibility of joint Korean team in Los Angeles Games.
10 May 1984	Samaranch telexes USSR NOC president Marat Gramov regarding communication of his NOC's decision and requests meeting with President Konstantin Chernenko.
	Press release issued by IOC stating that meeting with Chernenko had been requested.
	East Germany's NOC, under instructions from government to support Soviet boycott of Los Angeles Games, votes unanimously not to participate.
12 May 1984	DPRK refuses third north-south meeting to discuss joint team for Los Angeles Games.
14 May 1984	USSR delegation visits Samaranch in Lausanne to say that decision regarding Los Angeles is final and that Samaranch should consider this when considering any possibility of visiting Moscow; delegation states that its advice is not a formal reply to telex from Samaranch to Gramov.
15 May 1984	Antonin Himl, president of Czechoslovakian NOC, advises Samaranch of meeting of Socialist Ministers of Sport to be held in Prague on May 24 and invites him to be present.
16 May 1984	Samaranch speaks with USSR NOC president Marat Gramov, who says political authorities were not involved in the decision not to participate in Los Angeles.
17 May 1984	Constantin Karamanlis, president of Hellenic Republic, renews offer to have permanent Olympic site in Greece.
18 May 1984	Extraordinary meeting of IOC Executive Board in Lausanne; USSR NOC and LAOOC delegations also present. LAOOC president Peter Ueberroth states that April 27 meeting with USSR Foreign Ministry was low level on part of U.S. State Department and that he had been assured by

U.S. secretary of state George Shultz that United States would support the decisions of April 24 meeting.

ROK requests third north-south meeting to discuss possibility of joint team for Los Angeles Games on May 23.

23 May 1984 DPRK proposes such meeting be held on May 25.

Samaranch attends thirty-third meeting of Socialist Ministers of Sport in Prague, Czechoslovakia, May 23–24; though main purpose of meeting is matter of Los Angeles boycott and nonparticipation of socialist bloc, many delegates criticize choice of Seoul as host city for 1988 Games.

24 May 1984 DPRK announces that, together with other socialist countries, it will not participate in Los Angeles Olympic Games.

25 May 1984 Third north-south meeting to discuss joint team for Los Angeles Games held at Panmunjom; meeting unsuccessful.

28 May 1984 IOC Executive Board agrees to change dates of Seoul Games to September 17–October 2, 1988.

29 May 1984 ROK proposes fourth north-south meeting to discuss participation in Los Angeles Games.

30 May 1984 Samaranch visits Moscow, May 30–31, in effort to persuade Soviets to participate in Los Angeles.

1 June 1984 DPRK rejects fourth meeting requested by ROK.

2 June 1984 DPRK officially confirms boycott of Los Angeles Games.

9 June 1984 SLOOC president Roh Tae Woo discounts press reports of possible withdrawal of Games from Seoul due to USSR boycott of Los Angeles as merely the private opinion of some IOC members.

23 June 1984 Samaranch reports to IOC Executive Board meeting at the Sorbonne on the ninetieth anniversary of the founding of the IOC, regarding his reception in the USSR as part of his efforts to avoid a boycott of the Los Angeles Games; situation is hopeless.

French NOC president Nelson Paillou suggests 1988 Olympics be moved from Seoul to Barcelona. Idea rejected by Samaranch (Paris and Barcelona are both candidates to host 1992 Olympic Games).

27 June 1984	Italian foreign minister Giulio Andreotti suggests to ROK foreign minister Lee Won Kyoung that cohosting by DPRK might be necessary for success of Games; ROK government responds that such collaboration is not possible.
June 1984	U.S. president Reagan considers personal invitation to USSR president Chernenko to attend Games; Secretary of State George Shultz convinces Reagan that this would damage U.S.-USSR relations.
1 July 1984	Vice president of SLOOC and Asian Games Organizing Committee Cho Sang Ho gives assurance that all participants will enjoy the same hospitality, particularly DPRK; objective is to showcase ROK as distinct from DPRK.
July 1984	ROK government advises IOC through its ambassador in United States that having DPRK as cohost would only create opportunities for sabotage of Games.
16 July 1984	ROK president Chun Doo Hwan writes to Samaranch prior to IOC Session in Los Angeles to express full support for 1988 Games, including matters of security and respect for Olympic Charter.
17 July 1984	Samaranch discounts rumors of changing site of 1988 Games during press interview in Los Angeles; suggests possibility of sanctions against NOCs that do not take part in the Games.
22 July 1984	SLOOC president Roh Tae Woo indicates that ROK is prepared to try to resume sports exchanges with USSR despite frigidity of relations following KAL downing by Soviet aircraft in September 1983.
17 Aug. 1984	ROK proposes fourth round of north-south talks at Panmunjom to discuss joint teams.
22 Aug. 1984	ROK president Chun Doo Hwan writes to IOC, guaranteeing that Olympic Charter will be respected, security will be assured, and nonexistence of diplomatic relations will be no problem for Games.
27 Aug. 1984	DPRK rejects fourth north-south meeting as suggested by ROK.
17 Sep. 1984	Horst Dassler, president of Adidas, tells ROK ambassador to France of meeting he had on August 19 with USSR

NOC president Marat Gramov, who said all nations could compete in Games if ROK gave several events to DPRK.

19 Sep. 1984 Samaranch visits Moscow, September 19–22; presides over symposium on Olympic Solidarity attended by presidents and secretaries-general of NOCs from Asia, Africa, and Latin America; meets with USSR NOC president Marat Gramov; also meets with DPRK NOC president Kim Yu Sun, who asks if he has heard of recommendation by Andreotti regarding sharing of Games; Samaranch says if recommendation made officially by DPRK, IOC may consider the possibility.

27 Sep. 1984 Samaranch visits Seoul for opening of main stadium; delegation from People's Republic of China is present; USSR is not represented. Samaranch states at press conference that he is ready to organize meetings between the North and the South in Lausanne or elsewhere; Samaranch explains political developments to SLOOC president Roh Tae Woo, who states he is prepared to review any recommendations made by Samaranch.

28 Sep. 1984 Beijing is designated as host city for 1990 Asian Games; indications given that Beijing might wish to host Olympic Games in 2000.

29 Sep. 1984 Official opening of main Olympic stadium in Seoul.

30 Sep. 1984 Samaranch visits Beijing, September 30–October 2; meets with prime minister and minister of sport.

4 Oct. 1984 South Korea again proposes fourth north-south meeting to discuss joint teams for Korea.

Oct. 1984 Samaranch sends copies of August correspondence with Chun to all NOCs and IFs.

ROK continues exchanges with PRC by sending athletes to Tenth Asian Women's Basketball Championship in Shanghai.

12 Oct. 1984 Samaranch meets with Kampuchea NOC president in Lausanne.

19 Oct. 1984 Soviet IOC members Konstantin Andrianov and Vitaly Smirnov complain bitterly in writing to IOC about Los Angeles and Seoul decisions by IOC; they later apologize and matter is not pursued.

	Sports officials from Communist bloc meet in Prague and issue statement of "concern" over staging 1988 Olympic Games in Seoul, calling on IOC to ensure "normal conditions" for participation of all countries.
31 Oct. 1984	*Izvestia* speculates whether it is possible to organize sports festival in country governed by dictatorship where there are permanent problems.
2 Nov. 1984	Series of articles in *Sovietsky Sport* critical of choice of Seoul as host city for 1988 Games and calls for change of venue.
3 Nov. 1984	Barcelona mayor Pasqual Maragall announces that Barcelona could be ready to host 1988 Games if Seoul unable to do so.
6 Nov. 1984	Soviet NOC continues protest against Los Angeles and Seoul at meeting of ANOC in Mexico City, November 6–10, supported by East Germany; ANOC votes overwhelmingly to support Seoul Games; Samaranch meets with DPRK NOC president Kim Yu Sun, who is ready to meet in Lausanne under IOC auspices to discuss organizing events in DPRK and having a united team; Samaranch passes recommendation to Roh Tae Woo.
7 Nov. 1984	Samaranch advises IOC Executive Board that he has received letter from DPRK NOC president and IOC member Kim Yu Sun asking if he was ready to state that 1988 Games would be held in both North Korea and South Korea and that forthcoming ANOC meeting will be held in Pyongyang instead of Seoul. He reports that he will make no announcement on Games and that site of ANOC meeting is not a decision for the IOC.
16 Nov. 1984	Czechoslovakia NOC president Antonin Himl states that choice of Seoul was a mistake, but that Soviet bloc will participate.
19 Nov. 1984	KASA and KOC president Roh Tae Woo calls for fourth north-south meeting.
21 Nov. 1984	Soviet NOC president Marat Gramov declares choice of Seoul as host city for 1988 Games is "inappropriate"; USSR cannot understand why the Games should take place in Seoul.

29 Nov. 1984	Press reports suggest secret discussions taking place to resume meetings between DPRK and ROK and that discussions include possibility of moving some Olympic events to DPRK.
	Fidel Castro sends letter to Samaranch complaining about PASO decision to award 1987 Pan American Games to Indianapolis instead of Havana and proposing that 1988 Olympic Games be shared equally between the North and the South.
30 Nov. 1984	IOC Executive Board agrees with Samaranch's idea of calling for a meeting of the NOCs of the two Koreas in Lausanne, without prior conditions.
2 Dec. 1984	Eighty-ninth IOC Session in Lausanne, December 1–2, changes rules regarding sending of invitations to participate in the Olympic Games: invitations will be sent by IOC, not host Organizing Committees; no sanctions will be applied to NOCs that do not participate in the Games; strong resolution in support of Seoul Games.
6 Dec. 1984	ROK sports minister Lee Yong Ho states in interview in Tokyo that no official request has come from DPRK to share the Games; he believes it would be easier to share Games than have joint team.
10 Dec. 1984	DPRK prime minister Kang Sung San supports letter from Castro dated November 29 and states Seoul cannot successfully host Olympics.
16 Dec. 1984	DPRK NOC circulates letter stating that Seoul unfit in every way to host Games; letter also states that DPRK does not want the Games in the North either.
1 Feb. 1985	Samaranch proposes north-south meeting in Lausanne in September, under IOC auspices.
25 Feb. 1985	At IOC Executive Board meeting in Calgary, Samaranch advises that he has sent confidential letter to ROK regarding joint meeting.
	Roh Tae Woo advises Samaranch that he has been asked to assume presidency of Democratic Justice Party in ROK.
5 March 1985	Samaranch congratulates Roh Tae Woo on new responsibilities and asks him to remain as president of SLOOC.

March 1985	Fidel Castro gives interview to U.S. congressman on 1988 Olympics, in which he is critical of IOC, the Games, and certain sports personalities.
11 March 1985	Mikhail Gorbachev becomes general secretary of Communist Party of the Soviet Union.
13 March 1985	KOC accepts IOC offer of Lausanne meeting.
29 March 1985	Rumors begin to circulate that USSR has made decision in principle to attend Seoul Games; speculation ties this to Gorbachev policy.
25 April 1985	Lee Yong Ho, ROK minister of sport, elected as president of SLOOC Executive Board, following appointment of Roh Tae Woo as chairman of Democratic Justice Party; Roh will remain as president of SLOOC.
1 May 1985	Kim Chong Ha succeeds Roh Tae Woo as nineteenth president of KOC.
17 May 1985	Economic cooperation discussions between ROK and DPRK resume.
28 May 1985	Wire service reports that USSR sports officials confirm that best USSR athletes will be sent to competitions in ROK and will compete in Seoul Olympics.
5 June 1985	ROK president Chun Doo Hwan expresses hope for DPRK participation in 1986 Asian Games and 1988 Olympic Games in Seoul.
	Samaranch presents Olympic flag to SLOOC president Roh Tae Woo during IOC Session in Berlin, to be kept by city of Seoul until end of Games in 1988.
July 1985	IOC vice president Ashwini Kumar of India visits Pyongyang at request of Samaranch to see if DPRK NOC will attend a joint meeting at invitation of IOC, to be held later that year.
6 July 1985	DPRK agrees to Lausanne meeting under IOC auspices in Lausanne.
12 July 1985	DPRK NOC sends a proposal by mail to the IOC for a joint hosting of the 1988 Olympic Games.
23 July 1985	Samaranch sends letter to Fidel Castro critical of Castro's

comments on the IOC in interview given by Castro in March 1985.

24 July 1985 IOC announces joint meeting between two Korean NOCs to be held in Lausanne, under IOC auspices, during 1985.

25 July 1985 KOC president urges DPRK NOC to agree to a further north-south bilateral meeting.

26 July 1985 Samaranch in Moscow for Spartakiade; meets DPRK NOC president Kim Yu Sun, who insists on sharing of Games between two Koreas; says DPRK participation in 1986 Asian Games not yet studied; KGB officer assigned to Samaranch during his posting as ambassador says Gorbachev will make important changes in USSR, especially now that Gromyko is no longer involved in foreign affairs; also says Gorbachev was one of those responsible for USSR decision to boycott Los Angeles Games in 1984.

27 July 1985 Samaranch visits Leningrad and discusses prospective bid by Leningrad for Olympic Winter Games in 1996 (this is before cycle of Olympic Winter Games changed by IOC) with Mayor Khodyrev; he leaves USSR reassured that USSR now back in the Olympic "fold."

28 July 1985 DPRK NOC visits Samaranch in Lausanne.

30 July 1985 DPRK deputy prime minister Chung announces that 1988 Olympic Games are "Korean" Games and should be equally divided.

31 July 1985 Samaranch acknowledges DPRK NOC letter of July 12, 1985, regarding joint hosting of Games and requests confirmation of meeting dates.

2 Aug. 1985 ROK sports minister energetically rejects claim by DPRK regarding division of Games.

Aug. 1985 DPRK allows Soviet warships into DPRK port for first time, but does not allow bases to be established; seen as part of continuing effort to play off USSR and PRC.

25 Aug. 1985 Samaranch visits Seoul, August 25–26, to discuss forthcoming joint meeting with Roh Tae Woo, SLOOC, and KOC; in private meeting with Samaranch, Roh is receptive to possibility of giving some small events of no importance to DPRK, but states cohosting should not be considered and DPRK should not be allowed to make propaganda state-

ments; Samaranch meets with Chun Doo Hwan at Blue House for lunch, then private meeting; Chun is completely closed to idea of events for DPRK and has very firm position that Olympic Charter to be respected; suggests to Samaranch that Roh may be his successor; Samaranch has further meeting with Roh, whose position is much more flexible and who agrees some sports can be given to DPRK and teams can march together.

28 Aug. 1985 Aide-mémoire of discussions prepared by Koreans at Samaranch's request, following subsequent meeting with Roh Tae Woo on that date.

6 Sep. 1985 Cuban media reports that foreign ministers of nonaligned nations have endorsed Cuban proposal that 1988 Olympics be jointly organized.

15 Sep. 1985 NOCs of USSR and United States sign agreement for cooperation in Indianapolis, in which they agree to do everything possible to ensure the participation of their teams in the Olympic Games.

19 Sep. 1985 PRC NOC president Zhong Shitong sends letter to Samaranch applauding idea of joint meeting and indicating that DPRK proposal is "worth serious consideration."

20 Sep. 1985 Limited number of people from each side of the Korean border allowed to meet relatives on the other side, in first encounter since Korean War.

28 Sep. 1985 Olympic Council of Asia awards 1990 Asian Games to Beijing.

30 Sep. 1985 DPRK NOC president Kim Yu Sun writes to Samaranch with proposal for cohosting the Games to be discussed at forthcoming joint meeting with IOC.

ROK president Chun Doo Hwan addresses nation on fourth anniversary of Games being awarded to Seoul and reminds people of Olympic ideals and meaning and goal of Seoul Olympics.

Oct. 1985 DPRK "intruder" craft designed to sail with only six inches visible above water, intercepted in ROK waters off port of Pusan, location of Olympic sailing events.

2 Oct. 1985 ROK announces delegation to Lausanne meeting.

6 Oct. 1985 IAAF proposes relay marathon in North Korea and South Korea as part of 1987 Seoul World Cup Marathon.

7 Oct. 1985 IOC meets separately with each Korean delegation prior to joint meeting the following day.

DPRK party newspaper *Rodong Shinmun* reports that Seoul incapable of holding 1988 Games and is using Games for sinister political plots; Seoul is colony and military base of U.S. imperialists; never before had colonial puppet been allowed to organize the Games.

8 Oct. 1985 First IOC sponsored north-south joint meeting in Lausanne begins.

11 Oct. 1985 Australian Olympic Federation objects to DPRK proposal to stage half the Games.

16 Oct. 1985 Samaranch reports on four visits to Korea at meeting of IOC Executive Board with Executive Council of ANOC; if political situation in the world is delicate in 1988, there could be problems for the Games.

21 Oct. 1985 In separate interviews in New York, DPRK foreign minister Kim Yong Nam says DPRK will urge Communist countries to boycott Seoul if events not divided evenly between North Korea and South Korea, and ROK chief of mission Kim Kyung Won states cohosting is technically and logistically impossible.

23 Oct. 1985 Samaranch writes to DPRK NOC regarding agenda for second joint meeting with IOC.

24 Oct. 1985 Samaranch begins twelve-day tour of African NOCs and concludes that with possible exceptions of Burkina Faso and Benin, all are ready to participate in Seoul Olympics; all are following closely IOC's efforts to achieve an agreement between the two Koreas.

26 Oct. 1985 At request of SLOOC, ROK police ban manufacture and sale of T-shirts and caps that criticize USSR (they have pictures of bleeding polar bears and 1983 downing of KAL flight 007) as contrary to government policy of attracting USSR and East European countries to take part in Games.

11 Nov. 1985 ROK sports minister Lee Yong Ho states before parliamentary commission in Seoul that sharing the organization of the 1988 Games with DPRK is "totally out of the ques-

tion"; ROK had offered, in spirit of national reconciliation, to share some preliminary events with DPRK.

14 Nov. 1985 Samaranch attends thirty-fourth meeting of Socialist Ministers of Sport, November 14–16, in Hanoi, Vietnam; communiqué issued following meeting urges IOC and IFs to seriously consider DPRK proposal.

16 Nov. 1985 In press conference following meeting in Hanoi, Samaranch states Games were awarded to Seoul and will be held in Seoul; if proposal to cohost the Games meant "to split the Games in two, the answer is no. That is not possible."

17 Nov. 1985 Samaranch issues press release of contents of his communication to U.S. president Reagan and USSR general secretary Gorbachev prior to Geneva summit meeting.

25 Nov. 1985 DPRK NOC president Kim Yu Sun writes to Samaranch regarding agenda but confirms delegation will attend second joint meeting with IOC.

1 Dec. 1985 In open letter to Samaranch, Fidel Castro attacks choice of Seoul as host city for 1988 Games and says Games should be split between North Korea and South Korea.

2 Dec. 1985 Park Chong Kyu, IOC member in ROK, dies.

DPRK urges ROK to join it in a confederation in which each side would continue to govern itself; *Rodong Shinmun* states that "the differences in system, ideology and idea can well be overcome if neither the north nor the south of Korea absolutize its ideology or try to force them on the other side, abiding by the principle of subordinating everything to the fulfillment of the nation's supreme task, the national reunification."

6 Dec. 1985 Samaranch meets with ROK sports minister Lee Yong Ho in Lausanne to discuss recent meeting of Socialist Ministers of Sport in Hanoi, replacement of Park Chong Kyu as IOC member in Korea, 1988 Scientific Congress in Seoul, torch relay, television negotiations, relations between the IOC and SLOOC, and north-south discussions.

13 Dec. 1985 ROK ambassador in Geneva meets with Samaranch in Lausanne to explore means by which relationships between IOC and Koreans can be improved.

18 Dec. 1985 President of Ethiopian NOC and commissioner for sports and physical culture Tsegaw Ayele warns of Olympic boycott if Games not cohosted, in address to African continental association of NOCs (ANOCA); Samaranch praises African participation at Los Angeles and warns African states to avoid being manipulated by "your adversaries" to stage Olympic boycotts.

19 Dec. 1985 ROK deputy foreign minister Lee Sang Ock advises Japanese counterpart Kensuke Yanagiya that ROK is ready to make some limited concessions to DPRK if DPRK accepts Seoul as principal site and host city of the Games; another Japanese official refers to cohosting as unrealizable.

20 Dec. 1985 *Sport Intern* indicates Samaranch's preference for new IOC member in South Korea as Kim Un Yong, president of WTF and vice president of SLOOC.

30 Dec. 1985 ROK advises IOC of composition of its delegation for second joint meeting to be held under IOC auspices in Lausanne.

Canton de Vaud issues authorization for Korean participants to attend and participate in second joint meeting.

3 Jan. 1986 IOC issues press release regarding second joint meeting in Lausanne.

6 Jan. 1986 Samaranch prepares notes for opening IOC address at second joint meeting.

Samaranch meets ROK ambassador in Lausanne.

7 Jan. 1986 ROK sports minister Lee Yong Ho dismissed from position as minister; he is replaced by Park Seh Jik.

Samaranch and Siperco meet with DPRK NOC representatives Kim Yu Sun and Chin Chung Guk in Lausanne.

8 Jan. 1986 Second IOC sponsored north-south joint meeting in Lausanne begins; Samaranch also meets separately with DPRK delegation.

9 Jan. 1986 Samaranch meets in morning with DPRK NOC delegation and agreement in principle seems to be reached for three sports (soccer, archery, and table tennis) to be held in the North; procedure will be for DPRK to accept invitation to

participate in Seoul and then IOC will contact IFs and SLOOC.

Samaranch meets with KOC delegation in evening.

12 Jan. 1986 Editorial in the *Korea Times* calls upon DPRK to accept principle that Games awarded to Seoul and to "be more reasonable and consistent with the norms of international practices, lest its wanton behavior defame the prestige of the Korean people as a whole in the international community."

13 Jan. 1986 DPRK NOC vice president Chin and Kim Deuk Il visit Samaranch in Lausanne wanting answers to questions on joint Korean team, name of the Games, and what sports will be held in Pyongyang; Samaranch says he will reply on January 14.

15 Jan. 1986 DPRK delegation returns to Lausanne; Samaranch tells it to come back the following week.

Samaranch sends Italian foreign minister Giulio Andreotti copies of minutes of first and second joint meetings and press releases, and asks for his comments.

20 Jan. 1986 DPRK returns to Lausanne; DPRK vice president Chin now wants eight sports; Samaranch insists on a joint team; Chin accuses Samaranch of being partial to ROK and of wanting to help the South; Siperco meets for three hours with Chin and delegation; Samaranch concludes there is no way of dealing with DPRK and that it would be better not to have any agreement, but to keep matters in suspense until the last moment.

23 Jan. 1986 Interview by IOC member in USSR, Konstantin Andrianov, in *Sovietskaya Rossiya* suggests that even though Soviets disagree with selection of Seoul, it is likely that they will participate ("The train has already gone too far"), since ROK government has given guarantees of security to all participants including socialist countries; Tass communiqué same date reiterates support for organizing Games in both the North and the South.

29 Jan. 1986 Willi Daume, IOC member in West Germany, in speech to Association of Berlin Traders and Industrialists, states that participation in Seoul depends on overall political situation, and East Germany will stand with USSR in event of boycott; describes position of power of U.S. television in terms

of "prospects of Orwellian dimensions" and concludes speech by stating, "There are more important things in the world than the Olympic Games."

4 Feb. 1986 Fidel Castro in speech given at Third Communist Party Congress in Havana states that Cuba will boycott 1988 Games unless DPRK and ROK cohost; also claims Cuba prevented from hosting 1987 Pan American Games by $25 million bribe from unidentified multimillionaire; reference thought to be to Mario Vazquez-Raña, president of PASO.

6 Feb. 1986 DPRK vice president Pak Sung Chol, in Havana for Third Congress of Cuban Communist Party, calls for other nations to "wage a dynamic struggle" for DPRK to get share of Games; ROK is inappropriate site because it is a country where human rights are "trampled" and where U.S. forces are based; predicts "very few" countries will be represented unless IOC changes its decision.

7 Feb. 1986 DPRK vice president Pak Sung Chol pays courtesy visit to Nicaraguan president Daniel Ortega in Havana, who says Nicaragua will not participate in Games if DPRK proposal for cohosting is not realized.

11 Feb. 1986 Samaranch advises IOC Executive Board that he has told DPRK delegation that he will not contact any IF until he has guarantee that DPRK will take part in the Games; asks for briefing on Chinese attitude with respect to Korean problems.

18 Feb. 1986 Ten Japanese passports stolen from group of tourists in Madrid; by late August 1988, fears develop that some of these passports may be used by Japanese Red Army in efforts to disrupt Seoul Games.

19 Feb. 1986 General William J. Livsey, commander of ROK-U.S. Combined Forces Command, in interview in *Army Times* warns that DPRK might stage armed provocation against Seoul to disrupt 1988 Olympic Games.

2 March 1986 ROK sports minister Park Seh Jik, attending Asian Winter Games in Sapporo, Japan, states that joint hosting of the Games is "out of the question."

4 March 1986 DPRK and ROK compete against each other in ice hockey at Asian Winter Games for first time in forty years.

5 March 1986	DPRK NOC vice president Pak Myong Chol at Asian Winter Games states DPRK expects positive response from ROK to DPRK cohosting proposal at third joint meeting.
7 March 1986	Samaranch and Siperco meet DPRK NOC and KOC delegations separately in Lausanne.
8 March 1986	Fidel Castro arrives in Pyongyang after attending Twenty-seventh Congress of Communist Party of the Soviet Union in Moscow.
11 March 1986	DPRK president Kim Il Sung addresses rally in honor of Fidel Castro, saying 1988 Games are a political issue, and DPRK will not sit idly by.
	In Havana, sports minister Conrado Martinez calls upon nonaligned countries to support DPRK demand to cohost Games.
13 March 1986	ROK sports minister Park Seh Jik named acting president of SLOOC.
20 March 1986	ROK defense minister Lee Ki Baek states there is danger that war could break out at any time between now and end of 1988.
26 March 1986	Television contract with NBC for U.S. television rights to Games signed in Lausanne for minimum of $300 million.
	Samaranch asks KOC president Kim Chong Ha for help in having Kim Un Yong elected as IOC member.
1 April 1986	Statement by ROK sports minister Park Seh Jik that DPRK is welcome at April meetings of NOCs and that if DPRK is unconditionally present, there could be meetings prior to the joint meeting scheduled for Lausanne in June.
3 April 1986	DPRK chargé de mission in Geneva meets with Samaranch in Lausanne.
6 April 1986	Secretariat of DPRK Committee for the Peaceful Reunification of the Fatherland publishes White Paper entitled "24th Olympics, Be Conducive to Peace in Korea and Her Peaceful Reunification," denouncing the U.S. imperialists and the South Korean puppet clique for their criminal schemes to use the 1988 Olympiad for a foul purpose.
9 April 1986	DPRK ambassador in Geneva meets with Samaranch in Lausanne.

10 April 1986 Ethiopian president Mengistu Haile Mariam states that Ethiopia will boycott Games if not cohosted by DPRK and ROK.

12 April 1986 ROK president Chun Doo Hwan arrives in Switzerland for break in European tour to Great Britain, West Germany, and France and visits IOC headquarters in Lausanne.

Cuban resolution calling for cohosting of Games is rejected after five hours of debate at economic meeting of non-aligned countries in New Delhi.

19 April 1986 Samaranch meets privately in Switzerland with ROK president Chun Doo Hwan, who gives extensive presentation on essential emptiness of DPRK threats.

22 April 1986 DPRK issues statement in Workers Party newspaper *Rodong Shinmun* declaring that holding of 1986 Asian Games and 1988 Olympic Games in Seoul is an "adventure" since war "might explode at any moment" in ROK; present situation in ROK stated to be reminiscent of situation in 1950 when ROK "fascist clique started a war of northward invasion, engineered by the U.S. imperialists."

At ANOC General Assembly in Seoul, ANOC president Mario Vazquez-Raña calls for support from all NOCs for SLOOC, IOC Executive Board, and Samaranch so that discussions between NOCs of the Koreas can come to an end.

23 April 1986 Acting SLOOC president Park Seh Jik in report to IOC Executive Board in Seoul advises IOC not to overreact to threats and pressure from DPRK nor to overestimate DPRK's position; discounts military intervention; assures capability of handling terrorism.

25 April 1986 Samaranch meets secretly with Roh Tae Woo and Park Seh Jik as well as senior ROK officials to discuss third joint meeting in Lausanne; Samaranch, Roh, and Park meet with ROK president Chun Doo Hwan; Samaranch gets agreement from Roh to offer two sports to DPRK, provided DPRK agrees to observe Olympic Charter, so that responsibility for a negative decision will fall on DPRK; Roh advises Samaranch he will be candidate for presidential elections and agrees to help with election of Kim Un Yong as IOC member.

26 April 1986 Samaranch advises IOC Commission for the Olympic Move-

ment that he is more optimistic about the outcome of the third joint meeting after his discussions the previous day and believes a worthwhile solution can be found; same statement made in press conference following meeting of IOC Executive Board with ANOC.

28 April 1986 Samaranch meets with PRC minister of sports and NOC president Li Menghua in Beijing to explain IOC efforts regarding events in DPRK as a special concession by IOC; Li does not wish to discuss details and will reply at later date; China will participate in 1986 Asian Games.

30 April 1986 ROK president Chun Doo Hwan agrees to constitutional revision discussions if Democratic Justice Party and opposition parties can agree on contents.

Deadline for applications for preliminary Olympic soccer tournament in Asia.

Samaranch meets in Beijing with DPRK NOC vice president Chin, who is very aggressive and wants entire Olympic soccer tournament to be staged in Pyongyang as well as for ROK to stop attacks on DPRK; Samaranch gives Chin copy of Radio Pyongyang broadcast full of lies and attacks on ROK; Samaranch meets further with Li Menghua and He Zhenliang to explain what happened with DPRK; both are very careful — they want to be in Seoul but do not want to have problems with DPRK.

6 May 1986 Samaranch suggests during interview in Evian, France, that he may have some new elements to propose to DPRK at forthcoming third joint meeting.

8 May 1986 DPRK Central News Agency (KCNA) announces that vast epidemic of AIDS affecting ROK makes Seoul unacceptable for 1986 Asian Games and 1988 Olympic Games; says some 600,000 persons in Seoul are affected.

9 May 1986 Samaranch meets with DPRK NOC president Kim Yu Sun in Moscow.

25 May 1986 U.S. sports columnist Howard Cosell publishes article in *Miami Herald* entitled "Why the '88 Olympics Won't Be in South Korea" and quotes former USOC president William E. Simon as saying "There is not a prayer of the Summer Games being held in South Korea."

26 May 1986 IOC issues press release with outline of third joint meeting.

27 May 1986 East German NOC president and minister of sport Manfred Ewald visits Samaranch in Lausanne.

28 May 1986 Samaranch sends author draft agreement to be signed with DPRK NOC if agreement reached on number of sports to be staged in DPRK and asks for comments.

29 May 1986 Lausanne police authorities confirm they will make the necessary arrangements regarding third joint meeting.

2 June 1986 Bulgarian NOC president and IOC member Ivan Slavkov visits Samaranch in Lausanne.

5 June 1986 USSR NOC president Marat Gramov writes to Samaranch urging him to reach an agreement to organize the Games in both parts of Korea.

6 June 1986 USSR NOC president Marat Gramov states in Moscow at press conference relating to Goodwill Games that he will "wait and see" what happens at third joint meeting in Lausanne; East Germany not in favor of Goodwill Games and will send minimum delegation to participate, for protocol purposes.

7 June 1986 Radio Pyongyang announces that DPRK has support of USSR, PRC, Poland, Cuba, and Ethiopia for cohosting proposal and that organization of Games only in South Korea would be intolerable defeat of sacred cause of reunification of Korea.

8 June 1986 Samaranch states in Paris that IOC has something new to offer to DPRK to help come to agreement in principle; fourth joint meeting may be required to come to complete agreement; fundamental condition will be full opening of border between ROK and DPRK.

9 June 1986 SLOOC vice president Kim Un Yong visits Samaranch in Lausanne.

Samaranch meets with DPRK delegation in Lausanne.

10 June 1986 Third IOC-sponsored north-south joint meeting in Lausanne begins; meeting concludes June 11; at press conference Samaranch states that important headway has been

made and that "the mediation role of the IOC has been a very important one."

11 June 1986 Samaranch writes to DPRK NOC and KOC reminding each of deadline of June 30, 1986, to accept in principle IOC's proposal, following which a fourth meeting would be convened to deal with organizational matters.

IOC issues press communiqué following third joint meeting.

Samaranch writes to USSR NOC president Marat Gramov and to president of Chinese Olympic Committee Li Menghua (both of whom are also sports ministers) following third joint meeting.

12 June 1986 Aide-mémoire prepared by KOC delegation following third joint meeting.

13 June 1986 IOC director of legal affairs sends Samuel Pisar draft copy of working document that might become agreement between IOC and DPRK NOC if agreement reached on sports to be held in DPRK.

15 June 1986 DPRK president Kim Il Sung issues statement that athletes, foreign journalists, officials, tourists, and guests would receive warm welcome if DPRK named cohost of Games; states that Games are not merely "a simple sports event. They are a serious political issue affecting the reunification of Korea"; he also states, "Participating in the Olympic Games in South Korea means approving the U.S. occupation of South Korea and encouraging the United States and the South Korean authorities that are scheming for 'two Koreas' and a permanent division of our country"; ROK not fit to be sole host because "danger of a new war is always present."

19 June 1986 ROK minister for national unification Park Ton Jin states in New York that ROK may respond favorably to IOC request that DPRK organize some events, out of respect for IOC and to create an "atmosphere of reconciliation by accommodating in some way" the DPRK.

21 June 1986 DPRK NOC vice president Kim Duk Jun issues statement calling for cohosting of 1988 Olympic Games and criticizing ROK position that KOC backed down in agreeing to allow two events to be organized in DPRK; states that "It was

not to hold one or two games in our area that we proposed the cohosting of the Olympics"; IOC proposal termed "preposterous."

23 June 1986 ROK ambassador to Geneva, Park Kun, sends Samaranch translation of DPRK statement of June 21.

24 June 1986 ROK soccer officials note that DPRK has applied to compete in regional preliminary rounds of Olympic soccer tournament, according to FIFA bulletin; draw to be made June 27 in Mexico during World Cup.

27 June 1986 ROK accepts IOC June 11 proposal for 1988 Games.

28 June 1986 DPRK NOC gives written agreement, in principle, to IOC proposal, under condition that greater number of sports be allocated to it.

30 June 1986 KOC president Kim Chong Ha replies to IOC proposal by letter; also sends identical message by cable.

ROK ambassador to Geneva, Park Kun, transmits response of KOC president Kim Chong Ha to IOC proposal.

Rodong Shinmun denounces ROK insistence on being sole host of Games and states that "the Olympic Movement must never be abused for the perpetuation of the division of Korea"; also states: "As we have already made clear, the 24th Olympic Games must be cohosted by the North and the South and, to this end, our elementary demand for such basic questions as the title of the Games, division of events, formation of the Organizing Committee and the Opening and Closing Ceremonies of the Games must be accepted."

2 July 1986 Samaranch meets separately with representatives of two Korean NOCs (North first, followed by South) in Lausanne.

ROK ambassador in Geneva, Park Kun, transmits copy of cable message of June 30 to Samaranch.

3 July 1986 Samaranch sends telex to reiterate question previously posed and requests clarification from DPRK NOC prior to July 15 regarding its exact position concerning IOC proposal; negative reply would make further meetings totally meaningless and unnecessary.

IOC issues press release announcing receipt of replies to

its proposal, stating it considers these positive, but has requested further information from DPRK as to interpretation of its reply.

9 July 1986 Samaranch meets DPRK NOC president Kim Yu Sun in Moscow; Kim repeats request as per letter of June 28 and Samaranch extends deadline for reply to July 20; Samaranch meets with USSR president Andrei Gromyko, who supports idea of staging some sports in DPRK.

Final Declaration of Second Conference of Ministers and Senior Officials in the Sphere of Physical Education and Sport in Pyongyang contains reference to cohosting Games and concern of "deep and irreversible crisis" to Olympic Movement if agreement not reached.

19 July 1986 DPRK NOC sends letter to IOC, stating agreement in principle for sports proposed, in addition to request for an increase in number of sports to be allocated to DPRK.

21 July 1986 DPRK delegation meets with Samaranch in Lausanne.

USSR general secretary Mikhail Gorbachev makes Vladivostok Declaration, expressing beginnings of new policy of détente.

22 July 1986 DPRK ambassador in Geneva, Kim Hyeung On, announces DPRK wishes to stage at least ten disciplines in 1988 Games.

25 July 1986 SLOOC president Park Seh Jik writes to Samaranch expressing concern regarding declaration made at sports ministers conference in North Korea and asking for assistance to keep this from becoming part of final report to summit meeting of nonaligned countries scheduled for August 25–September 7 in Harare, Zimbabwe.

28 July 1986 Samaranch sends letter to DPRK NOC urging acceptance of IOC proposal without conditions.

30 July 1986 Samaranch replies to Park Seh Jik's letter of July 25, agreeing to be present for opening of Asian Games, confirming that IOC has sent another letter to DPRK regarding acceptance of IOC proposal, but only notes he has read with interest the matter regarding nonaligned countries.

1 Aug. 1986 DPRK NOC sends letter to IOC requesting increase in

number of sports to be allocated to the North and requesting further meeting.

6 Aug. 1986 *Rodong Shinmun* publishes open letter from Fidel Castro stating that if Games are not cohosted by DPRK and ROK, Cuba will boycott.

7 Aug. 1986 IOC *administrateur délégué* Raymond Gafner sends memorandum to Alexandru Siperco, Samuel Pisar, and François Carrard with translation of DPRK response dated August 1 for comments concerning whether DPRK appears to understand differences between sports, disciplines, and events, in order to help interpret response.

13 Aug. 1986 DPRK ambassador in Geneva, Kim Hyeung On, meets in Lausanne with IOC *administrateur délégué* Raymond Gafner, in absence of Samaranch.

21 Aug. 1986 Samaranch proposes meeting with DPRK NOC president Kim Yu Sun or vice president Chin to clarify situation, since meetings with DPRK ambassador in Geneva were not fruitful.

25 Aug. 1986 Cuban boycott if Games not cohosted confirmed by Alberto Juantorena, Cuban delegate to IAAF Congress in Stuttgart.

1 Sep. 1986 Samaranch gets memorandum from West German minister Dr. Hans G. Wieck regarding political and security aspects of Seoul Games.

2 Sep. 1986 DPRK announces refusal to participate in 1986 Asian Games.

5 Sep. 1986 Kenya Olympic Association president Sam Kamau writes to Samaranch reporting on success of efforts to keep statement proposed by DPRK from final communication of nonaligned countries meeting in Harare; Cuban draft inclusion was much "softer."

8 Sep. 1986 DPRK NOC vice president Chin in Lausanne states that position of NOC has been given three times in relation to June 11 proposal and calls for fourth joint meeting; additional events can be discussed on that occasion. Samaranch requests official reply.

11 Sep. 1986 DPRK NOC vice president Chin reconfirms agreement in principle with IOC proposal of June 11, reiterates desire for fourth joint meeting, declares that his presence in Lau-

sanne obviates need for written response; Samaranch insists on written response; Chin agrees to transmit Samaranch's request.

14 Sep. 1986 Bomb explosion at Kimpo International Airport in Seoul; timing is less than a week prior to opening of Tenth Asian Games.

16 Sep. 1986 Student demonstrations in Seoul protesting Asian Games; numbers not significant, but considerable violence reported.

SLOOC president Park Seh Jik assures IOC Executive Board that security for Olympic Games will be increased, in light of Kimpo bombing two days earlier.

18 Sep. 1986 Samaranch states that DPRK must accept IOC proposal before further discussions can occur; DPRK boycott will not hurt 1988 Games and socialist countries will participate even without DPRK.

19 Sep. 1986 IOC delegation visits Panmunjom in visit organized by Swiss ambassador Bernard Freymond.

20 Sep. 1986 Tenth Asian Games begin in Seoul; only DPRK does not participate. (Chinese Taipei does not participate since it was not a member in time for it to do so; it will compete in Beijing in 1990.)

25 Sep. 1986 Samaranch attends Association of European National Olympic Committees (AENOC) Congress in Budapest, September 25–26 and is encouraged by attitude of USSR regarding IOC's efforts to find a solution regarding 1988 Games.

26 Sep. 1986 Viacheslav Koloskov, USSR vice president of FIFA, states that USSR is preparing soccer team for 1988 Games but actual participation will depend in part on "the general situation in the Olympic Family."

28 Sep. 1986 Samaranch and Primo Nebiolo meet with Fidel Castro, Jose R. Fernandez, Conrado Martinez, and Manuel Gonzalez Guerra (IOC member in Cuba and NOC president) in Havana.

29 Sep. 1986 Second meeting between Samaranch and Fidel Castro in Havana.

3 Oct. 1986 USOC secretary-general George Miller writes to Sama-

ranch regarding his meeting with Castro to discuss the 1988 Games.

10 Oct. 1986 Samaranch reports to IOC Executive Board that in meeting with Fidel Castro, Castro agreed to contact DPRK to encourage further meeting in Lausanne; IOC would be willing to make minor changes to proposal.

Oct. 1986 Ninety-first IOC Session agrees with proposal of IOC dated June 11, 1986, and delegates authority to Executive Board to reach appropriate agreements to implement this proposal; Albertville (France) and Barcelona (Spain) selected as host cities for 1992 Olympic Winter Games and 1992 Olympic Summer Games.

13 Oct. 1986 IOC spokesperson following ninety-first IOC Session announces that IOC will send request to DPRK NOC asking for acceptance of IOC proposal prior to September 17, 1987.

14 Oct. 1986 Vice president of DPRK NOC Chin Chung Guk demands eight sports be allocated to the North.

18 Oct. 1986 Samaranch has private meeting with DPRK NOC vice president Chin Chung Guk in Lausanne.

20 Oct. 1986 Samaranch meets in Lausanne with DPRK NOC vice president Chin; DPRK prefers to wait until after ROK presidential elections in December before continuing negotiations.

22 Oct. 1986 Iran states it may reappraise decision to participate in Seoul Games following defection of four athletes during Asian Games.

5 Nov. 1986 Kim Young Sam states in Bonn, West Germany, that 1988 Games would be endangered unless democratic government comes to power first; democratic government means direct presidential elections and revision of Constitution.

Nov. 1986 PASO designates Havana as host city for 1991 Pan American Games.

12 Nov. 1986 Samaranch meets East Germany's president Erich Honecker in Berlin, who says East Germans are preparing for 1988 Games.

13 Nov. 1986 Samaranch attends thirty-fifth meeting of Socialist Ministers of Sport in Berlin.

18 Nov. 1986 Samaranch states he is pleased with results of meeting of Socialist Ministers of Sport and says all socialist countries will attend the Games; Cuba's hosting of 1991 is "very good news for the Olympic Movement."

19 Nov. 1986 Hungarian sports minister Gabor Deak states that socialist bloc countries have common position supporting DPRK bid to cohost 1988 Games.

26 Nov. 1986 Polish sports minister and NOC president Boleslaw Kapitan states that Polish athletes are preparing for and will compete in 1988 Games.

East Germany names preliminary roster of 1988 Olympic team, but supports cohosting to avoid problems.

12 Dec. 1986 Samaranch reports to IOC Executive Board meeting in Lausanne that, with award of 1991 Pan American Games to Havana, it will be difficult for Cuba to justify a boycott of 1988 Games to American countries.

22 Dec. 1986 DPRK NOC president Kim Yu Sun writes to Samaranch pressing for fourth joint meeting.

1 Jan. 1987 ROK foreign minister Choi Kwang Soo urges USSR to refrain from military cooperation with DPRK and states that recent intensification of military assistance encourages DPRK "adventurism."

5 Jan. 1987 IOC announces it has not yet received December 22 letter from Kim Yu Sun.

11 Jan. 1987 DPRK NOC requests opportunity to meet with IOC Executive Board in February 1987.

17 Jan. 1987 Report on ROK president Chun Doo Hwan's New Year Policy Statement states that DPRK efforts to hinder Games are not supported by any country and that Asian Games had elevated status of homeland.

21 Jan. 1987 IOC announces that DPRK NOC will meet with IOC Executive Board to give explanations regarding its response to the IOC offer of events.

26 Jan. 1987 Iran is first country to announce it will participate in 1988 Olympic Games.

10 Feb. 1987 DPRK NOC meets with Samaranch and Siperco in Lausanne prior to appearance before IOC Executive Board.

11 Feb. 1987	IOC Executive Board meets in Lausanne; DPRK NOC present to meet with Executive Board on February 12 instead of scheduled date of February 11; assumption is that further consultations needed after meeting with Samaranch; principles leading to fourth joint meeting established.
12 Feb. 1987	DPRK NOC president Kim Yu Sun, at press conference following meeting between DPRK NOC and IOC, insists on more sports for DPRK, despite agreement "in principle" with IOC compromise proposal of June 1986.
13 Feb. 1987	Samaranch states at press conference that IOC cannot offer more to DPRK, that assurances received from highest levels from socialist countries they will participate, and that IOC will never "close the door to negotiations with the North Koreans."
	President of KOC Kim Chong Ha says no events can be hosted in DPRK unless DPRK stops making further unreasonable demands.
16 Feb. 1987	SLOOC announces there will be no official pre-Olympics, but instead a heavy schedule of international sports events in ROK to gain experience for 1988 Games, involving 3,800 athletes from 146 countries in fifteen events and thirteen sports.
17 Feb. 1987	ROK sports minister Lee Sei Kee states in Seoul that DPRK demand for more sports is unacceptable.
18 Feb. 1987	ROK sports minister Lee Sei Kee leaves for trip to Eastern European countries to promote participation in Seoul Games.
2 March 1987	Ethiopian head of state Colonel Mengistu Haile Mariam reportedly announces Ethiopia will not take part in Games unless cohosted by DPRK and ROK.
	In Reuters interview, Samaranch states that DPRK is not "measuring the value" of the IOC's offer, "but many other countries realize the IOC has made every effort to please the North Koreans."
3 March 1987	DPRK NOC vice president Chin Chung Guk demands cohosting of Games and allocation of eight sports to DPRK during press conference.

East German delegation including sport minister Manfred Ewald and IOC member Günther Heinze arrives in Seoul for meetings to discuss participation in Seoul Games.

DPRK letter to ROK prime minister Lho Shin Yong agrees to resume Red Cross and economic talks and discussions about Kumgangsan Dam simultaneously with political and military talks.

4 March 1987 DPRK Central News Agency quotes DPRK NOC vice president Chin Chung Guk as stating DPRK should be allowed to stage eight of twenty-three sports.

5 March 1987 ROK sports minister Lee Sei Kee returns to Seoul from fifteen-day tour of Czechoslovakia, Yugoslavia, and Hungary, and reports these countries as ready to participate in Seoul Games.

9 March 1987 *Wall Street Journal* editorial states objective of DPRK plan is to prevent world from seeing what ROK has to offer, with backup plan to take part of prestige of Games for itself.

13 March 1987 Press reports comment on DPRK refusal to play in Asian qualification rounds of Olympic soccer tournament on basis that it is cohost of Games and therefore does not have to qualify.

Samaranch telexes Ethiopian NOC president Tsegaw Ayele asking for text of declaration made by head of state in relation to potential boycott of Games by Ethiopia.

ROK assistant foreign minister Park Soo Gil states, in relation to DPRK acceptance "in principle" of IOC offer, "In diplomatic jargon, the terminology 'in principle' means virtual rejection."

14 March 1987 Press reports announcement by United States, immediately following return of Secretary of State George Shultz from visit to China, of possibility of direct talks between United States and DPRK.

18 March 1987 ROK prime minister Lho Shin Yong responds to DPRK prime minister Li Gun Mo concerning March 3 proposal for talks, agreeing to talks but only after "the minimum conditions for mutual trust have been created."

19 March 1987 DPRK Foreign Ministry issues statement that DPRK is pre-

pared to have contacts and dialogue with official persons of the United States.

24 March 1987 — Report monitored in Tokyo broadcast by Radio Pyongyang following visit by Nicaraguan president Daniel Ortega to Pyongyang claims Ortega declared to DPRK vice president and minister of foreign affairs that Nicaragua will not take part in Games unless they are cohosted by DPRK and ROK.

25 March 1987 — President of East Germany's People's Chamber, Horst Sindermann, at press conference in Tokyo declares that East Germany will participate in Seoul Olympics whether or not DPRK cohosts the Games.

26 March 1987 — FIFA Subcommittee for Matters of Emergency meets in Zurich and recommends that DPRK be excluded from Olympic soccer tournament due to failure to appear for qualifying matches in Kuala Lumpur.

28 March 1987 — Samaranch states Olympic authorities totally support FIFA decision to expel DPRK from Olympic soccer tournament, as a technical matter, outside jurisdiction of IOC.

3 April 1987 — United States proposes promotion of humanitarian trade with the North.

5 April 1987 — Cuban news agency reports, on basis of interview with DPRK president Kim Il Sung, that Kim believes more than one-third of sports should be allocated to DPRK as cohost of the Games.

IOC vice president Ashwini Kumar visits Seoul to review security preparations for Games.

6 April 1987 — International tennis tournament held in Seoul, April 6–10.

10 April 1987 — World Cup Marathon held in Seoul.

11 April 1987 — DPRK Football Association urges FIFA to reconsider its decision to exclude DPRK from Olympic soccer tournament.

International marathon event held in Seoul, April 11–12.

13 April 1987 — ROK president Chun Doo Hwan issues statement postponing any modifications to Constitution until after the Olympics, including negotiations with opposition parties, which will eventually lead to most serious crisis since he assumed power. This decision apparently taken upon advice of secu-

	rity authorities, including Chang Se Dong, then head of National Security Planning Agency (formerly KCIA), and without political input of Roh Tae Woo and his colleagues.
14 April 1987	DPRK NOC general secretary reported as agreeing to have both Opening and Closing Ceremonies in Seoul, but stating that DPRK wants more events.
18 April 1987	ROK student protesters clash with riot police.
	DPRK NOC president Kim Yu Sun telexes Samaranch attempting to confirm rumors that fourth joint meeting may be held in June 1987 and urging it be held as soon as possible.
22 April 1987	DPRK demands announced in Pyongyang by NOC vice president Chin Chung Guk on eve of KOC meeting with IOC; ROK sports minister Lee Sei Kee responds by stating that DPRK will not be offered more sports; KOC president Kim Chong Ha states KOC will stand by IOC formula.
	Samaranch announces fourth joint meeting will occur in Lausanne, July 14–15.
23 April 1987	Delegation from KOC meets with Samaranch in Lausanne.
26 April 1987	Samaranch telexes president of DPRK NOC that IOC has "taken note" of DPRK acceptance in principle of IOC's proposal of June 1986. Small IOC delegation will visit DPRK in May 1987, to inspect facilities and discuss preparations for fourth joint meeting.
28 April 1987	KOC president Kim Chong Ha urges DPRK to stop demanding more events or risk having none at all.
1 May 1987	In speech launching new political party (Party for Reunification and Democracy) Kim Young Sam compares Seoul Olympics to 1936 Olympics in Nazi Germany under Hitler.
May 1987	KOC president Kim Chong Ha strongly criticizes May 1 remarks of Kim Young Sam and warns opposition politicians not to use Games to try to create political tensions.
	Czechoslovakian NOC advises Samaranch it will be in Seoul for Games regardless of participation by DPRK.
6 May 1987	IOC announces hope to send delegation to Pyongyang in advance of fourth joint meeting in July and says it has asked

for permission to cross line of military demarcation by land as a "gesture" by DPRK.

7 May 1987 DPRK NOC issues statement demanding cohosting of Games, monitored in Tokyo, and citing clash between North Korea and South Korea as serious threat to Olympic Movement.

8 May 1987 DPRK NOC vice president Chang Ung announces the NOC will consider the possibility of a visit by an IOC delegation.

10 May 1987 SLOOC reports to ninety-second IOC Session in Istanbul.

11 May 1987 Park Seh Jik, president of SLOOC, announces that no further concessions beyond four sports already offered to DPRK will be considered.

12 May 1987 Samaranch states that IOC delegation would still go to Pyongyang even if it is not allowed to cross the line of military demarcation as requested by the IOC.

16 May 1987 DPRK NOC agrees to receive IOC delegation May 26–30; delegation will be unable to cross line of military demarcation. This matter can only be discussed once the question of cohosting is resolved.

17 May 1987 DPRK NOC repeats text of telex dated May 16 in letter to Samaranch; received by Samaranch on May 29.

18 May 1987 Anniversary of Kwangju uprising in 1980. ROK police crack down following protests.

19 May 1987 Samaranch telexes DPRK NOC expressing disappointment regarding refusal to allow IOC delegation to cross line of military demarcation, but will still send delegation via Beijing.

20 May 1987 IOC sends list of subjects to be discussed with DPRK NOC in forthcoming meeting with IOC delegation.

21 May 1987 DPRK NOC telexes Samaranch acknowledging telex of May 19, and indicates reply will be forthcoming.

DPRK president Kim Il Sung begins visit to PRC, May 21–26.

Cuban NOC issues declaration that its hosting of 1991 Pan American Games is not linked to its participation in 1988

Olympic Games and that in an offense to Cuba in 1985, it had been deprived of its right to host the 1987 Pan American Games.

22 May 1987 DPRK NOC telexes IOC regarding discontent with proposed list of questions to be discussed.

Samaranch replies to say that response from DPRK NOC is unacceptable in substance and in form.

Kim Il Sung is received by chairman of Chinese Communist Party, Deng Xiaoping.

23 May 1987 Kim Il Sung has three-hour meeting with PRC's premier, Zhao Ziyang, described as "cordial, friendly, and sincere."

25 May 1987 IOC issues press release on state of negotiations between the two Koreas, which recounts decision to have fourth joint meeting, refusal to allow IOC delegation to cross at Panmunjom, DPRK request for eight sports, and visit of IOC delegation, May 27–29.

26 May 1987 Soviet premier Nikola Ryzhkov tells Japanese religious leader Daisaku Ikeda that USSR supports DPRK's hosting of some events in 1988 Olympics and that USSR is preparing its athletes for the Games.

SLOOC president Park Seh Jik states that DPRK refusal to allow passage of IOC delegation through DMZ goes against the Olympic spirit.

27 May 1987 IOC delegation of Alexandru Siperco and Alain Coupat begins visit to DPRK on instructions of Samaranch to discuss matters in preparation for fourth joint meeting in Lausanne.

DPRK official newspaper *Rodong Shinmun* publishes reports of Kim Il Sung's visit to China, described as successful.

29 May 1987 IOC delegation prepares report of meetings in Pyongyang for Samaranch.

30 May 1987 IOC delegation leaves Pyongyang for Beijing.

2 June 1987 At meeting in Blue House, President Chun Doo Hwan advises Roh Tae Woo that Roh will be his candidate as successor and president.

8 June 1987 International soccer tournament held in Seoul, June 8–21.

9 June 1987 IOC member in PRC, He Zhenliang, sends Samaranch reports of visit by DPRK president Kim Il Sung.

10 June 1987 Chun Doo Hwan names Roh Tae Woo as his successor as head of the Democratic Justice Party and its presidential candidate in forthcoming elections. Party convention confirms nomination by overwhelming majority. Roh promises to use best efforts to initiate early discussions with opposition parties on constitutional amendments.

Period of severe political crisis begins for government of ROK president Chun Doo Hwan, including civil demonstrations in Seoul and throughout the country, with riots and confrontations with police. Electoral college system controlled by government virtually guarantees election of Roh as ROK president when Chun steps down.

Japanese prime minister Yasuhiro Nakasone calls on G-7 leaders meeting in Venice to help make Seoul Olympic Games a success.

Hungarian NOC delegation arrives in Seoul for six days of discussions with SLOOC, headed by Tibor Tomas, minister of youth and sports and NOC vice president.

11 June 1987 Samaranch proposes in letters to KOC president Kim Chong Ha and SLOOC president Park Seh Jik that IOC delegation visit Seoul later that month; in letter to Park, he requests that delegation be able to meet privately with Roh Tae Woo.

FIFA Executive Committee confirms decision of subcommittee to exclude DPRK from Olympic soccer tournament and imposes additional fine to be paid by July 31, 1987.

DPRK president Kim Il Sung makes no reference to unrest in South Korea during interview on occasion of nonaligned countries' Conference on Cooperation held in Pyongyang, June 9–13.

13 June 1987 DPRK minister of foreign affairs, Kim Yong Nam, makes no reference to political unrest in South Korea during interview with foreign delegates to nonaligned countries' conference in Pyongyang.

17 June 1987 Jesse Jackson, U.S. presidential candidate, suggests U.S.

boycott of Games may be called for unless South Korea makes significant progress in human rights and free elections.

USOC president Robert Helmick, returning from visit to Seoul, states that though he hopes those responsible for the Games will be successful, the United States will not participate in the Games if there is a security risk.

ROK president Chun Doo Hwan meets with Roh Tae Woo to discuss the political crisis.

Yugoslavian news agency Tanjug quotes DPRK officials as saying they were building facilities to host entire 1988 Olympics if political situation in the ROK deteriorates.

IOC announces there is no change in plans to hold 1988 Olympic Games in Seoul; announcement made by Samaranch from Toronto, Canada.

18 June 1987 Roh Tae Woo emerges as leader in search for a compromise in political crisis; tries to convince ROK president Chun Doo Hwan to reverse April 13 decision. Roh leads colleagues in confrontation with government leaders who advocated force and imposition of martial law to suppress demonstrations.

Seoul's most influential newspaper, *Dong-A Ilbo,* calls on Chun government to allow renewed debate and identifies April 13 decision to suspend talks as main cause of present political instability.

U.S. ambassador James Lilley delivers letter from U.S. president Ronald Reagan to ROK president Chun Doo Hwan, urging moderation in dealing with crisis.

U.S. secretary of state George Shultz urges end to eight days of protests and a resumption of dialogue.

Los Angeles mayor Tom Bradley offers Los Angeles as alternate site for 1988 Olympic Games if Seoul is abandoned because of political problems.

Samaranch writes to FIFA president Joao Havelange to enquire about decision to exclude DPRK from Olympic tournament.

Senator Edward Kennedy and four other legislators introduce draft legislation calling for economic sanctions against ROK; congressional leaders call instead for political dialogue between the government and the opposition parties.

19 June 1987 ROK president Chun Doo Hwan agrees to allow measures of democratization agreed between Democratic Justice Party and opposition parties.

21 June 1987 Roh Tae Woo chairs special meeting of Democratic Justice Party.

Author, appearing on NBC's *Meet the Press,* states there is no question of seeking alternate site for 1988 Games.

22 June 1987 Author, on ABC-TV's *Monday Sportsnite,* states IOC is confident that 1988 Games will be held in Seoul; that IOC is not looking for alternate site and should not be seen to be vacillating; confident political difficulties will be solved; Korean people united in desire to have Games.

Spokesman for International Amateur Wrestling Federation, Toshimisu Azuma, states that there will be no wrestling competitions in 1988 Olympics if they are to be held in the DPRK.

24 June 1987 ROK president Chun Doo Hwan agrees to meet opposition leader Kim Young Sam; meeting later described by Kim as a failure.

ASOIF (Association of Summer Olympic International Federations) president Primo Nebiolo meets with Samaranch in Lausanne to provide support for IOC efforts; press release issued by IOC.

SLOOC vice presidents Kim Un Yong and Kim San Hoon have secret meeting in Tokyo with USSR vice minister Viacheslav M. Gavrilin to agree on security for Soviet athletes and permission for Soviet ship to anchor in port of Inchon.

25 June 1987 Samaranch writes to Roh Tae Woo suggesting agreement with opposition parties regarding presidential elections during Olympic year; expresses concern about elections in year of Games and states that he has twice suggested to Chun Doo Hwan that elections be postponed until after Games.

Samaranch writes to all IOC members reminding them that choice of Seoul was IOC's decision, that responsibility for supervision of preparations belongs to the Executive Board, and that members should refrain from making statements other than that Games have been awarded to Seoul and will be held there.

26 June 1987 IOC delegation of Siperco and Coupat arrives in Seoul for visit with the SLOOC and ROK NOC, leaving on July 2.

Nationwide demonstrations in ROK.

29 June 1987 Roh Tae Woo proposes eight-point plan to end political crisis, including constitutional amendments leading to direct presidential elections before February 1988, when Chun Doo Hwan's term of office expires, and states that if proposals are not accepted by Chun, he will give up all public offices and not be a candidate in presidential elections; other elements in plan include restoration of political rights to political prisoners, lifting of press restrictions, protection of human rights, encouragement of local and campus autonomy, promotion of political parties, nationwide campaign against violent crime and corruption, and generalized call for "bold social reforms."

Roh Tae Woo writes to Samaranch acknowledging Samaranch's thoughts on the political situation in Korea and advising Samaranch of his declaration earlier that day; this will create solid foundation for Olympic Games and put an end to the negative publicity. ROK president Chun Doo Hwan concurs with letter's content.

IOC delegation of Siperco and Coupat meets with ROK sports minister Lee Sei Kee.

30 June 1987 Roh Tae Woo meets with IOC delegation of Siperco and Coupat, accompanied by Kim Chong Ha, Cho Sang Ho, and Kim Un Yong.

Memorandum prepared by IOC delegation containing position of ROK on IOC proposals and, indirectly, regarding demands from DPRK; also, memorandum to Samaranch prepared regarding discussions in Seoul.

1 July 1987 ROK president Chun Doo Hwan accepts Roh's proposals of June 29.

3 July 1987 FIFA secretary-general Josep Blatter writes Samaranch to

explain FIFA process and decision to exclude DPRK from Olympic soccer tournament.

8 July 1987 ROK sports minister Lee Sei Kee writes to Samaranch regarding rumors of change of site for Games and assures him that Koreans know how to solve their political problems.

9 July 1987 ANOC president Mario Vazquez-Raña confirms to Samaranch that he has sent messages to DPRK and ROK urging a compromise to enable Games to proceed in tranquillity.

Major student demonstrations in Seoul; Olympic flag removed from city hall but later replaced at request of the people.

10 July 1987 ROK president Chun Doo Hwan announces resignation as leader of Democratic Justice Party.

July 1987 1987 International Invitational Basketball Tournament held in Seoul.

11 July 1987 U.S. assistant secretary of state Gaston Sigur writes Samaranch regarding the Games, the ROK, and internal developments in ROK, all of which appear encouraging.

President of South African Non-Racial Olympic Committee, Dennis Brutus, writes to Samaranch expressing concern regarding police violence and denial of human rights in South Korea and states this will cause concern to African NOCs; SANROC is not a recognized NOC, and South Africa will not be invited to the Games.

13 July 1987 Prior to fourth joint meeting, KOC president Kim Chong Ha meets with Samaranch, who reveals strategy for the meeting.

14 July 1987 Fourth IOC sponsored joint north-south meeting begins in Lausanne and concludes July 15.

15 July 1987 IOC issues press communiqué on conclusion of fourth joint meeting.

16 July 1987 Samaranch sends IOC press communiqué following fourth joint meeting to all summer IFs, NOCs, ASOIF, ANOC, and continental associations of NOCs.

Primo Nebiolo, president of ASOIF, sends telex to Samaranch expressing support of the summer IFs.

Samaranch sends letters to DPRK NOC president Kim Yu Sun and KOC president Kim Chong Ha confirming proposal made at fourth joint meeting and requesting reply.

IOC member in West Germany, Willi Daume, writes to Samaranch advising that media reports of Berlin wanting to replace Seoul as site for Games and that IOC members in Germany support such a change are incorrect.

Samaranch writes ROK sports minister Lee Sei Kee acknowledging letter of July 8 and stating he is pleased with progress on political front in ROK.

Samaranch writes Mario Vazquez-Raña, president of PASO, concerning Cuban NOC declaration of May 21 regarding linkage of hosting 1991 Pan American Games and participation in Seoul.

23 July 1987 DPRK proposes that two Koreas and the United States meet in Geneva to discuss mutual arms reductions.

24 July 1987 IOC *administrateur délégué* Raymond Gafner telexes details of Soviet delegation to Kim Un Yong.

27 July 1987 DPRK ambassador to Beijing, Sin In Ha, gives press conference at DPRK embassy and states that USSR, China, and other Communist countries support DPRK's desire to cohost Games but have not promised to boycott if Games are held only in Seoul.

USSR NOC delegation in Seoul begins meetings with SLOOC officials and review of preparations for the Games, headed by Anatoli Kolessov, vice minister of sports and vice president of USSR Sports Committee, and Yuri Titov, NOC secretary-general and International Gymnastics Federation president.

28 July 1987 Samaranch acknowledges Daume's letter of July 16 and says matter of Berlin's hosting of Games has been well handled.

3 Aug. 1987 ROK assistant foreign minister Park Soo Gil proposes foreign ministers of two Koreas meet, but rejects DPRK agenda as "typical propaganda piece" and suggests New York as venue when both would be present in September for opening of UN; formal statement merely discusses the

points ROK wants to discuss and does not comment on DPRK agenda; Olympic Games not mentioned.

4 Aug. 1987 DPRK NOC indicates dissatisfaction with IOC proposal and demands fifth joint meeting prior to September 17.

5 Aug. 1987 Radio reports from Pyongyang monitored in Tokyo claim Syrian vice president Abdel Halim Khaddam declared to DPRK minister of foreign affairs Kim Yong Nam during latter's July visit to Syria that Syria might boycott the Seoul Games.

International basketball tournament held in Seoul, August 5–15.

6 Aug. 1987 ROK assistant foreign minister Park Soo Gil states that ROK is willing to accept proposals to transfer additional events to DPRK if it accepts IOC proposals made at fourth joint meeting in July 1987.

10 Aug. 1987 Letter from DPRK NOC demands that six sports (five full sports and one partial) be allocated to DPRK and that fifth joint meeting be held; reiteration of demand for full soccer tournament.

DPRK ambassador to Beijing gives press conference in Beijing for Communist journalists to explain the reduced demands by DPRK.

11 Aug. 1987 DPRK press conference indicates dissatisfaction with IOC proposal and demands fifth meeting.

15 Aug. 1987 ROK president Chun Doo Hwan, in 42nd Liberation Day message, calls for resumption of suspended north-south dialogue and urges DPRK to participate in 1988 Games.

17 Aug. 1987 KOC advises IOC that it accepts IOC proposal as revised at fourth joint meeting, provided DPRK withdraws assertion of cohosting and guarantees free entry and exit between the North and the South, and that its delegation participates in Opening and Closing Ceremonies in Seoul; decision communicated in two letters, one of which is completely unconditional, the other of which has preconditions referred to above.

21 Aug. 1987 ROK president Chun Doo Hwan warns he will not tolerate

any more major social or economic upheavals that might sully ROK's record of achievement under his administration.

22 Aug. 1987 President of International Amateur Cycling Federation (FIAC), Valery Syssoev (USSR), telexes Samaranch to state that because it has learned that DPRK had renounced holding any Olympic cycling events, the FIAC Congress scheduled for August 24 planned to advise all national federations that all competitions will take place in the South.

24 Aug. 1987 Samaranch advises DPRK NOC that reduced demands do not constitute response to most recent IOC proposal; no fifth joint meeting will be called unless there is full acceptance of IOC's "important and historical" proposal.

30 Aug. 1987 DPRK NOC president Kim Yu Sun telexes Samaranch (received August 31) urging fifth joint meeting be held as soon as possible; if not held before September 17, requests IOC postpone sending of invitations.

31 Aug. 1987 DPRK NOC holds press conference to request IOC to postpone sending of invitations to Games.

2 Sep. 1987 International shooting tournament held in Seoul, September 2–October 3.

International women's volleyball tournament held in Seoul, September 2–13.

3 Sep. 1987 Roh Tae Woo and Kim Young Sam agree on dates for direct presidential election.

4 Sep. 1987 Secretariat of Committee for the Peaceful Reunification of the Fatherland (CPRF), a semiofficial agency of the DPRK, issues information bulletin sharply critical of ROK "puppet" defense minister's request for continued support due to expected obstructionist activities leading up to Games.

Samaranch writes DPRK NOC president Kim Yu Sun suggesting meeting with IOC on October 7 to discuss points for agenda of a fifth joint meeting with IOC; states it is impossible to postpone sending of invitations, since date is prescribed in Olympic Charter.

9 Sep. 1987 *Rodong Shinmun* article published in DPRK warns of increasing tensions if Games are held only in the South.

10 Sep. 1987	DPRK indicates deadline for negotiations regarding Games may be January 17, 1988, instead of September 17, 1987.
	Report published by Korean Development Institute (in South Korea) states that failure to reach agreement on Olympics with DPRK could lead to limited DPRK military attack.
11 Sep. 1987	DPRK NOC president advises through DPRK central broadcast that he will send letter to KOC to be delivered September 12 at Panmunjom special conference room.
	Fidel Castro writes to Samaranch urging that solution be found and indicating he will help prevent DPRK from being "carried away from what is, after all, its obvious right."
12 Sep. 1987	Samaranch, in Syria, for Tenth Mediterranean Games, states that IOC will keep negotiating with DPRK and ROK and will not "close the door."
	DPRK NOC president Kim Yu Sun sends letter to KOC counterpart Kim Chong Ha requesting direct joint meeting between NOCs prior to fifth joint meeting.
	KOC President Kim Chong Ha advises DPRK NOC that he will pick up message in Panmunjom on September 15.
14 Sep. 1987	U.S. assistant secretary of state advises ROK foreign minister Choi Kwang Soo that during visit to Moscow the previous week he asked USSR officials to use their influence over DPRK to cause DPRK to accept the IOC's proposal to stage some events of the Games.
Sep. 1987	ROK president Chun Doo Hwan sends personal letter to Samaranch regarding DPRK proposal to negotiate directly with ROK, without IOC presence.
	KOC's conclusion on DPRK proposal to negotiate without IOC is that it is intended to weaken ROK's position.
15 Sep. 1987	DPRK NOC president Kim Yu Sun sends telex to Samaranch requesting delay in sending invitations pending outcome of direct discussion between NOCs.
	International tennis tournament held in Seoul, September 15–20.
16 Sep. 1987	SLOOC president Park Seh Jik assures IOC Executive

Board that preparations are well advanced and that all of Korea is enthusiastic about 1988 and the Games.

Sep. 1987 Seoul International Invitational Track and Field Meet held in Olympic Stadium.

17 Sep. 1987 IOC sends invitations to participate in Seoul Games to all NOCs, accompanied by a letter from Samaranch stating that negotiations between the two Koreas are continuing under IOC auspices and that the door is not closed.

ROK president Chun Doo Hwan sends letter to Samaranch assuring him of successful Olympics.

1987 International Invitational Yachting Competition held in Pusan, September 17–28.

1987 International Modern Pentathlon Championships held in Seoul, September 17–22.

18 Sep. 1987 1987 Seoul International Cycling Championships held in Seoul, September 18–20.

21 Sep. 1987 Samaranch attends thirty-sixth meeting of Socialist Ministers of Sport in Soukhoumi, USSR, September 21–23; has meeting with DPRK NOC president Kim Yu Sun.

DPRK NOC denounces the sending of the invitations to participate in 1988 Olympic Games in Seoul.

22 Sep. 1987 KOC president Kim Chong Ha indicates he will send message to the North on September 24.

23 Sep. 1987 ROK ambassador in Switzerland provides Samaranch with advance copy of letter to be sent by KOC on September 24 to DPRK NOC.

24 Sep. 1987 KOC letter urges DPRK NOC to agree to IOC's latest proposal.

26 Sep. 1987 DPRK president Kim Il Sung, in interview with leader of Japanese Socialist Party, indicates hope that direct dialogue with United States can occur.

27 Sep. 1987 World Cup shooting competition held in Seoul, September 27–October 3.

28 Sep. 1987 European Broadcasting Union advises Samaranch that organization of events in DPRK could have serious logistical and financial consequences for broadcasters.

30 Sep. 1987 International Canoe Federation Board of Directors meets in Seoul.

Oct. 1987 Japanese Red Army issues statement saying Games are being used as part of new Japanese imperialist strategy for Asia.

2 Oct. 1987 DPRK NOC president Kim Yu Sun indicates he will send letter to KOC on October 3 at Panmunjom.

KOC president advises DPRK NOC he will receive letter on October 12.

DPRK NOC president writes to Samaranch referring to letter included with invitations to 1988 Games and encloses copy of letter to KOC dated September 12.

3 Oct. 1987 1987 International Canoeing Championships held in Seoul, October 3–4.

6 Oct. 1987 DPRK NOC agrees to change date for receipt of its letter.

12 Oct. 1987 DPRK NOC letter received by KOC urges KOC to agree to second meeting between the two NOCs, as proposed by IOC; ROK generally not interested in having such a bilateral meeting.

15 Oct. 1987 KOC president Kim Chong Ha indicates he will send letter to DPRK NOC at Panmunjom on October 16.

KOC sends memorandum to Samaranch expressing thanks that he insists on acceptance of proposal before agreeing to have fifth joint meeting and expressing view that recent push by DPRK NOC for bilateral talks has ulterior motives (dividing KOC and IOC), since there is no "important information" as alleged by DPRK to be brought to IOC; wants no more events to be allocated to DPRK.

16 Oct. 1987 DPRK NOC indicates letter will be received October 20 in Panmunjom.

20 Oct. 1987 DPRK NOC vice president Chin meets with Samaranch in Lausanne and requests delay until after ROK presidential elections in December to answer IOC proposal of July 15, 1987.

KOC urges DPRK NOC to accept IOC revised proposal.

21 Oct. 1987	International hockey tournament held in Seoul, October 21–28.
23 Oct. 1987	DPRK NOC issues statement proposing to postpone negotiations for cohosting of Games until after ROK presidential elections (despite having asked Samaranch to treat this position as confidential).
6 Nov. 1987	International men's volleyball tournament held in Seoul, November 6–11.
7 Nov. 1987	International wrestling tournament held in Seoul, November 7–8.
15 Nov. 1987	Samaranch visits Seoul for three days.
16 Nov. 1987	Samaranch attempts to meet with opposition leaders, but this is not made possible.
17 Nov. 1987	Samaranch has secret meeting with Roh Tae Woo, Park Seh Jik, and Kim Un Yong.
18 Nov. 1987	IOC sends reminders to ninety-one NOCs that have not yet accepted IOC invitation to participate in Seoul Games.
20 Nov. 1987	Samaranch meets Kim Yu Sun, president of DPRK NOC, in Guangzhou; Kim promises answer to IOC proposal by mid-January 1987.
24 Nov. 1987	Osamu Maruoka, second in command in Japanese Red Army, arrested in Tokyo; his plans were to travel to ROK on December 7, via Osaka.
26 Nov. 1987	ROK NOC holds press conference to urge DPRK to accept IOC revised proposal.
29 Nov. 1987	KAL aircraft is bombed over Burma, and all 115 people aboard are killed. DPRK suspected as responsible; later investigation ties explosion to self-confessed DPRK agent.
7 Dec. 1987	Samaranch sends telegrams to Communist Party general secretary Mikhail Gorbachev and U.S. president Reagan on behalf of Olympic Movement on eve of their summit meeting.
8 Dec. 1987	Gorbachev and Reagan sign agreement to schedule removal of short- and medium-range nuclear missiles from European theater.

1987 Songgok Flag International Judo Championships held in Seoul, December 8–10.

9 Dec. 1987 U.S. secretary of state George Shultz explains that Olympic Games should be held without trouble and with participation of all countries; General Secretary Gorbachev says allocation of sports to DPRK could help Olympic Games to be held smoothly.

10 Dec. 1987 ROK opens commercial office in Hyatt Hotel in Budapest.

12 Dec. 1987 Suspected terrorist in November 29 bombing of KAL aircraft is extradited from Bahrain to ROK.

16 Dec. 1987 Presidential elections in ROK; Roh Tae Woo becomes president-elect of ROK with plurality of some 37 percent of vote; Kim Young Sam is runner-up.

Samaranch sends circular letter to IOC members outlining status of discussions with two Koreas, indicating the increasing difficulty of reaching agreement as time goes on.

18 Dec. 1987 IOC sends reminders to forty-nine NOCs that have not yet accepted invitation to participate in Seoul Games.

21 Dec. 1987 East Germany announces participation in Games.

22 Dec. 1987 Hungary announces participation in Games.

23 Dec. 1987 IOC member in Puerto Rico, German Rieckehoff, telexes Fidel Castro urging participation in Games; copy sent to Samaranch.

26 Dec. 1987 Roh Tae Woo writes Samaranch to assure him he will give utmost effort for the success of the Games.

27 Dec. 1987 USSR delegation in Seoul, December 27–30, agrees on accommodations to be allocated to USSR athletes and on consular functions; at dinner on December 28, Soviets predict 160 countries will participate in Games.

Jan. 1988 DPRK proposes conference in February 1988 between government ministers, representatives of political parties, and public organizations, in Panmunjom.

U.S. State Department, in annual report on human rights, names DPRK as worst violator in world.

4 Jan. 1988 USSR NOC president Marat Gramov announces in Frankfurt, at start of six-day visit to West Germany for meetings

with sports officials, that USSR does not intend to boycott Games; problem of DPRK remains to be solved, but IOC has left door open for further talks.

5 Jan. 1988 SLOOC states Yugoslavia has accepted invitation to participate.

Bulgaria and Poland announce participation.

IOC sends reminders to twenty-one NOCs that have not yet accepted invitation to participate in Seoul Games.

6 Jan. 1988 Samaranch has telephone conference with vice president of Cuban Council of Ministers, José R. Fernandez Alvarez, outlining IOC's efforts to ensure DPRK participation; Fernandez will discuss matter with Castro, but in view of privileged relationship with DPRK, will be difficult to accept anything short of sharing of Games between DPRK and ROK.

Samaranch sends telex to DPRK NOC president Kim Yu Sun requesting answer to IOC proposal not later than January 16.

Kim Young Sam, runner-up in December 1987 presidential elections, states his party will do its best to make Olympic Games "the greatest festival in the world."

Samaranch meets with Kim Un Yong and replies to Roh Tae Woo's letter of December 26.

7 Jan. 1988 Yugoslavia announces participation.

8 Jan. 1988 Romania and Mongolia announce participation.

Samaranch sends telex to Cuban minister José R. Fernandez Alvarez with copy of text of telex to DPRK NOC and number of acceptances to date and reminds Fernandez that latest offer made to DPRK had been based on recommendation made by Fidel Castro.

10 Jan. 1988 IOC sends reminders to ten NOCs that have not yet accepted invitation to participate in Seoul Games, stating that January 17, 1988, is last day to accept.

11 Jan. 1988 USSR and PRC announce participation; USSR statement still supports sharing of Games, but decision is to participate; number of sports to be allocated is for IOC to decide; DPRK situation not discussed by USSR NOC.

12 Jan. 1988 DPRK NOC issues statement of intention to boycott 1988 Olympic Games if hosted singly by ROK but will continue to make every effort to cohost; failure to reach agreement blamed on "obstinate objection" by ROK and continuation of military rule in ROK after elections; official letter is dated January 11, but is sent by mail and arrives only on January 26.

Seoul stock exchange rises 11.35 points upon news of USSR's decision to participate.

ROK announces it will permit USSR and other socialist countries with which it has no diplomatic relations to transport athletes and officials on their own planes or ships.

USSR will be permitted to bring ship to Inchon and to use it as "main supply base" for its Olympic athletes.

USSR publishes decision of DPRK not to participate in Games without comment.

ROK opposition parties join governing Democratic Justice Party in welcoming USSR's decision to participate.

U.S. State Department welcomes USSR's decision to participate in Games.

13 Jan. 1988 Cuba states it will not participate in Games unless Games are cohosted; decision contained in lengthy letter from Fidel Castro to Samaranch.

15 Jan. 1988 Czechoslovakia and Vietnam announce participation.

ROK displays Kim Hyun Hee to the press for the first time, during which she confesses to being DPRK agent responsible for bombing KAL flight on November 29, 1987; she states orders came directly from Kim Jong Il of DPRK.

16 Jan. 1988 PASO president Mario Vazquez-Raña states he believes 1991 Pan American Games will take place in Havana despite Cuban boycott of Seoul Games.

Nicaraguan NOC telexes IOC to state that it will not be participating in the Games.

17 Jan. 1988 One hundred sixty-one NOCs declare their intention to participate in Seoul Olympics by official deadline; Syria is 161st. Statistical distribution of acceptance dates is:

September 1987: 2
October 1987: 65
November 1987: 25
December 1987: 32
January 1988: 32
Later (officially): 5

Madagascar will eventually drop out, claiming its acceptance was conditional on cohosting of Games by DPRK.

Samaranch telexes Nicaraguan NOC regarding even symbolic participation; points out Nicaraguan participation in other sports events has not been affected by domestic situation.

18 Jan. 1988 Samaranch expresses criticism of DPRK and Cuba for refusal to accept invitation to participate in Games but says door is still open.

19 Jan. 1988 Park Seh Jik, SLOOC president, announces SLOOC will continue to keep door open to DPRK for the Games.

Samaranch praises Gorbachev and Reagan for their work in lowering superpower tensions, which contributed to record number of acceptances to Games.

Ethiopia issues statement that reason for nonacceptance of invitation to participate is the failure to have joint hosting of the Games; if Games are staged by DPRK and ROK together, will reconsider decision.

20 Jan. 1988 SLOOC hoists flags of 161 participating countries around plaza of Olympic Center.

IOC issues denial of DPRK's claim, made on January 15, that Madagascar will not participate in Games.

Cuban minister José R. Fernandez Alvarez claims there is no reason that Cuba should be sanctioned by either IOC or PASO for its decision not to participate in Seoul.

Samaranch meets USSR foreign minister Eduard Shevardnadze in Madrid to discuss the Games and enlist help in ensuring all countries can participate.

23 Jan. 1988 Samaranch indicates he would like to go to USSR to meet Mikhail Gorbachev to enlist his help in finding solution to DPRK participation.

28 Jan. 1988 Samaranch telexes DPRK NOC president Kim Yu Sun expressing disappointment concerning decision, but indicates he is still waiting for DPRK response to IOC proposal.

29 Jan. 1988 ROK president Chun Doo Hwan states he expects DPRK will gradually change its hard-line policy and agree to open peace talks as early as 1989, during Chun's first foreign media press conference since taking power in 1980.

6 Feb. 1988 DPRK NOC secretary-general Chang Ung in Calgary interview states that reunification is motivation for desire to cohost Games; issue cannot be discussed apart from larger discussion of issues dividing the two countries.

7 Feb. 1988 SLOOC vice president urges DPRK to take part in the Games.

8 Feb. 1988 United States announces it will send naval forces consisting of at least one carrier group for exercises in area of Korea (Sea of Japan) during Olympic period to discourage DPRK from attempts to disrupt Games.

10 Feb. 1988 SLOOC reports to ninety-third IOC Session in Calgary; IOC resolves to do everything in its power to ensure full attendance at Seoul Games; SLOOC will keep Olympic door open for remaining uncommitted NOCs.

Samaranch reminds DPRK member Kim Yu Sun that deadline for acceptance of invitation to participate was January 17, but that door would be kept open.

ROK ambassador to Canada, Roh Jae Won, says ROK expects more violence from DPRK, and this threat is justification for massive U.S. naval maneuvers planned around ROK during Games.

DPRK speed skaters refused U.S. visas to compete in short track World Championships in St. Louis due to U.S. State Department's placing of DPRK on restricted list for links to terrorism.

11 Feb. 1988 Former Japanese prime minister Yasuhiro Nakasone meets Roh Tae Woo in Seoul and pledges support for terrorism-free Olympics; also offers services to improve relations between China and ROK.

DPRK NOC secretary-general Chang Ung calls ROK ambassador to Canada an "idiot" for remarks made the previous day.

13 Feb. 1988 DPRK NOC secretary-general Chang Ung states that DPRK may reconsider its previous stance if proposed meeting requested by DPRK takes place on February 19.

ROK government issues statement requesting DPRK apology for KAL bombing of November 1987.

16 Feb. 1988 Roh Tae Woo confirms door open to DPRK until eve of Opening Ceremony to Games, but feels that possibility is slim it will take part; indicates that more flexible attitude will mark relations with Japan.

In the UN Security Council, Japanese ambassador Hideo Kagami supports case made by ROK foreign minister Choi Kwang Soo that blowing up KAL flight 858 was clear act of state terrorism.

Samaranch writes Fidel Castro regarding Cuba's decision to boycott Seoul; recounts that IOC offer to DPRK had been improved since his conversation with Castro; says willing to go to DPRK and asks for Castro's help for benefit of athletes.

25 Feb. 1988 Roh Tae Woo sworn in as president of ROK; in inaugural address, indicates ROK will keep door of dialogue open to DPRK for the sake of peace and unity of Korean peninsula.

1 March 1988 ROK president Roh Tae Woo expresses welcome to DPRK participation in Games, in Samil Independence Day message.

March 1988 Hungary opens commercial office in Seoul.

7 March 1988 U.S. assistant secretary of state Edward Derwinski confirms U.S. naval presence in region of ROK during the Games as "a very timely, practical coincidence" and will consist of one or two aircraft carriers.

18 March 1988 Suggestion voiced by Hungarian Yonhap News Agency that Cuba may be rethinking its position on Olympics.

21 March 1988 ROK foreign minister Choi Kwang Soo advises Japanese counterpart Sosuke Uno that ROK will continue efforts to ensure DPRK participation; Uno also meets with Roh Tae Woo and Prime Minister Lee Hyun Jae.

23 March 1988 — DPRK issues statement condemning annual Team Spirit exercises as serious threat to peace in Asia and rest of world.

24 March 1988 — Mario Vazquez-Raña, president of PASO, gets mandate from Executive Commmittee to try to persuade Cuba, Nicaragua, and DPRK to reverse decisions regarding participation in Games; U.S. Olympic Committee indicates it will likely attend 1991 Pan American Games even if Cuba does not participate in Seoul.

25 March 1988 — U.S. senator Ted Stevens writes to U.S. secretary of state George Shultz urging that joint statement be made by U.S. president Reagan and USSR general secretary Gorbachev expressing support for Olympic Movement.

26 March 1988 — Further suggestions come from Hungarian sports officials that Cuba may reconsider position on Games participation.

30 March 1988 — Samaranch writes to Giulio Andreotti to thank him for his help and information on Cuba, Albania, and Ethiopia and sends correspondence with Castro to him.

1 April 1988 — At 442d meeting between UN Command and DPRK forces, called by DPRK, DPRK major general Li Tae Ho protests against Team Spirit maneuvers, claims exercise can readily be switched to war when signal given, and states DPRK armed forces on full alert. U.S. rear admiral William Pendley states that if tension exists on peninsula, it is DPRK's fault.

7 April 1988 — U.S. commander in chief of forces in Japan, General James Davis, states he cannot neglect threat of DPRK action during Games, in view of unpredictable behavior of DPRK regime; he is ready to dispatch troops if necessary.

12 April 1988 — ROK announces that "Peace Dam" will be increased in size as necessary to neutralize Kumgangsan Dam in DPRK; convenient for ROK to portray it as "water bomb over Seoul" in ROK government booklet; admittedly some danger if DPRK construction is faulty; the area is also major earthquake zone.

April 1988 — Mario Vazquez-Raña, president of ANOC, visits Fidel Castro in Havana to discuss Cuban participation in Games and offers to go to DPRK.

21 April 1988 — ROK president Roh Tae Woo in first press conference fol-

lowing inauguration states that rest of his term will be devoted to paving way for peaceful reunification of Korea.

24 April 1988 Samaranch announces, following IOC Executive Board meeting, that while door is still open, is now too late for participation by NOCs who have not accepted invitation to Games in team sports.

25 April 1988 ROK and Japan begin two-day meeting in Tokyo to cooperate regarding terrorism at Games; liaison council was agreed between Roh Tae Woo and Noboru Takeshita in February.

26 April 1988 ROK elections for seats in National Assembly: Democratic Justice Party wins 125; People's Democratic Party wins 71; Party for Reunification and Democracy wins 59; New Democratic Republican Party wins 35; remaining seats in 299-seat assembly won by independents.

28 April 1988 Opposition leaders agree with Roh Tae Woo's call for an Olympic truce in ROK; though there are problems to be solved within ROK, there is no reason why some of them cannot wait until after the Games.

4 May 1988 Possible shift in ROK positioning noted when head of Olympic Security Coordination and Control Headquarters, Yook Wan Sik, states that there will be no provocation from DPRK and that security net will protect against terrorists.

7 May 1988 ROK ambassador to the United States, Park Ton Jin, in first address as ambassador, confirms to U.S. Olympic Committee support celebration in Seattle that door is still open for DPRK and Cuba; also predicts Asian Pacific Rim countries will constitute economic power as large as the United States and larger than Europe by the year 2000.

10 May 1988 Yashiro Shibata of Japanese Red Army arrested; newspaper reports say he recently visited DPRK.

14 May 1988 ROK riot police in Seoul disperse crowd of fifteen thousand students demanding cohosting of Games by DPRK; this is worst violence since Roh Tae Woo became president.

16 May 1988 SLOOC president Park Seh Jik offers to go to DPRK to brief officials on Games preparations if DPRK accepts IOC offer.

18 May 1988 Opposition party leaders urge government to resume talks aimed at persuading DPRK to participate in Games.

20 May 1988 DPRK delegation to Asian Table Tennis Championships, specially admitted to Japan despite ban on DPRK officials as a result of state terrorist activities, leaves in protest after refusal by Japanese authorities to permit attendance at political event.

21 May 1988 Kim Dae Jung forced to withdraw support of DPRK proposals for cohosting the games, made the previous day, after furor and massive criticism from government, sports leaders, and other opposition figures.

22 May 1988 Demonstrators arrested in Kwangju after demanding investigation into crushing of civil revolt eight years previously.

23 May 1988 U.S. secretary of state George Shultz responds to U.S. senator Ted Stevens regarding joint statement by Reagan and Gorbachev, saying he will urge Reagan to ask Gorbachev to join in statement of support for Olympic Movement.

ROK announces completion of first stage of "Peace Dam," designed to stop flood of water and channel it back to DPRK.

24 May 1988 Japanese foreign minister Sosuke Uno states that Japan will continue to urge DPRK to participate in Games despite boycott by DPRK of Asian Table Tennis Championships.

Kim Il Sung confirms DPRK boycott of Games and denies any intention to disrupt Games.

U.S. undersecretary of state Edward Derwinski states that DPRK terrorism poses an "extraordinary potential threat" to 1988 Games, but that security forces are prepared to prevent outbreaks of violence; states Cuba's decision to boycott reflects Castro's "screwed up" sense of priorities.

25 May 1988 DPRK announces plan to host meeting of socialist leaders on September 9 to celebrate fortieth anniversary of DPRK and plans to invite USSR general secretary Gorbachev as guest of Kim Il Sung; Western and Asian diplomats doubtful that Gorbachev will attend.

Cuban women's volleyball team scratched from Olympic event upon failure to enter qualifying tournament by deadline of May 24.

26 May 1988 Press reports state that U.S. spy satellites will be redeployed to keep special watch on DPRK military movements for signs of buildup or other potential threats.

Japanese prime minister Noboru Takeshita assures ROK ambassador Lee Won Kyong of Japanese cooperation to ensure safety of Games; Lee conveys message from Roh Tae Woo that talks in February between the two leaders were useful.

27 May 1988 DPRK president Kim Il Sung, on occasion of visit by general secretary of Czechoslovakian Communist Party, calls for cohosting of Olympic Games.

IOC issues press release containing substance of Samaranch's messages to U.S. president Reagan and USSR general secretary Gorbachev on eve of forthcoming summit meeting.

28 May 1988 ROK president Roh Tae Woo meets with opposition leaders and advises that his government will pursue a unification policy to create a national community in a way that all Koreans can live well.

30 May 1988 Samaranch arrives in Seoul for meeting with Roh Tae Woo, opposition leaders, and SLOOC officials.

1 June 1988 Joint statement by U.S. president Reagan and USSR general secretary Gorbachev issued in Moscow contains message of support for Olympic Movement, which promotes international cooperation and understanding through athletic competition.

ROK foreign minister Choi Kwang Soo announces that Olympic "attachés" from countries without diplomatic relations with ROK will be allowed to perform consular functions and will be granted like protection and supervision of property and citizens in addition to participation in Games functions.

Samaranch predicts Seoul Games will be the best ever.

Mario Vazquez-Raña, German Rieckehoff, and Mexican ambassador to Cuba meet with Fidel Castro in Cuba on evening of June 1 and early morning of June 2; visit to DPRK by Vazquez-Raña and Rieckehoff essentially arranged for them by Castro; Castro's personal opinion on solution to Games problem communicated to Kim Il Sung.

2 June 1988 Samaranch has meeting with ROK political leaders, at his request, and obtains statement of support for Games from them; at urging of ROK political leaders, statement by Samaranch reiterates call to DPRK to accept IOC's "unique and historical" offer; Samaranch announces willingness to visit DPRK.

Samaranch instructs IOC to send copy of statement and press release to DPRK NOC president Kim Yu Sun.

3 June 1988 ROK prime minister Lee Hyun Jae writes to DPRK counterpart Li Gun Mo proposing cabinet-level talks on trade and exchange visits as well as forthcoming Olympics in Seoul; DPRK refuses to accept letter at Panmunjom; letter made public by ROK.

'88 Seoul International Diving and Synchronized Swimming in Seoul, June 3–6.

4 June 1988 SLOOC president Park Seh Jik calls upon help of Japanese Socialist Party to deliver message to DPRK that door will be left open to last moment for DPRK participation.

DPRK NOC president Kim Yu Sun telexes Samaranch to say that he has been invited several times to visit Pyongyang but has never responded.

Radio Pyongyang broadcast states that Samaranch will not be invited to DPRK.

Mario Vazquez-Raña and German Rieckehoff report separately by telexes to Samaranch of being encouraged by visits to Cuba and DPRK; report Castro's personal opinion that DPRK more interested in symbology of having events in DPRK than in relative importance of the events.

6 June 1988 U.S. secretary of defense Frank Carlucci states that USSR has indicated it will do everything possible to prevent trouble during Games.

DPRK announces it is prepared to consider ROK proposal for cabinet-level talks between DPRK and ROK only as preparation for subsequent bilateral talks.

7 June 1988 Samaranch states he is still ready to go to DPRK to try to convince DPRK to participate in Games.

Spanish prime minister Felipe Gonzales pays courtesy visit to IOC headquarters in Lausanne.

International Table Tennis Federation revokes berths reserved for DPRK players in Olympic tournament.

Hiroshui Sensui, suspected member of Japanese Red Army, extradited from Philippines to Japan.

U.S. defense secretary Frank Carlucci, in Seoul for annual security conference, states U.S. armed forces will be used to crush any disruption of Seoul Games.

9 June 1988 At press conference in Barcelona, Samaranch states he believes DPRK and Cuba will boycott Games; choice of Seoul had helped to support democratic changes in ROK.

Statement from DPRK Central News Agency monitored in Tokyo says DPRK NOC will not participate in singly hosted Games and that it will continue to work for cohosting.

Japan and ROK hold second round of liaison council meetings in Seoul, June 9–10, to discuss safety measures concerning Games.

10 June 1988 Proposed student meeting between DPRK and ROK in Panmunjom blocked by police.

ROK foreign minister Choi Kwang Soo, speaking at special disarmament session in UN, calls on DPRK to participate in Games.

White House spokesperson confirms that USSR has been asked to use its influence to see that Games are not disrupted.

DPRK NOC president Kim Yu Sun telexes Samaranch to state that visit by Samaranch to Pyongyang would probably not be worthwhile until north-south dialogue completed.

Samaranch responds to telex reiterating that he is ready to visit but relies on DPRK NOC president Kim Yu Sun to find the right moment.

11 June 1988 DPRK ambassador to UN, Pak Gil Yon, states that ROK

has nothing to fear "because we are all brothers" but that scheduled military buildup by ROK and United States "will not go unchecked"; Seoul Games referred to as the "Olympics of war" and compared to 1936 Olympics in Berlin.

ROK ambassador to UN, Park Sang Yong, calls on boycotting countries to participate in Games.

13 June 1988 DPRK officials criticize "negative stand" of United States toward DPRK's proposals for peace talks with ROK.

Radical students in Seoul burn Olympic flags and throw incendiary bombs at Japanese cultural center and other public buildings.

ROK speaker of National Assembly, Kim Chae Sun, asks Japanese opposition party leader Saburo Tsukamotu (Democratic Socialist Party) for his party's support, with PRC, to persuade DPRK to participate in Games and in north-south dialogue.

Government and opposition parties agree to establish special committee in National Assembly to discuss question of unification.

Madagascar, according to DPRK sources, will boycott Games; previous acceptance had been conditional on cohosting by DPRK.

14 June 1988 Australian officials announce emergency evacuation plans for Olympic team in event of disturbances in Seoul.

DPRK NOC president Kim Yu Sun telexes Samaranch regarding possible visit and questions statements by Samaranch in June 9 press conference.

15 Jun 1988 Radical students protesting military training riot in Seoul; other riots in Taejon protesting breakup of planned student march June 10 to Panmunjom; minor firebomb attack on Democratic Justice Party headquarters in Seoul.

ROK president Roh Tae Woo states he would like to visit Japan and express his gratitude to various parties after Games are over.

Security officials of thirteen Asian and Pacific countries agree in Tokyo to cooperate regarding international terrorism that might affect Games.

	Chinese press reports that Communist Party of China politburo member Li Ruihuan has visited DPRK and has met with Kim Il Sung, to whom he delivered a diplomatic but firm message that Beijing very much wants the Seoul Games to run smoothly.
	U.S. secretary of state George Shultz announces that USSR authorities are certain that there will be no DPRK terrorist activities directed at the Games.
16 June 1988	Seoul officials agree to withdraw crackdown on street vendors, which had led to police clashes on June 13 and 15.
	FIFA president Joao Havelange states no longer possible for DPRK to stage any part of Olympic soccer tournament.
	Lottery for purchase of 20,800 Opening and Closing Ceremonies tickets in Seoul attracts 966,974 applicants.
	U.S. secretary of state George Shultz expresses concern about DPRK aggressive military moves, including deployment of SAM-5 anti-aircraft missiles within range of Seoul.
	Samaranch responds to June 13 telex from DPRK NOC president Kim Yu Sun.
17 June 1988	Samaranch meets UNESCO director general Frederico Mayor at IOC headquarters in Lausanne to discuss Seoul Games; Mayor agrees to help with acceptance of Madagascar.
	IOC advises DPRK NOC president Kim Yu Sun that his invitation as member of IOC to IOC Session in Seoul is being delivered to him through DPRK embassy in Geneva.
20 June 1988	ROK president Roh Tae Woo orders all government functions to be turned into an "emergency setup" to help ensure safety of Games.
	G-7 leaders, meeting in Toronto, support request made by Japanese prime minister Noboru Takeshita at behest of ROK president Roh Tae Woo to enlist the support of Western governments in successfully staging the Games.
21 June 1988	IOC hosts Olympism Against Apartheid meeting at IOC headquarters with African sports leaders to reaffirm IOC position against apartheid in sport.

DPRK rejects recent statements by Samaranch that DPRK refused to open its borders for the Games; states it was ready to do so if it were to cohost the Games.

24 June 1988 United States announces once again that naval presence off the coast of ROK will be increased; doubts that USSR expects SAM-5 missiles that it supplied will be used against its athletes.

Samaranch telexes DPRK NOC president Kim Yu Sun in discussion over meaning of "cohosting."

25 June 1988 Kim Un Yong, as president of GAISF (General Assembly of International Sports Federations) visits Moscow, June 25–July 3, and reports that USSR Foreign Ministry has decided to open temporary consular office in Seoul during Games and was planning to extend this initial contact to economic and cultural spheres.

27 June 1988 Japan announces that starting July 1, thorough immigration checks will be carried out at all airports and seaports to deter terrorists from entering and leaving Japan.

DPRK NOC president Kim Yu Sun telexes Samaranch complaining about attitude of ROK and wondering why Samaranch persists with questions.

29 June 1988 DPRK announcement from Pyongyang states that cohosting includes not only the events to be staged, but the name of the Games, the composition of the Organizing Committee, Opening and Closing Ceremonies, a joint team, and sharing of television revenues.

Representatives of seven countries announce measures for aviation security in connection with Games.

Samaranch telexes DPRK NOC president Kim Yu Sun responding to his questions in previous telex and asking why he persists in reference to cohosting.

30 June 1988 Samaranch sends letter to ROK president Roh Tae Woo containing political proposal prepared by Samuel Pisar.

2 July 1988 More than one hundred ROK members of National Assembly, including government members, introduce resolution urging DPRK to participate in Games, saying this will help reunification.

DPRK advises ROK that letter from DPRK students will be delivered at Panmunjom on July 4, concerning preparations for scheduled August 15 meeting between students.

4 July 1988 ROK government allows march of dissident students for first time in several years; usual slogans abound; no sign of public support for demonstrators.

Unidentified "senior official" of DPRK NOC claims ROK's refusal to accept its cohosting proposals is aimed at perpetuating division; accuses ROK of refusal to open borders.

5 July 1988 U.S. senator Ted Stevens writes to Samaranch with copies of his correspondence with U.S. secretary of state George Shultz regarding the inclusion of message of support for the Olympic Movement in the joint statement to be issued by U.S. president Ronald Reagan and USSR general secretary Mikhail Gorbachev; states he had also sent telegrams to Shultz and USSR foreign minister Eduard Shevardnadze the previous fall; asks Samaranch what can be done to get Soviets to depoliticize Olympic Games within its sphere of influence; suggests delegation of Olympic athletes go to ROK and meet with students to explain importance of Seoul Olympic Games to bring about peaceful relations between nations.

7 July 1988 ROK president Roh Tae Woo issues special declaration for National Self-Esteem, Unification, and Prosperity; this is a major policy address relating to inter-Korean relations.

DPRK NOC president Kim Yu Sun sends letter to Samaranch relating to cohosting and opening of border; letter reaches IOC on July 19.

9 July 1988 Twentieth plenary meeting of 142d Extraordinary National Assembly adopts resolution calling for participation by DPRK in Seoul Games.

Polls show significant majority of Koreans support Roh Tae Woo's declaration aimed at peace on Korean peninsula.

12 July 1988 USSR Olympic official confirms that Soviet athletes will live in Olympic Village, not on ships, during Olympic Games.

DPRK official representative in France states that DPRK will not disturb Games.

13 July 1988 ROK proposes resumption of suspended Red Cross Conference.

15 July 1988 UN Command accuses DPRK of trying to undermine Games in Seoul by making war threats and contriving tension.

ROK proposes meetings between education officials of ROK and DPRK.

16 July 1988 PRC announces it will send largest ever Olympic team to Seoul.

U.S. secretary of state George Shultz expresses confidence that Games will be safe and successful and says PRC and USSR have given assurances that DPRK would refrain from terrorist acts; Shultz will extol ROK for "impressively struggling to put this democracy on the road."

ROK foreign policy announced in follow-up to July 7 declaration, which contains elements of new policy regarding north-south relationship.

DPRK rejects ROK proposal to resume Red Cross Conference.

17 July 1988 USSR Olympic attaché Nikolai Lents says he is sure Games will be safe: "If we were not confident that the Games would be safe, we would not have decided to come here."

ROK house speaker Kim Chae Sun sends letter to DPRK counterpart containing ROK National Assembly resolution that DPRK participate in Seoul Games.

DPRK rejects ROK proposal for meetings between education officials.

18 July 1988 DPRK accepts letter containing text of ROK National Assembly resolution calling for its participation in Games, the first communication DPRK has accepted since Roh Tae Woo became president of ROK on February 25.

U.S. secretary of state George Shultz regrets delivery of Soviet missiles and military aircraft to DPRK, but does not believe they will affect security at the Games.

19 July 1988 Samaranch replies to DPRK NOC president Kim Yu Sun's letter dated July 7.

20 July 1988 ROK president Roh Tae Woo writes to Samaranch rejecting proposal prepared by Samuel Pisar and suggestion by Samaranch.

21 July 1988 DPRK Supreme People's Assembly proposes to National Assembly of ROK to hold joint north-south parliamentary meeting to resolve question of nonaggression.

ROK president Roh Tae Woo gives morale-boosting message and alert to Marine forces who will guard against attacks by sea.

24 July 1988 Samaranch reports to IOC Executive Board on progress with negotiations with the two Koreas and on visit by Mario Vazquez-Raña with Fidel Castro and trip to DPRK; Cuban participation unlikely, since message came from Castro himself; Samaranch would maintain contact with DPRK; developments in recent days might be helpful.

Samaranch acknowledges ROK president Roh Tae Woo's letter of July 20 and congratulates Roh on recent developments.

25 July 1988 Series of rumors from opposition parties and United States that apparent thaw in relations with DPRK may lead to participation in Games; U.S. State Department spokesman denies any evidence to this effect; ROK links had tied information to Edward Derwinski of U.S. State Department; similar links suggested Cuba and Angola might also participate.

26 July 1988 In letter from DPRK Supreme People's Assembly to speaker of ROK National Assembly, suggestion is made to include idea of cohosting Olympics in the proposed north-south parliamentary meeting.

Samaranch says he is happy at prospect of north-south dialogue and hopes Olympics may benefit from this.

27 July 1988 ROK agrees that Olympics can be included on agenda for proposed north-south talks.

28 July 1988 SLOOC president Park Seh Jik makes last-ditch appeal to DPRK and urges political dissidents and student activists to keep low profile during Games.

ROK Democratic Justice Party officials state that for all

practical purposes, it is now too late for events to be staged in DPRK.

DPRK president Kim Il Sung calls for legislators from both Koreas to meet at the "earliest date" and renews demand to cohost Games; denounces U.S. plans to reinforce military presence in and around ROK during Games.

Samaranch responds to U.S. senator Ted Stevens's letter of July 5, thanking him for his support in getting a statement in support of Olympic Movement included in the summit declaration; says he is not optimistic about finding solutions to the other problems.

1 Aug. 1988 ROK calls for preliminary meeting to discuss agenda for parliamentary talks between ROK and DPRK.

Samaranch reported as saying in interview with *L'Equipe* that it is too late for team events to be staged in DPRK even if IOC proposal accepted.

Aug. 1988 Cho Choong Kun, president of KAL, visits Moscow to seek permission for KAL to overfly Soviet airspace for flights with Olympic participants.

3 Aug. 1988 ROK foreign minister Choi Kwang Soo announces that Soviet Union will open consulate in Seoul to handle matters for Soviet delegation and states this will improve relations between Seoul and Moscow.

Special security measures announced for flights between Tokyo and Seoul until end of Games.

Radical student leaders deny report of Olympic "truce."

4 Aug. 1988 Press reports that IOC's request to change name of the Games to accommodate the DPRK were rejected at the highest level by ROK; speculation is that request made by Samaranch during visit to Seoul, late May–early June.

5 Aug. 1988 Law for Preservation of the Peace of the Olympics proclaimed in ROK.

6 Aug. 1988 Kim Un Yong, IOC member in ROK and SLOOC vice president, writes to Samaranch requesting assistance concerning permission for KAL overflights of USSR territory for Olympic participants.

Kim Un Yong writes to USSR NOC president Gramov to

	request assistance for KAL overflights of USSR (Siberian route) and provides list of flights requested.
	Japanese government announces it will invalidate passports of suspected terrorists who may attempt to disrupt Seoul Olympics; this is first time Japanese authorities take overt action in relation to passports that might be used in connection with terrorist actions affecting the Games and first time passports ordered returned for Japanese security interests.
7 Aug. 1988	In wake of declining public support for student demonstrations, student leaders indicate that demonstrations during Olympic period will be restricted to university campuses.
8 Aug. 1988	Radical students leave Seoul on cross-country march toward Panmunjom for unification talks with DPRK students, scheduled for August 15; DPRK students start their own march for same purpose.
	DPRK announces it will reply to ROK request for preparatory meeting on August 9.
9 Aug. 1988	DPRK accepts idea of preliminary meeting at Panmunjom on August 17 to discuss agenda for parliamentary meeting (preliminary meeting will eventually take place on August 19); continues to push for five-day meeting starting August 26.
10 Aug. 1988	ROK students clash with police over refusal to allow students to meet in Panmunjom with DPRK counterparts.
11 Aug. 1988	Samaranch, in IOC press release, calls for DPRK NOC participation in 1988 Olympic Games in Seoul and for joint parade of teams in Opening and Closing Ceremonies.
12 Aug. 1988	SLOOC president Park Seh Jik telexes Samaranch to support Samaranch's call for DPRK participation in Games; KOC agrees with IOC proposal.
	Seoul newspaper *Shinmun* reports that Cuba may soon announce its participation in Seoul Games.
	SLOOC president Park Seh Jik briefs ROK president Roh Tae Woo, opposition leaders, and other prominent figures on Games and gets assurance of cooperation and support for Games.

ROK president Roh Tae Woo calls for "cease-fire" on violent student demonstrations in period up to the Games; message is to pool wisdom for success of Olympics and put aside "family quarrels" until after Games.

13 Aug. 1988 ROK sports minister Cho Sang Ho confirms door still open for DPRK, but decision must be made by September 2.

14 Aug. 1988 ROK police take tougher approach to radical student demonstrations and break up rallies.

15 Aug. 1988 ROK president Roh Tae Woo speaking on forty-third anniversary of liberation from Japanese occupation calls for top leaders of DPRK and ROK to meet for a dialogue.

Roh also advises that people and government will not forgive violence that threatens Olympics.

Students prevented from marching to Panmunjom to meet with DPRK students; government posture is that north-south relationship is a matter for government to solve.

DPRK students wait for extra hour at Panmunjom for ROK students, then withdraw.

Press reports from Beijing suggest DPRK will not create problems for the Games.

16 Aug. 1988 DPRK NOC refuses IOC request for DPRK and ROK to march together in Opening and Closing Ceremonies; will contact IOC if results of north-south meeting on August 19 are good.

17 Aug. 1988 Cuban ambassador to DPRK, Ricardo Danza Sigas, reported to confirm nonparticipation by Cuba in speech at Wonsan, DPRK, at end of a month of "solidarity with the Cuban people."

DPRK agrees to meet in Panmunjom on August 19 to again discuss Olympic Games; this will be first time that government officials will have met since cessation of discussions some three years previously.

ROK proposes joint parliamentary meeting be held on August 27 instead of August 26.

Starting this day, holders of Olympic accreditation cards do not require visas to enter ROK; period will expire after November 2.

18 Aug. 1988 Japanese minister responsible for post, telegraph, and telephone announces special security measures relating to parcels destined for Korea.

Soviets ask if materials furnished for their team by ROK and Games sponsors, including buses, minivans, cars, photocopiers, and twenty other pieces of technical equipment can be taken back to the USSR following the Games.

19 Aug. 1988 Preliminary meeting between ROK and DPRK in Panmunjom to discuss agenda for parliamentary meeting; no progress made on Olympic matters.

20 Aug. 1988 Discussions continue in Panmunjom; ROK proposes meeting on August 29 in Pyongyang to settle DPRK demands relating to Olympics and participation by DPRK athletes in Games.

21 Aug. 1988 Concern expressed in Japan that passports stolen two years previously in Madrid may be used by Japanese Red Army.

22 Aug. 1988 DPRK rejects ROK offer to discuss Olympic matters in Pyongyang on August 29.

Special security measures put in place in Japan to guard foreign athletes training in Japan, as well as diplomatic establishments and VIPs.

23 Aug. 1988 Japanese Red Army publication *Political Review* (issue no. 29) criticizes cooperative ties between Japan, ROK, and United States on Olympics and calls for fight against such ties; publication was bimonthly since 1984, but had been suspended in August 1987.

KAL obtains permission from PRC for overflights of Chinese territory for Olympics-related flights to and from Tripoli and Zurich and continues to negotiate for such permission following the Games.

DPRK, on forty-five minutes' notice, requests resumption of discussions with ROK; ROK states it is impossible and suggests August 24 instead; DPRK agrees; meeting eventually held August 26.

Olympic flame lit at Temple of Hera in Olympia; torch relay begins to Panathenian Stadium in Athens.

Olympic "peace zones" established, within which no political rallies will be permitted, August 23–October 31.

Two U.S. activists arrested and ordered deported for participating in radical political meetings in ROK.

24 Aug. 1988 Samaranch telexes USSR sport minister Gramov to support request of ROK to allow KAL overflights of USSR for Olympic participants; points out that PRC has already given approval for similar flights.

U.S. undersecretary of state Edward Derwinski states that combination of public opinion and tight security will deter terrorists; Games will be a triumph; radical students do not appear to have public support.

25 Aug. 1988 Formal transfer of lighted torch to representatives of SLOOC occurs at Panathenian Stadium in Athens.

26 Aug. 1988 ROK student leaders indicate that demonstrations during Games period will be confined to university campuses.

ROK government declares Seoul to be a Peace Zone and prohibits unauthorized gatherings.

ROK and DPRK negotiators in Panmunjom unable to agree on Olympic matters and agree to meet again on October 13; DPRK delegates accuse ROK of deliberately blocking DPRK participation in Games.

27 Aug. 1988 Former director of the IOC, Monique Berlioux, whose employment with the IOC terminated in 1985, reported as stating that security measures in Seoul will "kill the very soul of the Games."

Olympic torch arrives at Cheju International Airport for welcoming ceremony and beginning of torch relay throughout ROK to arrive at Olympic Stadium during Opening Ceremony of the Games at 12:00 noon local time.

Japanese authorities increase security precautions at airports and place armed guards on ferries operating between Japan and ROK; 80 percent of coast guard patrol boats and planes will be assigned to Sea of Japan to prevent smuggling of arms and explosives into ROK.

Opposition leader Kim Young Sam demands stern measures from Roh Tae Woo against extreme rightists.

29 Aug. 1988	Samaranch telexes DPRK NOC president Kim Yu Sun urging him to attend IOC Session; expresses disappointment that no solution found, but IOC still ready to discuss agreement in the interest of athletes.
30 Aug. 1988	USSR NOC secretary-general Yuri Titov compliments preparations of SLOOC for Games in Soviet press.
1 Sep. 1988	Bolshoi Ballet performs in Seoul.
2 Sep. 1988	Olympic Village opens; Press Village opens.
	Four individuals, including Kaneko Eiko, an international terrorist, connected with DPRK and Japanese Red Army attempt to infiltrate ROK with forged passports; special action taken when advice received that DPRK plotting to bomb chartered planes transporting USSR and Chinese athletes to Seoul (per Park Seh Jik).
3 Sep. 1988	Main press center opens; training sites open.
	SLOOC president Park Seh Jik announces that no political asylum will be granted during Olympic period to any third world country nationals.
4 Sep. 1988	DPRK formally announces boycott of the Seoul Games and states it will do nothing to disrupt them.
	Individual traveling on Iranian diplomatic passport refuses to have baggage inspected; known to have bought batteries and wires during stay in Bangkok.
5 Sep. 1988	Samaranch arrives in Seoul; will stay until end of Games.
	DPRK NOC president Kim Yu Sun telexes Samaranch in response to August 29, 1987, telex, stating that DPRK had left no stone unturned to solve cohosting problem at north-south parliamentary meeting, but effort failed owing to unjust position of the South; DPRK will not participate in singly hosted Games.
6 Sep. 1988	First Soviet plane to land in ROK arrives in Seoul with part of Soviet delegation.
7 Sep. 1988	IOC announces that some Cuban journalists have been accredited for the Games, but that sport officials will not be accredited to the Games.
	ROK radical student leaders announce they will refrain

from street demonstrations but plan to topple Roh government by end of year.

IOC announces that door is still open for DPRK to participate in the Games.

China's *People's Daily* announces it will devote special page for reporting on Olympic events; up from a half page for Los Angeles Games in 1984.

8 Sep. 1988 In meeting with ROK president Roh Tae Woo, Samaranch confirms door to remain open for participation by DPRK until last moment of Games on October 2.

Samaranch has dinner meeting at Olympic Village with leaders of political parties: Yoon Giel Joong, Kim Dae Jung, Kim Young Sam, and Kim Jong Pil.

ROK student radicals battle police in rally against Olympics in Seoul, near IOC hotel, and in other cities.

Marat Gramov, president of USSR NOC and Soviet sports minister, urges all countries to participate in Seoul Olympics.

DPRK propaganda found in Olympic Village, raising concerns about security measures.

DPRK president Kim Il Sung calls for meeting with ROK president Roh Tae Woo to discuss reunification on a confederal basis (not a new proposal, but one dating back to 1980, in opposition to ROK proposal for reunification through democratic parliamentary elections).

Samaranch sends telex to DPRK NOC president Kim Yu Sun for delivery to Kim Il Sung on occasion of September 9 anniversary.

9 Sep. 1988 Final date for entries in athletics.

ROK Ministry of Culture and Information states that books brought in to ROK by eastern bloc athletes and tourists will not be confiscated and that new policy of ROK government is that publications on communism will be open to public unless contents violate the Constitution.

Mario Vazquez-Raña, president of ANOC, states he will use his best efforts to help sport exchanges between DPRK and ROK.

ROK radical students battle with police; vast majority of students take no part.

Mass rally in DPRK to mark fortieth anniversary; most socialist countries send heads of state; USSR sends lower-level director of KGB, General Viktor Chebrikov, instead of Andrei Gromyko, in what is regarded as a diplomatic "message" concerning Seoul Olympics.

Seoul Olympic Scientific Congress begins on Cheonan campus of Dankook University, September 9–15.

10 Sep. 1988 ANOC president Mario Vazquez-Raña describes Castro as "very, very sad" when talks with DPRK did not result in a solution for the Games; Castro urged him to visit DPRK to help with solution.

Samaranch in interview says it is time to concentrate on athletes who are in Seoul, rather than those who are not.

11 Sep. 1988 SLOOC reports to IOC Executive Board; Samaranch concerned about student demonstrations and says they are bad for the Games and for ROK; Park Seh Jik says only few students involved and would be unwise to attempt to prevent such actions on campuses; Samaranch nevertheless insists that IOC concerns be brought to attention of ROK government.

DPRK NOC expresses hope that socialist nations in Games will refrain from political activities that might be used by ROK for political advantage.

12 Sep. 1988 Ninety-fourth IOC Session begins in Seoul.

IOC agrees to allow broadcast of Games in DPRK, free of charge, through OIRT, the broadcast union in socialist countries.

13 Sep. 1988 SLOOC reports to ninety-fourth IOC Session in Seoul.

Samaranch urges Libyan president Mu'ammar Gadhafi to give necessary instructions to allow participation of Libyan Olympic team.

Mario Vazquez-Raña, president of ANOC, telexes Libyan leader Gadhafi, urging intervention for benefit of athletes, to enable them to participate in the Games.

Police statistics show dramatic decline in street demonstrations August 17–September 12 (about a fifth of number reported July 24–August 16).

ROK president Roh Tae Woo in interview with NBC says democracy likely following Games.

ROK and Hungary announce agreement to exchange permanent missions.

14 Sep. 1988 ROK radio broadcast says ROK will accept DPRK proposal to have talks in Pyongyang if no disruption of Games.

Cuba denies rumors it may participate in Games; 1991 Pan American Games not in doubt because Cuba did not exert pressure as did United States in 1980.

DPRK NOC president Kim Yu Sun replies to Samaranch telex of September 8, stating that symbolic participation in Games not possible; calls on Samaranch to get ROK authorities to change their position regarding cohosting.

15 Sep. 1988 IOC selects Lillehammer, Norway, as host city for 1994 Olympic Winter Games.

16 Sep. 1988 USSR general secretary Mikhail Gorbachev makes speech at Krasnoyarsk proposing seven-point peace plan for Asian and Pacific areas.

17 Sep. 1988 Opening Ceremony of Seoul Olympics.

19 Sep. 1988 Opening Ceremony for yachting events at Pusan Yachting Center.

Libyan Olympic team arrives in Seoul.

20 Sep. 1988 Arab countries consider boycott of Games due to inadvertent sign in Opening Ceremony stating that capital of Israel is Jerusalem; boycott averted at last minute by apology from SLOOC for inadvertent error.

24 Sep. 1988 Fidel Castro criticizes socialist countries for attending Games in Seoul.

27 Sep. 1988 Preventative action launched when advice received of departures of twenty Japanese Red Army terrorists from Lebanon to attack U.S. and Israeli athletes participating in Seoul (per Park Seh Jik).

USSR foreign minister Eduard Shevardnadze in speech to UN General Assembly announces de-ideologization of Soviet foreign policy; states that "class struggles have come to an end in the international society and ideology can no longer become the basic principle of international relations."

29 Sep. 1988 Closing Ceremony for yachting events at Pusan Yachting Center.

2 Oct. 1988 Closing Ceremony of Seoul Olympics begins at 7:00 P.M. local time.

3 Oct. 1988 Samaranch and Vazquez-Raña visit former ROK president Chun Doo Hwan at his private residence to thank him for his support of the Games.

4 Oct. 1988 Policy speech by ROK president Roh Tae Woo to National Assembly begins with lengthy references to Seoul Olympics and use of Games as stepping stone to further national and international progress; also calls for meeting with top leaders of DPRK.

7 Oct. 1988 Samaranch telexes General Secretary Gorbachev to congratulate him on Soviet team's successful Olympics and, in particular, his contribution to the internal aspects of such success as well as in the summits with the United States.

18 Oct. 1988 ROK president Roh Tae Woo addresses UN General Assembly, proposing north-south meeting of top leaders and Consultative Conference for Peace in Northeast Asia; speech includes several references to success of Seoul Olympics.

ROK president Roh Tae Woo addresses U.S. Congress and urges United States not to withdraw its troops from ROK; this is only second time ROK president has addressed U.S. Congress.

9 Nov. 1988 Samaranch attends thirty-seventh meeting of Socialist Ministers of Sport in Budapest, Hungary, November 9–11.

21 Dec. 1988 President Roh Tae Woo releases and restores civil rights of all those serving prison terms for staging antigovernment protests; hundreds of laws and decrees revised to promote basic human rights.

Feb. 1989 ROK establishes diplomatic relations with Hungary; these are followed by Poland, Yugoslavia, Bulgaria, Czechoslovakia, and Romania.

15 May 1989	USSR general secretary Mikhail Gorbachev visits Beijing.
11 Sep. 1989	DPRK rejects ROK proposal to reunify Korea as single commonwealth.
20 Sep. 1989	U.S. vice president Dan Quayle states during visit to Seoul that United States will not withdraw from ROK as long as DPRK threatens peace.
16 Oct. 1989	DPRK and ROK agree to permit family visits for only second time since 1945 (previous occasion was September 20–24, 1985).
26 Nov. 1989	ROK president Roh Tae Woo visits IOC headquarters in Lausanne.
8 Dec. 1989	ROK announces that partial consular relations have been established with USSR.
31 Dec. 1989	Former ROK president Chun Doo Hwan appears before National Assembly to respond to questions concerning abuses of power during his regime.
6 Jan. 1990	Opposition leaders Kim Young Sam and Kim Jong Pil announce they will form alliance for 1990 local elections.
7 Jan. 1990	United States objects to testimony of former ROK president Chun Doo Hwan before Korean parliamentary committee in which Chun accused the United States of involvement in 1979 assassination of ROK president Park Chung Hee and in 1980 Kwangju massacre.
10 Jan. 1990	ROK president Roh Tae Woo announces reduction in size of annual joint military exercise with United States.
22 Jan. 1990	Ruling Democratic Justice Party agrees to form conservative coalition with two opposition parties (Reunification Democratic Party and New Democratic Republican Party) for parliamentary actions.
28 May 1990	DPRK returns remains of U.S. servicemen killed in Korean conflict to U.S. congressional delegation at Panmunjom; first such meeting since 1954.
4 June 1990	ROK president Roh Tae Woo meets USSR president Gorbachev in San Francisco; first time any ROK president has met a Soviet leader; Roh says diplomatic relations are planned.

6 July 1990	DPRK government offers to open border with ROK on August 15, DPRK Independence Day.
20 July 1990	ROK president Roh Tae Woo announces border with DPRK will be opened at Panmunjom for five days in August; travel will be allowed for citizens of both countries; DPRK asks for removal of tank traps along border, repeal of laws that prohibit travel to DPRK, and formation of joint committee to resolve border issues; opposition members of National Assembly threaten to resign; Party for Peace and Democracy and Democratic Party agree to merge.
26 July 1990	Officials of ROK and DPRK agree to exchange of visits by prime ministers in September; DPRK will visit Seoul for first visit.
25 Sep. 1990	Seoul Peace Prize awarded to Samaranch at Sejong Cultural Center in Seoul.
30 Sep. 1990	Diplomatic relations established between USSR and ROK.
20 Oct. 1990	ROK and PRC agree to exchange trade offices, which are combined with de facto consular activities.
30 Dec. 1990	Former ROK president Chun Doo Hwan ends two years of (self-imposed) exile and returns to Seoul.
22 Jan. 1991	ROK agrees to lend USSR $3 billion for development projects, including importation of Korean products; ROK allowed to fish in USSR waters.
May 1991	DPRK drops opposition to joint entry of Koreas into UN after PRC indicates it will not use its Security Council veto to prohibit ROK from joining.
2–6 May 1991	All-Korean team competes in World Table Tennis Championships in Japan.
14–30 June 1991	DPRK and ROK field joint team at World Youth soccer tournament in Portugal.
Jan. 1992	U.S. president George Bush visits ROK; announcement of cancellation of 1992 joint military exercises.
17 Jan. 1992	Japanese prime minister Kiichi Miyazawa apologizes to Korean people for Japanese army's forcing of Korean women into prostitution during World War II in speech at ROK parliament.

24 Aug. 1992 Diplomatic relations established between ROK and PRC.

5 Oct. 1992 ROK president Roh Tae Woo resigns from Democratic Liberal Party to enable preparations to go forward for December election.

18 Dec. 1992 Kim Young Sam elected as president of ROK with 42 percent of popular vote (highest number of votes ever won in a Korean election), capping four decades of political activity; first civilian president in thirty-two years; Kim Jae Dung places second with 34 percent of vote.

21 Dec. 1992 ROK Ministry of Sports and Youth announces it will bid for 2002 World Cup soccer tournament and 1996 Asian Winter Games.

Index

ABC, 237
Afghanistan, 38*n*
  Soviet invasion of, 15–16, 33, 51, 55
African countries:
  apartheid issue and, 23, 25, 26, 31–32, 51
  Montreal Games boycotted by, 14, 25, 31–32
AIDS, 164
Albania, 38*n*, 276
Albertville Winter Games (1992), 203
An Bok Man, 104*n*, 134*n*, 176*n*
Andreotti, Giulio, 67*n*, 84*n*, 281, 328*n*
Andrianov, Konstantin, 20*n*, 34, 59–60, 158, 197*n*, 315*n*
Andropov, Yuri, 34, 52
Angola, 38*n*
ANOC. *See* Association of National Olympic Committees
apartheid, 22, 23, 31–32
  and expulsion of South Africa from Olympic Movement, 24–25, 26
  Olympism Against Apartheid meeting and, 300–301
archery, proposals for cohosting or sharing of, 113, 129, 131, 140, 147, 154, 160, 180, 182, 184–188, 190, 196, 198, 205, 210, 222, 243, 249, 252, 259
Asian Games:
  of 1966, 8*n*, 321
  of 1982, 72*n*
  of 1986, 8, 9*n*, 48, 49, 68–69, 74, 81, 83, 84*n*, 99, 128, 132–133, 164, 167, 202–203, 204, 206, 232, 262*n*, 313, 321–322, 324, 325
  of 1990, 69, 332
Asian Table Tennis Championships (1988), 284
Asian Winter Games (1986), 159*n*
Association of National Olympic Committees (ANOC), 9, 109, 124
  1986 meeting of, 67, 132, 159, 162–167, 171, 177, 178, 190, 206
Athletes Commission, 40
Attarabulsi, Bashir, 316
Australia, Melbourne Games in, 21–22
Australian Olympic Federation, 120*n*
Ayele, Tsegaw, 277*n*–278*n*
Azuma, Toshimisu, 259*n*

Barcelona, proposal to move 1988 Games to, 60*n*, 73–74
Barcelona Games (1992), 203, 286*n*, 338
Barnier, Michel, 203
basketball, proposals for cohosting or sharing of, 96, 140, 143, 186, 187, 222
Beaumont, Comte de, 43*n*
Beijing, 1990 Asian Games awarded to, 69
Beitz, Berthold, 109*n*, 176*n*, 241*n*
Berlin Games (1936), 19, 215*n*, 296
Berlioux, Monique, 43–44, 45, 77, 127*n*, 313*n*
Black September, 27
Blatter, Josep, 234
Bolshoi Ballet, 313
boycotts, 51–53
  Berlin Games and, 19
  and expenses incurred due to late withdrawal, 62
  ineffectiveness of, 51, 337
  invitation procedures and, 65–66

boycotts (*cont.*)
of Los Angeles Games, xi, 33–38, 44, 47, 52, 53, 55, 56, 58–65, 73, 99, 116, 262*n,* 286, 324, 327, 328, 332
of Melbourne Games, 21
of Montreal Games, 14, 25, 31–32, 51, 62
of Moscow Games, xi, 7, 16–17, 32–33, 51, 54–55, 327
and new schedule for entry process, 65
and possible legitimate reasons for nonparticipation, 61–62
proposed UN resolution and, 52
sanctions proposal and, 53, 59, 61–63, 64–65
of Seoul Games, 79, 121, 199*n,* 258*n,* 262*n,* 271–274, 276–278, 281, 285–286, 297–300, 304, 309, 311, 315, 316*n,* 324, 326, 327–328, 337, 338
Brezhnev, Leonid, 17, 34
Brinkley, David, 237
Brundage, Avery, 11, 24, 27, 28, 41, 43
Brunei, 38*n*
Buda, Istvan, 124
Bulgaria, 38*n*

Calgary Winter Games (1988), 127*n,* 146*n,* 279
Canada, 277*n*
"two Chinas" issue and, 13–14
see also Montreal Games
canoeing, proposals for cohosting or sharing of, 131, 230
Carlucci, Frank, 295
Carrard, François, 208*n,* 241*n*
Carraro, Franco, 60*n*
Carter, Jimmy, 16, 17, 33
Castro, Fidel, x, 125, 159*n,* 168, 205*n,* 277*n,* 289, 290*n*–291*n,* 305, 327–329, 337
boycott decision and, 189*n,* 273–274, 281, 286, 304, 315
and proposals for cohosting or sharing of Games, 67*n,* 68, 70, 74, 78, 79, 121*n,* 123, 189*n,* 199*n*
urged to participate in Seoul Games, 266–267
CBS, 237
Chang Choon Sik, 104*n,* 130, 136*n,* 177*n*
Chang Se Dong, 214
Chang Ung, 104*n,* 134*n,* 176*n,* 208*n,* 215*n,* 226, 242*n,* 254, 279, 280
Chebrikov, Viktor, 315
Chernenko, Konstantin U., 34, 35, 36, 52
Chin Chung Guk, 114, 128, 134*n,* 137–138, 153, 154–157, 160*n,* 174–175, 176*n,* 181–182, 187, 208*n,* 212, 220, 242*n,* 272
and proposals for cohosting or sharing of Games, 204, 205*n,* 213, 248–249, 256
China, People's Republic of (PRC), x, 79, 109, 226, 227, 251, 267, 286, 319, 327, 330–333
airlines allowed to overfly territory of, 312, 333
bid for 2000 Games made by, 332
economic experiments in, 332
Ethiopia and, 278
IOC-sponsored North-South talks and, 99–100, 331
1986 Asian Games and, 49, 68, 133, 203
Olympic Movement joined by, 13–15, 38
participation of, in Seoul Games, 265*n,* 270*n,* 308
and proposals for cohosting or sharing of Games, 84, 85, 100, 160, 175*n,* 196, 197–198, 258*n*
restraints placed on North Korea by, 169, 296–297, 323
Seoul ANOC meeting attended by, 167
Seoul Games supported by, 296–297, 304, 312
South Korean relations with, 69, 280, 333, 334
"two Chinas" issue and, 21, 22, 29–30, 41–43, 68–69
Ching-Kuo Wu, 43*n*
Chirac, Jacques, 74*n,* 203
Cho Choong Kun, 312*n*
Cho Myong Hwang, 104*n,* 134*n,* 176*n,* 242*n*
Cho Sang Ho, 9, 231*n,* 310
Choi Eun Hee, 72*n,* 74
Choi Kwang Soo, 264, 281, 287*n*
Chol Pak Song, 78–79
Choy Man Lip, 104*n,* 136*n,* 177*n*
Chun Doo Hwan, 93, 239, 240*n,* 261, 262, 264*n,* 270, 279, 329, 333*n*
bid for 1988 Games and, 10
constitutional reforms and, 214
coup led by, 7, 48, 320
domestic political unrest and, 224–225
expiration of presidential term of, 49, 91, 92, 168, 170–171, 225, 238*n,* 321
IOC-sponsored north-south talks and, 88*n,* 91
on military threat posed by North Korea, 169–170, 331
presidency assumed by, 9
and proposals for cohosting or sharing of Games, 94, 168–170, 171–173, 231
Roh's electoral reforms and, 235, 236
Samaranch's correspondence with, 75
Samaranch's meetings with, 167–173
Chung Ju Yung, 71–72, 116
Chung Jun Gi, 82, 99
Clark, William, 265
Closing Ceremony, in Seoul Games, 96, 98, 106, 223, 230, 231, 243–244, 269, 310

Commonwealth Games, 32
Congo, 31–32, 298
Congress, U.S., 329
constitution (South Korean), 214, 238
Cosell, Howard, 173
Coupat, Alain, 109*n*, 176*n*, 199, 208*n*, 231*n*, 241*n*
  in IOC delegation to Pyongyang, 217, 220–222
  in IOC delegation to Seoul, 229
Cuba, x, 213, 314, 327–329
  absent from Seoul ANOC meeting, 167
  bid for 1987 Pan American Games lost by, 122–123
  Los Angeles Games boycotted by, 38*n*, 328
  1991 Pan American Games in, 276–277, 281, 316*n*
  North Korean relations with, 168
  and proposals for cohosting or sharing of Games, 124, 169, 175*n*, 189, 199*n*, 271, 328–329
  Seoul Games boycotted by, 199*n*, 271, 273–274, 276–277, 281, 286, 304, 309, 311, 315, 316*n*, 327–328
  urged to participate in Seoul Games, 266–267
  see also Castro, Fidel
Cuban missile crisis (1962), 212*n*
cultural events, proposals for North Korean participation in, 97, 98, 110, 111, 115, 133, 137, 141–142, 145, 147–148, 149, 178, 185, 186, 244
cycling, proposals for cohosting or sharing of, 96, 98, 111, 141, 145, 147, 148, 178, 180, 184–188, 190–191, 198, 199, 200, 210, 243, 249, 251–252, 254, 259
Czechoslovakia, 38*n*, 213, 286

Daily Sports News, 173
Dassler, Horst, 68*n*
Daume, Willi, 40
Davis Cup, 333*n*
de Sales, A. O., 47*n*
Deak, Gabor, 205*n*
defections, of athletes, 313
demilitarized zone (DMZ), 6, 7, 70
Democratic Justice Party (South Korea), 91, 92, 93, 225, 234, 235, 250, 282, 321
Deng Xiaoping, 219, 227*n*, 332*n*, 333*n*
Derwinski, Edward, 35, 280, 286, 309, 312
deVarona, Donna, 285*n*
diving, 230
Drapeau, Jean, 13

East Germany. *See* Germany, Democratic Republic of
Egypt, 21
Eight Point Proposal, 234–236, 238–239, 240, 250*n*
Eiko, Kaneko, 313*n*
Ethiopia, 169, 175*n*, 276, 277–278
European Broadcasting Union, 264
Ewald, Manfred, 60, 270

fencing, 180, 184–186, 190
Fernandez Alvarez, José R., 267*n*, 277
FIAC, 259*n*–260*n*
FIFA, 160, 179, 182, 187*n*, 222, 253–254, 269, 297*n*
  North Korean expulsion from, 233–234, 246*n*, 247*n*, 248, 249, 254
FILA, 259*n*
Finland, Helsinki Games in, 20–21
FISU University Games, 251
FITA, 155, 162*n*
France, 21
Frank, Barry, 146*n*

Gadhafi, Muammar, 316
Gafner, Raymond, 77, 97, 98, 109*n*, 145, 176*n*, 199–202, 241*n*, 289–290
Ganga, Jean-Claude, 31–32, 298
Gavrilin, Viacheslav M., 226
Germany, 20
  Berlin Games in, 19, 215*n*, 296
  joint team for, 22, 72
Germany, Democratic Republic of (East Germany), 34*n*, 38*n*, 60, 109, 205*n*, 213
  first appearance of separate team from, 25–26
  participation of, in Seoul Games, 270
Germany, Federal Republic of (West Germany), Munich Games in, 25–27, 28
glasnost, x
Gnecchi-Ruscone, Francesco, 155*n*, 162*n*
Gonzales, Felipe, 203
Gonzales Guerra, Manuel, 273*n*
Gorbachev, Mikhail, x, 56–57, 85*n*, 99, 125, 198*n*, 265*n*, 266, 279, 286, 315, 316, 329, 330
Gosper, Kevan, 241*n*
Gramov, Marat, 54*n*, 167, 312*n*, 315
  and awarding of Games to Seoul, 66*n*, 197
  IOC-sponsored north-south talks and, 174*n*–175*n*
  Los Angeles Games and, 34–35, 36, 47
  and proposals for cohosting or sharing of Games, 67*n*, 68*n*, 189, 197–198
  at Socialist Ministers of Sport meeting, 123–124
  Soviet participation in Seoul Games and, 85*n*, 267*n*, 271
Great Britain, 20, 21, 26, 32
Greece, 339
Gromyko, Andrei, 34, 52, 99, 315

Gulf War, xi
gymnastics:
  proposals for cohosting or sharing of, 113, 140, 147, 160, 180, 184, 222
  rhythmic, 230

Hamlet (Shakespeare), 339
Hamzah Abu Samah, Datuk Setia Raja Tan Sri Datuk Seri, 269
Han Chang On, 104*n*, 134*n*, 176*n*, 188, 242*n*
handball, proposals for cohosting or sharing of, 96, 113, 140, 143, 184, 186, 187, 222, 230
Hassan, Moises, 271
Havelange, Joao, 234, 297*n*
He Zhenliang, 69, 160, 175*n*, 211, 219, 227, 278
Heinze, Günther, 47, 123
Helmick, Robert, 225
Helsinki Games (1952), 20–21, 114
Himl, Antonin, 61*n*, 66*n*, 123
Hitler, Adolf, 19
Honecker, Erich, 205
Hsu, Henry, 15, 41, 42*n*, 43*n*
Hull, Don, 68
Hungary, 21–22, 38*n*, 109, 213, 271, 316
  Soviet suppression of revolution in, 21, 51

Igaya, Chiharu, 246, 289
Innsbruck Winter Games (1964), 160*n*
International Amateur Athletics Federation (IAAF), 141
International Olympic Committee (IOC), xi–xii, 334–337
  as acknowledged leader of Olympic Movement, 39, 41
  draft contract between North Korea and, 174, 175
  Executive Board of, 63, 126
  history of political problems faced by, 18–38
  international respect for, 336, 338
  invitations to participate in Games issued by, 66
  management of, 63–64
  media relations and, 45–46, 63
  meeting of NOCs with Executive Board of (1986), 159, 162–167, 171, 177, 178, 190
  members of, 63
  1986 Session of, 203–205
  North Korean delegation's appearance before Executive Board of, 205–213
  north-south talks under auspices of. *See* north-south negotiations, IOC-sponsored
  political role historically avoided by, 334–335
  presidency of, 63–64, 335
  proactive role assumed by, 50–51, 57
  Pyongyang visited by delegation from, 215–222, 227, 244, 247–248, 251, 253
  as referee between OCs and international federations, 45
  Samaranch elected president of, 10–11, 12, 13
  Seoul awarded 1988 Games by, xi, 3–10, 17, 47–49, 58–60, 64, 65, 66*n*, 68, 70–71, 73–75, 108, 109–110, 121, 122, 143–144, 189*n*, 197, 198, 204, 241, 257, 324
  Seoul visited by delegation from, 224, 228–233
  shift in administration of, 43–44
  site selection process of, 5, 143*n*
  sites for 1992 Games selected by, 203
  SLOOC's relations with, 126–127, 146
  Soviet relations with, 54–57
  see also specific topics
International Table Tennis Federation, 180
invitations to Games:
  as invitation vs. command, 61–62, 64
  issued for Seoul Games, 227, 255, 258, 260–263
  procedures for sending of, 65–66
IOC. *See* International Olympic Committee
Iran, 38*n*, 203
Iraq, 21, 203
Israel, 21, 27, 180
Italy, Rome Games in, 22
Ivory Coast, 32

Jackson, Jesse, 225
Jahncke, Ernest Lee, 19*n*
Japan, 20, 84, 228, 251, 319, 333–334
  and Nagoya's bid for 1988 Games, 3–6, 7–8, 17, 47–48, 59
  North Korean relations with, 284
  Sapporo Games in, 4
  security assistance provided by, 280, 282–283, 296, 301, 309–313
  South Korean relations with, 5, 333–334
  Tokyo Games in, xi, 4, 22–23, 160*n*
Japanese Red Army, 264, 265, 313*n*
  Political Review of, 311–312
Jin Youn Myeung, 160*n*
Juantorena, Alberto, 199*n*
judo, proposals for cohosting or sharing of, 113, 140, 147, 160, 180, 184, 186, 222

Kang Sung San, 74–75
Kapista, Mikhail, 149*n*
Kapitan, Boleslaw, 205*n*
Kaunda, Kenneth David, 270
Kennedy, John F., 212*n*
Khaddam, Abdel Halim, 262*n*
Khodyrev (Leningrad mayor), 99

Khrushchev, Nikita, 212*n*
Killanin, Michael Morris, Lord, 10, 12, 16*n*, 17, 27, 28, 43, 44, 271, 335
apartheid issue and, 31–32
"two Chinas" issue and, 14–15, 29–30
Killy, Jean-Claude, 203
Kim Chong Ha (South Kim), 121–122, 196, 215*n*, 240*n*
domestic political unrest and, 250–251
and IOC delegation to Seoul, 229, 230–231
at IOC-sponsored north-south talks, 104*n*, 107–109, 110*n*, 111–112, 116–117, 118, 130–132, 136–138, 143–147, 150, 151–153, 177–179, 184–186, 190–191, 194, 245–246, 250–253, 254, 256
joint team proposal and, 116–117, 137–138, 143, 151–152
and proposals for cohosting or sharing of Games, 101, 108, 111–112, 117, 118, 131, 137, 143–145, 184–186, 190–191, 214, 230–231, 245–246, 251–253, 254
television rights and, 145–147
Kim Dae Jung, 235, 238, 284, 287
Kim Deuk Kil, 153, 160*n*, 208*n*
Kim Duk Jun, 196
Kim Hyeung On, 198*n*, 199–202
Kim Hyong, 165–166
Kim Il Sung, x, 83, 159*n*, 163, 169, 170, 225, 264, 265, 270, 305, 326, 329
boycott of Seoul Games and, 285–286
Chinese relations with, 219, 227, 296–297, 331*n*, 332*n*
fortieth anniversary celebrations and, 315, 316
and proposals for cohosting or sharing of Games, 195, 213, 272–273, 309
reunification and, 154, 268, 272–273, 307–308
U.S. involvement in South Korea and, 154, 268, 309
Kim Jong Il, x, 326*n*
Kim Jong Pil, 250, 287
Kim Pyong Hoon, 168*n*
Kim San Hoon, 226
Kim Un Yong, 126*n*, 171, 215*n*, 224, 226, 229, 231*n*, 265, 266*n*, 267, 287, 288*n*, 301
Kim Yong Nam, 225, 262*n*
Kim Young Sam, 215*n*, 225–226, 250, 261, 267*n*, 287
Kim Yu Sun (North Kim), 95*n*, 116*n*, 123, 153, 174–175, 267*n*, 280*n*, 315
and awarding of Games to Seoul, 47, 58, 70, 75
boycott decision and, 272–273
fourth trilateral meeting sought by, 198, 205–206, 209, 211, 213, 214, 216, 218–219
and IOC delegation to Pyongyang, 215–219, 220
at IOC-sponsored north-south talks, 104–107, 112–115, 118, 128–130, 134–136, 138–142, 147–150, 152, 176–177, 179–183, 186–189, 191–192, 193–194, 242–245, 248, 249, 252–256
joint team proposal and, 71, 124, 129, 135, 136, 138–140, 142–143, 147, 148, 160–162
at meeting of IOC Executive Board, 205–206, 208*n*, 209–213
in planning of trilateral talks, 76–82
and proposals for cohosting or sharing of Games, 66–67, 77–78, 80–81, 99, 101, 104, 106–107, 113–115, 118, 135, 136, 140–141, 147–150, 160, 177, 179–183, 186–188, 191–192, 196, 198–200, 204, 210, 212, 213, 214–219, 243–244, 248, 249, 252–256, 258–261, 263–264, 265, 291–295
Samaranch's correspondence with, 75, 80, 196, 198–199, 258–261, 263–264, 289–295, 313–314
Kimpo Airport, bombing at (1986), 202*n*, 325
Kiyokawa, Masaji, 8*n*, 53, 63*n*
Koloskov, Viacheslav, 233
Korea:
joint team proposed for, 67, 70–73, 74, 77, 83, 115–117, 119, 124, 126, 129, 130–131, 135, 136, 137–140, 142, 147, 148, 150–155, 157–158, 160–162, 199
reunification of, x, 78, 79, 81, 100, 101, 105, 138, 140, 141, 142, 152, 154, 163, 195, 197, 211, 243, 253, 279, 296, 301–303, 307–308, 319, 325, 326
Korea, Democratic People's Republic of (DPRK) (North Korea), x, 8, 38*n*, 323–327
and awarding of Games to Seoul, 47, 48–49, 58, 59*n*, 70–71, 74–75, 204, 324
bilateral South Korean talks with. *See* north-south negotiations, bilateral
Chinese restraints on, 169, 296–297, 323
cohosting or sharing of Seoul Games sought by, 66–68, 70, 76*n*, 77–86, 87, 89–90, 94–102, 104, 106–115, 117–125, 129–132, 134–137, 140–141, 143–145, 147–151, 154–157, 159*n*, 160, 161, 164–174, 177–193, 195–202, 204–224, 226–233, 241–261, 263–266, 269–273, 279, 283–284, 290*n*–291*n*, 291–295, 296, 298, 301, 325–326, 328–329, 330, 332
construction of sports facilities in, 160, 161, 210, 220, 221, 226, 244, 249
diplomatic status of, 323
draft contract between IOC and, 174, 175

Korea, Democratic People's Republic of (*cont.*)
encouraged to participate in Seoul Games, 111, 113, 134, 178, 301, 307, 308–309
FIFA expulsion of soccer team from, 233–234, 246*n*, 247*n*, 248, 249, 254
fortieth anniversary of founding of, 315, 316
free circulation guarantees and, 96, 172, 175, 179–184, 206, 207, 208, 214–218, 220, 221, 223, 226–227, 247, 251, 252–253
international terrorism ascribed to, 265, 280, 286, 327
IOC delegation's visit to, 215–222, 227, 244, 247–248, 251, 253
IOC-sponsored South Korean talks with. *See* north-south negotiations, IOC-sponsored
Japanese relations with, 284
1986 Asian Games and, 81, 99, 133, 202, 324, 325
nuclear facilities of, 326*n*
possible hostile actions of, 6–7, 159, 168, 169–170, 202, 279, 280, 282–283, 286, 320–321, 323, 331
preliminary IOC negotiations with, 76–82
proposal for separate Organizing Committee in, 160, 161, 165, 174, 175, 180–183, 186, 187–188, 191, 192, 206, 207, 209, 223, 230, 243–244, 252
Seoul Games boycotted by, 271–274, 281, 285–286, 309
South Korean relations with, 6–7, 54
Soviet pressure on, 264, 323
Soviet-made missiles in, 297
Korea, Republic of (South Korea), 319–323
assassinations and coups in, 7, 48, 320
bilateral North Korean talks with. *See* north-south negotiations, bilateral
Chinese relations with, 69, 280, 333, 334
Confucianism in, 320, 322
constitution of, 214, 238
democratization process in, ix–x, 250–251, 316, 320–323, 329
economic progress in, 319–320
Games' effects on, xi, 322
hierarchical structure in, 91–92
IOC-sponsored North Korean talks with. *See* north-south negotiations, IOC-sponsored
Japanese relations with, 5, 333–334
Kimpo Airport bombing and, 202*n*, 325
military in, 7, 202, 320–321, 323
National Assembly elections in, 282
North Korean relations with, 6–7, 54
political unrest in, 202, 224–225, 229, 236–239, 240, 250–251, 282, 283–284, 288*n*, 289, 296, 301–302, 309–314, 321
presidential elections in, 91, 93, 168, 170–171, 214, 225, 234–236, 238, 239, 250–251, 261, 266, 321
and proposals for cohosting or sharing of Games, 82–83, 84, 89–90, 94–97, 101, 108, 111, 121, 137, 143–145, 151, 159*n*, 167–173, 178, 183–186, 189–191, 195–196, 213–214, 228–233, 245–246, 251–253, 254, 269
Samaranch given authority to negotiate for, 89–91, 94
Soviet relations with, 309
Team Spirit military exercises in, 154, 268, 280*n*–281*n*, 282
U.S. troops in, 7, 48, 78, 122, 154, 195, 268, 295–296, 309, 323
see also Seoul; Seoul Games
Korean Airlines (KAL):
allowed to overfly China, 312, 333
Soviet downing of flight 007 and, 59*n*
terrorist bombing of flight 858 and, 265, 280
Korean War, 5*n*, 6
Kumar, Ashwini, 76–80, 109*n*, 166*n*, 176*n*, 208, 211
Kyoto News Agency, 82

Lake Placid Winter Games (1980), 16
Laos, 38*n*
Lebanon, 21
Lee Chong Ha, 104*n*, 136*n*, 177*n*
Lee Hyun Jae, 281
Lee Ki Baek, 163*n*
Lee Sang Ock, 128*n*, 266
Lee Sei Kee, 213–214, 229, 240*n*
Lee Won Kyong, 67*n*, 286
Lee Yong Ho, 67, 70, 82, 92, 125–127, 163
television rights and, 126–127
Li Chang Son, 226
Li Jong Ho, 226
Li Menghua, 175*n*, 197
Li Ruihuan, 296–297, 333
Li Tae Ho, 281–282
Li Xiannian, 227*n*
Libya, 38*n*, 170, 316
Lilley, James, 225
Livsey, William J., 159*n*
Los Angeles Games (1984), 43, 44–47, 59–60, 66, 114, 122, 226, 277
boycott of, xi, 33–38, 44, 47, 52, 53, 55, 56, 58–65, 73, 99, 116, 262*n*, 286, 324, 327, 328, 332
joint Korean team proposed for, 71–73, 74, 116
private funding of, 44–45, 46–47
sole candidacy for 1984 Games and, 44
strained media relations at, 46
television rights and, 146*n*, 147

Macmanaway, Norma, 29
Madagascar, 298–300
Maglione, Julio Cesar, 277
Manoliu, Lia, 123
Maragall, Pasqual, 60*n*, 74*n*
marathon, proposals for cohosting or sharing of, 141, 145
Martin, Paul-René, 103–104
Martinez, Conrado, 122–123, 124–125, 159*n*, 273*n*
Martinski, Trendafil, 123
Maruoka, Osamu, 265
Mayor, Federico, 298, 300
MBaye, Kéba, 211
media, 45–46
  skeptical about Seoul Games, 236
Meet the Press, 236
Melbourne Games (1956), 21–22
  Stockholm as site of equestrian events in, 114, 172–173, 180, 184
Mengistu Haile Mariam, 278
Mérode, Prince Alexandre de, 241*n*
Mexico City Games (1968), 23–24
Mexico Declaration (1984), 109
Miami Herald, 173
Miller, George D., 189
Mitterrand, François, 73
Mongolia, 38*n*
Montreal Games (1976), 13–14, 28–32, 44, 122, 226
  boycott of, 14, 25, 31–32, 51, 62
  financial problems of, 28–29
  "two Chinas" issue and, 29–30
Moscow Games (1980), 12, 39, 40, 44, 122
  boycott of, xi, 7, 16–17, 32–33, 51, 54–55, 327
  joint Korean team proposed for, 83
Munich Games (1972), 25–27
  terrorism at, 27, 28

Nagoya, bid for 1988 Games made by, 3–6, 7–8, 17, 47–48, 59
Nakasone, Prime Minister, 228, 280
Nam Joung Moon, 104*n*, 136*n*, 177*n*
National Conference of Literary Writers, 301
NATO, 16
NBC, 126–127, 145–147, 237
Nebiolo, Primo, 246
Netherlands, 21
New Zealand, 31–32, 51
Nicaragua, 271–272, 276, 281
Nigeria, 31–32
Nonproliferation Treaty, 326*n*
North Kim. *See* Kim Yu Sun
North Korea. *See* Korea, People's Democratic Republic of
north-south negotiations, bilateral, 159, 163–166, 261, 263–264, 268, 279
  secret, in 1984, 67, 69–74
  in summer 1988, 309–312
north-south negotiations, IOC-sponsored:
  authority to negotiate on behalf of South Korea given to Samaranch in, 89–91, 94
  basic strategy agreed on by Roh and Samaranch for, 94–99
  Chinese support for, 99–100
  delegations at, 104*n*, 109*n*, 134*n*, 136*n*, 176*n*, 177*n*, 241*n*, 242*n*
  failure inevitable in, 87
  first meeting in, 103–119
  fourth meeting in, 192, 241–257
  ground rules for, 87–88
  interpreters at, 100, 129*n*
  joint team proposal and, 115–117, 119, 124, 129, 130–131, 135–140, 142, 147, 148, 150, 151–152
  Lausanne as site of, 88–89
  North Korea's desire for fifth meeting in, 258*n*, 259, 260
  parties at table in, 88
  planning for, 76–77, 81–82, 86, 87–102, 127–132, 198, 200–202, 204–216, 218–220, 231–233
  press communiqués in, 101, 118–119, 150, 192–193, 256–257
  and proposals for cohosting or sharing of Games, 87, 89–90, 94–102, 104, 106–107, 108, 110, 111–115, 117–121, 123, 131–132, 134–137, 140–141, 143–145, 147, 148–150, 151, 177, 178, 179–193, 241–250, 251–257
  Samaranch as dominant force at, 89
  seating arrangements at, 100, 128
  second meeting in, 120–122, 133–153
  third meeting in, 149, 150, 152, 157, 159, 161, 164–165, 168*n*, 175–194
  worldwide interest in, 120–121

officials, from nonparticipating countries, 65
Ogimura, Ichiro, 226–228, 246
Olympic Charter, 62, 100, 102, 108, 109
  North Korean willingness to abide by, 167, 170, 171, 172
  and proposals for cohosting or sharing of Games, 78, 80, 81, 82, 112, 114, 140, 185
Olympic Congress:
  of 1973, 39
  of 1981, 39, 40–41
Olympic Council of Asia, 69
"Olympic Family," use of term, 183*n*
Olympic Games:
  permanent site suggested for, 339
  prestige gained by hosts of, 4
  as substitute for war, 324*n*
  values represented by, 50
  see also specific games

Olympic Movement, 104–105, 336, 337–338
Chinese support for, 332
delineation between sport in general and, 25
IOC acknowledged as leader of, 39, 41
South Africa expelled from, 24–25, 26
South Africa readmitted to, 301
Olympic Solidarity funds, 272
Olympic Stadium (Seoul), 108–109, 137
Olympic torch relay, in Seoul Games, 79, 96, 97, 98, 145, 148, 153, 154, 156
Olympism Against Apartheid, 300–301
Opening Ceremony, in Seoul Games, 77, 95, 96, 98, 106, 110, 111, 115, 129, 132*n*, 133, 136, 137, 138, 142, 143, 148, 149, 178, 185, 223, 230, 231, 243–244, 269, 310, 317
Ordia, Abraham, 31–32
Ortega, Daniel, 272*n*

Paillou, Nelson, 73
Pak Chun Il, 242*n*
Pak Gil Yon, 296
Pak Myong Chol, 159*n*
Pan American Games:
of 1987, 122–123, 271
of 1991, 276–277, 281, 316*n*
Panmunjom:
border crossing at, 215–218, 220, 221, 226–227, 247, 251, 253
student march to, 296, 301–302, 310*n*, 311
Park Chong Kyu, 8, 9, 92, 95*n*, 127*n*
death of, 125, 126, 224*n*
Park Chung Hee, 7, 9, 320
Park Kun, 130, 163–164, 196
Park Seh Jik, 9*n*, 88*n*, 93, 147, 163, 171, 173, 220*n*, 224, 237*n*, 265, 273*n*, 283, 287, 288*n*, 309, 310, 313
and IOC delegation to Seoul, 229, 230
and proposals for cohosting or sharing of Games, 159*n*, 167, 230–231
Park Soo Gil, 258*n*, 259*n*
Park Ton Jin, 195
PASO, 276–277, 281
Pendley, William, 282
pentathlon, modern, 230
Pisar, Samuel, 176*n*, 208*n*, 241*n*, 285*n*, 304–306
Poland, 38*n*, 109, 175*n*, 205*n*
Pound, Richard W., 241*n*
Primakov (Soviet official), 266
Pueblo incident, 221*n*
Pyongyang:
IOC delegation to, 215–222, 227, 244, 247–248, 251, 253
Samaranch's readiness to pay visit to, 289–291
separate Organizing Committee proposed for, 160, 161, 165, 174, 175, 180–183, 186, 187–188, 191, 192, 206, 207, 209, 223, 230, 243–244, 252

Radio Pyongyang, 175*n*, 262*n*, 272*n*, 290*n*
Randriamanantenasoa, Charles, 298–300
Rangoon bombing (1983), 71, 72, 74, 116*n*
Ratsiraka, Didier, 298, 299
Reagan, Ronald, 34, 35–36, 52, 125, 170, 225, 265*n*, 279, 329
Red Cross, 145, 207, 303*n*
Renke, Marian, 124
Rhodesia, 26, 27
rhythmic gymnastics, 230
Rieckehoff, German, 61*n*, 266–267
Roby, Douglas, 17
Rodong Shinmun, 154, 167*n*, 196, 199*n*
Roh Tae Woo, 7*n*, 10, 59*n*, 73, 91–99, 116*n*, 127, 147, 171, 173, 214, 224, 225–226, 231–232, 265, 267, 268*n*, 270, 280, 281, 282, 286, 287, 288, 297, 302–308, 316, 321, 322, 329
Eight Point Proposal of, 234–236, 238–239, 240, 250*n*
and IOC delegation to Seoul, 229
IOC-sponsored north-south talks and, 88*n*, 91, 94–99, 102, 110, 120*n*
Pisar proposal and, 303–307
political unrest and, 236, 237–239, 310–311, 314
presidential elections, and, 91, 93, 234–236, 238, 239, 261, 266
and proposals for cohosting or sharing of Games, 76*n*, 94, 95–96, 167, 232, 269
secret north-south talks and, 68*n*, 72*n*, 74
Special Presidential Declaration of, 302–303
television rights and, 146
Romania, 38, 56, 84*n*, 123
Romanov, Alexei, 20*n*
Rome Games (1960), 22
Roosevelt, Julian, 17

Sabah, Sheik Fahad Al-Ahmad Al-, 109*n*, 241*n*
Samaranch, Juan Antonio, xi–xii, 18, 45, 49–50, 64, 77, 85*n*, 159–175, 226, 258–275, 279, 281, 301, 310, 321*n*, 329, 330*n*, 335–336, 337, 338
acceptances of IOC invitations and, 270–275, 282
and appearance of North Korean delegation at meeting of IOC Executive Board, 205–212
and awarding of Games to Seoul, 3, 10, 17, 70, 73–74, 75, 109–110, 121
background of, 11–13
bilateral north-south talks and, 163, 164, 165–166

boycott of Seoul Games and, 276*n*, 277*n*, 278*n*, 297–298
at ceremony for sending of invitations, 262–263
change in South Korean leadership and, 91–94, 168, 170–171
Chun's meetings with, 167–173
deterioration of Lee's relations with, 125–127
elected IOC president, 10–11, 12, 13
and FIFA expulsion of North Korean soccer team, 233*n*, 234
IOC delegation sent to Pyongyang by, 215–222
and IOC policy toward boycotts, 52, 53, 62–63
IOC-sponsored north-south talks and, 76, 81–82, 89–91, 94–102, 103, 104, 107, 109–118, 120, 121–122, 127–128, 133–134, 138–153, 159, 161, 175–176, 179–194, 200–202, 206, 209, 211, 213, 214, 219, 241–242, 246–257
joint team proposal and, 115–117, 124, 129, 130–131, 136, 139–140, 142, 148, 151–152, 153, 154, 157, 161
Los Angeles Games and, 35, 36–37, 38*n*, 53, 62–63
at 1981 Olympic Congress, 39, 40–41
North Kim's correspondence with, 75, 80, 196, 198–199, 258–261, 263–264, 291–295, 313–314
organization of Seoul Games and, 75–76
pessimism of, 271*n*
Pisar proposal and, 303–307
political unrest in South Korea and, 225, 237–239, 240, 250–251, 312
press conferences given by, 121*n*
and proposals for cohosting or sharing of Games, 66–68, 70–71, 76*n*, 78, 80–81, 84, 89–90, 94–97, 100, 101, 102, 110, 111–115, 117, 125*n*, 129–132, 140–141, 143–145, 148–151, 154–157, 161, 164–174, 179–193, 196–202, 204, 206, 208, 212, 214–219, 231, 241–242, 246–261, 263–265, 270, 272, 273, 291–295
Seoul ANOC meeting and, 162–166, 171
Seoul visited by, 251, 264–265
shift in IOC administration and, 43–44
socialist countries courted by, 54–57, 122–125
South Korean confidence in, 89–91, 94
television rights and, 145–147
temperament of, 335
U.S.-Soviet summits and, 265*n*, 284–285
Sapporo Games (1972), 4
Senegal, 32
Seoul:
ANOC meeting in (1986), 67, 132, 159, 162–167, 171, 177, 178, 190, 206
IOC delegation to (1987), 224, 228–233
1986 Asian Games hosted by, 8, 9*n*, 48, 49, 68–69, 74, 81, 83, 84*n*, 99, 128, 132–133, 164, 167, 202–203, 204, 206, 232, 262*n*, 313, 321–322, 324, 325
Samaranch's pre-Games trips to, 251, 264–265, 286–289
Seoul Games (1988):
appellation of, 129, 151, 153, 154, 156, 157, 160, 180–188, 191, 192, 206, 207, 209, 223, 230–231, 243–244
archery in, 113, 180, 182, 184–188, 190, 196, 198, 205, 210, 222, 243, 249, 252, 259
basketball in, 96, 140, 143, 186, 187, 222
boycotting of, 79, 121, 199*n*, 258*n*, 262*n*, 271–274, 276–278, 281, 285–286, 297–300, 304, 309, 311, 315, 316*n*, 324, 326, 327–328, 337, 338
canoeing in, 131, 230
Closing Ceremony in, 96, 98, 106, 223, 230, 231, 243–244, 269, 310
courting of socialist countries before, 54–57, 122–125
cultural events during, 97, 98, 110, 111, 115, 133, 137, 141–142, 145, 147–148, 149, 178, 185, 186, 244
cycling in, 96, 98, 111, 141, 145, 147, 148, 178, 180, 184–188, 190–191, 198, 199, 200, 210, 243, 249, 251–252, 254, 259
diving in, 230
domestic political unrest and, 236–239, 240, 283–284
fencing, 180, 184–186, 190
guarantees made by South Korea for, 75–76
gymnastics in, 113, 140, 147, 180, 184, 222
handball in, 96, 113, 140, 143, 184, 186, 187, 222, 230
invitation procedures for, 65–66
judo in, 113, 140, 147, 180, 184, 186, 222
marathon in, 141, 145
media skepticism about, 173, 236
modern pentathlon in, 230
move to Barcelona proposed for, 60*n*, 73–74
new schedule for entry process adopted in, 65
North Korea encouraged to participate in, 111, 113, 134, 178, 301, 307, 308–309
Olympic Stadium for, 108–109, 137
Olympic torch relay in, 79, 96, 97, 98, 145, 148, 153, 154, 156

Seoul Games (1988) (*cont.*)
Opening Ceremony in, 77, 95, 96, 98, 106, 110, 111, 115, 129, 132*n*, 133, 136, 137, 138, 142, 143, 148, 149, 178, 185, 223, 230, 231, 243–244, 269, 310, 317
possibility of North Korean aggression during, 6–7, 159, 168, 169–170, 202, 279, 280, 282–283, 286, 320–321, 323, 331
proposals for cohosting or sharing of, 66–68, 70, 76*n*, 77–86, 87, 89–90, 94–102, 104, 106–115, 117–125, 129–132, 134–137, 140–141, 143–145, 147–151, 154–157, 159*n*, 160, 161, 164–174, 177–193, 195–202, 204–224, 226–233, 241–261, 263–266, 269–273, 279, 283–284, 290*n*–291*n*, 291–295, 296, 298, 301, 325–326, 328–329, 330, 332
requests for confirmation of North Korean participation in, 156, 161, 162, 165, 206, 207, 218
rhythmic gymnastics in, 230
security in, 202*n*, 262, 280, 282–283, 286, 295–297, 301, 309–313
selection of site for, xi, 3–10, 17, 47–49, 58–60, 64, 65, 66*n*, 68, 70–71, 73–75, 108, 109–110, 121, 122, 143–144, 189*n*, 197, 198, 204, 241, 257, 324
sending of invitations to, 227, 255, 258, 260–263
shooting in, 113, 129, 140, 147, 186
soccer in, 96, 111, 129, 137, 140, 143, 147, 154, 160, 179, 180, 182–187, 190, 191, 198, 199, 200, 210, 222, 230, 233–234, 243, 246*n*, 247*n*, 248, 249, 253–254, 259, 261, 297*n*
success of, ix–x
swimming in, 113
synchronized swimming in, 230
table tennis in, 113, 129, 131, 140, 147, 154, 180, 182, 184–188, 190, 196, 198, 205, 210, 222, 243, 249, 252, 259
television rights and, 92*n*, 107, 126–127, 145–147, 162–163, 223, 244, 264
terrorist threat during, 280, 282–283, 286, 296–297, 301, 309–313
track and field in, 113
"truce" during, 282, 305, 309–311, 312–313
U.S. naval exercises during, 279, 280
volleyball in, 96, 113, 137, 140, 143, 147, 182, 184, 186, 187, 222, 230, 248, 249, 251, 252, 254, 259, 286*n*
weight lifting in, 113, 140, 186
wrestling in, 113, 140, 147, 180, 184, 186, 222, 230, 259*n*
Seoul Olympic Organizing Committee (SLOOC), 184
IOC's relations with, 126–127, 146
presidency of, 91, 92, 93, 163, 173
proposed Pyongyang Organizing Committee and, 161*n*, 230
socialist countries' relations with, 267
television rights and, 146–147
Seychelles, 276
Shakespeare, William, 339
Shevardnadze, Eduard, 268*n*, 279, 316*n*
Shin Hyun Taek, 145
Shin Sang Ok, 72*n*, 74
shooting, proposals for cohosting or sharing of, 113, 129, 140, 147, 186
Shultz, George, 35–36, 265–266, 285*n*, 297, 308
Sigur, Gaston, 240
Simon, William E., 62*n*, 173
Sin In Ha, 258*n*
Sin Hyonrim, 164–165
Sindermann, Horst, 213
Siperco, Alexandru, 76–77, 109*n*, 128, 129, 154, 156–157, 159, 161, 166, 187, 189, 199, 200, 201, 206, 207, 208*n*, 241*n*
in IOC delegation to Pyongyang, 215, 217, 220–222, 244, 247*n*, 248
in IOC delegation to Seoul, 229, 231
SLOOC. *See* Seoul Olympic Organizing Committee
Smirnov, Vitaly, 8*n*, 59–60, 208, 211
soccer tournament:
failure of North Korean team to qualify for, 222, 233–234
proposals for cohosting or sharing of, 96, 111, 129, 137, 140, 143, 147, 154, 160, 179, 180, 182–187, 190, 191, 198, 199, 200, 210, 230, 243, 246*n*, 247*n*, 248, 249, 253–254, 259, 261, 297*n*
Socialist Ministers of Sport, 122–125, 205*n*, 263*n*
Solomon, Richard, 266
South Africa, 22, 23, 51, 60*n*
and boycott of Montreal Games, 31–32
expelled from Olympic Movement, 24–25, 26
readmitted to Olympic Movement, 301
South Kim. *See* Kim Chong Ha
South Korea. *See* Korea, Republic of
Soviet Union, x, 20, 66, 132, 198*n*, 286, 319, 328, 330, 331, 332
Afghanistan invaded by, 15–16, 33, 51, 55
and awarding of Games to Seoul, 59–60, 197
Hungarian revolution suppressed by, 21, 51
IOC relations with, 54–57
Los Angeles Games boycotted by, xi, 33–38, 52, 53, 55, 56, 58–59, 60, 61,

62–63, 64–65, 73, 99, 116, 262*n*, 286, 327, 328
Olympic Movement joined by, 20–21
participation of, in Seoul Games, 266, 267*n*, 270*n*–271*n*, 308
possible North Korean aggression and, 169, 333
and proposals for cohosting or sharing of Games, 68, 79, 84, 85, 149*n*, 175*n*, 189, 197–198, 258*n*, 263*n*, 264, 266, 268*n*, 270*n*
restraints placed on North Korea by, 264, 323
security concerns of, 226
Seoul ANOC meeting attended by, 167
Seoul Games supported by, 158, 278–279, 295, 296, 297, 304, 312*n*, 313
South Korean relations with, 309
Spanish relations with, 11–12, 21
"two Chinas" issue and, 41–42
U.S. relations with, 52, 54, 265–266, 284–285
see also Moscow Games
Spain, 21
Soviet relations with, 11–12, 21
Spartakiade (1985), 99
Squaw Valley Winter Games (1960), 55
State Department, U.S., 34, 35*n*, 36, 37, 48*n*, 271*n*, 295, 309
Stevens, Ted, 284*n*, 285*n*
Stockholm, equestrian events of Melbourne Games held in, 114, 172–173, 180, 184
student dissidents, 202, 236, 250, 282, 283–284, 288*n*, 289, 296, 309–314
Panmunjon march of, 296, 301–302, 310*n*, 311
Stupp, Howard, 176*n*, 241*n*
Suez crisis, 21
swimming, 113
Switzerland, 21
synchronized swimming, 230
Syria, 262*n*
Syssoev, Valery, 259*n*–260*n*

Ta Quang Chien, 122
table tennis, proposals for cohosting or sharing of, 113, 129, 131, 140, 147, 154, 160, 180, 182, 184–188, 190, 196, 198, 205, 210, 222, 243, 249, 252, 259
Taiwan, "two Chinas" issue and, 13–15, 21, 22, 29–30, 41–43, 68–69
Takeshita, Noboru, 282, 286, 297
Tanjug, 225
Team Spirit military exercises, 154, 268, 280*n*–281*n*, 282
television rights, 92*n*, 107, 126–127, 162–163, 223, 244, 264
terrorism:
ascribed to North Korea, 265, 280, 286, 327
downing of KAL flight 858 and, 265, 280
Kimpo Airport bombing and, 202*n*, 325
at Munich Games, 27, 28
Rangoon bombing and, 71, 72, 74, 116*n*
threat of, during Seoul Games, 280, 282–283, 286, 296–297, 301, 309–313
Tito (Josip Broz), 38
Titov, Yuri, 5, 313
Tokyo, 1940 Games awarded to, 20
Tokyo Games (1964), xi, 4, 22–23, 160*n*
track and field, 113
Trudeau, Pierre, 30
TWI International, 146*n*

Ueberroth, Peter, 45, 47, 173
Uganda, 32*n*
UNESCO, 60*n*
United Nations (UN), 12, 49, 52, 60*n*, 164, 280, 281–282, 296, 308, 311, 338
United States, x, xi, 14, 55, 154, 227–228, 259*n*, 264, 277*n*, 278–279, 312, 319, 324, 325, 329–330, 333, 337
Berlin Games and, 19
Cuba and, 328
Moscow Games boycotted by, 16–17, 32–33
naval exercises of, during Seoul Games, 279, 280, 297
and political crisis in South Korea, 225
possible North Korean aggression and, 169, 323
and proposals for cohosting or sharing of Games, 84
Soviet relations with, 52, 54, 265–266, 284–285
Squaw Valley Winter Games in, 55
troops from, in South Korea, 7, 48, 78, 122, 154, 195, 268, 295–296, 309, 323
see also Los Angeles Games
Uno, Sosuke, 281, 284
Upper Volta, 38*n*
Uruguay, 277

Vance, Cyrus, 16
Vazquez-Raña, Mario, 9, 67*n*, 123, 239–240, 246, 277*n*, 281, 315, 321*n*
Vietnam, 38*n*, 125
Vietnam War, 55
Vladivostok Declaration (1986), 198*n*
volleyball, proposals for cohosting or sharing of, 96, 113, 137, 140, 143, 147, 182, 184, 186, 187, 222, 230, 248, 249, 251, 252, 254, 259, 286*n*

Walter, Eric, 153*n*
Warsaw Pact countries, 59, 330
  IOC courting of, 54–57, 122–125
  Los Angeles Games and, 37–38
  see also specific countries
weight lifting, proposals for cohosting or sharing of, 113, 140, 186
Weinberger, Caspar, 170
West Germany. *See* Germany, Federal Republic of
Wieck, Hans G., 84*n*, 202
World Shooting Championships (1978), 8–9
World Table Tennis Championships (1979), 180
World War II, 20
Worrall, James, 30
wrestling, proposals for cohosting or sharing of, 113, 140, 147, 160, 180, 184, 186, 222, 230, 259*n*

Xu Yinsheng, 226

Yanagiya, Kensuke, 128*n*
Yemen, North, 125
Yemen, People's Democratic Republic of, 38*n*
Yim Tae Soon, 104*n*, 136*n*, 177*n*
Yonhap News Agency, 281
Yoo Chang Soon, 5–6
Yook Wan Sik, 283*n*
Yoon Gil Joong, 287
Yugoslavia, 38, 109, 213, 338

Zambia, 270
Zhao Ziyang, 219, 227*n*, 332*n*
Zhong Shitong, 99–100
Zia Ul Hag, 333*n*
Ziffren, Paul, 173